Fodor's

MAINE COAST

Welcome to the Maine Coast

The Maine Coast is several places in one. Classic New England townscapes with picturesque downtowns mingle with rocky shorelines punctuated by sandy beaches and secluded coves with sweeping views of lighthouses, forested islands, and the wide-open sea. So, no matter what strikes your fancy—a spontaneous picnic on the beach or a sunset cruise with a bottle of local wine, an afternoon exploring hidden tide pools or a dose of culture followed by shopping and dining in town—there's something to suit every disposition.

TOP REASONS TO GO

★ **Lobster and Wild Maine Blueberries:** It's not a Maine vacation unless you don a bib and dig into a steamed lobster with drawn butter, and finish with wild blueberry pie.

★ **Boating:** Maine's coastline was made for boaters so make sure you get out on the water.

★ **Hiking the Bold Coast:** Miles of unspoiled coastal and forest paths Down East make for a hiker's (and a bird-watcher's) dream.

★ **Cadillac Mountain:** Drive a winding 3½ miles to the 1,530-foot summit in Acadia National Park for the sunrise.

★ **Dining in Portland:** With more than 250 restaurants and counting, Forest City is a foodie haven.

Contents

MAPS

Fodor's Features

Chapter 1

EXPERIENCE THE MAINE COAST

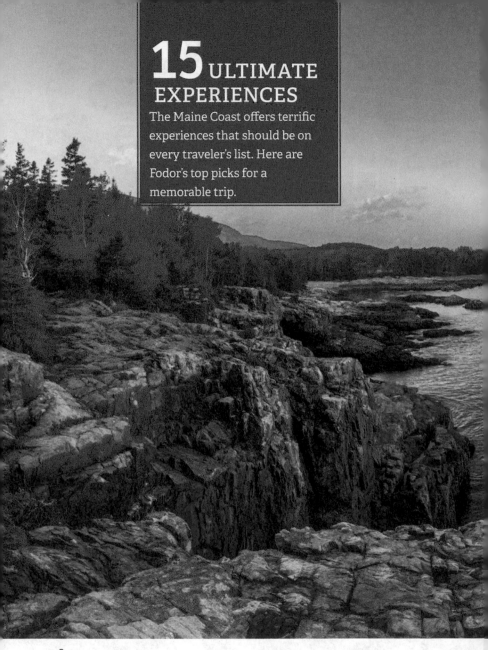

15 ULTIMATE EXPERIENCES

The Maine Coast offers terrific experiences that should be on every traveler's list. Here are Fodor's top picks for a memorable trip.

1 Explore Acadia National Park

At New England's only national park, drive or bike the 27-mile Park Loop Road, climb the 1,530-foot summit of Cadillac Mountain, or explore miles of trails and carriage roads. *(Ch. 8)*

2 Experience historic and hip Portland

Old Port and the East End offer eclectic restaurants and stylish boutiques, while the Arts District has the excellent Portland Museum of Art. *(Ch. 4)*

3 Eat a Maine lobster

A trip to Maine isn't complete without a meal featuring the state crustacean. Whether it's a lobster dinner, a bowl of lobster stew, or a lobster roll, bring your appetite.

4 Sail on a windjammer

Pretty Camden Harbor and nearby Rockland are home ports for a fleet of owner-operated schooners that take guests on voyages around Maine's rugged coast, peninsulas, and islands. *(Ch. 6)*

5 Eat your way through Portland

With renowned farm-to-table restaurants, waterfront seafood shacks, eclectic Asian and Latin eateries, and scads of artisan specialty food shops, Portland boasts a vibrant culinary scene. *(Ch. 4)*

6 Cruise Casco Bay

Via brightly painted ferries, take a narrated cruise on the Mailboat Run, or hop off to explore one of the larger islands on foot or by bike. *(Ch. 4, 5)*

7 Hop over the border to Campobello Island

From Lubec, it's just a 2-mile drive—which includes crossing a short international bridge (bring your passport!) to visit this international park, which preserves the summer cottage of FDR's family. *(Ch. 10)*

8 Shop at L.L. Bean

More than 3 million shoppers ply the aisles of the world-famous mail-order merchandiser's flagship store in Freeport. Visit any time—it's open 24 hours. *(Ch. 5)*

9 See the first sunrise in the U.S.

West Quoddy Head Light has stood at the nation's easternmost point of land since 1806. It's a majestic place to watch the country's earliest sunrise each morning. *(Ch. 10)*

10 Go lighthouse hopping

There are 65 lighthouses along Maine's coastline. Many of these historic and striking beacons are open for touring, or at least to stroll the grounds; some have overnight accommodations.

11 Paddle around in a kayak

With nearly 3,500 miles of coastline, renting a kayak or booking a guided paddle is one of the most memorable ways to explore Maine's colorful harbors, rocky ledges, and dramatic headlands.

12 Enjoy a towering view

Rising 437 feet, the sleek Penobscot Narrows Bridge has the world's tallest bridge observatory. You can also have fun next door at historic Fort Knox, the state's largest garrison. *(Ch. 6)*

13 Stop and smell the roses

Set on 300 acres in Boothbay, the Maine Coast Botanical Garden is New England's largest and a delightful place to admire spring blooms and fall foliage, and stroll among giant trolls. *(Ch. 5)*

14 Stroll along Marginal Way

The mile-long Marginal Way meanders atop a rocky promontory, connecting the dapper village of Ogunquit with the bustling lobster shacks and galleries of Perkins Cove. *(Ch. 3)*

15 Getting to know Andrew Wyeth's and Winslow Homer's Maine

In Prout's Neck, you can book a tour of Homer's studio through the Portland Museum of Art. In Rockland, don't miss the Wyeth Center at the Farnworth Art Museum. *(Ch. 3, 6)*

WHAT'S WHERE

1 The Southern Coast. Stretching north from Kittery to just outside Portland, this is Maine's most-visited region. Kittery, the Yorks, Ogunquit, and the Kennebunks abound with historic sites, sophisticated inns and restaurants, and miles of beaches.

2 Portland. Maine's largest city deftly balances its historic role as a working harbor with its newer identity as a center of art, shopping, dining, and lodging.

3 The Mid-Coast Region. North of Portland, from Brunswick to Monhegan Island, the craggy coastline winds its way around pastoral peninsulas and dozens of lighthouses. Its villages boast maritime museums, antique shops, and beautiful architecture.

4 Penobscot Bay. This region combines lively coastal towns with dramatic natural scenery. Camden, one of Maine's most picture-perfect towns, has antique homes and a historic windjammer fleet, and Rockland has a lively downtown and excellent museums.

5 Blue Hill Peninsula and Deer Isle. Art galleries are far more plentiful here in this less-developed swath of coastline than shops selling lobster T-shirts and lighthouse souvenirs. The entire region is ideal for biking, hiking, kayaking, and boating. For many, the Blue Hill Peninsula defines the silent beauty of the Maine Coast.

6 Acadia National Park. Travelers come by the millions to climb (mostly by car, but there's fantastic hiking, too) the miles of 19th-century carriage roads and well-marked trails leading to Acadia National Park's stunning peaks and vistas.

7 Acadia Region. Bar Harbor—where the wealthy built summer cottages in the 19th century—is now a visitor's haven abundant with restaurants and hotels, while Southwest Harbor and Bass Harbor offer quieter pleasures.

8 Down East Coast. Some say this is the "real" Maine. Thousands of acres of wild blueberry barrens, congestion-free coastlines, the winds and the winters, and the immense tides make the area strikingly beautiful.

Maine Coast Today

In recent decades, Maine's Congressional delegation has often been around 50–50—half Democrat and Republican, and half male and female, which somewhat resembles the makeup of the state. Voters legalized recreational marijuana in 2016, and retail pot shops began opening in 2020. Since 2000, Somali immigration has increased cultural diversity in Lewiston and Portland—in 2021, Deqa Dhalac was elected mayor of South Portland, making her the first Somali-American to become mayor of a U.S. city. As many paper mills have shuttered, farming is on the upswing, while the billion-dollar tourism industry struggles at times to find enough workers—especially following the pandemic. The state's soaring popularity with vacationers also continues to fuel rising real estate prices and rents up and down the coast.

THE PEOPLE

The vast majority of Maine's nearly 1.4 million residents live within 50 miles of the state's long, jagged, and picturesque coastline—the stretch from Kittery, at the New Hampshire border, to Bangor is the most populous. Nevertheless, outside of a few cities and more densely settled towns, much of the coast retains a verdant, semi-rural look and feel, especially compared with southern New England's generally more developed coast.

The idea of the self-reliant, thrifty, and often stoic New England Yankee has taken on almost mythic proportions in American folklore, but in parts of New England—especially in Maine—there still is some truth to this image. It makes sense—you need to be independent if you farm an isolated field, live in the middle of a remote forest, or work a fishing boat miles off the coast. As in any part of the country, there are stark differences between the city mice and the country mice of Maine. Both, however, are usually knowledgeable and fiercely proud of the region, its rugged beauty, and its contributions to the nation.

Though about 95% of the state's present population identifies as white, Maine is becoming steadily if slowly more diverse. About 80,000 Mainers are of some other race, and roughly 8,000 are direct descendants of coastal Maine's original inhabitants, the Wabanaki, who have foraged and hunted its fertile lands and fished its prolific waters. (navigating in sturdy canoes fashioned out of birchbark) for at least 12,000 years. This broader group historically comprises four specific tribes: the Penobscot, the Passamaquoddy, the Maliseet, and the Micmac.

THE LANGUAGE

True Mainers drop or soften their R's—making their favorite dish "lobstah"; they also often accentuate the vowel, so a one-word syllable can be pronounced like two, meaning "here" may become "hee-yuh."

A few words and phrases:

- **Chowdah**—always New England–style, *never* Manhattan-style

- **Grindah**—a submarine sandwich

- **Nor'eastah**—strong winter storm

- **Jimmies**—ice-cream sprinkles

- **Regulah coffee**—coffee with cream and sugar, not black

- **Wicked**—"very," added as a modifier (e.g., "wicked awesome," "wicked good")

SPORTS

Maine sports fans typically follow Massachusetts teams as if they were their own—Red Sox baseball, Bruins hockey, Celtics basketball, and Patriots football. But locals also fervently support Portland's professional minor league teams, such as baseball's Sea Dogs, an affiliate of the Red Sox; hockey's Mainers, an affiliate of the Bruins; and basketball's Maine Celtics, an affiliate of Boston's Celtics.

Coastal Mainers are generally drawn to the outdoors, too—hiking, sailing, kayaking, and bicycling are all favorite pastimes at or near the shore, and the region's many diehard skiers and snowboarders eagerly drive inland to Sunday River, Sugarloaf, and Saddleback Mountain during the winter months. But if you're seeking spectacular ocean views while enjoying a day on the slopes, look no further than Camden Snow Bowl, which overlooks West Penobscot Bay.

THE ECONOMY

Exports are a major part of the modern New England—and Maine—economy, consisting heavily of computers and other electronics, chemicals, and specialized machinery. Some towns are known for a particular export like L.L. Bean's home base of Freeport, and Bath, whose naval shipyards supply the military with high-tech ships and submarines. Farther inland in the state's densely wooded hills and mountains, a number of towns depend upon one of Maine's most important industries, the harvesting and processing of timber (in the form of wood, wood pulp, and paper).

On the coast, however, both seafood and tourism—two industries that share a sometimes complicated yet symbiotic relationship—dominate the economy. There are about 50 commercial fishing ports along the coast, and collectively they employ 26,000 people and typically generate upward of $750 million annually, although in 2021 the state's seafood industry netted (pardon the pun) nearly $900 million, a new record. You can probably guess most of the top revenue-producing products: about 80% of the yield is Maine's famously delicious lobster, with soft-shell clam, oysters, and scallops prolific as well. Menhaden, an oily species of herring, is another top catch—it's primarily used as lobster bait. Maine's third most valuable catch are elvers, aka baby eels, which are fished from rivers and exported mostly to Japan as seed stock. Some of these find their way back to Maine and other U.S. states in the form of unagi rolls at sushi restaurants. Maine is also known for a number of other food products, including maple syrup, blueberries, and cranberries.

Although Maine's ever-growing crop of tourists undoubtedly helps support the state's seafood and agricultural industries, it also contributes to soaring real estate costs in many port communities, which in turn threatens the economic sustainability of seafood companies and their workers. This balance is especially tenuous, for example, in Portland's Old Port maritime district, where the historic waterfront once dominated entirely by commercial wharves and dockyards is now a mix of industrial, residential, and leisure. Up and down the coast, as pleasure boats compete with fishing boats for valuable moorings and slips, and hotels, vacation condos, and upmarket restaurants and boutiques spring up alongside generations-old fishing commercial fishing operations, local officials continue to seek ways to strike a balance between development and preservation.

Maine's Best Seafood Shacks

BITE INTO MAINE, CAPE ELIZABETH, ME

This spot serves high-quality lobster rolls from a cart near Portland Head Light and has additional locations in Portland and Scarborough. The contemporary twists make the trip worth it, and the LBT (Lobster, Bacon and Tomato) sandwich is sheer heaven. *(Ch. 3)*

SHANNON'S UNSHELLED, BOOTHBAY HARBOR, ME

The namesake of this shack first got the idea to set up shop when her father posed the simple question: "Where can you buy a quick lobster roll in Boothbay Harbor?" The shack is now beloved for its grilled and buttered buns stuffed with whole lobsters and served with a side of garlicky, sea-salted drawn butter. *(Ch. 5)*

MUSCONGUS BAY LOBSTER, MUSCONGUS, ME

Locals and summer folks chow down on delicious seafood straight from the sea; if you can, grab a table on the deck overlooking the expansive bay. It's BYOB for now (a bar is planned for the future), so bring appropriate provisions. And, there's a kids menu. *(Ch. 5)*

BOB'S CLAM HUT, KITTERY, ME

With fresh (never frozen) shellfish and a cheery, old-school vibe, Bob's also serves up scrumptious, homemade sauces, including their tangy Moxie BBQ sauce, to smother over golden fried clams, alongside some of the creamiest New England clam chowder around. *(Ch. 3)*

THE LOBSTER SHACK, OGUNQUIT, ME

A fixture since 1947 in Ogunquit's bustling Perkins Cove, this cozy weathered-shingle lobster pound is just across from the oft-photographed footbridge. Choose from a 1/4- to a whopping 1-pound lobster roll, or try the delicious roll with hand-picked Maine crab meat. *(Ch. 3)*

FIVE ISLANDS LOBSTER, GEORGETOWN, ME
Located on a lively working wharf overlooking Sheepscot Bay, this cheerful spot welcomes hungry folks with its delicious seafood and stunning views. The family-friendly atmosphere extends to the menu, which also has plenty of "not from the sea" options. *(Ch. 5)*

THE CLAM SHACK, KENNEBUNKPORT, ME
For more than a half century, this shack has been known for speedy service and great takeout fare, like its traditional boiled lobster dinners and lobster rolls on freshly baked buns. Eat at one of several wooden picnic tables that overlook the Kennebunk River. There's even a lemonade stand to complete the experience. *(Ch. 3)*

THE HIGHROLLER LOBSTER CO., PORTLAND, ME
What many consider to be Portland's top lobster shop has plenty going for it, from the friendly service to the creative (try the lime-jalapeño mayo) takes on traditional lobster rolls. Be sure to give the tantalizing lobby pop—lobster tail on a stick—a try. *(Ch. 4)*

RED'S EATS, WISCASSET, ME
It's not uncommon to see hungry customers forming long lines outside this iconic red shack, which opened in 1938. The lobster roll (served with local butter) is a huge draw, but the menu features other staples like fried clams, shrimp, and scallops. Hot dogs, hamburgers, and grilled cheese round out the options. *(Ch. 5)*

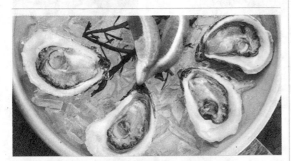

THE SHUCK STATION, NEWCASTLE, ME
There's a lobster roll on the menu, but here it's all about oysters— fried oysters, fried oyster tacos, oysters Rockefeller, oyster po'boys, BBQ oysters, and of course, raw oysters. This laid-back and family-friendly joint has a kids' menu and lots of local beers on tap. *(Ch. 5)*

Culinary Maine Musts

WHOOPIE PIES

Consisting of two soft moon-shape cakes and a creamy vanilla frosting, whoopie pies may have originated in a few possible northeastern locales. Maine leads the way in whoopie pie adoration, and gourmet shops offer up all kinds of fun flavors: think apple-spiced cakes with caramel cream, or chocolate cakes with peanut butter cream.

COFFEE

Another pillar of the state's craft beverage scene, artisan coffeehouses and roasters thrive here. Benbow's Coffee in Bar Harbor helped put the state on the premium-coffee map in the mid-'80s and remains a favorite. Other stellar showcases of well-crafted, complex espresso drinks include Coffee by Design in Portland and 44 North Coffee on Deer Isle.

APPLES AND CIDERS

Crisp fall days see a bounty of apple production throughout the state, from ubiquitous galas and honeycrisps to unusual heirloom and wild varieties. Gather your own supply at U-pick operations or stock up on artisan hard ciders that feature local apples and other Maine fruits at one of the state's two-dozen cideries.

PANCAKES AND MAPLE SYRUP

Maybe the most beloved of New England breakfasts, fluffy pancakes with local maple syrup are a year-round delight. Sure, Vermont and New Hampshire may be more famous for maple syrup, but Maine produces nearly 20% of the country's supply.

CRAFT BEER

New England has been a pioneer when it comes to innovative brewers, and in 2021, Maine overtook Vermont as having more craft producers per capita than any other state. From dry-hopped IPAs to tangy sours to barrel-aged saisons, the coast abounds with interesting ales and lagers.

BLUEBERRIES

From mid-July through mid-September, these berries proliferate throughout the region, at U-pick farms, of course, but also look for them in the wild when you're out along woodland trails. You can bring home a number of locally made products, like blueberry syrups, jams, sauces, and baked goods.

Saltwater taffy

SALTWATER TAFFY

Kid-approved since the 1880s, saltwater taffy stars among the many kinds of bulk candies you'll find at sweets shops situated in nearly ever good-size coastal village in Maine. Boxes of these chewy taffies in assorted flavors—from banana to maple to watermelon—make great gifts. Perkins Cove Candies in Ogunquit is a longtime favorite, but the Goldenrod in York Beach and Old Port Candy Company in Portland also have loyal followings.

FISH-AND-CHIPS

Maine shellfish—not just lobster but also clams, oysters, crab, and scallops—is justly famous the world over, but don't forget that the region's cool waters also yield fresh and flavorful fin fish, much of which makes its way into hearty platters of beer-battered, lightly fried fish (usually haddock) and chips. Standouts for this simple, traditional dish popularized in northern England in the mid-19th century include Pier 77 in Kennebunkport, and Robert's Maine Grill in Kittery.

ICE CREAM

Maine's quintessential road-tripping dessert, ice cream in these parts often features local ingredients. Long-running stands like Beal's Old Fashioned turn out classic flavors, from blueberry cobbler to Indian pudding. In more recent years, small-batch gourmet shops have made a splash with their inventive creations. Try matcha ginger–rhubarb jam at Rococo in Kennebunkport, or butterscotch-miso at Mount Desert Island Ice Cream in Bar Harbor and Portland.

For the Love of Lobster

Lobster mac and cheese

There's probably no more celebrated way to eat Maine's most sought-after crustacean than in the form of a lobster roll, but what kind of roll, you ask? The lobster roll is said to have been first served in the late 1920s by Perry's restaurant in Milford, Connecticut (which is far closer to New York City than to Boston, much less Maine). By the mid-20th century, the dish had become ubiquitous throughout coastal New England, and Maine (as well as Canada's Maritimes) in particular. Traditionally, it's consisted of lobster meat tossed lightly with mayonnaise and served cold in a hot dog (or similarly shaped) bun.

Red's Eats in Wiscasset, Maine is generally credited with having turned the

once humble sandwich into a genuine food craze in the 1970s. But it's Connecticut, yet again, where a number of restaurants are believed to have popularized the beloved version of the roll that's served hot, the lobster meat slathered in warm drawn butter and on a toasted roll—plenty of devotees consider this the only legit kind of lobster roll.

Easy portability is one of best attributes of a lobster roll, but throughout coastal Maine, at sit-down restaurants and even barebones shanties with weathered picnic tables, diners seeking a more leisurely, communal repast often prefer to order traditional lobster dinners. These full-scale feasts consist of fresh boiled lobster

served still in the shell, and thus requiring that you invest a little sweat equity into your meal: you'll be given sturdy leg-cracking utensils and tiny picking forks to surgically (or with reckless abandon, depending on your style) remove the tender bits from the knuckle, tail, big claw, and walking legs of your lobster. It can be a messy undertaking, hence the donning of lobster bibs.

Thankfully, many restaurants provide an alternate option to all this hard work: the so-called lazy lobster, consisting of all of that sweet claw and tail meat already picked from the shell and then sautéed in butter and served ready-to-devour. Either version comes with plenty of drawn butter, along with a rich assortment of sides—usually seafood chowder (or bisque), steamed clams, baked potato or fries, corn on the cob, and maybe coleslaw or potato salad.

In recent years lobster has begun appearing on menus in countless other formats: served atop or in salads, BLT sandwiches, pot pies, ravioli, mac and cheese, pizza, and various casseroles that you've probably already seen or maybe eaten yourself, even at restaurants well outside of New England. More unusual variations on the theme include lobster corn dogs, ramen, bao, banh mi, and—we're truly not sure what to think about this one—ice cream.

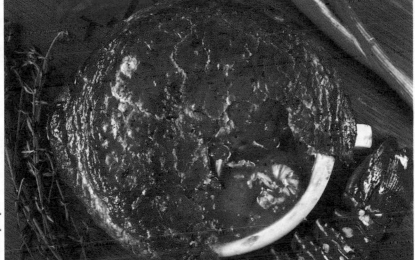

Lobster pot pie

When in Maine, and when staying in accommodations with kitchens (or even just outdoor grills), preparing lobster for yourself and ideally a group of family and friends presents the opportunity for a delicious culinary adventure. You can buy live lobster from countless seafood markets, and if you're new at preparing this dish, staff at these places are usually happy to provide instructions or at least give you a few pointers.

The most popular preparations are steaming and boiling (for which you'll need a pot of at least 3 quarts for every 2 pounds of lobster) and grilling. Boiling and steaming require a bit less work and take only about 12 to 15 minutes to produce a delicious pink crustacean ready to dig into. If you have access to fresh seawater, use that for boiling; otherwise, use very well-salted water to help preserve that fresh-from-the-sea flavor. Adherents of grilling prefer the slightly smoky, earthy flavor that the process imparts—but you'll need to kill your lobster first, and overcooking it can lead to tough, chewy meat, so take care. Allow about 12 minutes to grill a 2-pound lobster on a typical grill.

Whether you're just back from your trip and need to curb those seafood cravings or want to share your newfound love of lobster with someone back home, ordering fresh shellfish from Maine is easier than you might imagine. You can shop online from a number of reliable companies that will ship your delicious lobster—along with oysters, scallops, clams, crab, and cod—directly to your doorstep. **Maine Seafood** (⊕ *seafoodfrom-maine.com*) is your one-stop resource for finding a place to get the freshest Maine seafood to your table—they list nearly 40 online vendors. **Get Maine Lobster** (⊕ *getmainelobster. com*) and **The Lobster Guy** (⊕ *thelobsterguy.com*) are also popular mail-order options. The cost varies considerably, with some companies charging more for shipping but less for the product (generally a better choice for larger orders) and others charging little or nothing to ship orders over a certain amount but higher prices for the product itself. In general, for four live lobsters shipped overnight across the country, expect to pay around $150 to $200.

Maine's Best Beaches

FOOTBRIDGE BEACH, OGUNQUIT
This spot offers excellent swimming, beach combing, and bodysurfing opportunities, as well as a boat launch for kayaks, small boats, and standup paddleboards. Typically less crowded than Ogunquit Beach, it's reached by crossing a footbridge that runs over the Ogunquit River. *(Ch. 3)*

ROQUE BLUFFS STATE PARK, ROQUE BLUFFS
Largely sandy, with some pebbly spots thrown in for good measure, this ½-mile crescent beach offers bracing Atlantic Ocean swims as well as temperate dips in a 60-acre pond that backs up to the beach. *(Ch. 10)*

GOOSE ROCKS BEACH, KENNEBUNKPORT
A wildly popular beach in warmer months, Goose Rocks Beach is treasured for its long stretch of clean sand and close proximity to town. Parking can be tough and permits are required, but it's well worth the headache to get up early and snatch a spot. *(Ch. 3)*

JASPER BEACH, MACHIASPORT
Named after the many deep red pebbles scattered across its shore, this pocket beach tucked away in Howard Cove is definitely off the beaten path. Beach combers come to seek out the rare jasper stones among the equally red, volcanic rhyolite pebbles, while those seeking solitude find it in the salt marsh and fresh and saltwater lagoons. *(Ch. 10)*

SAND BEACH, ACADIA NATIONAL PARK
What this sandy beach lacks in size it's well compensated for by its commanding view of the mountains and craggy shores that draw millions of people to Mount Desert Island each year. Several trailheads dot the beach and lead up the surrounding cliffs, where you'll be rewarded with spectacular panoramas of the shore and beach below. *(Ch. 8)*

MOWRY BEACH, LUBEC
On the U.S.-Canadian border, this majestic beach has dramatic tides that produce excellent clamming conditions and superb beach runs at low tide. A small boardwalk leads out to the shore from where you can spy Lubec's famous lighthouse, as well as its Canadian neighbors. *(Ch. 10)*

REID STATE PARK, GEORGETOWN
One of the Pine Tree State's rare sandy beaches, Reid State Park is a surfer's and sunbather's paradise. Rarely crowded, even in summer, the beach stretches 1½ miles along the Atlantic, with large sand

Sand Beach, Acadia National Park

dunes and essential nesting areas for some of the state's endangered birds. *(Ch. 5)*

CRESCENT BEACH, CAPE ELIZABETH

This mile-long half-moon-shape swatch of sand has some of the state's warmest ocean currents, making it a favorite for swimming. *(Ch. 3)*

POPHAM BEACH, PHIPPSBURG

On a rugged peninsula just south of Bath, this hugely popular beach park is a great option for just about every shore activity: beachcombing, sunbathing, swimming, surf-casting, picnicking, kayaking, and even surfing. *(Ch. 5)*

OLD ORCHARD BEACH, OLD ORCHARD

Founded in the 1880s, Old Orchard Beach has been the state's premier family-resort destination for generations. Amusement parks, minigolf, midway games, and souvenir stands line the boardwalk and pier, and 7 miles of sandy oceanfront area popular for swimming and socializing. *(Ch. 3)*

BIRCH POINT STATE PARK, OWLS HEAD

Located near the mouth of West Penobscot Bay, this crescent-shaped beach is well-sheltered from the wind and tends to have a mild surf well-suited to swimming and tidepooling. *(Ch. 6)*

PEMAQUID BEACH, NEW HARBOR

Pemaquid Beach is a draw for families and couples looking for a quintessential beach day complete with an umbrella, sand bucket, and ice cream, all of which can be rented or purchased from the kiosk near the changing facilities and community center. *(Ch. 5)*

Stay in a Maine Lighthouse

Little River Lighthouse

Ever wondered what it would be like to stay at one of Maine's 65 lighthouses? Well, you're in luck because the following seven Maine lighthouses offer guests the unique opportunity to spend the night. *See the feature on Maine's Lighthouses at the end of this chapter for more lighthouse information.*

BURNT COAT HARBOR LIGHT STATION
Situated on the south shore of Swan's Island—a 6-mile ferry ride from Mount Desert Island—this 35-foot-tall white tower features a fairly spacious apartment in its red-roofed 1872 keeper's house, which is available on a weekly basis from June through October. ⊕ *burntcoatharborlight.com.*

GOOSE ROCKS LIGHTHOUSE
Make a minimum $600 donation to the nonprofit Beacon Preservation organization and you can spend the night at this 1890 sparkplug lighthouse with a dramatic offshore setting at the eastern entrance to the Fox Islands in Penobscot Bay. You enter this cast-iron structure's elegantly appointed

Seguin Island Lighthouse

accommodations (sleeps six) via a ladder. ⊕ *beaconpreservation.org*.

LITTLE RIVER LIGHTHOUSE
Located on an otherwise uninhabited 15-acre island at the mouth of a river in Coulter, less than 20 miles from the Canadian border, this iron tower affords sweeping sea vistas. Accommodations are in a cheerfully restored 1888 keeper's house with three guest rooms and a fully equipped kitchen. ⊕ *littleriverlight.org*.

PEMAQUID POINT LIGHTHOUSE
This nearly 200-year-old 80-foot brick cylinder lies at the tip of Pemaquid Neck. A popular attraction for day visitors, it's a great choice if you want relatively easy access to a quaint maritime village with restaurants

and galleries. Overnight stays are by the week in a one-bedroom suite on the second floor of the adjacent keeper's house. ⊕ *bristolmaine.org*.

SEGUIN ISLAND LIGHTHOUSE
Perched at the tip of a small island at the mouth of the Kennebec River, this cylindrical stone tower rises 52 feet above an already high headland. It's a short ferry ride from Phippsburg, and guest quarters in the keeper's house have two bedrooms and basic kitchen facilities. Camping is also permitted at the base of the lighthouse. ⊕ *seguinisland.org*.

WEST QUODDY STATION
Within walking distance of West Quoddy Lighthouse and Quoddy State Park, this complex of historic buildings—the original Station House, the Crews

Quarters, the Keepers Cottage, and the Meeting House—has been adapted into attractively furnished vacation homes that sleep four to nine guests. ⊕ *quoddyvacation.com*.

WHITEHEAD LIGHT STATION
This seven-bedroom keeper's house on 11 tranquil, wooded acres sits on secluded Whitehead Island, at the western mouth of West Penobscot Bay. It's an ideal haven for large groups and families, available by the week from June through October, and the house has a kitchen and extensive common spaces. Rates include transportation to the island in one of the station's boats. ⊕ *www.whiteheadlightstation.org*.

Maine with Kids

Coastal Maine—from small waterfront villages to bustling larger towns and even Portland—are hugely popular, especially in summer, with families. You'll have no problem finding reasonably priced, kid-friendly hotels and family-style restaurants, as well as museums, beaches, parks, and lighthouses. Many resorts offer lively children's programs, and farms that welcome overnight guests can also be great fun for children. Beach cottages, apartments, and family suites also abound. These can be especially economical, because most have kitchens—saving you the expense of restaurant dining for some or all meals.

ACADIA NATIONAL PARK, MOUNT DESERT ISLAND

Head out on a whale- and puffin-watching trip from Bar Harbor, drive up scenic Cadillac Mountain, swim at Echo Lake Beach, hike one of the many easy, novice-friendly trails. However you and your kids work up an appetite, don't forget to sample some wild blueberry pie.

MAINE NARROW GAUGE RAILROAD MUSEUM, PORTLAND

Fans of vintage trains embark on one of the scenic rides offered on these narrow-gauge trains. Ice Cream Trains offer a sweet adventure on certain Friday nights during the warmer months, and in the winter, kids can ride the *Polar Express*.

COASTAL MAINE BOTANICAL GARDENS, BOOTHBAY

This entire 295-acre wonderland of flora and fragrant flowers offers plenty to see and do for all ages, but the beautifully designed Children's Garden is an absolute must, with a treehouse, play cottage, story barn, and more. In the area, families also enjoy the Boothbay Railway Village and Maine State Aquarium.

SEA DOGS BASEBALL GAMES, PORTLAND

See the next David Ortiz or Dustin Pedroia while attending a minor league baseball game at Hadlock Field. The AA affiliate of the Boston Red Sox plays at this festive, kid-friendly ball field that even features a 37-foot-tall replica of Fenway Park's Green Monster.

OWLS HEAD TRANSPORTATION MUSEUM, OWLS HEAD

In the rural coastal community of Owls Head, just south of bustling Rockland, kids love checking out the colorful collection of carefully restored antique planes, cars, and even bicycles—the 1926 Ford Model T Snowmobile is a favorite.

FUNTOWN SPLASHTOWN USA, SACO

On warm summer days, kids of all ages can cool off and play for hours amid the thrill adventures, kiddie rides, waterslides, and play pools at this legendary amusement park on U.S. 1 in Saco.

PORTLAND FIRE ENGINE CO. TOURS, PORTLAND

These 50-minute narrated tours of Maine's largest city take place in a bright-red antique fire engine. Knowledgeable guides describe the local sights, and a large-screen TV on board shows photos of what Portland looked like generations ago.

MAINE MARITIME MUSEUM, BATH

At this historic 20-acre campus that preserves one of the East Coast's most important and historic shipyards, you can tour and even sail on a 1906 schooner, watch boatbuilders constructing vessels, view meticulously crafted ships' models, and take a nature or lighthouse cruise on the Kennebec River.

THE MAILBOAT RUN, CASCO BAY

Hop aboard this laid-back and scenic 2½- to 3½-hour cruise around Casco Bay. The world's long-running daily maritime mail service offers a unique perspective on Portland's working harbor and the bay's largest islands.

LIGHTHOUSE TOURS

Dozens of the state's iconic lighthouses dot the coast, and many of these are open for tours, typically in summer. Favorites in which you can climb to the top for sweeping water views include Wood Island Lighthouse in Saco Bay, Bug Light in South Portland, and Goat Island Lighthouse off the coast of Kennebunkport.

CHILDREN'S MUSEUM & THEATRE OF MAINE, PORTLAND

Attend a play at the nation's oldest continuously operating children's theater, or explore the imaginative exhibits at this state-of-the-art museum in Portland's West End. In winter, combine your visit with skating at the Rink at Thompson's Point, across the street.

BEST FAMILY-FRIENDLY LODGING OPTIONS

Cliff House, Cape Neddick *(Ch. 3)*

Stage Neck Inn, York Harbor *(Ch. 3)*

The Nonantum Resort, Kennebunkport *(Ch. 3)*

Black Point Inn, Scarborough *(Ch. 3)*

Higgins Beach Inn, Scarborough *(Ch. 3)*

The Press Hotel, Portland *(Ch. 4)*

The Inn on Carleton, Portland *(Ch. 4)*

Canopy by Hilton Portland Waterfront, Portland *(Ch. 4)*

Harraseeket Inn, Freeport *(Ch. 5)*

Sebasco Harbor Resort, Phippsburg *(Ch. 5)*

Cod Cove Inn, Edgecomb *(Ch. 5)*

Linekin Bay Resort, Boothbay Harbor *(Ch. 5)*

Spruce Point Inn, Boothbay Harbor *(Ch. 5)*

Newcastle Inn, Newcastle *(Ch. 5)*

The Tipsy Butler Bed and Breakfast, Newcastle *(Ch. 5)*

The Country Inn at Camden Rockport *(Ch. 6)*

Samoset Resort, Rockport *(Ch. 6)*

Lord Camden Inn, Camden *(Ch. 6)*

Whitehall, Camden *(Ch. 6)*

Lincolnville Motel, Lincolnville *(Ch. 6)*

Belfast Harbor Inn, Belfast *(Ch. 6)*

Fireside Inn & Suites, Belfast *(Ch. 6)*

The Castine Cottages, Castine *(Ch. 7)*

The Castine Inn, Castine *(Ch. 7)*

Under Canvas, Surry *(Ch. 7)*

The Oakland House Seaside Resort, Brooksville *(Ch. 7)*

Bar Harbor Grand Hotel, Bar Harbor *(Ch. 9)*

Harborside Hotel, Spa & Marina, Bar Harbor *(Ch. 9)*

Inn on Mount Desert, Bar Harbor *(Ch. 9)*

Salt Cottages, Hulls Cove *(Ch. 9)*

Terramor Outdoor Resort, Bar Harbor *(Ch. 9)*

Acadia Oceanside, Prospect Harbor *(Ch. 9)*

Pleasant Bay Bed & Breakfast, Addison *(Ch. 10)*

West Quoddy Station, Lubec *(Ch. 10)*

What to Read and Watch

IT BY STEPHEN KING

You won't find Derry, Maine on any map, but you can visit it via a number of chilling tales courtesy of horror writer Stephen King, including his 1986 novel *It*, which follows a group of friends who try to kill a monster that terrorizes their town. Note that the popular '90s TV miniseries and 2017 film were filmed outside of Maine, as have been most of film and TV adaptations of King's books, but the original (1989) *Pet Sematary* is the rare exception—it was shot in Ellsworth, Bangor, and Mount Desert Island.

CAROUSEL

One of the earliest major movies shot on location in Maine (in this case mostly in Boothbay Harbor), this lauded Rodgers and Hammerstein musical centers on the budding romance between a carousel barker (Gordan MacRae) and a mill worker (Shirley Jones). Filmed in 1956 in brilliant CinemaScope and featuring a haunting, memorable score, *Carousel* is often named among the greatest classic musicals.

LOBSTERMAN BY DAHLOV IPCAR

Dahlov Ipcar, who died at the age of 99 in 2017, is best remembered as a writer and illustrator of children's books, many of which took place in her home state of Maine. One such classic is *Lobsterman,* which portrays the day in the life of a lobsterman and his son as they work along the coast of Maine.

THE CIDER HOUSE RULES BY JOHN IRVING

This 1985 novel by John Irving was set in 1940s Maine, and the 1999 adaptation was filmed partly in Maine (along with New Hampshire, Vermont, and Massachusetts) and stars Kathy Baker, Michael Caine, and Tobey Maguire. The poignant and often funny saga depicts the father-son-like relationship that emerges between an orphan (Maguire), and the orphanage's doctor (Caine), who takes him under his wing.

EMPIRE FALLS BY RICHARD RUSSO

This Pulitzer Prize–winning 2001 novel is set in the fictional town for which it's named and likely modeled after some of interior Maine's hardscrabble mill communities. Russo's knack for handling both romance and tragedy with both empathy and comic wit shines through. The well-received 2005 TV miniseries—starring Ed Harris, Philip Seymour Hoffman, Helen Hunt, and Paul Newman—was shot in both on the coast (Ogunquit, Kennebunkport, Lincolnville) and a bit inland in Skowhegan, Waterville, Augusta, and elsewhere.

MISS RUMPHIUS BY BARBARA COONEY

The winner of two Caldecott Medals, Barbara Cooney authored and illustrated more than 100 children's books during her prolific career. She died in Damariscotta in 2000, where she had lived most of her adult life and set many of her tales, including *Miss Rumphius,* which earned her a National Book Award in 1983. Cooney based the book on a real-life figure, Hilda Hamlin, who planted colorful blue and purple lupines up and down the Maine coast.

IN THE BEDROOM

Adapted in 2001 into a critically acclaimed independent film from a short story called *Killings,* this emotionally taut and wrenching drama centers on a family tragedy set and filmed in and around Camden. It was nominated for five Oscars, including Best Picture, Best Actor (Tom Wilkinson), Best Actress (Sissy Spacek), and Best Supporting Actress (Marisa Tomei).

OLIVE KITTERIDGE BY ELIZABETH STROUT

Perhaps the most lauded of several contemporary novels by Portland-based novelist and short-story writer Elizabeth Strout, this Pulitzer Prize winner from 2008 is told through 13 short stories set in the fictional Maine college town of Crosby (which is said to be based on Brunswick), and the narrative is focused heavily on the eponymous lead character as well as her family and others in this small community. The HBO miniseries, starring Frances McDormand and Richard Jenkins, was filmed in 2014 in Massachusetts.

SALT & WATER

There are a number of podcasts recorded in Maine and touching on different aspects of the state, from the University of Maine's "Greater Good" to "From the Woodshed," which is based on the interior Maine reality TV stars of *Maine Cabin Masters*. Produced by the local cultural and heritage organization Experience Maritime Maine, "Salt & Water" is a six-part series of audio stories that shine a light on the people and places of Coastal Maine, from the female lobster fishers of Stonington to boatbuilders of Bath.

JUMANJI

This crowd-pleasing 1996 family adventure film starring Robin Williams, Bonnie Hunt, and a 12-year-old Kirsten Dunst was shot primarily in New Hampshire and Maine. Filming locations in the latter include Kennebunk and the Olde Woolen Mill in North Berwick.

MAINE'S LIGHTHOUSES

GUARDIANS OF THE COAST

By John Blodgett

Perched high on rocky ledges, on the tips of wayward islands, and sometimes seemingly on the ocean itself are the more than five dozen lighthouses standing watch along Maine's craggy and ship-busting coastline.

Marshall Point Light

LIGHTING THE WAY: A BIT OF HISTORY

Portland Head Light

Most lighthouses were built in the first half of the 19th century to protect vessels from running aground at night or when the shoreline was shrouded in fog. Along with the mournful siren of the foghorn and maritime lore, these practical structures have come to symbolize Maine throughout the world.

SHIPWRECKS AND SAFETY

These alluring sentinels of the eastern seaboard today have more form than function, but that certainly was not always the case. Safety was a strong motivating factor in the erection of the lighthouses. Commerce also played a critical role. For example, in 1791 Portland Head Light was completed, partially as a response to local merchants' concerns about the rocky entrance to Portland Harbor and the varying depths of the shipping channel. In 1789, the federal government created the U.S. Lighthouse Establishment (later the U.S. Lighthouse Service) to manage them. In 1939 the U.S. Coast Guard took on the job.

Maine's lighthouses were built in much-needed locations, but the points and islands upon which they sat were prone to storm damage. Along with poor construction, this meant that over the years many lighthouses had to be rebuilt or replaced.

LIGHTHOUSES TODAY

In modern times, many of the structures still serve a purpose. Technological advances, such as GPS and radar, are mainly used to navigate through the choppy waters, but a lighthouse or its foghorns are helpful secondary aids, and sometimes the only ones used by recreational boaters. The numerous channel-marking buoys still in existence also are testament to the old tried-and-true methods.

Of the 66 lighthouses along this far northeastern state, 57 are still working, alerting ships (and even small aircraft) of the shoreline's rocky edge. Government agencies, historic preservation organizations, and mostly private individuals own the decomissioned lights.

KEEPERS OF THE LIGHT

Some keepers also used bells and sirens, like this Fog Signal Station on Manana Island in 1898.

Pemaquid Point's fourth-order Fresnel lens

LIFE OF A LIGHTKEEPER

One thing that has changed with the modern era is the disappearance of the lighthouse keeper. In the early 20th century, lighthouses began the conversion from oil-based lighting to electricity. A few decades later, the U.S. Coast Guard switched to automation, phasing out the need for an on-site keeper.

While the keepers of tradition were no longer needed, the traditions of these stalwart, 24/7 employees live on through museum exhibits and retellings of Maine's maritime history, legends, and lore. The tales of a lighthouse keeper's life are the stuff romance novels are made of: adventure, rugged but lonely men, and a beautiful setting along an unpredictable coastline.

The lighthouse keepers of yesterday probably didn't see their own lives so romantically. Their daily narrative was one of hard work and, in some cases, exceptional solitude. A keeper's primary job was to ensure that the lamp was illuminated all day, every day. This meant that oil (whale or coal oil and later kerosene) had to be carried about and wicks trimmed on a regular basis. When fog shrouded the coast, they sounded the solemn horn to pierce through the damp darkness that hid their light. Their quarters were generally small and often attached to the light tower itself. The remote locations of the lights added to the isolation a keeper felt, especially before the advent of radio and telephone, let alone the Internet. Though some brought families with them, the keepers tended to be men who lived alone.

THE LIGHTS 101

Over the years, Fresnel (fray-NELL) lenses were developed in different shapes and sizes so that ship captains could distinguish one lighthouse from another. Invented by Frenchman Augustin Fresnel in the early 19th century, the lens design allows for a greater transmission of light perfectly suited for lighthouse use. Knowing which lighthouse they were near helped captains know which danger was present, such as a submerged ledge or shallow channel. Some lights, such as those at Seguin Island Light, are fixed and don't flash. Other lights are colored red.

DID YOU KNOW?

A lighthouse's personality shines through its flash pattern. For example, Bass Harbor Light (pictured) is on for three seconds, off for one second. Some lights, such as Seguin Island Light, are fixed and don't flash.

LIGHTHOUSE FINDER

Map labels:
Lubec, West Quoddy Head, Machias, Little River Lighthouse, Jonesport, Narraguagus, Prospect Harbor, Winter Harbor, Ellsworth, Old Town, Bangor, Newport, Farmington, 95, Fort Point, Searsport, Dyces Head, Belfast, Castine, Bar Harbor, Mt. Desert Is., Bass Harbor Head, Burnt Coat Harbor, AUGUSTA, Grindle Point, Camden, Goose Rocks Light, Rockland Breakwater, Rockland, Owls Head, Browns Head, Isle au Haut, Auburn, Lewiston, Harrison, Brunswick, Pemaquid Point, Marshall Point, Matinicus Rock, Freeport, Bath, Boothbay, The Cuckolds, Pond Island, Portland Head, Seguin, Monhegan Is., Portland, Cape Elizabeth (Two Lights), Goat Island, Kennebunk, Kennebunkport, Ogunquit, York, Cape Neddick (Nubble Light), Whaleback, Kittery, Portsmouth

KEY

🗼 Top Picks

West Quoddy Head

VISITING MAINE'S LIGHTHOUSES

As you travel along the Maine Coast, you won't see lighthouses by watching your odometer—there were no rules about the spacing of lighthouses. The decision as to where to place a lighthouse was a balance between a region's geography and its commercial prosperity and maritime traffic.

Lighthouses dot the shore from as far south as York to the country's easternmost tip at Lubec. Accessibility varies according to location and other factors. A handful are so remote as to be outright impossible to reach (except perhaps by kayaking and rock climbing). Some don't allow visitors according to Coast Guard policies, though you can enjoy them through the zoom lens of a camera. Others you can walk right up to and, occasionally, even climb to the top. Lighthouse enthusiasts and preservation groups restore and maintain many of them. All told, approximately 30 lighthouses allow some sort of public access.

SEEK OUT STATE PARKS

■ **TIP→ To get the full lighthouse experience your best bet is to visit one that is part of a state or local park.** These are generally well kept and tend to allow up-close approach, though typically only outside. While you're at the parks you can picnic or stroll on the trails. Wildlife is often abundant in and near the water; you might spot sea birds and even whales in certain locations (try West Quoddy Head, Portland Head, or Two Lights).

MUSEUMS, TOURS, AND MORE

Most keeper's quarters are closed to the public, but some of the homes have been converted to museums, full of intriguing exhibits on lighthouses, the famous Fresnel lenses used in them, and artifacts of Maine maritime life in general. Talk to the librarians at the **Maine Maritime Museum** in Bath (⊕ www.mainemaritimemuseum. org) or sign up for one of the museum's daily lighthouse cruises to pass by up to ten on the Lighthouse Lovers Cruise. In Rockland, the **Maine Lighthouse Museum** (⊕ www.mainelighthousemuseum.org) has the country's largest display of Fresnel lenses. The museum also displays keepers' memorabilia, foghorns, brassware, and more. Maine Open Lighthouse Day is the second Saturday after Labor Day; you can tour and even climb about two dozen lights usually closed to the public.

For more information, check out the lighthouse page at Maine's official tourism site: ⊕ visitmaine.com.

SLEEPING LIGHT: STAYING OVERNIGHT

Goose Rocks, where you can play lighthouse keeper for a week.

Want to stay overnight in a lighthouse? There are several options to do so. ■ **TIP→ Book lighthouse lodgings as far in advance as possible, up to one year ahead.**

Our top pick is **Pemaquid Point Light** (*L. Dewey Chase Rentals* ☎ 207/677-2100 ⊕ *newharborrentals.com*) because it has one of the most dramatic settings on the Maine coast. Two miles south of **New Harbor**, the second floor of the lighthouse keeper's house is rented out on a weekly basis early May through mid-November to support upkeep of the grounds. When you aren't enjoying the interior, head outdoors: the covered front porch has a rocking-chair view of the ocean. The one-bedroom, one-bath rental sleeps up to a family of four.

Situated smack dab in the middle of a major maritime thoroughfare between two Penobscot Bay islands, **Goose Rocks Light** (☎ 203/400-9565 ⊕ *www. beaconpreservation.org*) offers lodging for the adventuresome—the 51-foot "spark plug" lighthouse is completely surrounded bywater. Getting there requires a ferry ride from Rockland to nearby **North Haven**, a 5- to 10-minute ride by motorboat, and then a climb up an iron-rung ladder from the pitching boat—all based on high tide and winds, of course. There's room for up to six people. It's a bit more cushy experience than it was for the original keepers: there's a flat-screen TV with DVD player and a selection of music and videos for entertainment. In addition, a hammock hangs on the small deck that encircles the operational light; it's a great place from which to watch the majestic windjammers and the fishing fleet pass by.

Little River Lighthouse (☎ 877/276-4682 ⊕ *www.littleriverlight.org*), along the far northeastern reaches of the coast in **Cutler**, has three rooms available for rent from mid-June to September. You're responsible for food and beverages, linens, towels, and other personal items (don't forget the bug spray), but kitchen and other basics are provided. The lighthouse volunteers with Friends of Little River Lighthouse will provide a boat ride to the island upon which the lighthouse sits.

TOP LIGHTHOUSES TO VISIT

BASS HARBOR LIGHT

Familiar to many as the subject of countless photographs is Bass Harbor Light, at the southern end of **Mount Desert Island.** It is within Acadia National Park and 17 miles from the town of Bar Harbor. The station grounds are open year-round.

CAPE ELIZABETH LIGHT

Two Lights State Park is so-named because it's next to two lighthouses. Both of these **Cape Elizabeth** structures were built in 1828. The western light was closed in 1924 and eventually converted into a private residence; the eastern light, Cape Elizabeth Light, still projects its automated cylinder of light. The grounds surrounding the building and the lighthouse itself are closed to the public, but the structure is easily viewed and photographed from nearby at the end of Two Lights Road.

Cape Neddick

CAPE NEDDICK LIGHT

More commonly known as Nubble Light for the smallish offshore expanse of rock it rests upon, Cape Neddick Light sits a few hundred feet off a rock point in **York Beach.** With such a precarious location, its grounds are inaccessible to visitors, but close enough to be exceptionally photogenic, especially during the Christmas season.

MONHEGAN ISLAND LIGHT

Only the adventuresome and the artistic see this light, because **Monhegan Island** is accessible by an approximately one-hour ferry ride. To reach the lighthouse, you have an additional half-mile walk uphill from the ferry dock. The former keeper's quarters is home to the Monhegan Museum, which has exhibits about the island. The tower itself is closed to the public.

Portland Head

PORTLAND HEAD LIGHT

One of Maine's most photographed lighthouses (and its oldest), the famous Portland Head Light was completed in January 1791. At the edge of Fort Williams Park, in **Cape Elizabeth**, the towering white stone lighthouse stands 101 feet above the sea. The Coast Guard operates it and it is not open for tours. However the adjacent keeper's dwelling is now a museum.

WEST QUODDY HEAD LIGHT

Originally built in 1808 by mandate of President Thomas Jefferson, West Quoddy Head Light sits in **Lubec** on the easternmost tip of land in the mainland United States. The 49-foot-high lighthouse with distinctive red and white stripes, is part of Quoddy Head State Park.

West Quoddy Head

Chapter 2

TRAVEL SMART

Updated by
Andrew Collins

★ **CAPITAL:**
Augusta

♁ **POPULATION:**
1.381 million

💬 **LANGUAGE:**
English

$ **CURRENCY:**
U.S. Dollar

☎ **AREA CODE:**
207

⚠ **EMERGENCIES:**
911

🚌 **DRIVING:**
On the right

⚡ **ELECTRICITY:**
120–240 v/60 cycles;
plugs have two or three
rectangular prongs

🕐 **TIME:**
Eastern Time (same as New
York)

🌐 **WEB RESOURCES:**
visitmaine.com;
www.mainetourism.com

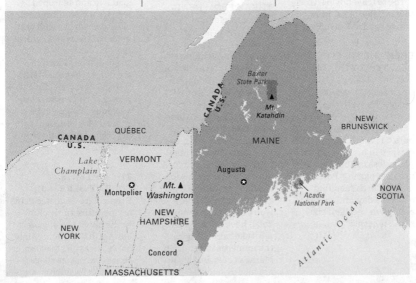

Know Before You Go

Maine has its fair share of regional character, color, and flavor—not to mention a few geographical and seasonal challenges. Here are some tips that will enrich your trip and ease your travels.

IT'S WICKED GOOD TO LEARN SOME LINGO

To avoid seeming like a chowdah-head (aka chowder head, aka idiot), brush up on some basic dialect. Want a big, long sandwich? Order a grinder, not a sub or a hero, and wash it down with a frappe or a tonic, not a milk shake or soda. At the hotel, grab the clickah (clicker) to change the TV station. At the supermarket, grab a carriage to shop for picnic sundries. If people direct you to a rotary, they mean traffic circle. And, even if you're traveling north toward, say, Bar Harbor, you're headed Down East.

EVEN THE BIG CITY IS RELATIVELY SMALL

Portland, Maine's biggest city, has 66,218 people. Despite its small size, it has a thriving cultural scene; amazing restaurants and bars; a few colleges; and it's steeped in history. Even if you're less inclined toward urban exploring, Portland is well worth spending at least a day, and there's enough to keep you busy here for several.

SMALL TOWNS RULE

You might have to dig a little deeper to sightsee along some parts of the Maine Coast, but it's worth the effort. Most villages have a Victorian- or Revolutionary-era homestead or site, small museum or historical society, and time-honored tavern or country store. Photo-worthy commons (open spaces once used for grazing livestock and around which towns were built) can be found in many small towns.

YOU CAN'T ALWAYS GET THEAH FROM HEAH

The shortest distance between two points isn't always a straight—or single—line. Finding the real Maine means driving (and getting lost on) its scenic byways. And GPS and cell-phone service can be spotty, especially on islands and some of the more bucolic peninsulas, so bring a physical map or save maps on your cell phone so that you're able to access them offline. There are a few places where you won't need a car, though. You'll have to take a ferry—few take cars—to access the numerous islands off Maine's coast, but most are bike-friendly so plan

accordingly. In Acadia National Park, other than driving along the main park road, you'll want to trade your car for hiking boots, a bike, or a carriage (an actual horse and buggy, not a shopping cart).

THE BEST FOOD IS FRESH AND LOCAL

Field-or-fishing-boat-to-table is the norm, with abundant local produce and seafood that includes lobster; quahogs or other clams; bay or sea scallops; rock or Jonah crabs; and pollack, hake, haddock, or cod (the latter two might appear on local menus as "scrod"). Lobster-roll meat is lightly dressed in mayonnaise; though you may also find it (many prefer it this way) drizzled with melted butter. Chowder is creamy and may contain bacon. Blueberries reign supreme and maple syrup adorns shaved ice (or snow!) and ice cream as well as pancakes; breakfast home fries are griddled and seasoned just so; and craft beer and cider pair just as well with boiled dinners and Yankee pot roast as they do with the delicious and often creatively prepared farm-to-table fare you'll find at plenty of restaurants up and down the coast. Be sure to try a Moxie, an "energizing," regionally unique tonic (aka soda).

THE WATER IS COLD UP HERE

Even in late August, ocean temperatures only climb to the upper 50s or lower 60s—still limb-numbingly chilly. Wet suits (and water shoes for rockier shores) are musts for surfing and standup paddleboarding. Obviously, the farther north you go, the shorter the beach season, with some properties reducing their hours or shuttering entirely between Labor Day and Memorial Day or July 4. The lakes may be a bit warmer with water temps hovering around the 70s, but once the sun goes down, it gets wicked chilly.

SOME OF THE FLIES BITE

First, it's the black flies, whose bites leave red, itchy welts. The season, which is particularly notorious in Maine, generally lasts three or four weeks and occurs in May or June—generally earlier the farther south you are. Then, in July, it's the deer flies. Summer also sees greenhead flies (aka saltmarsh greenheads) in some coastal areas. And how could we forget Maine's state bird—the mosquito? Keep insect repellent handy and spray liberally in the evening, especially when the sun begins to set. And don't forget to check for ticks.

YOU MIGHT SEE CANADA FROM YOUR HOTEL!

If you're so much as toying with the idea of traveling as far as Bar Harbor, definitely bring your passport, just in case you decide to venture into Canada. The province of New Brunswick is just across the border from the Maine villages of Lubec and Eastport. It's a fun and easy day trip—especially Campobello Island, St. Andrews, and Saint John. And there's high-speed ferry service from Bar Harbor to Yarmouth, Nova Scotia.

KNOW THE DO'S AND DON'TS OF BUYING CANNABIS

As with every other New England state except for New Hampshire, if you're age 21 or older you can purchase cannabis—in smoking and in edible forms—for recreational use in Maine. If you're wishing to partake recreationally, do buy only from a dispensary licensed to sell adult-use cannabis (some dispensaries are only licensed to sell medical cannabis, for which you'll need a prescription). Legally, you can only use cannabis on private property, not in public places, parks, restaurants, and other businesses. And do not leave Maine with cannabis products—recreational or medical—in your possession. Doing so is illegal and could land you in serious trouble.

WHEN IT COMES TO DRESS, LAYERS ARE BEST

The principal rule of weather in New England is that there are no rules. A cold, foggy spring morning often transitions to a bright, warm afternoon. A summer breeze can suddenly turn chilly, and rain can appear with little warning. Even in summer, be prepared for weather extremes along the coast, and sea spray can make things cool, too. Thus, the best advice on how to dress is to layer your clothing, peeling off or adding garments as needed. Bring long pants, a sweater or two, and a light jacket. A hat, sunscreen, a waterproof windbreaker or raincoat, and an umbrella should also be on your packing list. Dress in restaurants is generally casual, except at a handful of fancier coastal Maine restaurants, where sportier attire is expected. Casual sportswear—walking shoes and jeans or khakis—will take you almost everywhere, but swimsuits and bare feet will not.

IN THE LAND OF THE COUNTRY INN, IT'S BEST TO BOOK AHEAD

Although there are abundant chain hotels and several large, notable Victorians—seaside and near the slopes—smaller inns, often historical and privately owned, are among the best lodgings. Although the growth of Airbnb has made it easier to find rooms in charming old homes, it's still prudent to book well ahead, especially during peak seasons, when there might also be a two- or three-night minimum. And "peak seasons" vary. Leaf-peeping season is roughly late September to mid-October in Maine. In the ski areas, the season runs from November through April or even May.

NO SMOKING IN MAINE

Smoking (including electronic smoking devices such as electronic cigarettes and vaporizers) is banned in all indoor areas of workplaces, restaurants, hotels, bars, theaters, and music venues. It's also prohibited in outdoor dining areas, state parks, beaches, and historical sites.

Getting Here and Around

Air

Maine has two international airports, Portland International Jetport and Bangor International Airport, near the coast. Manchester–Boston Regional Airport in New Hampshire is about 45 minutes away from the southern end of the Maine coastline. Boston's Logan Airport is the only major international airport in the region; it's about 90 minutes south of the Maine's border with New Hampshire.

Boat

A number of ferries, some seasonal and some passenger-only, operate along the coast. Maine State Ferry Service provides ferry service to the islands of Mantinicus, Vinalhaven, North Haven, Islesboro, Swans Island, and Frenchboro. You can bring your car on the ferries to Islesboro, Vinalhaven, North Haven, and Mantinicus.

The CAT is a seasonal car ferry that travels between Yarmouth, Nova Scotia, and Bar Harbor, Maine. The trip takes about 3½ hours.

Casco Bay Lines connects the city of Portland with the islands of Casco Bay.

Bus

The seasonal Shoreline Explorer trolleys link southern Maine's beach towns from the Yorks to the Kennebunks, allowing travel in this region without a car. Service was suspended in 2022 due to staffing issues, but the company expects to resume operations in June 2023.

Concord Coach Lines has express service between Portland and Boston's Logan Airport and South Station. Concord operates out of the Portland Transportation Center (✉ *100 Thompson's Point Road*).

Car

Once you're here, the best way to experience the craggy Maine Coast, with its scenic and winding country roads, is in a car. There are miles and miles of roads far from the larger towns that have no bus service, and you won't want to miss the chance to discover your own favorite ocean vista while on a scenic drive. From the New Hampshire border through Portland to Brunswick, you can greatly cut down on travel time by following the dull but efficient interstates, I–95 and I–295; note that from York to Augusta, I–95 is a toll road.

If you're flying in, all the major car-rental agencies have counters at the two major airports (Bangor and Portland). When you reserve a car, ask about the cancellation penalties, taxes, drop-off charges (for one-way rentals), and surcharges (for being under or over a certain age, for additional drivers, or for driving across state or country borders or beyond a certain mileage). If you want car seats and extras such as GPS, request them when you book.

GASOLINE

There are numerous gas stations along the Maine Coast, but in smaller locales many close at 6 or 7 PM. Irving stations are among those open 24 hours; they have a convenience store, and pride themselves on the cleanliness of their restrooms. Nearly all gas stations are self-service, and allow you to pay with a credit card at the pump.

PARKING

Outside major cities, parking along the Maine Coast is neither difficult nor expensive, with the exception of larger beach towns in Southern Maine from spring through fall. Many of the coast's smaller towns have free street parking.

In Portland metered on-street parking is available, usually with a two-hour maximum; look for pay stations or download the PassportParking app. Street parking is free 6 pm–9 am Monday through Saturday, and all day Sunday and major holidays. Parking lots and garages can be found downtown, in the Old Port, and on the waterfront.

ROAD CONDITIONS

Most principal roads in Maine are well maintained and plowed and treated in winter before things get too messy. Secondary roads are another matter; beware of potholes and frost heaves. Watch out for deer and moose on the road; the number of accidents caused by moose is astonishingly high.

U.S. 1 is a well-maintained highway, but it's only two lanes wide for much of its length and can be quite slow in southern Maine and when passing through popular destinations like Camden. You may get more quickly to a destination like Bar Harbor by taking I–95.

RULES OF THE ROAD

The speed limit on the Maine Turnpike, or interstate, is 70 mph except where posted otherwise. The speed limit on secondary roads is 35 to 55 mph.

Maine has zero tolerance for driving under the influence of alcohol—the legal limit is.08—and penalties are severe. Car radars are legal, as are right turns on a red light. Pedestrians have the right of way at all marked crossings; you have to stop for them.

Taxis and Ride Shares

Taxis and rideshares (like Lyft and Uber) are available in most coastal towns, especially those closest to Portland. They are also widely available all around Portland.

There are also water taxis to get you to and from many of the state's islands.

Train

Amtrak offers regional service from Boston to Portland via its *Downeaster* line, which originates at Boston's North Station and makes six stops in Maine: Wells, Saco, Old Orchard Beach (seasonal), Portland, Freeport, and Brunswick.

Essentials

🏃 Activities

No visit to the Maine Coast is complete without some outdoor activity—on two wheels, two feet, holding two paddles, or pulling a bag full of clubs.

If your adventures find you swimming in the ocean or floating close to its surface on a kayak, be on the lookout for sharks. Their populations have rebounded in recent years following conservation and regulatory efforts. In summer 2020, off Bailey Island, a swimming woman was killed by a great white shark in Maine's first recorded shark fatality; authorities surmised her wet suit caused her to appear to be a seal, a favored prey of sharks.

BICYCLING
Both the Bicycle Coalition of Maine and Explore Maine by Bike are excellent resources for trail maps and other riding information.

HIKING
Exploring the Maine Coast on foot is a quick way to acclimate yourself to the relaxed pace of life here—and sometimes the only way to access some of the best coastal spots. Many privately owned lands are accessible to hikers, especially Down East. Inquire with locals or at your hotel to find out about unofficial hikes that may not appear on most maps.

KAYAKING
Nothing gets you literally off the beaten path like plying the inlets and seas—and even freshwater ponds and rivers—of coastal Maine in a graceful kayak.

🍴 Dining

Many breakfast spots along the coast open as early as 6 am, or sometimes even earlier, to serve local workers, fishermen, and the like. Lunch generally runs 11–2:30; dinner is usually served 5–9, although sometimes an hour later in some larger communities, especially on Friday and Saturday night. In larger towns, you can also usually find a bar or bistro with a limited menu available late into the evening.

Many restaurants in coastal Maine are closed Monday or Tuesday, although this is less often the case in resort areas in high season. Conversely, in the off-season, quite a few restaurants shut down entirely, and others keep very limited hours. Always check ahead.

Unless otherwise noted in reviews, restaurants are open daily for lunch and dinner.

Nearly all of the region's restaurants accept credit cards, but it's good to have some cash on hand just in case.

The signature meal on the Maine Coast is, of course, the lobster dinner. It typically includes a whole steamed lobster with drawn butter for dipping, a clam or seafood chowder, corn on the cob, coleslaw, and a bib. Lobster prices can vary greatly from day to day and restaurant to restaurant, but they've generally risen steadily over the past decade. Expect a full lobster dinner with all the fixings to cost around $35–$45, and a lobster roll to cost $28–$35.

➕ Health and Safety

Lyme disease, so named for its having been first reported in the town of Lyme, Connecticut, is a potentially debilitating disease carried by deer ticks. They thrive in dry, brush-covered areas, particularly in coastal areas. Always use insect repellent: the potential for outbreaks of Lyme disease makes it imperative that you protect yourself from ticks from early spring through summer and into fall. To prevent bites, wear light-color clothing and tuck pant legs into socks. Look for black ticks about the size of a pinhead around hairlines and the warmest parts of the body. If you have been bitten, consult a physician—especially if you see the telltale bull's-eye bite pattern. Flulike symptoms often accompany a Lyme infection. Early treatment is imperative.

Maine's most annoying insect pests are black flies and mosquitoes. The former are a phenomenon of late spring and early summer and are generally a problem only in densely wooded areas of the far north. Mosquitoes, however, are a nuisance just about everywhere from spring through early autumn. The best protection against both pests is repellent containing DEET; if you're camping in the woods during black fly season, you'll also want to use fine mesh screening in eating and sleeping areas and even wear mesh headgear. One pest particular to coastal areas, especially salt marshes, is the greenhead fly, which has a nasty bite and is hard to kill. It is best repelled by a liberal application of Avon Skin So Soft or a similar product.

Coastal waters attract seafood lovers who enjoy harvesting their own clams, mussels, and even lobsters; permits are required, and casual harvesting of lobsters is strictly forbidden. Amateur clammers should be aware that New England shellfish beds are periodically visited by red tides, during which microorganisms can render shellfish poisonous. To keep abreast of the situation, inquire when you apply for a license (usually at town halls or police stations) and pay attention to red tide postings as you travel.

Rural New England is one of the country's safest regions. Observe the usual precautions in cities: avoid out-of-the-way or poorly lighted areas at night; and keep handbags close to your body and don't let them out of your sight. Keep your valuables in the hotel or room safe. When using an ATM, choose busy, well-lighted places, such as bank lobbies.

If planning to leave a car overnight to make use of off-road trails or camping facilities, use designated parking areas and don't leave any valuables in sight; cars left at trailhead parking lots are sometimes a target for theft or vandalism.

COVID-19

Most travel restrictions, including vaccination and masking requirements, have been lifted across the United States except in healthcare facilities and nursing homes. Some travelers may still wish to wear a mask in confined spaces, including on airplanes, on public transportation, and at large indoor gatherings, but that is increasingly a personal choice. Be aware that some local mandates still exist and should be followed.

Essentials

🛏 Lodging

Beachfront and roadside motels, historic homes converted to B&Bs and inns, vacation rentals and Airbnbs, and a handful of more contemporary boutique hotels make up the majority of lodging along the Maine Coast. There are a few larger luxury resorts, such as the Samoset Resort in Rockport or the Bar Harbor Inn in Bar Harbor, but it's still easy to find unfussy, comfortable, and relatively inexpensive accommodations in most towns. You will find some chain properties in larger cities and towns, such as Portland, Freeport, and Bar Harbor. Many properties close during the off-season (mid-October–mid-May); those that stay open year-round often drop their rates dramatically after high season. A 9% state lodging tax is added to all room rates.

Hotel and restaurant reviews have been shortened. For full reviews visit Fodors. com. Hotel prices are the lowest cost of a standard double room in high season. Restaurant prices are the average cost of a main course at dinner or, if dinner is not served, at lunch.

💲 Money

It costs a bit more to travel in coastal Maine than it does in the rest of the country, the most costly areas being Portland and seaside resort towns. ATMs are plentiful, and large-denomination bills (as well as credit cards) are readily accepted in tourist destinations.

Driving in Coastal Maine	Miles	Time
Boston–Portland	110 miles	2 hours
Kittery–Portland	50 miles	50 minutes
Portland–Camden	82 miles	1 hour, 45 minutes
Portland–Bar Harbor	175 miles	3 hours
Portland–Lubec	240 miles	4–5 hours

📅 When to Go

Maine's dramatic coastline and pure natural beauty is a sight to behold year-round, but note that many smaller museums and attractions are open only in high season (around Memorial Day–mid-October), as are many waterside attractions and eateries.

Summer begins in earnest on July 4, and you'll find that many smaller inns, bed-and-breakfasts, and hotels from Kittery on up to Bar Harbor are booked a month or two in advance for dates through August. That's also the case come fall, when the fiery foliage draws leaf peepers. After Halloween, lodging rates drop significantly on the coast, although many properties shut down for the season.

Contacts

Air

Bangor International Airport. (*BGR*). ⊠ *287 Godfrey Blvd.* ☎ *207/992–4600* ⊕ *www.flybangor.com.* **Boston Logan International Airport.** ☎ *800/235–6426* ⊕ *www.massport.com/ logan-airport.* **Manchester-Boston Regional Airport.** ⊠ *1 Airport Rd.* ☎ *603/624–6539* ⊕ *www. flymanchester.com.* **Portland International Jetport.** (*PWM*). ⊠ *1001 Westbrook St., Portland* ☎ *207/774–7301* ⊕ *www. portlandjetport.org.*

 Bicycling

Bicycle Coalition of Maine. ☎ *207/623–4511* ⊕ *www. bikemaine.org.* **Explore Maine by Bike.** ☎ *207/624–3300* ⊕ *www.explore-maine.org/bike.*

Boat

Casco Bay Lines. ☎ *207/774–7871* ⊕ *www. cascobaylines.com.* **The CAT.** ☎ *877/762–7245* ⊕ *www.ferries.ca/thecat.* **Maine State Ferry Service.** ☎ *207/734–6935* ⊕ *www. maine.gov/mdot/ferry.*

Bus

C&J. ☎ *603/430–1100* ⊕ *www.ridecj.com.* **Concord Coach Lines.** ☎ *800/639–3300* ⊕ *www. concordcoachlines. com.* **Shoreline Explorer.** ☎ *207/459–2932* ⊕ *www. shorelineexplorer.com.*

⊙ Kayaking

Maine Association of Sea Kayak Guides and Instructors. ⊕ *www.maskgi.org.* **Maine Island Trail Association.** ☎ *207/761–8225* ⊕ *www.mita.org.*

⊟ Lodging

New England Inns & Resorts Association. ☎ *603/964–6689* ⊕ *www.newenglandinnsandresorts.com.*

⊕ Tours

American Queen Voyages. ☎ *833/583–1632* ⊕ *www. aqvoyages.com.* **Backroads.** ☎ *800/462–2848* ⊕ *www.backroads.com.* **Collette Tours.** ☎ *800/340–5158* ⊕ *www.gocollette. com.* **Maine Island Kayak Outfitters.** ⊠ *Portland* ☎ *207/766–2373* ⊕ *maineislandkayak.com.*

Maine Tour Connection. ☎ *800/554–6246* ⊕ *www. mainetour.com.* **New England EcoAdventures.** ⊠ *8 Western Ave.* ☎ *207/502–8040* ⊕ *www.newenglandecoadventures.com.* **Northeast Unlimited Tours.** ☎ *800/759–6820* ⊕ *www. newenglandtours.com.*

Train

Amtrak. ☎ *800/872–7245* ⊕ *www.amtrak.com.*

⊙ Visitor Information

DownEast and Acadia Regional Tourism. ☎ *207/707–2057* ⊕ *www. downeastacadia.com.* **Maine Beaches Association.** ⊕ *www.themainebeaches.com.* **Maine Office of Tourism.** ☎ *888/624–6345* ⊕ *www.visitmaine.com.* **Maine Tourism Association.** ☎ *800/767–8709* ⊕ *www.mainetourism. com.* **Maine's MidCoast & Islands.** ☎ *207/443–2067* ⊕ *www.mainesmidcoast. com.* **Visit Portland Maine.** ☎ *207/772–5800* ⊕ *www. visitportland.com.*

On the Calendar

January

New Year's Polar Plunges. What better way to brace yourself for the new year (or sober up from New Year's Eve festivities) than with an icy dip? Several Maine communities offer such events, and proceeds benefit charity. Look into the Lobster Dip in Old Orchard Beach; the Polar Bear Dip & Dash—featuring a 5K run, an icy plunge, or both—in Portland; and Freezin' for a Reason in Kennebunkport. ⊕ *www.visitmaine.net/maine-events.*

February

Paint the Town Red, Kennebunks. A month-long event that aims to entice people to the area in the middle of winter with discounts at local shops, restaurants, and accommodations. ⊕ *gokennebunks.com/paintthetownred.*

U.S. National Toboggan Championships, Camden. Started in 1991, this annual event is likely the country's only organized traditional wood toboggan race. ⊕ *camdensnowbowl.com/toboggan-championships.*

March

Maine Maple Sunday Weekend. Participating sugarhouses, all members of the Maine Maple Producers Association, offer tours, demonstrations, activities, and free samples. ⊕ *mainemapleproducers.com.*

April

Patriot's Day. Maine is one of six states that recognize the third Monday in April as a legal holiday or special day of remembrance honoring the first battles of the Revolutionary War. Parades, battle re-enactments, and other events are held in communities throughout the state.

Splash into Spring, Ogunquit. Over three weekends in late April (including one that coincides with Patriot's Day) and early May, this charming seaside village comes alive with treasure hunts, culinary showcases, parades, and historic reenactments. ⊕ *www.ogunquit.org.*

May

Down East Spring Birding Festival, Cobscook Bay. America's easternmost birding festival occurs during spring migration and nesting season. There are guided hikes, sightseeing boat rides, sunset cruises, and speakers. ⊕ *cobscookinstitute.org/birdfest.*

Kennebunk's May Day Festival, Kennebunk. Enjoy live music, a parade, kids activities, and arts, crafts, and food in this historic village the first weekend in May. ⊕ *kennebunkmaine.us.*

June

Summer Kickoff Weekend, Portland. Formerly known as Old Port Festival, this early-June event brings plenty of activity, music, and great food to the city's historic waterfront. ⊕ *www.portlandmaine.com.*

Windjammer Days, Boothbay Harbor. In late June and early July, check out this seaside town's fleet of historic ships over a week that also includes a boat parade, shipyard tours, and a pancake breakfast. ⊕ www.boothbayharborwindjammerdays.org.

July

Yarmouth Clam Festival, Yarmouth. This three-day celebration kicks off with a Friday-night parade and features crafts stalls, clam cook-offs, and great music performances. ⊕ www.clamfestival.com.

August

Machias Wild Blueberry Festival, Machias. Savor the state's tart-sweet berries with a blueberry-pancake breakfast, and attend a kids' parade and a fish fry during this fruit-filled, three-day celebration. ⊕ www.machiasblueberry.com.

Maine Antiques Festival, Union. Maine's largest antiques fair generally takes place in early or mid-August near Camden and Rockland. ⊕ www.maineantiquesfestival.com.

Maine Lobster Festival, Rockland. Stuff your face with lobster tails and claws during this three-day "lobstravaganza" that puts almost 20,000 pounds of delicious crustacean at your fingertips. ⊕ mainelobsterfestival.com.

September

Camden Windjammer Festival. Held Labor Day weekend, the region's fleet sails into the harbor and is open for tours. ⊕ www.facebook.com/WindjammerFestival.

Laudholm Nature Crafts Festival, Wells. Nearly 130 artisans showcase their creations at this juried, and highly respected, Labor Day weekend gathering. ⊕ www.wellsreserve.org.

October

Harvest on the Harbor, Portland. The state's top food-and-wine fest, held over a weekend late in October, is a great place to sample the latest creations of dozens of acclaimed chefs. ⊕ harvestontheharbor.com.

November

Christmas Prelude, Kennebunkport. Take part in the hat parade, shop at the crafts fair, see the fireworks, or watch for Santa arriving on a lobster boat—these are just a few of the activities at this 10-day annual event. ⊕ www.christmasprelude.com.

Lighting of the Nubble, York. The famous coastal Maine lighthouse gets all dressed up for the holidays in late November, and stays lit through New Years Day. ⊕ nubblelight.org.

December

Sparkle Celebration, Freeport. Embrace the good cheer of the holiday season with a Parade of Lights and other festivities. ⊕ www.visitfreeport.com/sparkle-celebration.

Great Itineraries

Highlights of the Maine Coast

Much of the appeal of the Maine Coast lies in its geographical contrasts, from its long stretches of swimming and walking beaches in the south to the cliff-edged, rugged rocky coasts in the north. And not unlike the physical differences of the coast, each town along the way reveals a slightly different character. With countless lighthouses, beaches, lobster shacks, and great waterways for kayaking and sailing, this rugged coastline has something for everyone. This tour reveals the region's highlights, but look to the book's individual chapters for more in-depth recommendations along the way.

Fly in: Portland International Jetport (PWM), Portland, Maine

Fly out: Bangor International Airport, (BGR), Bangor, Maine. Note that dropping off a rental car at a different location than where you picked it up can incur significant fees; it may be more economical to fly in and out of the same airport, even if that adds time to your drive. It's a two-hour drive via I–95 and I–295 between Bangor and Portland airports.

DAY 1: THE YORKS

Start your trip in **York Village** with a leisurely stroll through the seven buildings of the **Old York Historical Society,** getting a glimpse of 18th-century life in this gentrified town. Spend time wandering among the shops or walking the nature trails and beaches around **York Harbor.** There are several grand lodging options here, most with views of the harbor. If you prefer a livelier pace, continue on to **York Beach,** a haven for families with plenty of

entertainment venues. Be sure to stop and snap a phot of **Nubble Light.**

Logistics: 42 miles; via I–95 to exit 7; 45 minutes from Portland International Jetport (PWM).

DAYS 2 AND 3: OGUNQUIT

For well over a century, diverse **Ogunquit** has been a favorite vacation spot for those looking to combine the natural beauty of the ocean with a sophisticated, bohemian environment. Take a morning walk along the **Marginal Way** to see the waves crashing on the rocks. In **Perkins Cove,** have lunch, stroll the shopping areas, or sign on with a lobster-boat cruise to learn about Maine's most important fishery—the state's lobster industry supplies about 80% of the world's lobster market. See the extraordinary collection at the **Ogunquit Museum of American Art,** take in a performance at renowned **Ogunquit Playhouse,** or just spend time on the beach.

Logistics: 11 miles; via Rte. 1A and Shore Rd.; 30 minutes. Note that driving times throughout this itinerary are without stops, but that along Maine's scenic coast, you'll want to hop out and explore often. This 11-mile drive can take a few hours, for example, with stops for lunch, shopping, and strolling around.

DAY 4: THE KENNEBUNKS

Head north to the **Kennebunks,** allowing at least two hours to wander through the shops and historic homes of **Dock Square** in **Kennebunkport.** This is an ideal place to rent a bike and amble around the back streets, head out on Ocean Avenue to view the Bush estate, or ride to one of the several beaches to relax for awhile.

Logistics: 12 miles; via U.S. 1 and Rte. 9; 30 minutes.

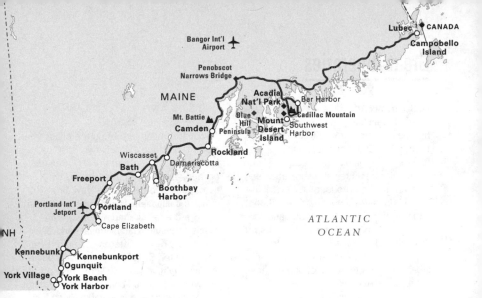

DAYS 5 AND 6: PORTLAND

You can easily spend several days in Maine's largest city, exploring its historic neighborhoods, shopping at hip boutiques, sipping at outstanding craft breweries, and eating at stellar restaurants in the **Old Port**, or visiting one of several excellent museums—the **Portland Museum of Art** is superb.

On your way from Kennebunkport, driving the longer but more scenic route through **Cape Elizabeth** takes you to **Portland Head Light**, Maine's first lighthouse, which was built in 1790–91. The lighthouse is on the grounds of Fort Williams Park, which is an excellent place to enjoy a picnic. Be sure to spend some time wandering the ample grounds. There are also excellent walking trails (and views) at nearby Two Lights State Park, home to the **Cape Elizabeth Light**, one of what was once a pair of lighthouses. If you want to take a boat tour while in Portland, get a ticket for Casco Bay Lines, and check out some of the scenic islands that dot the bay.

Logistics: 45 miles; via Rte. 9 to Biddeford, U.S. 1 to Scarborough, and Rte. 77 through Cape Elizabeth; 90 minutes.

DAYS 7 AND 8: FREEPORT TO BOOTHBAY HARBOR

Head north from Portland—perhaps stopping at the **L.L. Bean** flagship store in **Freeport**—to **Bath**, Maine's shipbuilding capital, and tour the fascinating **Maine Maritime Museum** or have lunch on the waterfront. Shop at boutiques and antique shops, or view the plentitude of beautiful homes. Continue on U.S. 1 north through the towns of **Wiscasset** and **Damariscotta**, where you may find yourself pulling over frequently for outdoor flea markets or intriguing antiques shops. Detour south from Wiscasset to visit the picturesque seaport village of **Boothbay Harbor**, and for a walk through the fragrant, and stunningly designed, **Coastal Maine Botanical Gardens**.

Logistics: 75 miles; via I–295 and U.S. 1, with side trip via Rte. 27 south to Boothbay Harbor; 2 hours.

DAYS 9 AND 10: ROCKLAND AND CAMDEN

In bustling **Rockland,** spend the day cruising on a majestic schooner or reserve a tee time at **Samoset Resort's** championship golf course overlooking Rockland Harbor. Save some time for the superb **Farnsworth Art Museum,** the **Wyeth Center,** and the **Center for Maine**

Great Itineraries

Contemporary Art. In the beautiful seaside town of **Camden,** stately inns occupy homes built from inland Maine's golden timber. Hundreds of boats bob in the harbor, and the colorful streets are lined with indie boutiques and sophisticated restaurants. The modest hills (by Maine standards, anyway) of nearby **Mt. Battie** offer great hiking, picnic spots, and coastal views. Camden is one of the hubs for the beloved and historic windjammer fleet—there is no better way to see the area than from the deck of one of these graceful beauties.

Logistics: 35 miles; via U.S. 1; 1 hour.

DAYS 11 AND 12: MOUNT DESERT ISLAND AND ACADIA NATIONAL PARK

Continue north along U.S. 1, letting your interests dictate where you stop—in Bucksport, the **Penobscot Narrows Bridge and Observatory Tower** and the adjacent **Fort Knox Historic Site** are good bets. Or head south to explore the **Blue Hill Peninsula.** You'll soon reach **Mount Desert Island,** where you can stay in the historic, affluent enclave of **Bar Harbor,** the busiest village in the area, or in the quieter **Southwest Harbor** area; either way, the splendor of the mountains and the sea surround you. Bar Harbor is less than 5 miles from the entrance to Mount Desert Island's 27-mile Park Loop Road, which winds through magnificent **Acadia National Park.** You could spend several days here boating or kayaking in the surrounding waters, biking the historic 45-mile carriage-road system, and driving to the summit of **Cadillac Mountain** for a stunning panorama.

Logistics: 75 miles; via U.S. 1 and Rte. 3; 1 hour and 45 minutes.

DAYS 13 AND 14: LUBEC AND CAMPOBELLO ISLAND

About 100 miles farther up the coast along U.S. 1 and "Way Down East" is **Lubec,** which is right at the U.S./Canada border—bring your passport to drive across the short bridge to New Brunswick's **Campobello Island,** where you can explore the fascinating history of **Roosevelt Campobello International Park.** Back in Lubec, on the easternmost tip of land in the United States, sits the **West Quoddy Head Light,** one of 60 lighthouses that dot Maine's rugged coastline. Depending on the time of year (and your willingness to get up very early), you may be lucky enough to catch the East Coast's first sunrise here.

Logistics: 104 miles; via Rte. 3, U.S. 1, and Rte. 189; 2½ hours. From Lubec, it's 115 miles (2½ hours) to the Bangor airport via Rtes. 192 and 9.

Maine Maritime History Tour

Maine's maritime leanings reach back into the early 17th century, and while many things have changed, the sea—via lobstering, fishing, and tourism—is still the backbone of the state's economy and culture. This tour provides a glimpse of how the sea has influenced the people, towns, and industries along the coastline to create the delightful and diverse region it is today. You can squeeze the Bath-to-Rockland portion into one day, and Searsport into one day as well if you prefer to complete this trip in just six days.

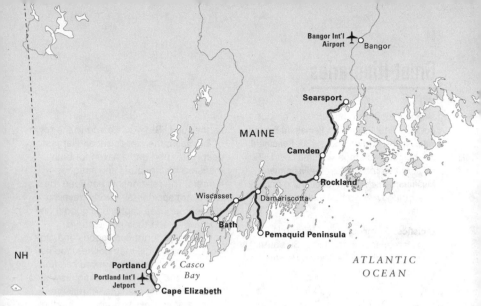

Fly in: Portland International Jetport (PWM), Portland, Maine

Fly out: Bangor International Airport, (BGR), Bangor, Maine. See the note about potentially expensive one-way car-rental dropoff fees in the Highlights of the Maine Coast itinerary.

DAYS 1 AND 2: PORTLAND AND CAPE ELIZABETH

A thriving, working harbor since the 17th century, **Portland** has maritime history written all over it. Take a step back in time at the **Fish Exchange,** where the day's catch is unloaded and auctioned off to worldwide markets just as it has been for centuries. For a more refined maritime experience, head to the **Portland Museum of Art** to see the impressive collection of sea-inspired art by such greats as Edward Hopper and Winslow Homer. Lighthouses still play an integral role in keeping Maine's coast safe and navigable. In nearby **Cape Elizabeth,** visit Fort Williams Park and Two Lights State Park to see the area's most famous lighthouses: **Portland Head Light** and **Cape Elizabeth Light.** For a more intimate view of the sea, try a boat cruise from Portland to the nearby islands in **Casco Bay.**

Logistics: 4 miles; via Rte. 22, from Portland International Jetport (PWM) to downtown Portland; it's a 30-mile round-trip side trip to Fort Williams Park and Two Lights State Park via Shore Rd. and Rte. 77 (allow 75 minutes without stops).

DAYS 3 AND 4: BATH AND THE PEMAQUID PENINSULA

From Portland, head north to **Bath,** Maine's current shipbuilding capital. The Bath Iron Works, which once built tall-masted wooden schooners, now builds destroyers for the U.S. Navy. Spend some time at the **Maine Maritime Museum** to get a sense of the area's longstanding prowess in the shipping industry. Wander the streets of Bath to see the grand mansions of 19th-century sea captains (some of which are now elegant B&Bs).

Head north on U.S. 1 to **Wiscasset,** a village that gained great wealth in the shipbuilding industry as evidenced by its stunning array of grand sea captains' and merchants' homes. Tour the **Nickels-Sortwell House** (1807) to get a glimpse of the wealth these seafaring business-men enjoyed. Continue on to **Damariscotta,** another town that found success in

Great Itineraries

shipbuilding. From here, take a detour down Route 130 to the **Pemaquid Peninsula.** At the end of Route 130, **Pemaquid Point Light** has stood watch since 1827. Adjacent to the light is the **Fishermen's Museum,** which has a fascinating display illustrating Maine's 400-year-old fishing industry.

Logistics: 70 miles; via I–295 and U.S. 1 to Damariscotta, then Rte. 30 south down through the Pemaquid Peninsula; 90 minutes.

DAYS 5 AND 6: ROCKLAND AND CAMDEN

Make your way north from Damariscotta to colorful **Rockland,** where you can tour the **Farnsworth Art Museum and Wyeth Center,** an excellent place to see maritime-inspired artworks. The fascinating **Maine Lighthouse Museum,** also in Rockland, displays many lighthouse and Coast Guard artifacts as well as other maritime curios. You can—and should—take a one-day or overnight cruise on a historic windjammer from either Rockland or nearby **Camden.** Sailing aboard one of these graceful schooners is the ideal way to see the coast.

Logistics: 50 miles; via Rte. 30 and U.S. 1; 75 minutes.

DAYS 7 AND 8: SEARSPORT

Farther up U.S. 1 you'll come to the town of **Searsport,** the state's second-largest deepwater port and a haven for both maritime history buffs and antiques hunters. The relationship between the two is not accidental—world-traveling 19th-century sea captains, a good many of whom made their homes here, constantly brought back goods and gifts from Europe to fill their houses. You never know what kind of gem you can find in one of the multitude of antiques shops and outdoor flea markets. A treasure of another sort exists here as well: the **Penobscot Marine Museum** is a complex brimming with fascinating sea history. You can easily spend several hours here.

Weekend traffic heading to the Maine Coast along its feeder roads, I–95 and U.S. 1, can be brutally frustrating. If you travel midweek instead (or outside of peak season), you won't find yourself nearly as stymied.

Logistics: 26 miles; via U.S. 1; 35 minutes. From Searsport, it's a 45-minute drive via U.S. 1A to Bangor International Airport or 2-hour drive via Rte. 3 and I–295 back to Portland International Jetport.

Chapter 3

THE SOUTHERN COAST

Updated by
Annie Quigley

◉ Sights	🍴 Restaurants	🛏 Hotels	💼 Shopping	🍸 Nightlife
★★★★★	★★★★★	★★★★★	★★★★★	★★★★☆

WELCOME TO THE SOUTHERN COAST

TOP REASONS TO GO

★ **Time travel:** Tour historic houses from Maine's early days at the Old York Historical Society—and duck inside an Old Gaol (jail) dating from 1656.

★ **Sand in your toes:** Ogunquit and Wells provide many miles of blissful beach walking.

★ **Sleeping like royalty:** Stay at one of Kennebunkport's luxurious and design-forward historic inns, like the Cape Arundel Inn and Resort.

★ **Harvesting the sea:** Head out on a lobster-boat excursion to glimpse one of Maine's largest industries, and take home some of the catch!

★ **Hot diggety dogs:** Chomp into a famous frankfurter at Flo's Steamed Hot Dogs, where they've been selling their dogs since 1959.

1 Kittery. Just across the border from New Hampshire, this town offers some of Maine's best shopping, as well as the first glimpses of the state's coastline.

2 The Yorks and Cape Neddick. From historic York Village to the bustling throwback of Short Sands Beach, there's plenty to explore in this cluster of seaside communities.

3 Ogunquit. Trendy boutiques and a thriving art scene define this quaint town, which sees a slew of visitors come summer.

4 Wells. Centered on Route 1, this town is known for its antiques stores, its miles of beaches, and, increasingly, its lively places to eat and drink.

5 Kennebunk, Kennebunkport, and Cape Porpoise. With picturesque cottages, shopping in Dock Square, and refined hotels, the Kennebunks are a destination all year round. Just north of Kennebunkport, the fishing village of Cape Porpoise has excellent restaurants.

6 Biddeford. Once a bustling mill town, this city 20 minutes south of Portland is Maine's newest foodie destination, with fine-dining establishments, breweries, and hotels giving new life to historic buildings.

7 Scarborough, Prout's Neck, and Cape Elizabeth. The draws here include state parks; lighthouses; hidden coves; and spectacular spots to walk, sit, or just take in the view.

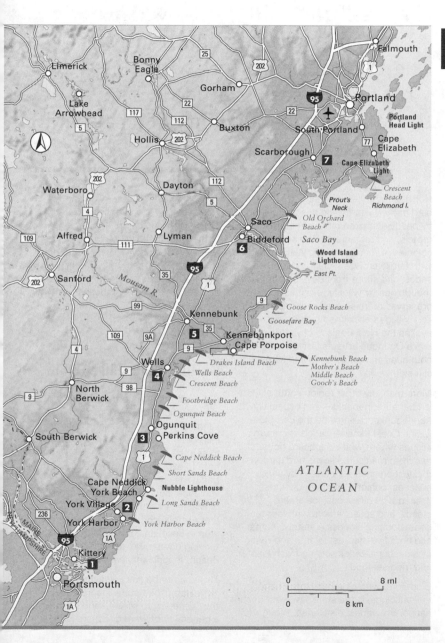

Falmouth

1

25

202

Bonny
Eagle

Limerick

Gorham

Lake
Arrowhead

117

22

95 Portland

22 South Portland

Portland
Head Light

5

112

202 Buxton

Scarborough

7

Cape
Elizabeth

77

Cape Elizabeth
Light

Hollis

Waterboro

202

Dayton

112

5

Saco

Prout's
Neck

Crescent
Beach
Richmond I.

Old Orchard
Beach

4

Alfred

Lyman

Biddeford

Saco Bay

109

111

6

Wood Island
Lighthouse

202

Sanford

Mousam R.

35

East Pt.

99

1

9

Goose Rocks Beach

95

Kennebunk

Goosefare Bay

109

9A

35

Kennebunkport
Cape Porpoise

Kennebunk Beach
Mother's Beach
Middle Beach
Gooch's Beach

5

4

9

Wells

Drakes Island Beach

4

9

Wells Beach

North
Berwick

98

Crescent Beach

Footbridge Beach

9

Ogunquit Beach

South Berwick

Ogunquit
Perkins Cove

3

Cape Neddick Beach

1

Short Sands Beach

Cape Neddick
York Beach

Nubble Lighthouse

York Village

Long Sands Beach

236

2

York Harbor

York Harbor Beach

95

1A

ATLANTIC
OCEAN

Kittery

1

Portsmouth

1A

0   8 ml

0   8 km

The Maine Coast's southernmost stretch features miles and miles of inviting beaches, beautifully preserved historic towns, and charming lighthouses. There is something for everyone here, whether you seek solitude in a kayak or the infectious conviviality of locals and fellow vacationers.

North of Kittery, long stretches of hard-packed white-sand beach are lined by nearly unbroken ranks of cottages, motels, and restaurants. The summer colonies of York Beach and Wells brim with family crowds, T-shirt and gift shops, and shore-front development, though nearby wildlife refuges and land preserves promise easy, quiet escapes. York Village's acclaimed historic district evokes the New England of yesteryear, while Ogunquit attracts visitors with its boutiques and art galleries and its paved cliff-side walk.

More than any other region south of Portland, the Kennebunks—and especially Kennebunkport—provide the complete Maine Coast experience: classic townscapes where white-clapboard houses rise from manicured lawns and gardens; rocky shorelines punctuated by sandy beaches; quaint downtown districts packed with gift shops, ice cream stands, and spas; harbors with lobster boats bobbing alongside stately yachts; and both five-star restaurants and rustic picnic-table eateries serving fresh lobster and fried seafood.

Biddeford, with its rehabilitated historic mill buildings, is the state's newest destination. Breweries, distilleries, thoughtful fine-dining establishments, inventive ice-cream shops, and one of the country's most acclaimed diners are just a handful of the bold, creative outposts that have revitalized the downtown. Farther north still, in Cape Elizabeth, the stunning landscape steals the show at any number of state parks and lighthouses.

Planning

Getting Here and Around

Although the Southern Coast makes up a mere portion of Maine's many thousands of miles of shoreline, it offers an incredible variety of sights. The best way to see the region is by car—taking the time to explore inviting byways. Summer traffic may be demanding and an inconvenience, but the beauty and diversity of Maine is worth a little patience. (Note that Amtrak, coming from Boston, does stop in Saco, an easy stroll to Biddeford's thriving downtown, and Old Orchard Beach, though service is infrequent.)

This chapter begins just across the New Hampshire state line in Kittery, the "Gateway to Maine," and heads in a general northward direction. Many of the sites and towns are off the main thoroughfares of U.S. 1 and I–95, so you can decide how quickly you want to pass from one town to the next.

From Kittery, a meandering drive takes you to the coastal towns of the Yorks, Ogunquit, and Wells. The town of Kennebunk is slightly inland, while its sister town of Kennebunkport is right on the water. Biddeford's thriving, historic downtown is inland, on the Saco River, though the classic summer communities of Biddeford Pool, Fortune's Rocks, and Ocean Park stretch along the coast.

Old Orchard Beach is a quintessential frolicking beach town with a historic pier and amusement park rides. Drive northward, and you'll discover the still-quiet and naturally spectacular sceneries of Scarborough and Cape Elizabeth.

AIR

Most visitors arriving by air fly into Portland International Jetport, which is 24 miles northeast of Kennebunk. Limited air service is also available from Portsmouth International Airport at Pease in New Hampshire, 25 miles south of Kennebunkport. Another option is Manchester-Boston Regional Airport in Manchester, New Hampshire, a 75-mile drive from Kennebunkport. Visitors flying into Boston's Logan International Airport can rent a car and be in the Kennebunkport area in about two hours (depending on traffic for the 92-mile drive).

CONTACTS Boston Logan International Airport. ☎ 800/235–6426 ⊕ www.massport.com/logan-airport. **Manchester-Boston Regional Airport.** ✉ 1 Airport Rd., Manchester ☎ 603/624–6539 ⊕ www.flymanchester.com. **Portsmouth International Airport at Pease.** ✉ 36 Airline Ave., Portsmouth ☎ 603/433–6536 ⊕ peasedev.org/travel.

BICYCLE

A bicycle can make it easy to get around the Kennebunks, the Yorks, and the Old Orchard Beach area, but the lack of shoulders on some roads can be intimidating. Ogunquit would seem like a good place for bikes, but traffic is hectic in the high season, making it a bit tricky. Biking around town is better, safer, and far more pleasant in the shoulder seasons (through spring or after Labor Day). Two good resources are the Facebook page of the Bicycle Coalition of Maine and the Maine Department of Transportation (⊕ exploremaine.org/bike).

BUS

Biddeford—Saco—Old Orchard Beach Transit is a localized bus service with routes connecting those communities as well as Scarborough, South Portland, and Portland.

For car-free travel from the Yorks to Kennebunkport and over to Sanford, the Shoreline Explorer Network connects private and public transportation options—mainly trolleys and buses. Each segment has its own timetable and fare schedule, but it's easy enough to get around using the network.

CONTACTS Shoreline Explorer. ☎ 207/459–2932 ⊕ www.shorelineexplorer.com.

CAR

U.S. 1 from Kittery is the shopper's route north; other roads hug the coastline. Interstate 95 is usually a faster route for travelers headed to towns north of Ogunquit. Exits on the turnpike coincide with mileage from the border. Northward, Route 9 winds from Kennebunkport to Cape Porpoise and Goose Rocks Beach.

In summer, parking can be hard to find in Maine's small town centers, particularly in the Ogunquit and Perkin's Cove areas, where paid lots can be pricey, as well as in Kennebunkport. In the latter, try the municipal lot behind Alisson's Restaurant in Dock Square ($4 an hour from May through October) and 30 North Street (free year-round).

TRAIN

Amtrak offers rail service on the *Downeaster* from Boston to Portland, with stops in Wells and Saco and a seasonal stop in Old Orchard Beach.

TROLLEY

Maine's classic trolleys have largely shifted from a means of transportation to tours only in recent years, a result of the pandemic and labor shortages. A trolley fleet still serves the major tourist areas and beaches of Ogunquit from Memorial Day through early October, and Biddeford–Saco–Old Orchard Beach Transit operates a seasonal summer service that connects points in Saco, Old Orchard Beach, and Scarborough. Scheduled trolley tours, meanwhile, are available in the Yorks and the Kennebunks.

CONTACTS Biddeford–Saco–Old Orchard Beach Transit. ☎ *207/282–5408* ⊕ *bsoobtransit.org.*

Hotels

The variation in lodgings along the Maine Coast has a lot to do with individual zoning laws. Towns like the Kennebunks, York Harbor, and Ogunquit have a much higher number of small inns and bed-and-breakfasts, while York Beach, Old Orchard Beach, Wells, and Kittery seem to be filled with one hotel-motel complex after another. U.S. 1 is famous (or infamous, depending on how you look at it) for its rampant commercialism, and its lodging options usually show it.

A stay in one of the restored mansions will cost you quite a bit more than a night at a sprawling hotel, but almost all lodging establishments offer off-season price reductions and special package rates. Minimum-stay requirements are common for weekends and July through Labor Day. Expect to pay the most in Kennebunkport, Ogunquit, and the Yorks.

Restaurants

Portland has become a true food destination, and the spread of excellent, innovative eateries and breweries continues south all along the coast. Restaurants range from the casually eclectic to the formal prix-fixe—and everything in between. There are, increasingly, excellent international restaurants, though these are still few and far between.

Given that Maine has more than 5,000 miles of shoreline, many restaurants specialize in local seafood—and there is plenty of it to choose from, including the state's mascot crustacean. Indeed, Maine produces well over 80% of the nation's lobsters, so it's no surprise that it's often featured on menus. Though steamed or boiled lobster is still a mainstay, creative chefs have gone well beyond traditional preparations with seemingly endless variations.

HOTEL AND RESTAURANT PRICES

Hotel and restaurant reviews have been shortened. For full information, visit Fodors.com. Hotel prices in the reviews are the lowest cost of a standard double room in high season. Restaurant prices are the average cost of a main course at dinner, or if dinner is not served, at lunch.

What It Costs In U.S. Dollars			
$	$$	$$$	$$$$
RESTAURANTS			
under $10	$10–$30	$31–$40	over $40
HOTELS			
under $200	$200–$400	$401–$600	over $600

Great Itineraries

If You Have 3 Days

A three-day trip to the Southern Coast can give you a good taste of regional flavor. Spend your first two days in Kittery and the Yorks. In Kittery, enjoy local brews and an excellent meal. If the weather cooperates, bring a picnic, a kayak, or your walking shoes for an afternoon of enjoying the vistas and trails of Ft. Foster. From Kittery, follow U.S. 1 north to York. Take Route 1A and explore the historic sites of York Village. Continue the few miles to lively York Beach, where you can swim, bowl, or play arcade games until after dark.

On your second day, continue north on Route 1A and spend the night and your third day in Ogunquit. Here you can walk the Marginal Way and spend several hours exploring the shops of both Perkins Cove and the village of Ogunquit. If you're visiting in summer, save some time to relax at Ogunquit Beach.

If You Have 5 Days

Start in Kittery, an area rich in history and natural beauty that's also a shopper's mecca, and follow the three-day itinerary. On Day 4, leave Ogunquit and continue on U.S. 1 through Wells, a town known for its 7-mile stretch of pristine beaches. If you'd like to do some hiking or bird-watching, you can wander along the Cutts Island Trail in the Rachel Carson National Wildlife Refuge. Otherwise, follow scenic Route 9 to Kennebunk-port, a good place to have a bite to eat and spend the night. If you have time and the weather cooperates, visit nearby Kennebunk Beach or poke into the shops in bustling Dock Square.

On Day 5, continue north on Route 9 to the up-and-coming mill town of Biddeford. Spend your last day eating your way through its innovative restaurants, bakeries, and breweries.

When to Go

Summer crowds converge on the Southern Coast, booking up hotel rooms, campgrounds, and dinner reservations at top restaurants and clogging the roads (don't expect speedy jaunts down U.S. 1). Still, July, August, and September are the best months to vacation here. The weather is warm, and every town has its share of festivals, outdoor concerts, and gatherings. Midweek tends to be a little quieter than weekends.

The brilliance of fall foliage brings another round of visitors, though it's not quite as busy as in the summer. The prime time for leaf-peeping here is usually the first week of October (check the state's weekly updated site: ⊕ www.mainefoliage.com).

Many accommodations and restaurants stay open throughout the year, though they do have limited hours come winter. In the off-season, rates are lower, and you won't be waiting in line anywhere. Some areas host winter festivals and events, like Kennebunkport's Christmas Prelude (⊕ www.christmasprelude.com) that see quaint towns decked out in lights and winter charm—and draw crowds, too.

Early morning light at Kittery Point.

Kittery

60 miles north of Boston, 4 miles north of Portsmouth, New Hampshire.

Known as the "Gateway to Maine," Kittery has become primarily a major shopping destination thanks to its massive complex of factory outlets. Flanking both sides of U.S. 1 are more than 120 stores, which attract serious shoppers year-round. But Kittery has more to offer than just retail therapy: head east on Route 103 to the area around Kittery Point to experience the great outdoors.

Here you'll find hiking and biking trails, as well as fantastic views of Portsmouth, New Hampshire, Whaleback Light, and, in the distance, Isles of Shoals. The isles and the light, along with two others, can be seen from two forts near this winding stretch of Route 103: Fort McClary State Historic Site (closed to vehicles off-season) and Fort Foster, a town park (with vehicle access to parking lots in the off-season, except in the case of ice or snow).

The Kittery Visitor Information Center is an excellent place to get information for mapping out your tour of Maine (and for a quick photo op with Smokey the Bear). Sometimes local organizations are on hand selling delicious homemade goodies for the road.

GETTING HERE AND AROUND

Three bridges—on U.S. 1, U.S. 1 Bypass, and Interstate 95—cross the Piscataqua River from Portsmouth, New Hampshire, to Kittery. Interstate 95 has three Kittery exits. Route 103 is a scenic coastal drive through Kittery Point to York.

VISITOR INFORMATION

CONTACTS Kittery Visitor Information Center. ⊠ *U.S. 1 and I–95, at Maine mile marker 3.5 on I–95 northbound, Kittery* ☎ *207/439–1319* ⊕ *www.mainetourism. com.*

Sights

Fort McClary State Historic Site

MILITARY SIGHT | FAMILY | Given the clear line of sight down to the Piscataqua River from here, it's easy to understand why this has been considered a strategic locale since the 1600s. The fort was named for Andrew McClary—an Irish immigrant whose family settled in New Hampshire prior to the Revolution and who was reportedly the last Continental Army soldier killed at Battle of Bunker Hill—and although it never saw a major conflict, it was manned and developed during several of them, including the War of 1812 and the Civil War. The remaining fortifications showcase the history of American military architecture and include the Magazine Building (circa 1808) and the iconic Blockhouse (1846), a large, hexagonal structure set atop an imposing granite-block foundation. Wandering the grounds or along a short trail here is, given the original purpose of the site, an ironically peaceful way to pass an afternoon. ✉ *Pepperrell Rd., Kittery Point* ☎ *207/439–2845* 🌐 *www.maine.gov/dacf/parks* 🎫 *$4* 🕒 *Closed mid-Oct.–late May.*

Tributary Brewing Company

BREWERY | There's nothing like a cold brew on a hot summer's day. Here you can enjoy your suds on the sunny patio or in the cool, navy-blue, industrial-style tasting room. The knowledgeable staff can guide you through the selection of the offerings brewed on site, whether you want to sample several in flight or just have one 12-ounce pour. You're welcome to bring your own food, perhaps even something from the nearby Chauncey Creek Lobster Pier. ✉ *10 Shapleigh Rd., Kittery* ☎ *207/703–0093* 🌐 *www.tributarybrewingcompany.com* 🕒 *Closed Mon.*

Restaurants

Anju Noodle Bar

$$ | ASIAN FUSION | With a cozy, open-plan dining area and a laid-back atmosphere, Anju Noodle Bar serves up reimagined versions of traditional dishes such as house-made, slow-roasted pork-shoulder buns, spicy miso ramen, inspired local seafood dishes, and seasonal vegetarian options. This is one of the few places in the Pine Tree State outside Portland where you'll find fresh and innovative Asian-inspired cuisine done really well. **Known for:** sake heaven; free-style dishes; house-made kimchi. [$] *Average main: $18* ✉ *7 Wallingford Sq., Unit 102, Kittery* ☎ *207/703–4298* 🌐 *www.anjunoodlebar.com* 🕒 *Closed Mon.*

The Black Birch

$$ | MODERN AMERICAN | This artful bar in happening Kittery Foreside district has an excellent selection of mostly local brews on tap, as well as a rotating menu of fun cocktails. Equally praiseworthy is its upscale-but-still-approachable pub fare, which includes buffalo fried oysters, ratatouille, and bar snacks like deviled eggs with pickled watermelon rind. **Known for:** right in the heart of Kittery Foreside; Maine's best brews and small-batch, organic, natural wines; upgrades on gastropub classics. [$] *Average main: $20* ✉ *2 Government St., Kittery* ☎ *207/703–2294* 🌐 *theblackbirch.com* 🕒 *Closed Sun. and Mon. No lunch.*

Chauncey Creek Lobster Pier

$$ | SEAFOOD | FAMILY | From the road you can barely see the red roof hovering below the trees, but chances are you can see the line of cars parked at this popular outdoor restaurant that has been serving up fresh lobster for more than 70 years. Brightly colored picnic tables fill the deck, and enclosed eating areas sit atop the high banks of the tidal river, beside a working pier, which delivers fresh seafood straight to your plate. **Known for:** classic lobster dinners; BYOB; ocean-to-plate. $ *Average main: $25* ✉ *16 Chauncey Creek Rd., Kittery* ☎ *207/439–1030* ⊕ *www.chaunceycreek. com* ☾ *Closed Mon. post-Labor Day–Columbus Day. Closed post-Columbus Day–Mother's Day.*

Robert's Maine Grill

$$ | SEAFOOD | New American surf or turf dishes made with locally sourced, farm- or fishing-boat-to-table ingredients are the hallmarks of this restaurant in a navy-blue clapboard building with a striking, red-and-white-striped lighthouse replica on one end of it. Lobster—in a roll, in risotto, or in mac and cheese—takes comfort-food pride of place, but the haddock Reuben sandwich and the barbecue steak tips in a sauce made with Moxie (a New England soft drink) are creative alternatives. **Known for:** fish-and-chips featuring an Allagash-beer batter; raw bar with oysters, jumbo shrimp, and littleneck clams; a mindful culinary approach. $ *Average main: $26* ✉ *326 Rte. 1, Kittery* ☎ *207/439–0300* ⊕ *robertsmainegrill.com.*

☕ Coffee and Quick Bites

Bob's Clam Hut

$$ | SEAFOOD | FAMILY | With fresh (never frozen) shellfish and a cheery, old-school vibe, Bob's also serves up scrumptious, homemade sauces to smother over golden fried clams, alongside some of the creamiest New England clam chowders around. **Known for:** retro-coastal decor; a classic stop since 1956; tangy Moxie barbecue sauce. $ *Average main: $16* ✉ *315 U.S. 1, Kittery* ☎ *207/439–4233* ⊕ *www. bobsclamhut.com.*

★ Lil's

$ | CAFÉ | This Kittery Foreside café is named for the woman who worked the register at nearby Bob's Clam Hut for two decades, but you'll find no shellfish here—just excellent pastries and breads, made on-site daily. Don't miss the

top-notch old-fashioned crullers, and duck into the vault in back—filled with vintage records—while you're at it. **Known for:** chill spot to refuel between explorations; lots of parking; a variety of excellent house-made crullers. $ *Average main: $6* ✉ *7 Wallingford Sq., Unit 106, Kittery* ☎ *207/703–2800* ⊕ *lilscafe.com* ☾ *No dinner.*

Shopping

Kittery Outlets

OUTLET | FAMILY | Along a several-mile stretch of U.S. 1 in Kittery you can find just about anything—often at deep discounts. Among the stores are Crate & Barrel, Eddie Bauer, Banana Republic, Kate Spade New York, and J. Crew; spend a rainy afternoon hunting for deals, or head to the nearby Kittery Trading Post (301 U.S. 1), a destination for fishing, boating, camping, and other types of outdoor accoutrements. ✉ *U.S. 1, Kittery* ⊕ *www.thekitteryoutlets.com.*

Kittery Trading Post

SPORTING GOODS | FAMILY | Akin to Freeport's L.L. Bean for camping, this destination stocks fishing, boating, camping, and other types of outdoor accoutrements. In business since 1938, the company continues to grow and offers various outdoor seminars and instruction. ✉ *301 Rte. 1, Kittery* ☎ *207/439–2700* ⊕ *www.kitterytradingpost.com.*

Activities

HIKING AND WALKING

Cutts Island Trail

HIKING & WALKING | For a peek into the Rachel Carson National Wildlife Refuge, this scenic 1.8-mile upland loop trail leads into the 800-acre Brave Boat Harbor Division and is a prime bird-watching area. There's a restroom and an information kiosk at the trailhead. The trail is open dawn–dusk year-round; dogs are not allowed. ✉ *Seapoint Rd., Kittery* ☎ *207/646–9226* ⊕ *www.fws.gov/refuge/ rachel-carson/visit-us.*

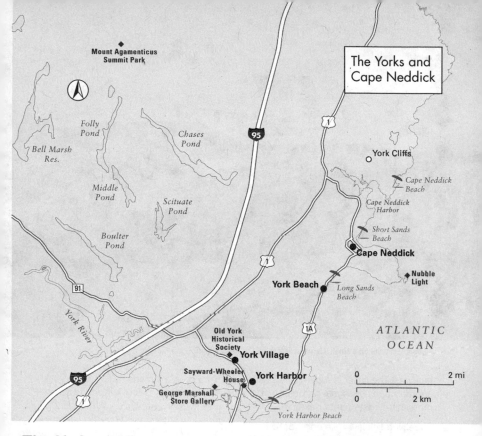

The Yorks and Cape Neddick

8 miles north of Kittery via I–95, U.S. 1, and U.S. 1A.

Spending an afternoon in York Village is like going back in time—and you really only need a couple of hours here to roam the historic streets of this pint-size but worthwhile town. One of the first permanent settlements in Maine, the village museums detail its rich history. York is also home to the flagship store of Stonewall Kitchen, one of Maine's signature gourmet-food purveyors; the store has a café, too. There's also a cluster of vibrant contemporary-art galleries.

A short distance from the village proper, York Harbor opens to the water and offers many places to linger and explore. The harbor itself is busy with boats of all kinds, while the sandy harbor beach is good for swimming. Much quieter and more formal than York Beach to the north, this area has a somewhat exclusive air. Perched along the cliffs on the north side of the harbor are huge "cottages" built by wealthy summer residents in the late 1800s, when the area became a premier seaside resort destination with several grand hotels.

York Beach is a real family destination, devoid of all things staid and stuffy, and a throwback to nostalgic summers past: kids are welcome here. Just beyond the sands of Short Sands Beach are a host of amusements, from bowling to indoor minigolf and the Fun-O-Rama arcade. Nubble Light is at the tip of the peninsula separating Long Sands and Short Sands

Nubble Light sits on a small island just off the tip of Cape Neddick.

beaches. The latter is mostly lined with unpretentious seasonal homes, with motels and restaurants mixed in.

Cape Neddick is 1 mile north of York Beach via U.S. 1A. It's still one of the less developed of York's areas, and there's no distinct village hub, though it's become something of an elevated destination, with acclaimed restaurants and trendy lodgings popping up. Cape Neddick Harbor is at its southern end, beyond York Beach village.

GETTING HERE AND AROUND

York is Exit 7 off I–95; follow signs to U.S. 1, the modern commercial strip. From here, U.S. 1A will take you to the village center and on to York Harbor and York Beach before looping back up to U.S. 1 in Cape Neddick. After passing through York Village to York Harbor (originally called Lower Town), U.S. 1A winds around and heads north to York Beach's village center, a 4-mile trip.

It's a scenic 6 miles to York Beach via the loop road, U.S. 1A, from its southern intersection with U.S. 1. Although 2 miles longer, it's generally faster to continue north on U.S. 1A to Cape Neddick and then U.S. 1A south to the village center, home to Short Sands Beach. Here U.S. 1A is known as Ocean Avenue as it heads north from York Harbor along Long Sands Beach en route to York Beach village and Short Sands Beach.

You can get from beach to beach on a series of residential streets that wind around Nubble Point between these beaches. Also, from late June through Labor Day, the bright-red vehicles of the York Trolley Company link Short Sands Beach in York Beach village with nearby Long Sands Beach, running along U.S. 1A, making a number of stops. Maps can be picked up throughout York; fares are $2 one-way, $4 round-trip, cash only (payable to driver upon boarding). You can also connect with a shuttle service to Ogunquit.

TRANSPORTATION York Trolley Co.. ⊠ *York* ☎ *207/363–9600* ⊕ *www.yorktrolley.com.*

VISITOR INFORMATION

CONTACTS Greater York Region Chamber of Commerce. ⊠ *1 Stonewall La., off U.S. 1, York* ☎ *207/363–4422* ⊕ *www.gateway-tomaine.org.*

◉ Sights

George Marshall Store Gallery

ART GALLERY | The storefront windows and bead-board trim at the George Marshall Store Gallery (built in 1867) pay homage to its past as a general store, but the focus here is on the present. Changing exhibits, installations, and educational programs focus on prominent and up-and-coming regional artists. Stop in on weekends or by appointment through summer and fall. ⊠ *140 Lindsay Rd., York Village* ☎ *207/351–8200* ⊕ *www.george-marshallstoregallery.com* ☉ *Closed Mon.–Wed. and Jan.–Apr.*

Mount Agamenticus Summit Park

MOUNTAIN | A park sits atop this humble summit of 692 feet, one of the highest points along the Atlantic seaboard. That may not seem like much, but if you choose to hike to the top, you will be rewarded with incredible views all the way to the White Mountains in New Hampshire. If you don't want to hoof it (though it's not very steep), there is parking at the top. If you bring your pup, make sure to keep them leashed. ⊠ *21 Mt. Agamenticus Rd., Cape Neddick* ☎ *207/361–1102* ⊕ *www.agamenticus. org* 🎟 *Free; donations appreciated.*

★ Nubble Light

LIGHTHOUSE | On a small island just off the tip of Cape Neddick, Nubble Light is one of the most photographed lighthouses on the globe. Direct access is prohibited, but the small Sohier Park right across from the light has parking, historical placards, benches, and a seasonal information center that shares the 1879 light's history. ⊠ *11 Sohier Park Rd.,* *York* ☎ *207/363–3569 May 1–mid-Oct.* ⊕ *www.nubblelight.org.*

Old York Historical Society

HISTORY MUSEUM | FAMILY | Nine historic 18th- and 19th-century buildings, clustered on York Street and along Lindsay Road and the York River, highlight York's rich history, which dates from the early colonial period. Start your visit at the museum's visitor center in the Remick Barn at the corner of U.S. 1A and Lindsay Road. The Old Gaol (established 1656) was once the King's Prison for the Province of Maine; step inside for a look inside its dungeons, cells, and jailer's quarters. The 1731 Elizabeth Perkins House reflects the Victorian style of its last occupants, the prominent Perkins family. ⊠ *Old York Museum Center, 3 Lindsay Rd., York Village* ☎ *207/363–1756* ⊕ *www.oldyork.org* 🎟 *$10* ☉ *Closed Nov.–Memorial Day.*

Sayward-Wheeler House

HISTORIC HOME | FAMILY | Built in 1718, this waterfront home was remodeled in the 1760s by Jonathan Sayward, a local merchant who had prospered in the West Indies trade. By 1860, his descendants had opened the house to the public to share the story of their Colonial ancestors. Accessible only by guided tour (first and third Saturday, June through mid-October, 11–4 with the last tour at 3), the house reveals the decor of a prosperous New England family and the stories of the free and enslaved people who lived here at the outset of the Revolutionary War. The parlor—considered one of the country's best-preserved Colonial interiors, with a tall clock and mahogany Chippendale-style chairs—looks pretty much as it did when Sayward lived here. ⊠ *9 Barrell La. Ext., York Harbor* ☎ *207/384–2454* ⊕ *www.historicnewengland.org/ property/sayward-wheeler-house* 🎟 *$10* ☉ *Closed mid-Oct.–June.*

Beaches

Cape Neddick Beach

BEACH | FAMILY | With a sheltered location just north of Short Sands Beach and at the mouth of the Cape Neddick River, this small rocky beach is the perfect place for wading and tide-pooling. **Amenities:** none. **Best for:** swimming; walking. ⊠ *Cape Neddick.*

Long Sands Beach

BEACH | FAMILY | In the peak of summer, each day sees thousands of visitors along this swath of white sand, which stretches for more than a mile. They come to sunbathe, surf (in designated areas), play volleyball, and explore tide pools. You can rent umbrellas and rafts here, but you'll have to walk to nearby restaurants for a bite to eat. Dogs are allowed (however, between late May and late September, only before 8 am and after 6:30 pm). **Amenities:** lifeguards (seasonal); parking (fee); toilets. **Best for:** surfing; swimming; walking. ⊠ *189 Long Beach Ave., Rte. 1A, York Beach.*

Short Sands Beach

BEACH | FAMILY | Rocky cliffs bookend this ¼-mile sandy beach. It's amid Ellis Park, which has a playground, basketball courts, a paved walkway, and free concerts in summer. Leashed pets are allowed, though, dog-walking hours are limited between late May and late September. Shops, restaurants, and other attractions are all nearby. **Amenities:** lifeguards (seasonal); parking (fee); toilets. **Best for:** swimming; walking. ⊠ *Ocean Ave., Rte. 1A, York Harbor.*

York Harbor Beach

BEACH | FAMILY | This small, somewhat secluded stretch with gentle surf is favored by locals, particularly families. It's near a shady park, the Cliff Walk, restaurants, and other attractions. Between late May and late September leashed dogs are allowed only before 8 am and after 6:30 pm. **Amenities:** lifeguards (seasonal); toilets. **Best for:** swimming; walking. ⊠ *York St., Rte. 1A, York Harbor.*

 Restaurants

Dockside Restaurant

$$ | SEAFOOD | On an islandlike peninsula overlooking York Harbor, this restaurant has plenty of seafood on the menu. Floor-to-ceiling windows in the stepped modern dining space transport diners to the water beyond—every seat has a water view. **Known for:** "drunken" lobster (lobster and seared scallops in an Irish-whiskey cream); decadent seafood chowder and lobster bisque; lively, dockside vibe with spectacular views. $ *Average main: $25* ⊠ *22 Harris Island Rd., off Rte. 103, York Harbor* ☎ *207/363–2722* ⊕ *www. dockside-restaurant.com* ⊙ *Closed Tues. in summer and late Oct.–mid-May.*

Frankie & Johnny's Restaurant

$$$ | ECLECTIC | If you've had about all the fried seafood you can stand, try this intimate spot that focuses on creative cuisine served with flair. There are lots of seafood, poultry, and meat options, homemade pasta choices, and always a few vegetarian dishes (special requests like gluten-free are happily accommodated). **Known for:** thoughtfully made dishes, like homemade pasta; intimate dinner-party atmosphere; full bar and wine list. $ *Average main: $35* ⊠ *1594 U.S. 1, Cape Neddick* ☎ *207/363–1909* ⊕ *www.frankie-johnnys.com* ⊙ *No lunch. Closed Dec. 15–Apr. 15; Mon.–Wed. Apr. 15–July 1 and Sept. 1–Dec. 15; and Mon. and Tues. July and Aug.*

The Goldenrod

$$ | AMERICAN | FAMILY | People line the windows to watch Goldenrod Kisses being made the same way they have since 1896—and thousands of pounds are made every year at this York Beach classic. Aside from the famous taffy (there's penny candy, too), this eatery is family-oriented, very reasonably priced, and a great place to get homemade

ice cream from the old-fashioned soda fountain. **Known for:** laid-back, kid-friendly atmosphere; breakfast served all day; classic American fare, like burgers, hot dogs, and baked dinners. [$] *Average main: $10* ✉ *2 Railroad Ave., York Beach* ☎ *207/363–2621* 🌐 *www.thegoldenrod.com* ⏲ *Closed mid-Oct.–mid-May.*

☕ Coffee and Quick Bites

Flo's Steamed Hot Dogs

$ | **AMERICAN** | Yes, it seems crazy to highlight a hot-dog stand, but this is no ordinary place—who would guess that a hot dog could make it into *Saveur* and *Gourmet* magazines? There is something grand about this shabby, red-shingle shack, where the classic dog has mayo and a special sauce—consisting of, among other things, onions and molasses (you can buy a bottle to take home, and you'll want to). **Known for:** family-owned and-operated; in business since 1959; lines out the door (but efficient service means waits aren't that long). [$] *Average main: $3* ✉ *1359 U.S. 1, Cape Neddick* ☎ *No phone* 🌐 *www.floshotdogs.com* 💳 *No credit cards* ⏲ *Closed Wed. No dinner.*

🛏 Hotels

★ Cliff House

$$$ | **HOTEL** | **FAMILY** | At this luxurious hotel overlooking the Atlantic Ocean, you can watch the white crests smash the craggy bluffs below while nestled in a hooded flannel robe on your balcony. **Pros:** the views; rooms have private terraces; plenty of activities to keep everyone busy. **Cons:** no in-room coffee setups (only one communal coffee station per floor to help reduce waste); meals not included; central location means a drive to the nearest town centers. [$] *Rooms from: $600* ✉ *591 Shore Rd., Cape Neddick* ☎ *207/361–1000* 🌐 *www.cliffhousemaine.com* 🔑 *226 rooms* 🍴 *No Meals.*

Inn at Tanglewood Hall

$$ | **B&B/INN** | This 1880s shingle-style "cottage" is a haven of antiques, art, and eclectic decor—artfully painted floors, lush wallpaper, and meticulous attention to detail are the fruits of a former designation as a designers' showcase home. **Pros:** authentic historic lodging; short walk to beaches; fireplaces in all rooms. **Cons:** no water views; dated decor (though it's in keeping with a historic property); no pets or children under 12. [$] *Rooms from: $225* ✉ *611 York St., York Harbor* ☎ *207/351–1075* 🌐 *www.tanglewoodhall.com* 🔑 *6 rooms* 🍴 *Free Breakfast.*

★ Stage Neck Inn

$$ | **RESORT** | **FAMILY** | A family-run operation that is now in the competent hands of the second generation, this resort hotel takes full advantage of its gorgeous harborside location, with Adirondack chairs, chaise longues, and a fire pit on the surrounding lawns; water views from most guest rooms; and floor-to-ceiling windows in the common spaces. **Pros:** elaborate breakfast buffet with scrumptious baked goods; poolside service and snack bar in season; rooms have balconies or deck areas and most have water views. **Cons:** spa is on the small side; some rooms have only partial water views; rooms with two beds have doubles rather than queens. [$] *Rooms from: $300* ✉ *8 Stage Neck Rd., off U.S. 1A, York Harbor* ☎ *800/340–1130, 207/363–3850* 🌐 *www.stageneck.com* ⏲ *Closed 1st 2 wks in Jan.* 🔑 *60 rooms* 🍴 *Free Breakfast.*

Union Bluff Hotel

$$ | **HOTEL** | This massive, turreted structure still looks much the same as it did when it opened in the mid-19th century, and the proximity to the beach can't be beat—just don your suit and step outside. **Pros:** many spectacular ocean views; in the middle of the action; spacious balconies. **Cons:** rooms lack any charm or character that would reflect the inn's origins;

not for those who want a quiet getaway; decor in need of an update. [$] *Rooms from: $290* ✉ *8 Beach St., York Beach* ☎ *207/363–1333* 🌐 *www.unionbluff.com* 🛏 *71 rooms* 🍴 *No Meals.*

York Harbor Inn

$ | **B&B/INN** | A mid-17th-century fishing cabin with dark timbers and a fieldstone fireplace forms the heart of this historic inn, which now includes several neighboring buildings. **Pros:** many rooms have harbor views; close to beaches, scenic walking trails; kid-friendly. **Cons:** rooms vary greatly in style, size, and appeal; no ocean views at the Chapman Cottage; only Harbor Crest Inn is pet-friendly. [$] *Rooms from: $199* ✉ *480 York St., York Harbor* ☎ *207/363–5119* 🌐 *www.yorkharborinn.com* 🛏 *65 rooms* 🍴 *Free Breakfast.*

Shopping

The Gateway York Farmers' Market

MARKET | **FAMILY** | Bring your own bag for morning shopping at the Gateway York Farmers' Market, held in the back lot at the Greater York Region Chamber of Commerce on Saturday in summer (mid-May–mid-November, 9–1). You'll find fresh, locally grown produce and flowers; lots of baked goods, pies, and artisanal breads; local meat and eggs; and handcrafted items like soaps, jewelry, pottery, and candles. It's a good place to gather the makings for a beach picnic or to stock up on holiday gifts. ✉ *1 Stonewall La., off U.S. 1, York* ☎ *207/363–4422* 🌐 *www.gatewayfarmersmarket.com.*

Ocean Fire Pottery

CERAMICS | This artist-owned and-operated studio and gallery features unique wheel-thrown stoneware. Stop in for keepsake souvenirs; just call ahead to make sure the studio is open during the off-season. ✉ *23 Woodbridge Rd., York Village* ☎ *207/361–3131* 🌐 *www.oceanfirepottery.com.*

Stonewall Kitchen

FOOD | **FAMILY** | You've probably seen Stonewall Kitchen's jars of chutneys, jams, jellies, salsas, and sauces in specialty stores back home. This complex houses the expansive flagship store, which has a viewing area of the bottling process. Sample all the mustards, salsas, and dressings you can stand, or have lunch at the café, then meander through the stunning gardens to the Stonewall Home Company Store, offering candles, hand lotions, and essentials for the garden and home. ✉ *2 Stonewall La., off U.S. 1, York* ☎ *207/351–2712* 🌐 *www.stonewallkitchen.com.*

Activities

BIKING

Berger's Bike Shop

BIKING | This former auto garage and full-service bike shop rents hybrid bikes for local excursions and sells bikes of all kinds. ✉ *241 York St., York* ☎ *207/363–4070.*

FISHING

The State of Maine Department of Marine Resources (🌐 *www.maine.gov/dmr/home*) has information on both saltwater and freshwater recreational fishing.

Eldredge Bros. Fly Shop

FISHING | This shop offers various guided fishing trips and private casting lessons. In the off-season, check out its fly-tying or rod-building seminars. ✉ *1480 U.S. 1, Cape Neddick* ☎ *207/363–9269* 🌐 *www.eldredgeflyshop.com.*

Shearwater Charters

FISHING | Shearwater offers light-tackle and fly-fishing charters in the York River and along the shoreline from Kittery to Ogunquit. Bait-fishing trips are also available. Departures are from Town Dock #2 in York Harbor; just note that trips are capped at three people. ✉ *Town Dock #2, 20 Harris Island Rd., York* ☎ *207/363–5324* 🌐 *www.mainestripers.net.*

Ogunquit's Perkins Cove is a pleasant place to admire the boats (and wonder at the origin of their names).

HIKING AND WALKING
Cliff Walk and Fisherman's Walk

TRAIL | Two walking trails begin near Harbor Beach. Starting in a small nearby park, the Cliff Walk ascends its granite namesake and passes the summer "cottages" at the harbor entrance. There are some steps, but, as signs caution, tread carefully because of erosion. Fisherman's Walk, on the other hand, is an easy stroll. Starting across Stage Neck Road from the beach, it passes waterfront businesses, historic homes, and rocky harbor beaches on the way to York's beloved Wiggly Bridge. This pedestrian suspension bridge alongside Route 103 (there is minimal parking here) leads to Steedman Woods, a public preserve with a shaded loop trail along the York River estuary's ambling waters. You can also enter the preserve near the George Marshall Store in York Village. ⊠ *Stage Neck Rd., off U.S. 1A, York.*

Ogunquit

7 miles north of the Yorks via U.S. 1.

A resort village since the late 19th century, Ogunquit made a name for itself as an artists' colony. Today it has become a mini Provincetown, with a population that swells in summer, boutique shops and galleries, and many inns and small clubs that cater to an LGBTQ+ clientele.

Nightlife in Ogunquit revolves around the precincts of Ogunquit Square and Perkins Cove, where people stroll, often enjoying an after-dinner ice-cream cone or espresso. For a scenic drive, take Shore Road from downtown to the 175-foot Bald Head Cliff; you'll be treated to views up and down the coast. On a stormy day the surf can be quite wild here.

GETTING HERE AND AROUND

Parking in the village and at the beach is costly and limited, so leave your car at the hotel or in a public parking space and hop the trolley. It costs $5 per trip and

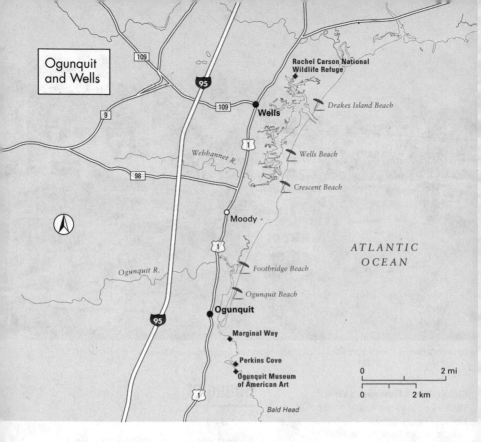

runs Memorial Day weekend–Columbus Day, with weekend-only service during the last few weeks, after Labor Day. From Perkins Cove, the trolley runs through town along Shore Road and then down to Ogunquit Beach; it also stops along U.S. 1.

TRANSPORTATION Shoreline Explorer.

☎ 800/965–5762 ⊕ www.shorelineexplorer.com.

VISITOR INFORMATION
CONTACTS Ogunquit Chamber of Commerce. ✉ 36 Main St., Ogunquit ☎ 207/646–1279 ⊕ www.ogunquit.org.

 ## Sights

Marginal Way
PROMENADE | FAMILY | This mile-plus-long, paved footpath hugs the shore of a rocky promontory just beyond Ogunquit's downtown. Thirty-nine benches along the easygoing path allow you to appreciate the open sea vistas. Expect heavy foot traffic, even in the off-season—which is the only time of the year that dogs are allowed. ✉ Perkins Cove Rd., Ogunquit ⊕ www.marginalwayfund.org.

★ Ogunquit Museum of American Art
ART MUSEUM | FAMILY | Ogunquit has long been an important site for artists, and this stellar museum—the only one in Maine focused solely on American art—continues that legacy. The collection includes 3,000 early modern and contemporary paintings, sculptures, drawings, and more, including works with ties to Ogunquit's once-famous artist colony. The main gallery offers sweeping views of Perkins Cove. Leave time to stroll around the 3-acre seaside sculpture park in good weather. ✉ 543

Shore Rd., Ogunquit ☎ *207/646–4909* 🌐 *ogunquitmuseum.org* 🎫 *$12* ⏲ *Closed Nov. 1–Apr. 30.*

Perkins Cove

OTHER ATTRACTION | FAMILY | This neck of land off Shore Road in the lower part of Ogunquit village has a jumble of sea-weathered fish houses and buildings that were part of an art school. These have largely been transformed by the tide of tourism into shops and restaurants, including the classic Barnacle Billy's seafood spot. When you've had your fill of browsing, stroll out along the mile-long Marginal Way. ✉ *Perkins Cove Rd., off Shore Rd., Ogunquit.*

Beaches

Footbridge Beach

BEACH | FAMILY | This spot offers excellent swimming, beach combing, and bodysurfing opportunities, as well as a boat launch for kayaks, small boats, and standup paddleboards. Typically less crowded than neighboring Ogunquit Beach, it's reached by crossing a footbridge that runs over the Ogunquit River. Dogs are welcome from September through March. **Amenities:** food and drink; lifeguards; parking (fee); toilets. **Best For:** solitude; sunrise; sunset; surfing; swimming; walking; windsurfing. ✉ *Ocean St. and Ocean Ave., Ogunquit* 🌐 *www.ogunquit.org/our-beaches* 🎫 *Parking $30 a day (mid-Apr.–Oct.).*

Ogunquit Beach

BEACH | FAMILY | Perfect for just about every beach fan—sunbathers to beachcombers and bodysurfers—this 3-mile-long, sandy beach is located between the Atlantic Ocean and the Ogunquit River. Beach chairs and umbrellas are available for rent seasonally. Dogs are welcome from September through March. **Amenities**: food and drink; lifeguards; parking (fee); toilets. **Best For:** sunset; swimming; walking. ✉ *Ogunquit* ✣ *End of Ocean Ave.* 🌐 *www.ogunquit.org/our-beaches* 🎫 *Parking $35 a day (mid-Apr.–Oct.).*

Restaurants

Barnacle Billy's

$$$ | SEAFOOD | Overlooking Perkins Cove, Barnacle Billy's has been serving up fresh, local seafood since 1961. Place your order at the counter before settling into a table on the deck to await delivery of your clam chowder, fried clams, broiled scallops, or lobster roll. **Known for:** lobster rolls and chowder; takeout counter and ice cream; deck seating overlooking Perkins Cove. [$] *Average main: $38* ✉ *50–70 Perkins Cove Rd., Ogunquit* ☎ *207/646–5575* 🌐 *www.barnbilly.com* ⏲ *Closed late Oct.–late Apr.*

The Lobster Shack

$$ | SEAFOOD | A fixture since 1947 in Ogunquit's bustling Perkins Cove, this cozy, weathered-shingle lobster pound is just across from the oft-photographed footbridge. Choose from a ¼- to a whopping 1-pound lobster roll, or try the delicious roll with hand-picked Maine crab meat. **Known for:** Maine beers on tap; lobsters rolls; chowder. [$] *Average main: $26* ✉ *110 Perkins Cove Rd., Ogunquit* ☎ *207/646–2941* 🌐 *www.lobster-shack.com.*

★ Northern Union

$$ | CONTEMPORARY | From the moment you walk into Northern Union you know you're going to be in very good hands. A genuine, welcoming staff and laid-back yet elegant design scheme put you in the mood for a slow, very memorable dinner of seasonally inspired small plates like braised pork belly or duck confit and rotating entrées like seared scallops and lobster fettuccine—all available with spot-on wine pairings that you won't find anywhere else in the area. **Known for:** almost everything is made in-house; dishes that can easily be shared; a terrific selection of cured meats and cheese boards with a local, seasonal bent. [$] *Average* *main: $27* ✉ *261 Shore Rd., Ogunquit* ☎ *207/216–9639* 🌐 *www.northern-union.me* 🕒 *No lunch.*

Coffee and Quick Bites

Backyard Coffeehouse and Eatery

$ | AMERICAN | FAMILY | This eager-to-please coffee shop is centrally located and a good stop for hot or iced coffee accompanied by a scone or bagel. For something more substantial, choose from a selection of breakfast or lunch sandwiches. **Known for:** locally sourced coffee, tea, and bagels; close to Marginal Way walking path; the North Country bacon, egg, and cheese breakfast sandwich. [$] *Average main: $5* ✉ *178 Main St., Ogunquit* ☎ *207/251–4554* 🌐 *www.backyardogunquit.com* 🕒 *Closed mid-Oct.–Apr.*

Performing Arts

Ogunquit Playhouse

THEATER | FAMILY | Over its nearly century-long history, this classic summer theater has brought some the country's best talent to its stage. The stately green-and-white building feels like a relic from an old-time summer resort, and with an average of five productions each season, the Playhouse offers a good reason to take a break from the beach and spend an evening indoors. ✉ *10 Main St., Ogunquit* ☎ *207/646–5511* 🌐 *www.ogunquit-playhouse.org* 🎫 *Show tickets: from $47* 🕒 *Closed Nov.–May.*

Wells

6 miles north of Ogunquit via U.S. 1.

Lacking any kind of discernible village center, Wells could be easily overlooked as nothing more than a commercial stretch of U.S. 1 between Ogunquit and the Kennebunks. But look more closely: this is a place where people come to enjoy some of the best beaches on the coast. Until 1980 the town of Wells incorporated Ogunquit, and today this family-oriented beach community has 7 miles of densely populated shoreline, along with nature preserves, where you can explore salt marshes and tidal pools.

GETTING HERE AND AROUND

Amtrak's *Downeaster* train stops at Wells Transportation Center, but from there, this town is best explored by car. U.S. 1 is the main thoroughfare, with antiques stores, shops, and diners lining both sides. Venture down the roads that branch off U.S. 1 to the east (and the coast), like Mile Road, which has spots to eat and drink and leads to Wells Beach. Just north, where U.S. 1 intersects with Route 9, is the Rachel Carson National Wildlife Refuge.

VISITOR INFORMATION

CONTACTS Wells Chamber of Commerce. ✉ *136 Post Rd., Wells* ✣ *At intersection of Post Rd. (U.S. 1) and Kimballs La.* ☎ *207/646–2451* 🌐 *www.wellschamber.org.*

Sights

Rachel Carson National Wildlife Refuge

WILDLIFE REFUGE | FAMILY | At the headquarters of the Rachel Carson National Wildlife Refuge, which has 11 divisions from Kittery to Cape Elizabeth, is the Carson Trail, a 1-mile loop. The trail traverses a salt marsh and a white-pine forest where migrating birds and waterfowl of many varieties are regularly spotted, and it borders Branch Brook and the Merriland River. ✉ *321 Port Rd., Wells* ☎ *207/646–9226* 🌐 *www.fws.gov/refuge/rachel_carson.*

Beaches

Crescent Beach

BEACH | FAMILY | Lined with summer homes, this sandy strand is busy in the summer, but the beach and the water are surprisingly clean, considering all

The 2-miles-long Wells Beach is popular with families and surfers.

the traffic. The swimming's good, and beachgoers can also explore tidal pools and look for seals on the sea rocks nearby. **Amenities:** lifeguards; parking (fee); toilets. **Best for:** swimming. ✉ *Webhannet Dr., south of Mile Rd., Wells.*

Drakes Island Beach

BEACH | **FAMILY** | Smaller and quieter than the other two beaches in Wells, Drakes Island Beach is also a little more natural, with rolling sand dunes and access to salt-marsh walking trails at an adjacent estuary. The ice-cream truck swings by regularly in the summer. **Amenities:** lifeguards; parking (fee); toilets. **Best for:** walking. ✉ *Island Beach Rd., via Drakes Island R. off of U.S. 1, Wells.*

Wells Beach

BEACH | **FAMILY** | The northern end of a 2-mile stretch of golden sand, Wells Beach is popular with families and surfers, who line up in the swells and suit up on the boardwalk near the arcade and snack shop. The beach's northern tip is a bit quieter, with a long rock jetty perfect for strolling. **Amenities:** food and drink; lifeguards; parking (fee); toilets. **Best for:** surfing; walking. ✉ *Atlantic Ave., north of Mile Rd., Wells.*

🍴 Restaurants

★ Batson River Fish Camp

$$ | **AMERICAN** | This outpost of the popular Batson River brewing and distilling company channels the feel of a trendy lakeside camp (think vintage thermoses and prize catches mounted on the walls) all year round. The menu includes standout cocktails, well-done bar fare, and beers brewed on-site, just behind Fish Camp. **Known for:** limited-edition brews; throwback camp decor; fun spot for a well-made cocktail after a day at the beach. $ *Average main: $20* ✉ *73 Mile Rd., Wells* ☎ *207/360–7255* 🌐 *batsonriver.com/wells-maine* 🕒 *Closed Wed. No lunch.*

Billy's Chowder House

$$ | **SEAFOOD** | **FAMILY** | Locals and vacationers head to this roadside seafood restaurant and bar in the midst of a salt marsh en route to Wells Beach. The menu features classic seafood dishes like lobster rolls and chowders, but there are plenty of nonseafood choices, too. **Known for:** views of the Rachel Carson National Wildlife Refuge; generous lobster rolls; one of the oldest waterfront restaurants in Wells. $ *Average main: $24* ✉ *216 Mile Rd., Wells* 🕾 *207/646–7558* ⊕ *www. billyschowderhouse.com* ⊗ *Closed mid-Dec.–mid-Jan.*

★ Bitter End

$$ | **SEAFOOD** | Pete and Kate Morency, the duo originally behind the ever-popular Pier 77 and the Ramp Bar and Grill in Kennebunkport, are also the masterminds behind this seafood spot, where Mediterranean and American classics are given brilliant, contemporary twists. The fabulous decor consists of an unlikely marriage of old-school American sports memorabilia and something that might be described as shabby ballroom chic—crystal chandeliers hang above old leather boxing gloves, and shiny trophies (including a 1961 Miss Universe cup) and black-and-white photos of sports icons line the bar. **Known for:** cuisine fusion and a rotating menu; outdoor seating area with firepit; superbly curated bevy of liquors. $ *Average main: $24* ✉ *2118 Post Rd., Wells* 🕾 *207/360–0904* ⊕ *www. bitterend.me* ⊗ *Closed Tues.*

Maine Diner

$$ | **AMERICAN** | One look at the 1953 exterior, and you'll start craving diner food, but be prepared to get a little more than you bargained for: after all, how many greasy spoons make an award-winning lobster pie? There's plenty of fried seafood in addition to the usual diner fare, and breakfast is served all day. **Known for:** classic diner fare; wild Maine blueberry pie; sources a lot of produce from its very own vegetable garden. $ *Average main: $15* ✉ *2265 Post Rd., Wells* 🕾 *207/646–4441* ⊕ *www.mainediner. com* ⊗ *No dinner. Closed Wed. and at least 2 wks in Jan.*

Spinnakers

$$ | **SEAFOOD** | **FAMILY** | Plenty of seafood shacks dot U.S. 1, but this roadside joint is really worth the stop, even if it's just to grab some takeout and escape the steady flow of summer traffic. Simple but pleasing contemporary design makes for a cheerful space to enjoy loaded lobster rolls, burgers, sandwiches, and a decidedly unholy lobster poutine consisting of hand-cut fries covered in a delicious mess of local cheese curds topped with lobster gravy. **Known for:** pick-and-choose seafood basket combos; quick bites that pack a punch and scream Maine; eat in or grab and go. $ *Average main: $20* ✉ *139 Post Rd., Wells* 🕾 *207/216–9291* ⊕ *spinnakersmaine.com.*

☕ Coffee and Quick Bites

Congdon's Doughnuts

$ | **AMERICAN** | **FAMILY** | These superior doughnuts have been made by members of the same family since 1945 and at the same location since 1955. Congdon's has about 40 different varieties, some seasonal, though the plain variety really gives you an idea of just how good these doughnuts are: it's the biggest seller, along with the honey dipped and black raspberry jelly. **Known for:** Congdon's After Dark features food trucks and live music nightly in summer; outrageously good, classic doughnuts; perfect spot to start a rainy day. $ *Average main: $3* ✉ *1090 Post Rd., Wells* 🕾 *207/646–4219* ⊕ *www. congdons.com* ⊗ *No dinner. Closed Wed. in season and Mon.–Wed. off-season; check website for details.*

🛏 Hotels

Haven by the Sea

$$ | **B&B/INN** | Once the summer mission of St. Martha's Church in Kennebunkport, this exquisite inn, just a block from the beach, has retained many details from its former life, including cathedral ceilings and stained-glass windows. **Pros:**

rotating breakfasts that cater to dietary restrictions without compromising taste; nightly happy hour with complimentary appetizers and sherry, port, and brandy; beach towels and beach chairs available. **Cons:** not an in-town location; distant ocean views; $50 cancellation fee no matter how far in advance. $ *Rooms from: $260* ✉ *59 Church St., Wells* ☎ *207/646–4194* 🌐 *www.havenbythesea.com* 🛏 *9 rooms* 🍴 *Free Breakfast.*

Activities

Wheels N Waves

WATER SPORTS | FAMILY | Rent surfboards, wet suits, boogie boards, kayaks, standup paddleboards, bikes and e-bikes, and all sorts of other outdoor gear at Wheels N Waves, Maine's oldest surf shop—in business since 1974. ✉ *365 Post Rd., U.S. 1, Wells* ☎ *207/646–5774* 🌐 *www.wheelsnwaves.com* 🎟 *$15 for 4-hr surfboard or bike rental; $30 for 4-hr paddleboard rental; $65 per day for e-bikes* 🕒 *Closed Jan. and Feb.*

Kennebunk, Kennebunkport, and Cape Porpoise

6 miles north of Wells via Rte. 9.

The town centers of Kennebunk and Kennebunkport are separated by 5 miles and two rivers, but, what are probably best described as the Hamptons of the Pine Tree State are united by a common history and laid-back seaside vibe. Kennebunkport has been a resort area since the 19th century, and its most recent residents have made it even more famous: the dynastic Bush family is often in residence on its immense estate, which sits dramatically out on Walker's Point on Cape Arundel. Newer homes have sprung up alongside the old, and a great way to take them all in is with a slow drive out Ocean Avenue along the cape.

Sometimes bypassed on the way to its sister town, Kennebunk has its own appeal. Once a major shipbuilding center, Kennebunk today retains the feel of a classic New England small town, with an inviting shopping district, steepled churches, and fine examples of 18th- and 19th-century brick and clapboard homes. There are also plenty of natural spaces for walking, swimming, birding, and biking, and the area's major beaches are along its shores.

Just north of Kennebunkport is the fishing village of Cape Porpoise, with a working lobster pier, spectacular views of the harbor and lighthouse, and excellent restaurants.

GETTING HERE AND AROUND

Kennebunk's main downtown sits along U.S. 1, extending west from the Mousam River. The Lower Village is along routes 9 and 35, 4 miles down Route 35 from downtown, and the way between is lined on both sides by mansions, making it a spectacular drive.

To reach the beaches of Kennebunk, continue straight (the road becomes Beach Avenue) at the intersection with Route 9. If you turn left instead, Route 9 will take you across the Kennebunk River, into Kennebunkport's touristy downtown, called Dock Square (or sometimes just "the Port"). Here you'll find the most activity (and crowds) in the Kennebunks, thanks to restaurants, shops, galleries, and boats that offer cruises.

The Intown Trolley runs narrated jaunts in season, passing Kennebunk's beaches and Lower Village as well as neighboring Kennebunkport's scenery and sights. The main stop is at 21 Ocean Avenue in Kennebunkport, around the corner from Dock Square.

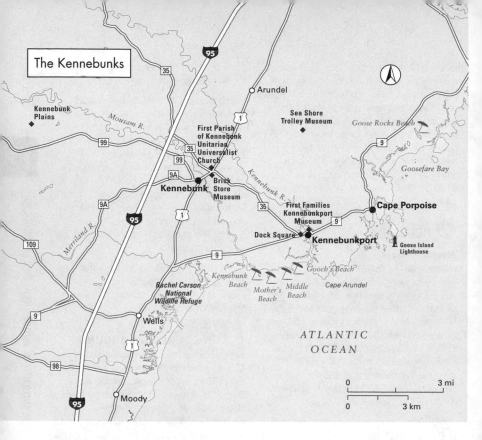

The Kennebunks

Arundel

Kennebunk Plains

Mousam R.

First Parish of Kennebunk Unitarian Universalist Church

Sea Shore Trolley Museum

Goose Rocks Beach

Goosefare Bay

Kennebunk

Brick Store Museum

Kennebunk R.

First Families Kennebunkport Museum

Cape Porpoise

Dock Square

Kennebunkport

Goose Island Lighthouse

Merriland R.

Rachel Carson National Wildlife Refuge

Kennebunk Beach

Mother's Beach

Middle Beach

Gooch's Beach

Cape Arundel

Wells

ATLANTIC OCEAN

Moody

0   3 mi

0   3 km

TRANSPORTATION Intown Trolley. ✉ Kennebunkport ☎ 207/967–3686 ⊕ www. intowntrolley.com.

WALKING TOURS

To take a little walking tour of Kennebunk's most notable structures, begin at the Federal-style Brick Store Museum at 117 Main Street. Head south on Main Street (turn left out of the museum) to see several extraordinary 18th- and early-19th-century homes, including the **Lexington Elms** at No. 99 (1799), the **Horace Porter House** at No. 92 (1848), and the **Benjamin Brown House** at No. 85 (1788).

When you've had your fill of historic homes, head back up toward the museum, pass the 1773 **First Parish Unitarian Church** (its Asher Benjamin–style steeple contains an original Paul Revere bell), and turn right onto **Summer Street.** This street is an architectural showcase, revealing an array of styles from Colonial to Federal. Walking past these grand beauties will give you a real sense of the economic prowess and glamour of the long-gone shipbuilding industry.

At noon on Thursday and Saturday from June through October (or by appointment off-season), the museum offers a guided architectural walking tour of Summer Street. You can also purchase a $4.95 map that marks historic buildings or a $15.95 guidebook, *Windows on the Past.*

For a dramatic walk along Kennebunkport's rocky coastline and beneath the views of Ocean Avenue's grand mansions, head out on the **Parson's Way Shore Walk,** a paved 4.8-mile round-trip. Begin at Dock Square and follow Ocean Avenue along the river, passing the Colony Hotel and St. Ann's Church, all the way to Walker's Point. Simply turn back from here.

VISITOR INFORMATION

CONTACTS Kennebunk-Kennebunkport Chamber of Commerce. ⊠ *16 Water St., Kennebunk* ☎ *207/967–0857* ⊕ *www. gokennebunks.com.*

Sights

Brick Store Museum

HISTORY MUSEUM | FAMILY | The cornerstone of this block-long preservation of early-19th-century commercial and residential buildings is William Lord's Brick Store. Built as a dry-goods store in 1825 in the Federal style, the building has an openwork balustrade across the roofline, granite lintels over the windows, and paired chimneys. Exhibits chronicle the Kennebunk area's history, art, and culture for kids and adults alike. In addition, museum staffers lead walking tours of Kennebunk's National Historic District (at noon on Thursday and Saturday from June through October) and of the town's beaches (at 11 on Saturday from July through September). ⊠ *117 Main St., Kennebunk* ☎ *207/985–4802* ⊕ *www.brickstoremuseum.org* ⊠ *$5* ⊗ *Closed Mon.*

★ Dock Square

PLAZA/SQUARE | Restaurants, art galleries, clothing boutiques, and other shops—both trendy and touristy—line this bustling square and nearby streets and alleys. Walk onto the drawbridge to admire the tidal Kennebunk River; cross to the other side and you are in the Lower Village of neighboring Kennebunk. ⊠ *Dock Sq., Kennebunkport.*

First Families Kennebunkport Museum

HISTORIC HOME | FAMILY | Also known as White Columns, this imposing Greek Revival mansion with Doric columns is furnished with the belongings of four generations of the Perkins-Nott family. From mid-July through mid-October, the 1853 house is open for guided tours and also serves as a gathering place for village walking tours. It is owned by the Kennebunkport Historical Society, which has several other historical buildings, including an old jail and schoolhouse, a mile away at 125–135 North Street. ⊠ *8 Maine St., Kennebunkport* ☎ *207/967–2751* ⊕ *www.kporths.com* ⊠ *$10.*

First Parish of Kennebunk Unitarian Universalist Church

CHURCH | FAMILY | Built in 1773, just before the American Revolution, this stunning church is a marvel. The 1804 Asher Benjamin–style steeple stands proudly atop the village, and the sounds of the original Paul Revere bell can be heard for miles. ⊠ *114 Main St., Kennebunk* ☎ *207/985–3700* ⊕ *www.uukennebunk.org.*

Kennebunk Plains

NATURE PRESERVE | FAMILY | For an unusual experience, visit this 650-acre grasslands habitat that is home to several rare and endangered species and managed, in part, with controlled burns. Locals call it Blueberry Plains, and a good portion of the area is abloom with the hues of ripening wild blueberries in late July; after August 1, you are welcome to pick and eat all the berries you can find. The area is maintained by the Nature Conservancy. ⊠ *Webber Hill Rd., Kennebunk* ✛ *4½ miles northwest of town* ☎ *207/251–2256* ⊕ *www.nature.org* ⊠ *Free.*

Seashore Trolley Museum

OTHER MUSEUM | FAMILY | This fun, visitor-favorite museum is an homage to transport from years past. Get an up-close look at trolleys from major metropolitan areas worldwide—from Boston to Budapest, New York to Nagasaki, and San Francisco to Sydney—beautifully restored and displayed (and, sometimes, operational). Best of all, you can take a nearly 4-mile ride on the tracks of the former Atlantic Shore Line Railway, with a stop along the way at the museum restoration shop, where trolleys are transformed from junk into gems. The outdoor museum is self-guided. ⊠ *195 Log Cabin Rd., Kennebunkport* ☎ *207/967–2800* ⊕ *www.trolleymuseum.org* ⊠ *$13* ⊗ *Closed weekdays in May and Mon.*

Did You Know?

The iconic "Welcome to Kennebunkport" sign is located on the Lanigan Bridge between Kennebunk and Kennebunkport.

and Tues. June 1–Oct. 31. Closed Nov.–Apr. except 1st 2 weekends in Dec.

Beaches

★ Goose Rocks Beach

BEACH | **FAMILY** | Three-mile-long Goose Rocks, a 10-minute drive north of Kennebunkport, has a good long stretch of smooth sand and plenty of shallow pools for exploring. It's a favorite of families with small children. Pick up a $25 daily parking permit at one of two kiosks along the beach: one outside of Goose Rocks Beach General Store at 3 Dyke Road and the other at the Proctor Avenue beach path. Dogs are allowed (on a leash), but only before 9 and after 5 during the summer season. There is one porta potty behind the General Store, but otherwise no facilities are available at the beach. **Amenities:** parking (fee). **Best for:** walking; swimming. ✉ *Dyke Rd., off Rte. 9, Kennebunkport* 🌐 *www.kennebunkportme.gov.*

Kennebunk Beach

BEACH | **FAMILY** | Kennebunk Beach has three distinct stretches, one after another, along Beach Avenue, which is lined with cottages and old Victorians. The southernmost **Mother's Beach** is popular with families. Rock outcroppings lessen the waves, and a playground and tidal pools keep kids busy. This is followed by the stony **Middle Beach.** The most northerly, and the closest to downtown Kennebunkport, is **Gooch's Beach,** the main swimming beach. **Amenities:** lifeguards; parking (fee); toilets. **Best for:** walking; swimming. ✉ *Beach Ave., south of Rte. 9, Kennebunk.*

Restaurants

The Boathouse Restaurant

$$$ | **SEAFOOD** | You can't get more up-close and personal with Kennebunkport's harbor than at this stunning waterside restaurant and bar that serves dressed-up, contemporary takes on classic Maine fare, alongside staples such as perfectly shucked local oysters, lobster tacos, and hearty clam and corn chowder. The inside spaces are warm and welcoming, with a maritime theme that's not too over-the-top. **Known for:** amazing waterside location; top-notch cocktails on the wraparound deck; great seafood. [$] *Average main: $31* ✉ *21 Ocean Ave., Kennebunkport* ☎ *207/967–8225* 🌐 *boathouseme.com/kennebunkport-maine-restaurants.*

The Burleigh

$$$ | **SEAFOOD** | Nautical accents give this trendy restaurant a laid-back vibe that is the perfect transition from time spent out on the water (or at the beach) to a relaxed end-of-the-day meal. While fresh seafood plays a central role, you can't go wrong with one of the excellent burgers or pork chops paired with one of the many rotating local craft-beer choices. **Known for:** Burleigh burger (prime beef patty, cheddar cheese, smoked bacon, lettuce, tomato, onion, pickles, hand-cut fries); craft cocktails that will knock you off of your feet; excellent happy hour in the inn's Garden Social Club. [$] *Average main: $32* ✉ *1 Dock Sq., Kennebunkport* ☎ *207/967–2621* 🌐 *kennebunkportinn.com/dining* ⏲ *No lunch. Closed Mon. and Tues.*

★ The Clam Shack

$$ | **SEAFOOD** | **FAMILY** | For more than a half century, this shack has been known for speedy service and great takeout fare, like its traditional boiled lobster dinners and lobster rolls on freshly baked buns. Eat at one of several wooden picnic tables that overlook the Kennebunk River. **Known for:** clam chowder; lobster rolls and fried clams; ships lobster nationally. [$] *Average main: $17* ✉ *2 Western Ave., Kennebunk* ☎ *207/967–3321* 🌐 *www.theclamshack.net.*

★ Earth at Hidden Pond

$$$ | **FUSION** | Each and every meal feels like a special occasion at his splurge-worthy place, which offers thoughtful attention to flavor and texture and uses the freshest locally sourced ingredients. The seasonally inspired menu is always in flux, but you can be sure that even hard-core foodies will be delighted with this culinary experience. **Known for:** woodfire surf-and-turf dishes; ingredients culled from its own garden; private dining sheds and cabanas for special occasions and groups. $ *Average main: $38* ⊠ *354 Goose Rocks Rd., Kennebunkport* ☎ *207/967–6550* ⊕ *hiddenpondmaine. com/earth.*

Mabel's Lobster Claw

$$$ | SEAFOOD | FAMILY | Since the 1950s, this tiny spot on Ocean Avenue has been serving lunches and dinners featuring lobster (baked and in rolls), clam chowder, and other seafood, as well as homemade pies. The decor includes paneled walls, wooden booths, and autographed photos of various TV stars (and members of the Bush family), and there's outside seating. **Known for:** blueberry pie; Lobster Savannah: split and filled with scallops and shrimp, and baked in a Newburg sauce; takeout window for food and ice cream. $ *Average main: $35* ⊠ *124 Ocean Ave., Kennebunkport* ☎ *207/967–2562* ⊕ *mabelslobster.com* ☽ *Closed Nov.–early Apr.*

★ Ocean

$$$ | SEAFOOD | Large picture windows make this one of the best places in town to watch the sun set (or rise) over the Atlantic. The intimate dining space features a touch of seaside elegance coupled with captivating, original local art, and Maine seafood and other local ingredients are used in contemporary takes on classic dishes such as lobster Thermidor, foie gras, swordfish, and seafood velouté. **Known for:** equally perfect for a romantic evening or a gathering of friends; gracious, old-world service; ridiculously indulgent desserts that you may want to eat first. $ *Average main: $40* ⊠ *208 Ocean Ave., Kennebunkport* ☎ *855/346–5700* ⊕ *capearundelinn.com/ dining* ☽ *No lunch.*

★ Old Vines Wine Bar

$$ | MODERN AMERICAN | Housed in a historic barn, this wine bar and its front patio get busy in summer, and for good reason: artisan cocktails and flavorful small plates are expertly made, and, as the name suggests, the wine list is stellar. Except for a six-week break in midwinter, it's open year-round and cozy on cold nights, too. **Known for:** regular entertainment by Maine musicians; wine list featuring small vineyards and unique varietals; lively Yard Bar open outdoors in summer. $ *Average main: $24* ⊠ *173 Port Rd., Kennebunk* ☎ *207/967–2310* ⊕ *oldvineswinebar.com* ☽ *No lunch. Closed for 6 wks in Feb. and Mar.*

★ Pier 77 Restaurant

$$ | AMERICAN | Here, phenomenal views share center stage with a sophisticated menu that emphasizes seafood. The ground-level restaurant's large windows overlook Cape Porpoise harbor, ensuring that every seat has a view of the water; tucked around the corner, the tiny but funky and fun Ramp Bar & Grill pays homage to a really good burger, fried seafood, and other pub-style classics; and, up a flight of stairs, Ramp Up offers crow's-nest harbor views and a place to wait for your table when lines to get in are long. **Known for:** live music in summer; great spot for cocktails on the water while watching boats and sea life pass by; a packed house almost every meal in the summer (reservations highly recommended). $ *Average main: $25* ⊠ *77 Pier Rd., Cape Porpoise* ☎ *207/967–8500* ⊕ *www.pier77restaurant.com.*

★ The Tides Beach Club Restaurant

$$$ | SEAFOOD | Maritime accents and a crisp color palette help to make this unfussy, beachside restaurant a good place to relax and enjoy a prebeach bite or a post-beach sit-down meal. The menu features lighter seafood fare and salads alongside heartier options, such as lobster rangoons, crispy fried-chicken sandwiches, and burgers. **Known for:** no

Maine's rocky coastline stretches for about 3,400 miles including Kennebunkport.

dress code—think beach-hair-don't-care chic; delicious craft cocktails; exceptional service that isn't cloying. $ *Average main: $35* ⊠ *930 Kings Hwy., Kennebunkport* ☎ *207/967–3757* ⊕ *tidesbeachclubmaine.com/food.*

Coffee and Quick Bites

Dock Square Coffee House
$ | AMERICAN | European-style coffee drinks, tea, pastries, smoothies, and other seasonal snacks are on the menu at this small café built over a tidal river in the midst of Dock Square. The coffee is sourced from Portland-based and nationally recognized Coffee By Design, one of the state's best. **Known for:** locally sourced coffee, pastries and breakfast sandwiches; quiet place to sit amid the bustle of Dock Square; central location. $ *Average main: $5* ⊠ *18 Dock Sq., Kennebunkport* ☎ *207/967–4422* ⊕ *www. docksquarecoffeehouse.biz* ⊗ *Closed Jan.–Mar.*

★ Rococo Ice Cream
$ | ICE CREAM | FAMILY | Have an open mind and an adventurous palate when you walk inside this tiny shop as you won't find plain vanilla or chocolate on the menu. Rococo's has a rotating rooster of internationally inspired flavors that range from olive oil, rosemary, caramel, and pepitas to goat cheese, blackberry, and Chambord. **Known for:** Maine whoopie-pie ice cream; unique ingredient combinations; ships ice cream around the country. $ *Average main: $5* ⊠ *6 Spring St., Kennebunkport* ☎ *207/835–1049* ⊕ *rococoicecream.com.*

🛏 Hotels

Cape Arundel Inn and Resort
$$$ | B&B/INN | This shingle-style, 19th-century mansion, originally one of the area's many summer "cottages," commands a magnificent ocean view that takes in the Bush estate at Walker's Point; its location is just far enough from the bustle of town to truly feel like you've gotten away from it all. **Pros:** exceptional

staff that is gracious and discreet; luxurious beds and linens that will make you feel like a spring chicken upon waking; champagne on arrival. **Cons:** not for the budget-minded; clubhouse amenities are ½ mile away from main house; not all rooms have ocean views. $ *Rooms from: $469 ⊠ 208 Ocean Ave., Kennebunkport ☎ 800/514–0968 ⊕ capearundelinn.com ⌚ Closed Jan. ⇄ 29 rooms ¡○¡ Free Breakfast.*

★ Hidden Pond

$$$$ | RESORT | Tucked away on 60 wooded acres near Goose Rocks Beach, this resort enclave has hiking trails, two pools, a sumptuous spa, a phenomenal restaurant, a working farm and a variety of lodging options—from luxurious one-bedroom bungalows and two-bedroom cottages to rustic-chic lodges with interconnected suites and studios. **Pros:** use of beach facilities at nearby Tides Beach Club and free beach shuttle and beach-cruiser bikes; lots of on-site activities for adults and children; guests can cut fresh flowers and harvest vegetables from the property's many gardens. **Cons:** steep prices; away from the center of town; no dogs allowed. $ *Rooms from: $1050 ⊠ 354 Goose Rocks Rd., Kennebunkport ☎ 207/967–9050 ⊕ hiddenpondmaine.com ⌚ Closed Nov.–Apr. ⇄ 46 units ¡○¡ No Meals.*

The Inn at English Meadows

$$ | B&B/INN | A stone's throw from the bustle of Kennebunkport and just a mile from the beach, this charming boutique B&B is housed in a gorgeously restored, 1860s farmhouse and carriage house. **Pros:** luxurious bathroom amenities including rain showers and toiletries by Malin + Goetz; gas fireplaces in many rooms; home-baked goods available every afternoon. **Cons:** no pool; no water view; not wheelchair accessible. $ *Rooms from: $359 ⊠ 141 Port Rd., Kennebunk ☎ 207/967–5766 ⊕ englishmeadowsinn.com ⌚ Closed Mon.–Wed mid-Dec.–Mar. ⇄ 11 rooms ¡○¡ Free Breakfast.*

★ Kennebunkport Captains Collection

$$ | B&B/INN | The four historic inns and houses in this Lark Hotels collection were painstakingly restored in 2020 and 2021, and each was given its own sumptuous, traditional-meets-modern twists. **Pros:** complimentary bikes; easy walk into town; fireplaces in the guest rooms. **Cons:** the nontraditional resort layout may not be everyone's ideal; no pool; no elevators (as these are historic homes). $ *Rooms from: $349 ⊠ 6 Pleasant St., Kennebunkport ☎ 207/967–3141 ⊕ www.larkhotels.com/hotels/kennebunkport-captains-collection ⇄ 45 rooms ¡○¡ Free Breakfast.*

The Nonantum Resort

$$$ | RESORT | FAMILY | Hands down the most family-friendly resort in the Kennebunks, this place is a dream for parents who want to have a quality family vacation without stress. **Pros:** comfortable beds from local Portland Mattress Makers; seasonal, Maine-centric childrens' activities; friendly, service-oriented staff. **Cons:** wedding events add to bustle; heavy visitor traffic; no indoor pool. $ *Rooms from: $449 ⊠ 95 Ocean Ave., Kennebunkport ☎ 207/967–4050 ⊕ nonantumresort.com ⌚ Closed mid-Dec.–late Apr. ⇄ 109 rooms ¡○¡ Free Breakfast.*

★ Sandy Pines Campground

$ | RESORT | The "glamping" (glamorous camping) tents, camp cottages, and A-frame hideaway huts on wheels at Sandy Pines Campground deliver every bit as much comfort and luxury as a fine hotel (with a few caveats, including communal bathing areas), but give you a chance to get up close and personal with nature. **Pros:** the glamping areas of Sandy Pines are quiet zones; nightly bonfires under the stars without roughing it; all lodgings equipped with outdoor sitting area, picnic table, and fire ring. **Cons:** expect all that comes with being in nature; glamping options are not pet-friendly; three-night minimum stay (seasonal). $ *Rooms from:*

$109 ✉ 277 Mills Rd., Kennebunkport ☎ 207/967–2483 🌐 sandypinescamping.com ⏲ Closed mid-Oct.–mid-May 🛏 60 units 🍴 No Meals.

The Tides Beach Club
$$$$ | B&B/INN | The stately building that houses the Tides Beach Club is a charming grande dame from the Gilded Age heyday of seaside "cure" retreats. **Pros:** use of the common spaces (pools, spa, garden) at the very exclusive Hidden Pond; beach service for a relaxed lunch or dinner on the sand; most rooms have ocean views and balconies. **Cons:** definitely will lighten your purse; a lot of activity in and around the inn; not pet-friendly. *[$] Rooms from: $629 ✉ 930 Kings Hwy., Kennebunkport ☎ 207/967–3757 🌐 tidesbeachclubmaine.com ⏲ Closed Nov.–Apr. 🛏 21 rooms 🍴 Free Breakfast.*

The Wanderer Cottages
$$ | MOTEL | This cluster of tidy, well-appointed cottages opened in summer 2022 in a quiet area that's still a stone's throw from beaches and Dock Square. **Pros:** serene, nicely landscaped setting; heated saltwater pool; private, spacious-feeling cottages, some with sitting areas. **Cons:** no food or bar on-site; no kids allowed; 1.5 miles from Dock Square and 1.2 miles from Parson's Beach. *[$] Rooms from: $349 ✉ 195 Sea Rd., Kennebunk ☎ 207/849–7400 🌐 wanderercottages.com 🛏 17 cottages 🍴 Free Breakfast.*

★ White Barn Inn, Auberge Resorts Collection
$$$$ | RESORT | At this intimate, exclusive property, no detail has been overlooked in the meticulously appointed cottages and rooms, most of which blend contemporary comforts with classic elements and have fireplaces, marble soaking tubs, and double walk-in showers. **Pros:** romantic and indulgent; amenities include a farm-to-table restaurant and an elegant spa; over-the-top service. **Cons:** prices are steep; not directly on a beach; you pay for what you get here. *[$] Rooms from: $1475 ✉ 37 Beach Ave., Kennebunk ☎ 207/967–2321 🌐 aubergeresorts.com/whitebarninn 🛏 27 units 🍴 No Meals.*

★ The Yachtsman Hotel and Marina Club
$$$ | HOTEL | These chic bungalows at this water-side property a short walk from town have a hip beach-vibe design, private lawns that blur the distinction between indoors and outdoors, and harbor views. **Pros:** lots of amenities included in the rate; free shuttle service around town; large marble showers and luxe toiletries from Malin + Goetz. **Cons:** not on the beach; private lawns aren't exactly private with all the boats passing by; not family-friendly, but two rooms are pet-friendly. *[$] Rooms from: $549 ✉ 59 Ocean Ave., Kennebunkport ☎ 207/967–2511 🌐 yachtsmanlodge.com ⏲ Closed Nov.–Apr. 🛏 30 bungalows 🍴 Free Breakfast.*

Shopping

★ Daytrip Society
SOUVENIRS | FAMILY | The impossibly hip and well-selected array of goods at this modern-design shop makes it an excellent place for both window-shopping and finding gifts for just about anyone on your list (including yourself). A refreshing departure from the rest of the somewhat stodgy gift shops in the village, this boutique is chock-full of eye candy, most of which is also functional. There are many locally sourced and contemporary products, from hats and jewelry to novelty books, home decor, and outdoor adventure essentials. Check out Daytrip Jr., its equally hip children's store around the corner. *✉ 4 Dock Sq., Kennebunkport ☎ 207/967–4440 🌐 www.daytripsociety.com.*

★ Farm + Table
HOUSEWARES | This delightful shop is housed in a bright-red Maine barn filled with household items both useful and pleasing to the eye. Browse the collection of ceramics, linens, kitchen essentials, and more by small-batch

makers, and pick up a few artisan treats, too. ✉ *8 Langsford Rd., Cape Porpoise* ☎ *207/604–8029* ⊕ *www.farmtablekennebunkport.com.*

Maine Art Hill

ART GALLERIES | Maine Art Hill's centerpiece is a two-story gallery showcasing works by artists from Maine and elsewhere in New England. There's also a sculpture garden, complete with copper wind designs and whirligigs. Just steps behind are the Studios, a cluster of cottages, each housing the work of a different artist, photographer, or creator. ✉ *14 Western Ave., Kennebunk* ☎ *207/967–2803* ⊕ *www.maine-art.com.*

Port Canvas

HANDBAGS | Since 1968, Port Canvas has been hand-crafting sporty, customizable canvas totes and duffels perfect for lugging your souvenirs home. Other products range from raincoats to keychains. Each stitcher puts their initials inside the bag ensuring authenticity and quality. ✉ *39 Limerick Rd., Kennebunkport* ☎ *207/985–9767* ⊕ *www.portcanvas.com* ⊘ *Closed Fri.–Sun.*

★ Snug Harbor Farm

HOUSEWARES | Don't let the name fool you: although there are ducks, chickens, and even peacocks wandering around the quaint grounds of this Kennebunk spot, it's far more charming than rustic. Wander through the gardens, or stop into the shop, housed in a 19th-century farmhouse, for one-of-a-kind terra-cotta pots and elevated gifts for the garden, home, and bath. ✉ *87 Western Ave., Kennebunk* ☎ *207/967–2414* ⊕ *snugharborfarm.com.*

 Activities

FISHING

Cast-Away Fishing Charters

BOATING | **FAMILY** | Private half- and full-day charters are available, as is a two-hour children's charter trip where kids can try lobstering for the day and haul in the traps. ✉ *Performance Marine, 4 Western Ave., Kennebunk* ☎ *207/284–1740* ⊕ *www.castawayfishingcharters.com* ☜ *From $300.*

***Rugosa* Lobster Tours**

BOATING | **FAMILY** | Lobster-trap hauling trips aboard the *Rugosa* in the scenic waters off the Kennebunks run daily, from Memorial Day through Columbus Day. ✉ *Nonantum Resort, 95 Ocean Ave., Kennebunkport* ☎ *207/468–4095* ⊕ *www.rugosalobstertours.com* ☜ *$49 per person for a group tour.*

WHALE-WATCHING

First Chance

WILDLIFE-WATCHING | **FAMILY** | This company leads whale-watching cruises on the 87-foot *Nick's Chance*. Scenic lobster cruises are also offered aboard the 65-foot *Kylie's Chance*. Trips run daily in summer and on weekends in the shoulder seasons. ✉ *Performance Marine, 4 Western Ave., Kennebunk* ☎ *207/967–5507* ⊕ *www.firstchancewhalewatch.com.*

★ The Pineapple Ketch

SAILING | **FAMILY** | One terrific way to get out on the water and see some marine life is aboard a classic 38-foot, Downeaster ketch steered by a knowledgeable captain and crew. Tours last 90 minutes, and soft drinks are provided. You'll have to bring your own snacks, as well as wine, beer, or cocktails, which are especially good to have on hand during the sunset cruises. ✉ *95 Ocean Ave., Kennebunkport* ☎ *207/888–3445* ⊕ *pineappleketch.com* ☜ *From $55 per person* ⊘ *Closed mid-Oct.–late May.*

Biddeford

11 miles north of Kennebunkport, 18 miles south of Portland.

Biddeford is waking from a deep sleep, having devolved into something of a ghost town for a good deal of the past half century. Chefs and small-business owners who have relocated from Portland are giving Biddeford's beautiful old-mill-town architecture a new lease on life. Developers have taken note as well, revamping many historic buildings, including the imposing 233,000-square-foot Lincoln Mill. Today, Biddeford is filled with art galleries and quirky boutiques, a distillery, an art school, and top-notch restaurants.

GETTING HERE AND AROUND

From I–95, get off at Exit 32 and follow Alfred Street to Biddeford's downtown. U.S. 1 also runs right through town. Amtrak's *Downeaster* train stops at Saco; the train station is just steps from Biddeford's mill buildings, breweries, and restaurants.

VISITOR INFORMATION

CONTACTS Biddeford-Saco Chamber of Commerce. ✉ *28 Water St., Biddeford* ☎ *207/282–1567* 🌐 *www.biddefordsacochamber.org.*

👁 Sights

Round Turn Distilling

DISTILLERY | There's a reason why all the good craft cocktail bars in Maine stock Bimini Gin, the flagship spirit of this distillery, located in a 150-year-old textile mill on the Saco River. Learn more about the best small-batch gin in the Pine Tree State, and be sure to take a peek at the production area: the distillery uses steam to power its modern steel-and-copper still. Finish up in the well-designed bar for a gin tasting or cocktail and snacks, or pick up a bottle of house-made spirits to go. ✉ *32 Main St., Bldg. 13W, Suite 103, Biddeford* ☎ *207/370–9446* 🌐 *roundturndistilling.com.*

Wood Island Lighthouse

LIGHTHOUSE | FAMILY | The 42-foot stone lighthouse and attached two-story keeper's house are on the 32-acre, uninhabited Wood Island off the coast of Biddeford. The island is closed to the public except for two-hour guided tours hosted by Friends of Wood Island Lighthouse. Tours are offered several times a week in July and August and on Maine Lighthouse Day in September, and reservations can be made starting in June. Boats leave from Vine's Boat Landing in Biddeford Pool. Note that people wearing flip-flops will not be allowed to board. ✉ *20 Yates St., Biddeford* ☎ *207/200–4552* 🌐 *woodislandlighthouse.org* 🎟 *$35* 🕒 *Closed Oct.–June.*

🍴 Restaurants

★ Elda

$$$$ | MODERN AMERICAN | Award-winning chef Bowman Brown is behind this restaurant, situated in an old mill building—transformed with exquisite, Scandinavian-style decor—and offering just two tasting-menu seatings (at 5 and 8:30) a night. This is one of Maine's most highly regarded and splurge-worthy dining experiences, featuring meticulously prepared, seasonally inspired dishes, but if your budget is tight, note that the first-floor Jackrabbit Cafe serves small plates and pastries for a fraction of the tasting-menu price. **Known for:** unhurried, indulgent dining (meals often last three hours); focus on locally sourced ingredients; impeccable, modern-meets-original design, with an old vault serving as bar. [$] *Average main: $160* ✉ *14 Main St., 2nd fl., Biddeford* ☎ *207/602–0359* 🌐 *www.eldamaine.com* 🕒 *No lunch. Closed Sun.–Tues. and for 2-wk break in spring.*

★ Goldthwaite's Pool Lobster

$$ | SEAFOOD | FAMILY | This classic spot has been a go-to in the seaside hamlet of Biddeford Pool for over 100 years. Now part general store, part takeout spot, it's a one-stop-shop for sunscreen, wine and beer, and locally made pies; the kitchen offers a bevy of Maine classics (including lobster dinners and fresh lobster rolls), sometimes with a twist (like haddock tacos with ginger-cucumber salsa or a blueberry cream cheese tart for dessert). **Known for:** award-winning clam chowder; decadent desserts made in-house;

reasonable prices with million-dollar views. $ *Average main: $22* ✉ *3 Lester B. Orcutt Blvd., Biddeford* ☎ *207/284–5000* ⊕ *poollobster.com* ◔ *General store closed mid-Sept.–mid-May; restaurant closed Labor Day–early June.*

Magnus on Water

$$ | **MODERN AMERICAN** | The small, shareable plates at this restaurant are excellent (think littleneck clam toast, locally made sourdough, and fresh plates of cheeses and greens), but the cocktails, that incorporate inventive ingredients (like a foam made from seawater collected from nearby Fortune's Rocks beach) aren't to be missed. Grab a spot on the spacious, laid-back granite patio in summer or inside at the intimate bar in colder months. **Known for:** creative, photo-worthy cocktails; approachable sharing plates (order as much or as little as you like); summer dining on a spacious, beautifully landscaped, granite patio. $ *Average main: $22* ✉ *12 Water St., Biddeford* ☎ *207/494–9052* ⊕ *magnusonwater.com* ◔ *No lunch. Closed Sun.–Tues. and for winter break in Feb.*

★ **Palace Diner**

$$ | **AMERICAN** | Everything about this diner, set in an old-fashioned train car just off Main Street, is retro except the food. Hop on a stool at the counter (that's all there is), enjoy the Motown tunes, and tuck into one of the deluxe sandwiches for breakfast or lunch. **Known for:** diner food that's anything but standard; delicious fried-chicken sandwich with cabbage slaw and French fries; fantastic collaboration with local chefs from regional restaurants. $ *Average main: $12* ✉ *18 Franklin St., Biddeford* ☎ *207/284–0015* ⊕ *www.palacedinerme.com* ▭ *No credit cards* ◔ *No dinner.*

 Coffee and Quick Bites

Elements: Books, Coffee, Beer

$ | **CAFÉ** | You could easily while away an entire day at this cozy spot. Enjoying Elements' own Biddeford-roasted coffee is a great way to start the day, to fuel an afternoon of reading, or to perk up in the early evening, especially on nights when there's a poetry reading or live local music performance. **Known for:** part café, part bookstore, part pub; great coffee and beer; live music. $ *Average main: $5* ✉ *265 Main St., Biddeford* ☎ *207/710–2011* ⊕ *www.elementsbookscoffeebeer.com.*

Hotels

★ **The Lincoln Hotel**

$$ | **HOTEL** | A far cry from Maine's coastal bed-and-breakfasts and quaint inns, this hotel in the massive, revitalized Lincoln Mill has a distinctly urban feel. **Pros:** cool base for exploring Biddeford's many watering holes; gas fireplaces in every room; soaring ceilings and huge windows with city views. **Cons:** not close to beaches or outdoor activities; no room service (only grab-and-go food in the lobby); trendy vibe might not appeal to some. $ *Rooms from: $299* ✉ *17 Lincoln St., Biddeford* ☎ *207/815–3977* ⊕ *www.lincolnhotelmaine.com* ⇆ *33 rooms* ❍ *No Meals.*

Scarborough, Prout's Neck, and Cape Elizabeth

Scarborough and Prout's Neck: 10 miles northeast of Biddeford. Cape Elizabeth: 10 miles southeast of Scarborough, 8 miles southeast of Portland.

Among the noteworthy attractions in the affluent Portland bedroom community of Cape Elizabeth are the famed Portland

Old Orchard Beach

Located between Kennebunkport and Portland, Old Orchard Beach was a classic, upscale, place-to-be-seen resort area in the late 19th century, when the railroad brought wealthy families looking for entertainment and the benefits of fresh sea air. During the 1940s and '50s, the pier had a dance hall where stars of the time performed. Although the luster has dulled and Old Orchard is now a little tacky (though pleasantly so) these days, it remains a good place for seaside entertainments.

The center of the action is a 7-mile strip of sand beach that's accompanied by Palace Playland, New England's only boardwalk amusement park (think Coney Island or Seaside Heights). Fire claimed the end of the pier—at one time it jutted out nearly 1,800 feet into the sea—but rides, miniature golf, midway games, and souvenir stands still line both sides. Despite the peak-season crowds and fried-food odors, the atmosphere is captivating; the town even sponsors a fireworks display every Thursday night in the summer. Places to stay range from cheap motels to cottage colonies to full-service seasonal hotels. You won't find free parking, but there are ample lots. Amtrak has a seasonal stop here, too.

For even more family fun, Saco's Funtown Splashtown USA is just 10 minutes from the Old Orchard Beach Pier. Kids of all ages can cool off and play for hours amid the thrill adventures, kiddie rides, waterslides, and play pools.

Head Light and the Cape Elizabeth Light, the subject of a well-known Edward Hopper painting.

Speaking of famous artists, Winslow Homer painted many of his famous oceanscapes from a tiny studio on the rocky peninsula known as Prout's Neck, a now-exclusive gated community 7 miles south of Cape Elizabeth. The studio is open to tours only through the Portland Museum of Art. The only other way to access Prouts Neck is by parking outside the gates and walking along a popular cliff trail.

GETTING HERE AND AROUND

The somewhat rural landscapes of Scarborough, the hamlet of Prout's Neck, and Cape Elizabeth are best explored by car. From Route 1 North, Routes 207 and 77 travel along the coast; most of the state parks, preserves, and vistas are along this route. From Portland, take the Casco Bay Bridge and continue onto Route 77 South.

Sights

Cape Elizabeth Light

LIGHTHOUSE | FAMILY | This was the site of twin lighthouses erected in 1828—and locals still call it Two Lights—but one of the lighthouses was dismantled in 1924 and converted into a private residence. The other half still operates, and you can get a great photo of it from the end of Two Lights Road (note that it's not quite visible from the nearby Two Lights State Park). The lighthouse itself is closed to the public, but you can explore the tidal pools at its base, looking for small, edible snails known as periwinkles, or just "wrinkles," as they're sometimes referred to in Maine. Picnic tables are also available. ⊠ *At end of Two Lights Rd., across from The Lobster Shack at Two Lights (225 Two Lights Rd.), Cape Elizabeth.*

The white-stone Portland Headlight was commissioned by George Washington in 1790.

★ Portland Head Light

LIGHTHOUSE | FAMILY | Familiar to many from photographs and the Edward Hopper painting *Portland Head-Light* (1927), this lighthouse was commissioned by George Washington in 1790. The towering, white-stone structure stands over the keeper's quarters, a white home with a blazing red roof, today the Museum at Portland Head Light. The lighthouse is in 90-acre Fort Williams Park, a sprawling green space with walking paths, picnic facilities, a beach and—you guessed it—a cool old fort. ⊠ *1000 Shore Rd., Cape Elizabeth* ☎ *207/799–2661* ⊕ *www. portlandheadlight.com* ⊠ *Museum $2* ⊙ *Museum closed mid-Oct.–late May.*

Scarborough Marsh Audubon Center

NATURE PRESERVE | FAMILY | You can explore this Maine Audubon Society–run nature center on foot or by canoe and on your own or as part of a guided walk or paddle. Canoes and kayaks are available to rent and come with a life jacket and map. The salt marsh is Maine's largest and is an excellent place for bird-watching and peaceful paddling along its winding ways. The center has a discovery room for kids, programs for all ages ranging from basket making to astronomy, and a good gift shop. Tours include birding walks. ⊠ *92 Pine Point Rd., Scarborough* ☎ *207/883–5100* ⊕ *www.maineaudubon. org* ⊠ *Free* ⊙ *Center closed Labor Day– Memorial Day. Trails open year-round.*

★ Winslow Homer Studio

HISTORIC HOME | FAMILY | The great American landscape painter created many of his best-known works in this seaside home between 1883 until his death in 1910. It's easy to see how this rocky, jagged peninsula might have been inspiring. The only way to get a look is on a tour with the Portland Museum of Art, which leads 2½-hour strolls through the historic property. ⊠ *5 Winslow Homer Rd., Scarborough* ☎ *207/775–6148* ⊕ *www. portlandmuseum.org* ⊠ *$65* ⊙ *Closed Nov.–Apr.*

Beaches

Crescent Beach

BEACH | FAMILY | Just off scenic Route 77, this ½-mile-long, half-moon-shape swatch of sand has some of the warmest ocean currents in the state, making it a favorite for swimming. **Amenities**: food and drink; lifeguards; parking; showers; toilets; water sports. **Best for**: swimming; walking. ✉ *Crescent Beach State Park, Bowery Beach Rd., Cape Elizabeth* ☎ *207/799–5871* 🌐 *www.maine.gov.*

Restaurants

★ Bite Into Maine

$$ | SEAFOOD | FAMILY | Hands down Maine's best lobster roll is found at this food truck that overlooks the idyllic Portland Head Light in Cape Elizabeth. Traditional rolls smothered in ungodly amounts of drawn butter are delicious, but you've also got the option to get out of the lobster comfort zone with rolls featuring flavors like wasabi, curry, and chipotle. **Known for:** quick and informal spot for a bite; unbeatable view over the ocean; always fresh lobster. [$] *Average main: $24* ✉ *1000 Shore Rd., Cape Elizabeth* ☎ *207/289–6142* 🌐 *www.biteintomaine.com* 🕒 *Closed mid-Nov.–mid-Apr.*

★ The Lobster Shack at Two Lights

$$ | SEAFOOD | FAMILY | A classic spot since the 1920s, you can't beat the location—right on the water, below the lighthouse pair that gives Two Lights State Park its name—and the food's not bad either. Enjoy fresh lobster whole or piled into a hot-dog bun with a dollop of mayo, or opt for the delicious chowder, fried clams, or fish-and-chips. **Known for:** picnic tables with unparalleled views; family-friendly environment; mini-homemade blueberry pies. [$] *Average main: $25* ✉ *225 Two Lights Rd., Cape Elizabeth* ☎ *207/799–1677* 🌐 *www.lobstershacktwolights.com* 🕒 *Closed late Oct.–late Mar.*

★ Shade Eatery at Higgins Beach Inn

$$ | SEAFOOD | FAMILY | This charming neighborhood restaurant and bar just steps from the beach serves up generous, deeply satisfying dishes filled with locally sourced ingredients. Seafood plays a big role in the menu, with lobster rolls brimming with fresh meat; fish tacos stuffed with cilantro, lime crema, and coleslaw; a seafood chowder; and a lobster tostada. **Known for:** family-friendly environment; three-season-porch dining; casual and perfect for a postbeach bite. [$] *Average main: $24* ✉ *Higgins Beach Inn, 36 Ocean Ave., Scarborough* ☎ *207/883–1479* 🌐 *www.higginsbeachinn.com/dining* 🕒 *Breakfast daily and dinner Wed.–Sun. mid-May–mid-Oct. Lunch daily Memorial Day–Labor Day.*

★ The Well at Jordan's Farm

$$$$ | MODERN AMERICAN | This off-the-beaten-path spot takes farm-to-table dining very literally. The fresh-grown produce—much of it from the grounds at Jordan's Farm—needn't travel far: prix-fixe dinners are served, family- or tasting-menu style on the intimate "chef's porch" or in private screened gazebos tucked among the flower fields, yours for the whole night. **Known for:** only one seating per night, so once you're seated, you can kick back; fresh-from-the-fields dishes; intimate, private-dinner-party feel. [$] *Average main: $85* ✉ *21 Wells Rd., Cape Elizabeth* ☎ *207/831–9350* 🌐 *thewellatjordansfarm.com* 🕒 *No lunch. Closed Oct.–May.*

Hotels

Black Point Inn

$$$ | RESORT | FAMILY | Toward the tip of the peninsula that juts into the ocean at Prout's Neck stands this stylish, tastefully updated, 1878 resort inn with spectacular views up and down the coast. **Pros:** dramatic setting; geothermally heated pool; discounts in shoulder seasons. **Cons:** non-Atlantic views a little underwhelming; rooms have an older, more stately feel to them; children are asked to only eat in pub area. [$] *Rooms from: $490* ✉ *510 Black Point Rd., Scarborough* ☎ *207/883–2500* 🌐 *www.blackpointinn.com* 🕒 *Closed late Oct.–early May* 🛏 *25 rooms* 🍴 *Free Breakfast.*

★ Higgins Beach Inn

$$ | **B&B/INN** | **FAMILY** | Decidedly "new Maine," this lovingly renovated 1892 inn with a laid-back, summer-casual kind of nonchalance is just steps from the surfer's paradise that is Higgins Beach. **Pros:** very family-friendly; exceptionally efficient and warm service; small touches (beach towels, sparkling-water dispenser) that make a difference. **Cons:** no pets allowed; a short walk to the beach; limited common areas. [$] *Rooms from: $269* ✉ *34 Ocean Ave., Scarborough* ☎ *207/883–6684* 🌐 *www.higginsbeach-inn.com* 🕒 *Closed Oct.–Apr.* 🛏 *23 rooms* 🍴 *Free Breakfast.*

★ Inn by the Sea

$$$$ | **B&B/INN** | With a location on stunning Crescent Beach, some of the state's most gracious service, and a top-notch restaurant that delights at every meal, you might never want to leave the aptly named Inn by the Sea. Each accommodation choice is impeccably maintained and equipped with luxe bedding. **Pros:** amenities like a spa and an outdoor pool with water views; hands down the most dog-friendly accommodations in Maine; direct access to Crescent Beach with chic beach chairs, towels, and umbrellas on hand. **Cons:** a little removed from Portland's food scene; not for the budget-minded; minimum stays in the high season. [$] *Rooms from: $719* ✉ *40 Bowery Beach Rd., Cape Elizabeth* ☎ *207/799–3134* 🌐 *www.innbythesea.com* 🛏 *62 rooms* 🍴 *No Meals.*

Chapter 4

PORTLAND

Updated by
Alexandra Hall

◉ Sights	🍴 Restaurants	🛏 Hotels	🛍 Shopping	🍸 Nightlife
★★★★★	★★★★★	★★★☆☆	★★★☆☆	★★★★☆

WELCOME TO PORTLAND

TOP REASONS TO GO

★ **Extraordinary food:** Eat your way through award-winning menus, in unpretentious and welcoming restaurants where "farm to table" has been always been the philosophy and practice.

★ **Natural beauty:** Take in iconic views of the rough coastline and bright white sails juxtaposed against a gray-blue sea from the lighthouse at Portland Head Light.

★ **Adventure:** Sail to one of the nearby islands aboard a Casco Bay Lines ferry or take a whale-watching or schooner cruise from Portland Harbor.

★ **History:** Experience the style of Colonial Maine at the Tate House, a grand 1775 home built by an English sea captain.

★ **Art:** Pay homage to Winslow Homer, Edward Hopper, Andrew Wyeth, and others at the Portland Museum of Art.

★ **Shopping:** Discover handmade crafts, new artists, or gear up for an outdoor adventure at the shops, galleries, and outfitters in and around Old Port.

1 **Old Port and Waterfront.** The city's retail and culinary core abuts the working waterfront.

2 **The Arts District.** Home to museums, galleries, and theaters.

3 **The East End, Munjoy Hill, and Washington Avenue.** Includes the Eastern Prom, the Portland Observatory, and Washington Avenue's eclectic and lauded eateries.

4 **The West End.** Victorian mansions, a sprawling park, and a cluster of cool gastropubs.

5 **Back Cove.** A residential slice of the city with terrific waterfront biking and walking trails.

6 **Bayside.** A magnet for hipsters and artists with breweries, diners, and bowling.

7 **Riverton, Stroudwater, and Parkside.** Thompson's Point, the Tate House Museum, and breweries; Hadlock Field and Deering Oaks Park; and Industrial Way's excellent breweries.

8 **South Portland.** Off the beaten path, you'll find lighthouses, beaches, forts, museums, and the state's biggest mall.

9 **Casco Bay Islands.** A collection of quiet islands just a ferry ride from Portland.

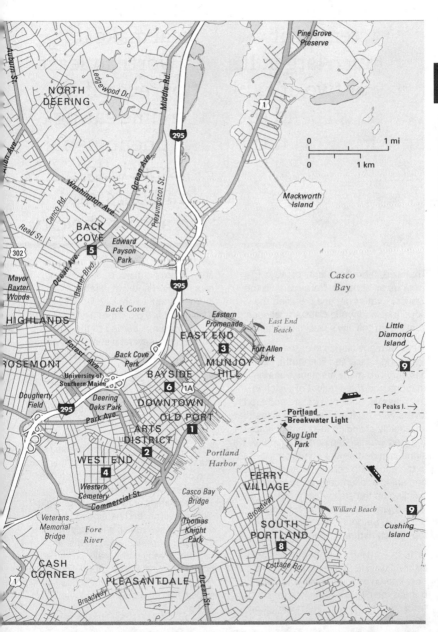

Pine Grove
Preserve

NORTH
DEERING

Ledgewood Dr.

Auburn St.

Middle Rd.

Washington Ave.

Presumpscot St.

Ocean Ave.

Allen Ave.

295

1

0   1 mi
0   1 km

Mackworth
Island

BACK
COVE 5

302

Canco Rd.

Read St.

Edward
Payson
Park

Casco
Bay

Mayor
Baxter
Woods

Ocean Ave.

Baxter Blvd.

Back Cove

HIGHLANDS

Forest Ave.

Eastern
Promenade

East End
Beach

EAST END
3

Little
Diamond
Island

9

ROSEMONT

University of
Southern Maine

Back Cove
Park

Fort Allen
Park

MUNJOY
HILL

BAYSIDE

Dougherty
Field

Deering
Oaks Park

6   1A

295

Park Ave.

DOWNTOWN

OLD PORT

1

Portland
Breakwater Light

To Peaks I. →

ARTS
DISTRICT 2

WEST END
4

Bug Light
Park

Portland
Harbor

FERRY
VILLAGE

9

Western
Cemetery

Commercial St.

Casco Bay
Bridge

Broadway

Willard Beach

9

Veterans
Memorial
Bridge

Fore
River

Thomas
Knight
Park

SOUTH
PORTLAND

Cushing
Island

CASH
CORNER

PLEASANTDALE

Cottage Rd.

8

1

Broadway

Ocean St.

Maine's largest city may be considered small by national standards—its population is just 66,000—but its character, spirit, and appeal make it feel much larger. It's well worth at least a day or two of exploration, even if all you do is spend the entire time eating and drinking at the many phenomenal restaurants, bakeries and specialty dessert shops, craft cocktail bars, and microbreweries scattered across the city.

That said, there are plenty of ways to work up an appetite, from roaming the working waterfront and perusing the boutiques and world-class art galleries, to soaking up the city's fascinating history.

A city of many names over the centuries (including Casco and Falmouth), Portland has survived many dramatic transformations, the most recent of which is the massive influx of hipsters and food lovers who have opened businesses that are rapidly changing the city's character. Blessed with a deep port, Portland was a significant settlement right from its start in the early 17th century. Settlers thrived on fishing and lumbering, repeatedly building up the area while the British, French, and Native Americans continually sacked it. Settlers came regardless, to tap its rich natural resources.

In 1632 Portland's first home was built on the Portland Peninsula in the area now known as Munjoy Hill. The British burned the city in 1775 when residents refused to surrender, but it was rebuilt and became a major trading center. Much of Portland was destroyed again in the Great Fire on July 4, 1866, when a boatyard fire grew into a conflagration; 1,500 buildings burned to the ground. These days, several distinct neighborhoods reveal a city that embraces its history as well as its art, music, and culinary scenes. The most visited section, the restored Old Port, features a working waterfront where emblematic lobster boats share ports with cruise ships, ferries, and sailing yachts. Stately homes built by ships' captains line the streets of the Western Promenade; artists, artisans, and other businesses have taken over many renovated redbrick warehouses. The nightlife is active here, with nightclubs, taverns, and bars pouring out the sounds of live music and lively patrons. Exceptional restaurants, shops, and galleries, many with locally produced goods, abound. Water tours of the harbor and excursions to the Casco Bay islands depart from the piers of Commercial Street.

Portland's busy harbor is full of working boats, pleasure craft, and ferries headed to the Casco Bay Islands.

Downtown Portland has emerged from a years-long on-again, off-again funk, during which much retail commerce was lost to suburban shopping malls. Its burgeoning Arts District centers on a revitalized Congress Street, which runs the length of the peninsular city from alongside the Western Promenade in the southwest to the Eastern Promenade on Munjoy Hill in the northeast. Washington Street, home to some of the city's newest and most exciting restaurants, runs through the East End and Munjoy Hill. Congress Street is peppered with interesting shops, eclectic restaurants, and excellent museums.

Just beyond the Arts District is the West End, an area of extensive architectural wealth. Predominantly residential, it's filled with stunning examples of the city's emphasis on preserving this past.

Planning

Getting Here and Around

From Interstate 95, take Interstate 295 to get to the Portland Peninsula and downtown. Commercial Street runs along the harbor, Fore Street is one block up in the heart of the Old Port, and the Arts District stretches along diagonal Congress Street. Munjoy Hill is on the eastern end of the peninsula and the West End on the opposite side.

Portland is wonderfully walkable; an able-bodied explorer can easily take in the Old Port, the Arts District, and the West End. Narrated trolley tours are also available. To get to many islands in Casco Bay, hop aboard a waterfront ferry.

AIR
The Portland International Jetport serves flights on American Airlines, United Airlines, Delta, Elite Airways, Frontier Airlines, JetBlue, Southwest, and Sun

Country Airlines. It offers direct flights to many destinations, all of which are domestic. It's about a 20-minute drive from Old Port, by either rental car or ride share. There is also a bus service between the Jetport and downtown Portland via the Greater Portland Transit District METRO (see Bus for more information); the website has routes and schedules.

AIRPORT Portland International Jetport. (*PWM*) ✉ *1001 Westbrook St., Portland* ☎ *207/774–7301* ⊕ *www.portlandjetport. org.*

BICYCLE

The craggy fingers of land that dominate this part of the coast are fun for experienced cyclists to explore, but the lack of shoulders on many roads combined with heavy tourist traffic can be intimidating.

Two good resources are the Bicycle Coalition of Maine and Explore Maine by Bike, which provide information on trails and bike shops around the state.

CONTACTS Bicycle Coalition of Maine. ✉ *38 Diamond St., Arts District* ☎ *207/623–4511* ⊕ *www.bikemaine.org.* **Explore Maine by Bike.** ☎ *207/624–3300* ⊕ *www.exploremaine.org/bike.*

BUS

Greater Portland's METRO runs bus routes in Falmouth, Portland, South Portland, and Westbrook. The fare is $2; exact change is required. The website has maps, schedules, and routes.

Regionally, Concord Coach Lines offers direct service to Boston, with continuation to points north of Portland. Fares are $26 one-way; schedules and tickets are available online. *See the Contacts section of the Travel Smart chapter for more information.*

CONTACTS Greater Portland Transit District METRO. ✉ *Portland* ☎ *207/774–0351* ⊕ *gpmetro.org.*

CAR

Several car-rental options are available at the Portland International Jetport; others are dispersed around the South Portland area, just outside the main city limits.

Congress Street leads from I–295 into the heart of Portland; the Gateway Garage on High Street, off Congress, is a convenient place to leave your car downtown. North of Portland, U.S. 1 brings you to Freeport's Main Street, which continues on to Brunswick and Bath. East of Wiscasset you can take Route 27 south to the Boothbays, where Route 96 is a good choice for further exploration. To visit the Pemaquid region, take Route 129 off U.S. 1 in Damariscotta; then pick up Route 130 and follow it down to Pemaquid Point. Return to Waldoboro and U.S. 1 on Route 32 from New Harbor.

Metered on-street parking is available in Portland at $2.50 per hour, with a two-hour maximum. Even more convenient is the Passport Parking App, which Portland widely offers as alternative to meters. Download the app, create an account, and enter the zone number provided on signs at or near the parking spot you find. On most blocks you can pay for up to two hours of parking (at $2–$2.50 per hour, depending on the neighborhood), and then later extend your time on the app, as necessary. The App alerts you when you as your initial two-hour window is about to end. Parking lots and garages can be found downtown, in the Old Port, and on the waterfront; most charge between $3.50 and $6 per hour or $8–$15 per day.

TAXIS AND RIDESHARES

Though sometimes bustling, Portland is still a small city, so taxis do not rush about as they do in locales that are more populous. Your best bet is to call ahead rather than wait to flag down a driver. Meter rates are $1.90 for the first 1/10 mile, 30¢ for each additional 1/10 mile throughout Portland. Rideshare companies such as Lyft and Uber are also widely available all around the city.

There are also water taxis to get you to and from the islands of Casco Bay. Rates for one-way trips range from $30 to $110, depending on the destination.

WATER TAXI Fogg's Water Taxi and Charters. ⊠ Portland ☎ 207/415–8493 ⊕ foggswatertaxi.com.

TRAIN

Amtrak runs the Downeaster train service from Boston to Portland, with stops (some seasonal) along the coastal route. See the Contacts section of the Travel Smart chapter for more information.

Activities

When the weather's good, just about everyone in Portland heads outside, whether for boating on the water, lounging on a beach, or walking and biking the promenades. There are also many green spaces nearby Portland, including Crescent Beach State Park, Two Lights State Park, and Fort Williams Park, home to Portland Head Light. All are on the coast south of the city in suburban Cape Elizabeth and offer walking trails, picnic facilities, and water access.

Various Portland-based skippers offer whale-, dolphin-, and seal-watching cruises; excursions to lighthouses and islands; and fishing and lobstering trips. Board the ferry to see nearby islands. Self-navigators can rent kayaks or canoes.

Beaches

The only public beach in Portland proper is East End Beach, a pretty and sandy swath sitting at the bottom of the hill of the Eastern Promenade. Come for the panoramic views of Casco Bay and the convenience—there's parking nearby, picnic tables, a boat launch, and lots of benches.

In nearby South Portland is Willard Beach, a 4-acre, sand-and-pebble stretch that's dog-friendly and has plenty of tidal pools for kids. Swimming is as popular as boating (both recreational and commercial) here, and even those staying on land can enjoy the beach's terrific views of Casco Bay.

Hotels

As Portland's popularity as a vacation destination has increased, so have its options for overnight visitors. Though several large hotels—geared toward high-tech, amenity-obsessed guests—have been built in the Old Port, they have in no way diminished the success of smaller, more intimate lodgings. Inns and B&Bs have taken up residence throughout the West End, often giving new life to the grand mansions of Portland's wealthy 19th-century merchants. For the least expensive accommodations, you'll find chain hotels near the interstate and the airport.

Expect to pay at least $200 or so per night for a pleasant room (often with complimentary breakfast) within walking distance of the Old Port during high season, and more than $400 for the most luxurious of suites. At the height of summer, many places are booked; make reservations well in advance, and ask about off-season specials.

PRICES

Prices are the lowest cost of a standard double room in high season. Hotel reviews have been shortened. For full information, visit Fodors.com.

What It Costs In U.S. Dollars			
$	$$	$$$	$$$$
FOR TWO PEOPLE			
under $200	$201–$300	$301–$399	over $400

Nightlife

Portland's nightlife scene is largely centered on the bustling Old Port and a few smaller, artsy spots on Congress Street. There's a great emphasis on live music from local bands and pubs serving award-winning local microbrews. Several cool bars have cropped up, serving appetizers along with a full array of specialty wines and serious craft cocktails. Portland is a fairly sleepy city after midnight, but you can usually find a couple of bars and restaurants open, even after the clock strikes 12.

Performing Arts

Art galleries and studios have spread throughout the city, infusing many beautiful, old abandoned buildings and shops with new life. Many are concentrated along the Congress Street downtown corridor; others are hidden amid the boutiques and restaurants of the Old Port and the East End. A great way to get acquainted with the city's artists is to participate in the First Friday Art Walk, a free self-guided tour of galleries, museums, and alternative-art venues that happens—you guessed it—on the first Friday of each month.

Restaurants

America's "Foodiest Small Town" is how one magazine described Portland, which is practically bursting at the seams with restaurants fabulous enough to rival those of any major metropolis. It's worth it to splurge and try as many as possible while visiting. Fresh seafood, including the famous Maine lobster, is still popular and prevalent, but it is being served up in unexpected ways that are a far cry from the usual bib and butter. There is a broad spectrum of cuisines to be savored, and many chefs are pushing the envelope in their reinventions of traditional culinary idioms. Long before it became a national movement, Portland (actually, all of Maine) has emphasized local meats, seafood, and organic produce as much as possible; changing menus reflect what is available in the region at the moment. Even the many excellent food trucks that have popped up across the city—several of which remain open in the off-season—reflect this trend. As sophisticated as many of these establishments have become in the way of food and service, the atmosphere is generally laid-back; with a few exceptions, you can leave your jacket and tie at home—just not your appetite.

■TIP→ Smoking is banned in all restaurants, taverns, and bars in Maine.

PRICES

Prices are per person for a main course at dinner, or if dinner is not served at lunch. Restaurant reviews have been shortened. For full information, visit Fodors.com.

What It Costs In U.S. Dollars			
$	$$	$$$	$$$$
AT DINNER			
under $10	$10–$20	$21–$30	over $30

Shopping

Exchange Street is great for arts and crafts and boutique browsing. Art galleries are scattered around the city, but are most prevalent (and high-end) around Old Port. Meanwhile Commercial Street caters to the souvenir hound—gift shops are packed with nautical items, and lobster and moose emblems are emblazoned on everything from T-shirts to shot glasses.

Tours

BIKE TOURS
Portland Trails

BIKING | FAMILY | For local biking and hiking information, contact Portland Trails. The staff can tell you about designated paved and unpaved routes that wind along the water, through parks, and beyond. ⊠ *305 Commercial St., The Old Port and the Waterfront* ☎ *207/775-2411* ⊕ *www.trails.org.*

BOAT TOURS
Casco Bay Lines

BOATING | FAMILY | Casco Bay Lines operates ferry service to the seven bay islands with year-round populations. Summer offerings include music cruises, lighthouse excursions, and a trip to Bailey Island with a stopover for lunch. Round-trip fees range from $7.70 to $11.55, depending on which island you're visiting.

Peaks Island is the only island to allow cars to be transported by ferry, and those car reservations are often tough to get during the busy summer months. On most islands, bikes and/or golf carts are available for rent close to the ferry terminal. You can bring along your own bike on the ferry for $6.50 per adult and $3.25 per child. ⊠ *Maine State Pier, 56 Commercial St., The Old Port and the Waterfront* ☎ *207/774-7871* ⊕ *www. cascobaylines.com.*

Lucky Catch Cruises

BOATING | FAMILY | Set sail in a real lobster boat: This company gives you the genuine experience, which includes hauling traps and the chance to purchase the catch. ⊠ *Long Wharf, 170 Commercial St., The Old Port and the Waterfront* ☎ *207/761-0941* ⊕ *www.luckycatch.com* ⊠ *From $25* ⊗ *Closed Nov.–Apr.*

Odyssey Whale Watch

BOATING | FAMILY | From mid-May to mid-October, Odyssey Whale Watch leads whale-watching and deep-sea-fishing excursions. ⊠ *Long Wharf, 170 Commercial St., The Old Port and the Waterfront* ☎ *207/775-0727* ⊕ *www. odysseywhalewatch.com* ⊠ *From $29* ⊗ *Closed Nov.–Apr.*

★ Portland Schooner Co.

BOATING | FAMILY | May through October this company and its efficient crew offers daily two-hour windjammer cruises aboard the beautiful vintage schooners, *The Bagheera, Timberwind,* and *Wendameen.* The sunsets alone are worth the sail, but breezes on a hot summer day and views of the islands put the experience over the top. You can also arrange private charters. ⊠ *Maine State Pier, 56 Commercial St.* ☎ *207/766-2500* ⊕ *www.portlandschooner.com* ⊠ *Prices vary according to time of sails* ⊗ *Closed Nov.–Apr.*

BUS TOURS
Portland Discovery Land and Sea Tours

BUS TOURS | FAMILY | These informative trolley tours detail the city's historical and architectural highlights, Memorial Day–October. It's one of the best ways to tour the harbor and Casco Bay, including an up-close look at several lighthouses. Options include combining a city tour with a bay or lighthouse cruise. ⊠ *Long Wharf, 170 Commercial St., Portland* ☎ *207/774-0808* ⊕ *www.portland-discovery.com* ⊠ *From $23* ⊠ *Closed Nov.–Apr.*

Maine Duck Tours

SPECIAL-INTEREST TOURS | This 60-minute, history-based sightseeing tour travels through the streets of Portland and into the waters of Casco Bay in a modernized U.S. Coast Guard-approved amphibious vehicle built for both land and sea. Along the way, see and learn about attractions such as Portland Observatory, the working waterfront in Old Port, the Wadsworth-Longfellow Home, and the Arts District. ⊠ *The Blue Lobster Gift Shop, 177 Commercial St., Portland* ☎ *207/774-3825* ⊕ *www.maineducktours.com* ⊠ *From $38* ⊗ *Closed Oct.–May.*

Portland Fire Engine Co. Tours

SPECIAL-INTEREST TOURS | FAMILY | See Portland on a vintage Fire Engine on these narrated, 50-minute tours that highlight the city's lighthouses, civil war forts, and historical buildings, and architecture. Tours leave from the waterfront and circle through the city, passing everything from the Maine State Pier and East End Beach to Longfellow Square, Portland Museum of Art, and Monument Square. ✉ *180 Commercial St., Old Port, Portland* ☎ *207/252–6358* ⊕ *portlandfiretours.com* ✆ *From $30* ☉ *Closed Nov.–May.*

WALKING TOURS

Greater Portland Landmarks

WALKING TOURS | FAMILY | Take 1½-hour walking tours of Portland's historic West End June–October, with Greater Portland Landmarks. Tours past the neighborhood's Greek Revival mansions and grand Federal-style homes begin at the group's headquarters and cost $10. You can also pick up maps for self-guided tours of the Old Port or the Western Promenade. ✉ *93 High St., Portland* ☎ *207/774–5561* ⊕ *www.portlandlandmarks.org* ✆ *From $10.*

Maine Foodie Tours

SPECIAL-INTEREST TOURS | Learn about Portland's culinary history and sample such local delights as lobster tacos, organic cheese, and the famous Maine whoopie pie. The culinary walking tours include stops at fishmongers, bakeries, and cheese shops that provide products to Portland's famed restaurants. From summer into early fall, you can also take a chocolate tour, a bike-and-brewery tour, or a trolley tour with a stop at a microbrewery. Tours begin at various locales in the Old Port. ✉ *320 Fore St., Portland* ☎ *207/233–7485* ⊕ *www.mainefoodietours.com* ✆ *From $29.*

Portland Freedom Trail

SELF-GUIDED TOURS | FAMILY | The Portland Freedom Trail offers a self-guided tour of sites associated with the Underground Railroad and the antislavery movement.

Cannabis in Vacationland

Though Maine voters approved legalizing the recreational use and sales of marijuana in November 2016, various delays prevented retail shops from opening until October 2020. Since then a deluge of outlets has opened in the Greater Portland area, and although availability has expanded statewide, Portland is by far the place to find the most retail options.

✉ *Portland* ⊕ *www.mainehistory.org/PDF/walkingtourmap.pdf* ✆ *Free.*

Visitor Information

CONTACTS Downtown Portland. ✉ *549 Congress St., Portland* ☎ *207/772–6828* ⊕ *www.portlandmaine.com.* **Greater Portland Convention and Visitors Bureau.** ✉ *14 Ocean Gateway Pier, Portland* ☎ *207/772–4994* ⊕ *www.visitportland.com.*

When to Go

Winters are long in Maine, so the city celebrates the warmer months (roughly May through October) with a full schedule of outdoor events, including concerts, farmers' markets, and festivals. The many happenings are testament to this small city's large and lively spirit.

Increasingly, visitors are opting to come in the shoulder seasons (spring and fall), to experience the city without the summer crowds, and to take advantage of lower rates on hotels, and better chances of scoring coveted restaurant reservations.

Great Itineraries

If You Have 1 Day
Spend the morning wandering the streets and shops of the Old Port. Break for a harborside lunch along Commercial Street. In the afternoon, hit the museums in the Arts District. Architecture buffs will want to take a drive or stroll through the West End neighborhood. End the day with a drive up Congress Street to the Eastern Promenade for sweeping hilltop views of Casco Bay.

If You Have 3 Days
Spend your first day in the Old Port and the Arts District. Art lovers will want several hours inside the Portland Museum of Art. Take an hour or so to walk the West End neighborhood, with its stunning Colonial Revival and Victorian homes, then head to Hadlock Field for a baseball game or spend the night downtown. On your second day, take a morning boat ride to Eagle Island or another to Casco Bay island. In the afternoon, drive to Cape Elizabeth and visit Portland Head Light and Two Lights. Return to Portland for the night. On your third day, head north to Freeport, where you can shop at various outlets and L.L. Bean.

If You Have 5 Days
Spend your first two days in Portland. Be sure to linger in the Old Port and stroll through the architectural splendor of the West End. You can leave your car at your hotel for both days and easily get around on foot. See the islands via a Casco Bay Lines ferry, vintage schooner, whale-watch or other theme cruise, or opt for a sportfishing adventure.

On Day 3 take a ferry to one of the islands in Casco Bay and prepare to relax. You'll have left your car in Portland; rent a bicycle on the island or just explore its quiet roads (many of which are unpaved) by foot. Take a guided kayak trip; or sign up for a golf-cart tour. Grab dinner on the island or head back to Portland.

On Day 4 head out in your car for several hours of touring, including a visit to nearby Cape Elizabeth to see Portland Head Light. The park is a great place for a picnic lunch. Continue your scenic drive, stopping at any of several state parks for hiking and beachcombing, before making your way to Prouts Neck. Here you can stroll along the Cliff Walk. Head back to the interstate and continue north to Freeport for some shopping at L.L. Bean.

Spend Day 5 browsing the outlets, hiking through Wolfe's Neck Woods State Park (for beautiful sea views, including osprey nests), or taking a scenic harbor cruise. On the way back to Portland, stop at Day's Crabmeat & Lobster in Yarmouth for a bona fide Maine lobster roll.

Old Port and the Waterfront

A major international port and a working harbor since the early 17th century, Portland's Old Port and the Waterfront bridge the gap between the city's historic commercial activities and those of today. It is home to fishing boats docked alongside whale-watching charters, luxury yachts, cruise ships, and oil tankers from around the globe. Commercial Street parallels the water and is lined with brick buildings and warehouses that were built following

The cobblestone Wharf Street in Portland's Old Port is a hidden gem worthy of a stroll.

the Great Fire of 1866. In the 19th century, candle makers and sail stitchers plied their trades here; today specialty shops, art galleries, and restaurants have taken up residence.

GETTING HERE AND AROUND

As with most of the city, it's best to park your car and explore the Old Port on foot. You can park at the city garage on Fore Street (between Exchange and Union streets) or opposite the U.S. Custom House at the corner of Fore and Pearl streets. It can be difficult to find street parking in the busy summer months, but if that's your goal, there are often spots can be found on side streets, and almost all use the Passport Parking App to pay, which allows two hours of parking and can be extended as you need. Allow a couple of hours to wander at leisure on Market, Exchange, Middle, and Fore streets. The city is very pedestrian-friendly. Maine state law requires vehicles to stop for walkers in crosswalks, and many benches allow for rest and a grand dose of people-watching.

Sights

Harbor Fish Market

STORE/MALL | A Portland favorite since 1968, this freshest-of-the-fresh seafood market ships lobsters and other Maine delectables almost anywhere in the country. A bright-red facade on a working wharf opens into a bustling space with bubbling lobster tanks and fish, clams, and other shellfish on ice; employees are as skilled with a fillet knife as sushi chefs. There is also a small retail store. ✉ *9 Custom House Wharf, The Old Port and the Waterfront* ☎ *207/775–0251* ⊕ *www.harborfish.com* ✉ *Free.*

Portland Fish Exchange

STORE/MALL | You may want to hold your nose as you take a dip into the Old Port's active fish business at the 20,000-square-foot Portland Fish Exchange. Peek inside coolers teeming with cod, flounder, and monkfish, and watch fishermen repairing nets outside. ✉ *6 Portland Fish Pier, The Old Port and the Waterfront* ☎ *207/773–0017* ⊕ *www.pfex.org* ✉ *Free.*

🍴 Restaurants

★ Blyth & Burrows

$$ | **CONTEMPORARY** | There are craft cocktails, and then there is Blyth & Burrows, where the alchemy of spirits is taken to the next level with creative concoctions that include the unholy integration of gorgeous (albeit unusual) ingredients such as absinthe foam, house-made black-lime cordial, blackstrap maple-chipotle syrup, and uncommon liqueurs and spirits. Delicious and inspired small plates, like squid ink bao stuffed with tuna tartare, tenderloin with chimichurri, and local meat and cheese boards keep you from falling under the table. **Known for:** knock-you-under-the-table cocktails; nautical-theme atmosphere filled with antique ships and mermaid figureheads; adventurous food that goes well with cocktails. [$] *Average main: $12* ✉ *26 Exchange St., The Old Port and the Waterfront* ☎ *207/613–9070* 🌐 *www.blythandburrows.com.*

★ Central Provisions

$$ | **CONTEMPORARY** | Small plates take center stage at Old Port's award-winning, always-busy bôite, with chef Chris Gould, who co-owns the place with his wife Paige Gould, cheekily pairing stalwart Maine ingredients with luxurious and global ones. Witness creations like the confit of tomato salad with smoked duck, rice noodles, and Lanzhou oil, or the bone marrow toast with red onion jam, horseradish cream, and fontina. **Known for:** use of local ingredients; a busy and excellent brunch; creative small plates. [$] *Average main: $18* ✉ *414 Fore St., The Old Port and the Waterfront* ☎ *207/805–1085* 🌐 *www.central-provisions.com.*

El Rayo Taqueria

$ | **MEXICAN** | For some of the best Mexican food in town, head to this fun, hip spot where the flavors are as vibrant as the turquoise, yellow, and fuchsia decor and the guacamole and salsas are made fresh daily. Wash down achiote-seasoned fish tacos or a citrus-and-cumin-marinated chicken burrito with a lemon-hibiscus *refresca* (cold drink) or a house margarita. **Known for:** quick bites such as grab-and-go burritos daily until 11 am; Mexican corn on the cob with chipotle mayo and cotija; a killer key lime pie. [$] *Average main: $10* ✉ *26 Free St., The Old Port and the Waterfront* ☎ *207/780–8226* 🌐 *www.elrayotaqueria.com.*

★ Evo Kitchen + Bar

$$$$ | **MIDDLE EASTERN** | Take a bounty of Maine ingredients, add an ever-changing Middle Eastern menu, and a chef that knows how to subtly blend the two, and you've got Evo. Chef Matt Ginn opened this swanky, two-story spot housed in the Hyatt in 2015, and has since earned a following for dishes like bluefin tuna with avocado toum, Fresno, and turmeric. **Known for:** terrific Middle Eastern classics with a Maine twist; a chic bar scene; a menu that changes daily with ingredients' availability. [$] *Average main: $31* ✉ *443 Fore St., The Old Port and the Waterfront* ☎ *207/358–7830* 🌐 *www.evoportland.com.*

Flatbread

$$ | **PIZZA** | **FAMILY** | Families, students, and bohemian types gather at this popular New England chain flatbread-pizza place where two massive wood-fire ovens are the heart of the soaring, warehouselike space. Waits can be long on weekends and in summer, but you can call a half-hour ahead to put your name on the list, or grab a drink from the bar and wait outside with a view of the harbor. **Known for:** unfussy, kid-friendly atmosphere; outdoor dining on a deck that overlooks the working waterfront; dogs allowed on outside deck. [$] *Average main: $18* ✉ *72 Commercial St., The Old Port and the Waterfront* ☎ *207/772–8777* 🌐 *www.flatbreadcompany.com.*

★ Fore Street

$$$ | **MODERN AMERICAN** | One of Maine's most legendary chefs, Sam Hayward, opened this much-lauded restaurant in a renovated warehouse on the edge

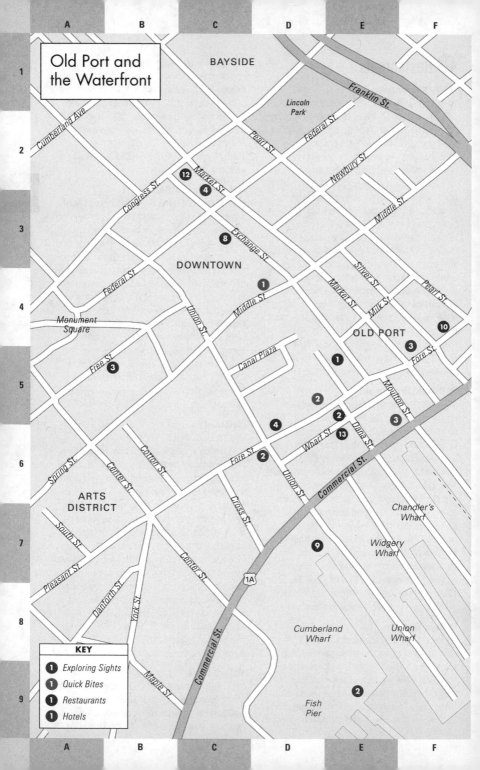

EAST END

Newbury St.

Middle St.

India St.

Fore St.

Thames St.

1A

Franklin St.

Commercial St.

1A

Marine
State Pier

Custom
House
Wharf

Portland
Pier

Long
Wharf

To Peaks Island,
Little Diamond Island
& Great Diamond Island

Portland Harbor

To Cushing Island →

0   200 m

0   500 ft

Sights ▼
1 Harbor Fish Market................ **G5**
2 Portland Fish Exchange............ **E9**

Restaurants ▼
1 Blyth & Burrows.................... **E5**
2 Central Provisions.................. **E5**
3 El Rayo Taqueria................... **B5**
4 Evo Kitchen + Bar................... **D5**
5 Flatbread........................... **H4**
6 Fore Street......................... **G3**
7 Gilbert's Chowder House......... **G5**
8 Highroller Lobster Co.............. **C3**
9 Liquid Riot Bottling Company..... **D7**
10 Mami............................... **F4**
11 Scales.............................. **H5**
12 Union............................... **C2**
13 Via Vecchia......................... **E6**

Quick Bites ▼
1 Bard Coffee **D4**
2 Gelato Fiasco...................... **D5**
3 The Holy Donut..................... **E5**
4 Standard Baking Co **G3**

Hotels ▼
1 Hilton Garden Inn Portland
Downtown Waterfront........... **H3**
2 Portland Harbor Hotel............. **D6**
3 The Portland Regency
Hotel and Spa **F4**
4 The Press Hotel.................... **C2**

4

Portland OLD PORT AND THE WATERFRONT

of the Old Port in 1996; today every copper-top table in the main dining room has a view of the enormous brick oven and soapstone hearth that anchor the open kitchen. The menu changes daily to reflect the freshest ingredients from Maine's farms and waters, as well as the tremendous creativity of the staff. **Known for:** turnspit roasted meats; handmade charcuterie; last-minute planners take heart: a third of the tables are reserved for walk-ins. $ *Average main: $30* ✉ *288 Fore St., The Old Port and the Waterfront* ☎ *207/775-2717* ⊕ *www.forestreet.biz* ⊙ *No lunch.*

Gilbert's Chowder House

$$ | SEAFOOD | FAMILY | This is the real deal, as quintessential as old-school Maine dining can be. Clam rakes and nautical charts hang from the walls of this unpretentious waterfront diner, and the flavors come from the depths of the North Atlantic, prepared and presented simply: fried scallops, haddock, clams and extraordinary clam cakes, and fish, clam, and seafood chowders (corn, too). **Known for:** family-friendly environment; classic lobster rolls, served on toasted hot-dog buns bursting with claw and tail meat; an ice-cream parlor to round out your meal; chalkboard daily specials. $ *Average main: $19* ✉ *92 Commercial St., The Old Port and the Waterfront* ☎ *207/871-5636* ⊕ *www.gilbertschowderhouse.com.*

Highroller Lobster Co.

$$ | SEAFOOD | FAMILY | Opened in early 2018, this high-energy spot serves lobster numerous ways—in a roll, on a stick, on a burger, over a salad, or even with your Bloody Mary. If you're feeling adventurous, try one of the sauces (lime mayo, lobster ghee) on your roll, and wash it all down with a beer from the ever-changing menu, which depends on availability from local breweries. **Known for:** origins as a food cart; the lobby pop (a lobster tail on a stick); Highroller whoopie pies baked by the owner's mom. $ *Average main: $15* ✉ *104 Exchange St., The Old Port and the Waterfront* ☎ *207/536-1623* ⊕ *highrollerlobster.com.*

Liquid Riot Bottling Company

$$ | AMERICAN | Part gastropub and part brewery, Old Port's cool-but-comfortable hangout is popular for its high-energy vibe, and brews made on-site by brothers Eric and Ian Michaud. The creative comfort food is also a draw (tempura eggplant with whipped ricotta and crab hushpuppies, anyone?), as are libations like tiki cocktails and newfangled classics like the Old Port Painkiller. **Known for:** craft beers; good bar food; a buzzy nightlife scene. $ *Average main: $14* ✉ *250 Commercial St., The Old Port and the Waterfront* ☎ *207/221-8889* ⊕ *liquidriot. com* ⊙ *No lunch.*

★ Mami

$$ | JAPANESE | Japanese street food takes center stage at this cozy locale. The menu rotates regularly, but you're likely to find uncommon takes on burgers and soba noodles as well as some form of *okonomiyaki*—a savory pancake filled with crazy-delicious flavor and texture combinations. **Known for:** ramen; steamed buns; grilled rice balls. $ *Average main: $15* ✉ *339 Fore St., The Old Port and the Waterfront* ☎ *207/536-4702* ⊕ *mamiportland.com* ⊙ *Closed Sun. and Mon.*

★ Scales

$$$$ | SEAFOOD | Seafood purists and adventurers alike find bliss in chef Fred Elliot's menu of superb pan-roasted, smoked, and grilled fish; fresh-as-can-be seafood crudos; and fried shellfish. Perched on Maine Wharf directly over the harbor, the contemporary-but-comfortable restaurant was opened by two local culinary heroes, restaurateur Dana Street and chef Sam Hayward, in 2016, and has since become one of Portland's most beloved. **Known for:** beautiful waterfront location; excellent pan-roasted and grilled seafood; fun bar scene. $ *Average main: $39* ✉ *68 Commercial St., The Old Port and the Waterfront* ☎ *207/8050444* ⊕ *www. scalesrestaurant.com* ⊙ *Closed Mon.*

Holding court in Old Port since 1996, Fore Street was one of the forerunners in Portland's dining renaissance.

★ Union

$$$ | **MODERN AMERICAN** | **FAMILY** | In the Press Hotel, Union Restaurant has a sophisticated but unpretentious air that is reflected in its menu, which focuses on local ingredients, many of which are foraged and fished, or gathered from its on-site greenhouse. Most dishes are modern comfort food; breakfast and brunch are a treat: you'll find maple *pain perdu* served alongside smoked-salmon tartines and classic dishes like eggs Benedict. **Known for:** sustainable ingredients; decadent "chef's table," a multicourse meal with wine pairings of the chef's choice; signature truffle beef pot roast. [$] *Average main: $30* ✉ *Press Hotel, 390 Congress St., The Old Port and the Waterfront* ☎ *207/808–8700* 🌐 *www.unionportland.com.*

★ Via Vecchia

$$$ | **MODERN ITALIAN** | Sparkling and gigantic crystal chandeliers aren't exactly the first thing you'd expect to greet you in a brick-and-ivy building tucked into a cobblestoned street, yet here they are—along with myriad other unapologetically glamorous touches. Settle into a green velvet booth and order up a meticulously made craft cocktail, or tuck into small Italian-inspired plates such as juicy lamb belly skewers or bucatini with spicy 'nduja cream. **Known for:** people-watching; Italian small plates; an excellent craft cocktail program. [$] *Average main: $29* ✉ *10 Dana St., The Old Port and the Waterfront* ☎ *207/407–7070* 🌐 *www.vvoldport.com* 🕒 *Closed Mon.*

☕ Coffee and Quick Bites

Bard Coffee

$ | **CAFÉ** | The beans sourcing this shop's delicious brew are bought from a handful of small growers—you can read their bios on the website—and roasted in-house. Enjoy your brew hot, cold, or iced with a locally made baked good. **Known for:** close relationships with sources; passionate, knowledgeable baristas; bulk coffee and tea. [$] *Average main: $5* ✉ *185 Middle St., The Old Port and the*

Waterfront ☎ *207/899–4788* 🌐 *www.bardcoffee.com.*

★ Gelato Fiasco

$ | **CAFÉ** | **FAMILY** | Proper Italian gelato and *sorbetto* here come in traditional flavors as well as more offbeat varieties like torched marshmallow s'more, mascarpone pistachio caramel, and mint brownie cookie. There are new flavors every day, along with espresso and other hot drinks. **Known for:** you can try every single flavor before deciding on what you'll get; long lines out the door in the summer; multigenerational bonding spot. [$] *Average main: $5* ✉ *425 Fore St., The Old Port and the Waterfront* ☎ *207/699–4314* 🌐 *www.gelatofiasco.com.*

The Holy Donut

$ | **CAFÉ** | **FAMILY** | Don't pass up a chance to try these sweet and savory, all-natural, Maine potato-based doughnuts glazed in flavors such as dark chocolate–sea salt, maple, pomegranate, triple berry, and chai, or stuffed with delicious fillings like bacon and cheddar, or ricotta. There are always new inventions, too, such as salted chocolate caramel and key lime pie. **Known for:** long lines, but worth the wait; shop closes for the day once all the doughnuts are sold; vegan and gluten-free options are available. [$] *Average main: $5* ✉ *177 Commercial St., The Old Port and the Waterfront* ☎ *207/331–5655* 🌐 *www.theholydonut.com.*

★ Standard Baking Co.

$ | **BAKERY** | **FAMILY** | You'd be hard-pressed to find a more pitch-perfect bakery in the Pine Tree State, but you'll have to pop by early (or put in an order in advance) to get your mitts on these delectable baked goods. The perfectly airy croissants, crusty baguettes, beguiling tarts, dainty Madeleines, and creative breads incorporate locally sourced grains and are nothing short of revelations. **Known for:** good selection of locally roasted coffees; amazing galettes and brioches; creative scones. [$] *Average main: $3* ✉ *75 Commercial St., The Old Port and the Waterfront* ☎ *207/772–5519* 🌐 *www.standardbakingco.com.*

🛏 Hotels

Hilton Garden Inn Portland Downtown Waterfront

$$$ | **HOTEL** | This bright, clean, and modern hotel is a perfect base for exploring on foot the adjacent Old Port and nearby East End, and it's only a walk across the street to catch a ferry to the Casco Bay islands. **Pros:** heated saltwater lap pool; central location for exploring; some rooms with harbor view. **Cons:** no pets; no self-parking; some rooms face neighboring businesses. [$] *Rooms from: $379* ✉ *65 Commercial St., The Old Port and the Waterfront* ☎ *207/780–0780* 🌐 *www.hilton.com/en/hilton-garden-inn* 🔑 *120 rooms* 🍴 *No Meals.*

Portland Harbor Hotel

$$ | **HOTEL** | Extensively renovated in 2017, this nautically themed hotel is in walking distance of both the waterfront and the Old Port. **Pros:** amid the action of the Old Port; pet-friendly ($50 per pet fee); courtesy car covers 4-mile radius. **Cons:** no pool; rooms facing Union Street pick up lively street noise; no water view. [$] *Rooms from: $299* ✉ *468 Fore St., The Old Port and the Waterfront* ☎ *207/775–9090, 888/798–9090* 🌐 *www.portlandharborhotel.com* 🔑 *101 rooms* 🍴 *No Meals.*

The Portland Regency Hotel and Spa

$$ | **HOTEL** | Not part of a chain despite the "Regency" name, this brick building in the center of the Old Port served as Portland's armory in the late 19th century. **Pros:** easy walk to sites; pet-friendly ($75 nonrefundable cleaning fee); full-service spa with lounges, saunas, steam rooms, hot tub, and an array of luxurious treatments. **Cons:** no pool; busy downtown location; not all rooms have noteworthy views. [$] *Rooms from: $300* ✉ *20 Milk St., The Old Port and the Waterfront* ☎ *207/774–4200, 800/727–3436* 🌐 *www.theregency.com* 🔑 *95 rooms* 🍴 *No Meals.*

★ The Press Hotel
$$$ | HOTEL | FAMILY | In a former newspaper building, this boutique hotel is part of Marriott's Autograph Collection; the hotel feels both broadly cosmopolitan and distinctly Maine. **Pros:** Frette bed linens and Maine-made Cuddledown comforters and bed throws; sparkling-clean rooms with a modern-design feel; art gallery and excellent public spaces with tasteful furnishings. **Cons:** right next to the fire department; valet parking can be expensive; some rooms have underwhelming views. [$] *Rooms from: $375* ✉ *119 Exchange St., The Old Port and the Waterfront* ☎ *877/890–5641* 🌐 *www.thepresshotel.com* 🛏 *110 rooms* 🍴 *No Meals.*

Nightlife

Bull Feeney's
PUBS | For nightly specials, plenty of Guinness, and live entertainment, head to Bull Feeney's, a lively two-story Irish pub and restaurant. ✉ *375 Fore St., The Old Port and the Waterfront* ☎ *207/773–7210* 🌐 *bullfeeneys.com.*

Gritty McDuff's Portland Brew Pub
BREWPUBS | Maine's original brewpub serves fine ales, British pub fare, and seafood dishes. There are between six and eight rotating ales on tap, and there's always a seasonal offering. ✉ *396 Fore St., The Old Port and the Waterfront* ☎ *207/772–2739* 🌐 *www.grittys.com.*

★ Novare Res Bier Café
CAFÉS | At tucked-away Novare Res Bier Café, choose from some three dozen rotating drafts and about 500 bottled brews. Relax on an expansive deck, munch on antipasti, or share a meat-and-cheese plate. Maine craft beers occupy at least eight of the taps at any given time, and the rest span the globe, with an emphasis on Belgian and Trappist ales. ✉ *4 Canal Plaza, off Exchange St., The Old Port and the Waterfront* ☎ *207/761–2437* 🌐 *www.novareresbiercafe.com.*

★ Portland Hunt and Alpine Club
BARS | Scandinavian-inspired dishes and serious craft cocktails drive this hip locale that also offers excellent charcuterie and seafood boards. If it's free, grab a seat in the intimate alpine-style hut, off to the side of the main room. And don't miss the excellent happy hour, weekdays 1–6. ✉ *75 Market St., The Old Port and the Waterfront* ☎ *207/747–4754* 🌐 *www.huntandalpineclub.com.*

Rí Rá
PUBS | This happening Irish pub has live music Thursday–Saturday night and a pub quiz on Tuesday. For a more mellow experience, settle into a couch at the upstairs bar. ✉ *72 Commercial St., The Old Port and the Waterfront* ☎ *207/761–4446* 🌐 *www.rira.com.*

Three Dollar Deweys
BARS | Opened in 1980 under Alan Eames, Three Dollar Deweys was reputed to be the very first place in town to pour a pint. The cozy, brick-lined bar changed hands a number of times since then—including ownership by famed actor Judd Nelson—and even closed once in 2018, only to be reopened again under the current owner. The tap lines have now been extended to 36 and eats like pizza, and nachos have been added to the menu. ✉ *241 Commercial St., The Old Port and the Waterfront* ☎ *207/772–3310* 🌐 *threedollardeweys.com.*

Shopping

ACCESSORIES

★ Sea Bags
OTHER SPECIALTY STORE | The brand's flagship location displays totes in every shape and size made from recycled sailcloth and decorated with bright, graphic patterns. Check out the display that shows you exactly how a sail is used to create all the different bags and accessories. The factory store, located just a few blocks away on the Custom House Wharf, is where the bags are actually

sewn; you can find some factory sales as well. ✉ *123 Commercial St., The Old Port and the Waterfront* ☎ *207/835–0096* ⊕ *www.seabags.com.*

ART AND ANTIQUES

Abacus Gallery

ANTIQUES & COLLECTIBLES | This appealing crafts gallery has gift items in glass, wood, and textiles, as well as fine modern jewelry. ✉ *44 Exchange St., The Old Port and the Waterfront* ☎ *207/772–4880* ⊕ *www.abacusgallery.com.*

Greenhut Galleries

ANTIQUES & COLLECTIBLES | The contemporary art at this gallery changes with the seasons. Artists represented include David Driskell, an artist and leading art scholar. ✉ *146 Middle St., The Old Port and the Waterfront* ☎ *207/772–2693* ⊕ *www.greenhutgalleries.com.*

BOOKS

Longfellow Books

BOOKS | This shop is known for its good service, author readings, and excellent selection of new and used books and magazines. Even if you go in looking for something specific, you'll almost certainly stumble on something even better you didn't know about before. ✉ *1 Monument Way, The Old Port and the Waterfront* ☎ *207/772–4045* ⊕ *www. longfellowbooks.com.*

★ Sherman's Maine Coast Book Shops

BOOKS | Open since 1886, Sherman's is Maine's oldest bookstore chain. The Portland store has an impressive stock of well-selected books interspersed with excellent gift choices, such as stationery, candles, and holiday decor, as well as a fun array of toys. It's a good place to spend a cold or rainy day perusing the selection. ✉ *49 Exchange St., The Old Port and the Waterfront* ☎ *207/773–4100* ⊕ *www.shermans.com.*

CLOTHING

★ Joseph's

MEN'S CLOTHING | A smart menswear boutique (and mainstay of the Old Port) that will have you looking suave in no time. Most impressive is the shop's balance of contemporary, casual pieces and custom men's suiting. ✉ *410 Fore St., The Old Port and the Waterfront* ☎ *207/773–1274* ⊕ *www.josephsofportland.com.*

★ Judith

WOMEN'S CLOTHING | Owned and operated by a former fashion designer, this stunning, well-curated concept boutique features women's apparel, shoes, accessories, and contemporary housewares. The stock can be quite pricey, but these are high-quality investment pieces meant to build a wardrobe around. ✉ *131 Middle St., The Old Port and the Waterfront* ☎ *207/747–4778* ⊕ *www.shopjudith.com* ☾ *Closed Tues.*

HOME AND GIFTS

Blanche + Mimi

HOUSEWARES | Your kitchen may never be the same after visiting this veritable trove of cooking and home accessories. Mismatched, vintage flatware, glasses, and plates provide the makings of a whimsical dining table, and equally charming block-printed pillowcases, handmade quilts, gauzy blankets, and hand-turned wooden candlesticks are the kind of gifts you wind up keeping for yourself. The baby clothing section is equally irresistible, filled with muslin sunhats, organic sleeping sacs covered in sailboats, and woolen mobiles of hovering storks. ✉ *184 Middle St., The Old Port and the Waterfront* ☎ *207/7743900* ⊕ *www. blancheandmimi.com.*

Fitz & Bennett

HOUSEWARES | FAMILY | Shelves here are covered in inspired finds—from ornately printed tea towels and handmade lavender-oat soap to graphic and colorful dinner plates made of bamboo. The baby section teems with unusually darling items—gingham bonnets, quilted bibs in pretty prints, and print-covered footies. ✉ *43 Silver St., The Old Port and the Waterfront* ☎ *207/835–0485* ⊕ *fitzandbennetthome.com.*

Lisa Marie's Made in Maine

SOUVENIRS | Here you'll find an excellent selection of locally sourced items from soaps and candles to dish towels, pottery, and jewelry, all made in the great state of Maine. ⊠ *35 Exchange St., The Old Port and the Waterfront* ☏ *207/828–1515* ⊕ *www.lisamariesmadeinmaine.com.*

TOYS

★ Treehouse Toys

TOYS | FAMILY | An instant mood-lifter, this shop is chock-full of offbeat toys and novelty items that are certain to delight children of all ages. ⊠ *47 Exchange St., The Old Port and the Waterfront* ☏ *207/775–6133* ⊕ *www.treehousetoys.us.*

SPECIALTY SHOPS

Fire On Fore

OTHER SPECIALTY STORE | The high-quality, recreational cannibis sold here is acquired through local, independent growers and producers. The shop sells everything from vape pens and edibles to topicals and concentrates—and sees to it that the growers are diligent in providing only clean products, without any additives, pesticides, or molds. ⊠ *367 Fore St., The Old Port and the Waterfront* ☏ *207/805–1870* ⊕ *www. fireonfore.com.* Cannibis

East End, Munjoy Hill, and Washington Ave.

These three sections of town are often referred to independently, but they also overlap in large parts; Washington Avenue runs through both areas, and Munjoy Hill is part of the East End. The latter includes the Eastern Promenade, East End Beach, and the Portland Observatory. Meanwhile, Washington Avenue has become one of the most concentrated areas of fantastic food in all Maine. From authentic Thai fixings and ultrafresh oysters to creative barbecue and locally made kombucha, it's all here.

Sights

East End Beach

BEACH | FAMILY | Portland's only public beach, it's set at the bottom of the hill of the Eastern Promenade. Its panoramic views of Casco Bay make it a popular summer spot, as do amenities like convenient parking, picnic tables, and a boat launch. **Amenities:** food and drink; parking (fee); toilets; water sports. **Best for:** sunrise; sunsets; swimming; walking. ⊠ *Cutter St., East End.*

Eastern Prom Trail

TRAIL | FAMILY | To experience the city's busy shoreline and take in the grand views of Casco Bay, walkers, runners, and cyclists head out on the 2.1-mile Eastern Prom Trail.

Beginning at the intersection of Commercial and India Streets, this paved trail runs along the water at the bottom of the Eastern Promenade, following an old railbed alongside the still-used railroad tracks of the Maine Narrow Gauge Railroad Co. & Museum. There are plenty of places with benches and tables for a picnic break along the way. From the trailhead, it's about 1 mile to the small East End Beach.

Continuing along the trail, you'll pass underneath busy Interstate 295, and emerge at the Back Cove Trail, a popular 3½-mile loop you can connect with for a long trek. To return to the Old Port, backtrack along the trail or head up the steep path to the top of the promenade. Here you can continue along the promenade sidewalk or take the trails through this 68-acre stretch of parkland to the lovely picnic area and playground.

Continuing along the sidewalk toward the Old Port, a gazebo and several old cannons to your left indicate you're at the small Fort Allen Park. Use one of the coin-operated viewing scopes to view Civil War–era Fort Gorges, which never saw action.

The Portland Observatory is the country's last remaining historic maritime signal station; guided tours are available from June through mid-October.

Where the Eastern Prom becomes Fore Street, continue on for a few blocks to India Street and take a left, which will bring you back to where you started. Or, continue into the Old Port.

Plan at least an hour to walk the trail with brief stops, or two if you continue along the Back Cove Trail. But if you can, make time for the Prom—it's truly an urban jewel. ✉ *Eastern Prom Trail, Portland* ⊕ *easternpromenade.org/ the-eastern-promenade.*

Eastern Promenade

PROMENADE | FAMILY | Between the city's two promenades, this one, often overlooked by tourists, has by far the best view. Gracious Victorian homes, many now converted to condos and apartments, border one side of the street. On the other is 68 acres of hillside parkland that includes Ft. Allen Park and, at the base of the hill, the Eastern Prom Trail and tiny East End Beach and boat launch. On a sunny day the Eastern Prom is a lovely spot for picnicking, snacking (there are always a few top-notch food trucks),

and people-watching. ✉ *Washington Ave. to Fore St., East End.*

Maine Narrow Gauge Railroad Museum

TRAIN/TRAIN STATION | FAMILY | Whether you're crazy about old trains or just want to see the sights from a different perspective, the railroad museum has an extensive collection of locomotives and rail coaches, and offers scenic tours on narrow-gauge railcars. The 3-mile jaunts run on the hour, at 10, 11, noon, 1, 2, and 3 every day in the operating season. Rides take you along Casco Bay, at the foot of the Eastern Promenade. The operating season caps off with a fall harvest ride (complete with cider), and during the Christmas season there are special Polar Express rides, based on the popular children's book. ✉ *58 Fore St., East End* ☎ *207/828–0814* ⊕ *www.mainenarrowgauge.org* ✐ *Museum $5, train rides $12* ☾ *Closed Nov.–Apr.*

Portland Observatory

OBSERVATORY | FAMILY | This octagonal observatory on Munjoy Hill was built in 1807 by Captain Lemuel Moody, a retired sea captain, as a maritime signal tower.

Moody used a telescope to identify incoming ships, and flags to signal to merchants where to unload their cargo. Held in place by 122 tons of ballast, it's the last remaining historic maritime signal station in the country. The guided tour leads all the way to the dome, where you can step out on the deck and take in views of Portland, the islands, and inland toward the White Mountains. ⊠ 138 Congress St., East End ☎ 207/774–5561 ⊕ www.portlandlandmarks.org 🖱 $10 ⊗ Closed mid-Oct.–late May.

Root Wild Kombucha

BREWERY | When owner (and self-titled "boochmaster") Reid Emmerich looked around Portland and realized that lots of locals were drinking kombucha but none of it was being made locally, he set his sights on fixing that in 2018. These days the funky tasting room-cum-brewery (it's technically licensed as the latter, since all kombucha contains at least a small amount of alcohol) gets filled with fans in to try Emmerich's latest flavors—which change with whatever ingredients are in season, since he forages many of them himself—and hang out with fellow boochlovers in the process. ⊠ 135 Washington Ave., Portland ☎ 207/303–9043 ⊕ www.rootwildkombucha.com.

🍴 Restaurants

★ Công Tử Bột

$$ | **VIETNAMESE** | Follow the scent of chili and sizzling scallions to this highly regarded Vietnamese joint, where the dishes are as authentic as they are adventurous. Beyond the requisite pho (and for the record, theirs is flavorful and addictive) are dishes ready to push your repertoire of Vietnamese cuisine: cold caramel vermicelli with caramel pork and fish sauce; Khmer sour beef sausage; and stir-fried turnips with oyster mushrooms and fermented tofu. **Known for:** excellent Vietnamese food; big flavors and the friendly service; national recognition and award nominations. 💲 Average

main: $16 ⊠ 57 Washington Ave., Portland ☎ 207/221–8022 ⊕ www.congtubot.com ⊗ Closed Tues. and Wed.

★ Duckfat

$$ | **MODERN AMERICAN** | **FAMILY** | Even in midafternoon, this small, casual, and cool panini-and-more shop in the Old Port is packed. The focus here is everyday farm-to-table fare: the signature Belgian fries are made with Maine potatoes cooked, yes, in duck fat and served in paper cones, and standards include meat loaf and the BGT (bacon, goat cheese, tomato). **Known for:** decadent poutine with duck-fat gravy; hopping atmosphere—waits for a table can be long; thick milk shakes prepared with local gelato by Gelato Fiasco. 💲 Average main: $12 ⊠ 43 Middle St., East End ☎ 207/774–8080 ⊕ www.duckfat.com ⊗ Closed Wed.

★ East Ender

$$$ | **AMERICAN** | **FAMILY** | The emphasis at this cozy neighborhood restaurant is on the superb food rather than the atmosphere, which isn't surprising, given that the owners formerly served their tasty, no-fuss fare from a truck. Lunch and dinner feature locally sourced, sustainable ingredients in dishes that reflect the seasons. **Known for:** mouthwatering house-smoked bacon; crispy, thrice-cooked fries; brunch cocktails that incorporate ingredients from local distilleries and house-made cordials. 💲 Average main: $24 ⊠ 47 Middle St., East End ☎ 207/879–7669 ⊕ www.eastenderportland.com ⊗ Closed Sun. and Mon.

★ Eventide Oyster Co.

$$ | **SEAFOOD** | Not only does Eventide have fresh, tasty oysters from all over Maine and New England, artfully prepared with novel accoutrements like kimchi, ginger ices, and cucumber-champagne mignonette, it also serves delicious crudos and ceviches with unique ingredients like blood orange and chili miso. The menu constantly changes, depending on what's in season. **Known for:** brown-butter lobster rolls; a decent selection of alternatives for nonseafood lovers; teaming up with other local restaurants for special cook-offs and menus. $ *Average main: $15* ✉ *86 Middle St., East End* ☎ *207/774–8538* ⊕ *www.eventideoysterco.com.*

The Honey Paw

$$ | ASIAN FUSION | Come for the salty wontons, piping-hot broths, and wok-fried noodles; stay for the turntable music, the well-stocked cocktail bar, and the soft-serve ice cream that comes in flavors like orange curd, moxie, and charred corn. If you order one thing here, make it one of the daily fresh fish creations—à la bluefin tuna tartare with miso, shiso, and fermented chili; or the halibut crudo with rhubarb and Meyer lemon. **Known for:** sister restaurant to Eventide Oyster Co.; house-made noodles; rotating wines on tap and an excellent selection of sake. $ *Average main: $15* ✉ *7 Middle St., East End* ☎ *207/774–8538* ⊕ *www.thehoneypaw. com* ◷ *Closed Tues.*

The Shop at Island Creek Oysters

$ | SEAFOOD | This no-fuss counter-service spot, opened by longtime wholesale purveyors of Island Creek Oysters (from Duxbury, Massachusetts), serves seriously fresh shellfish and excellent Maine microbrews (and wine) on tap. A clutch of imported, tinned fish and house-made pickled items that pair very well with oysters are also available. **Known for:** laid-back, family-friendly environment; impeccably scrubbed and shucked oysters; house-made mignonettes. $ *Average main: $10* ✉ *123 Washington Ave., East End* ☎ *207/699–4466* ⊕ *portland.islandcreekoysters.com* ◷ *Closed Mon.*

Terlingua

$$ | BARBECUE | FAMILY | New England—and especially Maine—may not be known for its barbecue, but Terlingua is one of the exceptions. Pitmaster/owner Piny Reynolds started the fire in steel smokers here in 2015, applying what he learned while living in Austin to Maine

foods, and he continues to smoke up a gorgeous brisket (to say the least), as well as smoke lobster tails to make tostadas. **Known for:** top-notch Texas-style barbecue; barbecuing seafood into delicious dishes; strong, well-balanced margaritas. $ *Average main: $19* ✉ *40 Washington Ave., Portland* ☎ *207/956–7573* ⊕ *www. terlingua.me* ◷ *Closed Tues.*

★ Twelve

$$$$ | CONTEMPORARY | One of the splashiest restaurants in town (Executive Chef Colin Wyatt returned to Portland to open Twelve after sharpening his knives for years at Daniel and Eleven Madison Park in New York City), this is a place to indulge in some of the best food Maine has to offer. Don't let the pedigree, the beautiful dining room, or the gastronomically ambitious menu fool you, either; Wyatt's dedication to real Maine ingredients and the purest of flavors shines in dishes like monkfish with trout rose and whey broth, and the spectacular cherry galette with almond and crème frâiche. **Known for:** local ingredients sourced; fine dining; a beautiful dining room and celebratory atmosphere. $ *Average main: $82* ✉ *115 Thames St., Portland* ☎ *207/910–7400* ⊕ *www.twelvemaine. com* ◷ *Closed Sun. and Mon. No lunch.*

☕ Coffee and Quick Bites

★ Coffee By Design

$ | CAFÉ | Housed in a former bakery building, this small and local coffeehouse company pours specialty coffee employing unusually high standards for environmental and economic sustainability. Flavor-wise, the sturdy coffee is brewed from beans they roast themselves, which have become a staple in many locals' home kitchens. **Known for:** among Portland's original artisanal coffee roasters; community commitment; three locations citywide. $ *Average main: $6* ✉ *67 India St., East End* ☎ *207/780–6767* ⊕ *www.coffeebydesign.com.*

🛏 Hotels

AC Hotel by Marriott
Portland Downtown/Waterfront

$$$$ | HOTEL | Though it's located a brief walk from many of Portland's most popular sites—from East End Beach and Casco Bay Lines to shopping in Old Port—it isn't just the location that brings many guests back to this hotel. **Pros:** convenience store on-site; on-site fitness center; new modern design. **Cons:** some rooms are a bit cramped; many rooms lack good views; expensive valet parking. 💲 *Rooms from: $449* ✉ *158 Fore St., Portland* ☎ *207/747–1640* ⊕ *www.marriott.com* ⇨ *191 rooms* ❍| *No Meals.*

🎭 Performing Arts

Mayo Street Arts

ARTS CENTERS | FAMILY | An alternative-arts venue for the innovative and up-and-coming, Mayo Street Arts often features intimate concerts, contemporary exhibitions, and offbeat puppet shows in a repurposed church. ✉ *10 Mayo St., East End* ☎ *207/879–4629* ⊕ *www.mayostreetarts.org.*

👜 Shopping

FOOD
Onggi

FOOD | Fermentation is the name of the entire game at this quirky and Onggi (pronounced "Ong-gee"), named after the Korean vessels in which fermentations like soy sauce, kimchi, and rice wine are made. Owned by a young trio of self-titled "fermentation nerds," the friendly shop peddles an array of fantastic—and mostly small-batch—products: the likes of Taiwanese soy pastes; preserved Moroccan Meyer lemon paste; ponzu sauces with yuzu; and mushroom ale vinegars. ✉ *131 Washington Ave., Portland* ☎ *207/352–3528* ⊕ *www.onggi.com* ⊘ *Closed Mon. and Tues..* Food

HOUSEHOLD ITEMS/FURNITURE
Angela Adams

HOUSEWARES | Maine islander Angela Adams specializes in simple but bold geometric motifs parlayed into dramatic rugs (custom, too), canvas totes, bedding, and other home accessories. The shop also carries sleek wood furniture from her husband's woodshop. ✉ *71 Cove St., East End* ☎ *207/774–3523* ⊕ *www.angelaadams.com* ⊘ *Closed weekends.*

🏃 Activities

BIKING
Cycle Mania

BIKING | FAMILY | Rent hybrid bikes downtown at Cycle Mania. The $40 per day rate includes a helmet and lock. ✉ *65 Cove St., East End* ☎ *207/774–2933* ⊕ *www.cyclemania1.com.*

BOATING
Portland Paddle

KAYAKING | FAMILY | Run by a pair of Registered Maine Guides, Portland Paddle leads introductory sea-kayaking clinics along with guided trips between the Casco Bay islands June through September. Two-hour sunset paddles ($45) are a fave, as are the full-moon standup paddleboard tours ($45). Kayak and SUP rentals are available. ✉ *Eastern Promenade, East End Beach, off Cutter St., East End* ☎ *207/370–9730* ⊕ *www.portlandpaddle.net* ⊘ *Closed Nov.–May.*

The Arts District

This district starts at the top of Exchange Street, near the upper end of the Old Port, and extends west past the Portland Museum of Art. Congress Street is the district's central artery. Much of Portland's economic heart is here, including several large banking and law firms. It's also where Maine College of Art and the Portland Public Library make their homes. Art galleries, specialty stores,

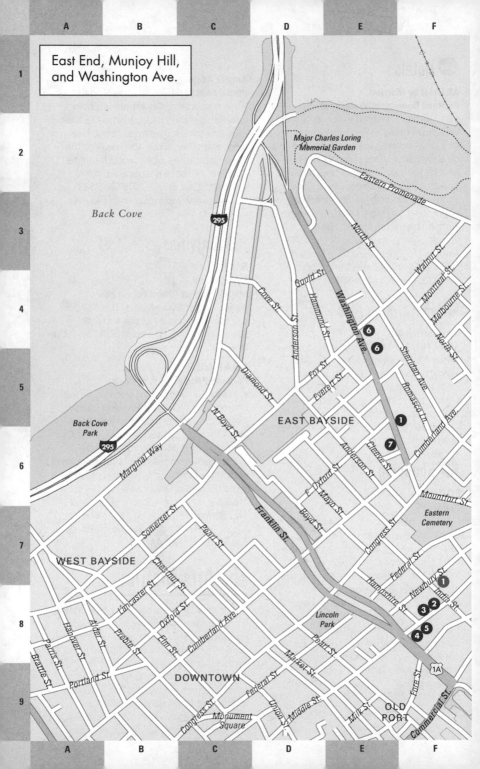

East End, Munjoy Hill, and Washington Ave.

Back Cove

Major Charles Loring Memorial Garden

Eastern Promenade

295

Back Cove Park

295

North St.

Walnut St.

Montreal St.

Melbourne St.

Gould St.

Hammond St.

Cove St.

Anderson St.

Diamond St.

Washington Ave.

Sheridan Ave.

North St.

Romasco Ln.

Cumberland Ave.

Fox St.

Everett St.

6

6

EAST BAYSIDE

1

Cleeves St.

7

Mt. Boyd St.

Marginal Way

Anderson St.

E. Oxford St.

Mayo St.

Mountfort St.

Eastern Cemetery

Somerset St.

Pearl St.

Franklin St.

Boyd St.

Congress St.

WEST BAYSIDE

Chestnut St.

Federal St.

Newbury St.

India St.

Lancaster St.

Oxford St.

Cumberland Ave.

Hampshire St.

1

3 **2**

Alder St.

Preble St.

Elm St.

Lincoln Park

Pearl St.

5

4

Hanover St.

Paris St.

Brattle St.

Portland St.

DOWNTOWN

Market St.

Fore St.

1A

OLD PORT

Congress St.

Monument Square

Union St.

Middle St.

Federal St.

Milk St.

Commercial St.

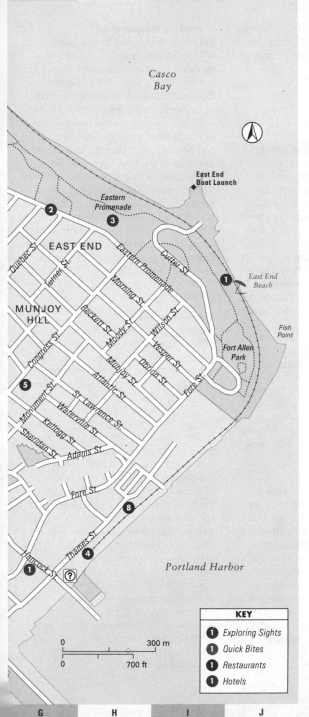

4

Portland THE ARTS DISTRICT

and a score of restaurants line Congress Street. Parking is tricky; two-hour meters dot the sidewalks, but there are several nearby parking garages.

Sights

★ Maine Historical Society and Longfellow House

HISTORIC HOME | The boyhood home of the famous American poet was the first brick house in Portland and the oldest building on the peninsula. It's particularly interesting, because most of the furnishings, including the young Longfellow's writing desk, are original. Wallpaper, window coverings, and a vibrant painted carpet are period reproductions. Built in 1785, the large dwelling (a third floor was added in 1815) sits back from the street and has a small portico over its entrance and four chimneys surmounting the roof. It's part of the Maine Historical Society, which includes an adjacent research library and a museum with exhibits about Maine life. After your guided tour, stay for a picnic in the Longfellow Garden; it's open to the public during museum hours. ✉ *489 Congress St., Arts District* ☎ *207/774–1822* ⊕ *www.mainehistory. org* ✆ *House and museum $15, gardens free* ⊙ *Closed Nov.–Apr.*

Neal Dow Memorial

HISTORIC HOME | The mansion, once a stop on the Underground Railroad, was the home of Civil War general Neal Dow, who became known as the "Father of Prohibition." He was responsible for Maine's adoption of the anti-alcohol bill in 1851, which spurred a nationwide temperance movement. Now a museum, this majestic 1829 Federal-style home is open for guided tours that start on the hour. ✉ *714 Congress St., Arts District* ☎ *207/773–7773* ⊕ *www.nealdowmemorial.org* ✆ *$10.*

★ Portland Museum of Art

ART MUSEUM | Maine's largest public art institution's collection includes fine seascapes and landscapes by Winslow Homer, John Marin, Andrew Wyeth, Edward Hopper, Marsden Hartley, and other American painters. Homer's *Weatherbeaten*, a quintessential Maine Coast image, is here, and the museum owns and displays, on a rotating basis, 16 more of his paintings, plus more than 400 of his illustrations (and it offers tours of the Winslow Homer Studio in nearby Prouts Neck). The museum has works by Monet and Picasso, as well as Degas, Renoir, and Chagall. I.M. Pei's colleague Henry Cobb designed the strikingly modern Charles Shipman Payson building. ✉ *7 Congress Sq., Arts District* ☎ *207/775–6148* ⊕ *www.portlandmuseum.org* ✆ *$18 (free Fri. 4–8 pm)* ⊙ *Closed Mon. and Tues.*

Victoria Mansion

HISTORIC HOME | Built between 1858 and 1860, this Italianate mansion is widely regarded as the most sumptuously ornamented dwelling of its period remaining in the country. Architect Henry Austin designed the house for hotelier Ruggles Morse and his wife, Olive. The interior design—everything from the plasterwork to the furniture (much of it original)—is the only surviving commission of New York designer Gustave Herter. Behind the elegant brownstone exterior of this National Historic Landmark are colorful frescoed walls and ceilings, ornate marble mantelpieces, gilded gas chandeliers, a magnificent 6-foot-by-25-foot stained-glass ceiling window, and a freestanding mahogany staircase. A guided tour runs about 45 minutes and covers all the architectural highlights. Victorian era–themed gifts and art are sold in the museum shop, and the museum often has special theme events. ✉ *109 Danforth St., Arts District* ☎ *207/772–4841* ⊕ *www.victoriamansion.org* ✆ *$18* ⊙ *Closed Nov.–Apr.*

🍴 Restaurants

★ Leeward

$$$ | ITALIAN | With nods from critics far and wide, one of the state's most celebrated restaurants is also one of its newest. This high-ceilinged, Italian-centric restaurant comes from husband and wife team Jake and Raquel Stevens who turn out exquisite handmade pasta like the spaghettini Nero laced with squid, serrano chile, pork brood, white wine, and bread crumbs—a revelation of flavors both strong and soothing. **Known for:** thoughtfully chosen wine list; delicious handmade pastas; happening bar scene on weekend nights. [$] *Average main: $25* ✉ *85 Free St., Arts District* ☎ *207/8088623* 🌐 *www.leewardmaine.com* 🕒 *Closed Sun. and Mon. No lunch.*

Local 188

$$$ | SPANISH | There's an infectious vibe at this eclectic, Spanish-inspired Arts District hot spot that's accentuated by its 2,000-square-foot space, lofty tin ceilings, worn maple floors, and mismatched chandeliers. Regulars chat with servers about which just-caught seafood will decorate the paella or which organic veggies will star in the tortillas, one of several tapas choices. **Known for:** large bar area; some 150 different wines, mostly from Europe; a lively crowd and warm environment. [$] *Average main: $25* ✉ *685 Congress St., Arts District* ☎ *207/761–7909* 🌐 *www.local188.com.*

★ Pai Men Miyake

$$ | JAPANESE | Some of the richest, most flavorful ramen this side of Tokyo is served at this Japanese gastropub, brought to Portland by chef and sushi wizard Masa Miyake; He's shuttered his nearby fine dining sushi restaurant, Miyake, for renovations and no reopening date has been set. And while yes, there is indeed terrific sushi also being rolled at this, his more casual outpost, it's the cooked stuff that brings in the crowds. **Known for:** terrific ramen; creative sushi; a fun, casual vibe. [$] *Average main: $18* ✉ *188 State St., Arts District* ☎ *207/541–9204* 🌐 *www.miyakerestaurants.com/paimen* 🕒 *Closed Sun.*

☕ Coffee and Quick Bites

Speckled Ax Wood Roasted Coffee

$ | CAFÉ | The Speckled Ax serves up a seriously delicious coffee, whether cold brewed or piping hot with frothy milk. The secret to the richness of the beans is the painstaking roasting process, using a vintage Italian Petroncini roaster fired with local hardwood—ask to take a peek at that contraption while you wait for your drink. **Known for:** pastries and other baked goods; local gathering space; a hip vibe. [$] *Average main: $4* ✉ *567 Congress St., Arts District* ☎ *207/660–3333* 🌐 *www.speckledax.com.*

🛏 Hotels

The Inn on Carleton

$$ | B&B/INN | FAMILY | This 1869 Victorian-era town home has a curved mahogany staircase to the third floor, a bay window overlooking the street from the front parlor beneath a gleaming crystal chandelier, and gleaming pumpkin-pine floors. **Pros:** most rooms have electric fireplaces; English garden with fountain; attentive resident innkeeper. **Cons:** no elevator; a short walk to the center of it all; no pets or children under 18. [$] *Rooms from: $210* ✉ *46 Carleton St., Arts District* ☎ *207/775–1910* 🌐 *www.innoncarleton.com* 🔑 *6 rooms* 🍴 *Free Breakfast.*

The Westin Portland Harborview

$$ | HOTEL | This imposing structure was New England's largest hotel, the Eastland, when built in 1927 and is a well-known part of the Portland skyline. **Pros:** the views from the rooftop bar and lounge; pet friendly; on-site laundry. **Cons:** rooms with city views cost more; not all rooms have harbor views; often bustling with event attendees. [$] *Rooms from: $254* ✉ *157 High St., Arts District*

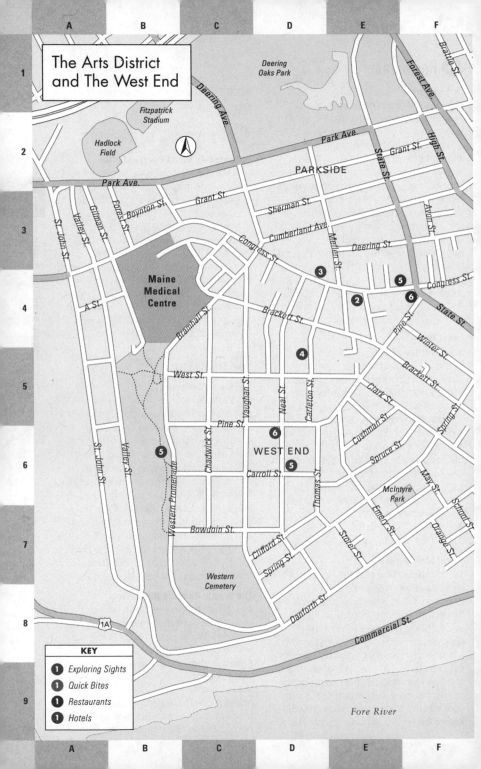

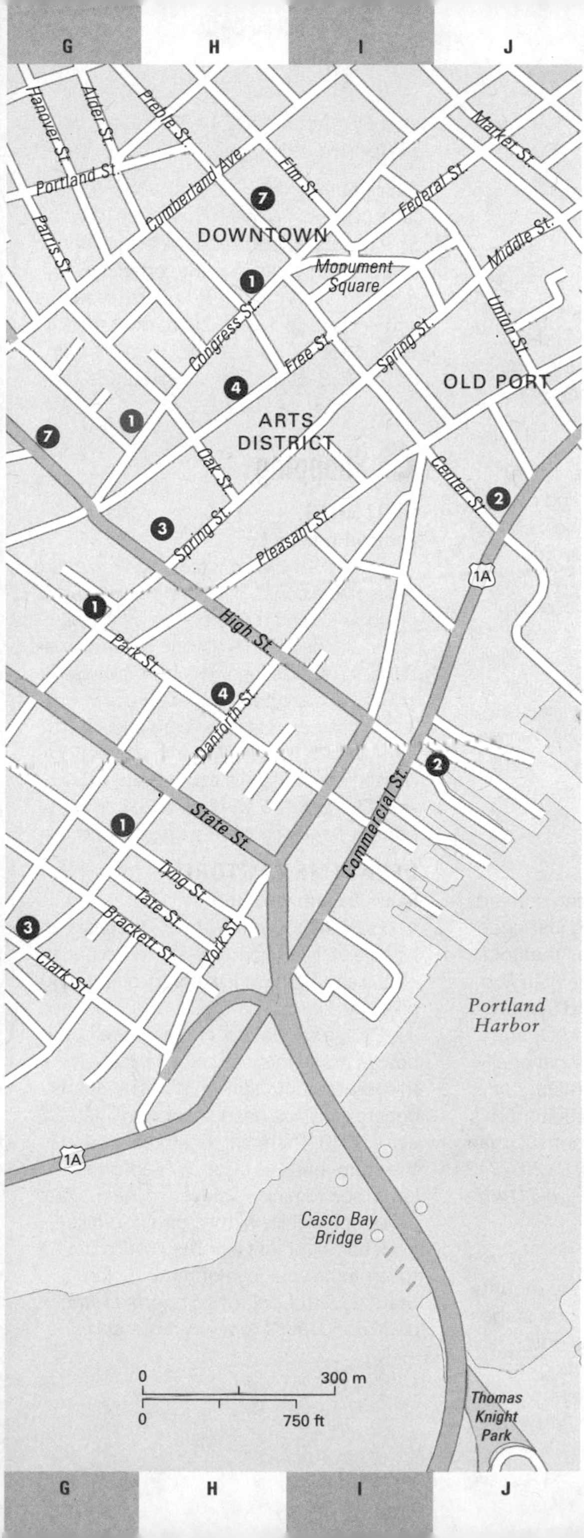

G
H
I
J
Hanover St.
Alder St.
Preble St.
Portland St.
Cumberland Ave.
Elm St.
Market St.
Federal St.
Parris St.
DOWNTOWN
Monument Square
Middle St.
Congress St.
Union St.
Free St.
Spring St.
OLD PORT
ARTS DISTRICT
Oak St.
Center St.
Spring St.
Pleasant St.
1A
High St.
Park St.
Danforth St.
Commercial St.
State St.
Tyng St.
Tate St.
Brackett St.
York St.
Clark St.
Portland Harbor
1A
Casco Bay Bridge
0
300 m
0
750 ft
Thomas Knight Park

Sights

1 Maine Historical Society and Longfellow House H2
2 Neal Dow Memorial....... E4
3 Portland Museum of Art....... H3
4 Victoria Mansion....... H5
5 Western Promenade....... B6

Restaurants

1 BaoBao Dumpling House....... G4
2 Becky's Diner....... J5
3 The Danforth....... G6
4 Leeward....... H3
5 Local 188....... F4
6 Pai Men Miyake....... F4
7 Slab Sicilian Street Food....... H1

Quick Bites

1 Speckled Ax Wood Roasted Coffee....... G3

Hotels

1 Blind Tiger....... G5
2 Canopy by Hilton Portland Waterfront....... J3
3 The Francis....... D4
4 The Inn on Carleton....... D5
5 Pomegranate Inn....... D6
6 West End Inn....... D6
7 The Westin Portland Harborview....... G3

🕾 *207/775–5411* ⊕ *www.marriott.com*
🛏 *289 rooms* ⦿| *No Meals.*

🍸 Nightlife

★ The Jewel Box

COCKTAIL LOUNGES | This hip, craft cocktail–centric hole-in-the-wall has tons of charm and a speakeasy vibe (indeed, there's no sign on the door). Sip a dainty glass of potent French absinthe, or one of the many creative concoctions on the ever-changing cocktail list. Rotating bar snacks include things like house meatballs, turmeric pickles, and candied popcorn with bacon butter and cayenne pepper. Once named "The Bearded Lady's Jewel Box," the bar's bearded owner has been known don beautiful dresses. Check out the massive and ornate, hand-painted mural on the wall that pays homage to that, depicting some elegant bearded ladies ✉ *644 Congress St., Arts District* 🕾 *207/747–5384* ⊕ *www.jewelboxportlandmaine.com/.*

Performing Arts

Merrill Auditorium

CONCERTS | **FAMILY** | This soaring concert hall, built in 1912 and holding just under 2,000 seats, hosts numerous theatrical, comedy, and musical events–including performances by the Portland Symphony Orchestra and the Portland Opera Repertory Theatre, and many nationally and internationally touring artists. Ask about organ recitals on the auditorium's huge 1912 Kotzschmar Memorial Organ. ✉ *20 Myrtle St., Arts District* 🕾 *207/842–0800* ⊕ *www.portlandmaine.gov/1144/Merrill-Auditorium.*

Portland Stage

THEATER | **FAMILY** | This company mounts theatrical productions on its two stages September through May. Recent productions have included lots of new plays, mixed in with well-known works and musical shows. ✉ *25–A Forest Ave.,*

Arts District 🕾 *207/774–0465* ⊕ *www.portlandstage.org.*

Space Gallery

ARTS CENTERS | **FAMILY** | Space Gallery sparkles as a contemporary art gallery and alternative arts venue, opening its doors to everything from poetry readings and art fairs to live music to documentary films. ✉ *538 Congress St., Arts District* 🕾 *207/828–5600* ⊕ *www.space538.org* ⦿ *Closed Sun.–Wed.*

Shopping

CLOTHING

Portland Trading Co.

WOMEN'S CLOTHING | Vintage clothing enthusiasts find a constantly evolving collection of women's and men's pieces on these racks, alongside new numbers—linen maxi skirts, silk tunics, and flowing kimonos—from local designers. The apothecary section carries retro manicure and beard trimming sets, as well as fragrances from Maison Louis Marie. ✉ *83 Market St., Arts District* 🕾 *207/899–0228* ⊕ *www.portlandtradingco.com* ⦿ *Closed Mon.*

DEPARTMENT STORE

Renys Department Store

DEPARTMENT STORE | With its emphasis on high-value merchandise—from Timberland shoes and Carhartt jackets to locally made products like Maine Chefs Wild Blueberry Jam, Raye's Mustard, and bamboo cutting boards made into a map of Maine—this third-generation family-run Maine-centric department has been serving Mainers since 1949. There are 17 stores around the state, but this location is an excellent place to pick up clever souvenirs, a sweater for chilly nights, gifts for folks back home, or just a home accessory to reinforce your love of the Pine Tree State. ✉ *540 Congress St., Arts District* 🕾 *207/553–9061* ⊕ *www.renys.com.*

The West End

A leisurely walk through Portland's West End, beginning at the top of the Arts District, offers a real treat to historic architecture buffs. Elaborate building began in the mid-1800s, encouraged by both a robust economy and Portland's devastating fire of 1866, which leveled nearly one-third of the city. The neighborhood, on the National Register of Historic Places, reveals an extraordinary display of architectural splendor, from High Victorian Gothic to lush Italianate, Queen Anne, and Colonial Revival.

GETTING HERE AND AROUND

A good place to start is at the head of the Western Promenade, which has parking, benches, and a nice view. From the Old Port, take Danforth Street all the way up to Vaughn Street; take a right and then an immediate left onto Western Promenade. You pass by the Western Cemetery, Portland's second official burial ground, laid out in 1829 (inside is the ancestral plot of famous poet Henry Wadsworth Longfellow); just beyond that is the parking area. Once on foot, you can happily get lost on side streets, each lined with statuesque homes.

You could easily spend an hour or two wandering the backstreets of the West End; longer if you bring a picnic to enjoy in the grassy park alongside the Promenade. If you're interested in the particular history of individual homes, download or pick up a brochure from Greater Portland Landmarks *(see Tours in the chapter planner).* A map is included, as well as the stories of some of the more prominent homes. The group also offers a guided house tour on Friday morning, July through September.

Sights

Western Promenade
PROMENADE | FAMILY | Developed beginning in 1836 and landscaped by the Olmsted Brothers, this 18-acre park is one Portland's oldest preserved spaces. It offers wonderful sunset views in spots, as well as a network of wooded trails, places to sit and people-watch, and paths that pass by the neighborhood's historic homes.

A good place to start is at the head of the Western Promenade, which has benches and a nice view. From the Old Port, take Danforth Street all the way up to Vaughn Street; take a right on Vaughn and then an immediate left onto Western Promenade. Pass by the Western Cemetery, Portland's second official burial ground, laid out in 1829—inside is the ancestral plot of poet Henry Wadsworth Longfellow—and look for street parking. ✉ *Danforth St. to Bramhall St.*

🍴 Restaurants

BaoBao Dumpling House
$$ | ASIAN | FAMILY | In a historic town house with traditional Asian decor (a 30-foot copper dragon watches over diners) in Portland's quaint West End, this dumpling house serves deeply satisfying Asian-inspired comfort food in an intimate setting. Start with the house-made Asian slaw, then move to dumplings filled with tried-and-trues such as pork and cabbage or something less traditional, like beef bulgogi or shrimp and bacon. **Known for:** dishes integrating local, seasonal ingredients; tap takeovers by local brewmasters; dishes other than the namesake dumplings. [$] *Average main: $12* ✉ *133 Spring St., at Park St.* ☎ *207/772–8400* 🌐 *www.baobaodumplinghouse.com* 🕒 *Closed Mon. and Tues.*

Becky's Diner
$$ | DINER | FAMILY | You won't find a more local or unfussy place—or one more abuzz with conversation at 4 am—than this waterfront institution way down on the end of Commercial Street. The food is cheap, generous in proportion, and has that satisfying, old-time-diner quality. **Known for:** classic Maine diner food featuring many seafood dishes; very

Landscaped by the Olmsted Brothers, the 18-acre Western Promenade is one of Portland's oldest preserved spaces with wonderful sunset views.

lively atmosphere commingling locals and visitors; parking is easy—a rarity in Portland. [$] *Average main: $14* ✉ *390 Commercial St., The Old Port and the Waterfront* ☎ *207/773–7070* 🌐 *www.beckysdiner.com.*

The Danforth

$$$$ | **AMERICAN** | A posh hangout space for neighborhood locals and visitors to mingle, nosh, and sip, The Danforth is part restaurant, part craft cocktail heaven. The kitchen makes its mark with imaginative takes on local oysters (with coconut and horseradish) and plates of cosseting half chicken in smoked butter pan sauce and Calabrian chili, and any given night sees a roster of at least 10 specialty cocktails, making it a choice spot for aperitifs, nightcaps, or both. **Known for:** a comfortable, swish atmosphere; terrific craft cocktails; local oyster dishes. [$] *Average main: $36* ✉ *211 Danforth St., Portland* ☎ *207/536–0361* 🌐 *www.thedanforth.me* 🕓 *Closed Tues. No lunch.*

★ Slab Sicilian Street Food

$$ | **PIZZA** | **FAMILY** | Let the fact that this incredibly popular outfit doesn't even bother to call its signature foodstuff "pizza" (but instead, "Sicilian street food") be your first hint that the pie here is a different animal altogether. And while there are perfectly good sandwiches on offer, almost everyone's here for the pillowy, chewy, old world–style pizza, by turns smothered in mushrooms or meats, freshly chopped herbs, or graced with a dollop of blue cheese dip. **Known for:** good sandwiches; dough and pizza fixings to make at home; excellent thick- and thin-crust pizzas. [$] *Average main: $14* ✉ *25 Preble St., Portland* ☎ *207/245–3088* 🌐 *www.slabportland.com* 🕓 *Closed Tues. and Wed.*

🛏 Hotels

★ Blind Tiger

$$$$ | **B&B/INN** | Housed in an 1823 Federal-style mansion with a rooftop cupola, Blind Tiger is an enclave of both historic elegance and personalized comfort. **Pros:**

fireplaces in all but one guest room; loaner picnic baskets; complimentary breakfast spread. **Cons:** a bit or a walk from the Old Port; rooms can be hard to get in high season. [$] *Rooms from: $403* ✉ *163 Danforth St., Portland* ☎ *207/8798755* 🌐 *www.larkhotels.com/hotels/blind-tiger* 🛏 *9 rooms* 🍴 *Free Breakfast.*

Canopy by Hilton Portland Waterfront
$$$$ | **HOTEL** | **FAMILY** | One of the newest additions to Portland's hotel landscape, there's a soft contemporary feel throughout the property—abstract carpets, plenty of warm lighting, textured headboards, compact tables, and multimedia artwork give guest rooms a nice mix of sleekness and coziness. **Pros:** pet-friendly room available; two good on-site restaurants; well-equipped fitness center. **Cons:** no self-parking available; a short walk from Old Port; valet parking is $38. [$] *Rooms from: $460* ✉ *9 Center St., Portland* ☎ *207/791–5000* 🌐 *www.hilton.com* 🛏 *135 rooms* 🍴 *No Meals.*

★ The Francis
$$$ | **HOTEL** | In the beautifully restored Mellen E. Bolster House, this charming boutique hotel has a mid-century-modern vibe that seamlessly compliments the building's immaculately preserved historical design elements. **Pros:** bars in rooms; smart spa on second floor; guest rooms feature custom-built furniture. **Cons:** only 15 rooms; some rooms not accessible by elevator; no bathtubs. [$] *Rooms from: $300* ✉ *747 Congress St., Portland* ☎ *207/772–7485* 🌐 *www.thefrancismaine.com* 🛏 *15 rooms* 🍴 *No Meals.*

Pomegranate Inn
$$$ | **B&B/INN** | The classic facade of this handsome 1884 Italianate in the architecturally rich Western Promenade area gives no hint of the splashy, modern (but cozy) surprises within. **Pros:** funky, modern decor; many rooms have gas fireplaces; close to Western Promenade. **Cons:** 15- to 20-minute walk to the Old Port; not pet-friendly; no elevator. [$] *Rooms from: $329* ✉ *49 Neal St., Portland* ☎ *207/772–1006, 800/356–0408* 🌐 *www.pomegranateinn.com* 🛏 *8 rooms* 🍴 *Free Breakfast.*

West End Inn
$$ | **B&B/INN** | Set among the glorious homes of the Western Promenade, this 1871 Georgian displays much of the era's grandeur, with high pressed-tin ceilings, intricate moldings, and ceiling medallions. **Pros:** fireplace library is a cozy place to relax; neighborhood is a historical walking tour; generous breakfast featuring local ingredients. **Cons:** 15- to 20-minute walk downtown; mostly street parking; some rooms without bathtubs. [$] *Rooms from: $279* ✉ *146 Pine St., Portland* ☎ *207/772–1374* 🌐 *www.westendbb.com* 🛏 *6 rooms* 🍴 *Free Breakfast.*

🍸 Nightlife

Luna Rooftop Bar
COCKTAIL LOUNGES | Sophisticated and blessed with stunning views of the city and waterfront, Luna has plenty to recommend as a spot to grab drinks before or after an evening stroll around the city. Perched atop the Canopy by Hilton Portland Waterfront, its talented bar staff pour creative cocktails and the kitchen turns out enough filling small plates to snack on or make a dinner out of. (The eclectic menu spotlights petite lobster rolls; tuna tataki; Korean BBQ beef sliders; and desserts like ricotta lavender fritters.) ✉ *Canopy Portland Waterfront, 285 Commercial St., Portland* ☎ *207/791–0011* 🌐 *lunarooftopbarmaine.com.*

Bayside

Bordered by Forest Avenue to the west, 295 to the north, Congress Street to the south, and Franklin Street to the east, Bayside is home to Whole Foods, Trader Joe's, Bayside Bowl, and the Bayside Trail.

Sights

Austin Street Brewery

BREWERY | Relax in the tasting room or on the patio and soak up the buzz on this block of Fox Street, peering up to Munjoy Hill. Ales like the Original Maine and the selection of IPAs—sessions, double, and traditional—are all on tap, and cans are also available of favorites like Austin Street's saison, Moses. Another location is found in the warehouse on Industrial Way in the Riverton neighborhood, alongside Allagash, Foundation, and Battery Steele Breweries. ✉ *115 Fox St., Bayside* ☎ *207/358–0492* 🌐 *www.austinstreetbrewery.com* 🕑 *Closed Tues.*

Lone Pine Brewing Company

BREWERY | Cozy and friendly, the tasting room buzzes with regulars and visitors—most here to try new brews as well as downpours of old favorites like the light and citrusy Portland Pale Ale. The mezzanine-style tasting room overlooks the production area, and well-behaved and leashed dogs are welcome. ✉ *219 Anderson St., Bayside* ☎ *207/536–4952* 🌐 *lonepinebrewery.com.*

Rising Tide Brewing Company

BREWERY | **FAMILY** | Local ingredients take the spotlight at this family-owned brewery, with sprawling indoor and patio spaces and even bigger list of seasonal creations (like blueberry sour ales and Marzen-style lagers) and year-round beers like Ishmael, a malty and sweet ale. There's also wine and kombuchas on offer. ✉ *103 Fox St., Bayside* ☎ *207/370–2337* 🌐 *www.risingtidebrewing.com/.*

Restaurants

★ Batson River Brewing & Distilling

$$$ | **AMERICAN** | **FAMILY** | The design and overall atmosphere here—part rustic Maine hunting lodge, part chic ski Aspen lodge, all beneath soaring ceilings and in front of a real roaring fire—keep crowds coming back, but the craft beer is very good (pale ales, IPAs, pilsners—you name, they're pouring it), as are the cocktails (the carefully made spirits include a slightly sweet vodka made from corn; a bourbon, and a gin, among others). And, the food deserves kudos, too—snacks like duck fat cornbread with hot honey, and mains, like the lobster mac 'n cheese with Boursin, do not miss. **Known for:** part Maine hunting lodge, part Aspen ski lodge atmosphere; very good brews and spirits; festive, sophisticated atmosphere. [$] *Average main: $26* ✉ *82 Hanover St., Bayside* ☎ *207/800–4680* 🌐 *batsonriver.com.*

★ Miss Portland Diner

$$ | **DINER** | **FAMILY** | A local institution (it's been here since 1949, and Portland's historic preservation department even helped restore it), Portland's beloved gem housed in a Worcester dining car is as authentic as they come. The menu's full of diner staples—lots of homemade pies, daily soups, big breakfasts, BLTs, and thick specialty milkshakes (in flavors like grasshopper and s'mores). **Known for:** authentic diner car history; friendly staff; creative milk shakes. [$] *Average main: $13* ✉ *140 Marginal Way, Bayside* ☎ *207/210–6673* 🌐 *www.missportlanddiner.com* 🕑 *No dinner.*

Coffee and Quick Bites

★ Two Fat Cats Bakery

$ | **BAKERY** | **FAMILY** | A regular stop for pie lovers around the city, Two Fat Cats bakes up delectable bourbon pecan, sour cherry, and coconut cream masterpieces. Meanwhile, the bakery's whoopie pies rely on light and fluffy, hand-scooped chocolate cake batter and a filling that's based on whipped vanilla buttercream, not the more typical marshmallow. **Known for:** delicious homemade pies; celebration cakes; whoopie pies. [$] *Average main: $6* ✉ *195 Lancaster St., Bayside* ☎ *207/347–5144* 🌐 *www.twofatcatsbakery.com.*

Nightlife

★ Bayside Bowl

BOWLING | FAMILY | This 12-lane bowling alley sprang out of a survival technique among a group of friends for getting through Maine's harrowing winters. A community-minded locale that often puts on concerts and other events, Bayside Bowl also serves up some seriously delicious cocktails and local craft beers and snacks like fries and smoked chicken wings; the Rooftop, which has a food truck that serves killer tacos, has one of the best views of the city (and the sunset) in town. ⊠ *58 Alder St., Bayside* ☎ *207/791–2695* ⊕ *www.baysidebowl. com.*

Shopping

ART AND ANTIQUES

Portland Architectural Salvage

ANTIQUES & COLLECTIBLES | A fixer-upper's dream, Portland Architectural Salvage has four floors of unusual finds from old buildings, including fixtures, hardware, and stained-glass windows, as well as assorted antiques. ⊠ *131 Preble St., Bayside* ☎ *207/780–0634* ⊕ *www.portlandsalvage.com* ⊘ *Closed Sun.–Tues.*

Portland Flea-for-All

ANTIQUES & COLLECTIBLES | FAMILY | Friday through Sunday, head to the city's Bayside neighborhood for the Portland Flea-for-All, where you'll find all sorts of vintage eye candy from an ever-rotating array of antiques, original art, and goods from artisan vendors—a fun excursion, whether or not you actually buy anything. ⊠ *585 Congress St., Bayside* ☎ *207/370–7570* ⊕ *www.portlandfleaforall.com* ⊘ *Closed weekdays.*

Back Cove

The Back Cove neighborhood is on the north side of 295 near the city's Back Cove basin—you'll hear some locals refer to it colloquially as Back Bay—which has a lovely 3½ mile trail around it. Its borders are Forest Avenue to Washington Avenue, and Canco Road to the Cove.

 Sights

★ Back Cove Trail

TRAIL | FAMILY | One of the city's most relaxing outdoor spaces, Back Cove Trail is a 3.6-mile paved loop with gorgeous views of the Cove, harbor, and downtown. It's a favorite route for walking, running, biking, and dog walking. Several benches and seasonal water fountains can be found along the trail. ⊠ *Back Cove* ✛ *From I–295 take Exit 6B U.S. 302/ME-100/Forest Ave. and turn right on Forest Ave. Take your next right on Baxter Blvd. and your next right to Preble St. The trail can be accessed anywhere on Baxter Blvd.* ⊕ *trails.org/our-trails/back-cove-trail/.*

Restaurants

★ Tipo

$$ | ITALIAN | FAMILY | Named for the finest grade of flour milled in Italy and owned by the same husband-and-wife duo behind Old Port's wildly popular Central Provisions, Tipo is a Back Cove gem and a neighborhood favorite. The Italian flour is put to excellent use in homemade pastas (like the buccatini with local mussels, fennel, and preserved lemon) and brick-oven pizzas (don't bypass the Casablanca, loaded with merguez sausage and roasted tomato). **Known for:** handmade pastas; creative cocktail program; refined but rustic wood-fired pizzas. ⓢ *Average main: $18* ⊠ *182 Ocean Ave., Back Cove* ☎ *207/358–7970*

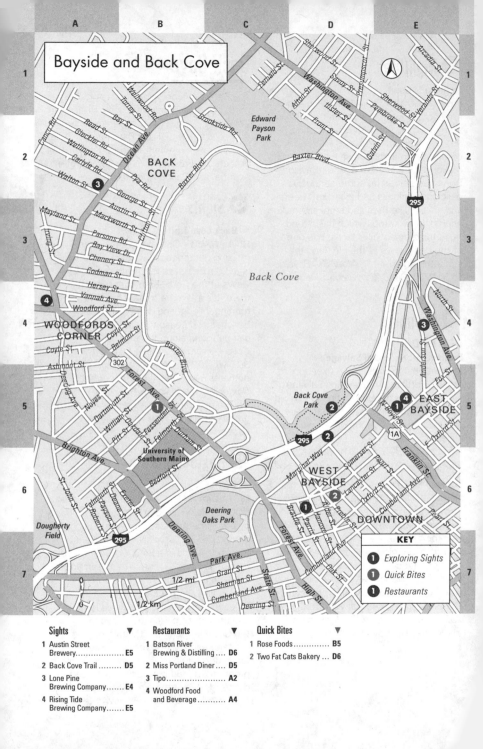

Bayside and Back Cove

Sights ▼

1 Austin Street
   Brewery **E5**
2 Back Cove Trail **D5**
3 Lone Pine
   Brewing Company **E4**
4 Rising Tide
   Brewing Company **E5**

Restaurants ▼

1 Batson River
   Brewing & Distilling **D6**
2 Miss Portland Diner **D5**
3 Tipo **A2**
4 Woodford Food
   and Beverage **A4**

Quick Bites ▼

1 Rose Foods **B5**
2 Two Fat Cats Bakery ... **D6**

KEY

1 Exploring Sights
1 Quick Bites
1 Restaurants

🌐 *www.tiporestaurant.com* 🕒 *Closed Sun. and Mon. No lunch.*

★ Woodford Food and Beverage

$$ | MODERN AMERICAN | The casual, retro vibe at this charming restaurant about 2 miles north of the Old Port makes it worth the journey, as do chef Courtney Loreg's superb offerings—all of them spotlighting locally sourced ingredients from land and sea. There's something for everyone on the menu, including steak tartare, sumptuous deviled eggs, croque madames and monsieurs, homemade pâtés and charcuterie, and killer brisket burgers that are to die for. **Known for:** family-friendly environment; laid back but efficient service; pâté du jour. [$] *Average main: $18* ✉ *660 Forest Ave., Back Cove* ☎ *207/200–8503* 🌐 *www.woodfordfb.com* 🕒 *Closed Tues. and Wed.*

☕ Coffee and Quick Bites

★ Rose Foods

$$ | SANDWICHES | FAMILY | In opening this pitch-perfect bagel shop, chef-owner Chad Conley filled a long-neglected gap in Portland's food scene. Here you'll find spot-on New York-style bagels (made in-house every morning) with both expected and unusual add-ons, including pastrami nova, chopped liver, and whitefish salad. **Known for:** family-friendly, neighborhood environment; house-cured gravlax; general-store-style shop items including books, games, and specialty food items. [$] *Average main: $11* ✉ *428 Forest Ave., Back Cove* ☎ *207/835–0991* 🌐 *www.rosefoods.me* 🕒 *No dinner.*

🛍 Shopping

SPECIALTY SHOPS

Sweet Dirt

OTHER SPECIALTY STORE | Clean and high-quality recreational cannabis—in forms ranging from edibles and concentrates to topicals—is the focus of this local company, started in 2015 by a husband-and-wife team. Sustainability is also a concern; the duo champions organic growing practices, growing plants in living soil, rich in organic matter and beneficial microbes, with clean water. ✉ *1207 Forest Ave., Back Cove* ☎ *207/248–8685* 🌐 *www.sweetdirt.com.* Cannibis

Riverton, Stroudwater, and Parkside

Beyond those Portland neighborhoods most frequented by visitors, the city is home to a handful of communities that range from quiet and residential to bustling—and many have worthy attractions. In Libbytown/Stroudwater you'll find concert venue Thompson's Point, along with the historic Tate House Museum, and destination breweries/distilleries; Parkside is home to highlights like Hadlock Field and Deering Oaks Park; and in Riverton is Industrial Way, the site of several excellent breweries—Allagash Brewing Company and Foundation Brewing Company—that may just convince you to spend the better part of a day.

👁 Sights

Battery Steele Brewing

BREWERY | The latest addition to the warehouse on Industrial Way filled with three quite-good breweries, Battery Steele started in an old barn in South Portland and has since moved to these well-trafficked digs. The tasting room offers a roster of rotating brews on tap—usually 10 or so. Highlights include pours like the double IPA, Avalon, and sours (if it's available, try a glass of Enjoy The Ride). ✉ *1 Industrial Way, Unit 12, Riverton* ☎ *207/749–5035* 🌐 *batterysteele.com/.*

Children's Museum and Theatre of Maine

CHILDREN'S MUSEUM | FAMILY | Kids can pretend they are lobstermen, veterinarians, shopkeepers, or actors in a play at Portland's small but fun Children's Museum. Most exhibits, many of which have a Maine theme, are hands-on and best for kids 10 and younger. Have a Ball! teaches about the science of motion, letting kids build ramps that make balls speed up, slow down, and leap across tracks. Don't miss the life-size inflatable humpback whale rising to the ceiling at the whale exhibit. The outdoor pirate-ship play area is a great place for a picnic lunch. Camera Obscura, an exhibit about optics, provides fascinating panoramic views of the city; it's aimed at adults and older children, and admission is therefore separate. ✉ *Thompson's Point, 250 Thompson's Point Rd., Stroudwater* ☎ *207/828–1234* ⊕ *www.kitetails.org* 🍽 *From $12* ⊘ *Closed Tues.*

Deering Oaks Park

CITY PARK | FAMILY | A lovely 55-acre space designed by the Olmsted Brothers, Deering Oaks is frequented for its sparkling pond, playground, and games at its baseball diamond. It's also the summer home of the Portland Farmer's Market, and you'll find its playground and water features enjoyed by kids on any warm day. A well-kept rose garden and wide clusters of native trees are draws for gardeners and botanists. ✉ *Parkside* ⊕ *www.deeringoaks.org.*

Hadlock Field

SPORTS VENUE | FAMILY | Baseball doesn't get much more authentic, close up, or old school than at Hadlock, home to The minor league Portland Sea Dogs. Whether you've come for the excellent sight lines, to watch a specific player (the team is a feeder for The Boston Red Sox, after all), or just to soak up the old school thrill of watching a mascot throw prizes to kids in the crowd, you're in for a few hours of smiles and vintage America-na. ✉ *271 Park Ave., Parkside, Portland* ☎ *207/874–9300* ⊕ *www.milb.com/portland* 🍽 *Tickets from $11.*

Tate House Museum

HISTORIC HOME | Astride rose-granite steps and a period herb garden overlooking the Stroudwater River on the outskirts of Portland, this magnificent 1755 house was built by Captain George Tate. Tate had been commissioned by the English Crown to organize "the King's Broad Arrow"—marking and cutting down gigantic trees, which were shipped to England to be fashioned as masts for the British Royal Navy. The house has several period rooms, including a sitting room with some fine English Restoration chairs. With its clapboard siding still gloriously unpainted, its impressive Palladian doorway, dogleg stairway, unusual clerestory, and gambrel roof, this house will delight all lovers of Early American decorative arts. ✉ *1267 Westbrook St., Stroudwater, Portland* ☎ *207/774–6177* ⊕ *www.tatehouse.org* 🍽 *$15* ⊘ *Closed Nov.–May.*

★ Thompson's Point

PERFORMANCE VENUE | FAMILY | Most visitors stumble on this stunning performance venue thanks to its national and international musical acts—and indeed, it's an ideal size and structure for that with a 3,000- to 8,000-person capacity; it's spacious but not too big to enjoy the show. But that's just the beginning of what the peninsular, waterfront spot offers, from ice skating in the winter to local craft fairs throughout the year. And on select Thursdays and Fridays from 4 pm till sunset in the summer, entry is free, dogs are welcome, and live music and lawn games are on offer with some of the city's best food trucks lining up to feed the happy crowd. ✉ *Thompsons Point Rd., Stroudwater* ☎ *207/747–5288* ⊕ *www.thompsonspoint.com/.*

🍴 Restaurants

★ Allagash Brewing Company

$ | AMERICAN | FAMILY | Arguably the best-known among all of Maine's many outstanding breweries, Allagash was one of the state's pioneers, first opening in the '90s with its signature Belgian-style wheat beer, Allagash White. There are plenty of other styles to discover at the brewery, including wilds, sours, barrel-aged brews

Allagash Brewing Company is arguably the best-known among all of Maine's many outstanding breweries. Stop by the taproom for an Allagash White and a bite to eat.

and special seasonal concoctions on tap, and when hunger strikes, there's a Bite Into Maine's food truck on-site, where you'll find burgers and excellent Maine staples like lobster rolls and whoopie pies. **Known for:** Bite Into Maine Food truck offerings; one of Maine's brewing pioneers; home of Allagash White. $ *Average main: $9* ✉ *50 Industrial Way, Riverton* ☎ *207/878–5385* 🌐 *www.allagash.com* 🕒 *Closed Tues. and Wed.*

Bissell Brothers Brewing Company

$$ | **AMERICAN** | Perched on Thompson's Point (a quick walk away from the busy entertainment venue of the same name), Bissell Brothers is in a perfect place—a 100-year-old former railway building, to be exact—to wow the crowds before and after the shows. It also draws crowds of its own for its hoppy ales (The Substance Ale, for instance), for regular releases available on tap and in cans, and a kitchen serving big salads full of local veg, wings covered in any of three sauces, and charcuterie from a nearby farm. **Known for:** hoppy ales; locally sourced ingredients; convenient to Thompson's Point events. $ *Average main: $13* ✉ *38 Resurgam Pl., Stroudwater* ☎ *207/808–8258* 🌐 *www.bissellbrothers.com.*

Foundation Brewing Company

$$ | **AMERICAN** | The biggest of three breweries sharing space in an industrial warehouse, Foundation welcomes visitors (and their fur babies—inside and out) to its tasting room with a roster of craft brews that pair well with their Detroit-style pizzas and snacks like giant pretzels, available Thursday through Monday. Foundation's best-known brew is the Double IPA Epiphany, but the ever-changing list of beers on tap includes pilsners like Riverton Flyer and wheaty brews such as Radiant Waves. **Known for:** food available Thursday–Monday; the Double IPA Epiphany; a large list of craft brews on tap. $ *Average main: $14* ✉ *1 Industrial Way #5, Riverton, Portland* ☎ *207/370–5180* 🌐 *foundationbrew.com/* 🕒 *Closed Tues.*

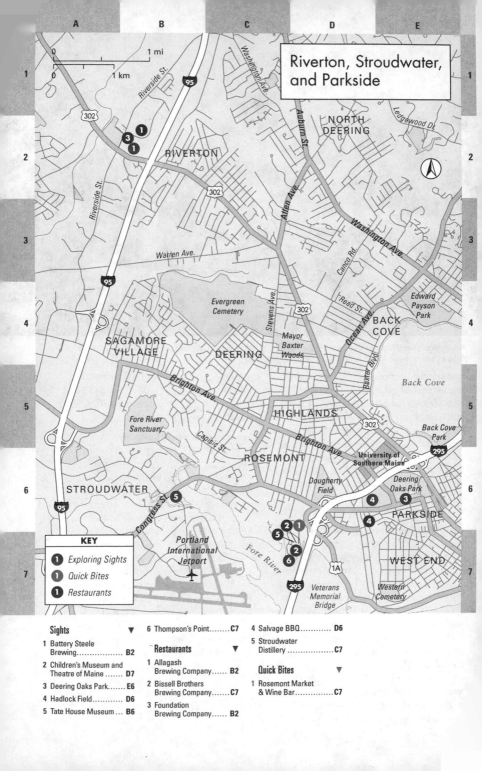

Riverton, Stroudwater, and Parkside

Salvage BBQ

$$$ | **BARBECUE** | **FAMILY** | Trays heaped with St. Louis–style ribs and brisket fly around Salvage's expansive room, as diners wait for orders to arrive at communal or dinette tables. The deep-flavored meats benefit from time in the outfit's smoker, custom-built from an old propane tank and fueled by Maine red oak, and sides like collard greens, delicious cornbread, and hush puppies round out the Southern-style feast. **Known for:** weekly events like bingo, quiz nights, and live music; Southern-style sides like cornbread and collard greens; St. Louis–style barbecue. [$] *Average main: $26* ✉ *919 Congress St., Parkside* ☎ *207/553–2100* 🌐 *salvagebbq.com/* 🕒 *Closed Mon. and Tues.*

Stroudwater Distillery

$$ | **AMERICAN** | A large and style-conscious, multiroom tasting room, Stroudwater centers on a long bar mixing up craft cocktails spotlighting the Distillery's spirits—gin, vodka, bourbon, tequila, rum, and rye. The menu features tasty burgers with homemade dijonnaise sauce and "make-your-own" flatbread pizzas and a few kid-friendly options like chicken tenders and grilled cheese. **Known for:** convenient to Thompson's Point; trendy, low-key atmosphere; craft cocktails. [$] *Average main: $17* ✉ *Thompsons Point, 4 Thompsons Point, Stroudwater, Portland* ☎ *207/536–7811* 🌐 *stroudwaterdistillery.com.*

☕ Coffee and Quick Bites

★ **Rosemont Market & Wine Bar**

$ | **AMERICAN** | **FAMILY** | A fantastic small local chain of markets based around the superb creations of its bakery, this location practices the same locovorism as the rest of the company, but also offers a place to enjoy its creative sandwiches. Expect the likes of turkey with goat cheese, roasted red peppers on puffy focaccia), sushi, and homemade soups, as well as a wine bar for sampling the well-curated vino program. **Known for:** local specialties; pick up picnic fixings for Thompson's Point events; great lunch spot before or after the Children's Museum. [$] *Average main: $9* ✉ *Thompson's Point, 42 Resurgam Pl., Stroudwater, Portland* ☎ *207/956–7341* 🌐 *rosemont-market.com* 🕒 *Closed Sun. and Mon.*

🍸 Nightlife

Vena's Fizz House

BARS | The old-fashioned soda fountain gets a modern update at Vena's Fizz House, where flavors like cucumber mint, chocolate-cherry cordial, and frothy blood orange go into delicious, fizzy "mocktails," while the cocktails feature artisanal ingredients such as Maine pine bitters, saffron syrup, and ghost pepper extract. Just as interesting as the beverages is the space itself; it's housed in a beautifully renovated church. ✉ *15 Chestnut St., Parkside* ☎ *207/747–4901* 🌐 *www.venasfizzhouse.com.*

South Portland

Though it isn't the magnet for visitors that Portland proper is, South Portland offers plenty of reasons to take a detour—from the recreational (lighthouses, breweries, several good eateries, a good beach, and reputable cannabis dispensaries) to the practical (Maine's biggest mall is here, and the area has easy access to the airport).

GETTING HERE AND AROUND

South Portland is a sprawling city and, unless, you're staying just around the immediate area of The Maine Mall, is not walkable. It's best to drive, use ride shares services, or use The City of South Portland bus service ($2), which runs about every hour on weekdays, between South Portland's Willard Square and Downtown Portland.

TRANSPORTATION South Portland - City Bus Services. ☎ *207/767–5556* 🌐 *www.southportland.org.*

VISITOR INFORMATION

Though it's technically a city, South Portland feels much more like a suburb. The largely coastal area is spread out over just under 13 miles, and tends to be thought of as two sections: the commercial and retail western half where you'll find The Maine Mall and many a strip mall, and the eastern half, home to Willard Beach, a community college, and parks.

Sights

Bug Light Park

LIGHTHOUSE | The relatively small size of Bug Light (it's officially known to the U.S. coastguard as South Portland Breakwater Light) is what gave it its nickname, and then the name of the 9-acre park surrounding it followed. Bug Light was originally built in 1855 and rebuilt with plates and Corinthian columns in 1875, and stands today as both a landmark and a terrific place to catch views of Casco Bay and Munjoy Hill. ✉ *Madison St., South Portland* 🌐 *www.southportland.org.*

Fore River Brewery

BREWERY | **FAMILY** | A laid-back brewery with a focus on IPAs and sour ales, Fore River has plenty of brews to sample and plenty to do while hanging at the fire pit, playing corn hole or dog frisbee (canines are welcome in the yard), or listening to live music. Specialties from various food trucks are here as well; call ahead or visit the website to see what trucks are scheduled. ✉ *45 Huntress Ave.* ☎ *207/370–0629* 🌐 *www.foreriverbrewing.com.*

Beaches

Willard Beach

BEACH | A 4-acre beach that swarms on hot summer days with residents and visitors, Willard Beach offers easy swimming and boating, as well as views of Fort Gorges. Convenient and free parking, lifeguards, a snack shack, and restrooms all add to its popularity. Dogs are permitted after sundown in the summer or all day in the off season. **Amenities:** food and drink; lifeguards; parking (free); showers; toilets; water sports. **Best for:** sunsets; swimming; walking; windsurfing. ✉ *44 Willow St., South Portland* ☎ *207/767–3201* 🌐 *www.southportland.org.*

Restaurants

Foulmouthed Brewing

$$ | **AMERICAN** | With a full and lively roster of brews on drafts and in cans, this small brewpub housed in an old auto garage is a friendly place to spend an afternoon. From their citrus-y IPAs and sours to wheat saisons with green tea and local Maine wildflower honey, the creations range from classic to niche. **Known for:** laid-back atmosphere in an old auto garage; very friendly staff; above average comfort food. [$] *Average main: $13* ✉ *15 Ocean St., South Portland* ☎ *207/618–6977* 🌐 *www.foulmouthedbrewing.com.*

Tuscan Table

$$$ | **ITALIAN** | **FAMILY** | One of two large locations (the other is in Freeport), this stylishly decorated, locally owned, and family-friendly trattoria-inspired spot specializes in wood-fired pizzas and hearty (mostly Italian) entrées. There are also seafood options like Maine mussels and oysters as well as a selection of Maine beers on tap. **Known for:** good option if you're at the Maine Mall; family-friendly atmosphere; wood-fired pizzas. [$] *Average main: $21* ✉ *Maine Mall, 390 Gorham Rd., South Portland* ☎ *207/536–0240* 🌐 *www.tuscantablemaine.com.*

Hotels

Hampton Inn Portland-Airport

$$$ | **HOTEL** | **FAMILY** | For a place to sleep that's convenient to both the Portland International Jetport and The Maine Mall, this Hampton Inn location is a comfortable bet. **Pros:** close to the Portland International Jetport; pet-friendly; indoor swimming pool. **Cons:** not ideal for vacation-length stays; not in a scenic area.

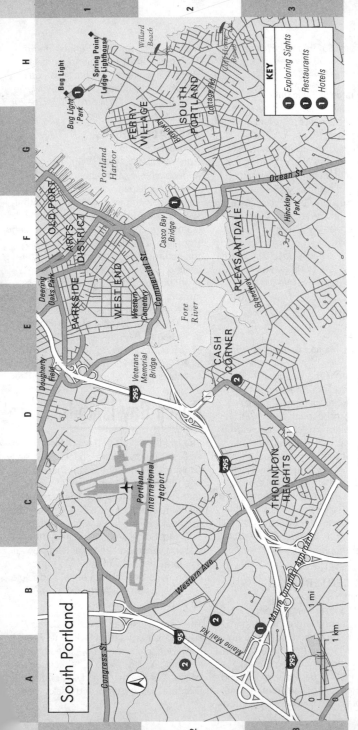

South Portland

KEY

1 Exploring Sights
1 Restaurants
1 Hotels

Bug Light

Bug Light Park

Spring Point
Ledge Lighthouse

Willard Beach

FERRY VILLAGE

SOUTH PORTLAND

Bug Light Park

Cottage Rd

Cliff House
Beach

Portland Harbor

Ocean St.

OLD PORT

ARTS DISTRICT

Casco Bay Bridge

Hinckley Park

Deering Oaks Park

PARKSIDE

WEST END

Western Cemetery

Commercial St.

Fore River

PLEASANTDALE

Bridewalk

Dougherty Field

Veterans Memorial Bridge

295

CASH CORNER

Portland International Jetport

295

THORNTON HEIGHTS

Western Ave.

Maine Turnpike

Maine Mall Rd.

95

295

Congress St.

1 mi

1 km

0

0

Sights ▶

1 Bug Light Park...............**H1**
2 Fore River
   Brewery..........................**D2**

Restaurants ▶

1 Foulmouthed Brewing....**F2**
2 Tuscan Table....................**B2**

Hotels ▶

1 Hampton Inn
   Portland-Airport............**B3**
2 Portland Sheraton
   at Sable Oaks.................**A2**

[$] *Rooms from: $329* ✉ *171 Philbrook Ave.* ☎ *207/773–400* 🌐 *www.hilton.com* 🛏 *129 rooms* 🍴 *Free Breakfast.*

Portland Sheraton at Sable Oaks

$$ | **HOTEL** | **FAMILY** | Just 2.4 miles from Portland International Jetport and close to the Maine Mall, South Portland's recently renovated Marriott now sports sharp, contemporary design with funky industrial lighting fixtures, ergonomic furnishings, and tech perks like free Wi-Fi. **Pros:** close to Maine Mall; close to airport; recently renovated. **Cons:** not ideal for more than a night or two; very few good views from rooms. [$] *Rooms from: $229* ✉ *200 Sable Oaks Dr., South Portland* ☎ *207/871–8000* 🌐 *www.marriott.com* 🛏 *226 rooms* 🍴 *No Meals.*

Shopping

FOOD

Cape Whoopies, Maine's Gourmet Whoopie Pie

FOOD | Maine leads the way in whoopie pie adoration, and gourmet shops like this one offer up all kinds of imaginative flavors including chocolate cakes with chocolate hazelnut and cayenne cream, vanilla cakes with maple cream, or seasonal options like pumpkin cakes with cream cheese cream and Granny Smith apple spiced cake with caramel cream. There are even gluten-free options. And the best part? They can be shipped all over the continental United States. ✉ *185 Cottage Rd., South Portland* ☎ *207/409–0957* 🌐 *capewhoopies.com* 🕒 *Closed Sun.*

SHOPPING CENTERS

The Maine Mall

MALL | **FAMILY** | Maine's largest shopping mall (and the second largest in northern New England) is enclosed and has a full stable of the expected national and international retail shops including Pottery Barn, Apple, Banana Republic, H&M, and Sephora. Mixed in, however, are regional and local stores, too. Department stores include Macy's and JC Penney, and the food court offers healthier options like Red Mango and a Mediterranean grill on top of the usual fast food. ✉ *364 Maine Mall Rd., South Portland* ☎ *207/828–2063* 🌐 *www.mainemall.com.*

SPECIALTY SHOPS

Seaweed Co.

OTHER SPECIALTY STORE | With a knowledgeable crew of "budtenders," Seaweed Co.'s flagship location is unusually spacious, with plenty of room to gather with fellow enthusiasts or the staff and learn more about the products that range from flower to sleep aids and edibles to tinctures. The bright and sunny store is lined in blonde woods and tables filled with products, and sitting areas indoors and out. Food trucks, live music, and events sometimes make a showing. There is a second, smaller location in Portland's Bayside neighborhood. ✉ *185 Running Hill Rd., South Portland* ☎ *207/819–4114* 🌐 *seaweedmaine.com.* Cannabis

Casco Bay Islands

The islands of Casco Bay are also known as the Calendar Islands, because an early explorer mistakenly thought there was one for each day of the year (in reality there are only 140 or so). These islands range from ledges visible only at low tide to populous Peaks Island, a suburb of Portland. Some are uninhabited; others support year-round communities, as well as stores and restaurants. Ft. Gorges commands Hog Island Ledge, and Eagle Island is the site of Arctic explorer Admiral Robert Peary's home.

The brightly painted ferries of Casco Bay Lines are the islands' lifeline. There is service to the most populated ones, including: Bailey Island, Chebeague Island, Cliff Island, Great Diamond / Little Diamond, Long Island, and Peaks Island.

The Chebeague Island Inn, reachable by ferry or personal boat, is a great place to watch the sunset.

There is little in the way of overnight lodging on the islands—the population swells during the warmer months due to summer residents—and there are few restaurants or organized attractions other than the natural beauty of the islands themselves. Meandering about by bike or on foot is a good way to explore on a day trip.

GETTING HERE AND AROUND

Casco Bay Lines provides year-round ferry service from Portland to the following islands in Casco Bay: Little Diamond and Great Diamond; Chebeague; Bailey; Cliff; Peaks; and Long Islands. Boats leave from the terminal in Old Port, and schedules vary according to season—ferries leave more often in summer, less so in fall and spring, and only several times per day in the winter. Islands also have different schedules; Peaks Island, the closest to Portland and the most populated, has the most frequent ferries. On-island transportation should be planned for. Peaks Island is the only one allowing cars to be transported by ferry, and if your aim is to do that, plan in advance, as ferries fill up fast in the summer. On most of the islands, you can rent a bike or a golf cart as soon as you get off the ferry terminal. You can also bring your own bike on the ferry to all islands; rates are $6.50 per adult bike and $3.25 per child's bike. Pets can tag along, too, for an additional $4.10 round-trip.

Specialty cruises are offered (also with differing schedules and prices according to season) passing by various islands, depending on the theme. There's a Moonlight Run, Sunset Run, Sunrise Run, and the popular Mailboat Run, which lets passengers join as the working ferry delivers real mail to Little Diamond, Great Diamond, Long, Cliff, and Chebeague Islands.

CONTACTS Casco Bay Lines. ⊠ *56 Commercial St., Portland* ☎ *207/774–7871* ⊕ *www.cascobaylines.com.*

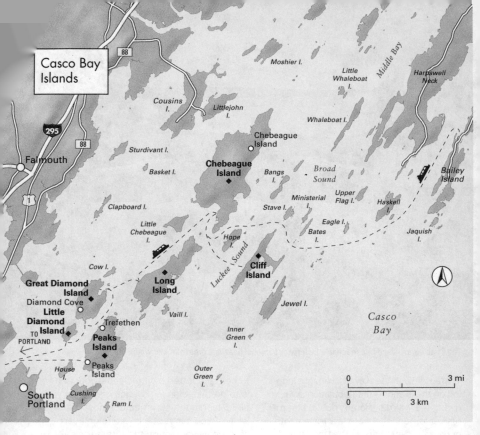

Casco Bay Islands

Moshier I.

Little Whaleboat I.

Middle Bay

Harpswell Neck

Cousins I.

Littlejohn I.

Whaleboat I.

Chebeague Island

Sturdivant I.

Chebeague Island

Bangs I.

Broad Sound

Bailey Island

Falmouth

Basket I.

Ministerial I.

Upper Flag I.

Haskell I.

Clapboard I.

Stave I.

Eagle I.

Jaquish I.

Little Chebeague I.

Hope I.

Bates I.

Cow I.

Cliff Island

Luckee Sound

Great Diamond Island

Long Island

Jewel I.

Casco Bay

Diamond Cove

Little Diamond Island

Trefethen

Vaill I.

Inner Green I.

TO PORTLAND

Peaks Island

House I.

Peaks Island

Outer Green I.

South Portland

Cushing I.

Ram I.

0 ——— 3 mi

0 ——— 3 km

◉ Sights

Don't expect sights and entertainment in the traditional sense. The islands are peaceful places with beaches to walk on, rocky shores to explore, and bikes (or golf carts) to rent.

History buffs take note: Casco Bay was the headquarters for Commander Destroyer Force, Atlantic (ComDesLant) during WWII. Officers' quarters were on Great Diamond; Long Island was home to the US Navy Fuel Annex, Torpedo Control Officers School, and the US Naval Air Facility Casco Bay; and Peaks Island had more than 50 military structures including two major gun batteries. Many of the structures still dot the islands.

For more info on Bailey Island and what to do there, see the Harpswell section of the Mid-Coast Region (Ch. 5).

Chebeague Island

ISLAND | FAMILY | About 5 miles long and 1½ miles wide, Chebeague (pronounced shah-big) has a year-round population of about 390, which more than quadruples in the summer season. Originally used as a fishing ground by Abenaki Indigenous people, the island later became a place known for stone slooping—those workers who carried ballast and granite for 19th-century ships, to be used in grand buildings. The island has a number of impressive Greek Revival homes built by them. There are a couple of small beaches, but most visitors come to spend time at The Chebeague Island Inn, where there's golf and tennis to play, and a very good restaurant open for lunch, dinner, or just drinks. ✉ *Portland* ☎ *207/846–3148* ⊕ *www.townofchebeagueisland.org.*

Cliff Island

ISLAND | FAMILY | Little wonder that the farthest island from Portland served by ferry service is also the most secluded and natural. Roads are unpaved, and most of the woods and beaches here are conservation land. Food isn't always easy to find here; there is but one store, and hours can be limited, so bring a lunch if you're looking to picnic. If a beach is on your agenda, head toward Stone Beach for great views of the nearby islands. ✉ *Portland.*

Great Diamond Island and Little Diamond

ISLAND | FAMILY | Though most of Great Diamond is closed to the public, the Inn at Diamond Cove welcomes visitors and offers plenty to do. Housed in what was once Fort McKinley, a United States Army coastal defense fort built in the late 1800s and retired in the 1940s, It's a combination resort, with several eateries as well as private residences. Guests can play tennis and indoor basketball, lounge at the pool, or use the complimentary bikes. Visitors often take the ferry just for the day, or for dinner at the property's fine dining establishment, Diamond's Edge. The area is car-free, so if you're not staying at the Inn, be prepared to explore on foot or bring your own bike.Meanwhile, Little Diamond can be accessed on foot at low tide via Lamson Cove, and is filled with private residences, many of which can be rented during the summer months. ✉ *Portland.*

Long Island

ISLAND | FAMILY | Three miles long and one-mile wide, Long Island lives up to its name in shape, and is home to 200 year-round residents (many of whom work in the fishing industry) and 1,000 summer dwellers. There are a few lovely beaches here, including South Beach, Andrews Beach, and Fowler Beach. A few country stores and a bakery can supply you with vittles for a picnic. Bike rentals are not available, so bring your own over on the ferry or rent a golf cart close to the ferry landing when you arrive. ✉ *Portland* 🌐 *townoflongisland.us/wp/.*

Peaks Island

ISLAND | FAMILY | Nearest to Portland (only a 15-minute ferry ride away), this is the most developed of the Calendar Islands, but it still allows you to experience the relaxed pace of island life. Explore an art gallery or an old fort, and meander along the alternately rocky and sandy shore on foot, or rent a kayak, bike, or golf cart once off the ferry. A number of spots are open for both lunch and dinner.

The Fifth Maine Museum, a small museum with Civil War artifacts, open only in summer, is maintained in the building of the 5th Maine Regiment. (🎟 *$8;* ☎ *207/766–3330,* 🌐 *www.fifthmainemuseum.org*). When the Civil War broke out in 1861, Maine was asked to raise a single regiment to fight, but the state came up with several (the number eventually totaled 40), and sent the 5th Maine Regiment into the war's first battle, at Bull Run. The museum also offers guidebooks for a two-hour self-guided tour of the World War II Peaks Island Reservation. ✉ *Portland* 🌐 *peaksisland.info.*

🍴 Restaurants

★ Crown Jewel

$$ | MODERN AMERICAN | Forget New England nautical; Crown's Jewel's owners went in a completely different design direction when they created it, and instead leaned into Latin American and Miami vibes. And in fact, the flamingos and palm trees dotting the decor here embody the whimsical spirit of the entire place, found in its partylike feel as well as the fun cocktails and in delicious dishes like mussels escabeche and lobster arancini. **Known for:** a popular happy hour; creative deviled eggs; food for sharing. [$] *Average main: $17* ✉ *255 Diamond Ave., Portland* ☎ *207/766–3000* 🌐 *www.crownjewelportland.com* 🕒 *Closed Mon. and Tues. June–Aug.; Mon.–Thurs. Sept.; and Oct.–May.*

★ Diamond's Edge Restaurant and Marina

$$$$ | **SEAFOOD** | Whether you dine on the large, airy deck or out on the lawn that stretches to the water, you're in for a real treat: creative surf-and-turf dishes featuring locally sourced, seasonal ingredients. Start with a few items from the excellent selection of hot and chilled seafood—the scallop crudo is superb—and then move on to one of the extremely fresh entrées, which include a bouillabaisse filled with mussels, fresh catch, salmon, cod, shrimp, scallops. **Known for:** gorgeous views; slow food prepared on island time; house-made desserts featuring delicious house gelato. $ *Average main: $32* ✉ *Diamond Cove, Portland* ☎ *207/766–5850* ⊕ *www.diamondsedgerestaurantandmarina.com* ◔ *Closed Nov.–June.*

Hotels

Chebeague Island Inn

$$$$ | **B&B/INN** | **FAMILY** | The focal point of Chebeague Island's activity, the Inn is a destination in its own right for golfers, tennis players, and food lovers looking to try the creations of 2018 Food Network Chopped award-winner, chef Matt Ginn. **Pros:** top-notch food from an award-winning chef; individually decorated rooms; stunning ocean views and sunsets. **Cons:** not a lot of other options on the island; no air-conditioning; no televisions. $ *Rooms from: $488* ✉ *61 South Rd., Portland* ☎ *207/846–5155* ⊕ *www.chebeagueislandinn.com* ◔ *Closed Oct.–May* ⮌ *21 rooms* ¶◯¶ *No Meals.*

Inn at Diamond Cove

$$$$ | **B&B/INN** | **FAMILY** | Transformed from Fort McKinley, an 1800s United States Army coastal defense fort, into a modern and swanky inn, this sprawling property welcomes guests for overnight stays or for dinners and lunches. **Pros:** an outdoor pool; lots of amenities, from tennis and biking, a game room, a pool; luxury rooms and suites, many with fireplaces. **Cons:** your arrival and departure is determined by the ferry schedule; not a lot of other options on the island; complimentary bikes don't always work. $ *Rooms from: $409* ✉ *22 McKinley Court, Portland* ☎ *207/805–9836* ⊕ *www.innatdiamondcove.com* ◔ *Closed Oct.–May* ⮌ *44 rooms* ¶◯¶ *No Meals.*

Inn on Peaks Island

$$$ | **B&B/INN** | **FAMILY** | Boasting spacious rooms with water views and Jacuzzi tubs in many of them, this year-round favorite blends a relaxed, island style with a dash of luxury; rooms are decked out in simple but pretty linens and soft patterns. **Pros:** easy walk from the ferry terminal; Jacuzzi bathtubs in many rooms; most rooms have water views. **Cons:** wedding season tends to monopolize the rooms; arrival and departure dictated by the ferry schedule; limited services offered in the off-season. $ *Rooms from: $343* ✉ *33 Island Ave., Portland* ☎ *207/766–5100* ⊕ *www.innonpeaks.com* ⮌ *8 suites* ¶◯¶ *No Meals.*

Chapter 5

THE MID-COAST REGION

Updated by
Mimi Steadman

⊙ Sights   🍴 Restaurants   🛏 Hotels   🛍 Shopping   🍸 Nightlife

★★★★★   ★★★★★   ★★★★★   ★★★★★   ★★★★★

WELCOME TO THE MID-COAST REGION

TOP REASONS TO GO

★ **Delectable seafood:** From waterside lobster shacks to celebrated contemporary restaurants, it's all here. Of course, there's lobster, but don't miss the oysters!

★ **Scenic drives:** Head north on Route 1 to find rockbound peninsulas that reach into the sea and working fishing villages.

★ **Sightseeing cruises:** Excursion boats, both power and sail, depart from numerous harbors, taking you past stalwart lighthouses and rock-rimmed islands, into rivers and inlets, and up close to lots of wildlife.

★ **Outdoor adventure:** Activities abound including kayaking, sailing, hiking, and rock climbing. Expert-led trips, as well as gear rentals, are offered in several towns.

★ **A shipbuilding heritage:** Shipbuilding has long been a part of the Mid-Coast, and the wealth it generated is evidenced by beautiful towns graced with elegant old mansions.

1 Yarmouth. Inviting, upscale old town near Portland.

2 Freeport. Home of L.L. Bean and historical neighborhoods.

3 Brunswick. Buzzing college town.

4 Harpswell. A scenic string of bridge-connected islands.

5 Bath. Shipbuilding heritage and the Maine Maritime Museum.

6 Wiscasset. The "prettiest village in Maine" has great lobster rolls.

7 Boothbay Harbor. A traditional fishing village turned tourist destination.

8 Damariscotta. Filled with upscale, locally owned shops and restaurants.

9 Pemaquid Point. Stunning lighthouse perched atop wave-dashed rocks.

10 Waldoboro. Popular with artists and artisans.

11 Thomaston. Handsome sea captains' homes in a historic district.

12 Tenants Harbor and Port Clyde. Sweet, serene fishing village and salty, end-of-the-road hamlet.

13 Monhegan Island. Rugged, rustic, heart-stealing place.

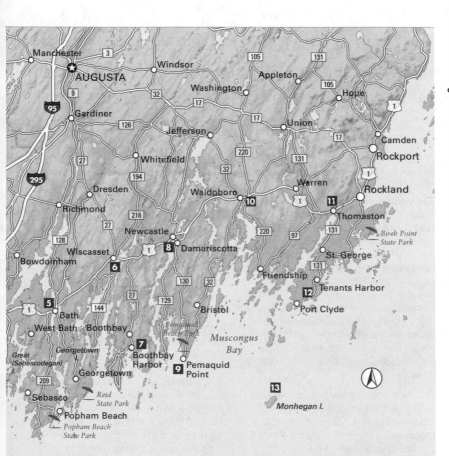

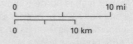

Lighthouses dot the headlands of Maine's Mid-Coast region, where thousands of miles of coastline wait to be explored. Defined by chiseled peninsulas stretching south from U.S. 1, this area has everything from the sandy beaches of Reid State Park and Popham Beach to the outer cliffs of remote Monhegan Island.

The sightseeing and charter boats that leave many of the harbors offer memorable views of the rockbound coast and the chance to glimpse a whale or hook a trophy-worthy fish. In midsummer, you can even visit an island to see puffins. To explore secluded coves, however, kayaks are your best bet. There are unlimited places to put in, and you can rent equipment in Harpswell, Boothbay Harbor, Damariscotta, Port Clyde, and other harbor towns. Protected inland rivers on many peninsulas offer more leisurely paddles.

Tall ships often visit Maine, sometimes sailing up the Kennebec River for a stopover at Bath's Maine Maritime Museum, on the site of the old Percy & Small Shipyard. Just up the road from the museum, Bath Iron Works still builds the U.S. Navy's Aegis-class destroyers. An impressive fleet gathers in Boothbay Harbor every June for the annual Windjammer Days celebration.

Along U.S. 1, charming towns, all of them unique, offer an array of attractions. One of the larger communities is Brunswick, which is home to Bowdoin College and has rows of historic brick and clapboard homes. Bath is known for its maritime heritage. Wiscasset offers some of the best antiques shopping in the state, as well as a couple of well-known lobster shacks. Damariscotta, too, is worth a stop for its shopping opportunities and seafood restaurants. (You'd be hard-pressed to find better-tasting oysters than those plucked fresh from the Damariscotta River.)

South along the peninsulas, the scenery opens to glorious vistas of working harbors and broad stretches of the bay. It's here you find old-fashioned dockside restaurants where you might even see your lunch come right off the boats. Boothbay Harbor is one of the most popular towns along the Mid-Coast—a busy tourist destination come summer, with lots of little stores that are perfect for window-shopping. It's one of three towns from which you can take a ferry to Monhegan Island, an artsy enclave for more than a century. Here you'll see painters in their studios and at their easels, intent on capturing the windswept cliffs, seascapes, and weathered homes with colorful gardens.

Planning

Getting Here and Around

Concord Coach Lines buses run from Boston's South Station and Logan Airport to Portland, with Mid-Coast stops in Brunswick, Bath, Wiscasset, Damariscotta, and Waldoboro. Amtrak's *Downeaster* passenger train between Boston's North Station and Portland stops in Freeport and Brunswick. To fully explore the region, however, you really need a car, as there is little local public transportation between or within the Mid-Coast's communities.

AIR

The Portland Jetport is convenient to the Mid-Coast region, only 30 minutes from Brunswick via the Maine Turnpike or I–295. Manchester International Airport, in New Hampshire, is two hours from the Mid-Coast region. Bangor International Airport is also about two hours away, but be aware that there are frequent cancellations at this small airport.

BICYCLE

There are two major bike routes in the Mid-Coast region. The Coastal Route tour runs from Brunswick to Ellsworth, a distance of 187 miles along the rocky coastline, with some stretches along heavily traveled roads. You need not go the full distance. In Brunswick, for instance, a mostly level 5-mile round-trip ride begins on Water Street at the west end of the Androscoggin River Bike Path. There are restrooms along the way and shady spots to rest along the river.

The 60-mile Merrymeeting Tour, traversing small hills and one major climb, originates in Bath and travels round-trip to Wiscasset. Along the way, you can see the Kennebec River and Merrymeeting Bay, famous for its variety of birds, including several types of ducks. For maps and info about the trail, visit ⊕ *www.krrt.org*.

BOAT

You can charter boats and go on scenic tours from almost any town in the Mid-Coast. Three towns also have regular boat service to Monhegan Island. Port Clyde is the point of departure for one-way trips of just over an hour aboard the *Elizabeth Ann* or the *Laura B*. The *Balmy Days II* makes the 90-minute sail from Boothbay Harbor daily at 9:30 am from Memorial Day through Columbus Day. Hardy Boat Cruises leave daily at 9 am from May through October and at 9 am and 2 pm in summer. The trip from Shaw's Wharf in New Harbor takes an hour.

CAR

While driving in the Mid-Coast region, you may encounter fog, especially on the peninsulas and points of land. It's best to leave headlights on. Fog may stay around all day, or it may burn off by late morning.

Snow and ice can make winter driving a challenge. "Black ice" is a special hazard along the coast, as the road may appear clear but is actually covered by a nearly invisible coating of ice. All-wheel-drive vehicles are recommended for driving in winter.

Hotels

Mid-Coast accommodations range from oceanfront and woodsy cabins to elegant bed-and-breakfasts and seaside resorts. The most interesting choices are often in former sea captains' or shipbuilders' homes, beautifully restored and furnished with period pieces.

Most accommodations have air-conditioning and cable TV, as well as good Wi-Fi (though it can be spotty on the islands and in other more remote places). At the lower end of the scale, you can still find clean, comfortable rooms with basic amenities, though the rates can still be on the high side. The good news is that stunning views can be found at just about every property.

Prices increase between the end of May and early September; they're at their highest from July 4 to Labor Day. Many of the high-end places require a two-night minimum stay, especially on weekends. Places book up early and reservations are strongly advised. Note, too, that most lodgings in Maine do not allow smoking on the property.

Restaurants

Although the Mid-Coast has experienced a boom in the number of restaurants offering sophisticated dining, for most visitors, casual places serving seafood, especially lobster, remain the main draw. At harborside eateries, the catch is often hauled right off the boat and stored in saltwater tanks, or pounds, just waiting for you to pick which lobster you want for dinner. For the true Maine experience, tuck into a shore dinner complete with lobster, steamer clams, and corn on the cob. At some point, you'll want to have a lobster roll or crab roll—or two—as well.

The area's burgeoning oyster-farming industry has put the delicate bivalves on numerous menus. Indeed, some people refer to the Damariscotta River area, where Maine oyster farming began, as the "Napa Valley of oysters." The Mid-Coast is also famous for its haddock sandwiches, chowders, crab cakes, lobster bisque, fried clams, and scallops. Of course, steak and prime rib appear on menus here, too, as do pork and lamb. Much of the meat on offer is raised locally.

Large servings, the norm here, may be daunting to light eaters, but most restaurants also offer smaller portions. Casual dress is fine in all the restaurants covered in this chapter. In summer, when business is brisk, many restaurants accept reservations; at some places, they are very strongly recommended. Call ahead to check. Note, too, that some restaurants—especially those serving lobster on the dock—close during the off-season.

HOTEL AND RESTAURANT PRICES

Hotel and restaurant reviews have been shortened. For full information, visit Fodors.com. Hotel prices in the reviews are the lowest cost of a standard double room in high season. Restaurant prices are the average cost of a main course at dinner, or if dinner is not served, at lunch.

What It Costs In U.S. Dollars			
$	$$	$$$	$$$$
RESTAURANTS			
under $18	$18–$24	$35–$35	over $35
HOTELS			
under $200	$200–$299	$300–$399	over $399

When to Go

In summer, temperatures often reach the 80s and occasionally the 90s. But be prepared for them to occasionally dip into the 60s or even 50s, especially at night. Pack layers if you're planning to go on a windjammer cruise or even a sightseeing boat trip of only a few hours; it's always noticeably cooler out on the water.

In autumn the humidity is gone, the days are often sunny and warm, and the nights are crisp, dropping into the 40s and 50s. In October, the foliage in the Mid-Coast region is spectacular, with brilliant reds and oranges bursting from maple trees and yellows illuminating the birch trees, all set against blue seascapes.

Sea storms can be dramatic in November and December. For winter visits, though, you don't have to reserve months ahead to score a room in a country inn or bed-and-breakfast—though some do close during the off-season.

April temperatures often don't reach above the 40s; the days gradually warm up in May. In spring, the hotels and restaurants are not yet crowded either. Many businesses remain closed until early or mid-May, but you shouldn't have trouble finding a few antiques shops, boutiques, and art galleries that are open. With Maine's dynamic dining scene, fewer restaurants close in the off-season than in the past.

Yarmouth

12 miles northeast of Portland.

Despite its proximity to Portland, Yarmouth remains a picturesque small town graced by centuries-old homes and commercial buildings. Exceptional restaurants and appealing shops, both in the historic downtown and out on Route 1, draw visitors from Portland and beyond. Yarmouth also has fine hiking trails, and frontage on both fresh and saltwater makes it a good boating destination. Unlike Freeport, its neighbor to the north, it's usually pretty quiet here, except during the annual Clam Festival.

GETTING HERE AND AROUND
The 12-mile drive on I–295 from Portland to Yarmouth takes about 15 minutes. The Metro Breez bus makes several 30-minute trips between the Portland Transportation Center and Yarmouth Town Hall every day except Sunday.

CONTACTS Metro Breez Buses. ⊠ *Portland* ☎ *207/774–0351* ⊕ *gpmetro.org.*

VISITOR INFORMATION
CONTACTS Maine State Visitor Information Center-Yarmouth. ⊠ *1100 U.S. Rte. 1, Exit 17 off I–295, Yarmouth* ☎ *207/846–0833.*

Yarmouth Chamber of Commerce. ⊠ *305 Main St., Yarmouth* ☎ *207/846–3984* ⊕ *yarmouthmaine.org.*

 Restaurants

Day's Crabmeat & Lobster
$$ | SEAFOOD | FAMILY | People have been stopping at this roadside lobster pound for a century, buying live or cooked lobsters to take home, or ordering a lobster or crabmeat roll, lobster stew, lobster dinner, steamed or fried fresh clams, and other local seafood to enjoy at a picnic table overlooking a serene salt marsh. It's just a few miles down the road from Freeport's Main Street shops, but it feels a world apart. **Known for:** fresh seafood at fair prices; low-key, old-fashioned atmosphere; wetlands views. $ *Average main: $20* ⊠ *1269 U.S. 1, Yarmouth* ☎ *207/846–5871* ⊕ *daysmaine.com* ⊗ *Closed Sept.–mid-Apr.*

★ The Garrison
$$$$ | MODERN AMERICAN | Christian Hayes—a champion on the TV show, *Chopped,* and a seventh-generation Mainer whose family has a deep history in the local fishing and farming industries—is the chef-owner of this bistro. He uses pure and simple ingredients to create complex dishes such as meaty sautéed mushrooms in bright, silky egg yolk or slow-braised pork belly with chili, cucumber, garlic-scape kimchi, quail egg, and cashew powder. **Known for:** creative ice cream or sorbet for dessert; contemporary setting; daring dishes made with Maine ingredients. $ *Average main: $38* ⊠ *81 Bridge St., Yarmouth* ☎ *207/847–0566* ⊕ *www.thegarrison-maine.com.* The Garrison

Great Itineraries

If You Have 3 Days

On the first day, visit Bath, setting aside a good half day for the Maine Maritime Museum. In addition to studying the ship models, paintings, and other artifacts on the 25-acre property, reserve a spot on one of the scenic river cruises that depart from here. You can also sign up for a trolley ride and boat trip to learn about neighboring Bath Iron Works, where huge ships are built for the Navy. ■ TIP→ **These tours to BIW almost always sell out, so book them well in advance through the museum.**

Spend the rest of the day on one of the two peninsulas to the south. On the Georgetown Peninsula, you can head to the broad beach at Reid State Park to climb up a tall outcropping and look out to Seguin and other islands. Or set your course for Popham Beach State Park on the Phippsburg Peninsula, where the Kennebec and Morse rivers meet the sea. Arriving at or near low tide allows you to roam miles of tidal flats and walk across to Fox Island. You also can make a 2-mile trek along the beach to Fort Popham, a Civil War–era fortification that is fun to explore.

On Day 2, drive up U.S. 1 to the pretty little village of Wiscasset, set beside the Sheepscot River. Budget an hour or two for shopping in charming boutiques, galleries, and antiques shops. For lunch, have a bulging lobster roll from either of two waterfront shacks on opposite sides of the street. Red's Eats is the best-known and busiest, but Sprague's offers fine lobster rolls at a slightly reduced cost.

In the afternoon, cross the Sheepscot River, turn onto Route 27, and head to Boothbay Harbor, a touristy but scenic town. Prowl the many shops, or just enjoy an ice cream cone as you stroll the boardwalk. Alternatively, take a sightseeing cruise of the harbor or out to one of the nearby islands.

On Day 3, drive about 18 miles north on U.S. 1, and turn off to Newcastle. Cross a small bridge to Damariscotta and browse a variety of appealing shops before having lunch on picturesque Main Street or overlooking the harbor. In the afternoon, head down Route 130 to beautiful Pemaquid Point and its iconic lighthouse. Climb the tower if it's open, stop at the small museum, and scramble around on the dramatic rocky shoreline. For lunch or dinner, you have a choice of quaint lobster eateries, including the Sea Gull Shop and Restaurant at Pemaquid Point, Shaw's in New Harbor, and two spots on the dock in Round Pond.

If You Have 5 Days

If you have five days for the Mid-Coast, you have time for a day or overnight (make lodging reservations well in advance) trip to Monhegan Island. Follow the three-day itinerary, and sleep in New Harbor on the third night. On your fourth day, rise early and hop on the 9 am ferry to Monhegan Island, where you can hike out to the bluffs and picnic with the circling seagulls. In addition to numerous trails, the island has a small museum and a couple of shops.

Spend some or all of Day 5 exploring the western side of the Pemaquid Peninsula at South Bristol, crossing the swing bridge onto Rutherford Island, and dining at a restaurant overlooking Christmas Cove.

Freeport

6 miles northeast of Yarmouth.

Boston may be called Beantown, but Freeport could easily lay claim to the moniker: L.L. Bean put the town on visitors' radar. The company's flagship store and impressive campus dominate Main Street, and a plethora of outlets and specialty stores edge both the main drag and nearby streets. But those who visit Freeport only to shop are missing out.

Lovely old clapboard houses line the town's shady backstreets, and, a few miles away, South Freeport's pretty harbor sits on the Harraseeket River. In addition, the area's nature preserves have miles of walking trails.

GETTING HERE AND AROUND

Interstate 295 has three Freeport exits and passes by on the edge of the downtown area. U.S. 1 is Main Street here. Note that parking in Freeport is free. The Amtrak *Downeaster* stops in the heart of town, and the Metro Breez bus travels between Portland and Freeport several times every day except Sunday.

CONTACTS Metro Breez Buses. ✉ *Portland* ☎ *207/774–0351* ⊕ *gpmetro.org.*

VISITOR INFORMATION

CONTACTS Visit Freeport. ✉ *115 Main St., Freeport* ☎ *207/865–1212* ⊕ *www. visitfreeport.com.*

Sights

Desert of Maine

OTHER ATTRACTION | FAMILY | It's not really a desert, as the climate isn't truly arid, but this 40-acre expanse of sand, a glacial deposit created during the last Ice Age, is nevertheless intriguing. In the 1800s, erosion caused by farming removed the thin layer of top soil and revealed the dune field, which has been a popular roadside tourist attraction since the 1920s. More than 40 interpretive signs along a

Yarmouth Clam Festival

Yarmouth is renowned for its multiday, mid-July clam festival. Join the crowd and chow down on fried clams and steamers (6,000 pounds are served), lobster rolls, and shore dinners, plus homemade blueberry pie and strawberry shortcake. Browse more than 100 artists' and artisans' tents, listen to dozens of music performances, and take a spin on the Ferris wheel and other carnival rides. There are clam-shucking contests, a parade, and road races, too. It's a summer tradition and it's lots of fun. Learn more at ⊕ *www.clamfestival.com.*

mile-long, self-guided walk explain the geology, history, and ecology. You can dig for fossils using the tools and techniques employed by paleontologists. Kids love the gemstone village, with fairy houses and a hobbit house, where they can hunt for (and keep) polished gems hidden throughout a maze. Rounding out the offerings are a miniature golf course and occasional open-air theatrical productions. ✉ *95 Desert Rd., Freeport* ☎ *207/250–2550* ⊕ *www.desertofmaine.com* 🎟 *$16; minigolf $10; combo ticket $24.*

Freeport Historical Society

HISTORY MUSEUM | FAMILY | Pick up a village walking map and delve into Freeport's rich past through the exhibits at the Freeport Historical Society, located in Harrington House, a hybrid Federal- and Greek Revival-style home built in the 1830s. It's a good idea to call ahead to make sure it's open. The historical society also offers walking tours a few times a month in the summer. ✉ *45 Main St., Freeport* ☎ *207/865–3170* ⊕ *www. freeporthistoricalsociety.org* 🕑 *Closed Sat.–Mon.*

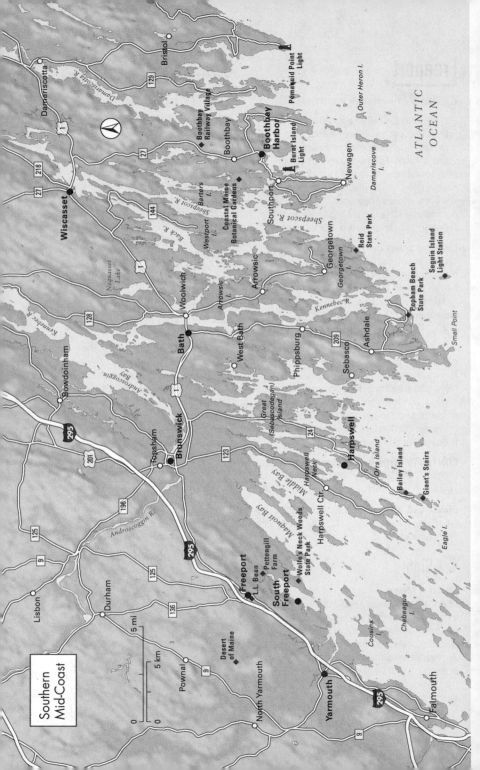

Open 365 days a year, 24 hours a day, L.L. Bean's giant flagship store is the anchor in the heart of Freeport's outlet-shopping district.

★ L.L. Bean

STORE/MALL | FAMILY | Founded in 1912 after its namesake invented the iconic hunting boot, L.L. Bean began as a mail-order merchandiser with a creaky old retail store. Today, the giant flagship store attracts more than 3 million visitors annually. Open 365 days a year, 24 hours a day, it is the anchor in the heart of Freeport's outlet-shopping district. You can still find the original hunting boots, along with cotton and wool sweaters; outerwear of all kinds; casual clothing, boots, and shoes for men, women, and kids; and camping equipment. Nearby are the company's home furnishings store and its bike, boat, and ski store. Don't miss the chance to snap a photo with the 16½-foot-tall statue of its signature rubber boot outside the main entrance, or visit its discount outlet, across the street in the Freeport Village Station mall. ⊠ *95 Main St., Freeport* ☎ *877/755–2326* ⊕ *www.llbean.com.*

Pettengill Farm

FARM/RANCH | FAMILY | The grounds of the Freeport Historical Society's saltwater Pettengill Farm—140 beautifully tended acres along an estuary of the Harraseeket River—are open to the public. It's about a 15-minute walk from the parking area down a farm road to the circa-1800 saltbox farmhouse, which is open by appointment. Little has changed since it was built, and it has rare etchings (called sgraffiti) of ships and sea monsters on three bedroom walls. ⊠ *31 Pettengill Rd., Freeport* ☎ *207/865–3170* ⊕ *www. freeporthistoricalsociety.org* ⊠ *Free (donations appreciated).*

Wolfe's Neck Woods State Park

STATE/PROVINCIAL PARK | FAMILY | A few minutes' drive from downtown Freeport, 5 miles of trails thread through this 200-plus-acre preserve, tracing the edges of Casco Bay, the Harraseeket River, and a salt marsh. It's an excellent place to view nesting ospreys. A park naturalist leads regularly scheduled, one-hour nature walks. There are picnic tables and a shelter with grills;

overnight camping is prohibited. In winter, the trails are great for snowshoeing and cross-country skiing. ✉ *426 Wolfe's Neck Rd., Freeport* ☎ *207/865–4465* 🌐 *www.maine.gov/dacf* 🎟 *$6.*

🍴 Restaurants

Broad Arrow Tavern

$$$ | AMERICAN | FAMILY | On the main floor of the Harraseeket Inn, this dark, wood-paneled tavern with mounted moose heads, decoys, snowshoes, and other outdoor sporty decor is known for both its casual nature and its menu. The chefs use organic, mostly Maine produce, meat, and seafood in all the dishes, including the pizzas made in a wood-fired oven. **Known for:** lively bar; cozy pub decor; award-winning lobster stew and clam chowder. [$] *Average main: $25* ✉ *162 Main St., Freeport* ☎ *207/865–1085* 🌐 *www.harraseeketinn.com.*

Harraseeket Lunch and Lobster Co.

$$ | SEAFOOD | FAMILY | Take a break from Main Street's bustle and drive 3 scenic miles to South Freeport, where this popular, bare-bones, counter-service place sits beside the town landing and serves up seafood baskets and lobster dinners. Save room for strawberry shortcake, blueberry crisp, bread pudding, whoopie pies, or another of the homemade desserts. **Known for:** great seafood; harbor views; picnic table dining inside or out. [$] *Average main: $18* ✉ *36 S. Main St., South Freeport* ☎ *207/865–3535, 207/865–4888* 🌐 *www.harraseeketlunchandlobster.com* 💳 *No credit cards* 🕒 *Closed mid-Oct.–May.*

Maine Beer Company

$$ | AMERICAN | FAMILY | Of the half dozen breweries in Freeport, the Maine Beer Company is a standout. Its beer is well crafted, as are its salads, charcuterie, and wood-fired pizzas, and you can dine indoors or out. **Known for:** delicious IPAs; beautiful bilevel space; community-spirited owners. [$] *Average main: $20* ✉ *525 U.S. 1, Freeport* ☎ *207/221–5711* 🌐 *www.mainebeercompany.com.*

☕ Coffee and Quick Bites

★ Met Coffee House

$ | CAFÉ | Sit at a table to enjoy a bagel, croissant, Belgian waffles, or quiche at breakfast or a cold or toasted sandwich or flatbread at lunch. At any time of the day, sink into a comfy chair or sofa to indulge in a great cup of regular coffee, an "artistic" latte (try the Heath Bar version), or one of 15 specialty hot chocolates, including almond joy and peppermint. **Known for:** 16 smoothie choices; relaxed atmosphere; decorated with art that's for sale. [$] *Average main: $13* ✉ *48 Main St., Freeport* ☎ *207/869–5809* 🌐 *www.metropolitancoffeehouse.com.*

When Pigs Fly

$ | AMERICAN | FAMILY | This outlet of a Kittery-based bakery sells unusual artisanal breads such as Sicilian green olive with hot cherry peppers or red pepper hummus with sesame seeds and garlic, as well as classic sourdough, whole-wheat, pumpernickel, rye, or oat-and-honey loaves. You can also grab a giant cookie or muffin-size cake to munch on while wandering between the outlet stores. **Known for:** all-natural ingredients with no preservatives; items baked daily; low-carb whole wheat loaf that's high on flavor and texture. [$] *Average main: $7* ✉ *21 Main St., Freeport* ☎ *207/865–6006* 🌐 *sendbread.com.*

🛏 Hotels

★ Harraseeket Inn

$ | HOTEL | FAMILY | The welcome is warm at this inn, where gas fireplaces glow in the lobby, and guest rooms—about half of them in a historic wing—have serene color schemes and reproduction Federal-style furnishings. **Pros:** generous breakfast buffet; amenities include an indoor pool and a gym; easy walk to shopping district. **Cons:** rooms in newer wings lack historic charm; not all rooms have a garden view; fireplaces only in select rooms. [$] *Rooms from: $179* ✉ *162 Main St., Freeport* ☎ *207/865–9377, 800/342–6423* 🌐 *www.harraseeketinn.com* 🛏 *84 rooms* 🍴 *Free Breakfast.*

James Place Inn
$$ | B&B/INN | Maine-inspired artwork and fresh flowers add to the simple elegance of this peaceful, Queen Anne–style inn, where guest rooms have colorful floral bedspreads, hooked rugs, and four-poster or other traditional-style beds. **Pros:** close to L.L. Bean and Main Street shopping; full breakfasts featuring many Maine products; cozy and welcoming. **Cons:** no pets; in-town location detracts from country feel; large, friendly resident dog may put some guests off. [$] *Rooms from: $249* ✉ *11 Holbrook St., Freeport* ☎ *207/865–4486* 🌐 *www.jamesplaceinn.com* 🛏 *7 rooms* 🍴 *Free Breakfast.*

Performing Arts

L.L. Bean Summer Concert Series
CONCERTS | FAMILY | Throughout the summer, L.L. Bean hosts free activities, including concerts, at the L.L. Bean Discovery Park, part of the company's large campus. It's set back from Main Street, along a side street that runs between the company's flagship and home furnishings stores. Additional offerings include family movie nights and wellness classes. ✉ *18 Morse St., Freeport* ☎ *877/755–2326* 🌐 *www.llbean.com* 🎟 *Free* ☞ *Bring chairs.*

Shopping

FOOD

Wicked Whoopies
FOOD | Sweeten your visit to Freeport with a taste of Maine's official state treat: the whoopie pie, consisting of two small cake rounds with a creamy filling. The selection here includes the classic chocolate cake with vanilla filling as well as some 20 enticing variations, including banana cream, mint, red velvet, and peanut butter. These discs of deliciousness come individually packaged, making them great for gifts as well as on-the-go snacks. ✉ *100 Main St., Freeport* ☎ *207/865–3100* 🌐 *www.wickedwhoopies.com.*

Wilbur's of Maine
CHOCOLATE | FAMILY | Calling all chocoholics! In a big, pumpkin-color house and barn at the lower end of Main Street, you'll find a wonderland of tempting treats, including chocolate-covered blueberries, turtles, almond butter crunch, truffles, fudge, and many more old-fashioned confections. They're all made by a dozen chocolatiers working in the adjacent barn; ask about taking a factory tour. Wilbur's has a second shop downtown on Bow Street. ✉ *174 Lower Main St., Suite 11, Freeport* ☎ *207/865–4071* 🌐 *www.wilburs.com.* Chocolate Confections

JEWELRY

R. D. Allen Freeport Jewelers
JEWELRY & WATCHES | This shop specializes in jewelry featuring brightly colored tourmaline and other gemstones mined in Maine. Most of the pieces are the work of Maine designers. Watermelon tourmaline—part pink, part green—is a specialty. ✉ *13 Middle St., Suite 1, Freeport* ✥ *2 blocks from L.L. Bean* ☎ *207/865–1818* 🌐 *www.rdallen.com* ⏲ *Closed Sun.*

SPECIALTY SHOPS

Bridgham & Cook, Ltd.
GENERAL STORE | If you're an Anglophile or a Brit missing Merrie Old England, this is the shop for you. Among the many shelves of imported goods are proper teapots, lots of English teas, Branston pickle and other condiments, Lyle's golden syrup, biscuits, sweets, and preserves. You'll also find tartan scarves, knitted sweaters, tweed caps, single-malt glasses, pint glasses, jewelry, and calendars. ✉ *123 Main St., Freeport* ☎ *207/865–1040* 🌐 *www.britishgoods.com.* British Goods

★ Thos. Moser Cabinetmakers

FURNITURE | The creations of this nationally recognized, local furniture company are displayed in a beautifully restored 19th-century home about a block from Bean's. The two-floor showroom is filled with artful, finely crafted wood pieces that have clean, classic lines. If you'd like to see how the furniture is made, ask about tours given on Wednesday and Friday at the large workshop 30 minutes away in Auburn (by appointment only). ⊠ *149 Main St., Freeport* ☎ *207/865–4519* ⊕ *www.thosmoser.com.*

 Activities

★ L.L. Bean Outdoor Discovery Programs

GROUP EXERCISE | **FAMILY** | It shouldn't come as a surprise that one of the world's largest outdoor outfitters also provides instructional adventures to go with its products. L.L. Bean's year-round Outdoor Discovery Programs include courses in canoeing, biking, kayaking, fly-fishing, snowshoeing, cross-country skiing, and other outdoor sports. Some last for only a few hours, while others are multiday experiences. Special offerings include women's-only adventures and team-building programs. ⊠ *11 Desert Rd., Freeport* ☎ *888/552–3261* ⊕ *www.llbean.com.*

Brunswick

10 miles north of Freeport.

Lovely brick or clapboard buildings are the highlight of Brunswick's Federal Street Historic District, which includes Federal Street, Park Row, and the stately campus of Bowdoin College. From the intersection of Pleasant and Maine streets, in the center of town, you can walk in any direction and discover an array of restaurants, bookstores, boutiques, and jewelers. Bowdoin's campus is home to several museums, and the college's performing-arts events are open to the public.

GETTING HERE AND AROUND

From I–295, take the Coastal Connector to U.S. 1 in Brunswick. The Concord Coach Lines bus that runs along the coast stops at the Brunswick Visitor Center, which is next to the train tracks and has a self-service ticket kiosk for Amtrak's *Downeaster* train. Brunswick Link buses can shuttle you around town and to Brunswick Landing and Cook's Corner every day (between 6:45 am and 6:30 pm) except Sunday.

CONTACTS Brunswick Link. ☎ *207/721–9600* ⊕ *brunswicklink.org.*

VISITOR INFORMATION

CONTACTS Brunswick Visitor Center. ⊠ *16 Station Ave., Brunswick* ☎ *207/721–0999* ⊕ *brunswickdowntown.org.*

 Sights

★ Bowdoin College Museum of Art

ART MUSEUM | **FAMILY** | This small museum housed in a stately building on Bowdoin's main quad features one of the oldest permanent collections of art in the United States. The more than 20,000 objects include paintings, sculpture, decorative arts, and works on paper. They range from Ancient, European, Asian, and Indigenous works to modern and contemporary art. The museum often mounts well-curated, rotating exhibitions and has programs for getting children excited about art. ⊠ *245 Maine St., Brunswick* ☎ *207/725–3275* ⊕ *www.bowdoin.edu/art-museum* 🖾 *Free* ⊙ *Closed Mon.*

Joshua L. Chamberlain Museum

HISTORIC HOME | **FAMILY** | The house where General Joshua Chamberlain resided for 50 years is now a museum documenting the life of Maine's most celebrated Civil War hero. In addition to playing an instrumental role in the Union Army's victory at Gettysburg, Chamberlain served as Maine's governor from 1867 to 1871 and as president of Bowdoin College from 1871 to 1883. There's also a statue of him across the street, on the edge of the

Bowdoin College campus. ✉ *226 Maine St., Brunswick* ☎ *207/725–6958* 🌐 *www.pejepscothistorical.org/chamberlain* 🎫 *$15* 🕒 *Closed mid-Oct.–late May.*

★ Peary-MacMillan Arctic Museum

HISTORY MUSEUM | Think Maine is cold in the winter? Try the Arctic, where two of Bowdoin's most famous alumni, Admiral Robert E. Peary (class of 1877) and explorer Donald B. MacMillan (class of 1898), spent considerable time. As a result, the college has both an Arctic Studies program and this museum, which is in the imposing Neo-Gothic Hubbard Hall.

Although controversy rages regarding whether it was Frederick Cook (in 1908) or Peary (in 1909) who first made it to the North Pole (or whether either man ever made it there at all), the museum has some of the principal artifacts from Peary's expedition, including his notebook page that reads "The pole at last!!!" and the American flag that he unfurled on reaching it. Among the many interesting things you'll learn is that Peary's assistant, an African American named Matthew Henson, was the only other man with him when he reached the pole—and Henson was actually in the lead.

MacMillan, who made more than 30 trips to the Arctic over the course of almost 50 years, extensively documented both the region and its peoples. He also named one of his expedition schooners after the college. (The is now the flagship training vessel of the Maine Maritime Academy in Castine). The museum's collection includes many of his photographs and films, as well as memorabilia, artifacts, and historical and contemporary Inuit, Yup'ik, and Iñupiat art. Changing exhibitions have showcased everything from changing Arctic climate conditions to Inuit music to traditional kayak construction. ✉ *255 Main St., Brunswick* ☎ *207/725–3416* 🌐 *www.bowdoin.edu/arctic-museum* 🎫 *Free* 🕒 *Closed Sat.–Mon.*

🍴 Restaurants

Fat Boy Drive-In

$ | **AMERICAN** | **FAMILY** | Pull your car up under the green awning and turn on your vehicle's lights to catch the attention of the servers at this retro drive-in restaurant. The eatery's BLT made with Canadian bacon is a longtime favorite that pairs well with onion rings and a frappe (try the blueberry), but baskets of fried clams and shrimp are also winners, and there are several burger options. **Known for:** thick milkshakes; old-school car-hop service; very friendly staffers. [$] *Average main: $9* ✉ *111 Bath Rd., Brunswick* ☎ *207/729–9431* 🌐 *www.fatboyofmaine.com.*

★ 555 North

$$$ | **AMERICAN** | Set within the gracious Federal hotel, 555 North is the rebirth of chef-owner Steve Corry's popular Portland restaurant, which closed in 2019 after an 18-year run. Diners will find the same exceptionally creative, seasonal approach to food as well as a sophisticated but relaxed atmosphere. **Known for:** imaginative menu; prominent, accomplished chef; attentive and polished service. [$] *Average main: $30* ✉ *10 Water St., Brunswick* ☎ *207/481–4535* 🌐 *555-north.com* 🕒 *Closed Tues. and Wed.*

Noble Kitchen and Bar

$$$ | **MODERN AMERICAN** | This inviting bistro at the Brunswick Hotel serves creative dishes like fingerling potato and frisée salad, mushroom galette, braised lamb shoulder, or seared diver scallops. For dessert, give the foie gras ice cream a try! **Known for:** well-prepared seasonal dishes; dining patio with a fire pit; delectable cocktails and desserts. [$] *Average main: $32* ✉ *Brunswick Hotel, 4 Noble St., Brunswick* ☎ *207/837–6565* 🌐 *www.noblekitchenbar.com* 🕒 *No lunch. Closed Sun.and Mon.*

Coffee and Quick Bites

Gelato Fiasco

$ | **ICE CREAM** | **FAMILY** | These days, you can buy this sinfully delicious gelato in food stores throughout New England and have it shipped to your door, but it all began in 2007 in this storefront in Brunswick. Stop in and pay homage to the history with a dish of ripe mango sorbetto, dark chocolate noir, or mascarpone pistachio caramel. **Known for:** free samples; "Netflix and Chill" with caramel, peanut butter cups, and brownie bites; lots of inventive flavors. [$] *Average main: $6* ✉ *74 Main St., Brunswick* ☎ *207/607–4262* 🌐 *www.gelatofiasco.com.*

Little Dog Coffee Shop

$ | **MODERN AMERICAN** | **FAMILY** | The coffee is freshly roasted and richly flavorful, the baked goods are straight from the oven, and the atmosphere is chill. Have a muffin or croissant, select from several toasties with imaginative fillings, or try the delicious avocado toast on homemade wheat bread. **Known for:** exhibits of local art; excellent light bites; grab-and-go burritos. [$] *Average main: $10* ✉ *87 Maine St., Freeport* ☎ *207/721–9500* 🌐 *www.littledogcoffeeshop.com.*

Hotels

★ The Federal

$$ | **HOTEL** | With a large modern wing attached to a historic Federal house, this refined hotel offers an airy, contemporary atmosphere blended with period-appropriate warmth. **Pros:** excellent on-site restaurant; personalized welcome; sophisticated decor. **Cons:** 20-minute walk to Bowdoin College campus; a bit tricky to find; no elevator to third floor in Federal House. [$] *Rooms from: $287* ✉ *10 Water St., Brunswick* ☎ *207/481–4066* 🌐 *www.thefederalmaine.com* 🛏 *30 rooms* 🍴 *No Meals.*

★ OneSixtyFive

$$$ | **B&B/INN** | An 1848 Greek Revival house has been transformed into this upscale boutique hotel, where the guest rooms, suites, and cottage are open, airy, and decorated with uncluttered traditional furnishings and serene color schemes. **Pros:** free on-site parking; delightful pub room for an end-of-day drink; perfect downtown location with a nonurban feel. **Cons:** steep stairs to second floor in main house (help with bags is available); no elevator; not on the water. [$] *Rooms from: $325* ✉ *165 Park Row, Brunswick* ☎ *207/729–4914* 🌐 *www.onesixtyfivemaine.com* 🛏 *17 rooms* 🍴 *No Meals.*

Shopping

Hatch on Maine

GENERAL STORE | This exceptional shop specializes in lovely, locally made wares, including jewelry, unusual gifts, and baby items. Just up the street, its sister store, Hatch Home, features new and antique accents for the home as well as a wide color selection of Chalk Paint by Annie Sloan. ✉ *96 Maine St., Brunswick* ☎ *207/373–0567* 🌐 *www.hatchonmaine.com.*

Nest

HOUSEWARES | It's hard to know where to look first when you enter this store filled with appealing home-decor accents. Shop for colorful pottery, tableware, candles, holiday ornaments, decorative birdhouses, textiles, and some packaged foodstuffs. ✉ *100 Maine St., Brunswick* ☎ *207/729–5599.*

Harpswell

10 miles south of Brunswick.

The town of Harpswell is divided between a peninsula called Harpswell Neck and, paralleling it just to the east, a string of three bridge-connected islands—Great (aka Sebascodegan), Orrs, and Bailey—which are part of the Casco Bay chain. Other, mostly private islets also dot the waters here.

On Harpswell Neck, coves shelter summer cottages tucked amid birch and spruce trees on the shore and lobster boats that bob in the water. The islands have fishing villages as well as their own charming coves, with places to picnic, hunt for beach glass, or put in a kayak.

Don't miss picturesque Cundy's Harbor on the eastern edge of Great Island. On Orrs Island, stop at Island Candy Company for handmade chocolates, fudge, candied fruit, or other old-time confections. To get from Orrs to Bailey island, you'll cross the world's only cribstone bridge. Pull over to take a photo. From afar, the "latticework" of the narrow structure looks delicate, but it's actually created by huge granite slabs laid, without any mortar, in a crisscross pattern with gaps. This ingenious design allows the tide to flow freely beneath the bridge.

On Bailey, the fishing harbor at Mackerel Cove is a scenic stop. For fabulous ocean views, especially at sunset, make the short drive to Land's End, on the island's southern tip. Don't miss the seven-foot-tall lobsterman statue there.

GETTING HERE AND AROUND

Route 123 runs from beside the Bowdoin campus in Brunswick all the way down Harpswell Neck. To get to the three islands, turn left part way down onto Mountain Road, which leads to a bridge that links to Orrs Island. You can also get to the islands via Route 24 south from Cook's Corner.

Sights

Bailey Island

ISLAND | FAMILY | One of three islands that make up the town of Harpswell, Bailey Island is connected to the mainland by the world's only cribstone bridge, made of enormous granite pieces of granite. So while you *can* take a ferry here, you can also just as easily drive. Come for the miles and miles of beautiful coastline; you can catch a gorgeous sunset (after a short hike) at the south end of the island, at Land's End Beach. Or seek out one of the local chartering companies and sign up for a day sail. Don't miss the rock formation known as the Giant's Stairs or the seven-foot-tall lobsterman sculpture by Victor Kahill. ⊠ *Bailey Island.*

Giant's Stairs

NATURE SIGHT | Near the tip of Bailey Island, a short side road takes you to a parking area and access to a mostly flat, graveled path along the ocean's edge to an intriguing cut in the rocky shoreline. The southern terminus of the trail leads across some rocky ledges. There is additional parking at that end. Known as an intrusive volcanic dike, the vertical rift looks like a staircase built for giants. The views are as compelling as the geology. ⊠ *19 Ocean St., Bailey Island* ☎ *207/721–1121* ⊕ *hhltmaine.org/get-outdoors/giants-stairs-mcintosh.*

Restaurants

Cook's Lobster and Ale House

$$$ | SEAFOOD | FAMILY | What began as a lobster shack in 1955 has grown into a large, well-known, family-style restaurant with a sizable menu that is predictably heavy on local seafood (lobster boats unload their catch at a dock here) but also has plenty of choices for landlubbers. A shore dinner will set you back close to $50, but you won't leave hungry after a 1¼-pound lobster, steamed clams, drawn butter, and corn on the cob. **Known for:** traditional Maine seafood fare prepared simply; great water views; live music and a festive atmosphere in the summer. $ *Average main: $26* ✉ *68 Garrison Cove Rd., Bailey Island* ☎ *207/833–2818* ⊕ *www.cookslobster. com* ⊘ *Closed Mon. and Tues.*

★ Dolphin Marina and Restaurant
$$$ | SEAFOOD | At the end of Harpswell Neck—next to the Dolphin Marina, where diners often arrive by boat—this popular restaurant serves one of the best fish chowders on the coast. Take in the excellent views through a wall of windows or from the outdoor deck as you enjoy your equally excellent chowder—or your lobster stew, crab or lobster roll, or chicken or beef entrée. **Known for:** spectacular seaside setting; exceptional food and service; blueberry muffins come with fish chowder and lobster stew. $ *Average main: $30* ✉ *515 Basin Point Rd. South, Harpswell, Harpswell* ☎ *207/833–6000* ⊕ *www.thedolphin.me* ⊘ *Closed Nov.–Apr.*

Hotels

Log Cabin Inn
$$ | B&B/INN | You may think you've arrived in the North Woods upon entering this lovingly maintained, 1940s-era, log structure—a family-run place with many repeat annual guests—but one look out the windows makes it clear that you're still on the Maine coast. **Pros:** full, hot breakfast; wonderful views from lawn and private decks; personalized lodging. **Cons:** close to road; must drive to restaurants; no elevator to second-floor rooms. $ *Rooms from: $299* ✉ *5 Log Cabin La., Rte. 24, Bailey Island* ☎ *207/833–5546* ⊕ *www.logcabin-maine.com* ⊘ *Closed late Oct.–Apr.* ⇌ *8 rooms* ♥ *Free Breakfast.*

Shopping

Island Candy Company
CHOCOLATE | FAMILY | Before crossing the cribstone bridge to Bailey Island, stop at this sweet little cottage—complete with a picket-fenced flower garden—for some old-fashioned confections. The brittle, bark, buttercreams, truffles, dipped candied fruit, and fudge that fill the glass cases are all made in the candy kitchen just behind the counter. There's ice cream, too! ✉ *1795 Harpswell Islands Rd., Rte. 24, Orrs Island* ☎ *207/833–6639* ⊕ *www.orrsislandcandy.com* ⊘ *Closed late Dec.–Apr.*

Seaside Creations
CRAFTS | Tucked down a driveway beside the trail to the Giant's Stairs, this tiny cottage is packed with carefully selected, Maine-made items created by nearly 100 artisans. The paintings, jewelry, soaps, clothing, textiles, and other wares make the perfect gifts or souvenirs. ✉ *47 Washington Ave., off Rte. 24, Bailey Island* ☎ *207/833–6645* ⊕ *www.seasidecreations.net* ⊘ *Closed Mon.–Wed.*

Activities

H2Outfitters
KAYAKING | FAMILY | Harpswell's corrugated shoreline is full of nooks and crannies waiting to be explored by kayak. H2Outfitters, at the southern end of Orrs Island just before the cribstone bridge to Bailey Island, is the place to get out on the water. It provides top-notch kayaking instruction, as well as half-, full-, or multiday (B&B or camping) trips near its home base and elsewhere in Maine. ✉ *1894 Harpswell Island Rd., Orrs Island* ☎ *207/833–5257, 800/205–2925* ⊕ *www.h2outfitters.com* ⊘ *Closed early Sept.–mid-June.*

From late May through late October, Maine Maritime Museum offers lighthouse cruises, ranging from 30 minutes to three hours, aboard the *Merrymeeting*, which travels along the scenic Kennebec River.

Bath

18 miles northeast of Harpswell Neck.

Bath's tradition of shipbuilding dates from 1607 with the construction of the pinnace *Virginia*, the first oceangoing ship built by Europeans in the Americas. (A full-size replica of the small sailing vessel was launched in June 2022.) It was a very lucrative industry, as evidenced by the historic district's architecture, including the 1820 Federal-style home at 360 Front Street; the 1810 Greek Revival, white-clapboard mansion at 969 Washington Street; and the raspberry-color Victorian gem at 1009 Washington Street. All three operate as inns.

In 1890, the venerable Bath Iron Works (BIW as it's known locally) completed its first passenger ship. During World War II, the company was capable of launching a new ship every 17 days. Today, BIW is one of the state's largest employers, with about 6,800 workers building destroyers for the U.S. Navy. (It's a good idea to avoid U.S. 1 on weekdays 3:15–4:30 pm, when a major shift change takes place.)

The must-see Maine Maritime Museum highlights shipbuilding history in Bath and elsewhere along the Maine Coast. It also offers tours to the perimeter of BIW's grounds (due to security concerns, it's a restricted property). Also, be sure to look up at City Hall, on Front Street: the bell in its tower was cast by Paul Revere in 1805.

Dangling to seaward of Woolwich, just east of Bath, Georgetown Island is connected to the mainland via a series of bridges. The island's exceptional beauty makes it well worth a detour. Along miles of corrugated shoreline, you'll find a few charming seafood eateries, old-fashioned lodging, and the natural jewel that is Reid State Park.

GETTING HERE AND AROUND

U.S. 1 passes through downtown and across the Kennebec River at Bath. Downtown is on the north side of the highway along the river. The Maine Maritime Museum is on the south side of the highway.

A stroll along the beach at Reid State Park on Georgetown Island is a popular pastime.

Concord Coach Lines bus service that runs along the coast stops in Bath.

VISITOR INFORMATION

CONTACTS Bath Regional Information Center. ⊠ *15 Commercial St., Bath* ☎ *207/443–1513* ⊕ *visitbath.com.*

 Sights

★ Maine Maritime Museum

HISTORY MUSEUM | FAMILY | No trip to Bath is complete without visiting the cluster of preserved 19th- and early 20th-century buildings that were once part of the historic Percy & Small Shipyard. Plan to spend at least half a day exploring them and the adjacent modern museum. Indeed, there's so much to see that admission tickets are good for two days.

During hour-long shipyard tours, you'll learn how massive wooden ships were built, and you might see shipwrights and blacksmiths at work. One of the vintage buildings houses a fascinating, 6,000-square-foot lobstering exhibit. In the main building ship models, paintings, photographs, and artifacts showcase maritime history. The grounds also contain a gift shop and bookstore; a seasonal café; and a huge, modern sculpture representing the 450-foot-long, six-masted schooner *Wyoming*, built right here and one of the longest wooden vessels ever launched.

From late May through late October, daily nature and lighthouse cruises, ranging from 30 minutes to three hours, are offered aboard the motor vessel *Merry-meeting,*which travels along the scenic Kennebec River. The museum also has guided tours of Bath Iron Works (June–mid-October). ⊠ *243 Washington St., Bass Harbor* ☎ *207/443–1316* ⊕ *www. mainemaritimemuseum.org* ⊠ *$18, good for 2 days within 7-day period.*

★ Popham Beach State Park

BEACH | FAMILY | At the tip of the Phippsburg Peninsula, Popham Beach State Park faces the open Atlantic between the mouths of the Kennebec and Morse rivers. At low tide, you can walk several miles of tidal flats and also out to small

Fox Island, where you can explore tide pools or fish off the ledges (pay attention to the incoming tide unless you want to swim back). Shifting sand and beach and sea dynamics have led to dramatic erosion here, and, in recent years, the sea has taken a big bite out of the beach. There are picnic tables, plus a bathhouse, showers, and toilets. About a mile from the beach, the road ends at the Civil War–era Fort Popham State Historic Site, an unfinished semicircular granite fort overlooking the sea. The site of the Popham Colony, an early 1600s English settlement, is also nearby. Enjoy beach views and some fresh seafood at nearby Spinney's Restaurant. ✉ *10 Perkins Farm La., off Rte. 209, Bath* ☎ *207/389–1335* 🌐 *www.maine.gov/pophambeach* 🎫 *$8.*

★ Reid State Park

BEACH | FAMILY | On Georgetown Island, this park's jewel is a gorgeous, unspoiled, mile-long beach framed by sand dunes; there's a second, ½-mile beach as well. Climb to the top of rocky Griffith Head to take in sea views that stretch to lighthouses on Seguin Island, Hendricks Head, and The Cuckolds. If you're swimming, be aware of the possibility of an undertow. Walking along the beach or following one of the hiking trails are popular pastimes as well. During a storm, this is a great place to observe the ferocity of the waves crashing onto the shore. In summer, parking lots fill by 11 am on weekends and holidays. ✉ *375 Seguinland Rd., Georgetown* ☎ *207/371–2303* 🎫 *$8* 🕒 *Closed sunset to 9 am.*

★ Seguin Island Light Station

ISLAND | FAMILY | Perched at the top of a small island off the mouth of the Kennebec River, this cylindrical stone tower is one of the state's prettiest and most imposing—it rises 52 feet above an already high headland. There's a small museum in the keeper's house, and the guest quarters can be rented. Camping is also permitted at the base of the lighthouse, and there are hiking trails. Access is by a short ferry ride from Fort Popham in Phippsburg. ✉ *Seguin Island, Phippsburg* 🌐 *seguinisland.org.*

🍴 Restaurants

★ Bath Brewing Company

$$ | MODERN AMERICAN | You'll feel right at home in this intimate modern pub, offering casual dining on two floors plus an upper outdoor deck. The beer ranges from IPAs to stouts and sours. **Known for:** surprising pub food; welcoming modern pub in the heart of downtown; tasty craft beers. $ *Average main: $20* ✉ *141 Front St., Bath* ☎ *207/389–6039* 🌐 *www.bath-brewing.com* 🕒 *Closed Mon. and Tues.*

★ Five Islands Lobster Company

$$ | SEAFOOD | Drive to the end of Route 127 and relax in the breezes off Sheepscot Bay in the tiny fishing village of Five Islands, not too far from Reid State Park. This award-winning lobster shack overlooks at least islands from its perch atop the working wharf, and you can watch lobstermen unload their traps onto the dock while you feast on fresh lobster rolls or a full lobster dinner and sample Maine-made ice cream. **Known for:** BYOB; authentic Maine setting with gorgeous scenery; excellent lobster rolls. $ *Average main: $24* ✉ *1447 5 Islands Rd., Georgetown* ☎ *207/371–2990* 🌐 *www.fiveislandslobster.com* 🕒 *Closed Wed. in summer; closed weekdays spring and fall; closed early May–early Oct.*

The Osprey

$$ | SEAFOOD | Simple, well-prepared dishes draw folks to this pleasant harborfront restaurant in the middle of a boatyard. On weekends, the full menu includes seafood and pub specialties as well as a selection of pizzas; on Thursday and Monday, only pizza is served. **Known for:** authentic Maine setting; open only in summer; views of a marina and an osprey nest. $ *Average main: $18* ✉ *340 Robinhood Rd., Georgetown*

☎ 207/371–2530 🌐 www.theospreyme.com ⏲ Closed Tues. and Wed.

Coffee and Quick Bites

Café Crème

$ | BAKERY | FAMILY | Located in the heart of downtown, this café with its own on-site bakery draws visitors and locals alike for delicious coffee paired with made-that-day goods served with a smile. The cinnamon roll with maple bacon is a savory Maine take on a classic sweet treat. **Known for:** sweet and savory stuffed croissants; creative coffee drinks; friendly staff. *[$] Average main: $7 ✉ 56 Front St., at Centre St., Bath ☎ 207/443–6454 🌐 www.cafecremebath.com.*

The Fountain Ice Cream & Deli

$ | ICE CREAM | FAMILY | From the red stools lined up at the soda fountain to the pressed-tin ceiling, this cute little place oozes nostalgia. Order a banana split, a shake, or just a cone, and enjoy your trip down memory lane. **Known for:** comfort-food specials; delicious pie (best when it's à la mode); great selection of deli sandwiches. *[$] Average main: $10 ✉ 110 Front St., Bath ☎ 207/389–4239 🌐 www.thefountainicecream.com.*

Mae's Cafe

$ | CAFÉ | This charming café offers several indoor spaces, plus a deck—built around a giant maple tree!—where you can enjoy homemade eggs Benedict, omelets, and breakfast sandwiches, as well as wraps, salads, soups, chowders, and smoothies. Everything is creative, and everything is homemade. **Known for:** breakfast served from opening till closing; grab-and-go baked goods; delicious pie. *[$] Average main: $15 ✉ 160 Centre St., Bath ☎ 207/442–8577 🌐 www.maescafeandbakery.com ⏲ Closed Tues.*

Hotels

Coveside Bed & Breakfast

$$$ | B&B/INN | Near the village of Five Islands on secluded and quiet-as-can-be Georgetown Island, this handsome shingled house sits on 5 secluded, waterfront acres along Gott's Cove. **Pros:** close to Reid State Park; quiet waterfront setting; great kayaking. **Cons:** 13-mile drive from town; may be too far from the action for some; can sometimes hear guests in other rooms or on their decks. *[$] Rooms from: $350 ✉ 6 Gotts Cove La., Georgetown ☎ 207/371–2807 🌐 www.covesidebandb.com 🛏 7 rooms 🍴 Free Breakfast.*

Grey Havens Inn

$$$ | B&B/INN | Perched above Harmon Harbor, this 1904, double-turreted inn truly is a haven from modern-day hustle and bustle—just head to the front porch, settle into a rocker, take in the amazing oceanfront panorama, and feel your stress melt away. **Pros:** stunning waterside setting; very good in-house restaurant; wonderful relaxing atmosphere. **Cons:** no elevator; rooms are on second and third floors; some rooms are small. *[$] Rooms from: $300 ✉ 96 Seguinland Rd., Georgetown ☎ 207/371–2616 🌐 www.greyhavens.com ⏲ Closed Nov.–late Apr. 🛏 13 rooms 🍴 Free Breakfast.*

The Inn at Bath

$$ | B&B/INN | An 1840s Greek Revival mansion in the heart of Bath's historic district is the setting for this welcoming, beautifully furnished (but unfussy) inn. **Pros:** excellent breakfasts; gracious atmosphere; short walk to Front Street shops and eateries. **Cons:** no elevator; breakfast served at communal table; not on the waterfront. *[$] Rooms from: $225 ✉ 969 Washington St., Bath ☎ 207/443–4294 🌐 www.innatbath.com ⏲ Closed Nov. 🛏 7 rooms 🍴 Free Breakfast.*

★ **Kennebec Inn Bed and Breakfast**

$$ | **B&B/INN** | Welcoming common spaces and immaculate, well-appointed guest rooms—with tasteful maritime decor touches and luxe bedding and towels—await you at this hidden gem in a historic captain's home. **Pros:** feels like an exclusive retreat; delicious, multicourse breakfast you can enjoy at your leisure; knowledgeable, warm innkeeper. **Cons:** only four rooms; a short walk into center of town; no pets. [$] *Rooms from: $275* ✉ *696 High St., Bath* ☎ *207/443–5324* 🌐 *www.kennebecinn.com* 🛏 *4 rooms* 🍴 *Free Breakfast.*

Mooring Bed & Breakfast

$$ | **B&B/INN** | Originally the home of Walter Reid, who donated the land for gorgeous Reid State Park (just down the road), this inn has stayed in his family for three generations. **Pros:** Reid State Park and its broad beach is just down the road; lovely oceanside setting; sweeping views. **Cons:** it's a drive to restaurants and shops; 11 miles from Bath; it may be too quiet for some. [$] *Rooms from: $260* ✉ *132 Seguinland Rd., Georgetown* ☎ *866/828–7343* 🌐 *www.themooringsb-b.com* 🛏 *5 rooms* 🍴 *Free Breakfast.*

Sebasco Harbor Resort

$$$$ | **RESORT** | **FAMILY** | This nearly century-old resort on 450 water-side acres at the western side of the Phippsburg Peninsula is a good choice for both couples and families. **Pros:** very good on-site restaurant; children's activities and an array of lawn games; golf course, tennis courts, and heated saltwater pool. **Cons:** no sandy beach; heavy traffic and large number of rooms can diminish quality and service; golf fee not included in stay. [$] *Rooms from: $420* ✉ *29 Kenyon Rd., off Sebasco Rd., Phippsburg* ☎ *207/389–1161, 866/389–2072* 🌐 *www.sebasco.com* ⏲ *Closed late Oct.–mid-May* 🛏 *89 rooms* 🍴 *No Meals.*

Shopping

BOOKS

★ **Mockingbird Bookshop**

BOOKS | This independent, community-minded bookstore is a great place to browse, discover new books, and settle into a wing chair or sofa to read for a bit. There's a good selection of works by Maine authors, and book signings are often held for new releases. ✉ *74 Front St., Bath* ☎ *207/389–4084* 🌐 *www.mockingbirdbookshop.com.*

CLOTHING

Over the Moon Boutique

LINGERIE | This welcoming boutique specializes in beautiful lingerie, shapewear, and loungewear—and in helping you find the best size and fit. Locally made CBD products are also available. ✉ *98 Front St., Bath* ☎ *207/442–9999* 🌐 *www.overthemoonmaine.com.*

Pitter Patter Inc.

CHILDREN'S CLOTHING | **FAMILY** | Grandmothers take note! This sweet shop sells lovely babies' and children's clothing, accessories, and toys. The quality is high, so don't expect bargain-store prices. ✉ *94 Front St., Bath* ☎ *207/443–9870* 🌐 *www.pitterpatterinc.com.*

HOUSEWARES

Now You're Cooking

HOUSEWARES | This emporium is a candy store for anyone who enjoys spending time in the kitchen. Chances are you'll find any utensil, pot, gadget, or machine might need—as well as some things you didn't know you needed. There's a good selection of cookbooks, plus spices and condiments, and wines and craft beers, too. ✉ *49 Front St., Bath* ☎ *207/443–1402* 🌐 *www.acooksemporium.com.*

MSDCo SHOP

HOUSEWARES | To complement its interior design services, Maine Street Design fills a storefront with carefully selected decor accents, lamps, tableware, and furniture. Much of the merchandise is

Maine made. There are also cookbooks and condiments. ⊠ *160 Front St., Bath* ☎ *207/541–9187* ⊕ *www.mainestreetdesign.com.*

SOUVENIRS

★ Lisa-Marie's Made in Maine

SOUVENIRS | If you'd like to take home a piece of Maine, this is the place to shop. Everything in this large store was created by the state's finest artisans and artists. There's lots of jewelry, plus clothing, home decor, art, kids' items, and much more. ⊠ *170 Front St., Bath* ☎ *207/443–2225* ⊕ *www.lisamariesmadeinmaine.com.*

Wiscasset

10 miles north of Bath.

Settled in 1663, Wiscasset sits on the bank of the Sheepscot River. It bills itself as "Maine's Prettiest Village," and it's easy to see why: it has graceful churches, old cemeteries, and elegant sea captains' homes (many converted into antiques shops and galleries).

This is where everyone wants to stop for a lobster roll. Red's Eats gets all the publicity—and the resulting long, long lines—for its positively overflowing rolls. At Sprague's, just across the street, the quality is just as high, and although they don't stuff the rolls with quite as much lobster, you do pay a few dollars less.

GETTING HERE AND AROUND

U.S. 1 becomes Wiscasset's Main Street. Traffic often slows to a crawl in summer, as everyone traveling along the coast here must funnel onto a two-lane bridge across the Sheepscot River. The speed limit is reduced in town, and there are several stop lights, both of which further slow things down. There's no parking on Main Street in front of the shops, but there are several free nearby lots to either side of the main drag. The Concord Coach Lines bus that goes along the coast stops in Wiscasset.

 # Sights

Castle Tucker

HISTORIC HOME | Learn about Wiscasset through the history of a prominent shipping family—the Tuckers—generations of whom lived in this mansion over the course of 150 years. Situated atop a hill overlooking the Sheepscot River, the house was built in 1807, when this was the busiest port town east of Boston. Originally constructed in the Federal style but transformed into an Italianate villa in the mid-1800s, the property has extravagant architectural details, including a freestanding elliptical staircase, and Victorian appointments. ⊠ *2 Lee St., Wiscasset* ☎ *207/882–7169* ⊕ *www.historicnewengland.org/property/castle-tucker* ⊡ *$15* ⊘ *Closed Mon.–Thurs. and mid-Oct.–June.*

Nickels-Sortwell House

HISTORIC HOME | This imposing white mansion on Main Street was built in 1807 by Captain William Nickels to show off the wealth he'd amassed in shipbuilding and international cargo shipping, which brought prosperity to Wiscasset in the early 19th century. The high Federal-style structure went on to become a hotel until it was bought and restored by the Sortwell family at the beginning of the 20th century. Furnished with fine period antiques, its beautifully carved woodwork and flying staircase are testament to the artistic skills of Captain Nickels' shipwrights. ⊠ *121 Main St., Wiscasset* ☎ *207/835–5887* ⊕ *www.historicnewengland.org/property/nickels-sortwell-house* ⊡ *$15* ⊘ *Closed Mon.–Thurs. and mid-Oct.–early June.*

Red's Eats, a little red shack at the bottom of Wiscasset's Main Street, just before the bridge across the Sheepscot River, is said to have one of the Maine Coast's best lobster rolls.

🍴 Restaurants

Maine Tasting Center

$ | **AMERICAN** | **FAMILY** | Cheeses, charcuterie, seafood, breads, and more from Maine's premier food producers and artisans go into the selection of small plates on the menu, which also features craft beers, wines, ciders, spirits, and Maine-made sodas. Open every afternoon from spring through fall, the center not only showcases the bounty of Maine, it also offers classes, workshops, and meet-the-producer events throughout the season. **Known for:** fun classes and workshops; tips on Maine's best foods; delicious small plates. [$] *Average main: $15* ✉ *506 Old Bath Rd., Rte. 1, Wiscasset* ☎ *207/558–5772* 🌐 *www.mainetastingcenter.com* 🕓 *Closed Nov.–late May.*

★ Red's Eats

$$$ | **SEAFOOD** | **FAMILY** | The customers lined up beside this little red shack at the bottom of Wiscasset's Main Street, just before the bridge across the Sheepscot River, have come from far and wide for one of the Maine Coast's best lobster rolls—namely, a perfectly buttered and griddled split-top roll that's absolutely, positively stuffed with fresh, sweet meat and served with melted butter and mayo on the side. Devotees swear that the wait (up to two hours!) is worth it, and it helps that staffers hand out ice water, popsicles, umbrellas to protect from rain or hot sun, and even dog biscuits for the pups. **Known for:** more than a whole lobster goes into each roll; the unholy "Puff Dog," a hot dog loaded with bacon and cheese and deep-fried; long lines in summer, especially on weekends. [$] *Average main: $25* ✉ *41 Water St., Wiscasset* ✣ *Corner of U.S. 1* ☎ *207/882–6128* 🌐 *www.redseatsmaine.com* 💳 *No credit cards* 🕓 *Closed late-Oct.–mid-Apr.*

Sprague's Lobster

$$ | **SEAFOOD** | Just across the road from Red's, Sprague's serves excellent lobster rolls, too. Indeed, many locals prefer to come here—though the rolls aren't quite as stuffed as at Red's, they usually cost a couple of dollars less, and the waits

are not nearly as long. **Known for:** picnic tables on a wide pier; menu includes chowder and full lobster dinners; great lobster rolls without the long lines. $ *Average main: $24* ✉ *22 Main St., U.S. 1, Wiscasset* ☎ *207/882–1236* ⊕ *www. facebook.com/spragueslobster* ۞ *Closed late Oct.–early May.*

★ Water Street Kitchen and Bar
$$$ | **MEDITERRANEAN** | Step into this welcoming, airy space, and settle at a table with a view of the Sheepscot River to enjoy local seafood, meats, and produce. Many of the pastas, paellas, and risottos have a Mediterranean flavor; other dishes showcase the chef's creative approach to modern American cuisine. **Known for:** eclectic menu; raw bar; pleasant atmosphere. $ *Average main: $25* ✉ *15 Water St., Wiscasset* ☎ *207/687–8076* ⊕ *www. waterstreetkitchen.com.*

☕ Coffee and Quick Bites

Treats
$ | **AMERICAN** | What started as a candy shop over 30 years ago has grown into a Wiscasset staple featuring baked goods, coffee, wine, craft beer, cheese, and more. All of the "treats"—scones, cookies, croissants, muffins, cakes, sweet buns, babka, coffee cake—are baked right here every day. **Known for:** scones made from owner's nana's recipe; a morning gathering spot for locals; locally sourced ingredients. $ *Average main: $5* ✉ *80 Main St., Wiscasset* ☎ *207/882–6192* ⊕ *www.treatsofmaine. com* ۞ *Closed Mon.*

🛏 Hotels

Cod Cove Inn
$$ | **MOTEL** | **FAMILY** | This hill-top, two-story motel complex makes an excellent base for exploring Boothbay Harbor and Damariscotta as well as Wiscasset. **Pros:** personalized hospitality; heated pool; rooms with river-view balconies or patios. **Cons:** there may be traffic noise from

Route 1; more of a motel than an inn; not on the water. $ *Rooms from: $279* ✉ *22 Cross Rd., Edgecomb* ✛ *Just off U.S. 1 and Rte. 27* ☎ *207/882–9586* ⊕ *www. codcoveinn.com* ⇌ *28 rooms* ◯ *Free Breakfast.*

Shopping

ART GALLERIES
★ Wiscasset Bay Gallery
ART GALLERIES | This fine-art gallery specializes in American and European paintings—often featuring Monhegan Island seascapes and landscapes—from the 18th, 19th, and 20th centuries. Featured artists include Rockwell Kent, William Zorach, and Abraham Bogdanove. Also on display are the brightly hued paintings by gallery owner Keith Oemig, whose work is included in the collection of the Portland Museum of Art. ✉ *75 Main St., U.S. 1, Wiscasset* ☎ *207/882–7682* ⊕ *www.wiscassetbay- gallery.com* ۞ *Closed Jan.–Mar. except by appointment.*

CERAMICS
Edgecomb Potters
CERAMICS | Just across the river from Wiscasset, this pottery is renowned for its vibrantly colored, exquisitely glazed porcelain, which is also sold at shops in Portland and York but is all made right here—the original location. The store also carries a fine selection of jewelry, glassware, and glass sculptures. ✉ *727 Boothbay Rd., Rte. 27, Edgecomb* ☎ *207/882–9493* ⊕ *www.edgecombpot- ters.com* ۞ *Closes briefly in winter.*

★ Sheepscot River Pottery
CERAMICS | You can peek into the workshop next door to see potters create this shop's beautiful plates, vases, and other vessels—often decorated with lighthouses, pine trees, lupine, chickadees, or other Maine-centric illustrations. The merchandise also includes home accessories, jewelry, and other items made by local artisans. There's a second shop

in downtown Damariscotta. ✉ *34 U.S. 1, Edgecomb* ☎ *207/882–9410* ⊕ *www. sheepscotriverpottery.com.*

CLOTHING
In the Clover

WOMEN'S CLOTHING | There's something charmingly old-school about this pretty boutique, with its warm and friendly service and fine displays of women's clothing, accessories, and beauty products. Geared toward elegant but no-fuss women of every age, the shop stocks clothing items such as fine cashmere shawls; pretty but not froufrou lingerie; and sophisticated loungewear as well as a good selection of natural beauty products and fragrances, unique jewelry, and inspiring books. ✉ *85A Main St., Wiscasset* ☎ *207/882–9435* ⊕ *inthecloverbeauty. com* ⊙ *Closes briefly in winter.*

GIFTS AND HOUSEWARES
Rock Paper Scissors

STATIONERY | Decidedly contemporary, with a Scandinavian bent, this well-curated boutique stocks offbeat cards and letterpress stationery, locally handcrafted goods, jewelry, and one-of-a-kind objects for the home. ✉ *68 Main St., Wiscasset* ☎ *207/882–9930* ⊙ *Closed Mon.*

Boothbay Harbor

11 miles south of Wiscasset.

The shoreline of the Boothbay Peninsula is a craggy stretch of inlets where pleasure craft of all sizes and types bob alongside lobster boats and sightseeing vessels. Boothbay Harbor is something of a smaller version of Bar Harbor: touristy, but friendly and fun, with pretty, winding streets and lots to explore. Commercial Street, Wharf Street, Townsend Avenue, and the By-Way are lined with shops and ice-cream parlors.

Be sure to take in the coast and islands from the water aboard one of many sightseeing cruises. One of the biggest draws here is the stunning Coastal Maine Botanical Gardens, a short drive north in the town of Boothbay. Its more than 300 acres encompass spectacular plantings and natural landscapes, walking trails, and a delightful children's garden.

GETTING HERE AND AROUND

Soon after crossing the Sheepscot River bridge just east of Wiscasset, turn right onto Route 27 and follow it to Boothbay and all the way into the heart of Boothbay Harbor, just 2 miles farther south. For some incredible scenery, take Route 96 off Route 27 out to Ocean Point in East Boothbay.

Note that, in season, a daily boat to Monhegan Island leaves from a dock on Boothbay Harbor's Commercial Street.

VISITOR INFORMATION

CONTACTS Boothbay Harbor Region Chamber of Commerce. ✉ *192 Townsend Ave., Boothbay* ☎ *207/633–2353* ⊕ *www. boothbayharbor.com.*

Sights

Boothbay Railway Village

HISTORIC SIGHT | **FAMILY** | Beside Route 27, about a mile outside Boothbay Harbor, this charming recreation of a New England village has more than two dozen small, historic, and reconstructed Maine structures, including a general store, train station, blacksmith shop, firehouse, hardware store, toy shop, and covered bridge. More than 60 automobiles are also on display. Take a ride on the passenger train—pulled by a century-old, coal-fired steam locomotive—that loops through the 30-acre site on a narrow-gauge track. Activities might also include Model T rides, demonstrations by blacksmiths and other artisans, and special events on the village green. ✉ *586 Wiscasset Rd., Rte. 1, Boothbay* ☎ *207/633–4733* ⊕ *www. railwayvillage.org* 🎫 *$15* ⊙ *Closed Mon. and mid-Oct.–mid-June.*

★ Coastal Maine Botanical Gardens

GARDEN | FAMILY | Reserve your admission tickets in advance online (required), and set aside a couple of hours to explore New England's largest botanical garden, where, depending on the time of year, you can stroll amid the lupines, rhododendrons, or roses. Regardless of the season, you'll encounter the site's biggest (literally and figuratively) draws: the five gigantic and utterly irresistible trolls constructed by Danish artist Thomas Danbo using scrap wood and other found materials that are placed in wooded areas throughout the 323-acre grounds.

The children's garden is a wonderland of stone sculptures, rope bridges, small teahouse-like structures with grass roofs, and even a hedge maze. Children and adults alike adore the separate woodland fairy area. The Garden of the Five Senses lets you experience flora through much more than just sight. Inside the main building are a café, grab-and-go market, shop, and resource library. During the holiday season, the gardens mount a dazzling, nighttime Gardens Aglow show, with 650,000 LED bulbs lighting up the darkness.

Comfortable walking shoes are a must, but, if you'd prefer not to walk everywhere, there's free shuttle service to several key locales. In addition, free, hour-long, docent-led tours of the central gardens leave from the visitor center at 11 each day from May through October. There's also a one-hour golf cart tour ($10; free on Wednesday). ✉ *132 Botanical Gardens Dr., off Rte. 27, Boothbay* ☎ *207/633–8000* 🌐 *www.mainegardens.org* 🎫 *$22* 🕓 *Closed late Oct.–May 1, except for holiday season Gardens Aglow extravaganza* ✍ *Reservations required.*

🍴 Restaurants

Boathouse Bistro Tapas Bar and Restaurant

$$ | TAPAS | Austrian-born chef-owner Karin Guerin dishes up intriguing, tapas-style small plates—from mojito ginger wings to Madagascar beef skewers—as well as full-size risotto, vegetarian, vegan, and seafood entrées. Be sure to try the fried oysters in vichyssoise sauce with flying-fish roe. **Known for:** great views from rooftop dining area and bar; internationally inspired tapas; unusual preparations of local seafood. [$] *Average main: $22* ✉ *12 The By-Way, Boothbay Harbor* ☎ *207/633–0400* 🌐 *www.theboathousebistro.com* 🕓 *Closed Thurs. and mid-Oct.–mid-Apr.*

Boothbay Lobster Wharf

$$$ | SEAFOOD | FAMILY | This is the real deal—a working lobster wharf where fishermen unload their catch to be sold at the on-site fish market or incorporated into the lobster rolls, crab rolls, or fried seafood dishes that are served to diners on the dock and in the enclosed dining room. If you opt for the steamed lobster dinner, you get to choose your crustacean from a saltwater tank. **Known for:** great harbor views; ultrafresh seafood; buck-a-shuck oysters on Friday and Saturday night. [$] *Average main: $25* ✉ *97 Atlantic Ave., Boothbay Harbor* ☎ *207/633–4900* 🌐 *www.boothbaylobsterwharf.com* 🕓 *Closed early Oct.–late May.*

Coastal Prime

$$$$ | AMERICAN | Yachts in the marina nose right up against the outdoor dining deck, and large windows frame the harbor in the elegant indoor dining room and casual bar. Complementing the views are the exceptional sandwiches, salads, pizzas, and tacos served at lunch and the oysters, lobster, sushi, and steaks served at dinner. **Known for:** special-occasion choice; smart-casual harborside dining;

Did You Know?

The Coastal Maine Botanical Gardens is the largest botanical garden in New England. It's also home to five gigantic and captivating trolls constructed by Danish artist Thomas Danbo.

surf-and-turf with Wagyu strip steak and butter-poached lobster. $ *Average main: $40* ✉ *35 Atlantic Ave., Boothbay Harbor* ☎ *207/633–4455* ⊕ *www.boothbayharboroceansideresort.com/coastal-prime* ☷ *Closed late Oct.–May.*

★ The Deck Bar & Grill

$$ | **AMERICAN** | Located at Linekin Bay Resort, this casual, mostly outdoor restaurant offers a serene waterside setting coupled with fresh lobster rolls, haddock BLTs, mussels, crab cakes, crudo yellowfin tuna, fish tacos, and clams linguine. There are plenty of meat, gluten-free, and vegan options, too. **Known for:** stunning view down Linekin Bay; live music on weekends; a wonderful escape from the bustle. $ *Average main: $20* ✉ *92 Wall Point Rd., Boothbay Harbor* ☎ *207/633–2494* ⊕ *www.linekinbayresort.com/dining* ☷ *Closed mid-Oct.–mid May.* at Linekin Bay Resort

Harborside 1901 Bar & Grill

$$$ | **SEAFOOD** | You just might want to eat dessert first when you spy the display case of cheesecakes, mousses, and profiteroles. But there are lots of savory temptations, too, including a large selection of sushi, tacos (lobster, shrimp, octopus, or haddock), and land and sea dinner entrées. **Known for:** seafood boils (lobster, crawfish, mussels, or king crab); harbor views; jewel-like minipastries. $ *Average main: $30* ✉ *12 Bridge St., Boothbay Harbor* ☎ *207/315–6043* ⊕ *www.harborside1901.com.*

Ports of Italy

$$$ | **ITALIAN** | Tucked above a shop in downtown Boothbay Harbor, this smart-casual restaurant combines attentive service with well-prepared, traditional Italian cuisine. Choose from antipasti, salads, and house-made pastas, as well as such *secondi* as osso buco and veal scallopine. **Known for:** Caprese salad served in a crunchy basket made of Parmesan cheese; extensive wine, spirits, and liqueur list, including grappa; authentic porchetta. $ *Average main:*

$25 ✉ *47 Commercial St., Boothbay Harbor* ☎ *207/633–1011* ⊕ *www.portsofitaly.com/boothbayharbor* ☷ *Closed Jan. 2–Apr.*

Robinson's Wharf

$$$ | **SEAFOOD** | **FAMILY** | On Southport Island, across an old-fashioned swing bridge from Boothbay Harbor and overlooking the waters of Townsend Gut, this lively local favorite often has waits for its tables on summer weekends. Head inside or sit at a picnic table out on the dock, where you can watch lobstermen deliver their catch while enjoying a lunch or dinner featuring one of the well-prepared seafood dishes, many of them fried. **Known for:** crispy haddock bites or tacos and raw-bar oysters; on-site fish market; lobster straight off the boat. $ *Average main: $25* ✉ *20 Hendricks Hill Rd., Southport, Boothbay Harbor* ☎ *207/633–3830* ⊕ *www.robinsonswharf.com* ☷ *Closed Tues. and Nov.–late May.*

★ Shannon's Unshelled

$ | **SEAFOOD** | **FAMILY** | The namesake of this shack first got the idea to set up shop when her father posed the simple question: "Where can you buy a quick lobster roll in Boothbay Harbor?" Unable to answer, Shannon's Unshelled was born, and the shack is now beloved for its grilled, buttered buns stuffed with whole lobsters and served with a side of garlicky, sea-salted, drawn butter. **Known for:** fried seafood features gluten-free batter; seaweed salads; trap-to-table lobster. $ *Average main: $16* ✉ *23 Granary Way, Boothbay Harbor* ☎ *207/350–7313* ⊕ *www.shannonsunshelled.biz* ☷ *Closed Sun. and Wed.*

☕ Coffee and Quick Bites

Brisetto's Second Cup

$ | **CAFÉ** | **FAMILY** | Stop in here for a hot or cold coffee drink, a smoothie, or fresh juice. If you'd like to linger for a while, take your drink upstairs and settle in with your laptop. **Known for:** friendly owner hails from Romania; fruit milk shakes; feel-good vibes. [$] *Average main: $6* ✉ *41 Commercial St., Boothbay Harbor* ☎ *207/315–6377* 🌐 *www.brisettos.com* 🕓 *Closed mid Oct.–early May.*

★ Downeast Ice Cream Factory

$ | ICE CREAM | FAMILY | Stop in at this cute little house next to the boardwalk and order an ice-cream cone to enjoy at a nearby picnic table or as you stroll along the waterfront. You'll probably want to make it a two-scooper, so you can try at least two of the many flavors, all made right here in Boothbay Harbor. **Known for:** more than 50 flavors; super-premium ice cream; vegan sorbets. [$] *Average main: $6* ✉ *1 By-Way, Boothbay Harbor* ☎ *207/315–6670* 🌐 *www.downeasticecreamfactory.com* 🕓 *Closed Nov.–mid-May.*

Eventide Specialties

$ | SANDWICHES | FAMILY | Just up the hill from the harbor, this goodie-filled shop is the ideal place to pick up picnic supplies. Large, made-to-order sandwiches (the chicken salad with apples and cranberries is divine) come on a choice of freshly baked breads, including sourdough, anadama, and three-Italian cheese. **Known for:** wonderful breads baked on-site; sandwiches come with a chocolate!; extensive cheese and wine selection. [$] *Average main: $12* ✉ *5 Boothbay House Hill, Boothbay Harbor* ☎ *207/350–4244* 🌐 *www.eventidespecialties.com* 🕓 *Closed Sun. and Mon.*

Hotels

Five Gables Inn

$$ | B&B/INN | This beautifully restored Victorian inn, set amid delightful gardens on a side road in East Boothbay, is one of the last of the many turn-of-the-20th-century hotels that once welcomed guests to the area. **Pros:** views of Linekin Bay; lovely secluded spot; delicious breakfasts and afternoon tea. **Cons:** waterfront is across the road; rooms under the gables have slanted ceilings and low headroom; must drive to restaurants and shops. [$] *Rooms from: $259* ✉ *107 Murray Hill Rd., East Boothbay, Boothbay Harbor* ☎ *207/687–1396* 🌐 *www.fivegablesinn.com* 🕓 *Closed mid-Oct.–mid-May* 🛏 *16 rooms* 🍴 *Free Breakfast.*

Harbor House Inn

$$ | B&B/INN | Built in the early 1800s by Captain Mitchell Reed, this yellow, mansard-roofed inn sits atop McKown Hill in the heart of Boothbay Harbor. **Pros:** lovely views; short walk to shops, restaurants, and the waterfront; personalized care. **Cons:** two-night minimum for weekend stays; steep, short walk back up the hill to the inn; not on the water. [$] *Rooms from: $281* ✉ *80 McKown St., Boothbay Harbor* ☎ *207/633–2941* 🌐 *www.harborhouse-me.com* 🕓 *Closed Jan.–Mar. except by advance reservation* 🛏 *8 rooms* 🍴 *Free Breakfast.*

Linekin Bay Resort

$$$ | RESORT | FAMILY | On the edge of its namesake bay and just a few minutes from downtown Boothbay Harbor, this secluded, 20-acre, wooded resort has accommodations that range from rustic cabins to modern waterfront suites. **Pros:** feels like a true Maine summer retreat; excellent casual on-site restaurant; lots of amenities for paddlers and sailors. **Cons:** a little difficult to find; no TV in the more rustic cabins; Saturday weddings can interfere with restaurant service. [$] *Rooms from: $350* ✉ *92 Wall Point Rd., Boothbay Harbor* ☎ *207/633–2494* 🌐 *www.linekinbayresort.com* 🕓 *Closed late Oct.–mid-May* 🛏 *51 rooms* 🍴 *Free Breakfast.*

Spruce Point Inn

$$$ | RESORT | FAMILY | Since 1892, this refined seaside resort has welcomed guests, including members of the Kennedy family, to its own sea-lapped point at the eastern side of the outer harbor. **Pros:** two on-site restaurants; private boat tour of harbor; lots of included amenities and activities. **Cons:** a few private residences close to premises; no elevators; some of the more-historic buildings have quirks. [$] *Rooms from: $300* ✉ *88 Grandview Ave., Boothbay Harbor* ☎ *207/633–4152, 800/553–0289* 🌐 *www.sprucepointinn.com* 🕓 *Closed mid-Oct.–mid-May* 🛏 *63 rooms* 🍴 *No Meals.*

★ Topside Inn

$$$$ | B&B/INN | Dating from 1865 and once the home of a wealthy sea captain, this grand, hilltop inn has an immense lawn dotted with Adirondack chairs, a wraparound porch, and a fireside lounge with a stylish bar. **Pros:** knockout harbor views; exceptional breakfasts; walking distance to downtown. **Cons:** two-person maximum per room; books up quickly in summer; steep, short walk back up the hill from town. [$] *Rooms from: $550* ✉ *60 McKown St., Boothbay Harbor* ☎ *207/633–5404* 🌐 *www.topsideinn.com* 🕓 *Closed late Oct.–early May* 🛏 *22 rooms* 🍴 *Free Breakfast.*

Shopping

★ Abacus Gallery

ART GALLERIES | This well-established gallery showcases artwork that captures the beauty of Maine, including Dana Heacock's brightly colored giclèe prints, cards, and Abacus calendars. Well-executed, often entertaining home-decor items and delicate or statement pieces of jewelry also make excellent souvenirs of your visit to Boothbay Harbor. ✉ *12 McKown St., Boothbay Harbor* ☎ *207/633–2166* 🌐 *www.abacusgallery.com.*

Ae Home Store

HOUSEWARES | The selection of strikingly glazed ceramics, including oyster-shape dishes, for sale here are handmade on-site by owner Alison Evans. You can also shop for home goods, local art, and cashmere clothing. ✉ *93 Townsend Ave., Boothbay Harbor* ☎ *207/315–6221* 🌐 *www.aehomestore.com* 🕓 *Closed weekends Oct.–May.*

★ Gleason Fine Art

ART GALLERIES | In a restored 1800s farmhouse in the center of town, this gallery showcases exceptional paintings and sculptures from the 19th, 20th, and 21st centuries. The focus is on artists inspired by Maine's beauty, especially those who have painted on Monhegan Island. Among those represented are Rockwell Kent, James Fitzgerald, Andrew Winter, Carroll Thayer Berry, and Charles Woodbury. Contemporary artists include Andrea J. Peters, Kevin Beers, and Henry Isaacs. ✉ *31 Townsend Ave., Boothbay Harbor* ☎ *207/633–6849* 🌐 *www.gleasonfineart.com* 🕓 *Closed Sun. in winter.*

Activities

BOAT TOURS

★ Balmy Days Cruises

BOAT TOURS | To truly appreciate the Boothbay region, you need to get out on the water. This fleet of tour boats includes the *Balmy Days II*, which carries passengers to and from Monhegan Island every day; the *Novelty*, offering harbor and lighthouse sightseeing; and *Miss Boothbay*, which takes anglers mackerel fishing. Some trips include a visit ashore to Burnt Island Light. There's also sailing aboard the classic Friendship sloop, *Bay Lady*. ✉ *42 Commercial St., Pier 8, Boothbay Harbor* ☎ *207/633–2284* 🌐 *www.balmydayscruises.com* 🎟 *From $24* 🕓 *Closed early Oct.–early June.*

Cabbage Island Clambakes

BOAT TOURS | FAMILY | Climb aboard the *Bennie Alice* for a Boothbay Harbor sightseeing cruise combined with a traditional Downeast lobster bake served on an island in Linekin Bay. You won't leave hungry: each person receives two lobsters (!), fish chowder, steamed clams, potato, onion, egg, and corn on the cob, all steamed the old-fashioned way in seaweed on a tarp-covered fire. There's blueberry cake, too. Beer, wine, and cocktails are available. The entire experience, including island feast and round-trip boat cruise, takes four hours. ✉ *22 Commercial St., Pier 6, Boothbay Harbor* ☎ *207/633–7200* ⊕ *www.cabbageislandclambakes.com* ✉ *$84* ⊘ *Closed early Sept.–mid-June.*

Cap'n Fish's Cruises

BOAT TOURS | **FAMILY** | If you're keen to see puffins or whales, this is the tour-boat fleet for you. The *Pink Lady II* travels to Eastern Egg Rock while puffins are nesting there in early and midsummer. The *Harbor Princess* goes farther out, visiting offshore whale-feeding grounds. Marine biologists are on board to provide expert commentary. Harbor cruises to see lighthouses and lobstering, plus a longer trip up the Kennebec River, are also offered. On all these trips, there's a good chance you'll also see seals, seabirds, and perhaps porpoises. ✉ *42 Commercial St., Boothbay Harbor* ☎ *207/613–6638* ⊕ *www.boothbayboattrips.com* ✉ *From $30.*

HIKING

★ Boothbay Region Land Trust

HIKING & WALKING | **FAMILY** | This exceptional organization manages 26 public preserves with more than 35 miles of hiking trails in the Boothbay region. It's headquartered in an early-1800s farmhouse at Oak Point Farm, where there's a visitor center and a gentle 1-mile loop through fields, forest, and along the water. Part of the trail is universally accessible. Among the many preserves under the trust's purview, Ovens Mouth is especially beautiful, with more than 5 miles of trails on two side-by-side peninsulas linked by a footbridge. The hikes meander through woodlands and along a rocky shore. If you have access to a private boat, consider a trip to fascinating Damariscove Island, offshore from Boothbay Harbor. ✉ *60 Samoset Rd., Oak Point Farm, Boothbay Harbor* ☎ *207/633–4818* ⊕ *www.bbrlt.org.*

KAYAKING

Tidal Transit Kayak Co.

KAYAKING | Whether you prefer to poke around inshore or set out for islands in open water, the Boothbay region offers plenty of places to paddle. Tidal Transit Kayak provides kayak and paddleboard rentals ranging from an hour to multiple days. Gear, basic instruction, and tips on where to go come with every rental. There is also a retail store. Those with their own boats are welcome to launch here. ✉ *18 Granary Way, Boothbay Harbor* ☎ *207/633–7140* ⊕ *www.kayakboothbay.com* ✉ *From $20* ⊘ *Closed mid-Sept.–late May.*

Damariscotta

18 miles northeast of Boothbay Harbor.

Near the head of the Damariscotta River, and flanked by the Boothbay and Pemaquid peninsulas, this vibrant little town has a bevy of shops, many tucked into 150-year-old brick buildings in the three-block-long National Historic District. This is also the place to slurp your fill of freshly plucked oysters.

Indigenous peoples summered on these shores millennia ago, leaving behind huge, still-visible, oyster-shell middens. By the late 1800s, the shellfish had disappeared. A century later, aquaculture programs spawned new enterprises, and today some of the country's most prized oysters come from the clear, clean Damariscotta River. Some say this is the Napa Valley of oyster growing.

Damariscotta is also the commercial hub of an eponymous region made up of several communities along the rocky coast. The closest is Newcastle, just a stroll across the bridge. It was settled in the early 1600s and later had shipyards and mills. The oldest Catholic church in New England, St. Patrick's, is here, and it still rings its original Paul Revere bell. South of Damariscotta on the Pemaquid

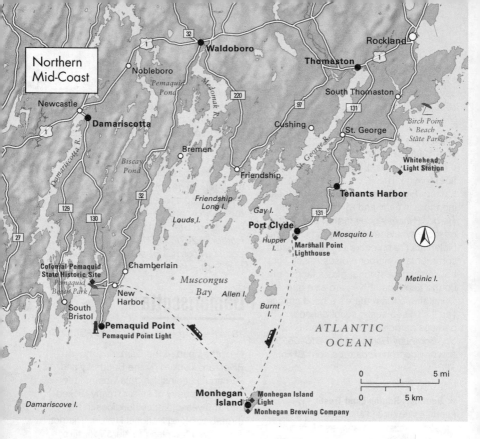

Northern Mid-Coast

Peninsula are the towns of Bristol, South Bristol, Round Pond, New Harbor, and Pemaquid Point.

Thousands descend on Damariscotta every October over Indigenous Peoples Day/Columbus Day Weekend for the zany Pumpkinfest, whose events include pumpkin-boat races on the harbor—yes, people actually race around in giant, tubby, tippy, paddle- and outboard-powered pumpkins.

GETTING HERE AND AROUND

From Boothbay Harbor follow Route 27 north to U.S. 1. Turn off U.S. 1 onto business U.S. 1, which runs through the village of Damariscotta.

At the northern end of downtown, Routes 129 and 130 lead south from business U.S. 1. In a few miles, 129 turns off to South Bristol and Christmas Cove.

Route 130 continues down to Bristol, New Harbor, and Pemaquid. From there, you can take Route 32 north up through New Harbor, Round Pond, and Bremen, returning to U.S. 1 in Waldoboro.

The Concord Coach Lines bus that travels the coast stops in Damariscotta daily.

VISITOR INFORMATION

CONTACTS Damariscotta Region Chamber of Commerce. ⊠ *67–A Main St., Damariscotta* ☎ *207/563–8340* ⊕ *www.damariscottaregion.com.*

Sights

Chapman-Hall House

HISTORIC HOME | What is thought to be the oldest house in Damariscotta was completed in 1754 by Nathaniel Chapman. Unlike nearby structures that have been remodeled, it retains much of its original design. Each room has been restored to represent a different era in the house's nearly three-century history. ✉ *270 Main St., Damariscotta* ☎ *207/882–6817* 🌐 *www.lincolncountyhistory.org/visit/museums/chapman-hall-house* 🎟 *$5* ⏲ *Closed weekdays and mid-Oct.–early June.*

🍴 Restaurants

Best Thai Restaurant

$$ | **THAI** | **FAMILY** | This aptly named, family-run restaurant serves all the standard Thai favorites, as well as some lesser-known options. Everything is prepared using fresh local fish, meats, and produce. **Known for:** exceptional Thai cooking; very friendly service; local ingredients. [$] *Average main: $18* ✉ *88 Main St., Damariscotta* ☎ *207/563–1440* 🌐 *www.bestthaimaine.com* ⏲ *Closed Mon.*

Damariscotta River Grill

$$$$ | **MODERN AMERICAN** | Even though it's not directly on the water, don't overlook this Main Street eatery. You can't go wrong with lobster cakes or Pemaquid oysters, but here you can also tuck into Thai fish stew, grilled hangar steak with a bourbon-brown-sugar glaze, or duck confit risotto. **Known for:** reliable, affordable wine list; well-established bar and grill; popular with locals. [$] *Average main: $40* ✉ *155 Main St., Damariscotta* ☎ *207/563–2992* 🌐 *www.damariscottarivergrill.com* ⏲ *Closed Sun.*

King Eider's Pub and Restaurant

$$$$ | **AMERICAN** | **FAMILY** | At this restaurant in an adorable building just off Main Street, the acclaimed crab cakes and the oysters fresh from the Damariscotta River are good bets, but so are the steak-and-ale pie, seafood stew, and fish-and-chips (made with fresh haddock that's sautéed rather than fried). With exposed-brick walls and low, wood-beamed ceilings hung with pottery beer mugs, the downstairs is a snug place to enjoy a Maine craft ale. **Known for:** live music in the pub; cozy atmosphere; extensive whiskey collection. [$] *Average main: $36* ✉ *2 Elm St., Damariscotta* ✣ *Just off Main St.* ☎ *207/563–6008* 🌐 *www.kingeiderspub.com.*

Newcastle Publick House

$$ | **AMERICAN** | **FAMILY** | In a large, historic, handsomely renovated brick building, Newcastle Publick House serves delicious comfort food in a pleasant dining room and welcoming bar. Specialties include fresh oysters prepared several ways, a selection of burgers, and one of the best French onion soups around. **Known for:** stacked burgers; cozy, old-school atmosphere; desserts and breads made by nearby Oysterhead Pizza Co.. [$] *Average main: $20* ✉ *52 Main St., Newcastle* ☎ *207/563–3434* 🌐 *www.newcastlepublickhouse.com* ⏲ *Closed Mon.*

Oysterhead Pizza Co.

$$ | **PIZZA** | **FAMILY** | Here, the dough and many of the toppings are made from scratch, so it's no surprise that the wood-fired pizzas often sell out before closing time. Keep it simple with red sauce, cheese, and pepperoni, or go for more sophisticated toppings such as wild mushrooms, duxelles, caramelized shallots, house-smoked chicken, or house-made fennel sausage. **Known for:** great bagels on weekend mornings; exceptional wood-fired pizza with creative toppings; indoor, outdoor, and take-out dining. [$] *Average main: $23* ✉ *189 Main St., Damariscotta* ☎ *207/563–6816* 🌐 *www.oysterheadpizzaco.com* ⏲ *Closed Mon. and Tues.*

★ River House

$$$ | **MODERN AMERICAN** | Perched on the bridge that spans the river between Damariscotta and Newcastle, this sweet little restaurant is passionate about growing or locally sourcing as many ingredients as possible. They're always fresh and top-quality, and shine in simply yet deftly prepared fish, chicken, and steak dishes. **Known for:** the finest

local ingredients; river views; dishes prepared on wood-fired grill. $ *Average main: $35* ⊠ *27 Main St., Damariscotta* ☎ *207/563–6156* ⊕ *www.riverhouseme. com* ☾ *Closed Sun. and Mon.*

Shuck Station

$$ | SEAFOOD | Shuck Station may be in a repurposed gas station, with umbrella-topped tables set on gravel beside a busy road, but its exquisite oysters elevate the dining experience here. Pull up a stool at the raw bar, and mix and match a dozen on the half-shell from various Maine oyster farms to compare the sweetness and brine. **Known for:** live music; wines that pair well with oysters; lively atmosphere. $ *Average main: $20* ⊠ *68 Main St., Newcastle* ☎ *207/682–0129* ⊕ *www.facebook.com/ShuckStation* ☾ *Closed Wed. and late Oct.–late May.*

☕ Coffee and Quick Bites

Barn Door Baking Company Cafe

$ | BAKERY | FAMILY | Connected to Sherman's Maine Coast Book Shop through an arched doorway, this little café turns out excellent coffee and hot and cold coffee drinks, plus fresh-from-the-oven sweet and savory baked items. It's hard to choose among the scones, slices of cake and pie, sinful cookies, cupcakes, and old-fashioned dessert bars. **Known for:** daily selection of irresistible baked goodies; good place to chill and catch up on email; friendly service. $ *Average main: $5* ⊠ *162 Main St., Damariscotta* ☎ *207/563–3662* ⊕ *www.barndoorbakingcompany.com.*

S. Fernald's Country Store

$ | SANDWICHES | FAMILY | Settle into the couch or sit at a table for breakfast and try the Eggs Bigelow (two eggs in a hole, bacon, cheddar, and locally baked sourdough) or grab a sandwich, wrap, or sub for lunch. The biggest challenge is deciding among the many breads and filling choices on the extensive menu. **Known for:** a local favorite; penny candy,

toys, and other nostalgic items; great for picnic provisions. $ *Average main: $10* ⊠ *50 Main St., Damariscotta* ☎ *207/563–8484* ⊕ *www.sfernalds.com* ☾ *Closed Sun. and Mon.*

Hotels

Mill Pond Inn

$ | B&B/INN | Rooms are comfortably furnished, warm, and inviting at this circa-1780 inn set beside the large, unspoiled Damariscotta Lake, where casual afternoon gatherings on the deck and hammocks-for-two overlooking the water make the most of the location. **Pros:** delightful owners; amenities include paddling equipment; quiet lakefront location. **Cons:** expected quirks with a house that's more than two centuries old; must drive to restaurants and shops; guests who stay up late might disturb others' sleep. $ *Rooms from: $175* ⊠ *50 Main St., Nobleboro, Newcastle* ☎ *207/563–8014* ⊕ *www.millpondinn. com* ▭ *No credit cards* ⤴ *5 rooms* ⏁ *Free Breakfast.*

★ Newcastle Inn

$$ | B&B/INN | FAMILY | A riverside location, tasteful decor, and lots of common areas (inside and out) make this an especially relaxing country inn. **Pros:** guests can order beer or wine; suites have sitting areas; water views from many rooms. **Cons:** flights of stairs to rooms on upper floors; not all rooms have water views; some rooms lack ample sitting areas. $ *Rooms from: $250* ⊠ *60 River Rd., Newcastle* ☎ *207/563–5685* ⊕ *www. newcastleinn.com* ⤴ *13 rooms* ⏁ *Free Breakfast.*

The Tipsy Butler Bed and Breakfast

$$ | B&B/INN | FAMILY | This large, century-old, white-columned house, tucked on a hillside not far from the heart of Newcastle, has large and comfortable rooms, appointed with period-appropriate furniture and equipped with modern conveniences like Nespresso machines,

high-speed Wi-Fi, and Blue-Ray players. **Pros:** very hospitable owners; EV car charging; large, airy rooms. **Cons:** a bit of a walk to Damariscotta's shops and restaurants; road noise from U.S. 1, which is near the back of the house; steep stairs to rooms on upper floors. [$] *Rooms from: $250* ✉ *11 High St., Newcastle* ☎ *207/653–4103* 🌐 *www.tipsybutler.com* 🛏 *4 rooms* 🍴 *Free Breakfast.*

Shopping

ART GALLERIES

★ Sarah Richards Lyn Snow Gallery

ART GALLERIES | Accomplished artist Sarah Richards specializes in horses and other animal subjects, capturing them in flowing swaths of color. In addition to original paintings and prints, Richards' gallery sells drinkware and clothing bearing some of her most popular images. Also here are lovely watercolors by her late mother, the talented floral artist Lyn Snow. ✉ *157 Main St., Damariscotta* ☎ *207/592–4036* 🌐 *www.sarahrichards.com.*

DEPARTMENT STORE

★ Renys

DEPARTMENT STORE | **FAMILY** | Renys is a beloved Maine institution—or, as their slogan says, "a Maine adventure." It has 17 locations throughout the state, and a visit to Maine truly isn't complete without browsing the endless bargains at at least one of them. Damariscotta is where it all started seven decades ago, and the original store—a quaintly crowded clothing store at 116 Main Street—is still going strong. Stop in there for bargains on Columbia, Carhartt, and other brands. Then cross the street and browse the larger outlet at 163 Main Street for great deals on housewares, nonperishable food items, seasonal goods, toys, and much more. You'll be amazed at what you find. And don't miss Waltz Soda Fountain, open during the summer at the left side of the building. It's been there since 1948. Order a malted, egg cream, lime rickey, or Moxie ice cream float at the counter, and slide into a booth to enjoy your sweet trip down memory lane. ✉ *163 Main St., Damariscotta* ☎ *207/563–3011* 🌐 *www.renys.com.*

GIFTS AND HOUSEWARES

The Beach Plum Company

HOUSEWARES | This visually pleasing shop stocks an array of treasures for the home and garden. There's a selection of personal accessories, toiletries, and children's books, too. ✉ *77 B Main St., Newcastle* ☎ *207/682–0181* 🌐 *www.beachplumcompany.com* 🕓 *Closed Sun. and Jan., Feb., and on a whim.*

Citizen Maine Home

HOUSEWARES | **FAMILY** | With an emphasis on interior design, this boutique stocks lovely bed linens, home-decor accents, and specialty soaps and toiletries. There's also a selection of kids' clothing no grandmother could resist. ✉ *93 Main St., Damariscotta* ☎ *207/682–0140* 🌐 *www.shopcitizenmaine.com.*

Gifts at 136

CRAFTS | Head to this gallery for fine pieces created by talented Mainers. It represents more than 75 of the state's artists and craftspeople, and its offerings include pottery, jewelry, glassware, artwork, and handmade chocolates. ✉ *136 Main St., Damariscotta* ☎ *207/563–1011* 🌐 *www.giftsat136.com.*

The Kingfisher & The Queen

HOUSEWARES | This appealing emporium brims with both vintage and new finds to embellish and enliven the home. There's also a selection of unusual gifts and sweet children's items. ✉ *79 Main St., Damariscotta* ☎ *207/563–1590* 🌐 *www.thekingfisherandthequeen.com* 🕓 *Closed Sun.–Tues.*

JEWELRY

ABOCA Beads

CRAFTS | **FAMILY** | This candy store for those who love stringing their own necklaces is filled with a dazzling array of beads in a range of prices. Staffers are always happy to lend assistance, and you can sit down and create jewelry on the spot if you'd like. ABOCA also offers classes in its workshop behind the store. ⊠ *157 Main St., Damariscotta* ☏ *207/563–1766* ⊕ *www.aboca.com.*

★ Stars Fine Jewelry

JEWELRY & WATCHES | This welcoming store carries everything from moderately priced costume jewelry to fine contemporary and estate pieces. Pick up a lovely souvenir of your Maine Coast visit, or select a treasure to be loved for years. The owners love to provide personal service, including help redesigning family heirlooms for today's style. ⊠ *65 Main St., Damariscotta* ☏ *207/563–5488* ⊕ *www.starsfinejewelry.com* ⊗ *Closed Sun. and Mon.*

Activities

★ Damariscotta River Cruises

BOAT TOURS | **FAMILY** | Climb aboard a 50-foot, bright-red powerboat called the *RiverTripper* for a two-hour cruise down the Damariscotta River. During the narrated tour, you'll spot such wildlife as harbor seals, osprey, and eagles; see oyster-farming operations (most Maine oysters are grown on this river); and learn about the area's rich history. There are also happy-hour tours with drinks and oysters available for purchase, as well as special oyster and wine-tasting cruises with a knowledgeable and entertaining sommelier. In the autumn, colorful foliage enhances the scenery. ⊠ *47 Main St., Damariscotta* ⚓ *Boarding at Damariscotta public ramp* ☏ *207/315–5544* ⊕ *www.damariscottarivercruises. com* 🚢 *From $35* ⊗ *Closed mid-Oct.–late May.*

Midcoast Kayak

KAYAKING | **FAMILY** | In a tiny building beside the bridge in Damariscotta, this full-service outfitter offers kayak, standup paddleboarding, and canoe rentals (and deliveries to your lodging if desired), as well as lessons and a variety of guided tours. Choose a paddle on the Damariscotta River to see wildlife and oyster-farming operations, or venture onto the open waters of nearby Muscongus Bay. All leaders and instructors are Registered Maine Guides. Midcoast Kayak also sells boats and gear. ⊠ *47 Main St., Damariscotta* ☏ *207/563–5732* ⊕ *www. midcoastkayak.com* ⊗ *Closed early Oct.–late May.*

Pemaquid Point

10 miles south of Damariscotta.

At the tip of its namesake peninsula, bordered by Muscongus and Johns bays, Pemaquid Point is home to a famous lighthouse that also shares its name. On the other side of the peninsula is Pemaquid Harbor, where you can walk the site of a European settlement established here in the 1600s, about the same time as the Plymouth Colony. Near the bottom of the peninsula, along Muscongus Bay, is the Nature Conservancy's small Rachel Carson Salt Pond Preserve.

GETTING HERE AND AROUND

At the top of the hill, just beyond the shops on U.S. 1B in Damariscotta, turn right and head south on Route 130 to Pemaquid Point.

Sights

Colonial Pemaquid State Historic Site

HISTORIC SIGHT | As you walk the gently sloping, waterfront meadow where Colonial Pemaquid was established by English colonists around 1620 (the same time as the Pilgrims were stepping ashore on Plymouth Rock), be sure to read signs describing the buildings that once stood here. Evidence that's been unearthed suggests there were some 40 structures—including houses, a forge, a tavern, a jail, and a customs house—set along a grid of dirt lanes. A replica of a

Pemaquid Point Lighthouse looks like it sprouted from the ragged granite outcroppings on which it stands.

fisherman's small cottage gives an idea of how the settlers lived. Nearby is a 1908 reproduction of a large stone tower, part of Fort William Henry, built in 1692 to protect the little community. Unfortunately, unlike Plymouth, Pemaquid was abandoned in the early 1700s. A small museum containing a diorama of the village and some 75,000 artifacts is open seasonally. ⊠ *Colonial Pemaquid Dr., New Harbor* ☎ *207/677–2423* ⊕ *www.maine.gov/dacf/parks* ✉ *$4* ⊙ *Closed Sept. 1–late May.*

★ Pemaquid Point Light

LIGHTHOUSE | FAMILY | At the very end of Route 130, this lighthouse at the tip of the Pemaquid Peninsula looks as though it sprouted from the ragged, striated granite outcroppings on which it stands. Most days in the summer you can climb the tower to the light. The former keeper's cottage is now the Fishermen's Museum, which displays historic photographs, scale models, and artifacts that explore commercial fishing in Maine. The original fog bell and bell house are also

here. Restrooms and picnic tables are available. ⊠ *3115 Bristol Rd., New Harbor* ☎ *207/677–2492* ⊕ *www.bristolmaine.org* ✉ *$3* ⊙ *Closed early Oct.–late May.*

Beaches

Pemaquid Beach Park

BEACH | FAMILY | Offering views down Johns Bay, this sandy beach is very popular with families. You can rent beach chairs, umbrellas, and boogie boards. A snack stand sells beverages, burgers, fish sandwiches, tacos, and salads. There are no lifeguards, however. **Amenities:** food and drink; parking (fee); showers; toilets. **Best for:** swimming. ⊠ *27 Pemaquid Beach Park, New Harbor* ☎ *207/677–2754* ⊕ *www.bristolmaine.org/parks-recreation/pemaquid-beach-park* ✉ *$5 (cash or check only)* ⊙ *Closed early Sept.–June.*

🍴 Restaurants

The Contented Sole

$$ | **SEAFOOD** | Whether you dine outside on the long, narrow dock, or inside, you'll enjoy the view, the vibe, and the food at this popular summertime eatery on Pemaquid Harbor. The fish tacos and fried-oyster tacos are exceptional, as are the lobster club sandwich, Korean barbecue smoked chicken, and the pizza. **Known for:** lively atmosphere; raw bar; great harbor setting. $ *Average main: $20* ✉ *Colonial Pemaquid Rd., New Harbor* ☎ *207/677–3000* ⊕ *www. thecontentedsole.com* ⏱ *Closed early Sept.–late May.*

Muscongus Bay Lobster

$$$ | **SEAFOOD** | **FAMILY** | The food here is guaranteed to be fresh, given that the lobster comes in off the boats just down the dock from the window where you order your meal. The menu also features scallops, oysters, crabmeat, and haddock, all prepared in a variety of tempting ways. **Known for:** laid-back atmosphere; kid-friendly; repeat visitors meet and greet here. $ *Average main: $25* ✉ *28 Landing Rd., Round Pond* ☎ *207/529–5528* ⊕ *www.mainefreshlobster.com* ⏱ *Closed mid-Oct.–mid-May.*

Round Pond Lobster

$$$ | **SEAFOOD** | This tiny, no-frills cook shack, operated by the lobstermen's co-op, is the place to come for a simple, old-fashioned feed, featuring fairly priced, cooked-to-order lobsters and steamers with corn on the cob and a few other sides. You're welcome to BYOB, soft beverages, and even other dishes or desserts to round out your meal. **Known for:** harbor views; family-friendly; dog-friendly. $ *Average main: $25* ✉ *25 Landing Rd.* ☎ *207/529–5725* ⊕ *www.facebook.com/ roundpondlobster* ⏱ *Closed Sun. and Labor Day–late-May.*

★ The Sea Gull Shop and Restaurant

$$ | **SEAFOOD** | **FAMILY** | Try for a table by the windows in the small dining room of this little landmark restaurant, perched beside Pemaquid Lighthouse at the very edge of the rocky shore. Blueberry pancakes with Maine maple syrup are the clear breakfast favorites; the lunch and dinner menu features fried fresh seafood, lobster and crab rolls, salads, and mouthwatering entrées like the shipwreck pie (lobster, crab, shrimp, and scallops sautéed in butter and topped with a cracker-crumb crust). **Known for:** spectacular sea views; gift shop with jams, condiments, and other great souvenirs; fresh, traditional Maine fare. $ *Average main: $20* ✉ *3119 Bristol Rd., New Harbor* ☎ *207/677–2374* ⊕ *www.seagullshop.com* ⏱ *Closed Mon. and Tues. and Dec.–mid-May.*

Shaw's Fish & Lobster Wharf

$ | **SEAFOOD** | **FAMILY** | At this old-fashioned lobster pound beside the water in New Harbor, you can choose from a large menu of coastal classics—shore dinners, fried shellfish dinners, seafood rolls, broiled fish and shellfish, and chowders. There are grilled steaks, too, and you can go all in with a surf-and-turf combo of rib eye and lobster tail. **Known for:** very fresh seafood; great views; large menu. $ *Average main: $15* ✉ *129 Rte. 32, Suite A, New Harbor* ☎ *207/677–2200* ⊕ *www.shaws-wharf.com* ⏱ *Closed late Sept.–mid-May.*

☕ Coffee and Quick Bites

The Cupboard Café

$ | **AMERICAN** | The cinnamon and sticky buns served at this little log cabin are the stuff of sweet dreams. Grab one while they last every morning, and pair it with Maine-roasted coffee or one of the espresso drinks. **Known for:** chocolate milk; grab-and-go lunch and dinner options; ships its buns to devotees nationwide. $ *Average main: $5* ✉ *137 Huddle Rd., New Harbor* ✛ *On way to Pemaquid Harbor* ☎ *207/677–3911* ⊕ *www.thecupboardcafe.com* ⏱ *Closed Sun.–Wed. and late Oct.–mid-June.*

🛏 Hotels

★ Bradley Inn

$$$ | B&B/INN | This gray-shingled, low-key yet refined inn—originally built as sea captain John Bradley's residence—has comfortable, tastefully decorated guest rooms painted in soothing colors. **Pros:** short walk to Pemaquid Point Light; elegant breakfasts; exceptional on-site restaurant and pub. **Cons:** restaurant only open Thursday through Saturday; not on water; a long drive to Damariscotta for dining and shopping. 💲 *Rooms from: $385 ⊠ 3063 Bristol Rd., New Harbor ☎ 207/677–2105 ⊕ www.bradleyinn.com ⇨ 15 rooms ⦿ Free Breakfast.*

Hotel Pemaquid

$ | B&B/INN | Step back in time at this restored 1888 summer hotel, where the decor in the main building remains Victorian and that in the cottages and bungalows is more contemporary. **Pros:** great location close to Pemaquid Point Light; old-fashioned atmosphere; reasonable rates. **Cons:** spotty Wi-Fi; not on the water; archaic reservation process. 💲 *Rooms from: $175 ⊠ 3098 Bristol Rd., New Harbor ☎ 207/677–2312 ⊕ www. hotelpemaquid.com ⊟ No credit cards ⦿ Closed early Oct.–late May ⇨ 38 rooms ⦿ No Meals.*

🛍 Shopping

★ Granite Hall Store

GENERAL STORE | FAMILY | Don't miss this charming little store in a sweet old mansard-roofed structure. The upstairs once served as a community dance hall, and the original piano is still on the stage. Kids will delight in the array of "penny candy" as well as fun small toys. There are also kitchen utensils, candles, gifts, pretty cards, and books. At an outdoor window on the side of the building, you can order an ice-cream cone to enjoy on a walk down to the harbor. ⊠ *9 Back Shore Rd., New Harbor ☎ 207/529–5864 ⊕ www.granitehallstore.com ⦿ Closed late Dec.–May 1.*

🏃 Activities

Hardy Boat Cruises

BOATING | FAMILY | From the dock in New Harbor, you can see Monhegan Island on the horizon, and Hardy Boat Cruises will take you there between mid-May and mid-October. The company also offers seal- and puffin-watching trips, as well as lighthouse and coastal autumn cruises. Dogs are welcome on board for $5. ⊠ *Shaw's Wharf, 132 Rte. 32, New Harbor ☎ 207/677–2026 ⊕ www.hardyboat. com ⊠ $50 ⦿ Closed mid-Oct.–mid-May.*

Waldoboro

10 miles northeast of Damariscotta.

Situated on the Medomak River, Waldoboro is an old seafaring town with a proud shipbuilding past. Its main drag is lined with houses representing numerous architectural styles: Cape Cod, Queen Anne, Stick, Greek Revival, and Italianate. The town was settled largely by Germans in the mid-1700s, and you can still visit the old German Meeting House, built in 1772.

Nowadays, Waldoboro attracts artists and skilled artisans who ply their talents in farmhouses tucked along the winding country roads. In the heart of the village, the charming old Waldo Theatre has been fully restored and once again shows films and hosts theatrical events and films.

GETTING HERE AND AROUND

From U.S. 1 North, veer off onto Main Street or down Route 220 or 32. The Concord Coach Lines bus that plies the coastal route stops in Waldoboro.

Sights

Waldoborough Historical Society

HISTORY MUSEUM | Three small historical buildings contain artifacts from the town's past, including photographs, models, and mementoes from some of the large schooners that slid down the ways here in the 1800s. The town lays claim to having built the first five-masted schooner, the 265-foot-long *Governor Ames,*which at the time of construction was the world's largest cargo vessel. You'll also see beautiful examples of antique Waldoboro hooked rugs, prized for their intricate workmanship and sculptural detail. Be sure to step into the one-room schoolhouse dating from 1857 and imagine sitting in one of the old student desks beside the wood stove. ✉ *1164 Main St., Waldoboro* ☎ *207/790–1307* 🌐 *www.waldoborohistory.us.*

Restaurants

★ Moody's Diner

$ | **DINER** | **FAMILY** | Whether you sit at a booth in the dining room or at the counter of this eatery, established in 1927, chances are, you'll soon be chatting with your neighbors. The multipage menu has all the breakfast standards (including fresh doughnuts every morning) and comfort-food lunch and dinner classics—from chowders, fish cakes, and lobster or crab rolls to chicken pot pie, meat loaf, and New England–style boiled dinners to wild Maine blueberry, custard, or apple pie. **Known for:** exceptional pies; landmark local favorite; breakfast served all day. [$] *Average main: $10* ✉ *1885 Atlantic Hwy., Waldoboro* ☎ *207/832–7785* 🌐 *www.moodysdiner.com.*

Odd Alewives Farm Brewery

$ | **AMERICAN** | **FAMILY** | Chosen as Maine's best tasting room by readers of *Down East* magazine in 2021, Odd Alewives is set in a beautifully restored old barn that's a cozily rustic place to grab a bite and brew, whether you're a beer aficionado or not. The beers—some of which feature herbs and flowers grown on the farm—range from saisons and farmhouse ales to a dark black ale; food offerings, which vary from week to week, include pizzas baked in a wood-fired oven, tacos, and meats cooked on an Argentinian wood-fired grill. **Known for:** delicious, wood-fired food; excellent, unusual beers; relaxing, welcoming atmosphere. [$] *Average main: $15* ✉ *99 Old Rte. 1, Waldoboro* ☎ *207/790–8406* 🌐 *oddalewives.com* 🕒 *Closed Mon.–Wed.*

Performing Arts

The Waldo Theatre

THEATER | Built in 1936 as a movie theater, this white-columned, Greek Revival building at the heart of Waldoboro has had its ups and downs over the decades, but, thanks to a restoration completed in 2021, its lights are glowing brightly again. It's now much more than a movie theater, thanks to a robust, year-round roster of concerts, plays, and dance performances. ✉ *916 Main St., Waldoboro* ☎ *207/974–6490* 🌐 *www.waldotheatre.org.*

Activities

★ Tops'l Farm

CAMPGROUND | Tops'l Farm is a lot of wonderful things rolled into one. It's a quiet, 83-acre oasis with spartan but glampy A-frames and cabins nestled in the woods. It's a gathering place for unusual, very memorable dining experiences offered both to overnight campers and others who come for the afternoon or evening. Guests bundle up for cold-weather feasts featuring raclette, wild game, or maple-syrup-centric dishes featuring local pork and root vegetables that begin outdoors around fire pits before moving into a handsome barn dining room. There are summertime barn dinners, too, and cookouts at a riverside yurt. And it's a place for special theme retreats. ✉ *365 Bremen Rd., Waldoboro* ☎ *207/832–1602* 🌐 *www.topslfarm.com.*

Thomaston

10 miles northeast of Waldoboro.

Thomaston is a delightful town, full of handsome and historic sea captains' homes. You can glimpse the town's rich past through a series of 25 Museum in the Streets signs placed throughout the National Historic District, which encompasses parts of High, Main, and Knox streets. Thomaston is also the gateway to two beautiful peninsulas and such picturesque harbors as Tenants Harbor and Port Clyde.

GETTING HERE AND AROUND

U.S. 1 is Main Street through Thomaston. Near the western end of town, Route 97 leads down the Cushing Peninsula and to Friendship. Near the eastern end of town, Route 131 runs from Route 1 down the St. George Peninsula to Tenants Harbor and Port Clyde.

👁 Sights

Knox Museum (Montpelier)

HISTORY MUSEUM | **FAMILY** | A true Revolutionary War hero, General Henry Knox was responsible for bringing key artillery equipment from Fort Ticonderoga to General Washington in Boston to end the siege of 1776. He also commanded troops at Brandywine, Valley Forge, and Yorktown. Following the war, Knox settled in Thomaston (where he is buried) and built a fine mansion called Montpelier beside the St. George River. Unfortunately, his descendants allowed it to fall into severe disrepair, and it was torn down. In 1931, a carefully researched replica was built nearby, and it is this grand white building that sits on a rise at the eastern end of town today. Tour guides tell the story of General Knox while leading you through the elegant interiors. ✉ *30 High St., Thomaston* ☎ *207/354–8062* 🌐 *knoxmuseum.org* 🎟 *$10* 🕒 *Closed Sun. and Mon. and Sept.–late May.*

🍴 Restaurants

★ The Block Saloon

$$ | **AMERICAN** | The menu at this late-afternoon-into-late-evening spot is limited and changes frequently, but it's always good. Order a small plate or charcuterie board, or go bigger with something like risotto, ramen, or seared pork shoulder with roasted shallots and toasted pistachios. **Known for:** intimate atmosphere; craft cocktails; creative, international menu. [$] *Average main: $20* ✉ *173 Main St., Thomaston* ☎ *207/354–5145* 🌐 *www.theblocksaloon.com* 🕒 *Closed Tues. and Wed.*

Station 118

$$ | **BARBECUE** | **FAMILY** | What was once a vintage gas station has been reborn as a casual dining spot with a Texas vibe. Moist, smoked barbecue is the star here, with offerings including brisket, pulled pork, and pork and beef ribs. **Known for:** fun atmosphere; excellent smoked meats; diet-busting desserts. [$] *Average main: $24* ✉ *118 Main St., Thomaston* ☎ *207/593–8208* 🌐 *www.station118.com* 🕒 *Closed Tues. and Wed.*

Thomaston Café

$$ | **AMERICAN** | **FAMILY** | With a welcoming, small-town atmosphere, this little café is popular with locals. Served at both lunch and dinner, the menu includes salads, sandwiches, burgers, and a few entrées such as fish-and-chips, baked stuffed haddock, and scallops au gratin. **Known for:** prime rib on Wednesday evening; friendly service; fresh seafood dishes. [$] *Average main: $20* ✉ *154 Main St., Thomaston* ☎ *207/354–8589* 🌐 *www.thomastoncafeme.com/* 🕒 *Closed Sun. and Mon.*

Coffee and Quick Bites

FlipSide Coffee
$ | **CAFÉ** | **FAMILY** | This local gathering spot sells a variety of hot and cold coffee and tea drinks, plus an appealing selection of light meals. Breakfast choices include a curried rice bowl, nachos, and avocado toast; at lunch, there are wraps and better-than-average salads. **Known for:** good spot to meet friends; casual atmosphere; a place to spend time on your laptop or phone. [$] *Average main: $10* ✉ *189 Main St., Thomaston* ☎ *207/354–5221* 🌐 *www.facebook.com/flipsidecoffeemaine.*

Laurel's Dolce Vita
$ | **BAKERY** | **FAMILY** | Billing itself as a classic Italian-American bakery, this little place across the street from the Maine State Prison Showroom turns out all sorts of sweet treats. The selection changes daily, but there's a good chance you'll find cupcakes, cookies, scones, sweet buns, tiramisu, Italian cream cake, savory foccacia buns, croissants, and pizzicati cookies. **Known for:** grab your favorite before it sells out; small-batch baking; classic Italian-American sweets. [$] *Average main: $6* ✉ *350 Main St., Thomaston* ☎ *207/354–5242* 🌐 *laurels-dolcevita.com* 🕒 *Closed Mon.*

Shopping

Maine State Prison Showroom
CRAFTS | Pop into the Maine State Prison Showroom for handcrafted wooden items ranging from beautiful cutting boards to furniture offered at very modest prices. Since 1824, prison inmates participating in the skills-building industries program have created wooden goods to be sold to the public; the proceeds fund the program. The store contains hundreds of items. Some, like ship models, have a nautical theme. Other items include toys, bowls, jewelry boxes, birdhouses, bureaus, and tables. They also sell metal fire pits. ✉ *358 Main St., Thomaston* ☎ *207/354–9237* 🌐 *www.facebook.com/MSPShowroom.*

Tenants Harbor and Port Clyde

Tenants Harbor is 10 miles south of Thomaston; Port Clyde is 5 miles south of Tenants Harbor.

The road down the St. George Peninsula from Thomaston meanders alongside the St. George River past meadows, farmhouses, and artists' studios (usually open to visitors in the summer). This is where generations of the Wyeth family of artists have summered for the past century, capturing the unspoiled scenery in their work.

Tenants Harbor is a quintessential coastal village tucked into the eastern edge of the serenely scenic peninsula. The town's harbor is filled with lobster boats, and its streets are flanked by clapboard houses, a church, and a general store. It's a favorite with artists, and galleries and studios welcome visitors.

In addition to being a busy lobstering harbor, Port Clyde, at the very tip of the peninsula, is home to Monhegan Boat Line's *Elizabeth Ann* and *Laura B,* which carry passengers—and the mail—to and from the island. Of the three Mid-Coast spots where you can catch a boat to Monhegan Island, it's the only one offering year-round service.

Turn off the main road to visit Marshall Point Light at the eastern entrance to the harbor. The views of the bay are lovely, and there's a small museum in the keeper's house.

GETTING HERE AND AROUND

From U.S. 1 at the eastern end of Thomaston, turn onto Route 131, and head down the St. George Peninsula to Tenants Harbor and continue all the way to Port Clyde at the tip.

Sights

★ Marshall Point Lighthouse

LIGHTHOUSE | FAMILY | About a mile from Port Clyde's town landing (turn off Route 131 at the sign), this 31-foot, granite and brick lighthouse has been in operation since it was erected in 1858 to replace an earlier tower whose beacon was fueled by lard. It is perhaps best known as the spot where Tom Hanks, aka Forrest Gump, concluded the eastern end of his very long cross-country run in the 1994 film adaptation of the book by the same name. As you walk out on the short footbridge to the light, resist the urge to shout, "Run, Forrest, Run!" There's also a small museum and gift shop, housed in the 1895 lightkeepers' house. Exhibits focus on local granite quarrying and lobstering as well as the lighthouse. The serene grounds have a few picnic tables and offer beautiful views of the sea; it's a perfect spot for watching pleasure and fishing vessels cruise in and out of Port Clyde harbor. ✉ *Marshall Point Rd., Port Clyde* ☎ *207/372–6450* 🌐 *www.marshallpoint.org.*

★ Whitehead Light Station

LIGHTHOUSE | The secluded 70-acre Whitehead Island, located in the western mouth of West Penobscot Bay, is home to this lighthouse, which was commissioned in 1803 and rebuilt in 1852 and which continues as a beacon for boaters. The seven-bedroom keeper's house can be rented on a weekly basis June through October, or adults can attend one of the onsite programs that are offered. Rates include transportation to the island in a light station boat. ✉ *Whitehead Island, Tenants Harbor* ☎ *207/200–7957* 🌐 *www.whiteheadlightstation.org.*

Restaurants

The Black Harpoon

$ | AMERICAN | FAMILY | Just off Route 131, this family-friendly eatery is a community favorite. You'll find good local fare, such as fish-and-chips, mussels, chowder, pastas, burgers, and a haddock Reuben. **Known for:** lively atmosphere; where the locals meet and eat; good prices. [$] *Average main: $15* ✉ *202 Drift Rd., Port Clyde* ✥ *On way to Marshall Point Light* ☎ *207/372–6304* 🌐 *www.theblackharpoon.com* ⏲ *Closed Sat.–Mon.*

The Causeway Restaurant

$$$ | AMERICAN | The restaurant at the atmospheric Craignair Inn—along a narrow lane in Spruce Head, about 8 miles northeast of Tenants Harbor—serves dinner four (winter) or five (peak season) nights a week. Enjoy your fresh, well-prepared seafood or meat dishes in the main dining room, in a gallery with a fireplace, or on an outdoor deck overlooking the water. **Known for:** sophisticated dinners; popular Sunday brunch; views of Wheeler's Bay and Clark Island. [$] *Average main: $30* ✉ *Craignair Inn, 5 3rd St., Spruce Head* ☎ *207/910–6622* 🌐 *www.craignair.com/maine-inn-restaurant* ⏲ *Closed Tues. and Wed. in summer; closed Mon., Tues., and Wed. in winter.* at the Craignair Inn

The Dip Net

$$ | SEAFOOD | FAMILY | You'll find the Dip Net behind the Port Clyde General Store, on a deck overlooking the harbor. Sit at a picnic table inside an enclosure or out in the sunshine and enjoy such local treats as fried oysters, lobster (of course), crab cakes, and fresh fish. **Known for:** a great summertime spot; very fresh lobster and other seafood; friendly, casual atmosphere. [$] *Average main: $18* ✉ *2 Cold Storage Rd., Port Clyde* ☎ *207/372–1112* 🌐 *www.thedipnet.co* ⏲ *Closed mid-Sept.–Memorial Day weekend.*

McLoon's Lobster Shack

$$ | SEAFOOD | FAMILY | You know that the lobster and other seafood is fresh at this quintessential shack, just east of Tenants Harbor and at the end of a scenic, winding shoreside byway—the owner's family owns the wholesale lobster company on the next wharf over, where local lobstermen tie up to deliver their catches. In addition to generously stuffed lobster rolls, the menu usually includes crab rolls, crab cakes, grilled clams, and a couple of nonseafood items. **Known for:** BYOB; views of a working harbor; Lobster Rolls Royce (with the meat of two lobsters). [$] *Average main: $20* ✉ *315 Island Rd., South Thomaston* ☎ *207/593–1382* 🌐 *www.mcloonslobster.com* ⏲ *Closed Wed. and late Sept.–late May.*

Coffee and Quick Bites

Squid Ink Coffee

$ | **CAFÉ** | Pop into this tiny café just beyond the Port Clyde General Store for a pick-me-up. Choose from excellent espresso drinks, brewed coffee and tea, and pastries. **Known for:** quick stop before hopping the boat to Monhegan Island; indoor and outdoor seating; harbor views. [$] *Average main: $5* ✉ *6 Cold Storage Rd., Port Clyde* ☎ *207/372–2088* 🌐 *www.facebook.com/SquidInkCoffeeOnTheDock* ⏲ *Closed late Sept.–late May.*

Hotels

Craignair Inn

$$$ | **B&B/INN** | Set on 4 acres overlooking Wheeler's Bay, about 8 miles northeast of Tenants Harbor, this atmospheric inn was built in 1930 as a boarding house for stonecutters working in the granite quarries on Clark Island, just across the way. **Pros:** great access to Clark Island trails and beaches; peaceful location; very good in-house restaurant. **Cons:** stairs to upper-floor rooms are steep; no TV in some rooms; small windows in water-view rooms. [$] *Rooms from: $300* ✉ *5 3rd St., Spruce Head* ☎ *207/910–6622* 🌐 *www.craignair.com* 🛏 *16 rooms* 🍴 *Free Breakfast.*

East Wind Inn

$$$ | **B&B/INN** | The main building of this charmingly old-fashioned inn dates from the 1800s—when it was built as a boatyard sail loft (where sails were made)—and is furnished with locally sourced antiques and nautical accents. **Pros:** cozy tavern that's open year-round; wonderful views of working harbor and islands; common areas include deck and wraparound porch. **Cons:** drive to shops and other restaurants; could be too quiet for some; no elevator to upstairs rooms. [$] *Rooms from: $300* ✉ *21 Mechanic St., Tenants Harbor* ☎ *207/372–6366* 🌐 *www.eastwindinn.com* 🛏 *19 rooms* 🍴 *Free Breakfast.*

Shopping

Port Clyde General Store

GENERAL STORE | **FAMILY** | Look for the green clapboard building with red trim a few steps to the right of the ferry landing. This is an old-time, honest-to-goodness general store, with wide-plank floors and an inventory that offers a little bit of everything: groceries, fresh pastries, candy, wines, liquor—even live lobsters. A great contraption makes fresh-squeezed OJ before your eyes. Outside, a sign touts the "Native Ice" for sale. The breakfast and lunch bar serves egg dishes, pancakes, sandwiches, pizzas, and smoothies. Hop on a stool, eat at a picnic table on the dock, or take your food with you. Above the store is a gallery dedicated to the art of three generations of the Wyeth family, which has long, deep connections to this area. Although you won't find any original paintings by N.C., Andrew, or Jamie here, there is a fine selection of prints, including some limited editions, and books for sale. ✉ *4 Cold Storage Rd., Port Clyde* ☎ *207/372–6543* 🌐 *www.portclydegeneralstore.com* ⏲ *Closed Jan.–May.*

🛶 Activities

★ Wyeths by Water

BOAT TOURS | This is Wyeth country, where three generations of the Wyeth family have summered and found ample inspiration for their art. On these boat tours aboard a restored, classic lobster yacht, you get to see the actual seascapes and landscapes that N.C., Andrew, and Jamie captured on canvas. Choose from three itineraries. One takes you up the St. George River to see the Olson House, setting for Andrew Wyeth's iconic "Christina's World." Another cruises past islands once owned by the Wyeths. The third travels along the eastern shore of the peninsula, which particularly inspired Andrew and Jamie. Along the way, you'll be shown how lobster traps are hauled. ✉ *4 Cold Storage Rd., Port Clyde* ☎ *207/372–6600* ⊕ *www.lindabeans-mainewyethgallery.com* ✉ *$65* ⊙ *Closed early Oct.–late May* ☞ *Board boat at dock behind Port Clyde General Store.*

Monhegan Island

East of Pemaquid Peninsula, about 10 miles offshore.

If you like the idea of a slow-paced vacation on a remote island, Monhegan is for you. What's more, if you're also an artist or an art aficionado, you might never want to leave: there's a reason this has been a haven for artists for over a century.

To get here you'll need to take a ferry. A tiny hamlet greets you at the harbor. There are no paved roads. It doesn't take long to grasp that Monhegan is the place where simple and artful living is the order of the day.

The island was known to Basque, Portuguese, and Breton fishermen well before Columbus discovered America. English fishermen spent summers catching cod here in the 1600s. About a century ago, Monhegan was discovered by some of America's finest painters—Rockwell Kent, Robert Henri, A.J. Hammond, and Edward Hopper among them—who sailed out to paint its open meadows, savage cliffs, wild ocean views, and fishermen's shacks.

In summer, the tiny village and its dirt lanes buzz with day trippers who've come to hike the island's trails, visit a few shops and artists' studios, lunch in a handful of eateries, and enjoy the unspoiled remoteness. The island has 17 miles of trails, and serenity awaits at the lighthouse atop the hill overlooking the harbor and at the high cliffs of White Head, Black Head, and Burnt Head. From these rugged headlands, you can gaze across the ocean, where the next landfall is Spain.

GETTING HERE AND AROUND

Excursion vessels transport passengers between three mainland harbors and Monhegan. The boat trip is almost as exhilarating as exploring the island itself. Be on the lookout for seals, porpoises, and perhaps even small whales. Note that visitors are not allowed to bring cars to the island, so be prepared to wander on foot.

The Port Clyde boat landing is home to Monhegan Boat Line's *Elizabeth Ann* and the *Laura B.* There are three round-trips daily mid-June through mid October, one trip daily in late fall and early spring, and three trips weekly in the winter. In season, Hardy Boat offers daily trips between New Harbor and Monhegan, while Balmy Days Cruises makes crossings from Boothbay Harbor. All three companies also offer a variety of regional sightseeing cruises.

CONTACTS Balmy Days Cruises. ✉ *42 Commercial St., Pier 8, Boothbay Harbor* ☎ *207/633–2284* ⊕ *www.balmydayscruises.com.* **Hardy Boat Cruises.** ✉ *129 State Rte. 32, New Harbor* ☎ *207/677–2026* ⊕ *hardyboat.com.* **Monhegan Boat Line.** ✉ *880 Port Clyde Rd., Port Clyde* ☎ *207/372–8848* ⊕ *www.monheganboat.com.*

Did You Know?

Monhegan Island's rugged cliffs of White Head, Black Head, and Burnt Head have amazing views across the ocean; some say you can see Spain on a very clear day.

◉ Sights

★ Monhegan Brewing Company

BREWERY | There's something to be said for enjoying a cold beer after a long hike. You can slake your thirst at a seasonal tap "room" (seating is actually outdoors beneath umbrellas and tents) of this tiny brewery owned by a local lobstering family. Options could include Crow's Nest IPA, Balmy Days Citra Kölsch, or Mad Cow Milk Stout. There might also be icy cold root beer, and you can get lunch to go at the on-site Bait Bag food trailer. ☒ *1 Boody La., Monhegan* ☎ *297/596–0011* ⊕ *monheganbrewing.com* ☉ *Closed mid-Oct.–late May.*

Monhegan Island Light

LIGHTHOUSE | FAMILY | Getting a close-up look at this squat stone lighthouse, which was automated in 1959, requires a ½-mile, slightly steep uphill walk from the island's ferry dock. The tower is open sporadically throughout the summer for short tours. In the former keeper's quarters, the small Monhegan Museum of Art & History provides a peek into island life past and present. It also exhibits works by artists with a connection to this special place. ☒ *Lighthouse Hill Rd., ½ mile east of dock, Monhegan* ☎ *207/596–7003* ⊕ *monheganmuseum.org* 🍽 *$10 (museum)* ☉ *Closed Oct.–late June.*

⑪ Restaurants

★ Fish House Market

$$ | SEAFOOD | Although everything served at this seafood shack and market beside Fish Beach is delicious and simply prepared, the crab roll—a large, split-top roll buttered and griddled and stuffed with fresh, sweet, mayo-tossed crabmeat—may just be the best on the Maine coast. Order at the window, carry your tray to a picnic table inches from the water, and lap up the view of lobster boats in the harbor. **Known for:** BYOB; outstanding fish chowder; lovely waterside location. 🛇 *Average main: $18* ☒ *98 Fish Beach La., Monhegan* ☎ *207/594–8368* ⊕ *www.facebook.com/fishhousemonhegan* ☉ *Closed late Sept.–late May.*

★ The Island Inn

$$$ | AMERICAN | FAMILY | The dining room at Monhegan's iconic Island Inn serves breakfast and dinner to the public as well as to guests. The breakfast menu includes eggs, pancakes, and granola. **Known for:** harbor views; well-prepared entrées featuring fresh Maine seafood; dishes for meat lovers and vegetarians, too. 🛇 *Average main: $35* ☒ *1 Ocean Ave., Monhegan* ☎ *207/596–0371* ⊕ *www.islandinnmonhegan.com* ☉ *Closed mid-Oct.–late May.*

☕ Coffee and Quick Bites

The Barnacle

$ | AMERICAN | On the wharf a few steps from the boat landing, The Barnacle serves espresso and a selection of coffees from Monhegan Coffee Roasters along with baked goods such as scones and brownies, and ice cream. For lunch, choose from prepared sandwiches, chowders, and salads, which you can eat at a picnic table or take with you. **Known for:** a place to wait for the ferry; eat outdoors or grab-and-go; locally roasted coffee. 🛇 *Average main: $15* ☒ *Monhegan Boat Landing, wharf, Monhegan* ☎ *207/596–0371* ⊕ *www.islandinnmonhegan.com/the-barnacle* ☉ *Closed mid-Oct.–late May.*

Hotels

★ The Island Inn

$$$ | B&B/INN | Perched on a bluff above the boat landing, this landmark summer hotel recalls an era when guests arrived with steamer trunks for extended island stays. **Pros:** great food; long porch with rocking chairs and great views; relaxing atmosphere. **Cons:** books up quickly (early reservations are essential); a few rooms share 4 hallway bathrooms; no a/c, no TVs in rooms, and limited Internet access. [$] *Rooms from: $300* ✉ *1 Ocean Ave., Monhegan* ☎ *207/596–0371* 🌐 *www.islandinnmonhegan.com* 🕒 *Closed mid-Oct.–late May* 🛏 *32 rooms* 🍴 *Free Breakfast* ☞ *Begins accepting reservations in Jan. for upcoming summer.*

Shining Sails

$$ | B&B/INN | The owners of this intimate B&B are friendly, the airy rooms—most with private, ocean-view decks—are kept cheery with fresh flowers, and the common room is stocked with games and has a wood stove. **Pros:** water views; in the middle of the village; choice of B&B, efficiency apartment, or rental cottages. **Cons:** not on the water; may be too cozy for some; furnishings are a bit dated. [$] *Rooms from: $225* ✉ *43 Monhegan Ave., Monhegan* ☎ *207/596–0041* 🌐 *www.shiningsails.com* 🛏 *11 rooms* 🍴 *Free Breakfast.*

Activities

***Balmy Days II* Sightseeing Cruise**

BOAT TOURS | FAMILY | The *Balmy Days II*, the excursion vessel that transports visitors between Monhegan Island and Boothbay Harbor, offers a 30-minute cruise all the way around the island every afternoon at 2, before returning to the mainland. (Anyone can take the tour, not just Boothbay Harbor–bound passengers.) The cost is just $5 cash, collected on board. It's a great way to learn a little island history while viewing its dramatic cliffs from the water. ✉ *Monhegan Boat Landing, Monhegan* ☎ *207/633–2284* 🌐 *www.balmydayscruises.com* 🎟 *$5* 🕒 *Close early Oct.–early June.*

Chapter 6

PENOBSCOT BAY

6

Updated by
Mimi Steadman

◉ Sights	🍴 Restaurants	🛏 Hotels	🛍 Shopping	🇹 Nightlife
★★★★★	★★★★★	★★★★★	★★★★★	★★★☆☆

WELCOME TO PENOBSCOT BAY

TOP REASONS TO GO

★ **Go windjamming:** Book a cruise of a few hours or a few days on a storied schooner sailing from Rockland and Camden.

★ **Historic sites:** Visit centuries-old lighthouses whose beacons still shine, venture into Bucksport's eerie, mid-1800s Fort Knox (not the one with all the gold), or stay at B&Bs in fine old mansions.

★ **Palate pleasers:** Authentic Maine "Shore Dinner" starring just-caught lobster, sweet and juicy lobster rolls, or masterfully prepared contemporary cuisine.

★ **Museum musts:** Rockland's Farnsworth Art Museum has works by prominent artists with ties to Maine; roll back time at the Owls Head Transportation Museum; and learn about Maine's proud maritime history at Searsport's Penobscot Marine Museum.

★ **Tower in the sky:** Near Bucksport, ascend 420 feet to the Penobscot Narrows Bridge Observatory, the world's highest public bridge observatory.

The shores of Penobscot Bay offer a distillation of all that is wonderful about the Maine Coast. There are rugged headlands, hidden harbors, sandy pocket beaches, gentle mountains, wildlife-filled woodlands, world-class boating waters, and unspoiled islands. Here you'll find the busy but delightful tourist destinations of Rockland and Camden, plus lovely, under-the-radar communities such as Lincolnville and Bucksport. Spend time in the must-visit spots—there's a good reason they're must-visits—but also head off the beaten path to discover the true essence of Maine in the quiet corners of this region.

1 **Rockland.** Old-fashioned Main Street with on-point restaurants, shops, and galleries alongside a historic windjammer homeport.

2 **Vinalhaven.** An island of tranquility perfect for hikers, kayakers, and those who want to jump into an old quarry swimming hole.

3 **Rockport.** Tucked between Rockland and Camden, with a couple of destination restaurants.

4 **Camden.** Shops, boat trips, charming B&Bs, and restaurants, all amid mountain-and-sea scenery overload.

5 **Lincolnville.** Tiny beach town with family-friendly sands.

6 **Islesboro.** A quiet island escape is just a 20-minute boat ride from Lincolnville.

7 **Belfast.** Artsy harbor town with terrific shopping and dining.

8 **Searsport.** Elegant old ship captains' homes and an excellent small museum showcasing the town's maritime heritage.

9 **Bucksport.** A reborn old mill town with a spectacular bridge-top observatory.

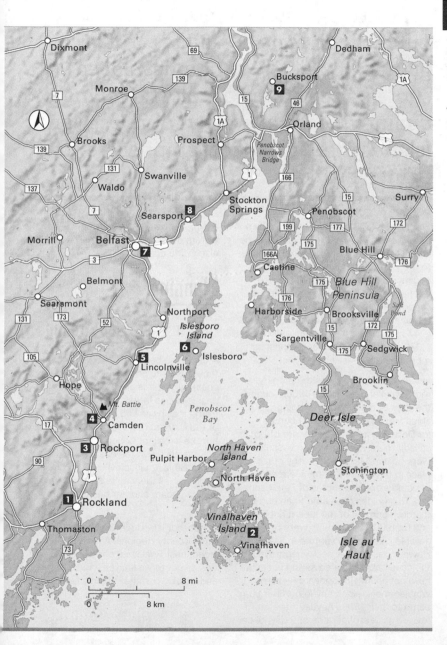

Few could deny that Penobscot Bay is one of Maine's most dramatically beautiful regions. Its more than 1,000 miles of coastline are made up of rocky granite boulders, often undeveloped shores, a sprinkling of colorful towns and quaint villages, and views of the sea and islands that are a photographer's (and painter's) dream.

Penobscot Bay stretches 37 miles from Port Clyde in the west to Stonington, the little fishing village at the tip of Deer Isle, to the east. The northern edge of the bay begins near Stockton Springs, where the Penobscot River, New England's second-largest river system, ends, and terminates in the Gulf of Maine, where it is 47 miles wide. It covers an estimated 1,070 square miles and encompasses more than 1,800 islands.

Initially, shipbuilding was the primary moneymaker here. In the 1800s, during the days of the great oceangoing tall ships and coasting cargo schooners (or Down Easters, as they were often called), more wooden sailing vessels were built in Maine than in any other place in the country. Many were constructed along the shores of Penobscot Bay. This golden age came to an end with the development of the steam engine, and by 1900, sailing ships were no longer a viable commercial venture in Maine. However, as you will see when traveling the coast, old-fashioned sailing vessels have not entirely disappeared—some windjammers, albeit tiny in number compared to their 1800s heyday, have been revived as passenger boats. Today, once

again, there are more tall ships plying the waters of Penobscot Bay than anywhere else in the country.

Planning

Getting Here and Around

A car is the best way to explore this area, though seeing some of Penobscot Bay's coast by water is also a very appealing possibility, as ferries travel back and forth from Lincolnville and Rockland to some of the islands. There is no train service, but the excellent Concord Coach Lines bus travels down the coast through Searsport, Belfast, Lincolnville, Camden, and Rockland, all the way to Portland. There, you can board another bus to Boston.

AIR
Penobscot Island Air, which flies out of Knox County Regional Airport in Owls Head, near Rockland, offers an alternate way to get to Vinalhaven, North Haven, and Islesboro, rather than by ferry.

AIRPORT Bangor International Airport.
(BGR) ⊠ 287 Godfrey Blvd., Bangor
☎ 207/992–4600 ⊕ www.flybangor.com.

AIRLINES Penobscot Island Air. ⊠ Knox
County Regional Airport, 21 Terminal La.,
Owls Head ☎ 207/596–7500 ⊕ www.
penobscotislandair.net.

BICYCLE

The most popular bike route on Maine's
Penobscot Bay is historic U.S. 1. But note
that for most of it, this is a two-lane highway, and tourists naturally are gawking
at the sights. Most of the highway does
have a designated bike lane—but you still
need to be very careful.

BOAT

Ferries travel back and forth from Lincolnville and Rockland to islands such as
Islesboro and Vinalhaven, and romantic
windjammer cruises sail from Camden
and Rockland along the coast to various
island coves and harbors.

CONTACTS Maine State Ferry Service. ⊠ 45
Granville Rd., Bass Harbor ☎ 207/244–
3254 ⊕ www.maine.gov/mdot/ferry.

BUS

Concord Coach Lines, an excellent bus
service that even shows movies, runs
two buses a day from the University of
Maine, at Orono, through Bangor, and
then down the coast through Searsport,
Belfast, Lincolnville, Camden, and
Rockland all the way to Boston's Logan
International Airport.

CONTACTS Concord Coach Lines.
⊠ Thompsons Point Rd., Portland
☎ 800/639–3317 ⊕ www.concordcoach-
lines.com.

CAR

The only route for exploring this region
is the historic two-lane U.S. 1, which
winds all the way along Penobscot Bay,
from Rockland to Bucksport and farther.
Although the distance from Rockland to
Bucksport is only 45 miles, the going is
slow; U.S. 1 is an old highway, and the
summer months bring heavily congested

traffic. There are some impressive coastal
views along the drive, but don't expect
to see the ocean continuously. The water
is blocked for a good part of the way by
woods, which are beautiful in their own
right. Driving the entire distance without
stopping should take about two hours,
but you'll probably want to stop along the
way and spend a day or two in some of
the more colorful towns.

If you're coming up I-95 to begin your
coastal tour of the Penobscot Bay area,
take the Augusta exit and follow signs to
take Route 3 (to Belfast) or Route 17 (to
Rockport and Rockland) and U.S. 1.

In winter the Maine Department of
Transportation keeps most major roads
plowed and graveled. However, you
should always drive with caution in
snowy conditions.

Hotels

Large hotels are few and far between
in this region; boutique hotels, motels,
B&Bs, AirB&Bs, and campgrounds are
more the norm. You'l find a range of
levels, from modest accommodations to
luxurious establishments with pampering
service and fine amenities. Many offer
delightful seaside locations. A good share
of the B&Bs are in historic Federal or
Colonial-style mansions that date back to
the mid-1800s and are filled with period
antiques.

Please note that while many of the smaller accommodations and B&Bs—as well
as some of the restaurants and museums—are not air-conditioned, ocean
breezes usually keep things amply cool.

If you're planning to come between
mid-May and mid-October, reservations
are recommended at least a month in
advance. If you have mobility concerns,
call ahead to confirm that a property can
accommodate you. Many B&Bs along the
Maine Coast do not have ramps.

Restaurants

Seafood is the name of the game along Penobscot Bay. "Lobstah" is, of course, a staple on most menus, and it comes cooked in myriad ways: whole lobster dinners (boiled or steamed in the shell), baked stuffed lobster, lazy man's lobster, broiled lobster tails, fried lobster, lobster stew, and lobster rolls. Local crabmeat, steamer clams, and scallops are other delectable specialties. Sweet, briny Maine-cultivated oysters have in recent years become a huge draw, and you'll find them on many menus, offered both on the half shell and cooked in a variety of ways.

Dining establishments are generally informal, and casual dress is almost always acceptable. Most restaurants are open for lunch and dinner, and some are open for breakfast. From June through August, reservations are always a good idea, particularly at the more celebrated or smaller restaurants.

For a truly authentic Maine experience, try the lobster pounds in Lincolnville, Belfast, and Spruce Head. Enjoy your meal right beside the water, or take home live lobsters or other fresh seafood to cook on your own.

HOTEL AND RESTAURANT PRICES

Restaurant and hotel reviews have been shortened. For full information, visit Fodors.com. Hotel prices in the reviews are the lowest cost of a standard double room in high season. Restaurant prices in the reviews are the average cost of a main course at dinner, or if dinner is not served, at lunch.

What It Costs In U.S. Dollars

	$	$$	$$$	$$$$
RESTAURANTS				
	under $18	$18–$24	$25–$35	over $35
HOTELS				
	under $200	$200–$299	$300–$399	over $400

Visitor Information

The Belfast Area Chamber of Commerce is the best source for information about lodging, dining, and activities in Belfast and surrounding towns, including Lincolnville, Northport, Searsport, and Stockton Springs.

CONTACTS Belfast Area Chamber of Commerce. ⊠ *14 Main St., Belfast* ☏ *207/338–5900* ⊕ *belfastmaine.org.* **Maine Windjammer Association.** ⊠ *Rockland* ☏ *800/807–9463* ⊕ *www.sailmainecoast.com.* **Penobscot Bay Regional Chamber of Commerce.** ⊠ *Visitor Center, 2 Public Landing, Camden* ☏ *207/236–4404, 800/562–2529* ⊕ *www.camdenrockland.com.*

When to Go

The busy season begins to ramp up in late May and continues through mid-October; high season is July, August, and September. Crowds are a bit thinner just before schools close in mid-June and just after they open in early September (except during fall foliage, when hordes of leaf peepers arrive, especially on the weekends). Though many residents enjoy the long, cold winter, it is not a busy tourist time on the coast. The Camden Snow Bowl—with its 11 downhill ski trails, a friendly, low-key atmosphere, and panoramic views of Penobscot Bay

Windjammer Excursions

Nothing defines the Penobscot Bay area better than its fleet of historic windjammers, and a sailing trip on one of these beauties, whether for just a few hours or a few days, is an unforgettable experience. Originally designed to carry cargo and built along the East Coast in the 19th and early 20th centuries, the wooden-hulled vessels once plied coastal waters in such trades as lumbering, granite, fishing, and oystering. Members of today's windjammer fleet range from as small as 46 feet, accommodating six passengers (plus a couple of crew members), to more than 130 feet, carrying 30 passengers.

In the past few years, nearly all of the windjammers have been passed on to new, young captain-owners who bring fresh energy as well as solid qualifications to their stewardship of these beloved tall ships.

On a windjammer excursion, passengers are welcome to participate in on-board tasks, be it helping to hoist a sail or taking a turn at the wheel. Exceptional meals help keep them fueled for the effort.

During the Camden Windjammer Festival (www.facebook.com/WindjammerFestival), held Labor Day weekend, crowds gather to watch the region's fleet sail into the harbor, and most boats are open for tours. The schooner-crew talent show later in the weekend is a bit more irreverent than the majestic arrival ceremony.

A windjammer cruise gives you a chance to soak up Maine's dramatic coast from the water. Overnight cruises can run anywhere from two to eight days; day trips—usually just a couple of hours long—feature a tour of the harbor and some lighthouse and wildlife sightseeing. Prices depend on trip length; overnight cruises include all meals. Trips leave from Camden, Rockland, and Rockport. You can find information on the fleets by visiting the individual vessels' websites or by contacting the Penobscot Bay Regional Chamber of Commerce (⊕ *amdenrockland.com*), the Maine Windjammer Association (⊕ *www.mainewindjammercruises.com*), or Maine Windjammer Cruises (⊕ *www.sailmainecoast.com*).

from atop the mountain—entices visitors in the winter months. The U.S. National Toboggan Championships weekend, which takes place at the Snow Bowl in February, is a popular draw for visitors. While communities remain vibrant throughout the winter, and most businesses remain open year-round, some motels, bed-and-breakfasts, restaurants, and other businesses close for at least part of the winter.

Rockland

25 miles north of Damariscotta via U.S. 1.

This town is considered the gateway to Penobscot Bay and is the first stop on U.S. 1 offering a glimpse of the often-sparkling and island-dotted blue bay. Though previously considered by visitors to be a place to pass through on the way to places like Camden, Rockland now gets lots of attention on its own. This is thanks to a great selection of small but excellent restaurants; a terrific Main Street lineup of shops and galleries;

Great Itineraries

If You Have 3 Days

On the morning of your first day, visit the Farnsworth Museum in Rockland with its wonderful collection of paintings by the Wyeth family. Then drive up to Camden, one of the most charming towns along the coast, and take a two-hour excursion on a schooner or sightseeing powerboat. Be sure to drive or walk to the top of Mt. Battie (in Camden Hills State Park) and take in sweeping views of Penobscot Bay. Consider staying at one of a handful of small hotels in the heart of the downtown or beside the harbor, or at one of many delightful, upmarket B&Bs.

On Day 2 drive on to Belfast, where you can wander around the downtown area, walk down to the harbor, and have a seafood lunch beside the harbor. In the afternoon, drive north on U.S. 1 to Searsport to visit the Penobscot Marine Museum or browse the antique shops and flea markets that flank the road. Plan on spending the night at a B&B. Good choices for dining are the Homeport Tavern, Rio's Spiked Cafe, Hey Sailor, and Anglers.

On Day 3 continue north on U.S. 1 to Bucksport to explore historic Fort Knox and ascend the elevator to the highest bridge observatory tower in America, atop the Penobscot Narrows Bridge. Have dinner at McLeod's restaurant or the Friar's Brewhouse Taproom.

If You Have 5 Days

Begin your itinerary in Rockland. Start with a morning visit to the Farnsworth Museum. Then head to Rockland's Maine State Ferry Terminal. Take the ferry (with your car) to Vinalhaven Island and spend the day exploring and watching the lobster boats and fishermen down by the harbor. Stay overnight at the Tidewater Motel (make advance reservations).

On Day 2 take the ferry back to Rockland and drive north to Camden, where you can explore the shops and galleries, try the excellent restaurants, and stay the night in a charming B&B. Spend your third day and night aboard a windjammer (arrange this ahead of time).

On your fourth day, drive to Belfast, where you can walk down the colorful main street, shop, and explore the harbor. For an authentic Maine dinner, take U.S. 1 across the bridge on the way to Searsport and turn right on Mitchell Avenue to reach Young's Lobster Pound. Stay overnight at the Belfast Harbor Inn nearby. On your last day, drive to Searsport and spend the morning exploring the Penobscot Marine Museum with its wonderful exhibits on the history of Penobscot Bay.

the renowned Farnsworth Art Museum and the Center for Maine Contemporary Art; and several popular summer festivals. Despite all of these developments, Rockland continues to be a fishing port and the commercial hub of this coastal area.

The best place to view Rockland's windjammers as they sail in and out of the harbor is the mile-long granite breakwater that protects Rockland Harbor. To get there, from U.S. 1, head east on Waldo Avenue and then right on Samoset Road; follow this short road to its end.

The mile-long walk to the Rockland Breakwater Light has been described as a walk into the sea without wet feet.

GETTING HERE AND AROUND

U.S. 1 runs along Main Street here. It is one way (headed north) as it goes through downtown. U.S. 1A curves through the residential neighborhood just west of the business district, offering a southbound route as well as a faster route if you are just passing through in either direction.

The Concord Coach Lines bus that runs along the coast stops in Rockland.

Ferries to the islands of Vinalhaven, North Haven, and Matinicus leave from the ferry terminal at the northern end of Main Street.

VISITOR INFORMATION

CONTACTS Penobscot Bay Area Chamber of Commerce. ✉ *Rockland* ☎ *207/596–0376, 800/562–2529* ⊕ *www.camdenrockland. com.*

WHEN TO GO

Late summer is an ideal time to visit Rockland—if you don't mind the crowds. The Maine Lobster Festival highlights the calendar in August. September is a beautiful month, with bright, clear skies and cooling breezes. In addition, it may be easier than it is at the height of summer to book a reservation at the many popular restaurants.

March is a dreary month. The skies are often gray, and it isn't too late in the season for snow. Some restaurants and shops that close in winter may not yet be open. But if you enjoy solitude, this is a great time for walking the shore, watching the waves, and searching for intriguing finds brought ashore by winter storms.

FESTIVALS AND EVENTS

Maine Lobster Festival

FESTIVALS | FAMILY | Rockland's annual Maine Lobster Festival, held in early August, is the region's largest annual event. About 10 tons of lobsters are steamed in a huge lobster cooker—you have to see it to believe it. The festival, held in Harbor Park, includes a parade, live entertainment, food booths, and, of course, the crowning of the Maine Sea Goddess. ✉ *Harbor Park, Main St., south*

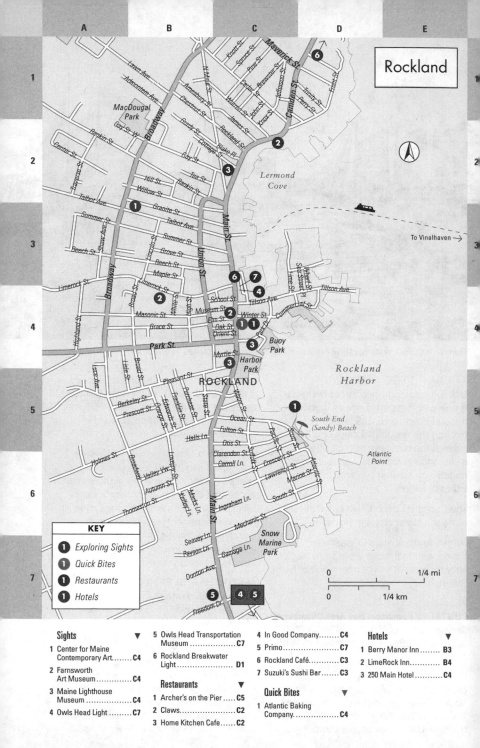

Rockland

KEY
- 🔵 Exploring Sights
- 🔵 Quick Bites
- 🔵 Restaurants
- 🔵 Hotels

Sights ▼
1 Center for Maine
  Contemporary Art........**C4**
2 Farnsworth
  Art Museum.............**C4**
3 Maine Lighthouse
  Museum **C4**
4 Owls Head Light **C7**
5 Owls Head Transportation
  Museum **C7**
6 Rockland Breakwater
  Light **D1**

Restaurants ▼
1 Archer's on the Pier **C5**
2 Claws....................**C2**
3 Home Kitchen Cafe......**C2**
4 In Good Company........**C4**
5 Primo....................**C7**
6 Rockland Café...........**C3**
7 Suzuki's Sushi Bar.......**C3**

Quick Bites ▼
1 Atlantic Baking
  Company.................**C4**

Hotels ▼
1 Berry Manor Inn **B3**
2 LimeRock Inn............**B4**
3 250 Main Hotel **C4**

of U.S. 1, Rockland ☎ 800/576–7512 ⊕ www.mainelobsterfestival.com.

North Atlantic Blues Festival

FESTIVALS | FAMILY | About a dozen well-known musicians gather for the North Atlantic Blues Festival, a two-day affair held the first or second full weekend after July 4. The show officially takes place at the public landing on Rockland Harbor Park, but it also includes a "club crawl" through downtown Rockland on Saturday night. Admission to the festival is $45 at the gate, $75 for a weekend pass. ⊠ *Public Landing, 275 Main St., Rockland* ☎ *207/596–6055* ⊕ *www. northatlanticbluesfestival.com.*

Sights

★ Center for Maine Contemporary Art

ART MUSEUM | The impressive Center for Maine Contemporary Art sprang from a 50-year legacy that originated in makeshift exhibitions in barns and a potato-barrel storage loft before settling Into a small, antique fire house in Rockport. Since 2016, this striking, light-filled building designed by Toshiko Mori has allowed the museum to showcase modern works by accomplished artists with a Maine connection in a space that befits the quality of the art. Expect envelope-pushing, changing exhibitions and public programs. Visitors are invited to drop into the museum's ArtLab to gain greater insight into current exhibitions by trying their own hand at making art inspired by the works on display. ArtLab is open weekends in summer; daily the rest of the year. ⊠ *21 Winter St., Rockland* ☎ *207/701–5005* ⊕ *cmcanow.org* ⌑ *$8.*

★ Farnsworth Art Museum

ART MUSEUM | FAMILY | One of the most highly regarded small museums in the country, the Farnsworth's collection is largely devoted to works by three generations of the famous Wyeth family, who have spent summers on the Maine Coast for a century. N.C. Wyeth was an accomplished illustrator whose works were featured in many turn-of-the-20th-century adventure books; his son Andrew was one of the country's best-known and-loved painters; and Andrew's son Jamie is an accomplished painter in his own right. Galleries in the main building always display some of Andrew Wyeth's works, such as *The Patriot, Witchcraft,* and *Turkey Pond.* Across the street, the Wyeth Center, in a former church, exhibits art by Andrew's father and son. The museum's collection also includes works by such lauded, Maine-connected artists as Fitz Henry Lane, George Bellows, Winslow Homer, Edward Hopper, Louise Nevelson, and Rockwell Kent. Changing exhlbits are shown in the Jamien Morehouse Wing.

Just across the garden from the museum, the Farnsworth Homestead, the handsome, circa-1850 Greek Revival home of the museum's original benefactor, retains its original lavish Victorian furnishings and is open late June–mid-October.

In Cushing, a village on the St. George River about 10 miles south of Thomaston (a half-hour drive from Rockland), the museum operates the Olson House. The large, weathered-shingle structure was the home of Christina Olson and her brother, Alvarez, who were good friends of Andrew Wyeth. He depicted them and their home in numerous works, including his famous painting *Christina's World.* It is open spring through fall. ⊠ *16 Museum St., Rockland* ☎ *207/596–6457* ⊕ *www. farnsworthmuseum.org* ⌑ *$15* ⊙ *Closed Tues. Nov.–Dec.; closed Mon. and Tues. Jan.–May; Wyeth Center closed Jan.–May.*

Maine Lighthouse Museum

HISTORY MUSEUM | FAMILY | The lighthouse museum has more than 25 Fresnel lighthouse lenses, as well as what's said to be the nation's largest collection of lighthouse and life-saving artifacts, and Coast Guard memorabilia. Permanent

Built in 1852, Owls Head Light sits on an 80-foot promontory at the southern entrance to Rockland harbor with amazing views of Penobscot Bay.

exhibits spotlight topics like lighthouse heroines—women who manned the lights when the keepers couldn't—and lightships. ⊠ *1 Park Dr., Rockland* ☎ *207/594–3301* ⊕ *www.mainelighthousemuseum.org* ✉ *$10.*

Owls Head Light

LIGHTHOUSE | FAMILY | Perched on an 80-foot promontory at the southern entrance to Rockland harbor, this white-brick tower built in 1852 provides broad views of Penobscot Bay. When volunteers are available, visitors may climb the tower to the small, glass-enclosed space at the top that houses the Fresnel lens, installed in 1856. In the 1930s, a light keeper's springer spaniel learned to pull the rope to ring the fog bell, and is said to have thereby saved vessels entering the harbor in poor visibility. A stone near the bell marks the dog's grave. In the small museum and gift shop, you can pick up a copy of a children's book that tells the story. The American Lighthouse Foundation is headquartered in the keeper's house. ⊠ *186 Lighthouse Rd.,*

Owls Head ✛ *5.6 miles southeast of downtown Rockland* ☎ *207/594-4174* ⊕ *www.lighthousefoundation.org* ✉ *$3 suggested donation* ⊙ *Closed Tues. and late Oct.–mid-May.*

Owls Head Transportation Museum

TRANSPORTATION | FAMILY | If you're fascinated by machines that move on wheels or wings, don't miss this impressive museum. You'll find more than 150 restored vintage automobiles, bicycles, motorcycles, and planes, as well as many related artifacts. The best part about this collection is that most of the vehicles are in operating condition, which means you may see them rolling along or flying overhead. ⊠ *117 Museum St., Owls Head* ✛ *3½ miles south of downtown Rockland via Rte. 73* ☎ *207/594-4418* ⊕ *www. owlshead.org* ✉ *$14.*

★ Rockland Breakwater Light

LIGHTHOUSE | FAMILY | First came the Rockland Breakwater, built in 1900 to protect ships in the harbor and structures on the shore from storm surge. But the breakwater itself was a navigational hazard, so the

25-foot-tall lighthouse was added to its far end in 1902. The mile-long breakwater offers an irresistible hike that's sometimes described as a walk into the sea without wet feet. Wear sensible shoes, though, and watch your step: there are gaps between the uneven granite blocks just waiting to trip you up. Stand beside the lighthouse for terrific views of passing windjammers and other marine traffic. (The lighthouse is not open to the public.)

To get to the landward end of the breakwater, go north on U.S. 1, turn right on Waldo Avenue, and right again on Samoset Road; go to the end of this short road. ⊠ *Rockland Breakwater Lighthouse, off Samoset Rd., Rockland* ⊕ *www.rocklandharborlights.org.*

Beaches

Birch Point Beach State Park
BEACH | FAMILY | Located near the mouth of West Penobscot Bay, this crescent-shape beach is well-sheltered from the wind and tends to have a mild surf well-suited to swimming and tidepooling. **Amenities:** parking (fee). **Best for:** swimming; walking. ⊠ *Birch Point Beach Rd., Owls Head* ✚ *10 miles south of downtown Rockland via Rte. 73* ☎ *207/941–4014* ⊕ *www.maine.gov.*

Restaurants

★ Archer's on the Pier
$$$ | SEAFOOD | FAMILY | Standing on the edge of the harbor, with dining decks on three sides, Archer's is the prime spot in Rockland for dining with a view—even when the weather keeps you indoors, there are plenty of windows. The large menu is heavy on traditional preparations of fresh, local seafood—including old-fashioned haddock cakes—but also includes plenty of contemporary dishes. **Known for:** welcoming atmosphere; great menu; broad harborside views. Ⓢ *Average main: $30* ⊠ *58 Ocean St., Rockland*

☎ *207/594–2435* ⊕ *www.archersonthepier.com* ⊙ *Closed Sun.*

Claws
$$$ | SEAFOOD | FAMILY | Set right beside the road at the northern end of town, this lobster shack gets consistently enthusiastic reviews—many say the overstuffed lobster roll is one of the best. The large menu includes all the usual suspects plus a great selection of "snacky things" and entrées, and even a taco bar—butter-poached lobster tacos, anyone? **Known for:** wild Maine blueberry shortcake; lobster rolls stuffed with a pound of meat; award-winning lobster bisque. Ⓢ *Average main: $25* ⊠ *743 Main St., Rockland* ☎ *207/596–5600* ⊕ *www.clawsrocklandmaine.com.*

Home Kitchen Cafe
$ | AMERICAN | FAMILY | There's a decidedly Mexican influence at this popular place, with breakfast choices including migas, huevos rancheros, and a burrito, and a list of tacos highlighted on the lunch menu. You'll also find a little Asian influence in the breakfast fried rice and a banh mi, as well as plenty of good old American dishes. **Known for:** just-baked sticky buns and "sinny" buns; lots of Mexican dishes; everything is housemade. Ⓢ *Average main: $13* ⊠ *650 Main St., Rockland* ☎ *207/596–2449* ⊕ *www.homekitchencafe.com* ⊙ *Closed Tues.*

★ In Good Company
$$$ | MODERN AMERICAN | As the name suggests, this is an excellent spot to slow down and catch up with good friends over a bottle of wine while savoring small, internationally flavored plates or a full meal. The creative blend of textures and flavors that comes out of the kitchen is exceptional. **Known for:** outside dining in summer; excellent wine pairings; pared-down aesthetic with a focus on the food. Ⓢ *Average main: $30* ⊠ *415 Maine St., Rockland* ☎ *207/593–9110* ⊕ *www.ingoodcompanymaine.com.*

★ Primo

$$$$ | MEDITERRANEAN | Chef Melissa Kelly has twice won the James Beard Best Chef: Northeast, and she and her world-class restaurant have been written up in such magazines as *Gourmet, Bon Appétit,* and *O*. Named for the chef-owner's Italian grandfather, Primo serves masterfully prepared pasta, fresh seafood, and local meats. **Known for:** house-made pasta; fresh Maine ingredients with Mediterranean influences; consistently excellent; $1 oysters every Sunday. [$] *Average main: $38* ✉ *2 N. Main St., Rockland* ☎ *207/596–0770* 🌐 *www.primorestaurant.com* 🕒 *Closed Tues.*

Rockland Café

$ | DINER | FAMILY | Famous for the size of its breakfasts—don't pass up the lobster or fish-cake Benedict—Rockland Café has been a local favorite for decades. The large menu includes plenty of lunch and dinner choices from the excellent clam, fish, and seafood chowder to fried haddock, clams, shrimp, and scallops or lobster, clam, shrimp, and scallop rolls. **Known for:** lots of traditional seafood dishes; classic liver and onions; lively place where locals come to catch up. [$] *Average main: $12* ✉ *441 Main St., Rockland* ☎ *207/596–7556* 🌐 *www.rocklandcafe.com.*

★ Suzuki's Sushi Bar

$$$ | SUSHI | Trained at the Tokyo Sushi Academy, Keiko Suzuki is an artist when it comes to preparing and presenting sushi—everything is almost too beautiful to eat. The fish is sweet and ultrafresh, and nothing on the menu is fried. **Known for:** authentic sushi with Keiko's creative touches; superfresh fish; beautiful presentations. [$] *Average main: $30* ✉ *419 Main St., Rockland* ☎ *207/596–7447* 🌐 *www.suzukisushi.com* 🕒 *Closed Sun.–Tues.*

Coffee and Quick Bites

★ Atlantic Baking Company

$ | AMERICAN | FAMILY | Classic European and American breads such as batards, baguettes, ciabatta, focaccia, sourdough boules, and rolls come out of French ovens every morning at this popular little spot. The cases are also filled with just-baked croissants, scones, muffins, cookies, and more. **Known for:** French macarons; apricot pistachio oat cookies; classic sourdough. [$] *Average main: $5* ✉ *351 Main St., Rockland* ☎ *207/596–0505* 🌐 *atlanticbakingco.com* 🕒 *Closed Sun.*

Hotels

Berry Manor Inn

$$$ | B&B/INN | Originally the residence of Rockland merchant Charles H. Berry, this 1898 shingle-style B&B sits in Rockland's National Historic District. **Pros:** guest pantry stocked with drinks, sweets, and treats—there's always pie; 10-minute walk to downtown and the harbor; some rooms can be combined to create two-room suites. **Cons:** view limited to gardens; somewhat fussy decor consistent with Victorian-era property; not pet-friendly. [$] *Rooms from: $350* ✉ *81 Talbot Ave., Rockland* ☎ *207/596–7696, 800/774–5692* 🌐 *www.berrymanorinn.com* 🛏 *18 rooms* 🍴 *Free Breakfast.*

LimeRock Inn

$$ | B&B/INN | Built in 1892 as a private home, the turreted LimeRock is perfectly located in Rockland's National Historic District. **Pros:** all rooms have TVs and DVD players; large in-town lot with gazebo; within easy walking distance of the Farnsworth Museum and many restaurants. **Cons:** not on the water; sometimes booked for weddings; not pet-friendly. [$] *Rooms from: $280* ✉ *96 Limerock St., Rockland* ☎ *207/594–2257, 800/546–3762* 🌐 *www.limerockinn.com* 🛏 *8 rooms* 🍴 *Free Breakfast.*

★ **250 Main Hotel**

$$$$ | **HOTEL** | Finely crafted by local shipwrights, this jazzy little boutique hotel is filled with stylish and colorful mid-century-modern design. **Pros:** heated bathroom floors; complimentary afternoon wine-and-cheese hour; walk to shops and restaurants. **Cons:** no pool; some noise from the street and from the harbor in the morning; parking (free) is across the street and down the hill. $ *Rooms from: $450 ✉ 250 Main St., Rockland ☎ 207/594–5994 ⊕ 250mainhotel.com ⇨ 26 rooms ⦿ Free Breakfast.*

 Performing Arts

The Strand Theatre

ARTS CENTERS | FAMILY | Originally built in 1923, The Strand was once only a movie theater, but it has evolved into an arts center hosting not only first-run and indy movies, but also live music, theater, simulcasts, and other events. Its interior has been fully renovated and its systems updated and modernized. The theater is centrally located on Main Street. Visit the website for a complete schedule. ✉ *345 Main St., Rockland ☎ 207/594–0070 ⊕ www.rocklandstrand.com.*

🛍 Shopping

ART AND ANTIQUES

★ **Archipelago**

CRAFTS | Run by the Island Institute, this inviting shop showcases an array of fine creations by Maine artists and artisans. On display are wooden goods, jewelry, soaps, books, housewares, clothing, fine art, and more. ✉ *386 Main St., Rockland ☎ 207/596–0701 ⊕ www.thearchipelago. net ⦿ Closed Sun.–Tues.*

★ **Harbor Square Gallery**

ART GALLERIES | This beautiful, multifloor gallery is nestled inside a jewel box of a building that was once a bank. Step inside, feast your eyes on fine contemporary paintings, beautifully wrought gold jewelry, sculpture, and perhaps purchase a new treasure. Be sure to go up to the rooftop sculpture garden. It's a delightful spot with views over the town to the harbor. ✉ *374 Main St., Rockland ☎ 207/594–8700 ⊕ www.harborsquare-gallery.com ⦿ Closed Mon.*

HOME AND GIFTS

Fiore Artisan Olive Oils & Vinegars

FOOD | It can be hard to choose your favorites from the fine olive oils, flavored olive oils, and balsamic vinegars displayed in large, spigoted containers all around the room here. Tasting a drop of a few of them is half the fun, and you'll soon know which ones you just have to add to your culinary repertoire. ✉ *503 Main St., Rockland ☎ 207/596–0276 ⊕ www.fioreoliveoils.com ⦿ Closed Sun.–Tues.*

The Grasshopper Shop

GENERAL STORE | This emporium is a longtime local favorite. Jewelry, candles, stylish clothing, shoes, toiletries, gifts, toys—you'll find all that and lots more here. ✉ *400 Main St., Rockland ☎ 207/596–6156 ⊕ www.grasshopper-shopofrockland.com.*

Ollie and David's

ANTIQUES & COLLECTIBLES | Tucked toward the back of the first floor of the Thorndike Building, this little shop brims over with delightful, one-of-a-kind home and garden decor. Many of the items are assemblages of upcycled vintage elements, put together by creative shop owner David Robichaud. His partner is Ollie, his English springer spaniel, who's usually in the shop on Saturday. ✉ *385 Main St., Thorndike Bldg., Rockland ☎ ⊕ instagram.com/ollieanddavids5/ ⦿ Closed Sun. and Mon.*

Trillium Soaps Ltd.

SKINCARE | Located at the very southern end of Main Street, this small shop-factory in a sweet house is a great place to pick up well-priced, lightly scented, 100% vegan soaps made from pure olive, palm, and coconut oils with such additional ingredients as aloe, lemongrass, rosemary, citrus, and rose petal; there are more than a dozen varieties. Place unwrapped squares of soap in provided small, waxy bags and save $2 off the price of gift-wrapped bars. The shop also sells gift-boxed soaps plus a small selection of white pottery goods and skincare accessories. ⊠ *216 Main St., Rockland* ☎ *207/593–9019* ⊕ *www.trilliumsoaps. com* ⊘ *Closed Sun.–Tues.*

Activities

BOATING

Schooner *American Eagle*

SAILING | FAMILY | Launched in 1930 as a fishing schooner, the *American Eagle* offers longer, farther-offshore voyages (up to 10 nights) as well as lots of shorter cruises in Penobscot Bay. She returns annually to compete in a race in her birthplace of Gloucester, Massachusetts, and sometimes sails way Down East to the Canadian border (she's the only windjammer licensed to sail internationally). She accommodates up to 26 passengers. Children aged 12 and up are welcome. ⊠ *North End Shipyard, 11 Front St., Rockland* ☎ *207/594–8007, 800/648–4544* ⊕ *www.schooneramericaneagle.com* ☜ *From $745* ⊘ *Closed early-Oct.–late May.*

Schooner *Heritage*

SAILING | FAMILY | Designed and built specifically for passengers, the 95-foot *Heritage* carries up to 30 guests. Both captains are musicians and enjoy playing their guitars for guests in the evening. Trips range from three to six nights in length, and children aged 10 and up are welcome. ⊠ *North End Shipyard, 11 Front St., Rockland* ☎ *207/594–8007, 800/648–4544* ⊕ *www.schoonerheritage.com* ☜ *From $780* ⊘ *Closed Oct.–early June.*

Schooner *J. & E. Riggin*

SAILING | FAMILY | The schooner *J. & E. Riggin*, originally an oyster dredger, offers multiday sailing cruises that thoroughly immerse passengers in traditional life under sail. Measuring 120 feet overall, the *Riggin* carries up to 24 overnight guests plus six crew. The experience is highlighted by three daily meals, plus snacks, all prepared using locally sourced seafood, vegetables, and other ingredients. ⊠ *Windjammer Wharf, 3 Captain Spear Dr., Rockland* ☎ *207/594–1875, 800/869–0604* ⊕ *www.mainewindjammer.com* ☜ *From $615* ⊘ *Closed early Oct.–late May.*

★ Schooner *Ladona*

SAILING | Unlike her windjammer sisters, which were built to work hard, the schooner *Ladona* began her career as a private racing yacht, though she was later called into duty during World War II. Built in 1922 (rebuilt in 1971), and restored from bow to stern before joining the windjammer fleet a few years ago, this graceful schooner takes guests on cruises of three to seven nights. The on-board experience recalls *Ladona*'s past as a private yacht, with greater comfort and luxury, as well as more elegant dining, than the other members of the windjammer fleet. All trips include breakfast, lunch, and dinner, as well as a selection of fine wines and beers every evening. One trip features daily wine tastings led by an experienced wine professional. ⊠ *40 Tillson Ave., Rockland* ☎ *800/999–7352, 207/594–4723* ⊕ *www.schoonerladona. com* ☜ *From $1108* ⊘ *Closed mid-Oct.–early June.*

Schooner *Stephen Taber*

SAILING | With a proud history that dates back to her launching in 1871, the *Taber* is the oldest documented sailing vessel in continuous service in the U.S. Always well maintained, she accommodates up to 22 guests. All trips include evening wine and fine cheeses, and special cruises offer such extras as live jazz, blues, or country music; a guest chef; and wine and chocolate. ⊠ *40 Tillson Ave., Rockland* ☎ *800/999–7352* ⊕ *www.stephentaber.com* ☜ *From $888* ⊘ *Closed early Oct.–late May.*

TOURS

★ Penobscot Island Air

AIR EXCURSIONS | FAMILY | There's nothing like taking in the breathtaking panorama of Penobscot Bay and its islands from above. Penobscot Island Air offers wonderful 30- and 60-minute "flightseeing" trips as well as providing regular service to the islands from its base at Knox County Regional Airport at Owls Head. Choose from several preplanned tours, including one featuring lighthouses, or request a custom route to include a special spot you'd like to see. ✉ *Knox County Regional Airport, 21 Terminal La., Owls Head* ☎ *207/596–7500* 🌐 *www.penobscotislandair.net* 🎫 *From $95 per person for 30- and 60-minute flights, depending on number of passengers.*

Vinalhaven

15 miles or 1 hour 15 minutes east of Rockland via Maine State Ferry.

Nearly 8 miles long by 5 miles wide, Vinalhaven is Maine's largest inhabited island, with about 1,200 year-round residents. That number burgeons with summer folk. Scalloped by harbors and coves, the stunningly beautiful, mostly wooded island is a quiet and rewarding day-trip destination.

Carver's Harbor's "downtown" is a short walk from the ferry dock. Along Main Street, you'll find a handful of shops and eateries where menus are heavy on freshly caught lobster and other local seafood. There's one small motel with comfortable rooms, perched over the water. (Reserve early for the summer season.)

In the early 1900s, there was a booming granite industry on the island. Today, the mostly abandoned quarries are great for swimming and picnicking. Many islanders work in the lobstering industry.

Despite being an island, Vinalhaven is relatively accessible. There are six ferry trips per day to and from the island in summer. The Maine State Ferry Terminal is right in the center of Rockland, on U.S. 1, across from the Navigator Motor Inn. The ferry runs throughout the year (except on major holidays), but the times change somewhat from the end of October through December, so it's best to call first or check their website. There is also regular ferry service to the island of North Haven, which lies just across the Fox Island Thorofare from Vinalhaven. These ferries are minimal in their amenities. You won't find a restaurant, snack bar, lounge, or even a vending machine on board.

If you'd like to explore the island beyond the village, bring a bike or a car. There is no public transportation on the island.

Within a mile of the ferry dock, you will find two town parks and a nature conservancy area a short walk beyond the village center. There is only one main road, so it's pretty easy to find your way around. Biking on the island can be fun, though there are no designated bike paths and the road can be a little rough outside the village.

Goose Rocks Lighthouse is located between North Haven and Vinalhaven.

🛏 Hotels

★ The Tidewater

$$ | MOTEL | This welcoming, third-generation family-owned motel is the only lodging option on the water and near the ferry dock. **Pros:** right in the village overlooking the working harbor; short walk from ferry dock; great views. **Cons:** may be too quiet for some; rooms book up far in advance during high season; the engines of early-departing lobster boats may disturb sleep. [$] *Rooms from: $220* ✉ *15 W. Main St., Vinalhaven* ☎ *207/863–4618* 🌐 *www.thetidewatervh.com* 🛏 *19 rooms* 🍴 *Free Breakfast.*

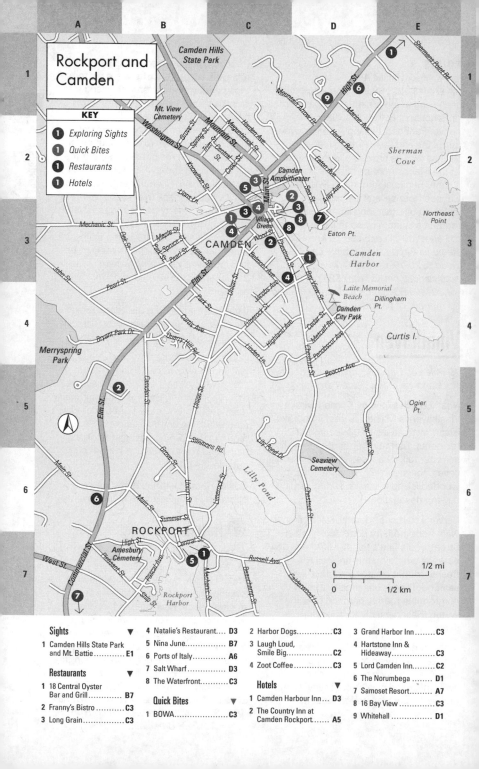

Rockport and Camden

KEY

1 *Exploring Sights*
1 *Quick Bites*
1 *Restaurants*
1 *Hotels*

Rockport

4 miles north of Rockland via U.S. 1.

Heading north on U.S. 1 from Rockland, you enter Rockport before you reach the tourist mecca of Camden. Hugging the harbor, Rockport Village is a short drive off U.S. 1. It's home to a handful of very good small restaurants.

Originally called Goose River, Rockport was part of Camden until 1891. The cutting and burning of limestone was once a major industry in this area. The stone was cut in nearby quarries and then burned in hot kilns; the resulting lime powder was used to create mortar. Some of the kilns can still be seen down on the harbor.

If you drive from Rockport to Camden on Union Street, you'll pass under the Camden-Rockport Arch at the town line. It has appeared in a number of movies, including *Peyton Place* and *In the Bedroom.*

GETTING HERE AND AROUND

Rockport is off U.S. 1 between Rockland and Camden. Turn on Pascal Avenue to get to the village center.

The Concord Coach Lines bus that runs along the coast makes a stop near Rockport village on Route 1 just over the town line in Camden.

🍴 Restaurants

★ 18 Central Oyster Bar and Grill

$$$ | **SEAFOOD** | 18 Central Oyster Bar and Grill produces excellent, creative dishes in a cozy spot high above Rockport's working harbor. Seasonally inspired, locally harvested seafood plus dishes with a hint of Southern comfort make up the backbone of the menu—think fried green tomatoes with local peekytoe crab, chili oil, and microgreens, or crispy fried chicken accompanied by collards and heirloom grits. **Known for:** evenly paced, well-balanced dinners transition gracefully from one course to the next; lively atmosphere encouraged by botanically infused cocktails; packed as soon as the door opens for dinner. $ *Average main: $30* ⊠ *18 Central St., Rockport* ☎ *207/466–9055* ⊕ *www.18central.com* ☉ *Closed Tues.–Thurs.* ☞ *Reservations strongly advised; credit card required to secure reservations for more than 4; max party size 8 people.*

Nina June

$$$ | **MEDITERRANEAN** | **FAMILY** | This lovely trattoria is known for its cheery harbor-view setting and frequently changing menus where locally sourced ingredients shine. Highly regarded chef-owner Sara Jenkins's fresh but authentic takes on Mediterranean-spanning dishes use seafood harvested along Maine's rocky coast, including local oysters, and everything from the pasta to the pickled veggies is made in-house; the presentation of each dish makes for sheer eye candy. Jenkins grew up in Italy and worked in restaurants both there and at her own New York City restaurants—in other words, she knows what she's doing. **Known for:** weekly five-course prix-fixe menu plus a small à la carte café menu; craft cocktails; harbor views, especially from outdoor deck; cooking classes with Sara Jenkins and guest chefs. $ *Average main: $26* ⊠ *24 Central St., Rockport* ☎ *207/236–8880* ⊕ *www.ninajunerestaurant.com* ☉ *Closed Sun.–Tues. No lunch.*

Ports of Italy

$$$ | **ITALIAN** | The sister establishment to Ports of Italy in Boothbay Harbor, this pleasant restaurant offers a selection of house-made pastas with traditional sauces, many featuring local seafood. Second-course choices include veal scaloppine, osso buco, and porchetta. **Known for:** appealing Sunday brunch menu; Caprese salad in a crisp Parmesan basket; well-prepared Italian classics. $ *Average main: $25* ⊠ *141 Commercial St., U.S. 1, Rockport* ☎ *207/236–1011* ⊕ *www.portsofitalyrockport.com.*

Hotels

The Country Inn at Camden Rockport
$$ | HOTEL | FAMILY | Set a bit back from the traffic on U.S. 1, this complex is a good choice for families—some of the 36 comfortable rooms have additional sleeping spaces to accommodate kids, and there's a large, heated indoor pool (plus hot tub and fitness room), and a minigolf course next door. **Pros:** large indoor heated pool; all rooms have private balconies or patios; minigolf right next door. **Cons:** not on water; drive to Camden restaurants and shops; drive to Rockport restaurants. [$] *Rooms from: $250* ✉ *8 Country Way, off Rte. 1, Rockport* ☎ *207/236–2725* 🌐 *www.countryinnmaine.com* 🛏 *47 rooms* 🍴 *Free Breakfast.*

Samoset Resort
$$$$ | RESORT | FAMILY | Located on the Rockland-Rockport town line along the edge of Penobscot Bay and the eastern side of Rockland harbor, this 230-acre resort offers luxurious rooms, suites, and cottages, all with a private balcony or patio and an ocean or garden view. **Pros:** sweeping ocean views; choice of restaurants on-site; a beautiful resort that seems to meet every need. **Cons:** not for those who prefer quiet, intimate lodging; not within easy walking distance of downtown Rockland or Camden; no beach. [$] *Rooms from: $400* ✉ *220 Warrenton St., off Rte. 1, Rockport* ☎ *207/594–2511* 🌐 *www.samosetresort.com* ⏲ *Closed weeknights Dec.–Apr.* 🛏 *178 rooms* 🍴 *Free Breakfast* ☞ *Daily $40 resort fee added to cost of room; dogs under 30 lbs. permitted ($75 per night per dog [does not apply to service dogs]; max 2 dogs).*

Performing Arts

★ Bay Chamber Concerts
CONCERTS | FAMILY | Every August, Bay Chamber Concerts mounts a three-week series of mostly classical concerts in the Rockport Opera House and in a variety of other venues, both indoors and out. Some events are free; others are ticketed, with discounted admission for young audience members. There's also a Bach for Breakfast series held in the Camden Amphitheatre. ✉ *Rockport Opera House, 6 Central St., Rockport* ☎ *207/236–2823* 🌐 *baychamber.org* 🎟 *$35* ⏲ *Closed Sept.–July.*

Shopping

★ Maine Sport Outfitters
SPORTING GOODS | FAMILY | Think of this store as a mini L.L. Bean, with a good selection of premier outdoor apparel and gear and knowledgeable staff to help with your selection. In addition, you can rent kayaks, canoes, SUPs, bikes, camping gear, and winter sports equipment. Maine Sport also offers a roster of guided fresh- and saltwater canoe, kayak, SUP, and fishing trips and tours, plus biking and hiking tours.

There is also a shop on Main Street in Camden, plus a third location in Rockland. ✉ *115 Commercial St., U.S. 1, Rockport* ☎ *207/236–7120* 🌐 *www.mainesport.com.*

Activities

BOATING

Schooner *Heron*
SAILING | FAMILY | Docked in the Rockport Marine Park, the lovely 65-foot, Alden-designed schooner takes passengers sailing on Penobscot Bay three times a day, weather permitting. She was built and is operated by a very experienced, qualified, and licensed couple who sail their schooner to the Caribbean every winter. In Maine from June through early October, they offer an Educational Eco Sail, a happy-hour sunset sail, and private morning charters. While underway, they share their knowledge of local maritime history, sea life, and lobstering. ✉ *Rockport Marine Park, Rockport* ☎ *207/236–8605* 🌐 *www.sailheron.com* ⏲ *Closed late Oct.–June.*

An aerial view of Camden's busy harbor.

Camden

8 miles north of Rockland.

Known as the Jewel of the Maine Coast, Camden is one of the region's most popular spots. The town's compact size makes it perfect for exploring on foot: shops, restaurants, and galleries line Main Street, as well as the side streets and alleys around the harbor. But be sure to include Camden's residential area on your tour. It is quite charming and filled with lovely period houses from the time when Federal, Greek Revival, and Victorian architectural styles were the rage among the wealthy; many of them are now B&Bs. The Chamber of Commerce, on the Public Landing, can provide you with a walking map.

Rising on the north side of town are the Camden Hills. Drive or hike to the summit of Mt. Battie, in Camden Hills State Park, to enjoy panoramic views of the town, harbor, and island-dotted bay. This perch is where Pulitzer-winning poet Edna St. Vincent Millay penned "Renascence," describing the view in the lines: All I could see from where I stood / Was three long mountains and a wood; / I turned and looked another way, / And saw three islands in a bay."

Camden's not only famous for its geography, but also for its fleet of windjammers—originals from the age of sailing as well as replicas—with their romantic histories and great billowing sails. If possible, sign up for a cruise, whether for a couple of hours or as much as a week.

GETTING HERE AND AROUND

U.S. 1 runs right through the middle of Camden. If you're driving from farther south on U.S. 1 and would like to bypass Thomaston and Rockland on your way to Camden, turn left off onto Route 90 in Warren and rejoin Route 1 at the other end of Route 90 in Rockport.

U.S. 1 has lots of names as it runs through Maine. Within Camden's town limits, it begins at the southern end of town as Elm Street, changes to Main

Street in the downtown area, and then becomes High Street.

The Concord Coach Lines bus that drives the coastal route stops on Route 1 in Camden, just south of town.

VISITOR INFORMATION

CONTACTS Penobscot Bay Regional Chamber of Commerce. ✉ *Visitor Center, 2 Public Landing, Camden* ☎ *207/236–4404, 800/562–2529* 🌐 *www.camdenrockland.com.*

WHEN TO GO

From June to September, the town is crowded with visitors, but that doesn't detract from its charm. Just make reservations for lodging and restaurants well in advance and be prepared for busy traffic on the town's Main Street. This is also the best time to book a windjammer excursion.

FESTIVALS AND EVENTS

★ Camden Windjammer Festival

FESTIVALS | FAMILY | One of the biggest and most colorful events of the year is the Camden Windjammer Festival, which takes place over Labor Day weekend. The harbor is packed with historic vessels, there are lots of good eats, and visitors can tour the magnificent ships. ✉ *Camden* ☎ *207/236–3438* 🌐 *www.facebook.com/WindjammerFestival/.*

Sights

★ Camden Hills State Park and Mt. Battie

HIKING & WALKING | Although the Camden Hills' height may not be much more than 1,000 feet, they are lovely landmarks for miles along the low, rolling reaches of the Maine Coast. The 5,500-acre Camden Hills State Park contains 25 miles of hiking trails, but the centerpiece is Mt. Battie. Hike or drive to its top for a magnificent view over Camden and island-studded Penobscot Bay. The panorama is so breathtaking it inspired Rockland native, poet Edna St. Vincent Millay to write in *Renascence,* "All I could see from where I stood / Was three long mountains and a wood; / I turned and looked another way, / And saw three islands in a bay." A plaque on the stone tower at the summit commemorates her. ✉ *280 Belfast Rd., Route 1, Camden* ☎ *207/236–3109* 🌐 *www.maine.gov/dacf* 🎫 *$6.*

Restaurants

★ Franny's Bistro

$$$ | BISTRO | This little bistro on a side street near the center of town is unassuming from the outside, but inside, the pleasantly cozy space features an ambitious menu flavored with hints of Asian, Italian, and modern American cuisines. Dishes are very well prepared, but service can be slow when the restaurant is full. **Known for:** inventive dishes with international flair; lobster fritters; intimate atmosphere. [$] *Average main: $30* ✉ *55 Chestnut St., Camden* ☎ *207/230–8199* 🌐 *www.frannysbistro.com* 🕓 *Closed Sun.–Tues. No lunch.*

★ Long Grain

$$ | ASIAN FUSION | The celebrated Thai chef at this Asian-fusion restaurant places an emphasis on authentic noodle and rice dishes. The atmosphere is casual and open, with rustic wood tables and bentwood chairs. **Known for:** chef Ravin Nakjaroen is a James Beard–nominated chef; consistently excellent; great take-out options. [$] *Average main: $20* ✉ *20 Washington St., Camden* ☎ *207/236–9001, 207/230–8735* 🌐 *www.longgrain-camden.com* 🕓 *Closed Sun. and Mon.*

★ Natalie's Restaurant

$$$$ | MODERN AMERICAN | Located in the stylish and elegant Camden Harbour Inn, this fine-dining restaurant serves imaginative, beautifully plated creations starring local seafood, meats, and other seasonal ingredients like vegetables and herbs from the property's garden. Probably the most sophisticated dining spot in Camden, Natalie's is the creation of Dutch owners Raymond Brunyanszki and Oscar Verest,

There are great views of Camden's harbor from Mount Battie.

who have brought in talented chefs to create splurge-worthy dishes that are served by a polished waitstaff. **Known for:** phenomenal service with true attention to detail; signature five-course lobster tasting menu; grand views of the Camden Hills, harbor, and bay. $ *Average main: $38* ✉ *Camden Harbour Inn, 83 Bay View St., Camden* ☎ *866/658–1542, 207/236–7008* 🌐 *www.nataliesrestaurant.com* 🕘 *Closed Sun. Nov.–May. No lunch.*

Salt Wharf

$$$ | MODERN AMERICAN | Opened in summer 2022, this lively, dockside bar-bistro on the eastern side of Camden harbor is a sweet spot to meet friends for drinks and small bites or for a full dinner. The sophisticated menu is complemented by lovely views of the boat-filled harbor and picturesque townscape across the way. **Known for:** lovely harborside setting; creative menu choices; fun atmosphere. $ *Average main: $25* ✉ *3 Wayfarer Dr., at Lyman-Morse, Camden* ☎ *207/230–8025* 🌐 *www.saltwharf.com* 🕘 *Closed Sun. and Mon.*

The Waterfront

$$ | AMERICAN | Come to this long-standing local favorite for a ringside seat on Camden Harbor; the best view, when the weather cooperates, is from the deck. The menu features fresh local seafood, but there are also beef and chicken entrées and salads. **Known for:** great salad choices; harborside dining, including outdoor deck; solid menu that never disappoints. $ *Average main: $20* ✉ *48 Bay View St., Camden* ☎ *207/236–3747* 🌐 *www.waterfrontcamden.com* 🕘 *Closed Tues.* ☞ *No groups larger than 8 people.*

☕ Coffee and Quick Bites

BOWA

$ | ASIAN | Under the same ownership as Long Grain around the corner, this tiny bistro—whose name is an acronym for "Best of What's Available"—serves a well-priced lunch menu of street food from Asia, the Middle East, and the Mediterranean. Popular menu items include bibimbap, pho, and a Mediterranean bowl and many options are or can be prepared vegan or gluten-free. **Known for:** yummy pastries; lively flavors; fresh, healthy take-out or eat-in. [$] *Average main: $13* ✉ *31 Elm St., Camden* ☎ *207/230–8292* 🌐 *www.bowacamden.com* 🕒 *Closed Sun. and Mon.*

Harbor Dogs
$ | **SEAFOOD** | **FAMILY** | A summertime fixture for five decades, the Harbor Dogs shack on the town landing is the perfect place to grab lunch to enjoy at a nearby bench beside the harbor or before or after a cruise. Hot dog toppings include southwestern, Asian, and Chicago, and there are also lobster and crab rolls, fish tacos, haddock Reubens, and fried-seafood platters. **Known for:** lengthy hot-dog menu; watching the sightseeing boats and sailboats coming and going; delicious takeout to enjoy on a harborfront bench. [$] *Average main: $15* ✉ *1 Public Landing, Camden* ☎ *207/230–9638* 🌐 *www.harbordogs.com* 🕒 *Closed Wed. and Thurs. and mid-Oct.–mid-May. No dinner.*

Laugh Loud, Smile Big
$ | **BAKERY** | **FAMILY** | You can't help but smile big when you feast your eyes on a case full of beautifully frosted cupcakes in this haven for sweets lovers. Enticing flavors change daily, but might include chocolate-peanut butter, raspberry-filled chocolate, blueberry compote-filled, red velvet, almond joy, pistachio, salted caramel, lemon curd, and wedding cake. **Known for:** amazing array of flavors; an inexpensive but extravagant treat; elegantly frosted and decorated cupcakes. [$] *Average main: $4* ✉ *38 Main St., Camden* ☎ *207/230–7001* 🌐 *www.laughloudsmilebig.com* 🕒 *Closed Sun.–Tues.*

Zoot Coffee
$ | **CAFÉ** | Locals and visitors alike are drawn to this community gathering spot by the irresistible aroma of freshly roasted coffee; it's a great spot to visit with friends or open your tablet to do some work. There's a wide selection of hot and cold coffee drinks, chai variations, and hot chocolate, as well as Italian ices and to-go choices that include porridge, yogurt, toast, soup, quiche, grilled cheese, pie, and even beans on toast! **Known for:** well-prepared coffee drinks; relaxed atmosphere; simple breakfast and lunch choices. [$] *Average main: $5* ✉ *5 Elm St., Camden* ☎ *207/236–9858* 🌐 *www.facebook.com/ZootCoffee* 🕒 *No dinner.*

🛏 Hotels

Camden Harbour Inn
$$$$ | **HOTEL** | Perched on a hill overlooking the harbor, not far from downtown, this luxurious retreat offers beautiful views of the water and the Camden Hills. **Pros:** excellent restaurant Natalie's is on-site; attentive service; elegant accommodations. **Cons:** uphill walk when returning from village center; expensive; not all rooms have water views. [$] *Rooms from: $800* ✉ *83 Bay View St., Camden* ☎ *207/236–4200, 800/236–4266* 🌐 *www.camdenharbourinn.com* 🕒 *Closed Jan.* 🔑 *20 rooms* 🍴 *Free Breakfast.*

★ **Grand Harbor Inn**
$$$$ | **HOTEL** | You can't get any closer to the harbor without being in the water—you can watch all the boats coming and going, including several classic schooners, from the windows or balconies—at this intimate boutique hotel that sits right on the dock next to the town landing. **Pros:** harborfront restaurants next door; right beside the harbor; all rooms have fireplaces and balconies. **Cons:** possible noise from people on docks; located beside a tight little parking lot; chilly breeze off water might make balconies uncomfortable. [$] *Rooms from: $659* ✉ *14 Bay View Landing, off Bay View St., Camden* ☎ *207/230–7177, 877/553–6997* 🌐 *www.grandharborinn.com* 🔑 *10 rooms* 🍴 *Free Breakfast.*

Hartstone Inn & Hideaway
$$$ | **B&B/INN** | Inside this circa-1835 mansard-roofed Victorian home at the southern edge of Camden's downtown

area is a plush, sophisticated retreat and a culinary destination. **Pros:** pet-friendly; extravagant breakfasts; some private entrances. **Cons:** not on water; no wheelchair access; not all rooms have fireplaces. [$] *Rooms from: $300* ✉ *41 Elm St., Camden* ☎ *207/236–4259* 🌐 *www.hartstoneinn.com* 🕒 *Restaurant closed Mon. and Tues.* 🛏 *22 rooms* 🍴 *Free Breakfast.*

Lord Camden Inn

$$ | HOTEL | FAMILY | If you want to be in the midst of the shops and not far from the harbor, this handsome Main Street brick building with bright blue-and-white awnings is the perfect choice. **Pros:** buffet breakfast with hot entrées; all rooms have mini-refrigerators and microwaves; most rooms have balconies. **Cons:** Main Street noise can drift up into front rooms; no on-site restaurant; $15/night parking unless room is booked directly with hotel. [$] *Rooms from: $299* ✉ *24 Main St., Camden* ☎ *207/236–4325, 800/336–4325* 🌐 *www.lordcamdeninn.com* 🛏 *36 rooms* 🍴 *Free Breakfast.*

★ The Norumbega

$$$$ | B&B/INN | With a commanding position overlooking the bay just north of downtown Camden, this impressive, turreted "castle" exudes Old World grandeur. **Pros:** beautiful views of both the ocean and the sloping, waterside lawn; eye-popping architecture; elegant rooms and suites. **Cons:** stairs to climb; a short drive from the center of town; no pets. [$] *Rooms from: $450* ✉ *63 High St., Camden* ☎ *207/236–4646* 🌐 *www.norumbegainn.com* 🛏 *11 rooms* 🍴 *Free Breakfast.*

16 Bay View

$$$$ | HOTEL | Tucked in among the shops on Bay View Street, just off Main Street, this boutique hotel is an ideal pied-à-terre for accessing all the pleasures of in-town Camden without needing a car. **Pros:** spectacular views from rooftop bar; fireplaces in all rooms; mere steps to harbor, shops, and restaurants. **Cons:** some street noise; small seating area in lobby; limited harbor views from rooms on lower floors. [$] *Rooms from: $439* ✉ *16 Bay View St., Camden* ☎ *207/706–7990, 844/213–7990* 🌐 *www.16bayview.com* 🛏 *21 rooms* 🍴 *Free Breakfast.*

Whitehall

$$$ | B&B/INN | FAMILY | Although the oldest part of the Whitehall is an 1834 white-clapboard sea captain's home, there's nothing stodgy about this historic hotel as the eclectic, midcentury-modern decor shakes things up with lots of red and other bright pops of color. **Pros:** fully renovated with surprisingly jazzy decor; small-plates breakfast choices; wonderful Edna St. Vincent Millay history. **Cons:** most rooms are upstairs; no elevator but help with bags; walls can be a bit thin; half-mile walk to in-town restaurants and shops. [$] *Rooms from: $379* ✉ *52 High St., Camden* ☎ *207/236–3391, 800/789–6565* 🌐 *www.whitehallmaine.com* 🕒 *Closed mid-Oct.–mid-May* 🛏 *36 rooms* 🍴 *Free Breakfast.*

Performing Arts

★ Camden Opera House

ARTS CENTERS | FAMILY | Throughout the year, Camden's historic opera house presents a full calendar of concerts, plays, and dance performances, as well as an annual film festival. ✉ *29 Elm St., Camden* ☎ *207/236–7963* 🌐 *www.camdenoperahouse.com.*

Camden Shakespeare Festival

THEATER | FAMILY | Every year, a professional troupe of actors presents a midsummer festival of Shakespeare plays beside the harbor. Held in Camden's beautiful amphitheater, the performances strive to engage audiences of all ages, including children. The festival is presented in association with the Camden Public Library. ✉ *Box 1206, Camden* ☎ *207/464–0008* 🌐 *camdenshakespeare.org* 🎟 *$28* 🕒 *Closed Aug.–June.*

Shopping

ART AND ANTIQUES

★ Ironbound Gallery

ART GALLERIES | A feast for the eyes, this lovely, two-floor gallery showcases a wide variety of beautifully wrought works, almost all of it created by Maine artists. There are paintings, sculptures large and small, carvings, unusual jewelry, cards, and more. ⊠ *37 Main St., Camden* ☎ *207/236–4100* ⊕ *www. ironboundgallery.com.*

Small Wonder Gallery

ART GALLERIES | If you're captivated by the beauty of the Maine Coast, come here to make a little of the scenery your own, in the form of a painting or other work of art created by excellent local artists. Rendered in a variety of media, there are landscapes, seascapes, and other compelling images that exude the mystique of Maine. ⊠ *1 Public Landing, Camden* ☎ *207/236–6005* ⊕ *www.small-wonder-gallery.myshopify.com.*

BOOKS

★ Owl and Turtle Bookshop and Café

BOOKS | **FAMILY** | This pint-size but well-stocked independent bookstore with a tiny café has been serving Camden for more than 50 years. The full menu of coffee drinks is based on locally roasted beans and includes a selection of homemade baked goods. It's closed Sunday and Monday. ⊠ *33 Bay View St., Camden* ☎ *207/230–7335* ⊕ *www.owlandturtle. com* ☉ *Closed Sun. and Mon.*

FOOD

Lily, Lupine and Fern

FLORIST | This full-service florist offers a wonderful array of gourmet foods, local charcuterie, chocolates, wines, craft beers, high-quality olive oils, and cheeses. There's a small deck where you can enjoy harbor views. ⊠ *11 Main St., Camden* ☎ *207/236–9600* ⊕ *www.lilylupine. com* ☉ *Closed Sun. and Mon.*

Uncle Willy's Candy Shoppe

CANDY | **FAMILY** | In this real-life candy land, you'll find anything your sweet tooth could be craving: "penny" candy, gummies, fudge, chocolates, truffles, jellybeans, taffy, hand-dipped chocolate strawberries, and so much more. Seasonal treats include hot-chocolate bombs and molded chocolates for every holiday. ⊠ *57 Bay View St., Camden* ☎ *207/230–2470* ⊕ *www.unclewillyscandyshoppe. com* ☉ *Closed Mon. and Tues.*

HOME AND GIFTS

Glendarragh Lavender

GENERAL STORE | The sweet scent of lavender will draw you into this petite shop. Many of the products, including lotions and sachets, are made using lavender from the owner's farm in the nearby countryside. Also on offer are candles, soaps, pottery, Italian and French cosmetics, and locally made and European clothing. ⊠ *22 Main St., Camden* ☎ *207/236–8151* ⊕ *www.mainelavender. com.*

★ Hearth and Harrow

HOUSEWARES | Featuring tea towels, napkins, the softest T-shirts, and other textiles hand-printed in Rockport with delightful animals and other nature themes, this inviting shop also stocks home goods, glassware, cards, cooking and gardening books, and plants. ⊠ *20 Main St., Camden* ☎ *207/252–9675* ⊕ *www.hearthandharrow.com.*

The Smiling Cow

GENERAL STORE | **FAMILY** | Jam-packed with gifts, souvenirs, fudge, books, cards, tote bags, home-decor items, jewelry, clothing, and so much more, this inviting, old-fashioned store has been a fixture on Main Street since 1940. Dogs are always welcome, and always get a biscuit. Don't miss the little back porch overlooking the harbor. Locals look forward to the annual half-price sale before the store closes in late October. ⊠ *41 Main St., Camden* ☎ *207/236–3351* ⊕ *www.smilingcow. com* ☉ *Closed late Oct.–May.*

★ Swans Island Company

CRAFTS | For luxurious handcrafted blankets, throws, pillows, wraps, and scarves, look no further. All products are made in Maine using natural, heirloom-quality yarns. The expert craftsmanship explains the hefty price tag. ⊠ *2 Bayview St., Camden* ☎ *207/706–7926* ⊕ *swansislandcompany.com.*

TOYS

Planet Toys

TOYS | **FAMILY** | With lots of great toys, plus books, games, and stuffed animals, this is the place for families, kids, people who wish they were kids, and grandparents. The quality of the products is well above average. ⊠ *10 Main St., Camden* ☎ *207/236–4410* ⊕ *www.facebook.com/ PlanetToysofMaine.*

Activities

BOATING

Angelique

SAILING | **FAMILY** | With distinctive tanbark sails, the *Angelique* is a ketch-rigged windjammer, the only one in the fleet that isn't a schooner. Three- to six-day Penobscot Bay cruise options aboard the *Angelique* include a photography workshop, a grandparents and grandkids trip, a yoga and wellness cruise, and trips focused on lighthouses and whales. ⊠ *Camden Harbor, Camden* ☎ *800/282– 9989* ⊕ *www.sailangelique.com* ✉ *From $950* ⊗ *Closed early Oct.–June.*

Lewis R. French

SAILING | Launched in 1871, the *French* is the oldest commercial sailing vessel in the country and a National Historic Landmark. She has, of course, been completely refitted for passengers, has modern navigational equipment, and is well-maintained. Cruises vary in length from three to six nights. Some center on such themes as kayaking, a Father's Day celebration, music, and schooner racing. ⊠ *Box 992, Camden Harbor, Camden* ☎ *207/542–1241* ⊕ *www.schoonerfrench.*

com ✉ *From $595* ⊗ *Closed mid-Oct.– Memorial Day* ☞ *10% discount for returning guests.*

Maine Windjammer Cruises

SAILING | **FAMILY** | Camden and Rockland are home to an impressive fleet of historic, cargo-carrying schooners that have been fully refitted and converted for use as passenger vessels. The schooners *Mercantile* and the *Grace Bailey* have both been designated National Landmarks. Built in 1882 and restored in 1990, the *Bailey* is 123 feet long and can carry up to 29 passengers. *The Mercantile*, built in 1916, is 115 feet long and also accommodates 29 passengers. Both sail from Camden Harbor out onto the waters of Penobscot Bay on cruises lasting up to a week. The fleet also includes the 60-foot *Mistress*, a newer, smaller sister to the other two that only carries up to six passengers. Unlike the larger vessels, she also has an inboard engine. ⊠ *Camden Harbor, Camden* ☎ *207/236–2938, 800/736–7981* ⊕ *www.mainewindjammercruises.com* ✉ *From $745* ⊗ *Closed late Sept.–late May.*

★ Mary Day

SAILING | **FAMILY** | Sailing for more than 50 years, the *Mary Day* was the first schooner in Maine built specifically for vacation excursions. Accommodating up to 28 guests and seven crew, she is continually maintained and upgraded. Cruise lengths range from one night to six nights. ⊠ *Camden Harbor, Atlantic Ave., Camden* ☎ *800/992–2218* ⊕ *www. schoonermaryday.com* ✉ *From $450* ⊗ *Closed Nov.–mid-June.*

Olad

SAILING | Captain Aaron Lincoln skippers two-hour sailing trips aboard the 57-foot *Olad* and the smaller *Owl*. Out on Penobscot Bay, passengers spot lighthouses, coastal mansions, seals, and the occasional red-footed puffin cousins known as guillemots. Either boat can also be chartered for longer trips. ⊠ *Camden Harbor, 1 Bay View Landing, Camden*

☎ 207/236–2323 ⊕ www.maineschoon-ers.com ✉ $55 ⊘ Closed Oct.–June 1 ☞ BYOB and snacks.

Schooner *Appledore II*

SAILING | FAMILY | After circumnavigating the world as a private yacht, this 86-foot, traditionally built schooner became a passenger sightseeing vessel and has been sailing out of Camden in the summer and Key West in the winter for decades. Camden's largest daysailer, the *Appledore II* welcomes passengers aboard for two-hour day sails and sunset sails on Penobscot Bay. ⊠ *18 Bay View Landing, Camden* ☎ *207/236–8353* ⊕ *www.appledore2.com* ✉ $55 ⊘ Closed Oct.–June.

Schooner *Lazy Jack II*

SAILING | FAMILY | Purpose-built by her owner/captain for daysailing cruises out of Camden, the 58-foot, gaff-rigged *Lazy Jack II* takes up to 21 passengers on two-hour trips on Penobscot Bay. As you sail, the captain will point out sea life, such as seals, porpoises, and ospreys. Friendly, well-behaved, leashed dogs are welcome on board. ⊠ *15 Bay View Landing, Camden* ☎ *207/230–0602* ⊕ *www. schoonerlazyjack.com* ✉ $50 ⊘ Closed Nov.–mid-May.

Surprise

SAILING | FAMILY | The graceful schooner *Surprise* was originally launched in 1918. Thanks to conscientious maintenance and loving care, she is still a strong and able vessel. Two-hour day sails take up to 18 passengers from Camden Harbor out onto Penobscot Bay where they often spot seals, bald eagles, and perhaps a porpoise. ⊠ *1 Bay View St., Camden Harbor, Camden* ☎ *207/236–4687* ⊕ *www. schoonersurprise.com* ✉ From $45 ⊘ Closed Nov.–May.

TOURS

Camden Harbor Cruises

BOAT TOURS | FAMILY | The classic Maine lobster boats *Lively Lady* and *Periwinkle* carry passengers out onto Penobscot Bay to see how lobster traps are

hauled and perhaps even help to bait and reset them. There are also wildlife eco-tours, lighthouse tours, and a Sunday excursion to the island of Islesboro to visit the museum at Grindle Point Lighthouse. Trips last from 1½- to 3 hours. ⊠ *Public Landing, Camden* ☎ *207/236–6672* ⊕ *www.camdenharborcruises.com* ✉ From $20 ⊘ Closed mid-Oct.–mid-May.

Maine Sport Kayak Tours

BOAT TOURS | FAMILY | Two-hour guided kayak tours launch from the town landing in downtown Camden and paddle out through the harbor and around Curtis Island and its lighthouse. Along the way, the guide points out wildlife, offers interesting facts about the historic schooners and fishing vessels, and shares tidbits of local history. There's also a half-day paddle from Camden to Rockport, with a stop for a picnic lunch. ⊠ *Camden Harbor, Camden* ☎ *207/236–7120* ⊕ *www. mainesport.com* ✉ From $50 ⊘ Closed Oct.–June.

Lincolnville

6 miles north of Camden via U.S. 1.

Lincolnville's area of most interest is Lincolnville Beach, where you'll find a few restaurants, the ferry to Islesboro, and a swimming beach that attracts folks from neighboring Camden and Belfast. The village is tiny, but it's worth stopping to check out a couple of shops and have a bite to eat. The village's history goes back to the Revolution, and you can see a small cannon (never fired) on the beach here, intended to repel the British in the War of 1812.

GETTING HERE AND AROUND

Lincolnville Beach is on U.S. 1, and the town of Lincolnville Center is inland on Route 173. The Concord Coach Lines bus that travels along the coast stops here.

Sights

★ Cellardoor Winery

WINERY | The beautiful 5-mile drive on Route 52 from downtown Camden alongside Megunticook Lake to Cellardoor Winery is itself a good reason to visit, but the winery is fun, too. To discover which wine is your favorite, sip a glass ($12) or a flight of four ($15) in the magnificent barn or on the porch with views to Levenseller Mountain. Reservations for self-guided tastings are not required but are prioritized; reservations for hosted tastings ($20) are required. Buy a bottle of wine, or choose some wine glasses or other accouterments from the shop. A cheese board and other nibbles are also available. ✉ *367 Youngtown Rd., Lincolnville* ☎ *207/763–4478* 🌐 *www.mainewine.com* 🕓 *Closed Tues. and Wed.*

Restaurants

Lobster Pound Restaurant

$$$ | **SEAFOOD** | **FAMILY** | A fixture since 1926, this is an authentic place to enjoy a classic Maine lobster dinner—a cup of clam chowder, steamed clams, a 1-1/8-pound lobster, corn on the cob, potato, and Maine blueberry pie. The large restaurant has rustic wooden picnic tables outside, an enclosed patio, and two dining rooms with a gift shop in between, as well as tanks where you can pick from hundreds of live lobsters for your dinner. **Known for:** family-friendly environment; so many seats you'll never have to wait; a solid selection of local craft beers. [$] *Average main: $25* ✉ *2521 Atlantic Hwy., Lincolnville* ☎ *207/789–5550* 🌐 *www.lobsterpoundmaine.com* 🕓 *Closed Sun.*

Whale's Tooth Pub

$$$ | **SEAFOOD** | **FAMILY** | Located in a historic old brick building with an interior that is reminiscent of an Old English pub—dark heavy woods, dark atmosphere, a wood-burning fireplace that takes four-foot-long logs, copper kettles—the restaurant and pub are basically one. Among the items on the menu are steamed lobsters, mussels, seared tuna, fried calamari salad, broiled scallops, and other seafood, as well as prime rib, charbroiled steaks, ribs—and the very popular British-style fish-and-chips. **Known for:** beachside setting; cozy atmosphere; good gastropub menu. [$] *Average main: $30* ✉ *2531 Atlantic Hwy., Lincolnville* ☎ *207/789–5200* 🌐 *www.whalestoothpub.com* 🕓 *Closed Tues. and Wed.*

Hotels

Inn at Ocean's Edge

$$$$ | **B&B/INN** | This inn on 11 acres has one of the loveliest settings in the area, with forest on one side and the ocean on the other, and the recently renovated and updated rooms offer a king-size bed, gas fireplace, and ocean views. **Pros:** infinity-edge, heated saltwater pool; gas fireplaces In all rooms; beautiful waterfront setting. **Cons:** on the pricey side; drive to Camden or Lincolnville Beach for shopping and dining; extra charge for breakfast if room isn't booked directly with inn. [$] *Rooms from: $439* ✉ *24 Stonecoast Rd., Lincolnville* ☎ *207/236–0945* 🌐 *www.innatoceansedge.com* 🕓 *Closed mid-Oct.–mid-May* 🛏 *32 rooms* 🍴 *No Meals.*

★ Inn at Sunrise Point

$$$$ | **B&B/INN** | At this serene and exclusive retreat, you'll feel as though you're staying on a private estate where every comfort has been arranged for you. **Pros:** right beside the water; beautiful accommodations; extremely quiet and private. **Cons:** expensive; a distance from restaurants and shops; small common areas to share with fellow guests. [$] *Rooms from: $800* ✉ *55 Sunrise Point Rd., off Rte. 1, Lincolnville* ☎ *207/236–7716* 🌐 *www.sunrisepoint.com* 🕓 *Closed Nov.–Apr.* 🛏 *12 rooms* 🍴 *Free Breakfast.*

★ Lincolnville Motel

$ | HOTEL | FAMILY | Turn back the calendar to the 1950s in these sweet, fully renovated, mid-century wooden cabins, plus a few motel rooms. **Pros:** outdoor swimming pool; ocean views from back decks; dog-friendly. **Cons:** no TVs; coffee, but no breakfast; light early-morning traffic noise. [$] *Rooms from: $160* ✉ *4 Sea View Dr., Lincolnville* ☎ *207/236–3195* 🌐 *www.lincolnvillemotel.com* 🕒 *Closed Oct.–Apr.* 🛏 *10 rooms* 🍴 *No Meals.*

The Spouter Inn

$$ | B&B/INN | The rooms in this large, restored 1832 Colonial-style home and an attached carriage house are beautifully furnished with antiques. **Pros:** two restaurants just across the road; very convenient to Islesboro ferry; every room has a view of the bay. **Cons:** some road noise from Route 1; walls are somewhat thin, so you may hear your neighbors; you must drive to Camden's or Belfast's restaurants and shops. [$] *Rooms from: $299* ✉ *2506 Atlantic Hwy., U.S. 1, Lincolnville* ☎ *207/789–5171* 🌐 *www.spouterinnbnb.com* 🛏 *8 rooms* 🍴 *Free Breakfast.*

Victorian by the Sea

$$ | B&B/INN | With nicely landscaped grounds and a quiet waterside location well off U.S. 1, the Victorian feels as if it's a world away from all the hustle and bustle of town. **Pros:** secluded and quiet, with ocean views; some rooms have fireplaces; generous breakfast. **Cons:** drive to town for restaurants and shops; a little difficult to find; extra charge for breakfast for cottage rental. [$] *Rooms from: $289* ✉ *33 Sea View Dr., off Rte. 1, Lincolnville* ✣ *Turn next to Lincolnville Motel* ☎ *207/236–3785* 🌐 *www.victorianbythesea.com* 🕒 *Closed Nov.–Apr.* 🛏 *7 rooms* 🍴 *Free Breakfast* ☞ *No children under 7.*

Shopping

Maine Artisans Collective

CRAFTS | This is a wonderful place to find meaningful souvenirs of Maine. Made by dozens of Maine artisans, the finely hand-crafted pieces include jewelry, pottery, paintings, fine photography, clothing, skincare products, preserves, and household items. ✉ *2518 Atlantic Hwy., Lincolnville* ✣ *On U.S. 1* ☎ *207/789–5376* 🌐 *www.maineartisanscollective.com* 🕒 *Closed Nov.–June.*

Windsor Chairmakers

FURNITURE | In a collection of 19th-century buildings, you'll find beautifully crafted Windsor-style beds, chests, china cabinets, tables, highboys, and chairs, as well as Shaker pieces. There are 18 rooms of furniture on display, but most items are made to order. Be sure to peep into the converted barn workshop to watch the skilled artisans at work. It's easy to understand why the cost of larger pieces reaches into the thousands. ✉ *2596 Atlantic Hwy., U.S. Route 1, Lincolnville* ☎ *207/789–5188* 🌐 *www.windsorchair.com* 🕒 *Closed Sun.*

Belfast

13 miles north of Lincolnville via U.S. 1.

Along with several other Maine communities, Belfast is a strong contender for being named the state's prettiest town. Old-fashioned street lamps set the streets aglow at night and there are handsome ship captain's mansions and a tantalizing selection of shops, galleries, and restaurants all along Main and adjacent streets as well as a lively arts scene. Take the time to stroll down one side of Main Street all the way to the harbor, and then back up the other side. Within a few blocks, you can enjoy not only fresh local seafood, but also a taste of Thai, Lao, Japanese, Italian, and Jamaican cuisines. It's a delightful place to spend a day or two.

Islesboro

If you would like to visit a Penobscot Bay island but don't have much time, Islesboro (⊕ *townofislesboro. com*) is a pleasant choice, as it's only a 20-minute ferry ride from Lincolnville Beach on the mainland. But do plan accordingly as the ferry terminal on Islesboro is miles from the heart of the island, so you'll need wheels—a car or a bike—to explore the 14-mile-long island that includes the tiny village of Dark Harbor. ■TIP→ **If you plan on simply walking, you won't have time before boarding the return ferry to see much other than a country road and the museum at the lighthouse (the ferry landing is right beside it)—if the museum is open.**

Round-trip ferry passage for a driver and one passenger plus car is $42. When you add a reservation for your car—optional but strongly recommended in-season to ensure space on the ferry for your car—the total comes to $82.

The drive along Islesboro's main road from one end of the island to the other is lovely, though, and a number of nature preserves offer hiking trails that wend through woodlands to bold shores. Most visitor-oriented businesses are open seasonally (Memorial Day to Labor Day) including the Dark Harbor Shop, which sells sandwiches and ice cream. You can also buy picnic supplies at two stores: the Island Market, on the main road a short distance from the road to the ferry terminal; and Durkee's General Store (✉ *867 Main Rd.*), 5 miles farther north. There are no full-service restaurants on the island. Next to the ferry terminal is the Grindle Point Lighthouse; the Sailor's Memorial Museum is in the keeper's house (open on summer weekends).

The Islesboro Ferry (⊕ *www.maine. gov/mdot/ferry/islesboro*), operated by the Maine State Ferry Service, makes nine daily round trips from Lincolnville April through October and seven daily trips November through March. Try to head out on one of the early ferries so you have enough time to drive around and get back without missing the last ferry. There are *no* public lodging accommodations on the island.

■TIP→ **As you walk around town, you will see a number of cream-color signs labeled THE MUSEUM IN THE STREETS. Be sure to read them. The signs present all sorts of interesting facts and factoids about the history of Belfast.**

GETTING HERE AND AROUND

As it traces the coast, U.S. 1 runs through Belfast, though the center of town is a short drive off the highway. If you're traveling Interstate 95, take U.S. 3 East in Augusta to get here. The highways meet in Belfast, heading north. Concord Coach Lines' coastal bus stops in Belfast.

VISITOR INFORMATION

The information center has a large array of magazines, guidebooks, maps, and brochures that cover the entire Mid-Coast. It also can provide you with a free walking-tour brochure that describes the various handsome, historic buildings.

CONTACTS Belfast Area Chamber of Commerce. ✉ *Belfast* ☎ *207/338–5900* ⊕ *www.belfastmaine.org.*

Built in 1879, the historic Belfast National Bank is located at Main and Beaver Streets in downtown Belfast.

Sights

Belfast is infused with a decidedly artistic atmosphere, thanks in part to its having been a magnet for artists, artisans, and back-to-the-landers in the late 20th century. Today, the streets are lined with eclectic and sophisticated boutiques as well as a surprising array of restaurants. And, there's still evidence of the wealth of the mid-1800s, as High Street and the residential area above it are lined with the Greek Revival and Federal-style mansions of business tycoons, shipbuilders, and ship captains. Indeed, the town has one of the best showcases of Greek Revival homes in the state. Don't miss the privately owned "White House," an especially imposing mansion that stands where High and Church streets merge, several blocks south of downtown. Built in 1840, it's named for James P. White, its original owner; while it also used to be painted white, it's actually more cream-colored these days.

Restaurants

Chase's Daily

$ | **VEGETARIAN** | **FAMILY** | For more than two decades, this Main Street mainstay has been serving farm-to-table food to an enthusiastic Belfast community. Straight from the Chase family's farm to their restaurant, everything on the menu is vegetarian, including many entrées that are rooted in Indian cuisine. **Known for:** excellent vegetarian cuisine; home-baked goods; fresh-from-the-farm produce. ⓢ *Average main: $15* ✉ *96 Main St., Belfast* ☎ *207/338–0555* ⊕ *www.chasesdaily.me* ☉ *Closed Sun. and Mon.*

Darby's Restaurant and Pub

$$ | **AMERICAN** | **FAMILY** | With pressed-tin ceilings, this charming, old-fashioned restaurant and bar—it's been such since 1865—is a perennial local favorite with a welcoming community feel to it. Pad Thai, chicken chili salad with cashews, a Buddha bowl, and a few Mexican-flavored items are signature dishes, but the menu also serves hearty, scratch-made

soups, sandwiches on homemade bread, and classic fish-and-chips. **Known for:** excellent happy hour; gluten-free menu choices; homemade breads. $ *Average main: $18* ☒ *155 High St., Belfast* ☏ *207/338–2339* ⊕ *www.darbys-restaurant.com* ⊘ *Closed Sun.*

Delvino's Grill & Pasta House

$$ | **ITALIAN** | Tucked among Main Street's lineup of small shops, this intimate bistro serves exceptional house-made pastas and other Italian favorites—try the eggplant fries to start. Among the entrées, the mushroom Sacchetti (pasta pockets filled with wild porcini, roasted portobello mushrooms, and cheeses) are especially popular, and on Tuesday, there's a special, budget-friendly menu for two. **Known for:** fresh pasta dishes; great service; mushroom sachetti. $ *Average main: $20* ☒ *52 Main St., Belfast* ☏ *207/338–4565* ⊕ *www.delvinos.com.*

Fon's Kitchen

$ | **THAI** | Diners are greeted by a friendly smile at this small and airy eatery. It serves a standard Thai menu—think pad Thai, tom kha, and chicken satay—with exceptional preparations. **Known for:** pleasant decor; well-prepared Thai dishes; friendly service. $ *Average main: $12* ☒ *132 High St., Belfast* ✛ *Just off Main St. in middle of town* ☏ *207/218–1007* ⊕ *www.fonskitchen.com* ⊘ *Closed Sun. and Mon.*

Marshall Wharf

$ | **AMERICAN** | A longtime stalwart in Maine's craft brewing movement, Marshall Wharf brews IPAs, Scottish ale, stouts, porters, and more. Their outdoor deck directly on the harbor is the perfect place to sample from as many as 20 excellent brews on draft that are perfectly complemented by the small menu of light bites. **Known for:** wide variety of beers; laid-back atmosphere with live music; oyster stout. $ *Average main: $6* ☒ *36 Marshall Wharf, Belfast* ☏ *207/338–2700* ⊕ *www.marshallwharfbrewing.com* ⊘ *Closed Mon.*

★ Young's Lobster Pound

$$$ | **SEAFOOD** | **FAMILY** | Right on the water's edge, across the harbor from downtown Belfast, this corrugated-steel building looks more like a fish cannery than a restaurant, but it's one of the best places for an authentic Maine lobster dinner, known here as the "shore dinner." Lobster rolls, surf-and-turf dinners, steamed clams, steak tips, and hot dogs are popular, too. As this is a real-deal lobster pound, with absolutely no frills, lobstermen tie up at the dock to unload their catch. **Known for:** "shore dinner": clam chowder or lobster stew, steamed clams or mussels, a 1½-pound boiled lobster, corn on the cob, and chips; family-friendly environment; BYOB. $ *Average main: $30* ☒ *2 Fairview St., off U.S. 1, Belfast* ☏ *207/338–1160* ⊕ *www.youngslobsters. com* ⊘ *Takeout only Jan.–Mar.*

☕ Coffee and Quick Bites

Belfast Co-op

$ | **CAFÉ** | **FAMILY** | Established back in 1976, the Co-op is a very special place in Belfast, and it's not unusual to hear the expression, "I'll meet you at the Co-op." As the name implies, this full-service market is a members' cooperative that sells organic, locally grown vegetables, and other provisions, but you don't have to be a member to shop here or visit the popular Co-op Café for coffee, tea, sandwiches, soups, prepared dishes, and homemade pastries. It's an excellent and inexpensive place for breakfast or lunch with one of the best selections of wines in town. **Known for:** coffee, tea, and to-go items at the Co-op Café; great selection of wine; excellent and inexpensive place for breakfast or lunch. $ *Average main: $10* ☒ *123 High St., Belfast* ☏ *207/338–2532* ⊕ *www.belfast.coop.*

Chocolate Drop Candy Shop and Dave's Old Fashioned Soda Fountain

$ | **DESSERTS** | **FAMILY** | The real focus of this little shop is an old-fashioned soda fountain, complete with Formica tops, red stools, and paper-hat-wearing soda jerks. Order an ice-cream soda or shake, and complete your stroll down memory lane with a selection of sweets from your childhood, such as candy cigarettes, jawbreakers, licorice, Chuckles, and even clove gum. **Known for:** old-fashioned soda fountain drinks; nostalgic candy selection; Maine-made ice cream. [$] *Average main: $5* ✉ *35 Main St., Belfast* ☎ *207/338–0566* 🌐 *www.belfastcandy.com.*

Must Be Nice Lobster

$$ | SEAFOOD | Not only does Sadie Samuels captain her own lobster boat, the *Must Be Nice*, but she also transforms her haul into lobster rolls that she sells—along with crab rolls, fries, hot dogs, and burgers—from a lunch wagon parked at the bottom of Main Street, just up from the harbor. There are outdoor tables plus indoor seating alongside a small shop of items Samuels crafts herself. **Known for:** made by a local lobsterwoman; award-winning lobster rolls; mini lobster rolls at half the price of the full-size rolls. [$] *Average main: $18* ✉ *2 Cross St., Belfast* ☎ *207/218–1431* 🌐 *www.mustbenicelobster.com* 🕒 *Closed Mon.*

The Only Doughnut

$ | AMERICAN | FAMILY | You can get anything here as long as it's on a doughnut (accompanied by hot or iced coffee, if you wish). Made in the Maine tradition with potato flour, the day's flavors might include salted caramel, buttermilk, and "full-tilt" blueberry with a glorious blueberry glaze. **Known for:** the "citrus" (orange zest in the dough, lemon juice in the glaze); the "sea smoke" (chocolate doughnut, maple glaze, smokey salt); the "chocolate toasted coconut" (chocolate doughnut, coconut milk glaze, toasted coconut). [$] *Average main: $3* ✉ *225 Northport Ave., Belfast* ☎ *207/218–1231* 🌐 *theonlydoughnut.com* 🕒 *Closed Mon. and Tues.*

★ The Scone Goddess

$ | BAKERY | FAMILY | In a petite gray Cape (look for the mini red-and-white-striped lighthouse beside it), the Scone Goddess makes what are almost certainly the best scones you've ever tasted. Tender and a little crumbly—they bear no resemblance to those stone-hard lumps so often passed off as scones—flavors, which change daily, include ginger lemon, wild Maine blueberry lemon, raspberry cream, and bacon cheddar. **Known for:** unusual flavors; lattes and other beverages; easy-to-mix-and-bake mixes. [$] *Average main: $4* ✉ *1390 Atlantic Hwy., Northport* ✢ *3 miles from downtown Belfast* ☎ *207/323–0249* 🌐 *www.thesconegoddess.com* 🕒 *Closed Sun. and Mon.*

Hotels

Belfast Harbor Inn

$$ | MOTEL | FAMILY | This recently refreshed motel on U.S. Route 1 is a quick drive away from downtown Belfast. **Pros:** water-side rooms have private balconies; walk to water's edge; continental breakfast often includes hot entrée. **Cons:** rooms on road side may hear road noise; rooms on road side do not have balconies; drive to shops and restaurants. [$] *Rooms from: $290* ✉ *91 Searsport Ave., on U.S. 1, Belfast* ☎ *207/338–2740* 🌐 *belfastharborinn.com* 🔑 *60 rooms* 🍴 *Free Breakfast.*

Fireside Inn & Suites

$$ | HOTEL | FAMILY | Located on the bay side of Route 1 just north of the turnoff to downtown Belfast, this large and pleasant motel is a budget-friendly choice for families. **Pros:** all rooms have broad bay views; all rooms have patio or balcony access; walk down broad lawn to water's edge. **Cons:** balconies and patios are not private; basic continental breakfast; rooms are somewhat small. [$] *Rooms from: $229* ✉ *159 Searsport Ave., U.S. 1, Belfast* ☎ *207/338–2090* 🌐 *www.belfastmainehotel.com* 🔑 *84 rooms* 🍴 *Free Breakfast.*

The Jeweled Turret Inn

$ | B&B/INN | Turrets, jewel-like stained-glass windows, columns, gables, and magnificent woodwork embellish this inn, built in 1898 as the home of a local attorney. **Pros:** two verandas; walking distance to downtown shops and restaurants; breakfast plus afternoon tea or lemonade. **Cons:** no TV in rooms; lots of steps and no elevator; Victorian decor may feel claustrophobic. [$] *Rooms from: $189* ✉ *40 Pearl St., Belfast* ☎ *207/338–2304* 🌐 *www.jeweledturret.com* 🛏 *8 rooms* 🍴 *Free Breakfast.*

Nightlife

Rollie's Bar & Grill

BARS | FAMILY | Just up from the harbor, Rollie's has been in business since 1972 and it's especially popular with sports fans who come to watch the big game. The food is good and very well priced and may just have the best hamburgers in the state. You'll see families crop up around dinnertime, but food is served until midnight on Friday and Saturday and there's an excellent happy hour weekdays 3–6. There's a deck for outside dining, too. The vintage bar came from a 19th-century sailing ship. ✉ *37 Main St., Belfast* ☎ *207/338–4502* 🌐 *www.rollies.me* 🕒 *Closed Mon. and Tues.*

Shopping

ART AND ANTIQUES

★ Parent Fine Art

ART GALLERIES | An anchor in downtown Belfast, this two-decade-old gallery showcases the work of a super-talented family: luminescent paintings by Joanne Parent; dreamlike, mixed-media creations by Lee Parent; and masterful, mostly black-and-white or sepia photographs of the Maine coast and its fishing vessels and traditional windjammers by Neal Parent. These are complemented by the work of a handful of other talented artists. ✉ *92 Main St., Belfast* ☎ *207/338–1553* 🌐 *www.parentfineart.com.*

BOOKS

Left Bank Books

BOOKS | Belfast is blessed with multiple small bookshops, including Left Bank Books, located in the historic opera house building just off Main Street in the heart of downtown. It's the sort of place where you begin seeing books you want as soon as you step in the door. And if you don't, the knowledgeable staff will find it for you or happily order it. Books by Maine authors—many of them autographed—are a specialty. ✉ *109 Church St., Belfast* ☎ *207/338–9009* 🌐 *www.leftbankbookshop.com.*

CLOTHING

City Drawers

LINGERIE | It's a surprise to find such an upscale lingerie shop in a small town. The experienced saleswomen specialize in personalized, professional, and respectful bra fittings. The inventory includes dozens of fine brands in a wide range of sizes. ✉ *105 Main St., Belfast* ☎ *207/338–9980* 🌐 *www.citydrawers.com* 🕒 *Closed Sun.*

Coyote Moon

WOMEN'S CLOTHING | You'll find multiple appealing women's clothing shops along Main Street, but this is one of the best and the oldest. The clothing is stylish yet comfortable, with some boho pieces. The shop also carries a nice selection of jewelry. ✉ *54 Main St., Belfast* ☎ *207/338–5659* 🌐 *www.coyotemoonmaine.com.*

HOME AND GIFTS

Brambles

OTHER SPECIALTY STORE | The irresistible assortment of adornments for garden and home spills out onto the sidewalk at this charming shop in a sweet building just off Main Street. You'll find everything from wrought-iron planters to beautiful cloth napkins. ✉ *2 Cross St., Belfast* ☎ *207/338–3448*

⊕ *www.mainstreetmaine.org/listing/ brambles-gift-shop-belfast-maine.*

The Green Store

GENERAL STORE | Calling itself "a general store for the 21st century," the Green Store stocks a wide variety of household items, clothing, cards, and many other products. Most of the goods in this inviting emporium come from organic sources and all emphasize sustainability and preservation of the environment. It's a great place to browse, and chances are you'll discover something you need, or didn't need but have to have. ⊠ *71 Main St., Belfast.*

Activities

BOATING
The *Back and Forth*

BOATING | **FAMILY** | Carrying up to six passengers, the *Back and Forth* is a converted wooden lobster boat offering a selection of trips ranging from a 30-minute "jaunt around the bay" (kids under 12 ride free) to a variety of longer experiences including a one-and-a-half-hour family treasure hunter and a daytime or sunset cruise with a stop at Young's Lobster Pound for a lobster roll. Depending on the cruise, the cost is per person or per boat. ⊠ *Belfast City Harbor Dock, Belfast* ✛ *At bottom of Main St.* ☎ *207/323–2566* ⊕ *www.thebackandforth.com* ⊠ *From $18* ⊘ *Closed late Oct.–late May.*

Searsport

6 miles north of Belfast via U.S. 1.

Searsport is well known as a great destination for antiques and flea-market finds, and with good reason: several high-end antiques shops flank the road. The Antique Mall alone, on U.S. 1 just north of town, is home to some 60 dealers, and flea markets (for trash and treasures) line both sides of U.S. 1 during the visitor season.

Searsport also has a rich history of shipbuilding and seafaring. In the early to mid-1800s there were 10 shipbuilding facilities in Searsport. The population of the town was about 1,000 people more than it is today, and jobs were plentiful. By the mid-1800s Searsport was home to more than 200 sailing-ship captains. The Penobscot Marine Museum does a wonderful job of bringing the maritime heritage to life through engaging exhibits in several handsome old buildings. You can also sleep in a sea captain's mansion, as a couple of the grandest are now upscale inns.

GETTING HERE AND AROUND
Downtown Searsport is right along U.S. 1, as is much of the town, which doesn't have many side streets. The broad harbor, not visible from U.S. 1, lies just behind Main Street. The Concord Coach Lines bus that runs along the coast stops here.

Sights

★ Penobscot Marine Museum

MUSEUM VILLAGE | **FAMILY** | On a strollable campus that feels like a mini–New England village, this fine museum just off Main Street explores the centuries-long maritime culture of the Penobscot Bay region and the Maine coast. Exhibits of artifacts and paintings are spread throughout six buildings, most dating to the first half of the 19th century; a former sea captain's home is appointed with period furnishings. The story of Maine's long connections to the sea can be traced in photos of local ship captains, model ships, lots of scrimshaw, navigational instruments, and objects brought home from world-spanning voyages. Exhibits of vintage tools speak of the area's history of logging, granite mining, and ice cutting. Outstanding marine art includes a notable collection of works by Thomas and James Buttersworth. There are also engaging exhibits just for kids. ⊠ *2 Church St., Searsport* ☎ *207/548–2529* ⊕ *www.penobscotmarinemuseum. org* ⊠ *$15* ⊘ *Closed late-Oct.–late-May.*

🍴 Restaurants

Anglers

$$ | SEAFOOD | FAMILY | This little restaurant has been around for a long time and has a large local following so it can be a little hard to get a table on a busy night, but it's worth the wait. The traditional seafood dishes (fried or broiled) are good, the prices are reasonable, many dishes may be ordered in a "minnow" portion, and there are also a few choices for those who don't enjoy seafood. **Known for:** welcoming atmosphere; traditional seafood dishes; friendly service—it's the kind of place where the waitresses call you "Hon". $ *Average main: $20* ✉ *22 E. Main St., Searsport* ☎ *207/548–2405* ⊕ *anglersseafoodrestaurant.com.*

Hey Sailor!

$ | INTERNATIONAL | Orange bar stools, dark walls with art deco–like horizontal stripes, and deep booths define this dimly lit "gastro dive bar" that lists cocktails under ports of call—Caribbean, New England, and the Pacific. The menu features tacos and a mostly Mexican-flavor selection of bar snacks, with a couple of dish detours to Thailand and the South. **Known for:** lively, edgy atmosphere; tasty small plates; creative cocktails and mocktails and a good craft beer selection. $ *Average main: $14* ✉ *25 E. Main St., Searsport* ☎ *207/306–9132* ⊕ *www.heysailorhey.com* ⊘ *Closed Tues. and Wed.*

★ Homeport Tavern

$$ | SOUTHERN | With tufted green leather settees and a wood-burning brick fireplace, the Homeport Tavern, part of the Homeport Inn, exudes an English-accented coziness. While bangers and mash and fish-and-chips give a nod to the old country and New England seafood is well represented, many dishes on the lunch and dinner menus have a distinctly Southern drawl. **Known for:** snug atmosphere; Louisiana comfort food; welcoming hosts. $ *Average main: $22* ✉ *121 E. Main St., Searsport* ☎ *207/548–2259*

⊕ *www.homeporthistoricinn.com* ⊘ *Closed Mon. and Tues.*

Rio's Spiked Café

$$ | MEDITERRANEAN | Don't be put off by Rio's unlikely location in a small roadside strip of businesses just south of downtown Searsport. The well-prepared, European-influenced menu offers a variety of tapas such as grilled octopus, pâté, Spanish Serrano ham, and chorizo, as well as entrées like roasted branzino, risotto, and local duck breast. **Known for:** creative weekend brunch choices; tapas; eclectic European and Southern dishes. $ *Average main: $20* ✉ *357 W. Main St., Searsport* ☎ *207/548–4016* ⊕ *www.riosspikedcafe.com* ⊘ *Closed Mon. and Tues.*

🛏 Hotels

★ Captain Nickels Inn

$$$$ | B&B/INN | Built in 1874 and listed on the National Register of Historic Places, this grand, elegantly restored mansion hails from an era when Searsport's shipyards launched more than 200 vessels and their captains sailed the world's trade routes, amassing fortunes along the way. **Pros:** full breakfast included; popular for weddings and corporate retreats; beautiful bayside setting. **Cons:** most bedrooms are up a steep staircase; some rooms are somewhat small; one bedroom's private bath is across the hall. $ *Rooms from: $400* ✉ *127 E. Main St., Searsport* ☎ *207/548–1104* ⊕ *captainnickelsinn.com* 🛏 *9 rooms* ❖ *Free Breakfast.*

★ The Homeport Inn

$$$ | B&B/INN | A top-to-bottom renovation and upgrade in 2022 has created a pleasing blend of period elegance and modern comforts at this grand 1861 sea captain's mansion, which is listed on the National Register of Historic Places. **Pros:** close to downtown Searsport; on-site tavern serving lunch and dinner 5 days a week; in-room espresso machines. **Cons:** some road noise from Route 1; breakfast not included in lodging cost; two rooms have

The 2,120-foot-long, cable-stayed Penobscot Narrows Bridge is taller than the Statue of Liberty.

shared bathroom. [$] *Rooms from: $350* ✉ *121 E. Main St., Searsport* ☎ *207/548–2259* 🌐 *www.homeporthistoricinn.com* 🛏 *9 rooms* 🍴 *No Meals.*

Shopping

★ Splendiferous Sweet Shoppe

CANDY | FAMILY | Said to be the world's only Alice in Wonderland–theme candy store, Splendiferous is tucked into a charmingly petite former bank building. You'll be greeted by the Queen of Hearts or Alice from behind a counter laden with excellent house-made chocolates. Choices include macaroons, macarons, turtles, filled chocolates, and needhams (an old-fashioned Maine coconut candy). A small, original vault is chockablock with "penny" candy. The ladies also serve ice cream that's churned just up the road in Ellsworth, and drinks made from locally roasted coffee. Ask to peek into the secret door at the end of the counter. ✉ *21 E. Main St., Searsport* ☎ *207/538–6729* 🌐 *www.splendiferoussweet-shoppe.com* 🕓 *Closed Tues. and Wed.*

Trove

CRAFTS | Proprietor Laura Brown displays beautifully handcrafted, sleek, and functional items for the home in an open and uncluttered space, drawing visitors in to browse and buy. The appealing selection ranges from handsome pottery and leather goods to textiles, soaps, and jewelry. Brown features rotating art shows in a gallery nook at the back of the shop. ✉ *36 E. Main St., Searsport* ☎ *207/548–4073* 🌐 *www.trovemaine.com* 🕓 *Closed Sun.–Tues.*

Bucksport

9 miles north of Searsport via U.S. 1.

Bucksport experienced a bumpy time following the closing a few years ago of a large paper mill that was a major employer. Happily, it is now experiencing a renaissance with new restaurants and shops popping up along Main Street. Just across from town, the stunning and graceful Penobscot Narrows Bridge and Observatory (the world's tallest public bridge observatory) stands taller than the Statue of Liberty. Take the time to ascend via elevator to the bridge-top observatory for sweeping views of land and sea. Fort Knox, Maine's largest historic fort, also overlooks the town from across the Penobscot River. Stroll the paved, garden-bordered riverfront walkway that edges Bucksport's downtown to take in magnificent vistas of both the imposing fort and the bridge.

GETTING HERE AND AROUND

Driving north on Route 1, pass over the spectacular Penobscot Narrows Bridge onto small Verona Island. Then cross a second bridge to Bucksport. Turn left to head down Main Street.

Sights

Fort Knox Historic Site
HISTORIC SIGHT | FAMILY | Next to the Penobscot Narrows Bridge is Fort Knox, Maine's largest historic fort. It was built of granite on the west bank of the Penobscot River between 1844 and 1869 when, despite a treaty with Britain settling boundary disputes, invasion was still a concern—after all, the British controlled this region during both the Revolutionary War and the War of 1812. The fort never saw any real action, but it was used for troop training and as a garrison during the Civil War and the Spanish-American War. Ghost hunters have reported a range of paranormal activities here. Visitors are welcome to explore the many rooms and passageways. Guided tours are given between 11 and 3 when volunteers are available. ✉ *740 Ft. Knox Rd., Prospect* ☎ *207/469–6553* 🌐 *www.fortknoxmaine.com* 🎫 *Fort $7; fort and observatory $9* 🕑 *Fort closed Nov.–Apr.*

★ Penobscot Narrows Bridge and Observatory Tower
VIEWPOINT | FAMILY | An "engineering marvel" is how experts describe this beautiful, cable-stayed, 2,120-foot-long Penobscot Narrows Bridge, which is taller than the Statue of Liberty. As one approaches, the bridge appears in the distance like the towers of a fairy-tale castle. The observatory, perched near the top of a 437-foot-tall tower and accessed by an elevator, is the tallest public bridge observatory in the world. Don't miss it—the panoramic views, which take in the hilly countryside and the Penobscot River as it widens into Penobscot Bay, are breathtaking. ✉ *711 Ft. Knox Rd., off U.S. 1, Prospect* ☎ *207/469–6553* 🌐 *www.maine.gov/mdot/pnbo* 🎫 *Fort and observatory $9* 🕑 *Closed Nov.–May.*

Restaurants

★ Friar's Brewhouse Taproom
$ | AMERICAN | FAMILY | You probably wouldn't expect to find an eatery run by Franciscan friars in this little town, but you'll be glad you did. Dressed in long brown habits, your hosts happily serve excellent European-style beers brewed in their nearby mountainside friary, which pair well with sandwiches on freshly baked baguettes, or hearty entrées that blend Maine and French Canadian flavors like family-recipe meat loaf, from-scratch soups, pâté, and fresh local fish dishes. **Known for:** fresh-baked breads; thoughtfully prepared dishes; warm and welcoming friars. [$] *Average main: $15* ✉ *84A Main St., Bucksport* ☎ *207/702–9156* 🌐 *www.facebook.com/friarbrew.hotmail/* 🕑 *Closed Sun. and Mon.*

MacLeod's Seafood & Steak House

$$ | SEAFOOD | FAMILY | A local favorite since 1980, MacLeod's serves a surprisingly wide variety of choices. Entrées include raspberry roasted duck, steak, ribs, broiled or fried local seafood, and a few Mexican-style options. **Known for:** fresh seafood, aged steaks; comfort food; great for families. [$] *Average main: $20* ✉ *63 Main St., Bucksport* ☎ *207/469–3963* 🌐 *www.macleodsrestaurant.com* 🕓 *Closed Sun.–Tues. No lunch.*

Verona Island Wine and Design

$ | CAFÉ | In an intimate courtyard hidden at the back of a historic brick house in the heart of downtown Bucksport, this weather-dependent outdoor dining space features Mediterranean tapas-style plates accompanied by good wines and beers. The adjacent retail shop sells an international selection of premium wines as well as products made from recycled wine barrels. **Known for:** pleasant outdoor setting; delicious light dishes; live music. [$] *Average main: $15* ✉ *77 Main St., Bucksport* ☎ *207/745–0731* 🌐 *www.veronawineanddesign.com* 🕓 *Closed Sun.–Tues. and Nov.–June and in inclement weather. No lunch.*

Chapter 7

BLUE HILL PENINSULA AND DEER ISLE

Updated by
Christine Rudalevige

◉ Sights	⑪ Restaurants	🛏 Hotels	🛍 Shopping	⛾ Nightlife
★★★★☆	★★★★☆	★★★★☆	★★★★☆	★★☆☆☆

WELCOME TO BLUE HILL PENINSULA AND DEER ISLE

TOP REASONS TO GO

★ **Seafood:** From the high-end tasting menu at Aragosta at Goose Cove on Deer Isle to the fry baskets at Bagaduce Lunch in Penobscot, fish is what's for dinner.

★ **Seascapes:** Admire Penobscot Bay from atop Caterpillar Hill. Watch the sunset over Wadsworth Cove in Castine. Observe maritime comings and goings in Stonington Harbor.

★ **Hiking:** Several heritage trusts maintain more than 50 hiking trails and preserves in this region.

★ **Local arts:** Catch everything from chamber music at Kneisel Hall to steel-drum bands. Explore galleries filled with paintings depicting area sea- and landscapes. Visit shops and studios to find an array of items made by local artisans.

★ **Kayaking:** Many places on the peninsula and the islands have public boat launches if you bring your own kayak, and several outfitters rent gear and offer instruction and guided tours.

To explore the Blue Hill Peninsula, the 20-mile-long finger of land that juts into the Penobscot Bay, you need a car, a good paper map (cell service is spotty), and a relaxed schedule. Just to the south of the peninsula, Little Deer Isle and Deer Isle are accessible by bridge; Isle au Haut, which is part of Acadia National park, can be reached by mail boat. The rest of Acadia is an easy day trip from the region.

1 Castine. Markers and museums detail this town's roles as a French and an English outpost during the colonial period, a port for trading ships and fishing vessels in the early 1800s, and a summer destination for the wealthy since the late 19th century.

2 Blue Hill. Snuggled between Blue Hill Mountain and Blue Hill Bay, this village is the place to shop for antiques, art, books, clothing, provisions, and toys.

3 Brooklin, Sedgwick, and Brooksville. Meandering farmland, pretty coves, and blueberry barrens surround these towns, each with its own draw. Brooklin has the Wooden Boat School, Sedgwick has the Eggemoggin Reach that separates it from Deer Isle, and Brooksville has intriguing restaurants.

4 Deer Isle. This center of this cute village, bounded by Northwest Harbor on one side and Mill Pond on the other, is a great place to grab coffee and pastry and find Maine-made, one-of-a-kind gifts.

5 Stonington. All roads lead to Stonington on the southern tip of Deer Isle. Although restaurants, boutiques, and galleries along Main Street cater to summertime visitors, the town remains a fishing community at heart.

6 Isle au Haut. Accessible by a 45-minute mail boat ride from Stonington, this island is ideal for day trippers who like to hike.

If unspoiled seascapes and an unhurried pace are your jam, then visit the Blue Hill Peninsula. Not much of it, or the Little Deer and Deer isles to its south, has been developed.

With few manmade distractions, you can focus on the many natural attractions while meandering the peninsula's labyrinth of well-paved roads. Excursions in Penobscot Bay—aboard the daily mail boat to Isle au Haut, on a motorboat cruise, or by kayak—are breezy seafaring ways to enjoy the peninsula and islands. If you're an experienced kayaker, you can paddle to an archipelago of uninhabited islands known as Merchant's Row and camp at secluded sites maintained by the Maine Coastal Heritage Trust.

Trails maintained by the Blue Hill Heritage Trust and the Island Heritage Trust offer their own unique perspectives. Many lead to vistas that have inspired generations of artists: hills covered with blueberry barrens, majestic granite formations, cascading farmland speckled with grazing livestock and hay wheels, pine-studded rocky coastlines, and the sea—always the sea.

You can sample regional bounty at roadside lobster shacks and farm stands, greasy spoon diners, and an increasing number of fine-dining restaurants and wine bars, many of which are part of historic inns. Galleries, studios, and shops showcasing art, pottery, and jewelry dot the region, highlighting the creativity of its residents.

Towns and villages such as Castine, Blue Hill, Brooksville, Sedgewick, and Stonington offer simple pleasures, like leisurely strolls through historic districts and explorations of time-honored waterfronts, where Maine fishermen and boat builders still work as hard as their forebears. Community bulletin boards in shops and other businesses are filled with posters announcing crab-roll lunches, pot-luck dinners, town-band concerts, daybreak yoga classes, and makers markets.

Topping it all off are magnificent sunrises on the eastern side of the peninsula and islands and brilliant sunsets on the western one. Both are just two more of Blue Hill's many unspoiled, unhurried experiences.

Planning

Getting Here and Around

AIR

Trenton's Hancock County–Bar Harbor Airport is near the Blue Hill Peninsula, but only two commuter airlines—CapeAir and JetBlue—fly between it and Boston. On clear days, this flight affords a bird's-eye views of the Maine Coast, but bad weather often makes arrivals and departures uncertain.

Most travelers to the peninsula prefer Bangor International Airport, which is an hour's drive from Blue Hill and which is served by American, Delta, and United. Major car rental companies have branches here, but it's best to book rental cars well in advance.

CONTACTS Bangor International Airport. (*BGR*) ✉ *287 Godfrey Blvd., Bangor* ☎ *207/992–4600* ✈ *www.flybangor.com.* **Hancock County–Bar Harbor Airport.** ✉ *115 Caruso Dr., Trenton* ☎ *866/227–3247* ✈ *www.bhbairport.com.*

BICYCLE

The Blue Hill Peninsula's winding roads rarely have adequate bike lanes, so be on your guard when exploring the region. Although there are a few bike-rental shops in the area, your best bet is to take your own bike, especially if you plan to cycle on Isle au Haut or other parts of Acadia National Park.

CONTACTS The Activity Shop. ✉ *139 Mines Rd., Blue Hill* ☎ *207/374–3600* ✈ *www.theactivityshop.com.*

BOAT

To get to and from Isle au Haut, the mail boat operated by Isle au Haut Boat Services is your best bet, with four trips a day Monday through Saturday and two trips on Sunday in summer. This company also offers regular puffin and lighthouse tours and private charters to Camden and Mt. Desert Island.

CONTACTS Isle au Haut Boat Services. ✉ *27 Seabreeze Ave., Stonington* ☎ *207/367–5193* ✈ *www.isleauhaut.com.*

BUS

Concord Coach Lines offers a bus from Boston's South Station to Bangor several times a day and drops passengers off across the street from the Bangor International Airport where car rentals are available.

CONTACTS Concord Coach Lines. ✉ *Blue Hill* ☎ *800/639–3300* ✈ *www.concordcoachlines.com.*

CAR

If you're traveling north up the coast on Route 1, you can get to the peninsula by picking up Route 15 about 4½ miles after passing through Bucksport. If you're traveling south, your best bet is to follow Route 172 toward Blue Hill, where it branches off near Ellsworth.

Little Deer Isle and Deer Isle are accessible by bridge. Route 15 brings you to the village of Deer Isle, where the road splits off with Route 15A. The former is the most direct route to Stonington, while the latter meanders along the islands western edge, terminating in Stonington as well. There, you can catch a ferry to Isle au Haut and Duck Harbor.

Hotels

You won't find grand, sprawling hotels on the Blue Hill Peninsula. Instead, the countryside is dotted with inns, bed-and-breakfasts, and small but distinguished hotels. Although summer days in August can get quite warm, ocean breezes will cool your room at night, so few accommodations have air-conditioning. Some places might not have in-room TVs or phones, but most will have Wi-Fi service of some type.

Restaurants

Dining options on the Blue Hill Peninsula and Deer Isle tend to fall into one of two categories: expensive restaurants where you can expect gourmet cuisine or more casual places where you can grab a fry basket, burger, or lobster roll. There are no fast-food chains in this part of the world. You can always count on finding fresh seafood, but many restaurants on the peninsula also proudly promote their locally raised produce and meats. This emphasis is not just on eating healthier foods; it's also a deliberate effort to support local farmers and fishermen.

HOTEL AND RESTAURANT PRICES

Hotel and restaurant reviews have been shortened. For full information, visit Fodors.com. Hotel prices in the reviews are the lowest cost of a standard double room in high season. Restaurant prices

Great Itineraries

If You Have 1 Day

For a comprehensive one-day tour of the Blue Hill Peninsula and Deer Isle, without spending all of it in an automobile, start with a stroll around Blue Hill's downtown followed by a hike up Blue Hill Mountain for 360-degree views. Then drive 45 minutes to Stonington—via panoramic Caterpillar Hill and the Deer Isle bridge—for some shopping in boutiques on Main Street.

In the afternoon, drive back to the mainland, taking scenic Route 175 through Sargentville, Sedgwick, and Brooklin before crossing the Blue Hill Falls bridge and driving west on Route 172 to Route 177 and South Penobscot. Continue to Castine to enjoy the historic architecture and have dinner on the deck of the Dennett's Wharf restaurant.

If You Have 3 Days

Stay in Blue Hill, and visit the town's shops and galleries on your first morning. In the afternoon visit neighboring Brooklin—home to the world-famous Wooden Boat School—Sedgwick, and Brooksville, where if you plan ahead, you can have pizza en plein air at Tinder Hearth Bakery. Alternatively, swing north and hit Bagaduce Lunch for dinner.

On Day 2, climb Blue Hill Mountain for 360-degree peninsula views, and then head to The Lobster Lady restaurant for a roll or a bowl of chowder. Drive on to Castine and take the town walking tour. Stop into the Compass Rose Books & Cafe for a browse and a caffeinated beverage or the Pentogoet Inn Wine Bar for a drink.

On your last day, head down to Deer Isle, starting the day off right with a cup of 44 North Coffee at its cafes in Deer Isle village or Stonington. Spend the rest of your time learning about the region's rocky past at the Deer Isle Granite Museum, taking in low tide passages to Barred Island Preserve, or visiting the less-austere but still bizarrely interesting sculpture garden at Nervous Nellies Jams and Jellies. You can grab a bite at The Harbor Café in Stonington.

are the average cost of a main course at dinner, or if dinner is not served, at lunch.

What It Costs In U.S. Dollars

	$	$$	$$$	$$$$
RESTAURANTS				
	under $18	$18–$24	$25–$35	over $35
HOTELS				
	under $200	$200–$299	$300–$399	over $399

Visitor Information

Deer Isle has numerous nature preserves and parks grouped under the stewardship of the Island Heritage Trust. Stop by the office for brochures and more information about the nature preserves listed below (as well as others).

CONTACTS Blue Hill Heritage Trust. ⊠ *157 Hinckley Ridge Rd., Blue Hill* ☎ *207/374-5118* ⊕ *bluehillheritagetrust.org.* **Blue Hill Peninsula Chamber of Commerce.** ⊠ *16 South St., Suite B, Blue Hill* ☎ *207/374-3242* ⊕ *www.bluehillpeninsula.org.* **Deer Isle–Stonington Chamber of Commerce.**

✉ *114 Little Deer Isle Rd., Deer Isle* ☎ *207/348–6124* ⊕ *www.deerisle.com.* **Island Heritage Trust.** ✉ *420 Sunset Rd., Deer Isle* ☎ *207/348–2455* ⊕ *www. islandheritagetrust.org.*

When to Go

Both the Blue Hill Peninsula and the Deer Isles are inhabited year-round, but the weather and tourist-centered businesses are most hospitable from late May through the middle of October. Outside of these months, you will find temperatures below freezing and many restaurants and inns closed for the season.

In summer, it's best to make reservations for accommodation, dining, and ferry services well in advance. Also in the summertime, galleries open their doors, concerts of all sorts enliven the evenings, and a handful of festivals attract locals and visitors alike.

FESTIVALS AND EVENTS

Wings, Waves and Woods. Held the third weekend in May, this birding festival on Deer Isle offers workshops, bird walks and boat tours so participants can see Atlantic puffins, razorbills, northern gannets, and up to two dozen species of warblers. ⊕ *www.islandheritagetrust.org*

Lupine Festival. This Deer Island–wide event in June includes trail walks on island preserves, boat tours, puffin boat trips, airplane rides, art exhibits, and kids' activities. ⊕ *www.deerisle.com*

Lobster Boat Races. Held in July, this race celebrates the Deer Isle's lobstering livelihood. ⊕ *www.deerisle.com*

Eggemoggin Reach Regatta. More than 100 wooden boats vie for bragging rights as they race off Naskeag Point in early August. ⊕ *www.erregatta.com*

Blue Hill Fair. Held Labor Day weekend, this old-time country fair inspired the fair featured in *Charlotte's Web,* written by E.B. White. It has agricultural exhibits, food, rides, and entertainment. ⊕ *www. bluehillfair.com*

Word. Although libraries and book stores hold book talks year-round, Blue Hill's late October literary festival makes reading and writing in Maine buzz-worthy. ⊕ *www.wordfestival.org*

Castine

22 miles south of Bucksport.

As one of the oldest towns in New England, Castine has a rich history. The Abanaki people inhabited the area long before the French established a trading post here, near Fort Pentagoet, in 1613. Given its strategic Penobscot Bay location and its importance to both the lucrative fur and timber industries, the French, English, and Dutch battled for control of it throughout the 17th and 18th centuries.

By the 19th century, Castine had become a port for trading ships and fishing vessels. Although train travel brought the town's prominence as a port to an end, in the late 1800s, some of the nation's wealthier citizens began summering here. In 1941, the state established the Maine Maritime Academy, a still-operating public college that sits on the hill above the town center and focuses on maritime science and engineering training.

With Federal- and Greek Revival–style architecture, spectacular Penobscot Bay views, and a peaceful setting, Castine is a good place to spend a day or two. Historical markers posted throughout town make it easy to do a self-guided walking tour. Consider parking your car at the public landing and walking up Main Street toward the white Trinitarian Federated Church. Among the white-clapboard buildings encircling the town common are the Ives House (once the summer home of poet Robert Lowell), the Abbott School, and the Unitarian Church with its whimsical belfry.

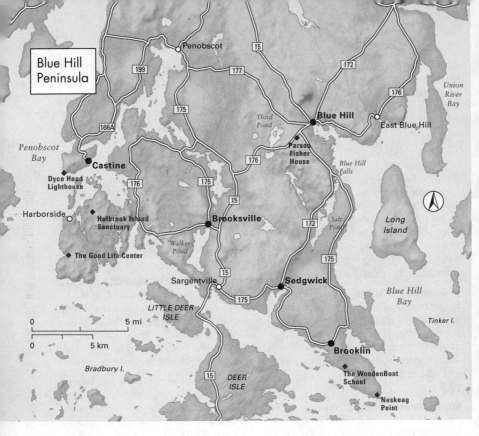

GETTING HERE AND AROUND

From Bucksport, Route 46 travels southeast to Orland. From there, Route 166 travels all way south to Castine.

Sights

Large signposts mark historical sights in Castine's lively harbor and village, where stops at shops and galleries add to the enjoyment of a stroll. You can also pick up a self-guided walking tour booklet at the Wilson Museum or the historical society, which offers guided outings on Mondays in summer. If you don't want to walk, head to the town dock and board the nonprofit Castine Touring Company's (⊕ castine-touring-company.business. site) roomy golf cart for a guided tour.

★ Castine Historical Society

HISTORY MUSEUM | This local museum digs into Castine's rich history with exhibitions and live reenactments that showcase important artifacts and ephemera from the past. It's newest exhibit features the work of world-renowned sculptor and Castine resident, Clark Fitz-Gerald. In addition, the society offers guided walking tours of the town on most Mondays during the summer. It's also a good place to get your bearings, find out what's going on in town, and maybe pick up a self-guided walking tour booklet. ⊠ 13 and 17 School St., Castine ☎ 207/326–4118 ⊕ www.castinehistoricalsociety. org ⊗ Closed Tues.–Thurs. in fall and mid-Oct.–early June.

Dyce Head Lighthouse

LIGHTHOUSE | FAMILY | Built in 1828 at the mouth of the Penobscot River in Castine Harbor to guide mariners upriver to the lumber port of Bangor, the light was discontinued in 1935. The tower was damaged in a storm but rebuilt in 2008. The original keeper's house, barn, and oil house still remain, but are privately owned. You can see them all from an adjacent public footpath, which is is short, steep (made less so by wooden stairs), and leads to a quiet view of the islands in the harbor. There's limited street parking available. ✉ *Dyce Head Rd., Castine* 🎟 *Free.*

★ Wilson Museum

HISTORY MUSEUM | FAMILY | The 4-acre campus of this museum has multiple historic structures. The main building houses anthropologist-geologist John Howard Wilson's collection of prehistoric artifacts from around the world. The **John & Phebe Perkins House** Is a restored 1763 residence originally built on what is now Court Street. The house fell into disrepair until the 1960s, when the Castine Scientific Society had it taken down piece by piece and reassembled on the grounds here. Inside, you can find Perkins family heirlooms and 18th- and early-19th-century furnishings. On the lower level, exhibits in the **Perkins Gallery** share stories and objects from 19th-century Castine, Penobscot, and Brooksville. The museum shop here features a curated selection of books for all ages, historical maps and prints, souvenirs, crafts, and educational toys.

The **Hutchins Education Center** offers year-round programs and seasonal exhibits. The **Blacksmith Shop** holds demonstrations showing all the tricks of this old-time trade. In addition to displays of small traditional boats, the **Wood Shop** has woodworking demonstrations and a workshop where boats are often under construction. The **Bagaduce Engine Company** showcases early firefighting memorabilia, including Castine's 1917 fire alarm, which still works! ✉ *120 Perkins St., Castine* ☎ *207/326–9247* 🌐 *www.wilsonmuseum.org* 🎟 *Free; Perkins House guided tours $5* 🕒 *Museum closed Oct.–late May.*

🍴 Restaurants

★ Dennett's Wharf

$$$ | AMERICAN | This well-established restaurant got a major overhaul in the spring of 2022 when formerly New York–based restaurateur Max Katzenberg took over and recruited Southern chef Taylor Hester. It offers Maine classics like Stonington Lobster Rolls and MDI mussels, as well littleneck clams linguine, New York strip steak au poivre, and family-size plates of Southern fried chicken. **Known for:** waterside deck; boating community favorite; lobster Cobb salad. [$] *Average main: $30* ✉ *15 Sea St., Castine* ☎ *207/326–5026* 🌐 *www.dennetts.co* 🕒 *Closed Mon.–Thurs. No lunch Fri.*

★ Pentagoet Inn Wine Bar

$$$ | MODERN AMERICAN | This upscale but relaxed place has a long list of farm- or sea-to-table small plates. Supplementing the well-curated selection of wines is a menu of craft cocktails and local beers. **Known for:** cheese and charcuterie boards; cozy, country inn setting; Maine blueberry crisp. [$] *Average main: $35* ✉ *26 Main St., Castine* ☎ *207/326–8616* 🌐 *www.pentagoet.com* 🕒 *Closed Nov.–Apr. and Sun. and Mon. May–Oct.*

Castine is home to the Maine Maritime Academy.

Hotels

The Castine Cottages

$$ | **HOUSE** | **FAMILY** | Built in the late 1950s, these six old-school (but Wi-Fi-equipped), two-bedroom log cottages offer an amazing view of both Blue Hill and the Bagaduce River, water access from a private dock, screened porches, and plenty of room to run around outdoors. **Pros:** well-behaved pets allowd; peaceful location; well-equipped and homey. **Cons:** weekly rentals; must drive to town; might be too rustic for some. [$] *Rooms from: $225* ✉ *33 Snapp's Way, Castine* ☎ *207/326–8003* 🌐 *www.castinecottages.com* 🛏 *6 cottages* 🍴 *No Meals.*

The Castine Inn

$$ | **B&B/INN** | **FAMILY** | Built in 1898, this elegant inn just a block from the harbor has a wraparound porch, an inviting sitting room, and a cozy pub where guests can enjoy a full bar. **Pros:** lovely perennial gardens; in the heart of town; tastefully appointed guest rooms. **Cons:** can book up with wedding parties; not all rooms have a/c; can be noisy when students are in town. [$] *Rooms from: $200* ✉ *33 Main St., Castine* ☎ *207/326–4365* 🌐 *www.castineinn.com* 🛏 *19 rooms* 🍴 *Free Breakfast.*

The Pentagoet Inn

$$ | **B&B/INN** | Nestled among majestic elm trees on a hill overlooking the village and harbor, this charming Queen Anne Victorian inn has a prominent three-story turret, gables, and a delightful wraparound porch lined with blossoming perennials. **Pros:** great views; some rooms are pet-friendly; good on-site wine bar with small plates. **Cons:** no a/c; breakfast needs improvment; atmosphere might be too staid for some. [$] *Rooms from: $280* ✉ *26 Main St., Castine* ☎ *207/326–8616* 🌐 *pentagoet.com* 🕒 *Closed Nov.–Apr.* 🛏 *16 rooms* 🍴 *Free Breakfast.*

♀ Nightlife

Danny Murphy's Pub
PUBS | An admirable beer selection, good pub grub, and a pool table are all on tap at this casual local hangout. ✉ *5 Sea St., Castine* ☎ *207/326–1004.*

Performing Arts

Annex Arts
ARTS CENTERS | Castine's hub for visual and performing arts hosts exhibitions, literary events, workshops, panel discussions, and film screenings. ✉ *8 Water St., Castine* ☎ *213/839–0851* ⊕ *annexarts.org.*

🛍 Shopping

Adam Gallery
ART GALLERIES | This is where husband-and-wife artists Susan and Joshua Adams display and sell their oil paintings primarily showcasing landscapes. ✉ *7 Main St., Castine* ☎ *207/326–7123* ⊕ *www.adamgalleryonline.com* ⊗ *Closed Oct.–May and Mon.–Wed. June–Sept.*

Analog Attic
MUSIC | Located above Mary Margaret's Mercantile, this record shop has vinyl, cassettes, CDs, and posters. ✉ *15 Main St., Castine* ☎ *207/326–5102* ⊗ *Closed Mon. and Tues.*

★ Compass Rose Bookstore & Café
BOOKS | The store is well stocked with books and tasteful gifts for all ages. The café has lovely pastries and top-notch coffee. ✉ *3 Main St., Castine* ☎ *207/326–9366* ⊕ *www.compassrosebookscastine.com* ⊗ *Closed Mon.*

Highlands Woodturning & Engraving
CRAFTS | Craftsman Temple Blackwood creates and sells wood-turned art and decorative items at his studio, where you can also sign up for a woodturning demonstration or workshop. ✉ *872 Castine Rd., Castine* ☎ *207/951–5086* ⊕ *www.highlandswoodturning.com* ☞ *Open by appointment only.*

Mary Margaret's Mercantile
GENERAL STORE | This elegant emporium sells clothing (for ladies and babies), hats, jewelry, yarn, and gifts (as well as lovely papers to wrap them in). ✉ *15 Main St., Castine* ☎ *207/326–5102* ⊕ *www.marymargaretsmercantile.com* ⊗ *Closed Sun. and Mon.*

Activities

Castine Kayak Adventures
KAYAKING | FAMILY | Castine Kayak Adventures offers customized sea-kayaking tours and instructional clinics for beginners and experienced paddlers alike. Registered Maine Guides lead small groups on exciting ecotours, exploring marine sea life, geology and Castine's rich history. Sign up for a half day of kayaking along the shore, a full day of kayaking in Penobscot Bay, or nighttime trips where paddling stirs up bioluminescent phytoplankton. The company offers overnight and multi-day kayak camping trips, custom kayak weddings, and kids' camps. It also rents kayaks, standup paddleboards, and bicycles. ✉ *17 Sea St., Castine* ☎ *207/866–3506* ⊕ *www.castinekayak.com* ⊗ *Closed Nov.–Apr.*

Castine Cruise Lines
CRUISE EXCURSIONS | FAMILY | Castine Cruises offers tours around Castine Harbor on *Lil' Toot* boat, a 26-foot Crosby Tug. Captains and guides work in tandem to give you a view of and information about Dyce Head Lighthouse, Revolutionary War naval battles, marine ecology, seals, and eagles. The 90-minute excursions depart several times a day in summer. You can also combine a tour with drop-off and pickup service at the Holbrook Island Sanctuary to get time ashore exploring island trails, beaches, and picnic spots. ✉ *Castine Town Dock, Main St., Castine* ☎ *207/701–1421* ⊕ *castinecruises.com* 🎫 *From $40* ⊗ *Closed Nov.–Apr.*

The seacoast village of Blue Hill is about 30 miles from Acadia National Park.

Blue Hill

20 miles east of Castine.

Nestled snugly between Blue Hill Mountain and Blue Hill Bay, the village of Blue Hill sits right beside Blue Hill Harbor. About 30 miles from Acadia National Park, the village is a good laid-back base for exploring the Mount Desert Island area, though summertime traffic can significantly increase out-and-back travel times.

Originally known for its granite quarries, copper mines, and shipbuilding, today Blue Hill has galleries, boutiques, and a modest but varied dining scene that offers everything from good coffee at Bucklyn's to fine dining at Arborvine. Tucked near the harbor, a charming little park explodes with sound on Monday nights in summer, when a renowned steel-drum band gives free concerts.

GETTING HERE AND AROUND

From Castine, take Route 166 to 166A. Turn right onto Route 199 North, and follow it to Route 175 South. Turn left onto Route 177 East, which takes you right into town.

 Sights

Parson Fisher House

HISTORIC SIGHT | FAMILY | Jonathan Fisher, the first permanent minister of Blue Hill, built this home from 1814 to 1820. It provides a fascinating look at his many accomplishments and talents, which included writing and illustrating books, painting, farming, and building furniture. Also on view is a wooden clock he crafted while a student at Harvard; the face holds messages about time written in English, Greek, Latin, Hebrew, and French. The site is on the National Register of Historic Places. ✉ *44 Mines Rd., Blue Hill* ☎ *207/374–2459* ⊕ *www. jonathanfisherhouse.org* ✉ *$5 suggested donation* ⊙ *Closed mid-Oct.–July.*

Shaw Institute

COLLEGE | Based here and in New York, this institute was founded in 1990 by environmental health scientist Dr. Susan Shaw to study how pollution affects humans, the oceans, and the planet. The institute has programs for all ages, including guided walks along the beach, as well environmental speakers series throughout the summer. ✉ *55 Main St., Blue Hill* ☎ *207/374–2135* 🌐 *www.shaw-institute.org* 🎫 *Free.*

🍴 Restaurants

★ Arborvine

$$$ | **MODERN AMERICAN** | Glowing gas fireplaces, period antiques, exposed beams, and hardwood floors covered with Asian rugs make the the candlelit dining areas in this historic house elegant but homey. The menu features dishes made with such ingredients as carrots and apples from Horsepower Farm; mesclun from Carding Brook Farm in Brooklin; and mussels, scallops, and clams from Blue Hill Bay. **Known for:** seasonal menus; fresh seafood dishes; farm-to-table ingredients. [$] *Average main: $34* ✉ *33 Tenney Hill, Blue Hill* ☎ *207/374–2119* 🌐 *www.arborvine.com* 🕒 *No lunch. Closed Sun.–Tues.*

Barncastle Restaurant

$ | **AMERICAN** | Enjoy this inn restaurant's small-plate dishes, local beers, and craft cocktails in the quiet dining room or the rustic pub. **Known for:** live music on weekends; contemporary twists on comfort food classics; deck seating in nice weather. [$] *Average main: $16* ✉ *Barncastle Inn, 125 South St., Blue Hill* ☎ *207/374–2300* 🌐 *www.barncastle.me* 🕒 *No lunch.*

Sandy's Blue Hill Café

$ | **AMERICAN** | **FAMILY** | Open for breakfast, lunch, and weekend brunch, this place has a mix of standard and surprising offerings, including a great falafel platter. If you want dinner, you can select from such house-made frozen dishes as beef stew, vegetable and cheese enchiladas, or Georgia onion pie. **Known for:** house-roasted coffee beans; house-made bagels; intriguing wine, beer, and cocktail lists. [$] *Average main: $15* ✉ *40 Main St., Blue Hill* ☎ *207/374–5550* 🌐 *www.sandysbluehillcafe.com* 🕒 *Closed Tues. and Wed.*

Siam Sky

$$ | **THAI** | The long menu has all the Thai favorites (some of them gluten-free), from pad Thai and noodle soups to traditionally prepared seafood, chicken, beef, and duck entrées. Dine in the bright and airy dining room or out on the deck with its bright red chairs and umbrellas. **Known for:** great lunch specials; wide selection of curries; open daily year-round. [$] *Average main: $20* ✉ *8 Mill St., Blue Hill* ☎ *207/374–7157* 🌐 *www.siamskyrestaurant.com/blue.*

☕ Coffee and Quick Bites

★ Bucklyn Coffee

$ | **CAFÉ** | This tiny, friendly shop serves big, flavorful coffee and interesting sweet and savory pastries. **Known for:** great place for a morning or early afternoon pick-me-up; Maine-roasted beans; coffee served anyway you like it. [$] *Average main: $9* ✉ *103 Main St., Blue Hill* ☎ *917/971–3246* 🌐 *bucklyncoffee.square.site* 🕒 *Closed Sun.*

★ The Co-Op Cafe

$ | **AMERICAN** | **FAMILY** | Housed in the Blue Hill Co-Op Community Market, this is a prime place for soups, sandwiches, and pastries. The bread selection alone is worth a stop. **Known for:** gluten-free and vegan options; eat in or takeout; great salad and hot-entrée bars. [$] *Average main: $11* ✉ *70 South St., Blue Hill* ☎ *207/374–2165* 🌐 *www.bluehill.coop/the-coop-cafe.*

Hotels

Barncastle

$$ | B&B/INN | The main building of this circa-1890 inn really does seem to be part barn and part castle, giving it a whimsical Loire-Valley-meets-Maine feel. **Pros:** open year-round; good restaurant on-site; spectacular turret suite. **Cons:** no elevator; not pet-friendly; tends to book up. [$] *Rooms from: $200* ✉ *125 South St., Blue Hill* ☎ *207/374–2330* 🌐 *www.barncastle.me* 🛏 *5 rooms* 🍴 *Free Breakfast.*

Blue Hill Inn

$$$ | B&B/INN | At this Federal-style inn, which was built as a home in 1835 and expanded into a lodging in the 1850s, wide-plank, pumpkin-pine floors perfectly complement the mix of antiques that fill the parlor, library, and guest rooms, several of which have working fireplaces, clawfoot tubs, and flower-garden views. **Pros:** plenty of charm; modern suites with kitchens in separate building; excellent service. **Cons:** narrow stairs; thin walls; only some rooms available in winter. [$] *Rooms from: $315* ✉ *40 Union St., Blue Hill* ☎ *207/374–2844* 🌐 *www.bluehillinn.com* 🛏 *13 rooms* 🍴 *Free Breakfast.*

Under Canvas

$$$$ | RESORT | FAMILY | Amid 100 acres on Union River Bay, this glamping property has luxury tents with king-size beds, bathrooms, organic toiletries, wood stoves, and other creature comforts. **Pros:** breathtaking coast and Cadillac Mountain views; lots of on-site amenities and activities; good base for Acadia National Park visits. **Cons:** some might find 10 pm quiet time restricting; pricey rates and food and activities cost extra; it still feels like camping. [$] *Rooms from: $620* ✉ *702 Surry Rd.* ☎ *888/496–1148* 🌐 *www.undercanvas.com/camps/acadia* 🕒 *Closed mid-Oct.–mid-May* 🛏 *63 tents* 🍴 *No Meals.*

Nightlife

The Brick Block

BARS | This is a great place to unwind with a late-afternoon or evening craft cocktail or local beer. While you're here, be sure to check the cool items for sale in the adjacent MOYO Boutique. ✉ *27 Water St., Blue Hill* ☎ *207/266–0967* 🌐 *www.moyobluehill.com/the-brick-block* 🕒 *Closed Mon.*

Performing Arts

Bagaduce Music

MUSIC | What started out as a lending library for printed sheet music has evolved into a nonprofit organization focused on music education and performances. Its online calendar lists all upcoming performance events. ✉ *49 South St., Blue Hill* ☎ *207/374–5454* 🌐 *www.bagaducemusic.org.*

Flash in the Pans Concerts

MUSIC | FAMILY | One of the country's largest community steel bands plays in the Blue Hill Town Park every Monday at 7:30 pm in summer. ✉ *113 Water St., Blue Hill* 🌐 *www.flashinthepans.org* 🎟 *Free.*

Kneisel Hall

CONCERTS | Kneisel Hall is a well-known venue for chamber music founded over 120 years ago by founder Franz Kneisel, who was also the founder the first fully professional string quartet in America. The organization's summertime festival school hosts promising young musicians and distinguished faculty and their rehearsals, masterclasses, and concerts are open to the public in July and August. ✉ *137 Pleasant St., Blue Hill* ☎ *207/374–2811* 🌐 *www.kneisel.org* 🎟 *Subscription and single ticket sales available* 🕒 *Closed Sept.–June.*

● Shopping

ART GALLERIES
Blue Hill Bay Gallery
ART GALLERIES | This gallery sells 19th-through 21st-century Maine and New England landscapes and seascapes by nationally recognized and emerging artists who work in a variety of media. It also carries the proprietor's own photography. ✉ *11 Tenney Hill, Blue Hill* ☎ *207/374–5773* ⊕ *www.bluehillbay-gallery.com* ◷ *Closed Sun. and Mon. Memorial Day–Labor Day and weekdays in off-season.*

Cynthia Winings Gallery
ART GALLERIES | This unassuming, two-story space focuses on contemporary painting and sculpture. The gallery is often used as a venue for performance art and poetry readings as well. ✉ *24 Parker Point Rd., Blue Hill* ☎ *207/204–4001* ⊕ *www.cynthiawiningsgallery.com* ◷ *Closed Sun. and Mon.*

★ Handworks Gallery
CRAFTS | Set in what was once a department store, this gallery sells fine art; contemporary fabric, metal, wood, glass, and ceramic decorative items and housewares; and jewelry and accessories. Everything is handcrafted by a diverse group of established and emerging Maine artists. ✉ *48 Main St., Blue Hill* ☎ *207/374–5613* ⊕ *handworksgallery.org* ◷ *Closed Sun.* ☞ *Limited hrs Jan.–Apr.*

Liros Gallery
ART GALLERIES | On exhibit here are oil and watercolor paintings, hand-color engravings, and woodcut birds and flowers. ✉ *14 Parker Point Rd., Blue Hill* ☎ *207/374–5370* ⊕ *www.lirosgallery.com* ◷ *Closed Sun. and Mon.*

BOOKS
★ Blue Hill Books
BOOKS | In addition to having a well-rounded selection of books, magazines, and stationary, this fabulous independent bookstore co-sponsors many literary events throughout the year. ✉ *26 Pleasant St., Blue Hill* ☎ *207/374–5632* ⊕ *bluehillbooks.com* ◷ *Closed Sun.*

GIFTS AND SOUVENIRS
5 Main Street
OTHER SPECIALTY STORE | This retail space sells gift items from Brooklin-based Leaf and Anna, an Art Box vending machine that offers tiny works form local artists, fun clothing and accessories from Hannah B. Designs, and refurbished art deco home goods from La Maison Rehash. ✉ *5 Main St., Blue Hill* ☎ *207/374–2575* ⊕ *linktr.ee/5mainstreet* ◷ *Closed Sun.*

MOYO Boutique
OTHER ACCESSORIES | The merchandise in this shop includes throw pillows and blankets, doormats, candles, pot holders, bath and body products, sweatshirts, T-shirts, baby onesies, hats, and bags. All of the items are sassy and equitably sourced. Take a break from shopping with a craft cocktail at The Brick Block, an adjacent bar. ✉ *27 Water St., Blue Hill* ☎ *802/236–4299 by text* ⊕ *www.moyo-bluehill.com* ◷ *Closed Sun.*

TOYS
Out on A Whimsey
TOYS | FAMILY | The toys in this trim, tidy shop are artfully arranged in colorful displays. There's something here for everyone, regardless of their age. ✉ *58 Main St., Blue Hill* ☎ *207/374–2313* ⊕ *out-on-a-whimsey-toys-blue-hill.business.site.*

WINE
★ Blue Hill Wine Shop
WINE/SPIRITS | In a restored barn and Cape-style house, one of Blue Hill's earliest residences, this shop carries more than 3,000 carefully selected wines, as well as cheeses, breads, groceries, local and imported beer, cider, cooking ingredients, and coffees and teas. ✉ *138 Main St., Blue Hill* ☎ *207/374–2161* ⊕ *www.bluehillwineshop.com* ◷ *Closed Sun.*

Activities

Blue Hill Falls

KAYAKING | Offering kayakers surfable currents when when the tide is running full force, Blue Hill Falls is a tide reversing waterway on Route 175 between Blue Hill and Brooklin. Water flowing in and out of the salt pond from Blue Hill Bay roars under Stevens Bridge. Take care when walking near the road here: the sound of the water drowns out the sound of on-coming cars. ⊠ *Rte. 175, Blue Hill* 🎫 *Free.*

Brooklin, Sedgwick, and Brooksville

Brooklin is 13 miles south of Blue Hill; Sedgwick is 5 miles northeast of Brooklin; Brooksville is 7 miles northeast of Sedgwick.

Winding through hills, the roads leading to this trio of villages take you past rambling farmhouses, beautiful coves, and blueberry barrens studded with occasional masses of granite. The towns themselves have tiny centers, each with a small cluster of businesses worth a look if you've have some time to stop.

The village of Brooklin, originally part of Sedgwick, established itself as an independent town in 1849. Today it's home to the world-famous Wooden Boat School. Incorporated in 1789, Sedgwick runs along much of Eggemoggin Reach, the body of water separating the mainland from Deer Isle, Little Deer Isle, and Stonington.

Brooksville, incorporated in 1817, is almost completely surrounded by water, with the Eggemoggin Reach, Walker Pond, and the Bagaduce River marking its boundaries. Cape Rosier, remote and cove-lined even for this off-the-beaten-path peninsula, is home to Holbrook Island Sanctuary, a state park with hiking trails and a gravel beach.

GETTING HERE AND AROUND

From Blue Hill, Route 175 runs along the bottom of the Blue Hill Peninsula, heading first to Brooklin, then through Sedgwick and Brooksville on its way to U.S. 1 in Orland. Route 176 traverses Sedgwick and Brooksville as it heads west from Blue Hill across the middle of the peninsula.

Because this wide peninsula has lots of capes, points, and necks, take care when driving to make sure you're continuing on the right road and not unintentionally looping around. Use a map (don't rely on GPS)—you can find a good one in the Blue Hill Peninsula Chamber of Commerce's visitors guide.

Sights

The Good Life Center

FARM/RANCH | The Good Life Center is on the site of Forest Farm, the historic homestead built in the 1950s by Helen and Scott Nearing, a back-to-the-land couple who practiced and advocated for simple, sustainable living. Sign up for one of the lectures or workshops, take a garden tour, or peace out in the meditation yurt. The center is open to the public from 1 to 5 pm, though opening days vary by season. ⊠ *372 Harborside Rd., Harborside* 🕿 *207/326–8211* ⊕ *goodlife. org* 🎫 *Free, but donations encouraged* ☉ *Closed mid-Oct.–mid-June; Tues. and Wed. mid-June–Labor Day; and weekdays Labor Day–mid-Oct.*

Holbrook Island Sanctuary

STATE/PROVINCIAL PARK | The 1,230-acre Holbrook Island Sanctuary protects the region's fragile ecosystem and has nine hiking trails (pick up trail maps in the parking lot), a gravel beach with splendid views, and a picnic area. There's a good chance you'll spot a blue heron, osprey, or bald eagle here. Note that the sanctuary, which is open from 9 am till sunset, is on the mainland; Holbrook Island itself is privately owned. ✉ *172 Indian Bar Rd., Brooksville* ☎ *207/326–4012* 🌐 *www.maine.gov/dacf* 🎟 *Free.*

Naskeag Point

BODY OF WATER | A few miles south of Brooklin, take Naskeag Point Road to a broken shell beach at the tip of the point. From there you'll have a view of the small islands of Jericho Bay while you sit on a bench dedicated to "all the fishermen who brave the sea." ✉ *649 Naskeag Point Rd., Brooklin* 🎟 *Free.*

The WoodenBoat School

SCHOOL | This school, which sits on a 60-acre oceanfront campus, is renowned for its weeklong woodworking and boatbuilding workshops. It also offers sailing and kayaking courses, as well as coastal-theme photography and art classes. The school is off the road to Naskeag Point, a sleepy, serenely beautiful spot at the end of the peninsula road with a small rock beach, a teeny park, and a lovely view across the harbor. ✉ *41 WoodenBoat La., Brooklin* ☎ *207/359–4651* 🌐 *www.thewoodenboatschool.com.*

🍴 Restaurants

★ Bagaduce Lunch

$ | SEAFOOD | FAMILY | This tidy little joint next to the reversing falls on the Bagaduce River is the perfect place for a lunch of clam, shrimp, haddock, or scallop baskets that come with onion rings or chips; there are also hot dogs, burgers, and chicken fingers. Picnic tables dot this nub of land surrounded on three sides by water, and you can walk onto the pier (or moor your kayak or boat there) for tidal estuary views and glimpses of seals, bald eagles, and ospreys. **Known for:** outdoor dining only; the views; fresh seafood. [$] *Average main: $17* ✉ *145 Franks Flat Rd., Penobscot* ☎ *207/326–4197* 🕒 *Closed mid-Sept.–late Apr. and Wed. in summer.*

★ Brooklin Inn

$$$ | CONTEMPORARY | Like the inn that houses it, this restaurant was modernized in 2021. Items on its changing menu feature local and seasonal produce and might include oysters with fish sauce mignonette, heirloom tomato gazpacho, or seared duck breast with polenta. **Known for:** garden seating; trendy but casual atmosphere; sophisticated fare. [$] *Average main: $25* ✉ *22 Reach Rd., Brooklin* ☎ *207/359–2777* 🌐 *www.thebrooklininn.com* 🕒 *No lunch* ☞ *Only serves pizza on Sun.*

Buck's

$$$$ | SEAFOOD | Follow the granite walkway to reach this fine-dining gem tucked behind Buck's Harbor Market, which is a good place to stock up on pantry staples and Maine-produced food products. The seasonal menu centers on seafood, but lamb and beef are regularly on offer. **Known for:** popular with boaters; offers gluten-free and vegetarian dishes; wine list with interesting, affordable options. [$] *Average main: $37* ✉ *6 Cornfield Hill Rd., Brooksville* ☎ *207/326–8688* 🌐 *www.bucksrestaurant.net* 🕒 *No lunch. Closed Sun.–Tues.*

El El Frijoles

$ | MEXICAN | FAMILY | Burritos, bowls, nachos, empanadas, and tacos filled with crab, fish, lobster, or meat and served with a full range of fiery accoutrement are made fresh daily at this taqueria, whose name is a play on L.L. Bean! **Known for:** festive, family-oriented atmosphere; local favorite; made-from-scratch Mexican classics. [$] *Average main: $14* ✉ *41 Caterpillar Rd., Sargentville* ☎ *207/359–2486* 🌐 *elelfrijoles.com* 🕒 *Closed Sat.–Tues.*

The Maine Lobster Lady Restaurant

$$ | SEAFOOD | FAMILY | This full-service restaurant replicates the famous food truck (a trailer, really) by the same name that is parked on Isle au Haut. The menu consists of yummy rolls, sandwiches, and baskets, most of them featuring seafood from local waters. **Known for:** wicked good lobstah; seasonal outdoor seating only; hand-breaded cheese curds. $ Average main: $18 ✉ 209 Caterpillar Hill Rd., Sedgwick ☎ 207/669–2751 ⊕ www.mainelobsterlady.com.

Strong Brewing & Kitchen

$ | **AMERICAN** | Good beer, pizza, and, occasionally, live music—it's a combination the fits perfectly into a lazy day of lazily exploring the Blue Hill Peninsula. **Known for:** wood-fired oven; outdoor dining; house-brewed porters, ales, and lagers. $ Average main: $16 ✉ 7 Rope Ferry Rd., Sedgwick ☎ 207/359–2687 ⊕ strongbrewing.com ⊗ Closed Tues.–Thurs.

★ Tinder Hearth

$$ | **BAKERY** | Tinder Hearth is well known in these part for its amazing pastries and wood-oven-baked breads, but it also makes pizza that's delicious enough to plan your whole week around—a must given that you have to reserve your pie days in advance. It's worth the bother, though, as the crust is thin but chewy, and the toppings are a mix of the classic and the inventive. **Known for:** elaborate pizza-reservation protocols; alfresco dining; changing list of toppings. $ Average main: $22 ✉ 1452 Coastal Rd., Brooksville ☎ 207/326–8381 ⊕ www.tinderhearth.com ⊗ Closed Sun.–Tues.

 Hotels

★ The Brooklin Inn

$$ | **B&B/INN** | This inn, which offers modern amenities while maintaining a conversation with the past, is where you want to stay if you're visiting from the other Brooklyn. **Pros:** streamlined, rustic-chic, coastal decor; good on-site restaurant and bar; a/c, fridge, and coffee/tea fixings in rooms. **Cons:** strict cancellation policies; bustling restaurant makes the inn less peaceful; rooms are on the small side. $ Rooms from: $250 ✉ 22 Reach Rd., Brooklin ☎ 207/359–2777 ⊕ www.

thebrooklininn.com ⊗ Closed Nov.–Apr. ⇥ 4 rooms ❘❍❘ No Meals.

The Maine Hideaway Guesthouse

$ | **B&B/INN** | Set in a former residence built in 1874, this inn's simply appointed rooms are all named after types of boats, a nod to the fact that it caters mainly to students at the nearby WoodenBoat School. **Pros:** full and delicious breakfasts; in-room a/c; friendly innkeepers. **Cons:** decor is nicer in some rooms than others; tends to book up; not all rooms have private baths. $ Rooms from: $195 ✉ 19 Naskeag Point Rd., Brooklin ☎ 207/610–2244 ⊕ www.themainehideaway.com ⊗ Closed mid-Nov.–late Feb. ⇥ 9 rooms ❘❍❘ Free Breakfast.

The Oakland House Seaside Resort

$$$ | **RESORT** | **FAMILY** | The coastal acreage on which the main inn, with its recently renovated rooms, and cottages are set was an original land grant by Great Britain's King George III in 1767 to John and Hannah Billings, direct ascendants of the current innkeepers, Rick and Robin Littlefield. **Pros:** private beaches; old-fashioned Maine hospitality; lots of outdoor activity options. **Cons:** do-it-yourself housekeeping; might feel too isolated for some; no on-site restaurant. $ Rooms from: $300 ✉ 435 Herrick Rd., Brooksville ☎ 207/359–8521 ⊕ www.oaklandhouse.com/ ⊗ Closed mid-Oct.–early Mar. ⇥ 21 units ❘❍❘ No Meals.

⬤ Shopping

Shopping in these towns requires purpose. There are lovely items to be found, but the shops dot, rather than cluster, along the winding roads. Be prepared to stop.

Brooklin Candy Co.

CANDY | **FAMILY** | Try the sea-glass hard candy and the coffee bark at this little shop offering small treats in a tiny town. ✉ 103 Bay Rd., Brooklin ☎ 207/479–5060 ⊕ brooklincandy.com.

Handmade Papers Gallery

ART SUPPLIES | Gigi Sarsfield makes fibrous papers that include things like tufts of cattail and small bits of lichen that she finds on walks in the woods or along the sea. You can buy individual sheets or blank books. Lampshades made from the paper are also for sale. ⊠ *113 Reach Rd., Brooklin* ☎ *207/359-8345* ⊕ *handmadepapersonline.com* ☞ *Open year-round by chance or appointment.*

Leaf and Anna

SOUVENIRS | This shop sells fun and functional wares—from aprons and tea towels to plush toys and puzzles—with a decidedly Maine theme. It's also a good place to stock up on Brooklin, Maine, caps, T-shirts, and mugs. There's also a branch in Blue Hill. ⊠ *12 Reach Rd., Brooklin* ☎ *207/359-5030* ⊕ *leafandanna.com* ⊙ *Closed Jan.–Apr.* ☞ *Second location in Blue Hill.*

Makers Market Shop and Studio

ART GALLERIES | It's well worth a stop here to spend part of an afternoon (it's not open in the morning) browsing items made by local photographers, seamstresses, fiber artists, and potters. ⊠ *33 Bagaduce Rd., Brooksville* ☎ *207/812-3703* ⊙ *Closed Sun.–Tues.*

Roaring Lion Farm and Market

FOOD | **FAMILY** | This farm hosts a weekend market featuring its own meat (including succulent Meishan pork), eggs, and produce, as well as items from other local producers and makers. You can also get breakfast sandwiches. ⊠ *160 Snows Cove Rd., Sedgwick* ⊕ *www.roaringlionfarm.com* ⊙ *Closed Mon.–Thurs.*

Activities

Buck's Harbor Marina Charters

BOAT TOURS | Charter a motor boat or yacht for a day or for a week to cruise around Maine waters. ⊠ *684 Coastal Rd., Brooksville* ☎ *207/326-8839* ⊕ *bucksharbor.com.*

Cooper Farm on Caterpillar Hill

HIKING & WALKING | The 134-acre Cooper Farm property lies on the sloping fields of Caterpillar Hill. Trails in the upper half of the property bring you through blueberry fields; those in the lower half run through a mixed mossy forest. Leashed dogs are allowed. There's parking off Cooper Farm Road. The Blue Hill Heritage Trust has a trail map on its website. ⊠ *Cooper Farm Rd., Sedgwick* ⊕ *bluehillheritagetrust.org* ⩛ *Free.*

Deer Isle

16 miles south of Blue Hill.

Reachable by a bridge, the thick woods of Deer Isle and Little Deer Isle give way to tidal coves at almost every turn. Stacks of lobster traps populate the backyards of shingled houses, and dirt roads lead to secluded summer cottages.

The village of Deer Isle is nestled between Northwest Harbor and Mill Pond. While it's only got one of each, it's got a great coffee shop, a lovely inn with a beer garden, an art gallery, and a quirky shop with all Maine-made books, toys, and crafts.

GETTING HERE AND AROUND

From Sedgwick, Route 15 crosses a 1930s suspension bridge onto Little Deer Isle and continues on to the larger Deer Isle.

Thick woods border tidal coves on Deer Isle.

VISITOR INFORMATION
CONTACTS Deer Isle–Stonington Chamber of Commerce. ✉ *114 Little Deer Isle Rd., Deer Isle* ☎ *207/348–6124* ⊕ *www.deerisle.com.* **Isle au Haut Boat Services.** ✉ *37 Seabreeze Ave., Stonington* ☎ *207/367–5193* ⊕ *isleauhaut.com.*

 Sights

★ Barred Island Preserve
NATURE PRESERVE | FAMILY | Famous landscape architect Frederick Law Olmsted once owned Barred Island Preserve. His grandniece, Carolyn Olmsted, donated it to the Nature Conservancy in 1969. The island is accessible only at low tide. The mile-long trail leading to the island offers great views of Penobscot Bay. Pick up a brochure at the Deer Isle–Stonington Chamber of Commerce for a map of the islands you can see from the area. The parking area fills quickly, so arrive early. ✉ *Goose Cove Rd., Deer Isle* 🎟 *Free.*

Edgar M. Tennis Preserve
NATURE PRESERVE | While enjoying miles of woodland and shore trails at the Edgar M. Tennis Preserve, you can look for hawks, eagles, and ospreys, and wander among old apple trees, fields of wildflowers, and ocean-polished rocks. ✉ *Tennis Rd., off Sunshine Rd., Deer Isle* ☎ *207/348–2455* ⊕ *www.islandheritagetrust.org* 🎟 *Free.*

Haystack Mountain School of Crafts
COLLEGE | Want to learn a new craft? This school 6 miles from Deer Isle Village offers one- and two-week courses for people of all skill levels in crafts such as blacksmithing, basketry, ceramics, jewelry making, printmaking, weaving, and writing. Artisans from around the world present free evening lectures throughout summer. Tours of the school and studios are available on Wednesday. ✉ *89 Haystack School Dr., off Rte. 15, Deer Isle* ☎ *207/348–2306* ⊕ *www.haystack-mtn.org* 🎟 *Lectures cost $8* ♿ *Tours require preregistration.*

Mariners Memorial Park

GARDEN | For picnics, bird-watching, or launching kayaks and canoes, visit Mariners Memorial Park, overlooking secluded Long Cove. There is a half-mile walking loop and a small garden maintained by the Evergreen Garden Club. ✉ *Fire Rd. 501 off Sunshine Rd., Deer Isle* 🌐 *www.evergreengarden.club/projects* 🎫 *Free.*

Shore Acres Preserve

NATURE PRESERVE | A mixture of hard and softwood trees makes an excellent habitat for songbirds at Shore Acres Preserve on the eastern edge of Deer Isle. Walk the perimeter trail to see light sparkling off Greenlaw Cove, native plants like juniper, blueberry, and cranberry, as well as mushrooms, mosses, and ferns. You might even spot a fox, a red squirrel, or a hawk. ✉ *Greenlaw District Rd., off Sunshine Rd., Deer Isle* 🎫 *Free.*

🍴 Restaurants

★ Aragosta at Goose Cove

$$$$ | **CONTEMPORARY** | Executive chef and proprietor Devin Finigan has created magic in this location with endless views of East Penobscot Bay and food that speaks to the prowess of this region's fishermen and farmers. Whether you're experiencing the chef's tasting menu—think scallops with sorrel and whey; Wagyu with ramps and new potato; and rhubarb with lemon and shortbread—Sunday a-la-carte brunch (seasonal), or a summer happy hour, you're in for a high-quality treat. **Known for:** seasonal tasting menu; delicious hand-crafted cocktails; locally sourced ingredients that dictate the menu. [$] *Average main: $150* ✉ *300 Goose Cove Rd., Deer Isle* ☎ *207/348–6900* 🌐 *aragostamaine.com* 🕒 *Closed Nov. and Dec. No lunch Mon.–Sat.*

LDI Lobster

$$$ | **SEAFOOD** | **FAMILY** | Whether you're stopping by on your way to Little Deer Island or on your way off it, the Maine lobster rolls and freshly fried seafood baskets are worth the detour (there is an additional fee for takeout). Enhanced by the view of the Deer Isle Bridge over Eggemoggin Reach, don't miss the daily specials, delicious milk shakes (worth the calories), or nonseafood items (like beef and veggie burgers). **Known for:** waterfront location; fresh seafood; Gifford's ice cream and milk shakes. [$] *Average main: $25* ✉ *202 Little Deer Isle Rd., Deer Isle* ☎ *207/348–2848* 🌐 *www.ldilobster.com* 🕒 *Closed late Oct.–early June and Mon.–Wed.*

☕ Coffee and Quick Bites

★ 44 North Coffee

$ | **BAKERY** | This place offers amazing (and equitably sourced) coffee and invites you to take a minute to have a conversation while you wait for your slow-pour brew to flow through a colorful, custom-built wooden drip bar. Grab a pastry supplied by a variety of local bakers—if there are any left when you arrive. **Known for:** no Wi-Fi; pastries from Brooksville's Tinder Hearth Bakery; great coffee. [$] *Average main: $15* ✉ *7 Main St., Deer Isle* ☎ *207/348–5208* 🌐 *44northcoffee.com* 🕒 *Closed Sun.*

Whale Rib Tavern Biergarten

$$ | **AMERICAN** | Run by the fine folks at The Pilgrim Inn, the tavern and its Biergarten are a great place to stop for a pint of one of the many Maine craft beers on tap. The menu features classic pub fare as well as fresh seafood and smoked barbecue. **Known for:** great place to watch the sunset; outside biergarten; family-friendly. [$] *Average main: $22* ✉ *20 Main St., Deer Isle* ☎ *207/348–6615* 🌐 *www.pilgrimsinn.com* 🕒 *Closed Sun. and Tues.–Thurs. and Oct.–May. No lunch.*

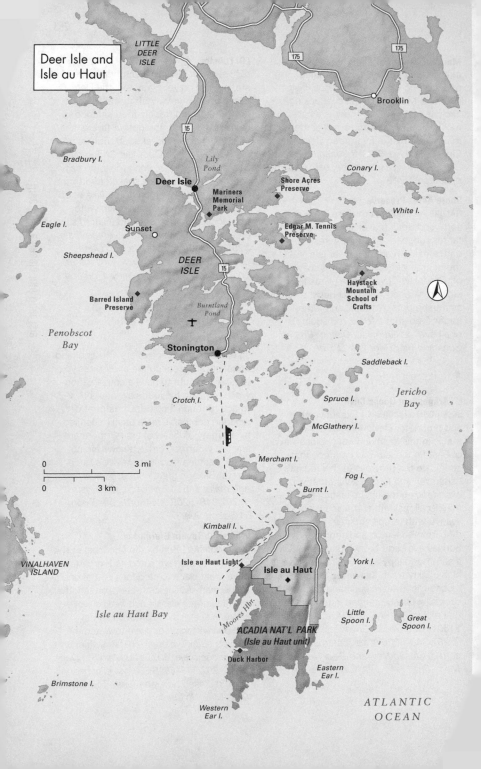

🛏 Hotels

★ Aragosta

$$$$ | **RESORT** | Nestled among spruces, moss-covered rocks, and the Barred Island Nature Preserve, Aragosta is one of Maine's most tranquil oceanfront complexes. **Pros:** excellent on-site restaurant; postcard-perfect location; cottages are dog-friendly. **Cons:** a car is a must; Wi-Fi is only available in the restaurant; suites are not dog-friendly. $ Rooms from: $500 ✉ 300 Goose Cove Rd., Deer Isle ☎ 207/348–6900 ⊕ aragostamaine.com ۵ Closed mid-Oct.–mid-May ⇆ 9 cottages, 3 suites ❑ Free Breakfast.

Pilgrim's Inn

$$ | **B&B/INN** | Built in 1893, this post-and-beam bed-and-breakfast has spectacular views of Northwest Harbor and the property's pond; it's listed on the National Register of Historic Places. **Pros:** well-cooked breakfast; quiet rooms; very attentive innkeepers. **Cons:** modern design fans will be at a loss here; breakfast has one item on the menu daily; lots of stairs. $ Rooms from: $270 ✉ 20 Maine St., Deer Isle ☎ 207/348–6615 ⊕ pilgrimsinn.com ۵ Closed mid-Oct.–mid-May ⇆ 12 rooms, 3 cottages ❑ Free Breakfast.

Inn at Ferry Landing

$$$ | **B&B/INN** | This inn, a farmhouse built in 1840, sits at the water's edge at the end of a quiet road with views of boats sailing in the Eggemoggin Reach. **Pros:** private beach provides a place to unwind; close to activities and town; idyllic setting. **Cons:** decor is dated; quiet location may not provide the excitement some are looking for on vacation; a car is necessary. $ Rooms from: $375 ✉ 77 Old Ferry Rd., Deer Isle ☎ 207/348–7760 ⊕ www.ferrylanding.com ۵ Closed Nov.–Apr. ⇆ 3 rooms, 1 cottage ❑ Free Breakfast.

🛍 Shopping

Deer Isle Artist Association

ART GALLERIES | This nonprofit gallery, fondly referred to as DIAA, comprises works from local artists with rotating exhibits every two weeks during the summer months. ✉ 15 Main St., Deer Isle ☎ 207/598–9656 ⊕ www.deerisleartists.com ۵ Closed Mon. and Nov.–May.

Nervous Nellie's Jams and Jellies

FOOD | **FAMILY** | Jams and jellies are made right on the property at Nervous Nellie's. There is a tearoom with homemade goodies, and also a fanciful sculpture garden with everything from knights to witches to a lobster and a flamingo. They are the works of sculptor Peter Beerits, who operates Nervous Nellie's with his wife. ✉ 598 Sunshine Rd., off Rte. 15, Deer Isle ☎ 207/348–6182 ⊕ www.nervousnellies.com ۵ Closed Sun. and Mon. and mid-Oct.–mid-May.

The Perwinkle

BOOKS | **FAMILY** | An eclectic collection of Maine-produced books, puzzles, toys, clothing, and art like carved birds and a myriad of alpaca items. Always call ahead or check the Facebook page for updated hours. ✉ 8 Maine St., Deer Isle ☎ 207/348–5277 ۵ Closed Sun. and Jan.–May.

The Turtle Gallery

ART GALLERIES | Started in 1982, the Turtle Gallery resides in the 1876 Centennial House and barn. Exhibits range from contemporary painting and sculpture to crafts. There's also an outdoor sculpture garden. ✉ 61 N. Deer Isle Rd., Deer Isle ☎ 207/348–9977 ⊕ www.turtlegallery. com ۵ Closed Mon.–Thurs. and mid-Oct.–mid-May.

Stonington Granite

Although you can see almost no sign of it today, the granite industry used to be a vital part of Stonington's economy. The first quarry was established in the 1860s, when the area known as Green's Landing had a population of approximately 300 people. From 1869 to 1969, area granite was used to build the Brooklyn Bridge, the Boston Museum of Fine Arts, the Smithsonian Institution, and other well-known sites. Demand was so high during the late 1800s that the town welcomed a wave of immigrants from Italy and Sweden, swelling the population to more than 5,000 people.

In 1897 Green's Landing split from Deer Isle and became known as Stonington. Since no bridge connected the area to the mainland until 1939, the community had to be completely self-sufficient. The boom was short-lived, however. With the rediscovery of concrete in the early 20th century, the granite industry ground to a sudden halt. Although one quarry reopened in the 1960s to fashion the granite blocks used in the Kennedy Memorial, it was unable to remain profitable. Today, Stonington's only remaining active quarry is on Crotch Island, just off the coast of Stonington. Its granite is shipped to Rhode Island, where it is cut for countertops and building facades.

🏃 Activities

Isle Au Haut Boat Services
BOAT TOURS | Tour options include scenic harbor tours that cruise the outer islands around Isle au Haut and Acadia National Park, Seal Island puffin tours, lighthouse tours, additional puffin tours, and lobster fishing opportunities. They also provide bike rentals on Isle au Haut as well as year-round passenger and mail service between Stonington and Isle au Haut, and seasonal service to the Acadia National Park landing at Duck Harbor. ✉ 27 Seabreeze Ave., Stonington ☎ 207/367–5193 ⊕ www.isleauhaut.com ⊙ Tours closed Oct.–May.

Stonington

7 miles south of Deer Isle village.

A charming seaside town with only 1,000 year-round residents, Stonington sits at the southern end of Route 15, which has helped retain its unspoiled small-town flavor. This picturesque working waterfront, where boats arrive overflowing with the day's catch, is Maine's largest lobster port. It's also a tranquil tourist destination with boutiques and galleries lining Main Street that cater mostly to out-of-towners.

Stonington includes the villages of Burnt Cove, Oceanville, Green Head, and Clam City. It also serves as the gateway to Isle au Haut, which is home to a remote section of Acadia National Park.

◉ Sights

Deer Isle Granite Museum
HISTORY MUSEUM | FAMILY | This tiny museum documents Stonington's quarrying tradition. The museum's centerpiece is a working model of quarrying operations on Crotch Island and the town of Stonington at the turn of the last century. Granite was quarried here for Rockefeller Plaza in New York City and for the John F. Kennedy Memorial in Arlington National Cemetery, among other well-known

Stonington's picturesque working waterfront is also Maine's largest lobster port.

structures. ✉ *51 Main St., Stonington* 📠 *207/367–6331 July and Aug. only* ⊕ *deerislegranitemuseum.wordpress. com* ✉ *Donations accepted* ◷ *Closed Sun., Tues., Thurs., and Fri. and Labor Day–Memorial Day.*

🍴 Restaurants

Fin and Fern

$$$ | AMERICAN | Perched on a hill overlooking Stonington Harbor, diners can watch lobster boats unload their daily haul and enjoy the sounds of seagulls and foghorns in the distance while dining on dishes made with fresh, seasonal ingredients. The appetizers and main courses center on seafood and the wood-fired pizzas coming out of the kitchen include the Garden Gnome (mushroom, caramelized onion, and ricotta) and the Seapig (scallop, applewood bacon, ricotta, and maple drizzle). **Known for:** year-round restaurant; delicious vegetarian options; beautiful outdoor deck. $ *Average main: $35* ✉ *25 Seabreeze Ave., Stonington* 📠 *207/348–3111*

⊕ *www.finandfernme.com* ◷ *Closed Mon.–Wed. No lunch.*

★ Harbor Cafe

$$$ | AMERICAN | FAMILY | This long-time Main Street greasy spoon got a face-lift and a menu upgrade when Brooklyn restaurateur Max Katzenberg reopened it in 2022. The breakfast menu has all the traditional offerings as as well a few extras like huevos rancheros and chicken and waffles, while the lunch and dinner menu features local seafood dishes and carnitas tacos, and fried chicken. **Known for:** great sandwiches and seafood rolls; centrally located; the portions are big. $ *Average main: $30* ✉ *36 Main St., Stonington* 📠 *207/367–5099* ⊕ *www.harborcafe.me/* ◷ *Closed Mon. No dinner Sun.*

🛏 Hotels

Inn on the Harbor

$$ | B&B/INN | Built in the 1880s, this inn is made up of four Victorian buildings with an expansive deck over the harbor that's a pleasant spot for morning coffee and

The Isle Au Haut Light was built in 1907 to guide fishing vessels into safe harbor during northeast storms.

afternoon cocktails. **Pros:** dogs allowed; great views from the property's harbor side; perfect place to unplug. **Cons:** not all rooms have great views or fireplaces; lobster boats wake up early and noisily; limited Internet and cell phone service in the area. [$] *Rooms from: $257* ✉ *45 Main St., Stonington* ☎ *207/367–2420* 🌐 *www.innontheharbor.com* 🍴 *No Meals.*

Shopping

Stonington has a variety of unique shops and galleries as well as a branch of 44 North Coffee (🌐 *44northcoffee.com*) on Main Street. If you happen to be in town on a Friday morning, check out the farmers' market located on School Street in the Community Center Parking Lot.

ART GALLERIES

gWatson Gallery

ART GALLERIES | Founded in 1998, the gallery sits on the edge of Stonington Harbor. It shows contemporary art and landscape paintings. Check out its Facebook page for upcoming events. ✉ *68 Main St., Stonington* ☎ *207/367–2900* 🌐 *www.gwatsongallery.com.*

Jill Hoy Gallery

ART GALLERIES | Artist Jill Hoy has summered on Deer Isle since she was 10. In 1986, she opened her own gallery to exhibit her contemporary landscapes that can also be seen at the Portland Museum of Art, Harvard Business School, and the Boston Public Library. ✉ *80 E. Main St., Stonington* ☎ *207/367–2777* 🌐 *www.jillhoy.com.*

BOOKS

Dockside Books & Gifts

BOOKS | Facing the harbor, this tiny shop stocks an eclectic selection of gifts and souvenirs from Maine and marine books to handcrafted and nautical items. ✉ *62 W. Main St., Stonington* · ☎ *207/367–2652.*

FOOD
Coldwater Seafood Market and Seacoast

FOOD | A bit out of town, this seafood market has an interesting collection of smoked and fresh local seafood, meats, and cheeses. Their signature offering is smoked mussels in honey mustard, salsa, chipotle, garlic and olive oil, and plain. They can also ship lobster anywhere in the continental United States. ✉ 100 N. Main St., Stonington ☎ 207/348–3084 ⊕ www.coldwaterseafoodmaine.com ✆ Closed Sun.

GENERAL STORES
The Dry Dock

GENERAL STORE | The Dry Dock offers clothing, gifts, and accessories (many made of Deer Isle granite) and is described by owner Janet Chaytor as "a creative department store." ✉ 24 Main St., Stonington ☎ 207/348–5528 ⊕ www.drydockstonington.com ✆ Closed mid-Oct.–mid-May.

Marlinespike Chandlery

OTHER SPECIALTY STORE | Inspired by chandleries, a sort of general store often found in seaside towns, the shop was born out of the owner's hobby of fancy marlinespike (marine) rope work. The shop is filled with a variety of marine artifacts, antiques, and other interesting items like beach stone and seaglass necklaces, rope and fiber boat fenders, and ditty bags (a canvas bag with marlinespike handles). ✉ 58 W. Main St., Stonington ☎ 207/460–6034 ⊕ www.marlinespike.com.

🏃 Activities

Driftwood Kayak

KAYAKING | These all-inclusive one-, two-, and three-day sea-kayaking trips are expertly guided throughout the small islands of Penobscot Bay with an emphasis on protecting the local ecosystems. Meals are made from local ingredients. ✉ 17 Hardy's Hill Rd., Deer Isle ☎ 617/957–8802 ⊕ www.driftwoodkayak.com/ ✆ Closed Oct.–May.

★ Isle au Haut Boat Services

BOATING | FAMILY | To get to and from Isle au Haut, the mail boat operated by this company is your best bet, with four trips a day Monday through Saturday and two trips on Sunday in summer. Parking is available at the Stonington ferry terminal and at several lots in town that are within walking distance. This company also offers regular puffin and lighthouse tours and private charters to Camden and Mt. Desert Island. ✉ 27 Seabreeze Ave., Stonington ☎ 207/367–5193 ⊕ www.isleauhaut.com 🚢 Mail boat: $20 each way. Tours: $80.

Stonington Sea Kayak

KAYAKING | This full-service sea-kayaking outfit offers gear rentals, instruction, and a variety of guided tours from Stonington's town boat launch. ✉ Merchant Row Bldg., 9 Thurlows Hill Rd., Stonington ☎ 207/266–2717 ⊕ upwestanddowneast.com.

Isle au Haut

6 miles south of Stonington.

Isle au Haut thrusts its steeply ridged back out of the sea south of Stonington. French explorer Samuel D. Champlain discovered Isle au Haut—or "High Island"—in 1604, but heaps of shells suggest that indigenous populations lived on or visited the island prior to his arrival.

The island is accessible only by mail boat, but the 45-minute journey is well worth the effort. As you pass between the tiny islands of Merchants Row, you might see terns, guillemots, and harbor seals. The ferry makes multiple trips a day between Stonington and the Town Landing from Monday to Saturday, and adds a Sunday trip from mid-May to mid-September. From mid-June to mid-September, the ferry also stops at Duck Harbor, located within Acadia National Park. The ferry will not unload bicycles, kayaks, or canoes at Duck Harbor, however.

Except for a grocery store, the Shore Shop gift shop, and a food co-op, Isle au Haut offers few opportunities for shopping. The island is ideal for day-trippers intent on exploring its miles of trails. There are no hotels or inns on the island at this point in time. You can secure a campsite in Duck Harbor if you book well in advance.

Sights

Duck Harbor

NATIONAL PARK | This half of Isle au Haut is part of Acadia National Park and has more than 18 miles of trails winding through quiet spruce woods, along beaches and seaside cliffs, and over the spin of the central mountain's ridge. The park's small campground, with several lean-tos, is open from mid-May to mid-October and fills up quickly. Reservations are essential. ✉ *Isle Au Haut* 🌐 *www.nps.gov/acad/planyourvisit/duckharbor.htm.*

Isle au Haut Light

LIGHTHOUSE | The Isle au Haut Lighthouse is best seen from the water, where the Isle au Haut mailboat passes within a hundred feet of the tower. Built in 1907 as the Robinson Point Fog Station, its purpose was to guide the New England ground fishing fleet into safe harbor during northeast storms. As the most modern of the 60 lighthouses along the Maine Coast, it introduced architectural advancements unseen in other stations and featured a behemoth 42-inch fog bell hanging over the water. In 1934, as a cost-saving measure during the Great Depression, the keeper's house was sold off. The lighthouse tower ownership was transferred from the federal government to the town in 1998. Today it is maintained by the town's Lighthouse Committee, while still serving as a registered aid to navigation. ✉ *Isle Au Haut.*

Restaurants

Maine Lobster Lady

$$$ | **SEAFOOD** | In summer, this former island innkeeper sells yummy and quick eats, many of them made with fish from local waters and her own organic garden produce. Her "food truck" (actually a tow trailer) is parked in the Island Store parking lot on Isle au Haut. **Known for:** everything prepared on-site; traditional Maine lobster rolls; whoopie pies. [$] *Average main: $25* ✉ *Off Main Rd., Isle Au Haut* ☎ *207/335–5141 in summer, 207/669–2751* 🌐 *www.mainelobsterlady.com* 🕒 *Closed mid-Sept.–early June.*

Chapter 8

ACADIA NATIONAL PARK

8

Updated by
Mary Ruoff

🏕 Camping	🏨 Hotels	🤸 Activities	👁 Scenery	👥 Crowds
★★★★☆	★★★★☆	★★★★★	★★★★★	★★★★☆

WELCOME TO ACADIA NATIONAL PARK

TOP REASONS TO GO

★ **Looping the park:** Get oriented along the 27-mile Park Loop Road, leaving plenty of time to stop at acclaimed locales like Sand Beach, Thunder Hole, and Otter Point.

★ **Unique roadways:** Acadia's 45 miles of crushed-stone carriage roads built and gifted by a famed philanthropic family can be enjoyed via two feet, two wheels, or horse-drawn carriage.

★ **A choice of flavors:** Many of the park's most popular attractions are on the east side of Mount Desert Island, including Park Loop Road, the carriage roads, and Cadillac Mountain. But Acadia's grand seascapes, forested lakes, and hiking trails also await on the "quiet" west side.

★ **Powerful popovers.** At the park's only restaurant, Jordan Pond House, gigantic popovers filled with strawberry jam have delighted visitors for more than 100 years.

★ **The parting sea:** Low tide exposes a land bridge between Bar Harbor and Bar Island—and an Acadia hike unlike any other.

Acadia National Park sprawls on both sides of Mount Desert Island.

1 East Side of Mount Desert Island. The busiest and largest part of Acadia National Park is near the amenities hub of Bar Harbor and home to many of its best-known attractions, including the carriage roads, Park Loop Road, Jordan Pond House, Cadillac Mountain, and Sieur de Monts. Hulls Cove Visitor Center is off Route 3, 3 miles from downtown Bar Harbor.

2 West Side of Mount Desert Island. Acadia also offers stunning scenery and great recreational opportunities on the island's "quiet side," where Southwest Harbor is a lower-key tourist hub and Bass Harbor lower yet. You can swim at the park's popular Echo Lake Beach, visit iconic Bass Harbor Head Light, and hike to the landmark Beech Mountain fire lookout tower.

3 Schoodic District. Visitors enjoy grand seascapes with a more secluded feel at the park's only mainland section at the bottom of this peninsula across Frenchman Bay from the east side of Mount Desert. Highlights include a loop road, bike paths, hiking trails, and the Schoodic Institute, an educational facility on the grounds of a former Navy base.

4 Isle au Haut. Acadia occupies half of this island out in the ocean 15 miles southwest of Mount Desert. It's accessible by ferry from Stonington on Deer Isle, itself reachable by bridge from the mainland west of Mount Desert. There's a small primitive campground, gravel roads for mountain biking, and hiking trails. Island amenities are meager.

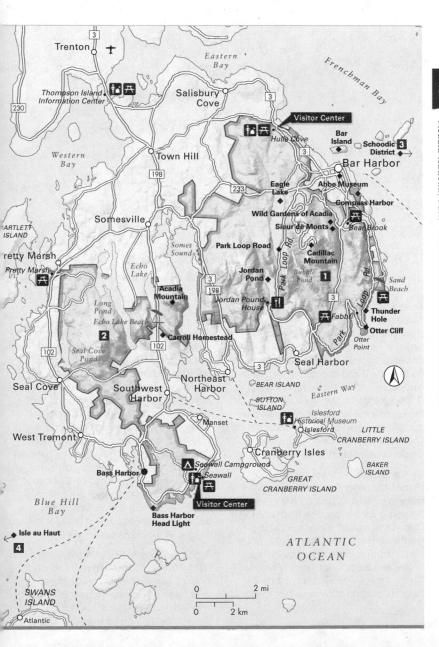

Mostly on Mount Desert Island, Acadia is among the nation's most popular national parks—4.07 million visits in 2021—and the only one in Maine. It also holds some of the most spectacular scenery in the eastern United States: a rugged surf-pounded granite coastline; an interior graced by glacially sculpted mountains, lakes, and ponds; and lush deciduous and conifer forests. Cadillac Mountain, the Eastern Seaboard's highest point, dominates the 47,000-acre park.

Acadia has more than 150 miles of hiking trails and 45 miles of finely crafted crushed-stone carriage roads—used by walkers, runners, bikers, and horse-drawn carriages—with elegant stone bridges. Built and later gifted by late philanthropist and part-time resident John D. Rockefeller Jr., the network wends on the island's busier eastern side, as does the 27-mile Park Loop Road. Sand Beach, Thunder Hole, and Otter Cliff, along its Ocean Drive section, are must-sees.

On the island's northeast corner, Bar Harbor, the main tourist hub located, has a few hamlets beyond the village. Bordering Bar Harbor, the Town of Mount Desert has several villages, including Northeast Harbor and Somesville. Southwest Harbor encompasses the village center and the smaller seaside Manset. On the "quiet side," Trenton is home to Bass Harbor and other small villages.

To truly appreciate the park you must experience it by walking, hiking, biking, rock climbing, paddling, boating, or carriage ride. Making that easier, and helping protect Acadia's environment, are seasonal free Island Explorer buses serving the park and nearby towns. Acadia also encompasses all or parts of 19 other islands. Most are uninhabited, but only one is closed to the public. There are ranger-led boat tours to two, Little Cranberry and Baker off the bottom of Mount Desert. Inhabited year-round and accessible by ferry, Little Cranberry is home to a small park museum about island life. Almost the entirety of the seasonally inhabited Baker Island is in Acadia, including its namesake light.

Acadia extends to half of remote Isle au Haut, out in the ocean 15 miles southwest of Mount Desert. Reachable by ferry from Stonington on Deer Isle (don't worry, a bridge gets you there from the mainland), it offers rugged trails,

AVERAGE HIGH/LOW TEMPERATURES					
Jan.	Feb.	Mar.	Apr.	May	June
32/17	34/19	40/27	50/36	59/44	67/52
July	Aug.	Sept.	Oct.	Nov.	Dec.
73/57	72/57	65/51	56/43	46/34	37/24

primitive camping, and unpaved roads. On the Schoodic Peninsula east of Mount Desert, Acadia's only mainland district has bike paths, hiking, camping, ranger programs, and a loop drive all its own, with views of Mount Desert—Maine's largest island.

Planning

When to Go

During the summer season, days are usually warm and nights cool—bring a jacket. July tops the charts with a comfortable average daily high of 73°F. But there are hot and humid spells, more so in recent years. Peak visitation is late spring through October. July and August are the busiest months, but September—when the heat and humidity of summer begin to taper off—is one of the most enjoyable, and also busy. The foliage season in the first few weeks of October bustles, too. While Memorial Day and Labor Day mark the traditional beginning and end of high season, nowadays many seasonal establishments stay open through Indigenous Peoples Day/ Columbus Day and some longer.

Consider coming in mid-spring when temperatures start to rise but crowds haven't yet formed. Be sure to check for seasonal closures due to ice, snow, or mud on Acadia's carriage roads, unpaved roads, and trails. For hardy souls, winter can be a wonderful time to visit. While many dining and lodging facilities are hibernating, you can still find good options. Just know that from December

through mid-April, paved park roads are closed to vehicles except for two short sections of Park Loop Road. For unpaved roads, it's mid-November to mid-May. When enough snow flies, folks head to the park to snowshoe and cross-country ski—many carriage roads are groomed. Snowmobilers take to Park Loop Road, drive up Cadillac Mountain, and hit unpaved roads.

Regardless of when you decide to go, it's best to book your accommodations in advance, especially if you have a particular type of lodging in mind or will be visiting on a holiday weekend. Visitors are advised not to travel to the Acadia area in peak season without a reservation.

Getting Here and Around

AIR

Bangor International Airport (BGR) in Bangor is the closest major airport to Acadia National Park. The driving distance from Bangor to Mount Desert Island is approximately 50 miles. Car rentals, taxi, bus, and shuttle service are available.

Farther south along the coast, Portland International Airport (PWM) is approximately three hours to the Mount Desert Island area. Renting a car is your best bet for getting to Acadia National Park from here.

The small regional Hancock County–Bar Harbor Airport (BHB) is in Trenton just minutes from the causeway to Mount Desert Island. Cape Air/JetBlue offer flights to and from Logan International Airport (BOS) in Boston. Car rentals and taxi service are available, and the airport is a stop for the free seasonal Island Explorer buses that serve Acadia and nearby towns.

CONTACTS Bangor–Bar Harbor Express Shuttle. ✉ Bangor ☎ 207/944–8429 ⊕ www.bangorbarharborexpressshuttle. com. **Bangor International Airport.** (BGR) ✉ 287 Godfrey Blvd., Bangor ☎ 207/992–4600 ⊕ www.flybangor.com. **Hancock County–Bar Harbor Airport.** (BHB) ✉ 143 Caruso Dr., Trenton ☎ 207/667–7329 ⊕ www.bhbairport.com.

BUS

Operating seasonally, Island Explorer buses serve Acadia and communities throughout Mount Desert Island as well as neighboring Trenton. Though touted as free, donations are requested to support the service. Island Explorer also serves the mainland district of Acadia and nearby villages, including Winter Harbor, on the Schoodic Peninsula. You can get to the park's Schoodic District from the seasonal Bar Harbor–Winter Harbor Ferry via an Island Explorer bus.

Bus service starts in late May on the Schoodic Peninsula and late June in the Mount Desert area and runs through Indigenous Peoples Day/Columbus Day. A reduced fall schedule starts in late August. Island Explorer's designated stops include many campgrounds and hotels. The buses also pick up and drop off passengers anywhere along the route where it's safe to stop.

Buses have bike racks, but they only hold four or six bicycles. So during the peak summer season, the Island Explorer Bicycle Express takes bikes and passengers by van from downtown Bar Harbor to Acadia's Eagle Lake Carriage Road. The vans can take tag-along bikes and small children's bikes but not tandem, fat-tire, or electric bikes. Island Explorer buses can't transport any of these specialty bikes (i.e., tag-along and small children's bikes).

CONTACTS Island Explorer. ☎ 207/667–5796 ⊕ www.exploreacadia.com.

CAR

Route 3 leads to Mount Desert Island and Bar Harbor from Ellsworth and circles the eastern part of the island. Route 102 is the major road on the west side. Acadia National Park's Hulls Cove Visitor Center is off Route 3, 3 miles from downtown Bar Harbor. Acadia's main thoroughfare, 27-mile Park Loop Road, is accessible from the visitor center as well as park entrances (Cadillac Mountain) near downtown Bar Harbor on Route 233, south of Bar Harbor proper on Route 3 (Sieur de Monts), and in Seal Harbor on Route 3 (Stanley Brook Road). Much of the road is one-way.

Shaped like an upside-down "U" (some liken it to a pair of lobster claws), Mount Desert is relatively easy to navigate, though it may take longer than expected to reach some points. Somes Sound, a fjard (less steep-sided than a fjord) that runs up the middle of Mount Desert Island, requires drivers at the ends of the "U" to travel quite a distance to get to a town that is close as the crow flies. Beyond the geographical barriers, summer traffic can slow your progress and make finding a parking space, especially in Bar Harbor or Acadia, difficult to nearly impossible. Avoid the problem by hopping on one of the seasonal free Island Explorer buses that serve the park and nearby towns.

Inspiration

In *Granite, Fire, and Fog: The Natural and Cultural History of Acadia,* ecologist and naturalist Tom Wessels intimately examines how nature, time and weather, and the humanity they attracted and influenced, all have interacted to create "a landscape that can be found nowhere else in the United States." In closing the book Wessels takes readers along on a favorite hike to help illustrate the natural and human history he related in previous chapters.

Who better than John D. Rockefeller Jr.'s granddaughter to tell the story of the famed carriage roads that he created, and have since delighted millions of Acadia National Park visitors? In *Mr. Rockefeller's Roads: The Untold Story of Acadia's Carriage Roads,* Ann Rockefeller Roberts relies on her family connection and her own personal enjoyment of the crushed-stone roads, stemming from childhood, to relate their history from behind the scenes.

The 1999 film *The Cider House Rules,* based on a 1985 novel of the same name by John Irving and starring Tobey Maguire, Charlize Theron, and Michael Caine, is primarily set in a fictitious Maine orphanage. While many scenes were filmed in New Hampshire and Massachusetts, some were shot at Acadia National Park's Sand Beach and on Bass Harbor at the bottom of Mount Desert Island.

Park Essentials

ACCESSIBILITY
Many Acadia National Park sights and amenities are at least partly accessible to those with accessibility challenges. Island Explorer buses (but not all bus stops), park visitor and information centers, and many picnic areas and camping sites are wheelchair accessible. Accessibility varies for scenic overlooks, trails, and carriage roads. Echo Lake Beach has wheelchair-accessible changing rooms; stairs to the water prevent wheelchair access at Sand Beach. The Sieur de Monts area of the park has a Nature Center with exhibits and an information desk at wheelchair height; a trailhead for the mostly wheelchair-accessible 1.5-mile Jesup Path and Hemlock Path Loop; a level if narrow path through Wild Gardens of Acadia; and a wheelchair-accessible water fountain and water bottle-filling station. Check the park website for information on accessibility.

PARK FEES AND PERMITS
A National Parks pass is required to enter Acadia year-round; display it on your dashboard when parking at trailheads or parking areas. An annual national park's pass ($80) and the Acadia weekly pass ($30 per vehicle) can be purchased online at ⊕ *www.Recreation.gov.*

Within the park, passes can be purchased at the Hulls Cove Visitor Center, the Sand Beach Entrance Station on Park Loop Road, and park campgrounds (except Isle au Haut). Automated fee machines in the Hulls Cove Visitor Center parking lot pavilion and at Acadia's mainland Schoodic District (inside the gatehouse at the entrance to Schoodic Institute) sell Acadia's weekly pass. Third-party sellers like local chambers of commerce and park concessionaires also sell Acadia weekly passes.

The park is free on Martin Luther King Jr. Day (third Monday in January); Great American Outdoors Day (August 4); first Monday of National Park Week in mid-April; National Public Lands Day (fourth Saturday in September); and Veterans Day, November 11.

PARK HOURS
The park is open 24 hours a day year-round, but paved roads within the park on Mount Desert Island close December–mid-April except for two small sections of Park Look Road: Ocean Drive and the section providing access to Jordan Pond. Unpaved roads are closed from mid-November–mid-May. Paved roads are open year-round at Acadia's mainland section on Schoodic Peninsula.

CELL PHONE RECEPTION
Depending on your cell phone carrier, you may not always be able to rely on your cell phone while visiting Mount Desert Island.

Hotels

Lodging is not available within Acadia National Park. Bar Harbor has the greatest variety and number of lodging facilities, but they are also found in other Mount Desert Island towns and villages. Northeast Harbor and Southwest Harbor having the largest concentration outside Bar Harbor. With short notice in high season the Ellsworth area might be your best bet. Visiting the Acadia area in peak season without a reservation is not advised.

Restaurants

The Jordan Pond House Restaurant is the only dining option within the park, serving lunch, tea, and dinner late May to late October; it also has a takeout place. There are a number of restaurants serving a variety of cuisines in Bar Harbor, while smaller coastal communities typically have at least one or two small eateries. Northeast Harbor and Southwest Harbor have the largest concentration outside the main tourist hub of Bar Harbor.

PRICES

Restaurant prices in the reviews are the average cost of a main course at dinner, or if dinner is not served, at lunch. Restaurant reviews have been shortened. For full information, visit Fodors.com.

What It Costs In U.S. Dollars

$	$$	$$$	$$$$
RESTAURANTS			
under $18	$18–$24	$25–$35	over $35

Visitor Information

Mount Desert Chamber of Commerce isn't an island-wide chamber; it serves the Town of Mount Desert (Northeast Harbor, Somesville, and a few other villages). The two other island chambers are Bar Harbor Chamber of Commerce and Southwest Harbor & Tremont Chamber of Commerce.

CONTACTS Acadia National Park.
☎ *207/288–3338* ⊕ *www.nps.gov/acad.*
Bar Harbor Chamber of Commerce. ✉ *2 Cottage St., Bar Harbor* ☎ *207/288–5103* ⊕ *www.visitbarharbor.com.* **Mount Desert Chamber of Commerce.** ✉ *41 Harbor Dr., Northeast Harbor* ☎ *207/276–5040* ⊕ *www.mtdesertchamber.org.* **Southwest Harbor & Tremont Chamber of Commerce.** ✉ *329 Main St., Southwest Harbor* ☎ *207/244–9264* ⊕ *www.acadiachamber. com.* **Thompson Island Information Center.** ✉ *1319 Bar Harbor Rd., Bar Harbor* ☎ *207/288–3338* ⊕ *www.nps.gov/acad/ planyourvisit/hours.htm.*

East Side of Mount Desert Island

10 miles south of Ellsworth via Rte. 3.

Many of Acadia National Park's best-loved features, including all of its carriage roads, Sand Beach, and Cadillac Mountain, are on this side of Mount Desert Island. So, too, is Bar Harbor, the island's largest town and your best bet for finding lodging and dining.

Sights

BEACHES
Sand Beach
BEACH | FAMILY | At this 290-yard-long pocket beach, hugged by picturesque rocky outcroppings, the combination of crashing waves and chilly water (normal range is 50–60°F) keeps most people

on the beach. You'll find some swimmers at the height of summer, when lifeguards may be on duty, but the rest of the year this is a place for strolling and snapping photos. In fact, when the official swimming season (mid-June to early September) ends, more activities are allowed, from fishing and surfing to dog walking and boat launching/landing. **Amenities:** parking; toilets. **Best for:** solitude; sunrise; walking. ⊠ *Ocean Dr. section of Park Loop Rd., Acadia National Park* ☎ *207/288–3338* ⊕ *nps.gov/acad.*

GEOLOGICAL FORMATIONS
Thunder Hole
CAVE | When conditions are just so at this popular visitor attraction, the force of pounding surf being squeezed into a narrow slot of cliffside pink granite causes a boom that sounds like thunder and often sends ocean spray up to 40 feet into the air—soaking observers standing nearby behind safety railings. Time your visit within an hour or two of high tide for the best chance to observe the phenomenon; at low tide, take the stairway down to a viewing platform for a peak at the water-carved walls of the tiny inlet. ⊠ *Ocean Dr. section of Park Loop Rd., Acadia National Park* ✛ *About 1 mile south of Sand Beach* ☎ *207/288–3338* ⊕ *nps.gov/acad.*

PICNIC AREAS
Bear Brook
OTHER ATTRACTION | FAMILY | This seasonally opened picnic area is located just past the entrance to Sieur de Monts along the one-way section of the Park Loop Road. Trees shade most of its 35 sites. A restroom is available. ⊠ *Park Loop Rd., Acadia National Park* ✛ *East of Sieur de Monts* ☎ *207/288–3338* ⊕ *nps.gov/acad.*

Fabbri
OTHER ATTRACTION | FAMILY | Open year-round, with 23 sites and restrooms, Fabbri is beyond Otter Point via the one-way section of Park Loop Road and also accessible from Otter Cliff Road. ⊠ *Park Loop Rd., Acadia National Park* ✛ *¾ mile west of Thunder Hole* ☎ *207/288–3338* ⊕ *nps.gov/acad.*

Thompson Island
CITY PARK | FAMILY | Stop by this 46-site picnic area with a water view after visiting Thompson Island Information Center. Both are along Route 3 on a small island just before the causeway onto Mount Desert Island. It's open seasonally and has a restroom. ⊠ *Rte. 3, Acadia National Park* ☎ *207/288–3338* ⊕ *nps.gov/acad.*

SCENIC DRIVES
★ Park Loop Road
SCENIC DRIVE | FAMILY | This 27-mile road provides a perfect introduction to the park. You can drive it in an hour, but allow at least half a day, so that you can explore the many sites along the way, including Thunder Hole, Sand Beach, and Otter Cliff. The route is also served by the free Island Explorer buses. Traffic is one-way from near the Route 233 entrance to the Stanley Brook Road entrance south of the Jordan Pond House. The 2-mile section known as Ocean Drive is open year-round, as is a small section that provides access to Jordan Pond from Seal Harbor. ☎ *207/288–3338* ⊕ *nps.gov/acad.*

SCENIC STOPS
Bar Island
ISLAND | FAMILY | Offering one of Acadia National Park's more unique experiences, Bar Island is only accessible by foot and during a three-hour window when low tide exposes a ½-mile gravel bar connecting Bar Island to Bar Harbor. The entire Bar Island trail offers an easy 1.9-mile round-trip hike; once on the island you can enjoy views of Bar Harbor and Frenchman Bay. Make sure to check the tide charts before setting out, because once covered by rising tidal waters it'll be another nine hours before the land bridge is once again exposed. ⊠ *Bar Harbor* ✛ *Access via West St. then Bridge St.* ☎ *207/288–3338* ⊕ *nps.gov/acad.*

★ Cadillac Mountain

MOUNTAIN | FAMILY | One of Acadia's premier attractions, 1,530-foot Cadillac Mountain is the Eastern Seaboard's tallest mountain. Stunning panoramic views sweep across bays, islands, and mountains on and off Mount Desert Island. You can see Bar Harbor below on the northeast side and Eagle Lake to the west. Low-lying vegetation like pitch pine and wild blueberry plants accent granite slabs in the "subalpine-like" environment. There's a paved summit loop trail and several hiking trails up Cadillac, named for a Frenchman who explored here in the late 1600s and later founded Detroit. From mid-May–mid-October, a vehicle reservation (done through ⊕ www. recreation.gov) is needed to drive to the summit. Sunrise slots are in high demand, as this is one of the first places in the country to see first light, not to mention the perfect spot to watch the sunset or stargaze in the spring and fall—Bar Harbor's light ordinance helps with that. ⊠ *Cadillac Summit Rd., Acadia National Park* ☏ *207/288–3338* ⊕ *www. nps.gov/acad* ⊡ *$6 per car in addition to park entrance fee (via www.recreation. gov)* ☽ *Access road closes at 10 pm in season and Dec.–mid-Apr.*

Compass Harbor

TRAIL | FAMILY | Just beyond Bar Harbor proper, this easy 0.8-mile round-trip trail through woods to the shore passes through land that belonged to George B. Dorr—Acadia National Park's first superintendent and a key player in its creation. Views extend to Ironbound Island across Frenchman Bay, and you can check out remnants of Dorr's estate, including the manor house's foundation, remains of a saltwater pool, stone steps to the ocean, and old gardens and apple trees. *Easy.* ⊠ *399 Main St., trailhead parking, Bar Harbor* ☏ *207/288–3338* ⊕ *nps.gov/acad.*

The Early Bird Gets the Sun

Many people believe the top of Cadillac Mountain is the first place in the United States to see the sunrise. It is, though only from early October to early March. To experience first light atop Cadillac's granite summit, plan to get up *very* early. A timed reservation ($6 per car in addition to the park entrance fee via ⊕ *www.recreation. gov*) is required to drive up the mountain from mid-May through mid-October; sunrise slots are especially popular.

Eagle Lake

MARINA/PIER | Located just east of Acadia National Park headquarters, 436-acre Eagle Lake is the largest freshwater lake on Mountain Desert Island. Swimming is not allowed, but kayaking, canoeing, boating, and fishing are, and the encircling 6.1-mile carriage road invites walkers and cyclists. ⊠ *Rte. 233, Bar Harbor* ⊹ *½ mile east of Acadia National Park headquarters* ☏ *207/288–3338* ⊕ *nps.gov/acad.*

★ Jordan Pond

BODY OF WATER | FAMILY | Soak up the mountain scenery, listen for the call of loons, and watch for cliff-nesting peregrine falcons along the 3.3-mile trail around this 187-acre tarn—a mountain lake formed by retreating glaciers—on Park Loop Road's two-way portion. Several carriage roads converge here, one marked by a fanciful gatehouse, one of two on the road network. Visitors kayak and canoe on the deep water (no swimming) and gaze down on Great Pond after hiking up nearby mountains. A popular choice is The Bubbles, with twin peaks whose distinct shape makes up for what they lack in size. They rise across the water from Jordan Pond House Restaurant, where folks come for popovers served with strawberry jam and tea, hoping for a table on the expansive lawn—a tradition started in the 1890s in the original Jordan Pond House, which burned in 1979. The rebuild has a two-story gift shop and, on the upper level, an observation deck and Carriage Road Carry Out, with to-go items like sandwiches and salads—or try the popover sundae. Parking lots here fill fast in high season; consider biking or taking the free Island Explorer bus. ⊠ *2928 Park Loop Rd. Seal Harbor ☎ 207/288–3338 ⊕ nps.gov/acad.*

Otter Cliff

NATURE SIGHT | Looming 110 feet above the crashing surf of the North Atlantic, Otter Cliff is the terminus of the popular Ocean Path walking trail, which starts 2 miles north at the Sand Beach parking lot. Don't fret If you're not up for the walk: you can still enjoy the view from the overlook just beyond the cliff, where you can often watch rock climbers on the cliff face. Nearby on the shore are thousands of round boulders of various sizes that have been smoothed into shape by many thousands of years of wave action. ⊠ *Park Loop Rd., Bar Harbor ✛ About ¾ mile south of Thunder Hole on Park Loop Rd. ☎ 207/288–3338 ⊕ nps.gov/acad.*

★ Sieur de Monts

NATURE SIGHT | FAMILY | The seasonal ranger-staffed Nature Center is the first major stop along the Park Loop Road. There are exhibits about the park's conservation efforts, as well as a park information center. The area is known as the "Heart of Acadia," which memorializes George Dorr, Acadia National Park's first superintendent, and includes walking trails, Sieur de Monts Spring, Wild Gardens of Acadia, and Abbe Museum (its main location is in downtown Bar Harbor), which honors the area's Native American heritage.

Book a Carriage Ride

Riding down one of the park's scenic carriage roads in a horse-drawn carriage is a classic way to experience Acadia. Carriages of Acadia (⊕ *www.acadiahorses. com,* ☎ 877/276–3622) offers rides out of Wildwood Stables in the park from late May to mid-October. Reservations are strongly recommended and can only be made by phone. There is a wheelchair-accessible carriage as well as a step stool to assist with boarding.

⊠ *Park Loop Rd., Bar Harbor ✛ Also accessible from Rte. 3 ☎ 207/288–3338 ⊕ nps.gov/acad ⊙ Nature Center closed mid-Oct.–mid-May.*

TRAILS

Cadillac Mountain North Ridge Trail

TRAIL | The mostly exposed 4.4-mile round-trip summit hike rewards with expansive views of Bar Harbor, Frenchman Bay, and the Schoodic Peninsula for much of the way. The trail is worth undertaking at either sunrise or sunset (or both!). Parking can be limited, especially in high season, so park officials recommend taking the Island Explorer bus for access via a 0.1-mile section of the Kebo Brook Trail. *Moderate.* ⊠ *Park Loop Rd., Bar Harbor ✛ Trailhead: Access is via Park Loop Rd. near where one-way travel to Sand Beach starts ☎ 207/288–3338 ⊕ nps.gov/acad.*

★ Ocean Path Trail

TRAIL | This easily accessible 4.4-mile round-trip trail runs parallel to the Ocean Drive section of the Park Loop Road from Sand Beach to Otter Point. It has some of the best scenery in Maine: cliffs and boulders of pink granite at the ocean's edge, twisted branches of dwarf jack pines, and ocean views that stretch to the horizon. Be sure to save time to stop at Thunder Hole, named for the sound the waves make as they thrash through a narrow opening in the granite cliffs, into a sea cave, and whoosh up and out. It's roughly halfway between Sand Beach and Otter Cliff, with steps leading down to the water to watch the wave action close up. Use caution as you descend (access may be limited due to storms), and also if you venture onto the outer cliffs along this walk. *Easy.* ✉ *Ocean Dr. section of Park Loop Rd., Acadia National Park* ✣ *Trailhead: Upper parking lot of Sand Beach* ☎ *207/288–3338* 🌐 *nps.gov/acad.*

VISITOR CENTERS

Hulls Cove Visitor Center

VISITOR CENTER | FAMILY | This is a great spot to get your bearings. A large 3D relief map of Mount Desert Island gives you the lay of the land, and there are free park and carriage road maps. The gift shop sells hiking maps, guidebooks, and a CD for a self-driving park tour and is well-stocked with books about Acadia. Ranger-led programs include guided hikes and other interpretive events, and there are Junior Ranger programs for kids, family-friendly campfire talks at campground amphitheaters (open to all visitors), and night sky talks at Sand Beach. ✉ *25 Visitor Center Rd., Bar Harbor* ☎ *207/288–3338* 🌐 *www.nps.gov/acad.*

🍴 Restaurants

Jordan Pond House Restaurant

$$ | AMERICAN | The only dining option within Acadia serves lunch, tea, and dinner as well as to-go items like sandwiches and salads. Most folks come for tea and popovers with strawberry jam on the lawn—a tradition started in the 1890s in the original Jordan Pond House—but the menu also includes chowders and entrees like a lobster dinner or the fresh catch of the day. **Known for:** popover sundae; lawn seating; popovers and strawberry jam. [$] *Average main: $20* ✉ *2928 Park Loop Rd., Acadia National Park* ☎ *207/276–3610* 🌐 *jordanpondhouse.com* ⏲ *Closed Nov.–late May.*

West Side of Mount Desert Island

8 miles east of Bar Harbor via Rte. 233 and Rte. 3.

On Acadia National Park's "quiet side" west of Somes Sounds, there's plenty to explore including Echo Lake Beach, which is the park's swimming beach with the warmest water, and Bass Harbor Head Light. Popular hiking trails adorn Acadia and Beech mountains.

👁 Sights

BEACHES

Echo Lake Beach

BEACH | FAMILY | A quiet lake surrounded by woods in the shadow of Beech Mountain, Echo Lake is one of Acadia's few swimming beaches. The water is considerably warmer, if muckier, than nearby ocean beaches, and dogs are allowed in the off-season. The surrounding trail network skirts the lake and ascends the mountain. A boat ramp is north of here along Route 102 at Ikes Point. **Amenities:** lifeguards (at times); parking; toilets. **Best for:** sunset; swimming; solitude. ✉ *Echo Lake Beach Rd., off Rte. 102 between Somesville and Southwest Harbor, Acadia National Park* ☎ *207/288–3338* 🌐 *nps.gov/acad.*

GEOLOGICAL FORMATIONS

Acadia Mountain

MOUNTAIN | FAMILY | This 681-foot peak is situated between Echo Lake to the east and Somes Sound to the west and is accessible via Route 102. The only mountain on Mount Desert Island that lies east–west rather than north–south,

it features a popular summit trail with outstanding and expansive views. ⊠ *Rte. 102, Acadia National Park* ☎ *207/288–3338* ⊕ *nps.gov/acad.*

HISTORIC SIGHTS

★ Bass Harbor Head Light

LIGHTHOUSE | **FAMILY** | Built in 1858, this is one of Maine's most photographed lighthouses; it's been a part of Acadia National Park since 2020. Now automated, it marks the entrance to Bass Harbor and Blue Hill Bay at the island's southernmost point nearly 2 miles below Bass Harbor village. You can't go inside, but a walkway brings you to a seaside viewing area with placards about its history. The small parking lot typically fills for sunset viewing in high season and parking isn't allowed on the entrance road or on Route 102A. The free Island Explorer bus doesn't serve the lighthouse. ⊠ *116 Lighthouse Rd., off Rte. 102A, Bass Harbor* ☎ *207/288–3338* ⊕ *www.nps.gov/acad* ▤ *A National Parks pass is required.*

Carroll Homestead

FARM/RANCH | **FAMILY** | For almost 100 years beginning in the early 1800s, three generations of the Carroll family homesteaded at this small-scale farm that was donated to the park in 1982. A few miles north of the village of Southwest Harbor, the weathered farmhouse still stands and is occasionally opened for ranger-led tours during the summer; check the park website for details. ⊠ *Acadia National Park* ⊹ *Turn off Rte. 102* ☎ *207/288–3338* ⊕ *nps.gov/acad.*

PICNIC AREAS

Pretty Marsh

OTHER ATTRACTION | **FAMILY** | The scent of fir and spruce trees mingle with the ocean's salty tang at this secluded seasonal picnic spot on the quiet western side of Mount Desert Island. A handful of picnic tables, including the park's only covered ones, are set close to a stairway leading down to the shore alongside Pretty Marsh Harbor. ⊠ *Rte. 102, Acadia*

National Park ⊹ *1½ miles north of Seal Cove* ☎ *207/288–3338* ⊕ *nps.gov/acad.*

Seawall

OTHER ATTRACTION | **FAMILY** | This 14-site picnic area, open year-round, has restrooms. Tables are perched along the shoreline with water views. The park's Seawall Campground is across the road. ⊠ *Rte. 102A, Acadia National Park* ⊹ *Across from Seawall Campground* ☎ *207/288–3338* ⊕ *nps.gov/acad.*

TRAILS

Beech Mountain

TRAIL | **FAMILY** | A unique payoff awaits on this 1.2-mile round-trip hike: a fire lookout tower where you can enjoy views of Somes Sound, Echo Lake, Acadia Mountain, and beyond from its platform. The forested and rocky trail is popular with sunset seekers, who are reminded to carry appropriate clothing and headlamps for the descent. *Moderate.* ⊠ *Beech Hill Rd., Southwest Harbor* ⊹ *Trailhead: 4 miles south of Somesville on Beech Hill Rd. off Rte. 102* ☎ *207/288–3338* ⊕ *nps. gov/acad.*

Ship Harbor Trail

TRAIL | **FAMILY** | Popular with families and birders, this 1.3-mile figure-8 trail loops through woods and follows a sheltered cove where you may spot great blue herons feeding in the mudflats during low tide. *Easy* ⊠ *Rte. 102A, Acadia National Park* ⊹ *Trailhead: 1.2 miles west of Seawall picnic area on Rte. 102A* ☎ *207/288–3338* ⊕ *nps.gov/acad.*

★ St. Sauveur and Acadia Mountain Loop

TRAIL | If you're up for a challenge, this is one of the area's best hikes. The 3.9-mile round-trip loop summits both St. Sauveur and Acadia mountains. Ascents and descents are steep and strenuous, but the views of Somes Sound and beyond are grand. The hike begins at the Acadia Mountain trailhead. For a shorter excursion, follow the fire road that connects with the Acadia Mountain Trail section of the loop. *Difficult.* ⊠ *Rte. 102, Mount*

Desert ✛ Trailhead (Acadia Mountain): Rte. 102 just after Ikes Pt. on Echo Lake (opposite side of road) ☎ 207/288–3338 ⊕ www.nps.gov/acad.

VISITOR CENTER
Seawall Ranger Station
VISITOR CENTER | This small information center is located at the park's Seawall Campground along Route 102A near the island's southernmost point. Stop here for park information and to purchase park passes. ✉ 664 Seawall Rd., Southwest Harbor ✛ Off Rte. 102A ☎ 207/288– 3338 ⊕ www.nps.gov/acad ☉ Closed mid-Oct.–mid-May.

Schoodic District

25 miles east of Ellsworth via U.S. 1 and Rte. 186.

Acadia National Park's 3,900-acre Schoodic District sits at the bottom of Schoodic Peninsula, east of Mount Desert Island and mostly in Winter Harbor. The landscape of craggy coastline, towering evergreens, and views over Frenchman Bay is breathtaking—and less crowded than over at the park on Mount Desert. A scenic loop road spurs to Schoodic Point, the experiential pinnacle. Schoodic Head, the literal one, also has spectacular views—of ocean as well as forested peninsula. Biking is popular on the loop road and 8.3 miles of wide, interconnected packed-gravel bike paths (no Class 2 or Class 3 e-bikes). Also used by walkers, they were added in 2015 along with the campground and additional hiking trails. Ranging from easy coastal treks to difficult ascents, most trails are part of a network that links with the bike path system, which has some challenging climbs. The Schoodic District has education programs for visitors, including Junior Ranger activities for the kiddos. A seasonal passenger ferry links Bar Harbor and Winter Harbor, where it connects with free seasonal Island Explorer buses serving the park and peninsular villages (see the Getting Here and Around section of the Chapter Planner for more information).

Sights

HISTORIC SIGHTS
Schoodic Institute
COLLEGE | FAMILY | Formerly apartments and offices for the U.S. Navy base that operated here for decades, this massive 1934 French Eclectic-style structure is on the National Registry of Historic Places. Today, the building is known as Rockefeller Hall, and its home to the Schoodic Institute, which is home base for many ranger-led programs and family-friendly activities at the park's Schoodic District, including public programs of its own (some have fees and require overnight stays; check the institute's website for more information); it's the largest facility of its kind at a national park. The Rockefeller Welcome Center is on the first floor. ✉ 1 Atterbury Circle, Winter Harbor ☎ 207/288–1310 ⊕ www.schoodicinstitute.org.

PICNIC AREAS
Frazer Point
OTHER ATTRACTION | FAMILY | Just before the start of the one-way section of the loop road, this serene spot has views across to Winter Harbor and out to nearby islands. Open year-round, it has 26 sites and a handicapped-accessible pier where you can fish, launch your canoe or kayak, or simply soak up the view. For the warm months, a float dock is attached to the pier. ✉ Schoodic Loop Rd., Winter Harbor ✛ Schoodic Loop Rd. ☎ 207/288–3338 ⊕ nps.gov/acad.

SCENIC DRIVES
Schoodic Loop Road
SCENIC DRIVE | FAMILY | Less than a mile from the entrance to Schoodic Woods Campground and Ranger Station, and just beyond Frazer Point Picnic Area, the only road into the park becomes one-way

and continues for about 6 miles to the park exit (no RVs are allowed on the road after the campground entrance). Edging the coast and sprinkled with pullouts, the first few miles yield views of Grindstone Neck, Winter Harbor, Winter Harbor Lighthouse, and, across the water, Cadillac Mountain. After a few miles, a two-way spur, Arey Cove Road, passes Schoodic Institute en route to Schoodic Point. Here, huge slabs of pink granite lie jumbled along the shore, thrashed unmercifully by the crashing surf, and jack pines cling to life amid the rocks. Continuing on the loop road, stop at Blueberry Hill parking area to look out on near-shore islands. The Anvil and Alder trailheads are near here. From the park exit, continue two miles to Route 186 in Birch Harbor. There's a biking path trailhead with parking at the exit and another one about midway to Route 186, both on your left. ⊠ *Schoodic Loop Rd., Winter Harbor* ☎ *207/288–3338* ⊕ *nps.gov/acad.*

SCENIC STOPS
Blueberry Hill

SCENIC DRIVE | About a half mile beyond the Schoodic Point spur on the scenic one-way loop drive, this spot looks out on nearby Little Moose and Schoodic islands and the ocean beyond. It's also where to park if you're planning to hike a loop consisting of the Alder and Anvil trails across the road from the parking lot. ⊠ *Schoodic Loop Rd., Winter Harbor* ✛ *About 1 mile east of Schoodic Point* ☎ *207/288–3338* ⊕ *nps.gov/acad.*

★ Schoodic Point

NATURE SIGHT | FAMILY | Massed granite ledges meet crashing waves at Schoodic Peninsula's tip, off the loop road at the end of Arey Cove Road. Dark basalt rock slices through pink granite, to dramatic effect. Look east for a close view of Little Moose Island; a bit farther away to the west is a sidelong view of Mount Desert Island; and to the south, an inspiring open ocean view. There are bathrooms and a good-size parking area. ⊠ *Arey*

Cove Rd., Winter Harbor ☎ *207/288– 3338* ⊕ *nps.gov/acad.*

TRAILS
Alder and Anvil Trails

TRAIL | Popular with birders, the Alder trail heads inland, passing fruit trees and alder bushes on an easy 1.2-mile out-and-back hike, but many hit the grassy path as part of a near-loop with the challenging 1.1-mile Anvil Trail, since trailheads for both are near the Blueberry Hill parking area on the loop road (you must cross the road to get to them). Steep and heavily rooted in sections as it climbs Schoodic Head, Anvil requires lots of rock climbing but rewards with wonderful water and island views from the rock knob overlook (side trail) for which it's named. After connecting with Schoodic Head Trail from Alder or Anvil, it's not far to the top of Schoodic Head, where expansive views of the surrounding seascape and landscape await. ⊠ *Schoodic Loop Rd., Winter Harbor* ✛ *Beyond turn for Schoodic Point* ☎ *207/288–3338* ⊕ *nps.gov/acad.*

Schoodic Head Ascents

TRAIL | FAMILY | You can drive up or walk up to the 440-foot summit —the highest point in these Acadia lands—along a narrow 1-mile gravel road. It's unmarked, so watch for it 2½ miles from the start of the one-way portion of Schoodic Loop Road. Prefer an actual hiking trail? You've got options: plot your course for an easier or longer way up, or down. Starting at Schoodic Woods Campground, Buck Cove Mountain Trail—Schoodic's longest at 3.2 miles—summits its namesake before climbing Schoodic Head's north face. On the southeastern side, the challenging 1.1-mile Anvil trail links with .6-mile Schoodic Head Trail to the summit, as does the easy 0.6-mile Alder Trail. Trailheads for both are along the loop drive near the Blueberry Hill parking area; hikers often combine them. A bit farther is a terminus for the ½-mile East Trail; this challenging, steep climb up

Schoodic Head's east face connects, near the summit, with Schoodic Head Trail. Regardless of your route, on a clear day atop Schoodic Head, spectacular views flow across the forested peninsula and island-dotted Frenchman Bay to Cadillac Mountain. ⊠ *Schoodic Loop Rd.* ☎ *207/288–3338* ⊕ *nps.gov/acad.*

VISITOR CENTERS
Rockefeller Welcome Center
VISITOR CENTER | FAMILY | This impressive 1934 structure resembles a mansion but was built as housing for personnel at the U.S. Navy base that operated on Schoodic Peninsula for decades. Now part of Schoodic Institute, an Acadia-affiliated research and education nonprofit, the first floor houses a seasonal park welcome center. You can get information, watch a video about Schoodic, and check out kid-friendly exhibits about this neck of Acadia and the navy base. There's a small gift shop area. An automated fee machine inside the gatehouse at the complex's entrance sells Acadia weekly park passes. ⊠ *1 Atterbury Circle, Winter Harbor* ✛ *Off Arey Cove Rd.* ☎ *207/288–3338* ⊕ *nps.gov/acad.*

Schoodic Woods Ranger Station
VISITOR CENTER | FAMILY | Built with materials from the surrounding region and opened in 2015 along with the campground here, this striking post-and-beam structure serves double duty as campground host and information center— Acadia passes and Federal Lands passes are sold. Inside, a large Schoodic District relief map centers the room, which has a gift shop area and exhibits, some hands-on, about the park. Comfy chairs flank a fireplace, inviting visitors to relax, pamphlet in hand, after chatting with a ranger or park volunteer. Outside, the setting is village-like, with walkways and handsome signage for bike paths that converge here, a stop for the free Island Explorer buses, and restrooms in a cabin-like building. Trailheads for 3.2-mile Buck Cove Mountain and 1.5-mile Lower

Harbor trails are nearby. A campground amphitheater hosts ranger programs for park visitors and campers. ⊠ *54 Farview Dr., Winter Harbor* ✛ *Off Schoodic Loop Rd.* ☎ *207/288–3338* ⊕ *nps.gov/acad* ⊗ *Closed late Oct.–mid-May.*

Isle Au Haut

6 miles south of Stonington via ferry.

French explorer Samuel D. Champlain discovered Isle au Haut—or "High Island"— in 1604, but native populations left heaps of oyster shells here prior to his arrival. The only ferry is a passenger-only "mail boat" out of Stonington, but the 45-minute journey is well worth the effort. Acadia National Park covers about half of the island, with miles of rugged trails, and the boat will drop visitors off in the park at Duck Harbor in peak season. The park ranger station (restroom) is a quarter mile from the Town Landing, and from there it's about 4 miles to Duck Harbor. To get there, hit the trail or walk (or bike) the unpaved road, a slightly longer but faster route. Isle au Haut has a small general store and a gift shop but no restaurants or inns, though there are vacation rentals. There's one main road: partly paved and partly unpaved, it circles the island and goes through the park.

 Sights

SCENIC STOPS
Duck Harbor
MARINA/PIER | Acadia National Park's most primitive (and therefore secluded) campground is here, as is a dock for the passenger-only ferry that serves Isle au Haut from Stonington. Duck Harbor (there's a composting toilet) is the best jumping off point for the 18 miles of trails in the park, which lead through woods and to rocky shoreline, marshes, bogs, and a freshwater lake. Note that the ferry only stops at Duck Harbor from early June through early October. Off-season or if you

miss the boat, you'll be hoofing it about 4 miles to the Isle au Haut Town Landing. Bring your bike or kayak for an extra fee or rent a bike from the ferry service. *Note: Kayaks and bikes are dropped off and picked up at the Town Landing only, not at Duck Harbor.* ✉ *Duck Harbor, Isle Au Haut* ☎ *207/288–3338* ⊕ *nps.gov/acad.*

Western Head

TRAIL | Located at the southern tip of remote Isle au Haut, Western Head is accessible by foot or bicycle from the Town Landing. There are no amenities, so be sure to pack plenty of water and snacks. Western Head Trail is most often hiked as a loop that includes Western Head Road and Cliff Trail (*bicycles are not allowed on trails*). Starting from Duck Harbor (*the ferry doesn't drop bikes off here, only at the Town Landing*) on the unpaved road, it's approximately 4 miles round-trip. Once off the wooded road, the trail alternates between forest and volcanic rock clifftop, with opportunities to go off-course and explore the rocky shoreline. Dramatic coastal cliff views are your reward for visiting perhaps the most remote corner of Acadia National Park. ✉ *Isle Au Haut* ☎ *207/288–3338* ⊕ *nps. gov/acad.*

Activities

The best way to see Acadia National Park is to get out of your vehicle and explore on foot or by bicycle or boat. There are 45 miles of carriage roads that are perfect for walking and biking in the warmer months and for cross-country skiing and snowshoeing in winter. There are more than 150 miles of trails for hiking; numerous ponds and lakes for canoeing, kayaking, standup paddle boarding, fishing, and boating; a handful of beaches for swimming; and steep cliffs for rock climbing.

BIKING

Exploring Acadia National Park on a bike can be heavenly, and there are a variety of surfaces from paved to gravel, inland to seaside; always check ahead of time for trail closures. A park pass is required to ride anywhere within park boundaries; be sure to carry your pass or leave it in view in your parked car. On carriage roads, bicyclists must yield to everyone, including horses, and not exceed 20 mph; in winter, bikes are not permitted on carriage roads groomed for cross-country skiing. Bikes are allowed on carriage roads; biking Park Loop Road during peak season is discouraged as it's narrow, often congested, and lacks shoulders. Cyclists must ride with the flow of traffic where the road is one-way. Seasonal Island Explorer buses that have four or six bike racks operate between Bar Harbor and Eagle Lake carriage road. Pick up a free carriage road map at the park's Hulls Cove Visitor Center or Nature Center, or download it from the website.

BIRD-WATCHING

Acadia National Park is for the birds— much to the enjoyment of birders of a feather from all corners. Famed ornithologist and avian illustrator Roger Tory Peterson is known to have deemed Mount Desert Island as "the warbler capital of the world." More than 20 species of the energetic and colorful songbirds breed here, while 300-plus bird species have been "encountered in or around the park," according to the National Park Service. The park's website outlines a dozen areas rich in birdwatching opportunities. Come fall, park rangers lead hawk watches from the summit of Cadillac Mountain, counting hundreds and even thousands of migrating raptors. In addition to its namesake tours, Bar Harbor Whale Watch Co. offers cruises that seek out the comically colorful seabird known as the puffin.

CAMPING

Acadia National Park's four campgrounds require advance registration at ⊕ *www. recreation.gov*. Note: Same-day and upon-arrival reservations are not allowed at any of the campgrounds. Check the park website (⊕ *www.nps.gov/acad/ planyourvisit/camping.htm*) for campground information. For reservations, call ☏ *877/444-6777* or visit ⊕ *www. recreation.gov*.

The park's campgrounds on Mount Desert Island—Seawall and Blackwoods—don't have water views, but the price is right, and the ocean is just a 10-minute walk from each. There are two campgrounds—Schoodic Woods and Duck Harbor—off Mount Desert Island in the park's Schoodic Peninsula and Isle au Haut sections, respectively.

Blackwoods Campground. Near star attractions like Sand Beach and Jordan Pond along Park Loop Road, this is Acadia's most popular campground, with mostly tent but also RV sites. Open early May to mid-October, it's well served by the free Island Explorer buses. *Rte. 3, Mount Desert Island, 5 miles south of Bar Harbor.*

Seawall Campground. At the bottom of Mount Desert's "quiet" western side, with tent and RV sites, Seawall is near the park's seaside picnic area of the same name and a natural seawall. Open late May to mid-October, it's served by the free Island Explorer buses. *Rte. 102A, Mount Desert Island, 4 miles south of Southwest Harbor.*

Duck Harbor Campground. These five primitive sites—each one a three-sided lean-to—are available mid-May to mid-October in the remote section of Acadia on Isle au Haut, accessible by ferry from Stonington, via a bridge from the mainland. *Duck Harbor, Isle au Haut.*

Schoodic Woods Campground. At the park's only mainland section, this Schoodic Peninsula campground mostly has RV sites—and lacks showers by design, even though it opened in 2015. Open late May to mid-October, it has a stop for the free Island Explorer buses. *OffS choodic Loop Rd., 1 mile south of Rte. 186, Winter Harbor.*

Some of the best campgrounds outside the park are conveniently located in the middle of Mount Desert on fjord-ish Somes Sound.

Mount Desert Campground. At the head of Somes Sound, sites are wooded, and many are on the waterfront. RVs and trailers longer than 20 feet are not allowed. You can rent canoes, kayaks, and standup paddleboards. Open late May to mid-October, it's an Island Explorer bus stop. The Gathering Place sells baked goods in the morning and ice cream in peak season. *Town of Mount Desert* ☏ *207/244-3710* ⊕ *www. mountdesertcampground.com.*

Somes Sound View Campground. Spread about the remains of a granite quarry on Somes Sound, some sites are shaded, others sunny, and a few perched on the water. Most accommodate tents and RVs; at some, granite forms a natural terrace. There are a few cabins, plus kayak rentals, a heated pool, and a playground. Open mid-May through October, an Island Explorer bus stop is nearby. *Town of Mount Desert* ☏ *207/244-8094* ⊕ *www.ssvc.info.*

EDUCATIONAL PROGRAMS

The National Park Service offers a variety of ranger-led programming and tours, including the popular Junior Ranger Program for kids and, unique to Acadia National Park, citizen science opportunities at the Schoodic Institute, based at the mainland section on Schoodic Peninsula. Two ranger-led boat tours depart from Mount Desert Island. Out of Northeast Harbor, Islesford Historic and Scenic Cruise travels Somes Sounds and stops at Islesford on Little Cranberry Island to tour the park's Islesford Historic

8

Acadia National Park ACTIVITIES

Museum. Departing from Bar Harbor, Baker Island Cruise follows the shoreline en route to Baker Island nine miles away. Passengers explore the island and check out its namesake light and an old homestead. Virtually all of Baker Island, including the lighthouse, is part of Acadia. Baker Island doesn't have a year-round population and like Little Cranberry is part of the Cranberry Isles. *Visit the park website for more information.*

FLIGHTSEEING

Viewing the Acadia National Park region from above is a great way to get your bearings for your on-the-ground (and on-the-water) explorations, and perhaps the easiest way to wrap your arms around the sheer variety of scenery and attractions.

★ Scenic Flights of Acadia

AIR EXCURSIONS | For $144 per person, Scenic Flights of Acadia offers a 35-minute tour around the shoreline of Mount Desert Island, plus three other tours and fall foliage trips that fly over some of the island but head inland for the best color. Trips are out of Hancock County–Bar Harbor Airport. You can make reservations online or by phone; in Bar Harbor tickets are sold at Acadia Stand Up Paddle Boarding (*200 Main Street*). ⊠ *1044 Bar Harbor Rd., Rte. 3, Trenton* ☎ *207/667–6527* ⊕ *www.scenicflightsofacadia.com.*

HIKING

Acadia National Park maintains more than 150 miles of hiking trails. Generally rocky and rooted, many are steep and require scrambling: most visitors find hiking here harder than expected. Even trails that aren't that difficult may take longer than you think. But there is a range of options, from easier strolls around lakes and mostly level paths to rigorous treks with climbs up rock faces and scrambles along cliffs. Whatever you have in mind, park rangers can help you plan hikes and walks that fit your abilities and time frame. Although trails are concentrated

on the east side of the island, where they often connect with the park's carriage roads, the west side has plenty of scenic ones, too. For those wishing for a longer trek, try hiking up Cadillac Mountain or Dorr Mountain; Parkman, Sargeant, and Penobscot mountains are also good options. Most hiking is done mid-May– mid-November. In winter, cross-country skiing and snowshoeing replace hiking, assuming enough snow flies. Melting snow and ice can create precarious conditions in early to mid-spring.

■ TIP→ **Every so often folks die in Acadia National Park, from falling off trails or cliffs or being swept out to sea. The rocky shore can be gravelly and slippery—so watch your step. In springtime, conditions may seem fine for hiking until you get on a trail where shade has kept ice and snow intact or mud lingers from snowmelt.**

MULTISPORT OUTFITTERS

Name just about any popular sporting activity—kayaking, cycling, rock climbing, cross-country skiing, and snowshoeing, to say nothing of hiking—and chances are you can do it at Acadia National Park. Cadillac Mountain Sports (⊕ *www. cadillacsports.com*), with locations in Bar Harbor and Ellsworth, sells what you need to do all of them, and their staff will be happy to answer your questions and offer advice for where to go to exert yourself.

SWIMMING

The park has three swimming beaches. Sand Beach on Park Loop Road and Echo Lake Beach off Route 102 are the largest and most popular, with changing rooms and sometimes lifeguards on duty. Neither are found at Lake Wood, but its small, secluded beach is near Hulls Cove Visitor Center (the access road to the beach doesn't open until June 1).

Chapter 9

ACADIA REGION

Updated by
Mary Ruoff

★ Sights ★★★★★ 🍴 Restaurants ★★★★☆ 🛏 Hotels ★★★★☆ 🛍 Shopping ★★★☆☆ 🍸 Nightlife ★★☆☆☆

WELCOME TO ACADIA REGION

TOP REASONS TO GO

★ **Unforgettable vistas:** Whether from the air, trail, water, or road, you'll gaze at rugged natural beauty, from mountains to rock-clad seashore to forested lakes and ponds. There's even a fjard (less steep-sided than a fjord).

★ **Get on the water:** Soak up the region's splendor by kayak, canoe, standup paddleboard, motorboat, charter boat, ferry, or windjammer. Fishing trips, whale-watching trips, scenic cruises, and even lobster boat tours depart from island towns.

★ **Masterful museums:** Bar Harbor's Abbe Museum explores the heritage, history, and culture of Maine's Wabanaki nations, while La Rochelle Mansion and Museum highlights local history during the Gilded Age.

★ **Quiet time:** Mount Desert Island's western "quiet side" has small museums, fishing villages, the slower-paced tourist hub of Southwest Harbor, and much of Acadia.

★ **Peninsular beauty:** The Schoodic Peninsula has remote beauty and a lack of crowds.

1 Ellsworth Area. Ellsworth has big box stores and a charming downtown. Trenton's souvenir shops and budget lodgings are on the only road to Mount Desert.

2 Bar Harbor. Mount Desert's main tourist hub has restaurants, hotels, shops, tours, and museums.

3 Northeast Harbor. Renowned public gardens and a year-round ferry to the Cranberry Isles.

4 Somesville. The island's oldest town has white clapboard homes and the oft-photographed white bridge over a pond.

5 Southwest Harbor. A relaxed tourist hub; Acadia's best swimming beach and popular Beech Mountain Trail are outside the village.

6 Bass Harbor. A picturesque fishing village; its namesake light, part of Acadia, is just beyond the village.

7 Hancock Area. Hancock and Sullivan have skilled artisans' galleries and the Schoodic National Scenic Byway.

8 Schoodic Peninsula. Home to Acadia's only mainland section, there are fishing villages like Winter Harbor, and the ocean is never far.

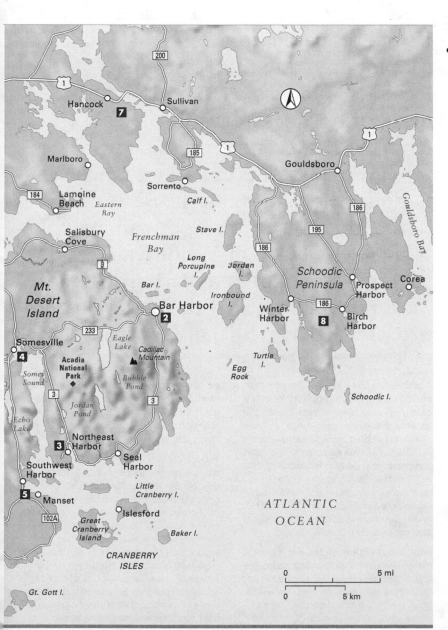

With some of the Maine Coast's most dramatic and varied scenery, and the state's only national park, Acadia, it's no wonder Mount Desert Island (pronounced "Mount Dessert" by locals) is Maine's most popular tourist destination. Rocky coastline rises starkly from the ocean, and more than 20 forested mountains tower here, including Cadillac, the highest on the Eastern Seaboard. Much of the approximately 15-mile-long by 13-mile-wide island is part of Acadia National Park. The largest, most popular swath of the park is in and near Bar Harbor, the main tourist hub.

Acadia offers seemingly endless hiking on 150-plus trails, with options for everyone, from easy level paths to challenging ascents with ladders and rungs; 45 miles of interconnected carriage paths, popular with bikers as well as walkers; and lakes and ponds that beckon for paddling, boating, and fishing. Along Park Loop Drive, spectacular seascapes and renowned locales like Sand Beach and Thunder Hole await. But there is also much for visitors to enjoy outside the park.

From summer through fall, Bar Harbor's many restaurants, hotels, and shops are abuzz, tourists crowd the sidewalks, and boat tours and pleasure craft come and go in the island-dotted harbor. There's a shore path, greens and parks, and two excellent museums: the Abbe Museum, exploring the heritage of Maine's Wabanaki tribes, and the historic La Rochelle Mansion and Museum, with exhibits on local history.

Though smaller and less crowded than Bar Harbor, the tourist hubs of Northeast Harbor and Southwest Harbor on opposite sides of Somes Sound have lots of choices for lodging, eating, and getting on the water. In Southwest Harbor, the Wendell Gilley Museum preserves and expands on the legacy of its namesake, a legendary bird carver. Northeast Harbor's Asticou Azalea Garden is one of three at a serene preserve. Smaller island villages also entice visitors with small museums, boat tours, ferries, sweeping ocean vistas, quintessential New England town centers, and scenic roads and lanes.

Parts of Acadia are in all four island towns, including those on the "quiet" western side. In the middle of the island, the Town of Mount Desert encompasses Northeast Harbor, Seal Harbor, Somesville, and three smaller villages. On the western half, Southwest Harbor is home to its namesake village, seaside Manset, and a few hamlets. Extending up the western shore from the island's southernmost part, Tremont has a handful of small villages, of which Bass Harbor is the largest. Bar Harbor has a few hamlets beyond the town proper.

Island gateway towns Ellsworth and Trenton have more affordable lodging choices and are good places to stock up before heading to Mount Desert. Acadia's only mainland section lies east of Ellsworth, below U.S. 1 at the bottom of Schoodic Peninsula. About an hour's drive from Bar Harbor, it's also accessible by a seasonal ferry and connecting bus. Schoodic offers bike paths, hiking, and dramatic seascapes along a loop drive that spurs to the rocky, wave-slapped peninsular point. Hancock is a quiet enclave between Ellsworth and the Schoodic Peninsula.

Planning

Getting Here and Around

AIR

Bangor International Airport (BGR) in Bangor is the closest major airport to Acadia National Park. Driving distance from here to Mount Desert Island is approximately 50 miles. Car rentals, taxi, bus, and shuttle service are available.

Farther south along the coast, Portland International Airport (PWM) is approximately three hours from the Mount Desert Island area. Renting a car is your best bet for getting to Acadia National Park from here.

The small regional Hancock County–Bar Harbor Airport (BHB) is in Trenton just minutes from the causeway to Mount Desert Island. Cape Air/JetBlue offer flights to and from Logan International Airport (BOS) in Boston. Car rentals and taxi service are available, and the airport is a stop for the free seasonal Island Explorer buses that serve Acadia and nearby towns.

CONTACTS Bangor–Bar Harbor Express Shuttle. ⊠ *Bangor* ☎ *207/944–8429* ⊕ *www.bangorbarharborexpressshuttle. com.* **Bangor International Airport.** (*BGR*) ☎ *207/992–4600* ⊕ *www.flybangor.com.* **Hancock County–Bar Harbor Airport.** (*BHB*) ⊠ *143 Caruso Dr., Trenton* ☎ *207/667–7329* ⊕ *www.bhbairport.com.*

BUS

CONTACTS Island Explorer. ☎ *207/667–5796* ⊕ *www.exploreacadia.com.*

Operating seasonally, Island Explorer buses serve Acadia and communities throughout Mount Desert Island as well as neighboring Trenton. Though touted as free, donations are requested to support the service. Island Explorer also serves the mainland district of Acadia and nearby villages, including Winter Harbor, on the Schoodic Peninsula. You can connect with an Island Explorer bus to the park from the seasonal Bar Harbor–Winter Harbor Ferry.

The bus service starts operating in late May on the Schoodic Peninsula and late June in the Mount Desert area and runs through Indigenous Peoples Day/Columbus Day. A reduced fall schedule starts in late August. Island Explorer's designated stops include many campgrounds and hotels. The buses also pick up and drop off passengers anywhere along the route where it's safe to stop.

Buses have bike racks, but they only hold four or six bicycles. So during the peak summer season, Island Explorer Bicycle Express ferries bikes and passengers by van from downtown Bar Harbor to Acadia's Eagle Lake Carriage Road. The vans can take tag-along bikes and small children's bikes but not tandem, fat-tire, or electric bikes. Island Explorer buses can't transport any of these specialty bikes, including tag-along and small children's bikes.

FERRY

The seasonal Bar Harbor–Winter Harbor Ferry makes daily round-trips on Frenchman Bay between the Mount Desert Island tourist hub and the Schoodic Peninsula town. In Winter Harbor passengers can connect to a free Island Explorer bus to Acadia National Park's mainland Schoodic District. On crossings, passengers are treated to stunning views of mountains, lighthouses, and wildlife. Visitors staying on the peninsula for a quieter vibe can venture by ferry to Bar Harbor and walk a few blocks to the Village Green to hop Island Explorer to the park. The ferry ($18 one-way) transports bikes (extra fee) as do the buses. Dogs ride free on the ferry but aren't allowed on Island Explorer buses.

Starting in 2022, ferry service between Bar Harbor and the Canadian city of Yarmouth, Nova Scotia, resumed—bringing back a tourism stalwart that operated from 1956 until 2009. Know as The CAT, the comfortable boat itself is a draw, with several restaurants, a gift shop, entertainment, and lots of seating. Crossing in 3½ hours, it departs Bar Harbor at 3 pm and Yarmouth at 9:30 am (Atlantic Time) spring through fall, though trips aren't daily in the shoulder seasons. Don't forget your passports or other government-approved ID. Fares start at $115 for a walk-on one-way ticket. You can bring your bike (extra fee); dogs ride free.

Seasonal and year-round passenger ferries serve Little Cranberry and Great Cranberry islands off the bottom of Mount Desert. Acadia's Islesford Historical Museum is in the village of the same name on Little Cranberry. Beal and Bunker Ferry "aka the Mail Boat" runs year-round between Northeast Harbor and the islands, which have year-round populations—unlike the three other Cranberry Isles ($15 one-way; $30 round-trip). Cranberry Cove Boating Company's seasonal ferry out of Southwest Harbor stops at Manset on Mount Desert on trips to and from the isles ($22 one-way, $32 round-trip). Along with providing wonderful mountain views from the water, the ferries allow day-trippers to enjoy time on both islands, since they run several round-trips daily. You can bring your bike (extra fee); dogs ride free.

Carrying vehicles and passengers, the Maine State Ferry Service's *Captain Henry Lee* ferries between Bass Harbor, at the bottom of Mount Desert, and two outer islands, Swans and Long, where it stops in the village of Frenchboro. Service to Swans Island (40-minute, 6-mile crossing) runs daily; and to Frenchboro (50-minute, 8½-mile crossing) on Wednesday, Thursday, and Sunday, plus passenger-only service on a smaller boat on Friday in summer. Both round-trips are $17.50 (passenger only) and $38.50 (car with driver) June–September and, respectively, $12.50 and $31 off-season. You can bring your bike (extra fee); dogs ride free.

CONTACTS Bar Harbor–Winter Harbor Ferry. ✉ *7 Newport Dr., Bar Harbor* ✛ *Departs from Bar Harbor Inn Pier (from Schoodic Marine Center, 88 Sargent St., in Winter Harbor)* ☎ *207/288–2984* ⊕ *www. barharborferry.com.* **Beal and Bunker Ferry Service.** ✉ *41 Harbor Dr., Northeast Harbor* ☎ *207/244–3575* ⊕ *www. bealandbunkerferry.com.* **The CAT.** ✉ *121 Eden St., Bar Harbor* ☎ *207/901–0077* ⊕ *www.ferries.ca.* **Cranberry Cove Ferry.** ✉ *110 Clark Point Rd., Southwest Harbor* ✛ *Departs from Upper Town Dock (next stop Manset Dock)* ☎ *207/244–5882* ⊕ *www.cranberrycoveferry.com.* **Maine State Ferry Service.** ✉ *45 Granville Rd., Bass Harbor* ☎ *207/244–3254* ⊕ *www. maine.gov/mdot/ferry.*

CAR

Route 3 leads to Mount Desert Island and Bar Harbor from Ellsworth and circles the eastern part of the island. Route 102 is the major road on the west side. Acadia National Park's Hulls Cove Visitor Center is off Route 3 3 miles from downtown Bar Harbor, and before it if driving from the causeway. Acadia's main thoroughfare, 27-mile Park Loop Road, is accessible from the visitor center as well as park entrances near downtown Bar Harbor on Route 233 (Cadillac Mountain), south of Bar Harbor proper on Route 3 (Sieur de Monts), and on Route 3 in Seal Harbor (Stanley Brook Road). Much of the road is one-way.

Shaped like an upside-down "U" (some liken it to a pair of lobster claws), Mount Desert is relatively easy to navigate, though it may take longer than expected to reach some points. Somes Sound—a fjard, which is less steep-sided than a fjord, as this was long considered—runs up the middle, requiring drivers at the ends of the "U" to travel quite a distance to get to a town that is close as the crow flies. Beyond the geographical barriers, summer traffic can slow your progress and make finding a parking space, especially in Bar Harbor or Acadia, difficult to nearly impossible. Avoid the problem by hopping one of the seasonal free Island Explorer buses that serve the park and nearby towns. They also operate on Schoodic Peninsula, home to Acadia's only mainland district, which is east of Mount Desert about an hour's drive via Ellsworth. A seasonal ferry links Bar Harbor and the peninsula's Winter Harbor, where you can connect with Island Explorer.

TAXIS

A handful of taxi companies cover Mount Desert Island and environs, with service to Bangor International Airport in Bangor and Hancock County–Bar Harbor Airport in Trenton. Ride services Lyft and Uber are not available in Bar Harbor.

Hotels

Whether you are looking for camp-grounds, bed-and-breakfasts, resort hotels, or well-run basic motels, there are lodging options to meet your needs on or near Mount Desert Island. However, prices are especially high in peak season in Bar Harbor, the island's largest and best-known community. Those looking to stay in a sprawling resort hotel or a beautifully appointed seaside inn should be prepared to pay top dollar, but even modest lodgings will cost a good bit more than they would elsewhere.

While shoulder season rates still exist at some establishments, and prices drop over the winter at the relatively few that stay open year round, many lodgings, even more modest ones, set prices based on real-time lodging availability in the area and don't have set rates. It's wise to check to see if you can get a better rate booking directly with the establishment. Many lodgings require a two-night minimum stay during the busy months, at least on weekends; visitors are advised not to travel here without a reservation in the summer and fall.

Bar Harbor is a good choice for being close to the park, shopping, dining, and nightlife, but other villages offer accom-modations that are equally—or even more—enticing, especially if you want a quieter lodging experience. Along Route 3 on and before the island, there are low-er-priced roadside motels and cabin-style accommodations. Acadia National Park offers two wooded campgrounds but no cabins or lodges.

Restaurants

With some of the nation's wealthiest families making Mount Desert Island their summer residence, a handful of restaurants cater to those seeking an upscale dining experience, with carefully prepared menus, many farm-to-table dishes, extensive wine lists, and impressive service. In Bar Harbor, and many nearby towns on and off the island, you'll find traditional lobster pounds and fun casual sit-down establishments that also source some of their foods from local waters and farms. Menu choices range from seafood to hamburgers and pub foods to more creative dishes to gluten-free options. You won't see fast-food chains, except on the mainland in Ellsworth, but you will find lots of Maine microbrews—from pale ales and brown ales to stouts—on draft or by the bottle.

HOTEL AND RESTAURANT PRICES

Hotel prices in the reviews are the lowest cost of a standard double room in high season. Restaurant prices in the reviews are the average cost of a main course at dinner, or if dinner is not served, at lunch. Restaurant and hotel reviews have been shortened. For full information, visit Fodors.com.

What It Costs In U.S. Dollars

	$	$$	$$$	$$$$
RESTAURANTS				
	under $18	$18–$24	$25–$35	over $35
HOTELS				
	under $200	$200–$299	$300–$399	over $399

Visitor Information

CONTACTS Acadia National Park. ☎ *207/288-3338* ⊕ *www.nps.gov/acad.* **Bar Harbor Chamber of Commerce.** ✉ *2 Cottage St., Bar Harbor* ☎ *207/288-5103* ⊕ *www.visitbarharbor.com.* **Mount Desert Chamber of Commerce.** ✉ *41 Harbor Dr., Northeast Harbor* ☎ *207/276-5040* ⊕ *www.mtdesertchamber.org.* **Southwest Harbor & Tremont Chamber of Commerce.** ✉ *329 Main St., Southwest Harbor*

☎ *207/244-9264* ⊕ *www.acadiachamber. com.* **Thompson Island Information Center.** ✉ *1319 Bar Harbor Rd., Bar Harbor* ☎ *207/288-3338* ⊕ *www.nps.gov/acad/ planyourvisit/hours.htm.*

When to Go

During the summer season, days are usually warm and nights cool—bring a jacket. July tops the charts with a comfortable average daily high of 73°, but there are hot and humid spells, more so in recent years. Peak visitation is late spring through October. July and August are the busiest months, but September—when the heat and humidity of summer begin to taper off, making it one of the most enjoyable—is right on their heels. The foliage season in the first few weeks of October bustles, too. While Memorial Day and Labor Day mark the traditional beginning and end of high season, nowadays many seasonal establishments stay open through Indigenous Peoples Day/Columbus Day and some longer.

Consider coming in mid-spring when temperatures start to rise but crowds haven't yet formed. Be sure to check for seasonal closures (always a good idea) due to ice, snow, or mud on Acadia's carriage roads, unpaved roads, and trails. For hardy souls winter can be a wonderful time to visit. While many dining and lodging facilities are hibernating, you can still find good options. Just know that from December through mid-April, paved park roads are closed to vehicles except for two short sections of Park Loop Road. For unpaved roads, it's mid-November to mid-May. When enough snow flies, folks head to the park to snowshoe and cross-country ski—many carriage roads are groomed. Snowmobilers take to Park Loop Road, drive up Cadillac Mountain, and hit unpaved roads. Yes, they're allowed.

Regardless of when you decide to go, it's best to book your accommodations in advance, especially if you have a particular type of lodging in mind or will be visiting on a holiday weekend. Visitors are advised not to travel to the Acadia area in peak season without a reservation.

FESTIVALS AND EVENTS

Acadia Oktoberfest. Held on Indigenous Peoples Day/Columbus Day weekend in October, the event offers music, food, crafts, and of course beer (some wine and hard cider, too). ⊕ *www.acadiaokto-berfest.com.*

Bar Harbor Music Festival. Held since the 1960s and one of New England's most acclaimed music festivals, young musicians in a variety of genres, including pops, jazz, opera, and string orchestra, perform at Bar Harbor's Criterion Theatre and other venues from late June through late July. ⊕ *www.barharbormusicfestival. org.*

July 4th. Events take place throughout the day, from a pancake breakfast and parade in the morning to concerts in the afternoon and evening. Fireworks light up the night sky over Frenchman Bay. ⊕ *www. visitbarharbor.com/july-4th.*

Schoodic Arts Festival. Art workshops, classes, and performances are held across Schoodic Peninsula for three weeks, from July into August. ⊕ *www. schoodicartsforall.org.*

Ellsworth Area

140 miles northeast of Portland, 28 miles south of Bangor.

Ellsworth is the main gateway to Acadia National Park making it a good spot for refueling—literally and figuratively. With two supermarkets, several good restaurants, and a range of shops, the city has nearly everything you need.

Big box stores are along Route 3 and there's a nice downtown area on Main Street with unique shops set in attractive brick buildings. From here you continue through to Trenton, where there are souvenir shops, roadside eateries, and less expensive lodgings before crossing onto Mount Desert Island. ■TIP➔ **Folks stay in Ellsworth and Trenton for the less expensive lodging.**

GETTING HERE AND AROUND

Ellsworth is the eye of the storm through which all vehicles traveling to Mount Desert Island must pass. As such, the few short miles of U.S. 1 that pass through the city can be gnarled with traffic in summer.

VISITOR INFORMATION

CONTACTS Ellsworth Area Chamber of Commerce. ✉ *151 High St., Ellsworth* ☎ *207/667–5584* ⊕ *www.ellsworthchamber.org.*

 Sights

Woodlawn Museum, Garden & Grounds
HISTORY MUSEUM | In the mid-1820s, Colonel John Black built an elegant Federal-style mansion with a distinct full-length front porch and balustrades on a 180-acre estate of fields and woods. Inside the Black House as it's known is an especially fine elliptical flying staircase and period artifacts from the three generations of the family who lived here. Outside, Woodlawn has a garden, 2 miles of walking trails that Colonel Black used as a bridle path, and a croquet court that's still in play (check the website for fees and availability). The trails and garden are open to the public year-round. Check the website for special events such as concerts and children's programming. ✉ *19 Black House Rd., Ellsworth* ☎ *207/667–8671* ⊕ *www.woodlawn-museum.org* 🎫 *guided tours $15; audio tours $10* 🕑 *Closed Nov.–May.*

Great Itineraries

If You Have 1 Day

If you only have one day on Mount Desert Island, spend it in Acadia National Park, saving Bar Harbor for dinner at Side Street Cafe or Geddy's. At Hulls Cove Visitor Center, get maps, information, and a park pass (if you don't have one). Then drive Park Loop Road, stopping at scenic spots like Sand Beach, Thunder Hole, and Otter Cliff; from late May to late October, a reservation is needed to drive up Cadillac Mountain. Save time to hike a trail, or to walk or bike the carriage roads—several converge at Jordan Pond on the loop road's two-way section.

If You Have 3 Days

If you have three days on Mount Desert Island, stay in Bar Harbor. There's lots to occupy you in the busy resort town on Day 1, from bustling boutiques to interesting museums to the Bar Harbor Shore Path. On Day 2, head to Acadia National Park, stopping at Hulls Cove Visitor Center for maps, information, and a park pass (if you don't have one). Drive Park Loop Road to get the lay of the land, leaving time for stops at scenic overlooks and renowned locales like Sand Beach and Thunder Hole. If you get a reservation (needed late May through late October), drive up Cadillac Mountain. On Day 3, rent

a bike and explore the network of carriage roads that crisscross the park. Head to Jordan Pond for a hike or at least to enjoy the view from the observation deck of the Jordan Pond House Restaurant, famous for its popovers. Other hiking options in this area of the park include The Bubbles, overlooking the lake, or for something more challenging, Penobscot Mountain. Or rent kayaks or take a guided kayak tour.

If You Have 5 Days

Follow the three-day itinerary above. On Day 4, drive to Northeast Harbor, the summer home of many of the country's wealthiest families. Their legacy lives on at the Land & Garden Preserve, which has three world-renowned public gardens (open seasonally), trails, and carriage roads (no bikes). If you're in Seal Harbor, you'll want to stop at the beach right along Route 3, even if it's just to savor the view for a bit. Northeast Harbor's village center has a nice cluster of restaurants, shops, galleries, and a small maritime museum. On your last day, make the trip to iconic Bass Harbor Head Light on the island's "quiet side." Hop on a whale-watch or scenic cruise; many boat tours depart from Bar Harbor, but there are also trips out of Bass Harbor, Southwest Harbor, and Northeast Harbor.

🍴 Restaurants

Airline Brewing Company

$ | BURGER | With red cushioned seating and wood walls around the bar, this cozy-as-can-be brew pub (the brewery itself is inland) right on Main Street has a decor and menu that reflects its British ownership. Several of the dozen or so

beers served are hand-pulled, and food options include steak and ale pie and bangers and mash. **Known for:** being a community gathering place; warm beer cheese appetizers; "signature toasties" (yes, British for toasted sandwiches). $ *Average main: $13* ⊠ *173 Main St., Ellsworth* ☎ *207/412–0045* ⊕ *www. abcmaine.beer/.*

Fogtown Brewing Company

$ | PIZZA | FAMILY | Though tucked back on an Ellsworth residential street, folks find this hip brewpub—yes, the brewery is right here—with a large, inviting beer garden, housed on the lower level of an old brick warehouse. The simple menu includes hotdogs and bratwurst, and pizza cooked in the outdoor oven. **Known for:** live music; seasonal pizza toppings; community gathering spot. $ Average main: $15 ✉ 25 Pine St., Ellsworth 🕾 207/370–0845 ⊕ www.fogtownbrewing.com ⊗ No lunch Closed Mon. from late May–mid-Oct. and Mon.–Wed. from mid-Oct.–late May.

Nightlife

The Grand

THEATER | FAMILY | A local art deco landmark on the National Register of Historic Places, the Grand opened as a movie theater in 1938, then fell into disrepair, sitting vacant for much of the '50s to the '70s. The theater reopened in 1975 and since then has staged plays, hosted concerts, and shown films. ✉ 165 Main St., Ellsworth 🕾 207/667–9500 ⊕ www.grandonline.org.

Shopping

John Edwards Market

FOOD | With a selection of organic and natural foods, and soup, sandwiches, salads, baked goods, and coffee to go, John Edwards Market is a pleasant option whether you're packing a picnic or stocking the kitchenette at your rental. Downstairs, a wine cellar and an art gallery showcase work by area artists. Wine tastings are on the first Friday of the month 5–7 pm. ✉ 158 Main St., Ellsworth 🕾 207/667–9377 ⊕ www.johnedwardsmarket.com.

Rooster Brother

HOUSEWARES | You should be able to find what you need for your kitchen at Rooster Brother. On the first floor of a towering Victorian building, specialty foods, fresh cheese, baked goods, wines (including a nice selection of sherry and port), and house-roasted coffee are on offer and samples are always available. Upstairs is a huge collection of cooking items and pretty much everything for your table. ✉ 29 Main St., Ellsworth 🕾 800/866–0054 ⊕ www.roosterbrother.com.

Bar Harbor

20 miles from Ellsworth via Rte. 3.

A resort town since the 19th century, Bar Harbor is the artistic, culinary, and social center of Mount Desert Island, providing visitors to nearby Acadia National Park with lodging, shops, and restaurants. Around the turn of the last century, the town was a premier summer haven for the very rich because of its cool breezes and stunning interplay of mountains and sea. Many of their lavish mansions in and near town burned down in the Great Fire of 1947. The business district—centered around Main, Mount Desert, Cottage, and West streets—was spared. You can stroll past mansions that survived the fire on the shore path and West Street, a national historic district.

Bar Harbor has a few excellent museums and numerous greens and parks. Some were the sites of grand hotels like Agamont Park overlooking the harbor, and the Village Green, a gathering spot with a piano (that anyone can play) under the gazebo. Spring through fall, scenic cruises and whale-watching trips come and go from the town pier, boats cluster in the harbor, and visitors linger on the many sidewalk benches. At low tide, folks walk to Bar Island.

GETTING HERE AND AROUND

Route 3 leads to Bar Harbor. Acadia National Park's Hulls Cove Visitor Center is off the highway three miles before downtown, near the oceanside hamlet of Hulls Cove. The Cadillac Mountain entrance for Acadia's Park Loop Road (two-way section) is on Route 233 just west of downtown. Continuing on Route 233 to its terminus at Route 198, turn left for Northeast Harbor or right to reach Route 102, which loops the western side of Mount Desert Island. A few miles from downtown Bar Harbor on Route 3 is an entrance for Acadia's Sieur de Monts section and the loop road (one-way section). A more scenic and only slightly longer route to Northeast Harbor is via Route 3. Tiny Otter Creek is about midway along the drive, which has hilly forested sections and ocean views in Seal Harbor and Northeast Harbor.

VISITOR INFORMATION
CONTACTS Bar Harbor Chamber of Commerce. ⊠ *2 Cottage St., Bar Harbor* ☎ *207/288–5103* ⊕ *www.visitbarharbor. com.*

Sights

★ Abbe Museum
HISTORY MUSEUM | FAMILY | This important museum dedicated to Maine's Indigenous tribes—collectively known as the Wabanaki—is the state's only Smithsonian-affiliated facility and one of the few places in Maine to experience Native culture as interpreted by Native peoples themselves. Spanning 12,000 years, the "core" exhibit, People of the First Light, features items such as birch bark canoes, basketry, and bone tools as well as photos and interactive displays. Changing exhibits often showcase contemporary Native American art. A birchbark canoe made at the Abbe anchors the free Orientation Gallery beside the gift shop at the entrance. Check the website for events, from basket weaving and boatbuilding demonstrations to author talks and family-friendly pop-up rainy days activities.

Opened in 1928, the Abbe's Acadia National Park location at Sieur de Monts is its original home. Longtime exhibits

in the small eight-sided building include artifacts from early digs on Mount Desert Island and dioramas of Native American life here before European settlement. ⊠ *26 Mount Desert St., Bar Harbor* ☎ *207/288–3519* ⊕ *www.abbemuseum. org* ☞ *$10* ⊘ *Closed Nov.–early May; Fri. and Sat. mid-May–Oct.*

★ La Rochelle Mansion and Museum
HISTORY MUSEUM | Stepping into the large foyer of this 1903 brick chateau, your view flows through glass doors on the opposite side, then across the piazza and flat lawn to a serene coastal expanse. A business partner of J.P. Morgan, George Bowdoin, and his wife, Julia, built this 13,000-square-foot, 41-room mansion near downtown Bar Harbor as their seasonal residence. Unlike many of the area's summer "cottages" of the nation's elite, it was spared from the Great Fire of 1947. In 2020, La Rochelle became Bar Harbor Historical Society's museum and the town's only Gilded Age mansion open to the public. While the Bowdoins' story weaves through displays, each room has themed exhibits on local history: in the foyer, baskets the Wabanaki made to sell to tourists; the dining room, grand hotels of yesteryear; the master bedroom, old maps (one shows where the fire raged); a guest room, the town's famous visitors; and so on. Under the elegant wishbone staircase, a "flower room" with a curved wall spotlights the famous landscape artist who created the long-gone sunken garden. In the servants' quarters on the third floor, their story is shared—don't miss the hallway callbox. ⊠ *127 West St., Bar Harbor* ☎ *207/288–0000* ⊕ *www. barharborhistorical.org* ☞ *$15* ⊘ *Closed Nov.–late May.*

🍽 Restaurants

Atlantic Brewing Co. Midtown
$ | AMERICAN | FAMILY | Glass walls let you see this busy craft brewery spot in action even before you enter, but look up or head up—there's rooftop seating with

The Abbe Museum is one of the few places in Maine where you can experience Native culture as interpreted by Native peoples themselves. It's a must-visit.

great Bar Harbor views. After ordering a flight or glass of beer, choose from a food menu offering soups, sandwiches, salads, and lobster and crab rolls. **Known for:** jumbo pretzel with cheese and mustard made with an English Brown Ale; Old Soaker natural blueberry soda and root beer for the kids; also selling beer to go. $ *Average main: $16* ⊠ *52 Cottage St., Bar Harbor* ☎ *207/288–2326* ⊕ *www. atlanticbrewing.com.*

Galyn's

$$$ | **AMERICAN** | Open much of the year and filled with Maine art, this large restaurant has a classic New England vibe, several dining rooms on two floors, and a large menu to match. Offerings range from sandwiches and small plates to lobster dishes, steak, and seafood, including a bouillabaisse with shrimp, scallops, fresh fish, and lobster, served with steamed mussels and grilled ciabatta bread. **Known for:** happy hour daily in cozy bar constructed with items salvaged from area estates; New England Indian

pudding; harbor views from some dining rooms. $ *Average main: $28* ⊠ *17 Main St., Bar Harbor* ☎ *207/288–9706* ⊕ *www.galynsbarharbor.com* ⊗ *Closed Thanksgiving–Easter.*

Geddy's

$$$ | **AMERICAN** | **FAMILY** | With a big menu that's big on seafood (there's a pick-your-own lobster tank), this lively longtime establishment would be easy to spot even without a lighted moose on the roof. Humor pervades inside: kids meals come on Frisbees; quirky plastic animals on sticks adorn the cocktails; and old photos, murals, signs, license plates, and other bric-a-brac fill the walls, adding a sense of coziness to a large restaurant with a large bar right in the middle. **Known for:** 98% gluten-free menu, including fried foods and chowders; "house specialty" fish-and-chips; build-your-own pizzas. $ *Average main: $27* ⊠ *19 Main St., Bar Harbor* ☎ *207/288–5077* ⊕ *www.geddys. com* ⊗ *Closed late Nov.–early Mar.*

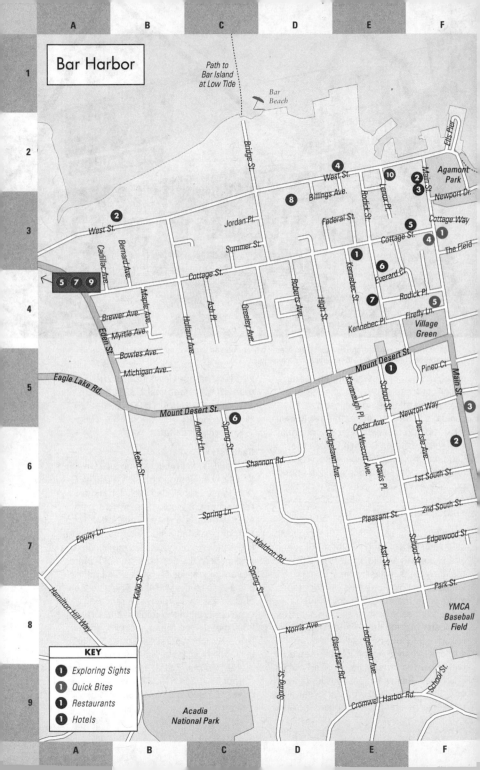

Bar Harbor

Path to Bar Island at Low Tide

Bar Beach

KEY

- **1** Exploring Sights
- **1** Quick Bites
- **1** Restaurants
- **1** Hotels

Acadia National Park

YMCA Baseball Field

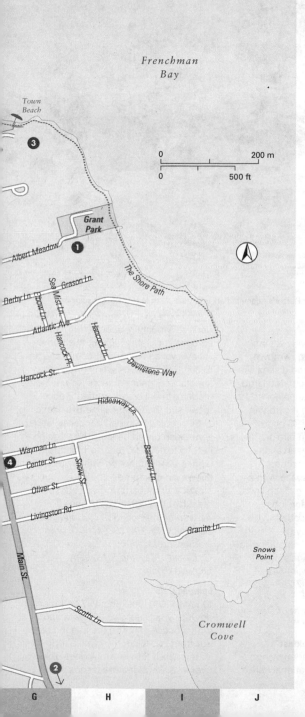

Sights ▼
1 Abbe Museum E5
2 La Rochelle Mansion and
  Museum B3

Restaurants ▼
1 Atlantic Brewing Co. Midtown E3
2 Galyn's F2
3 Geddy's F2
4 Havana............................... G7
5 Jeannie's Great Maine
  Breakfast F3
6 Lompoc Cafe E3
7 Side Street Cafe E4

Quick Bites ▼
1 Ben & Bill's
  Chocolate Emporium F3
2 Burning Tree G9
3 Choco-Latte Cafe F5
4 Downeast Deli &
  Boxed Lunch Co.................... F3
5 Mount Desert Island
  Ice Cream........................... F4

Hotels ▼
1 Balance Rock Inn.................. H4
2 Bar Harbor Grand Hotel........... F6
3 Bar Harbor Inn and Spa.......... G3
4 Harborside Hotel,
  Spa & Marina E2
5 Highbrook Motel................... A4
6 Inn on Mount Desert C5
7 Salt Cottages...................... A4
8 Sand Bar Cottage................. D3
9 Terramor Outdoor Resort A4
10 West Street Hotel.................. E2

With great waterfront views, Bar Harbor's Agamont Park is a great place to picnic in the summer.

★ Havana

$$$$ | LATIN AMERICAN | A lively yet intimate spot on the edge of downtown, Havana serves Latin-inspired dishes like seafood paella and panko-crusted lamb chops with lemon mojo sauce paired with robust wines from an award-winning, passionately curated 73-page wine list. In season, have a bite on "the Parrilla," the informal no-reservations patio (separate menu); year-round, dine in a pleasant indoor space with a modern aesthetic, featuring clean lines and cheery colors. **Known for:** lobster moqueca (a Brazilian seafood stew); a lively atmosphere fueled by great craft cocktails; knowledgeable waitstaff who help make this one of Maine's best restaurants. $ *Average main: $42* ✉ *318 Main St., Bar Harbor* ☎ *207/288–2822* ⊕ *www.havanamaine.com* ⊙ *No lunch. Closed Mon. and Tues. most of Dec.–Apr. Closed late Feb.–early Apr.*

Jeannie's Great Maine Breakfast

$ | AMERICAN | FAMILY | After enjoying the sunrise atop Acadia National Park's Cadillac Mountain, snuggle into a wooden booth or grab a table at this homey, yellow-walled eatery that opens at 6 am to catch the crowds who flock to the spectacle. Signature items include homemade oatmeal bread, stuffed French toast, and the Great Maine Breakfast, with three eggs, meat, pancakes, and vegetarian baked beans—the tradition here is to eat leftovers from Saturday night's bean supper on Sunday morning. **Known for:** gluten-free and vegan options; strawberry rhubarb fruit spread; serving breakfast through lunch (closes 1 pm). $ *Average main: $13* ✉ *15 Cottage St., Bar Harbor* ☎ *207/288–4166* ⊕ *www. jeanniesbreakfast.com* ⊙ *Closed mid-Oct.–early May and Tues. early May–mid-Oct. No dinner.*

Lompoc Cafe

$$ | AMERICAN | Tucked away on a lane-like downtown street, this laid-back spot with a bocce court on the shaded patio out front is back in the groove after two sisters, both former employees, took over in 2022. Signature dishes include seared scallops with Korean barbeque sauce, the falafel plate, and the peanut sauce and pita bread (both house-made) appetizer; new are weekly cocktail specials that, say, mix elderflower, blueberry shrub, vodka, and mint to honor a supermoon. **Known for:** occasional live music, Friday night DJ, karaoke on Sunday; Bang Bang fried chicken sandwich with aioli sauce, slaw, and honey and hot sauce; drinks served until 1 am, a rarity for Bar Harbor. $ Average main: $20 ⊠ 36 Rodick St., Bar Harbor ☎ 207/901–0004 ⊕ www. lompoccafe.com ⊙ No lunch. Closed from Jan.–March. Closed Mon.–Wed. from April–Dec.

★ **Side Street Cafe**

$ | AMERICAN | FAMILY | On a side street near the Village Green, this place (and its sister arm, The Annex) hops on busy summer evenings as folks line up for its comfort food like fish tacos and burgers. Outdoor and indoor dining spaces, one anchored by a horseshoe bar, flow together and exposed brick, and a cork wall and ceiling, add warmth to the welcoming, modern, family-friendly vibe; friendly dogs are allowed outside. **Known for:** handcrafted cocktails and live music nightly in The Annex; "signature" mac-and-cheese including lobster and meatball as well as "create-your-own"; margaritas. $ Average main: $14 ⊠ 49 Rodick St., Bar Harbor ☎ 207/801–2591 ⊕ www.sidestreetbarharbor.com ⊙ Main restaurant: closed late Oct.–early Apr.; The Annex: no lunch, closed mid-Oct.–late May.

☕ Coffee and Quick Bites

Ben & Bill's Chocolate Emporium

$ | ICE CREAM | FAMILY | Ogling the assorted goodies makes for a fun wait in the often long lines at this cheeky, old-fashioned candy and ice cream shop. Most of the candy, including numerous varieties of fine chocolates and fudge, is made right here, as is the ice cream (64 flavors) and gelato (8 flavors). **Known for:** lines out the door; buttercrunch candy; lobster ice

cream in a butter pecan base. $ Average main: $8 ⊠ 66 Main St., Bar Harbor ☎ 207/288–3281 ⊕ www.benandbills. com ⊙ Closed early Jan. and Feb.

★ **Burning Tree**

$ | AMERICAN | An early standout in Maine's farm-to-table movement, this acclaimed establishment not far from Bar Harbor in tiny Otter Creek sells to-go foods—prepared (including breakfast pastries) and ready-to-cook, all made on-site and largely featuring ingredients from the owners' extensive gardens. The retail side has a small gardenside outdoor eating area and also sells small-scale wines (natural, organic, and biodynamic) as well as ciders. **Known for:** crab cakes with jalapenos; inventive seasonal items like pickled plums; nice selection of vegetarian offerings. $ Average main: $10 ⊠ 69 Otter Creek Dr., Otter Creek ⊹ 5 miles from Bar Harbor, 7 miles from Northeast Harbor ☎ 207/288–9331 ⊕ www.theburningtreerestaurant.com ⊙ Closed late Oct.–late May; closed Tues. late May–late Oct.

Choco-Latte Cafe

$ | CAFÉ | This large year-round café features coffee from a local coffee roaster, but you can get much more than a cup of Joe—for breakfast, grab a breakfast sandwich or avocado toast; for lunch or dinner, a salad or taco. In a town without a lot of quick bite spots, it's a good choice for picking up lunch to enjoy in the park, at your lodging, or at a table here; in summer, some tables are out front. **Known for:** bagels made fresh daily at sister restaurant Havana; a local gathering spot; all sorts of coffee drinks. $ Average main: $10 ⊠ 240 Main St., Bar Harbor ☎ 207/801–9179 ⊕ www.choco-lattecafe.com.

Downeast Deli & Boxed Lunch Co.

$ | AMERICAN | Don't be fooled by this tiny takeout-only joint's no-frills storefront: many praise its lobster rolls as the best around. On summer mornings, the line often stretches around the corner by 10 am as folks come to get lobster rolls as well as wraps, sandwiches, salads, and slices of blueberry pie for outings to Acadia National Park and elsewhere around Mount Desert Island. **Known for:** taking orders the night before; several lobster roll options, including just plain "naked"; selling a few breakfast items, too. [$] *Average main: $13 ✉ 65 Main St., Bar Harbor ☎ 207/288–1001 🌐 www.downeastdeli.com 🕘 Closed late Oct.–early May.*

Mount Desert Island Ice Cream
$ | **ICE CREAM** | Madagascar Vanilla Bean has specks from beans scraped from vanilla pods—just one example of the prep work that goes into creating these heralded artisanal ice creams (and a few sorbets), made at a nearby production facility with as many local ingredients as possible. The shop's double doors open like a huge window, welcoming passers-by right in; grab a seat or head across the street to the Village Green to savor every bite. **Known for:** unique rotating flavors like Bay of Figs; locations in Portland, Maine; Washington, D.C.; and Japan; ice cream on menus at area restaurants. [$] *Average main: $5 ✉ 7 Firefly La., Bar Harbor ☎ 207/801–4007 🌐 www.mdiic.com 🕘 Closed late Oct.–early Apr.*

🛏 Hotels

Balance Rock Inn
$$$$ | **B&B/INN** | Along the shore path near downtown, spacious, gorgeously furnished rooms and suites are spread about the 1903 shingle-style main inn (originally a wealthy summer resident's "cottage"), a modern addition, and a pet-friendly carriage house. **Pros:** two suites and one room sleep up to five people; many rooms have amenities like a fireplace, deck, and dry sauna; upscale restaurant serves light fare by the firepit or in the piano bar, dinner on the veranda. **Cons:** some upper-level accommodations have limited elevator access; not all rooms have central air-conditioning; pricey room rates. [$] *Rooms from: $450 ✉ 21 Albert Meadows, Bar Harbor ☎ 207/288–2610, 800/753–0494 🌐 www.balancerockinn.com 🕘 Closed late Oct.–early May 🔑 27 rooms 🍴 Free Breakfast.*

Bar Harbor Grand Hotel
$$$ | **HOTEL** | **FAMILY** | Taking one of the well-appointed, modern rooms in this 2011 replica of Bar Harbor's famed Rodick House hotel puts you a stone's throw from the town's lively restaurants, cafés, and gift shops, and though it's a short walk to the waterfront, you can relax here with a dip in the hotel's heated pool or Jacuzzi. **Pros:** "extended stay" suites with kitchenettes; standard rooms have a king or two queens; courtesy full breakfast includes local pastries. **Cons:** summer street noise in front-facing rooms; no restaurant or bar on-site; not on or in sight of the ocean. [$] *Rooms from: $389 ✉ 269 Main St., Bar Harbor ☎ 888/766–2599, 207/288–5226 🌐 www.barharborgrand.com 🕘 Closed mid-Nov.–early Apr. 🔑 72 rooms 🍴 Free Breakfast.*

Bar Harbor Inn and Spa
$$$$ | **HOTEL** | Originally a men's social club, this elegant oceanfront hotel has rooms spread among three buildings on well-landscaped grounds: the historic 1887 main inn, which has a modern wing, and two buildings with exterior-entrance rooms. **Pros:** main inn's water-view two-room, two-bath suites are great for families; infinity ocean-view pool; on-site Reading Room is a terrific restaurant known for its lobster bisque. **Cons:** Ocean Lodge sits close to public Shore Path; pricey; no water views in Newport Building, but it was renovated in 2022. [$] *Rooms from: $679 ✉ 1 Newport Dr., Bar Harbor ☎ 207/288–3351, 844/814–1668 🌐 www.barharborinn.com 🕘 Closed late Nov.–mid-Mar. 🔑 153 rooms 🍴 Free Breakfast.*

Harborside Hotel, Spa & Marina
$$$$ | **HOTEL** | **FAMILY** | At this large waterfront hotel downtown, building facades, the large lobby, and granite walls, stairs, and benches imbue the Harborside with

the aesthetic of Bar Harbor's Gilded Age mansions; also designed in the Tudor style, the 1929 Bar Harbor Club, originally private, anchors resort amenities including a fitness center, full-service spa, clay tennis courts, and one of the two heated pools. **Pros:** "family rooms" with walled-off bunkbeds; most rooms have balconies or patios and water views; two pools plus access to adults-only rooftop affinity pool at sister hotel across the street. **Cons:** too large, busy, and bustling for some; $35 resort fee; chilly Maine weather can limit use of resort amenities. [$] *Rooms from: $750* ✉ *55 West St., Bar Harbor* ☎ *207/288–5033, 866/258–7253 for reservations* 🌐 *www.opalcollection.com/harborside* 🕒 *Closed late Nov.–early Apr.* 🛏 *193 rooms* 🍴 *No Meals.*

Highbrook Motel

$$$ | **MOTEL** | Run by the third generation of the family that's owned it since 1978, original mid-century features like porcelain tile and tubs and wood-framed screen doors to usher ocean breezes into guestrooms, don't show their age; the 24-hour access lobby shows the same meticulous attention to maintenance and cleanliness—even with free microwave popcorn available (and movie-style containers to put it in). **Pros:** rooms have an inside seating area (most have an outside one, too); Adirondack chairs at the Island Explorer bus stop on the street out front; one building has larger rooms and baths (adjoining dressing area). **Cons:** only one bed (king) per room; microwave in the lobby but not rooms; two-person room limit (no cots or cribs). [$] *Rooms from: $300* ✉ *94 Eden St., Bar Harbor* ☎ *207/288–3591* 🌐 *www.highbrookmotel.com* 🕒 *Closed from late Oct.–late May* 🛏 *26 rooms* 🍴 *Free Breakfast.*

Inn on Mount Desert

$$$$ | **HOTEL** | **FAMILY** | This midsize, year-round hotel on Mount Desert Street—with touches like rocking chairs on the front porch and a tranquil hillside garden with surprises like bocce and a tree swing—is reminiscent of Bar Harbor's Gilded Age mansions, but make no mistake, this is a thoroughly modern hotel with good-size rooms, and it's family-friendly, too. **Pros:** refrigerators and microwaves in all rooms; all rooms have kings or two queens; some rooms have balconies or terraces. **Cons:** harbor is a 10-minute walk from the hotel; no pool; no suites. [$] *Rooms from: $450* ✉ *68 Mount Desert St., Bar Harbor* ☎ *207/288–8300* 🌐 *www.staybarharbor.com* 🛏 *31 rooms* 🍴 *Free Breakfast.*

★ Salt Cottages

$$$$ | **MOTEL** | **FAMILY** | Renovated into a chic family-friendly resort in 2022, these 1940s-era roadside cottages surround a green that sweeps uphill across Route 3 from Hulls Cove beach just 3 miles from Bar Harbor—Acadia is even closer. **Pros:** stylish lodge where you can relax by the fireplace and go to Picnic, a takeout restaurant serving breakfast, lunch, and dinner; kids 12 and under stay free in cabins with adults; resort amenities include heated pool, hot tubs, bocce, lawn games, "game shed," and courtesy s'mores for the firepit. **Cons:** no courtesy coffee in the lodge (but provided for cottage coffeemakers); limited or no water views from inside most cabins; cabins aren't stocked with utensils or dishes. [$] *Rooms from: $480* ✉ *20 Rte. 3, Hulls Cove* ☎ *207/288–9918* 🌐 *www.saltcottagesbarharbor.com* 🕒 *Closed Nov.–mid-May* 🛏 *31 cottages* 🍴 *No Meals.*

Sand Bar Cottage

$$$$ | **B&B/INN** | A Bar Harbor hotelier gave this large, yellow shingle-style "cottage"—listed on the National Register of Historic Places—a stylish overhaul in 2021, so rooms and common spaces are fresh and updated yet blend perfectly with architectural features like moldings and fireplaces; guests staying in the property's three cottages and modern building out back also enjoy common spaces in the main inn and are served a full breakfast there. **Pros:** many lodging quarters have fireplaces; wraparound front porch, perfect for relaxing and people-watching; courtesy baked treats in the dining room in the afternoon. **Cons:** two rooms each have a bath (private) across the hall; only partial water views from some rooms; neighborhood too busy for some folks. $ *Rooms from: $550* ⊠ *106 West St., Bar Harbor* ☎ *207/288–3759* ⊕ *www.staybarharbor.com* ⇲ *19 rooms* ⚭ *Free Breakfast.*

★ Terramor Outdoor Resort

$$$$ | **RESORT** | **FAMILY** | Luckily for visitors to Acadia National Park, Kampgrounds of America transformed one of its traditional campgrounds into its first glampground in 2020; anchoring 64 tents (all with floors, beds, private fire rings, and hotel-like amenities) on well-shaded, well-spaced sites is an impressive lodge with a high sloped wood ceiling and restaurant (eat in or get items to go), bar, fireplaces, chic chairs and couches, and decks. **Pros:** activities galore, including yoga, stargazing, concerts, and lobster bakes; big fancy grill sites (fee; all you need is provided including food); covered sitting area by swank pool and hot tub. **Cons:** no "en tent" baths in four tents remaining from KOA campground (but baths are private and the price is right); not on the water; road noise at some sites. $ *Rooms from: $400* ⊠ *1453 Rte. 102, Bar Harbor* ☎ *207/288–7500* ⊕ *terramoroutdoorresort.com* ⊙ *Closed mid-Oct.–mid-May* ⇲ *64 units* ⚭ *Free Breakfast.*

★ West Street Hotel

$$$$ | **RESORT** | With only 85 mostly water-view rooms and suites, attention to detail comes naturally here, and the panoramic views from the fabulous adults-only infinity pool on the rooftop deck are hands down the best in town. **Pros:** each floor is equipped with guest pantries filled with snacks and goodies; one of Maine's most tastefully decorated boutique hotels; many rooms and suites have balconies. **Cons:** $35 daily resort fee; chilly Maine weather can limit use of resort amenities; near but not on the water. $ *Rooms from: $700* ⊠ *50 West St., Bar Harbor* ☎ *207/288–0825* ⊕ *www.opalcollection.com/west-street* ⊙ *Closed from late Oct.–early May* ⇲ *85 rooms* ⚭ *No Meals.*

 Performing Arts

Criterion Theatre

MUSIC | **FAMILY** | Opened in 1932 and run as a nonprofit since 2014 with help from a $2 million anonymous donation, this art deco gem with a floating balcony in the heart of downtown shows movies and hosts live performances. Depending on when you're in town, you may catch a drag show or a nationally known musician such as Christopher Cross. ⊠ *35 Cottage St., Bar Harbor* ☎ *207/288–0829* ⊕ *www.criteriontheatre.org.*

🛍 Shopping

ART

★ Argosy Gallery

ART GALLERIES | At this salon-inspired gallery, relax on antique furniture while gazing at framed paintings, mostly of island and coastal Maine scenes, that fill the dark walls. Opened in 1996 and representing approximately 30 artists of national renown who live, summer, or paint on Mount Desert Island, works range from $500–$10,000. The owner's background is in art history, and she warmly welcomes even those who are "just looking" and shares her art knowledge, especially the stories of painters who've been drawn to the island since the 1800s. ⊠ *6 Mount Desert St., Bar Harbor* ☎ *207/288–9226* ⊕ *www.argosygallery.com* ⊙ *Closed Nov.–mid-May.*

Island Artisans

ART GALLERIES | Works by more than 100 Maine artisans are sold here, including basketry, pottery, fiber work, embossed paper, wood bowls and objects, and jewelry. ⊠ *99 Main St., Bar Harbor* ☎ *207/288–4214* ⊕ *www.islandartisans. com* ⊗ *Closed Jan.–Apr.*

★ The Rock and Art Shop

HOUSEWARES | As advertised, there are both "rocks" and "art" for sale at this eclectic family-owned store. There are also taxidermied animals, fossils, home decor and plants, interesting jewelry, and bath products. There are also stores in Bangor and Ellsworth. ⊠ *23 Cottage St., Bar Harbor* ☎ *207/288–4800* ⊕ *www. therockandartshop.com* ⊗ *Closed Nov.–mid-May.*

FOOD

Bar Harbor Tea Co.

FOOD | Cozy up in this small store, filled with the company's elegantly packaged all-natural teas. Ingredients are blended right in town in small batches. Pots and tea accessories, and of course a large selection of cups, are also sold. ⊠ *150 Main St., No. 2, Bar Harbor* ☎ *207/288– 8322* ⊕ *www.barhabortea.com* ⊗ *Closed mid-Dec.–Apr.*

SPORTING GOODS

Cadillac Mountain Sports

SPORTING GOODS | One of the best sporting-goods stores in the state, Cadillac Mountain Sports has developed a following of locals and visitors alike. Here you'll find top-quality climbing, hiking, boating, paddling, and camping equipment, and in winter you can rent cross-country skis, ice skates, and snowshoes. ⊠ *26 Cottage St., Bar Harbor* ☎ *207/288–4532* ⊕ *www. cadillacsports.com.*

 Activities

BIKING

Bar Harbor Bicycle Shop

BIKING | FAMILY | Rent bikes for a half day, full day, or week at the Bar Harbor Bicycle Shop. The selection includes hybrid and Class 1 e-bikes as well as tag-alongs, child trailers, and car racks. ⊠ *141 Cottage St., Bar Harbor* ☎ *207/288–3886* ⊕ *www.barharborbike.com.*

BOATING

Coastal Kayaking Tours

GUIDED TOURS | FAMILY | This outfitter has been leading trips in the scenic waters off Mount Desert Island since 1982. Trips are limited to no more than 12 people. The season is mid-May–mid-October. ⊠ *48 Cottage St., Bar Harbor* ☎ *207/288– 9605* ⊕ *www.acadiafun.com.*

★ Downeast Windjammer Cruises

BOAT TOURS | FAMILY | Cruises among the islands of Frenchman Bay are offered on the 151-foot four-masted schooner *Margaret Todd* and 58½-foot two-masted *Bailey Louise Todd,* both with distinctive red sails, as well as 72-foot, two-masted Schooner *Joshua,* with traditional white sails. Trips run morning, afternoon, and at sunset for 1½ to 2 hours, except in the fall when sunset cruises are a bit shorter than usual. Whatever the season, these evening excursions feature live folk music. The tour operator often offers longer specialty cruises and does fishing and sailing charters. ⊠ *Bar Harbor Inn pier, 7 Newport Dr., Bar Harbor* ☎ *207/288–4585* ⊕ *www.downeastwind-jammer.com* 🎫 *From $44 per person* ⊗ *Closed mid-Oct.–mid-May.*

ROCK-CLIMBING

Atlantic Climbing School

ROCK CLIMBING | Accredited by the American Mountain Guides Association and a "guiding partner" with local retailer Cadillac Mountain Sports, this guide service has led climbs on Acadia National Park's cliffs for years. Individual, small group, family, and group courses are offered. Depending on the instructor-to-client ratio, the cost is $75 to $175 for a half-day and $115 to $310 for a full day. For family groups of four, it's $90 per person and $135 per person, respectively. In winter, the adventure continues—on ice and snow. Cross-country skiing and snowshoeing courses are available, too. ⊠ *67 Main St., 2nd fl., Bar Harbor* ☎ *207/288– 2521* ⊕ *www.climbacadia.com.*

TOURS
Acadia GEM

DRIVING TOURS | FAMILY | To catch sea breezes and be closer to the action—from autumn leaves turning in Acadia National Park to sidewalk scenes in Bar Harbor—folks usually cruise with the doors off these low-emission Global Electric Motorcars (GEMs). Holding two, four, or six passengers, rentals are one to three hours, half day, full day, multiday, and weekly. Easier to park and maneuver through traffic than a regular car, GEMs are only allowed on roads with 35 mph speed limits or less: that includes those in the park and within the village of Bar Harbor. A map highlighting suitable routes is provided (and on the website). GEM has a free shuttle to its garage for cruise ship passengers disembarking from tenders. ⊠ *195 Main St., Bar Harbor* ☎ *207/288–8983* ⊕ *www.acadiagem.com* ⊠ *From $55 an hr (per vehicle).*

Oli's Trolley

DRIVING TOURS | In business since 1992, these historic-looking red and green trolleys are part of the local scene. Departing from the harbor, narrated tours run April through October. Acadia National Park tours (2½ or 4 hours) are the most popular, but there's also a half-hour downtown one that's full of fun and interesting facts and helps visitors get oriented to the busy town. Private van tours (up to 10 passengers) are also offered, but availability is limited. ⊠ *1 West St., Bar Harbor* ☎ *207/288–9899* ⊕ *www.olistrolley.com* ⊠ *From $20.*

WHALE-WATCHING
Bar Harbor Whale Watch Co.

BOAT TOURS | FAMILY | This company has six boats, one of them a 130-foot jet-propelled double-hulled catamaran with spacious decks. There are lighthouse and puffin-watching, lobstering and seal-watching, whale-watching, nature, and sunset cruises. The Somes Sound trip takes in four lighthouses; one to Acadia National Park's Baker Island is led by a park ranger. ⊠ *1 West St., Bar Harbor* ☎ *207/288–2386, 888/942–5374* ⊕ *www.barharborwhales.com* ⊠ *From $43.*

Northeast Harbor

12 miles south of Bar Harbor via Rtes. 3 and 198.

A summer community for some of the nation's wealthiest families, Northeast Harbor on the eastern side of the entrance to Somes Sound has one of the best harbors on the Maine coast. Filled with yachts and powerboats, you can catch a cruise or hop the year-round ferry to the Cranberry Isles (see the Getting Here and Around section of the Chapter Planner for more information).

The small downtown—two blocks from the harbor on Sea Street—is nicely clustered with shops, galleries, and eateries. The village's extensive trail network (maintained by a village improvement association) provides access to Acadia National Park's Lower Hadlock Pond (you can hike around the pond or connect with other trails). Most of the Land & Garden Preserve, which stretches from Northeast Harbor to Seal Harbor, was formerly part of John D. Rockefeller Jr.'s summer estate; the preserve encompasses the world-renowned Asticou Azalea Garden, Thuya Garden, and the Abby Aldrich Rockefeller Garden.

GETTING HERE AND AROUND

After crossing onto Mount Desert Island, it's 11 miles via Route 198 to Northeast Harbor. Be sure to slowly cruise Sargeant Drive during your stay—about 4 miles long and well-shaded with a few small pullovers, this narrow scenic drive edges the fjord-like deep sound between its terminuses in the village center and at Route 198.

From Northeast Harbor, Route 3 travels eastward to Seal Harbor, affording lovely ocean views. Here, Acadia National

Park's Stanley Brook Road (closed off-season; about 2 miles long) connects to Park Loop Road where it becomes two-way near Jordan Pond. Continuing to Bar Harbor from Seal Harbor, Route 3 passes through Otter Creek and by lovely forested Acadia slopes. The 11½-mile route to Bar Harbor from Northeast Harbor via Route 198/Route 3 and Route 233 is only a few minutes faster and a half-mile shorter than the Route 3 way. Both routes pass through sections of Acadia.

VISITOR INFORMATION
CONTACTS Town of Mount Desert Chamber of Commerce. ⊠ *41 Harbor Dr., Northeast Harbor* ☏ *207/276–5040* ⊕ *mtdesertchamber.org.*

Sights

Land & Garden Preserve manages and cares for 1,400 acres in Northeast Harbor and Seal Harbor that encompasses the Abby Aldrich Rockefeller Garden, Asticou Azalea Garden, Little Long Pond Natural Lands, and Thuya Garden.

Parking areas at the Preserve's gardens are small and fill quickly at peak times; you may have to return later in the day. Thuya Garden also has a parking area below the garden on Route 3, from which you can ascend to the garden on a trail with granite stairs. In lieu of a day hike, consider walking up to Thuya and Asticou Azalea gardens from the village at the end of Route 198. It's about 2 miles from there to Asticou at the corner of Route 198/Route 3. Take the sidewalk all the way or hit the preserve's Asticou Stream Trail for the last leg. It's a 15-minute walk along Route 3 between Asticou and Thuya. You can also hike between them on a route that includes a side road and a bit of the sidewalk near Asticou (see the preserve map online or at parking area kiosks).

Abby Aldrich Rockefeller Garden
GARDEN | The Abby Aldrich Rockefeller Garden is the creation of its namesake and famed landscape designer Beatrix Farrand. An ever-present Narnia vibe begins on the drive up through the woods to the hilltop locale: leaf blowers keep the large mossy granite rocks free of leaves and needles, to magical effect. Even before entering on the Spirit Path, lined with Korean funerary statues, the garden's earthy pink high wall is entrancing as it resembles walls in Beijing's Forbidden City. The English-style main border garden has many colorful annuals; one side is more shaded so bed heights vary, adding whimsy to the symmetrical space. In smaller garden spaces nearby, you can rest on a bench, step through a pagoda, look out on Little Long Pond, and contemplate more Eastern sculptures, from seated Buddhas to guardian animals. An easy forest trail leads to the large terrace—with commanding extended ocean views—that fronted The Eyrie, the Rockefellers' massive summer "cottage," until it was torn down in 1962. ⊠ *Lawn & Garden Preserve, Seal Harbor* ⊕ *www.gardenpreserve.org/abby-aldrich-rockefeller-garden* ⊠ *$15* ⊙ *Closed early Sept.–early July* ⚠ *Reservations only.*

Asticou Azalea Garden
GARDEN | With many varieties of rhododendrons and azaleas, the Japanese-style garden is spectacular from late May to mid-June as the pink, white, and blue flowers not only bloom but reflect in a stream-fed pond. Whatever the season there's plenty to admire, especially in fall when the many native plants brighten the landscape. You can contemplate on a bench along the winding paths as intended, perhaps by the white sand garden—raked to evoke moving water. Created with azaleas from famed landscape designer Beatrix Farrand's Bar Harbor garden, Asticou was designed by Charles Savage, a self-educated garden designer

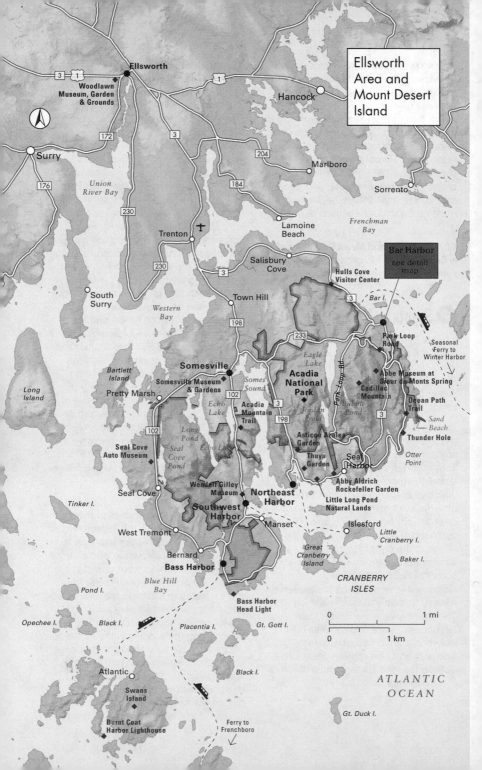

who managed his family's nearby Asticou Inn. ⊠ *Land & Garden Preserve, 3 Sound Dr., on corner of Rte. 3 and Rte. 198, Northeast Harbor* ☎ *207/276–3699* ⊕ *www.gardenpreserve.org/asticou-azalea-garden* 🎟 *$5 suggested donation* ⊗ *Closed Nov.–early May.*

Great Harbor Maritime Museum

HISTORY MUSEUM | FAMILY | Housed in the town's former fire station, this museum promotes and celebrates the Mount Desert Island region's maritime heritage. Inside, a map of the Great Harbor at the mouth of Somes Sound anchors a display that helps visitors orient themselves to the area as well as the museum. Interesting changing exhibits about local history have a nautical theme and include photographs and objects like ship models from the museum's collection as well as other area institutions. ⊠ *124 Main St., Northeast Harbor* ☎ *207/276–5262* ⊕ *www.facebook.com/greatharbormaritimemuseum* 🎟 *$5* ⊗ *Closed Sun. and Mon. and mid-Oct.–late June.*

Little Long Pond Natural Lands

NATURE PRESERVE |The Land & Garden preserve expanded greatly in 2015 when David Rockefeller, son of Acadia National Park founder John D. Rockefeller Jr., donated about 1,000 acres of largely forested land in Seal Harbor to the conversation group. The property includes 17 acres of meadows; 12 acres of marsh; a bog and streams; carriage roads and trails, some connecting with Acadia's trails; stone staircases on the Richard Trail, steep in sections, similar to those in Acadia; and a pond you can hike around and swim in (at designated areas). Upon David Rockefeller's death in 2017, the preserve was gifted the old estate's formal garden, the Abby Aldrich Rockefeller Garden.

Two of several preserve parking areas on Route 3 are for Little Long Pond Natural Lands. The one beside the pond across from Bracy Cove is small, so consider using the parking area west of here, where a 0.4-mile trail leads to the cove

and pond. ⊠ *Lawn & Garden Preserve, Rte. 3 Seal Harbor* ⊕ *www.gardenpreserve.org/little-long-pond.*

Thuya Garden

GARDEN | Hidden atop a hill above Route 3, this garden is part of what was once the summer home of Boston landscape designer and engineer Joseph Henry Curtis. Today the site is a peaceful and elegant spot to take in formal perennial gardens. Designed by Charles Savage and named for the property's majestic white cedars, Thuja occidentalis, the garden is filled with colorful blooms throughout summer. Walk the immaculately groomed grass paths or enjoy the view from a well-placed bench. You'll find delphiniums, daylilies, dahlias, heliotrope, snapdragons, and other types of vegetation. You can take a look at the sitting room in the Curtis home, which has a large collection of books compiled by Savage. Check the website for docent-led tours of the "lodge" as it's known. ⊠ *Land & Garden Preserve, 15 Thuya Dr., Northeast Harbor* ☎ *207/276–5130* ⊕ *www. gardenpreserve.org* 🎟 *$5 suggested donation* ⊗ *Closed mid-Oct.–mid-June.*

🍴 Restaurants

★ Abel's Lobster

$$$ | SEAFOOD | FAMILY | Located on a nub jutting into Somes Sound a few miles from Northeast Harbor, this place hums on summer nights as adults grab a drink from the outside bar, kids and dogs romp, and folks angle to watch lobsters cook in an open-air kitchen before eating at tables about the sloping lawn; the window-lined mid-century wood-walled dining room has views from every table. There are separate menus for each dining space though there is some overlap including the wood-fired boiled lobster, a lobster roll, fried clams, and the 9-ounce house burger. **Known for:** house-made cornbread; largely locally sourced menu; outside bar-type table curves above the

shore. [$] *Average main: $33* ✉ *13 Abels Lane Mount Desert* ☎ *207/276–8221* 🌐 *www.abelslobstermdi.com* ⏲ *Closed mid-Oct.-mid-May and Sun. and Mon. from mid-May–mid-Oct.*

Asticou Inn
$$$ | **AMERICAN** | **FAMILY** | Overlooking the water out back and practically hugging Route 3 out the front, this 1883 four-story gray-shingled restaurant and inn can't be missed nor is the opportunity to dine here and savor the spectacular view of picturesque Northeast Harbor, especially from the large deck fronting the classic old New England dining room. The menu offers a handful of entrées, including filet mignon, and lighter fare like fish tacos. **Known for:** popovers with strawberry jam; award-winning seafood chowder; lodging choices outside the main inn include funky six-sided 1960s cottages nicknamed "spaceships". [$] *Average main: $33* ✉ *15 Peabody Rd., Northeast Harbor* ☎ *207/276–3344* 🌐 *www.asticou.com* ⏲ *Closed Tues. and early Oct.–mid May.*

Hotels

★ Harbourside Inn
$$ | **B&B/INN** | Built in 1888 and once part of a summer colony, this hillside inn—run by the same family since 1977—is an easy base for exploring Acadia National Park, as you can connect from local trails here to get there. **Pros:** touches like courtesy dishes, glasses, and utensils (in the parlor but for use anywhere at the inn); guest parlor with working fireplace; delightful, window-lined breakfast porch where the continental breakfast is served (includes a fresh-baked treat and fresh fruit). **Cons:** close to but not on the water; no TVs in guest or common rooms; third floor rooms but no elevator. [$] *Rooms from: $275* ✉ *48 Harborside Rd., Northeast Harbor* ☎ *207/276–3272* 🌐 *harboursideinn.com* 🍴 *Free Breakfast.*

Shopping

The Kimball Shop
DEPARTMENT STORE | Fine china, and lots of it, is front and center at this upscale small department store in downtown Northeast Harbor. Many patterns are formal, yet one big seller is a line of dishes embellished with a red lobster or a blue octopus. Among the other impeccably arrayed offerings: kitchen items, toys, home decor, and children's clothing. A sister store with uber-nice women's apparel is down the street. ✉ *135 Main St., Northeast Harbor* ☎ *207/276–3300* 🌐 *www.kimballshop.com* ⏲ *Closed Fri.–Wed. late Dec.–Apr.*

The Naturalist's Notebook
TOYS | **FAMILY** | Filling two stories and a lower level, this one-of-a-kind and even out-of-this-world shop is chock full of books (for adults and kids), toys (many educational), and other items (of the gift variety), all relating to science and nature. But there's much more in this store, located in an old-fashioned commercial strip just up from Seal Harbor beach. Part museum, each room and space is fantastically painted and designed around a theme, like the moon, earth, or dinosaurs. Items for sale are grouped accordingly, as are exhibits, many of them interactive. Students from the College of the Atlantic in Bar Harbor were involved in creating the store. ✉ *16 Main St. Seal Harbor* ☎ *207/801–2777* 🌐 *www.thenaturalistsnotebook.com.*

Shaw Contemporary Jewelry
JEWELRY & WATCHES | Some 4,000 pieces of statement-making jewelry from artisans worldwide are displayed in this spacious store. Most pieces cost hundreds to thousands of dollars, but there are $10 items, and perhaps a $60,000 diamond necklace—you can always just look. Maine-made works include owner Sam Shaw's unique 18kt gold bracelets, rings, and necklaces created with birch twigs. On nice summer days, glass wall panels

open to a small "view garden" out back. Also come summer, the walls serve as an art gallery, with new shows and a Thursday evening opening every two weeks. ⊠ *128 Main St., Northeast Harbor* ☎ *207/276–5000* ⊕ *www.shawjewelry. com* ⊙ *Closed Jan.–Apr.*

Activities

Acadia Outdoor Center
KAYAKING | At this outfitter's hub just up from Seal Harbor beach, you can rent mountain bikes (from $34) to ride in nearby Acadia National Park and sign up for a coastal sea kayaking trip (from $99). Before or after your excursion, you can also grab an ice cream or gelato here and peruse the gift shop. ⊠ *18 Main St. Seal Harbor* ☎ *207/801–9343* ⊕ *www. acadiaoutdoorcenter.com.*

Sea Princess Cruises
BOAT TOURS | Both morning and afternoon cruises on Great Harbor at the entrance to Somes Sound include a stop at the fishing village of Islesford on Little Cranberry Island and a closeup look at cliffs on Somes Sounds. The narrator on the morning trip is often an Acadia National Park ranger. ⊠ *Northeast Harbor* ☎ *207/276–5352* ⊕ *barharborcruises.com* ⊠ *$35* ⊙ *Closed mid-Oct.–mid-May.*

Somesville

7 miles north of Northeast Harbor via Rte. 198.

Most visitors pass through Somesville on their way to Southwest Harbor. There isn't much amenities-wise in the well-preserved village, but it's well worth a stop—and not just to take a photo of, or a selfie on, the footbridge arching over a brook alongside Main Street (Route 102), as many do. This is Mount Desert Island's oldest village, though Maine's Wabanaki were living seasonally on the deep sound (and elsewhere on the island) before

Abraham Somes settled the town in 1761. Now lined with white-clapboard houses with black shutters and well-manicured lawns, its library (circa 1896) still sits prettily beside an old mill pond, a remnant of a once bustling commercial center.

GETTING HERE AND AROUND
Though a small village, because of its location in the center of Mount Desert Island atop Somes Sound, many roads lead here. Somesville is 5 miles south of the causeway onto Mount Desert Island on Route 102/Route 198, which separate in the village, with Route 102 continuing south and Route 198 east; 8 miles west of Bar Harbor via Route 198 and Route 233, which intersect slightly east of the village; 6 miles north of Southwest Harbor on Route 102; and 7 miles north and slightly west of Northeast Harbor on Route 198.

VISITOR INFORMATION
CONTACTS Mount Desert Chamber of Commerce. ⊠ *41 Harbor Dr., Northeast Harbor* ☎ *207/276–5040* ⊕ *www.mtdesertchamber.org.*

Sights

★ Seal Cove Auto Museum
HISTORY MUSEUM | FAMILY | About 65 immaculately maintained vehicles from the "Brass Era"—the beginning of auto production until about 1915—are displayed in this large warehouse-type space. There are gasoline, steam, and electric vehicles; each has a sign detailing its history. The big red 1914 Stanley Mountain Wagon was used to ferry passengers between the train station and lodging—the term "station wagon" derives from such vehicles. Enticing not only car buffs, the changing exhibit (new every two years) also highlights the impact of early automobiles on society and culture ("Engines of Change" explored how autos helped drive the suffragette movement). There are also

The Somesville Museum & Gardens are run by the Mount Desert Historical Society.

30-plus vintage motorcycles. Kids of all ages love hopping a ride on vehicles taken outside for "exercise" and a close-up look (catch-as-catch-can but call ahead to up the odds). On Tuesday, you can watch car mechanics at work. For Cars & Coffee on select Saturdays, folks head over in historic and unique vehicles; admission is free during the event, however you arrive, and always free for kids (under age 18). Check the website for information about other special events. ⊠ *1414 Tremont Rd., Seal Cove, Somesville* ☎ *207/244–9242* ⊕ *www.sealcoveautomuseum.org* ⌨ *$10* ⊗ *Closed Nov.–Apr.*

Somesville Museum & Gardens

HISTORY MUSEUM | FAMILY | Two small white buildings with changing exhibits about island history are clustered with heirloom gardens along Main Street at this Mount Desert Historical Society museum. The larger one isn't historic but has typical New England architectural touches. Hugging the road just beyond the footbridge over the mill stream, the tiny 1780s Selectmen's Building

was the Town of Mount Desert's office for many years. Herb and floral plants from the 19th and early 20th centuries bloom in the gardens. ⊠ *2 Oak Hill Rd., Somesville* ✛ *Along Main St. (Rte. 102) but turn onto Oak Hill Rd. for parking* ☎ *207/276–9323* ⊕ *www.mdihistory.org* ⌨ *$5 suggested donation* ⊗ *Museum closed early Sept.–late June and Mon. and Tues. late June–early Sept.*

Shopping

The Gallery at Somes Sound

ART GALLERIES | In a late 1800s commercial building on Main Street, natural light washes into both floors of this large rectangular gallery. Offering an arresting mix of paintings in a host of mediums and styles by nationally acclaimed contemporary artists, a specialty—not found at many such top-tier galleries—is fine art or sculpted furniture. There is also sculpture. ⊠ *112 Main St., Somesville* ☎ *207/610–4622* ⊕ *www.galleryatsomes-sound.com* ⊗ *Closed Nov.–mid-May.*

Southwest Harbor

6 miles south of Somesville via Rte. 102.

Southwest Harbor sits on the west side of the entrance to Somes Sound, which cuts up the center of the island. The town makes for a mellower Acadia base camp than Bar Harbor. Downtown is a fun place to poke around and shop for an afternoon, or swoop into the Wendell Gilley Museum, which pays homage to a local renowned bird carver. In summer, handsome yachts and towering sailboats bob in the harbor, while tour and charter boats come and go. The working waterfront is home to well-known boatbuilding companies, a major source of employment in the area. If you spot lots of pink flamingos about, you may have just missed the Harbor House Flamingo Festival (*www. harborhousemdi.org/ flamingo-festival*) in early July. North of town, trailheads at Echo Lake Beach and Fernald Point access some of Acadia National Park's less explored territory.

GETTING HERE AND AROUND

With Somes Sound cutting up the middle of Mount Desert Island and Southwest Harbor on the western side of its mouth, Route 102 is the only major road leading here; it's Main Street as it travels through town toward Trenton. Seal Cove Road travels west to Seal Cove from Southwest Harbor. A seasonal ferry serves the Cranberry Isles from Southwest Harbor (*see the Getting Here and Around section of the chapter planner for more information*).

VISITOR INFORMATION

CONTACTS **Southwest Harbor & Tremont Chamber of Commerce.** ⊠ *329 Main St., Southwest Harbor* ☎ *207/244–9264* ⊕ *www.acadiachamber.com.*

◉ Sights

Wendell Gilley Museum

OTHER MUSEUM | FAMILY | Wendell Gilley (1904–83), master plumber-turned-renowned bird carver from Southwest Harbor, hunted ducks and game birds for recreation and food. Aspiring to preserve them through taxidermy he instead took up bird carving, producing some 10,000 works (mostly basswood). He sold the fine and to-scale carvings at his "Bird Shop," a popular island tourist stop back in the day; his personal collection of 300-plus carvings—including ruffed grouse, upland sandpiper, American goldfinch, Atlantic puffin, and loon—is the foundation of the museum's collection. On a large corner near downtown, with bird sculptures and placarding outside, it showcases his carvings and others as well as avian art. One gallery has changing exhibits; you might catch a contemporary artist's show. A resident carver is at his workbench, not only carving but answering questions and helping visitors give it a go. Check the website for special events. You can buy carving kits in the museum workshop. ⊠ *4 Herrick Rd., Southwest Harbor* ☎ *207/244–7555* ⊕ *www.wendellgilleymuseum.org* ⌚ *$10* ⊘ *Closed Sun.–Thurs. Nov.–mid-May; Mon. and Tues. mid-May–Oct.*

🍴 Restaurants

Beal's Lobster Pier

$$$ | SEAFOOD | FAMILY | Watch lobstermen and fishermen haul their catch and pleasure craft come and go at this working pier with a large restaurant that's big on lobster, clams, and other seafood but also sells burgers, steak, and hot dogs for the kids. There's a roofed seating area with a bar, waterside bar tables for two along a covered pier walkway, indoor dining (upper level), and patio seating. **Known for:** lobster rolls: traditional (warmed in butter) or classic (served cold with mayonnaise); also a

lobster wholesaler, you can order the critters to go; in business since 1932. [$] *Average main: $33* ✉ *182 Clark Point Rd., Southwest Harbor* ☎ *207/244–3202* 🌐 *www.bealslobster.com* 🕘 *Closed mid-Oct.–mid-Apr.*

★ Red Sky Restaurant

$$$ | CONTEMPORARY | Whether you have a table in the dining room or a seat at the small bar, you'll feel comfortable at this longtime fine dining downtown restaurant, where yellow walls, white tablecloths, and the white brick fireplace add lightness and dark wood walls and ceilings and landscape paintings (for sale) add warmth. Along with entrées such as lobster risotto with asparagus and maple-glazed baby back ribs, grilled with crescendo after slowly braising, there's always a burger on the menu. **Known for:** scrumptious desserts including house-made ice creams; well-curated wine list; outdoor dining out back. [$] *Average main: $32* ✉ *14 Clark Point Rd., Southwest Harbor* ☎ *207/244–0476* 🌐 *www.redskyrestaurant.com* 🕘 *No lunch.*

Hotels

The Claremont Hotel

$$$$ | HOTEL | Though it was fully renovated in 2021, this 6-acre property still boasts a clapboard three-story 1884 inn with a wide porch that provides wondrous views of Somes Sound. **Pros:** cabin rentals are great for families; camp-style seaside eatery, full-service restaurant, snug pub, bakery/ice-cream shop; courtesy cruiser bikes. **Cons:** no cots or cribs for guest rooms; no elevator; only one bed (king) in main inn rooms. [$] *Rooms from: $605* ✉ *22 Claremont Rd., Southwest Harbor* ☎ *207/244–5036* 🌐 *www.theclaremonthotel.com* 🛏 *50 units* 🍴 *No Meals.*

Harbour Cottage Inn

$$ | B&B/INN | Built in 1870 as part of Mount Desert Island's first summer hotel, the elegant main inn has tastefully decorated rooms named after different kinds of boats and a two-bedroom suite; there's also a wing with two modern accommodations and a "carriage house" cottage. **Pros:** the inn's bar (open early evening only) sells "snackables" and drinks; fireplace and plenty of seating in well-appointed parlor-like common area; bottled wine and canned beer and soda sold to guests via the honor system. **Cons:** in three-bedroom suite, only bedrooms have air-conditioning; a short walk to harbor; no water views. [$] *Rooms from: $275* ✉ *9 Dirigo Rd., Southwest Harbor* ☎ *207/244–5738* 🌐 *www.harbourcottageinn.com* 🕘 *Closed Nov.–late May* 🛏 *11 rooms* 🍴 *Free Breakfast.*

Shopping

Southwest Harbor Artisans

CRAFTS | Right downtown, this welcoming shop sells an array of items—everything from jewelry and wood cutting boards to American Girl doll clothing and photography and paintings. Whoever waits on you can show you their own wares, as some of the 75 or so artisans and artists whose works are represented own and run the shop. ✉ *360 Main St., Southwest Harbor* ☎ *207/244–8370* 🌐 *www.southwestharborartisans.com* 🕘 *Closed late Oct.–early May.*

Activities

TOURS

Acadia Lobster Cruise

BOAT TOURS | FAMILY | A Down East native hauls, cooks, and serves lobster to passengers aboard his 1966 wooden lobster boat, and yes, there's a picnic table and the meal includes corn-on-the-cob and blueberry pie. Trips have a six-passenger limit and run midmorning and midafternoon; private charters are also offered. Families take note: the captain is known to fish and entertain the kids while mom and dad finish their meal! ⊠ *Dysart's Great Harbor Marina, 11 Apple La., Southwest Harbor* ☎ *207/370–7663* ⊕ *www.acadialobstercruise.com* 🍽 *From $150.*

Bass Harbor

9 miles south of Somesville via Rtes. 102 and 102A.

Tucked below Southwest Harbor at the bottom of Mount Desert Island, this small lobstering village doesn't bustle with seasonal tourists like larger island villages, but it does have a few restaurants. It's also the departure point for the ferry to Frenchboro and Swans Island (*see the Getting Here and Around section of the Chapter Planner for more information*).

Two miles south of Bass Harbor and part of Acadia National Park, Bass Harbor Head Light is the most popular attraction on the island's "quiet side" and one of the most photographed lighthouses in Maine. Acadia's Ship Harbor and Wonderland trails, both easy and under 1½ miles, are also nearby.

GETTING HERE AND AROUND
Bass Harbor is 2.7 miles from Southwest Harbor via Route 102 and Route 102A (Seawall Road), but many visitors travel between them on the 7-mile-long scenic route that loops below Route 102 on a coastal swath bordered by the ocean and both harbors: Southwest on the north and Bass on the west. The road provides access to several popular Acadia National Park attractions.

ESSENTIALS
CONTACTS Southwest Harbor & Tremont Chamber of Commerce. ⊠ *329 Main St., Southwest Harbor* ☎ *207/244–9264* ⊕ *www.acadiachamber.com.*

Sights

For more information on Bass Harbor Head Light, see the West Side of Mount Desert Island section of the Acadia National Park chapter.

Burnt Coat Harbor Lighthouse and Swans Island
LIGHTHOUSE | FAMILY | Swans Island is a picturesque 6-mile ferry ride from Bass Harbor at the bottom of Mount Desert Island. There are numerous outdoor activities, like hiking, swimming, fishing, and biking, but the 35-foot-tall white Burnt Coat Harbor Lighthouse on the south shore is not to be missed. Both the light and the keeper's house, which has history exhibits, an art gallery, bathrooms, and a small gift shop, are open from late June to early September. An apartment upstairs can be rented on a weekly basis from June through October. Aside from vacation rentals, there's only one lodging, the five-room Harbor Watch Inn (⊕ *www. harborwatchinnswansisland.com*). The Island Market & Supply (⊕ *www.tims-swans-island.com*) is a great place to get picnic supplies or other general store needs. ⊠ *Swans Island, Bass Harbor* ⊕ *www.burntcoatharborlight.com.*

🍴 Restaurants

Thurston's Lobster Pound
$$ | SEAFOOD | FAMILY | Right on Bass Harbor, Thurston's is easy to spot because of the bright yellow awnings covering much of its outdoor-only seating. You can order everything from a grilled-cheese crab sandwich, haddock chowder, or hamburger to a boiled lobster served with clams or mussels. **Known for:** selling fresh cooked or uncooked lobsters to go—it's also a lobster wholesaler; lobster

Visiting Bass Harbor Head Light is one of the highlights of a visit to Acadia National Park.

fresh off the boat sold in three size ranges; good place to watch sunsets. $ *Average main: $20* ✉ *9 Thurston Rd., Bernard* ☎ *207/244–7600* ⊕ *www.thurstonforlobster.com* ⊘ *Closed mid-Oct.–late spring; closed Sun. and Mon. late spring–mid-Oct.*

Seafood Ketch

$$$ | **AMERICAN** | **FAMILY** | About half the seating here is on a large patio within spitting distance from the water, though you can also enjoy the quintessential view of a working harbor through large windows inside this cheery establishment. Lobster—served not only boiled with a choice of sides but in dishes such as baked seafood casserole—is purchased fresh off the boat from the lobsterman next door. **Known for:** all breads made in-house, even rolls for burgers and lobster; baked stuffed haddock topped with lobster and seafood sauce; gorgeous pink and orange sunsets. $ *Average main: $25* ✉ *47 Shore Rd., Bass Harbor* ☎ *207/244–7463* ⊕ *www.seafoodketch.com* ⊘ *Closed mid-Oct.–mid-May.*

Shopping

Across from Bass Harbor, teeny Bernard is an unexpected shoppers' delight: in the village are two stores, each charming in a different way, run by local women.

Fernandez Gift Shop

CRAFTS | All over the world at Christmas, folks hang stockings knitted by the proprietor, who you're likely to find needles in hand at this homestead shop. There are large and small stockings and, yes, designs include a red lobster on a green background. Other craft items and used goods, including books, are also sold. From a long line of islanders, the owner displays old family photos and wood toys her great-grandfather made for sale to tourists. ✉ *41 Bernard Rd., Bernard* ☎ *207/244–7224.*

Slack Tide Shop

HOUSEWARES | In a cute tiny red building with a welcoming porch at the end of Bernard Road across from Thurston's Lobster Pound, this shop stays open into the evening. Smart, tasteful offerings include home decor, original art, body and bath products, jewelry, and summer clothing. Many items have sea or nautical themes, such as seashell earrings and float rope door mats. ⊠ *129 Bernard Rd.* ☎ *207/244–8035* ⊕ *www.facebook.com/ slacktideshopbernard* ⊗ *Closed early-Oct.–late May.*

Activities

TOURS
Bass Harbor Island Cruises
BOAT TOURS | **FAMILY** | Two-hour nature tours on a lobster boat-like *R.L. Gott* travel Bass Harbor and Blue Hill Bay, cruising up close to outer islands and the cliffs below Bass Harbor Head Light. Passengers spot wildlife and learn about local history and the fishing industry—a few lobster traps are hauled. Run by a local family since the 1990s, this tour operator also offers custom sailboat, fishing, and sightseeing trips. ⊠ *12 Little Island Way, Bass Harbor* ☎ *207/244–5785* ⊕ *www. bassharborcruises.com* 🖃 *From $40* ⊗ *Closed mid-Oct.–May.*

Hancock Area

9 miles north of Ellsworth via U.S. 1.

A triangular green with a Civil War monument marks the small village of Hancock on U.S. 1 and the turn for the summer colony at Hancock Point on Crabtree Neck. This reach of land isn't named for native trees but for Capt. Agreen Crabtree, a 1760s settler from Massachusetts who was a privateer during the American Revolution, seizing goods from British ships. In the Gilded Age, trains filled with residents of cities like New York and Philadelphia connected with ferries in Hancock for the final leg of the journey to Bar Harbor (known as Eden until 1918) across Frenchman Bay for the summer season. In Hancock, you can pick up items to have a picnic at one of the preserves sprinkled about the area. Another

option is Sullivan's Sumner Memorial Park, on U.S. 1 after it crosses the bridge over the Taunton River from Hancock. A tall sculpture there, like stacked blocks, is on the Maine Sculpture Trail. Throughout this area, signs along the highway point you down country roads to homestead artisan galleries in Hancock, Sullivan, and neighboring Franklin, where Taunton Bay protrudes inland.

GETTING HERE AND AROUND
U.S. 1 travels through Hancock. In the village, Point Road heads down from the highway to Hancock Point at the bottom of Crabtree Neck, passing through sleepy South Hancock en route. The gateway rest stop for the National Scenic Schoodic Byway (⊕ *www.schoodicbyway.org*) is in Hancock just before U.S. 1 crosses the Taunton River into Sullivan.

Down the road, in Gouldsboro, the byway turns onto Route 186 to loop the Schoodic Peninsula, home to Acadia National Park's Schoodic District. Don't miss the byway's premier roadside pullout a few miles from Hancock in Sullivan, with stunning views of Mount Desert Island's mountains across Frenchman Bay, and at the gateway, placards on local history.

Sights

Crabtree Neck Land Trust
NATURE PRESERVE | Descendants of the early Hancock settler for whom Crabtree Neck was named are among those behind Crabtree Neck Land Trust, which impressively has six preserves in and around this reach of land. They include the 3-mile Old Pond Railway Trail, with two trailheads near U.S. 1 (one is in the village just off the highway on Point Road across from Hancock town hall). It follows a railbed on which trains in an earlier era transported rusticators heading to (and later from) Bar Harbor, completing the last leg of the journey by ferry. The trust has also made it easier for folks to swim, walk, or simply enjoy views of

Frenchman Bay at Carters Beach down on the neck. To get there, drive about 4½ miles down Point Road and turn left onto Haskins Road, which soon ends at Carters Beach Road. Walk the unpaved shore-hugging road, aka Carters Beach Corridor, about a half mile north to the beach. Here, one of the trust-owned tracts along the road connects with Frenchman Bay Conservancy's Salt Pond Preserve (www.frenchmanbay.org). Yes, there's a salt pond near the beach. Salt Pond Trail is about a mile out and back. ✉ *Crabtree Neck Land Trust, Hancock* 🌐 *crabtreenecklandtrust.org.*

Tidal Falls Preserve
WATERFALL | FAMILY | One of New England's best-known reversing falls—the phenomenon is created when the current "reverses" en route from bay to harbor—roils just below the U.S. 1 bridge linking Hancock and Sullivan. Frenchman Bay Conservancy's 8-acre preserve (*no dogs*) beside the falls on the Hancock side is a great picnic spot, with tables strung along the waterfront. Two hours before and two hours after low tide is the best time for viewing the falls. The preserve has a viewing platform, and placards explain the area's rich history and ecology. Granite was quarried nearby and shipped in schooners over the falls, once the site of a ferry and train terminal for Bar Harbor visitors. The mingling of fresh and salt water creates an environment that attracts wildlife, especially birds and waterfowl. Free concerts are held at the preserve on Monday evenings in July and August; check the conservancy's website for information. At the site you can also learn about hiking opportunities at its many other preserves in the region, from the Union River in Ellsworth to Gouldsboro on the Schoodic Peninsula. ✉ *71 Tidal Falls Rd.* ✥ *Turn on East Side Rd. from U.S. 1* ☎ *207/422–2328* 🌐 *www.frenchmanbay.org/preserve/tidal-falls* 🎟 *Free* 🕒 *No vehicle access in winter.*

Hotels

The Crocker House Country Inn
$ | B&B/INN | Set amid towering fir trees on Hancock Point, this shingled lodging was built in 1884; the main inn holds comfortable rooms decorated with authentic antiques and country-style furnishings, while two modern accommodations in the carriage house are perfect for families, and the den there is for all inn guests to enjoy. **Pros:** hot tub off the den; short walk to Frenchman Bay; only lodging on exclusive Hancock Point. **Cons:** not on water and no water views; pitched ceilings in two third floor rooms; no elevator to third floor rooms. [$] *Rooms from: $165* ✉ *967 Point Rd.* ☎ *207/422–6806* 🌐 *www.crockerhouse.com* 🛏 *11 rooms* 🍴 *Free Breakfast.*

Shopping

Many artists and artisans have their own galleries in and near Hancock, often right at their home or homestead. To find some of the best, look for the yellow Artist Studio Tour Map pamphlet at area stores, inns, and so on.

Granite Garden Gallery & Stone Designs Inc.
ART GALLERIES | You can buy a vase or sailboat sculpture made of granite in the self-serve shop in one of the small buildings at this old granite quarry. If you blow the horn, as advised, owner Obadiah Bourne Buell may appear. His stone business, also here, makes practical and sculptural granite pieces for gardens and homes, "upcycling" the blocks of granite that are all about. Buell grew up and lives on this ethereal land, where rain long ago filled the old quarries, and has created a large year-round public garden (free, donations welcome) with granite sculptures large and small; granite benches, tables, fire pit, and pizza oven; and trails, flower beds, and charming signage (even when asking folks to stay back from the work area) and more. Ping pong anyone?

Ocean waves crash into the rocks on the scenic Maine coast at Schoodic Point.

Yes, the table is granite, and the paddles and balls are provided. ✉ *228 Whales Back Rd.* ☎ *207/664–9951* ⊕ *www.granitegardengallery.com.*

Gull Rock Pottery

HOUSEWARES | It's worth the trip down the long dirt drive to Gull Rock Pottery. Sculpture dots serene grounds with a knockout view of Cadillac Mountain across Frenchman Bay. The shop sells the owner's dishware and lamps, with either hand-painted blue and white depictions of local wildlife, flowers, and water scenes, or a rust-color or celadon glaze. The etchings, prints, and jewelry are made by the potter's husband, who also created most of the sculpture. Open year-round, but it's by chance or appointment in the off-season. ✉ *103 Gull Rock Rd., Hancock* ✛ *Off East Side Rd.* ☎ *207/664–3376* ⊕ *www.gullrockpottery.com.*

Hog Bay Pottery

HOUSEWARES | Heron-patterned dinnerware is one of the specialties at Hog Bay Pottery, which also sells knitted items and handspun and natural-died yarns.

A husband and wife run this year-round homestead shop: he's the potter, she's the knitter and spinner. ✉ *245 Hog Bay Rd., Franklin* ☎ *207/565–2282* ⊕ *www.hogbay.com.*

Spring Woods Gallery

ART GALLERIES | Ann and Paul Breeden's Spring Woods Gallery, nestled between their home and a large shade garden for visitors, is illuminated by a tall arched window. Local farm animals appear often in her colorful, playful oil paintings. His strikingly realistic acrylic paintings capture the intensity of the Maine Coast. Sculpture and paintings by their children are also sold at this welcoming gallery just off U.S. 1 in Sullivan. Folks are welcome to come just for the tranquil garden. ✉ *19 Willow Brook La., Sullivan* ☎ *207/422–3007.*

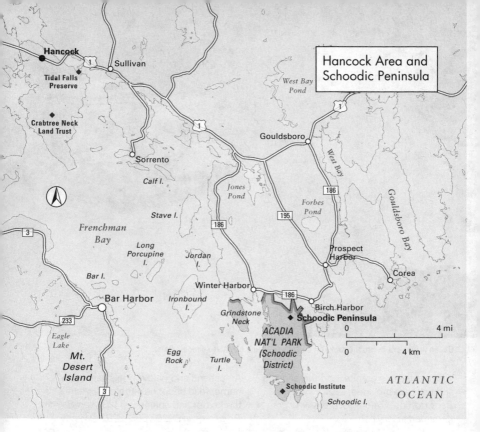

West Bay
Pond

Hancock

Sullivan

Tidal Falls
Preserve

Crabtree Neck
Land Trust

Gouldsboro

Sorrento

Calf I.

West Bay

Jones
Pond

186

Forbes
Pond

195

Stave I.

186

Frenchman
Bay

Long
Porcupine
I.

Jordan
I.

Gouldsboro Bay

Prospect
Harbor

Corea

Bar I.

Winter Harbor

186

3

Grindstone
Neck

Birch Harbor

Schoodic Peninsula

Bar Harbor

Ironbound
I.

ACADIA
NAT'L PARK
(Schoodic
District)

0   4 mi

233

Eagle
Lake

Egg
Rock

Turtle
I.

0   4 km

Mt.
Desert
Island

Schoodic Institute

ATLANTIC
OCEAN

3

Schoodic I.

Activities

Hancock Point Kayak Tours & Schoodic Maine Guide Snowshoe Tours

ADVENTURE TOURS | FAMILY | A Master Sea Kayak Guide/Registered Recreational Guide, in business since 2002, leads kayak tours in the waters off Hancock Point from May through October. Public tours are in the morning and include an island stop unless fog has rolled in. Trips then stay close to shore, immersing visitors in fog's otherworldly beauty. Custom trips are also offered. Guided snowshoe trips are on Hancock Woods Trail. ✉ *58 Point Rd., Hancock* ☎ *207/266–4449* ⊕ *www. schoodicmaineguide.com* ✉ *Kayak tours from $50 per person; snowshoe tours from $25 per person per hr.*

Schoodic Peninsula

25 miles east of Ellsworth via U.S. 1 and Rte. 186.

Acadia National Park's only mainland section sits at the bottom of Schoodic Peninsula, extending to its very tip. As at the park over on Mount Desert Island, visitors to the Schoodic District hike, bike, camp, and savor spectacular views. Crowds are smaller, though they are increasing, and it's here that you'll find Winter Harbor and Gouldsboro.

On the peninsula's western side, Winter Harbor's small but sweet downtown is en route to Grindstone Neck. Granite steps lead to rocky shorefront on tucked-away street ends in the wealthy summer community, which gives an inkling of Bar Harbor before a 1947 fire destroyed many mansions there. Surrounding Winter Harbor, Gouldsboro is also a proud lobstering and fishing community, sprinkled with coastal villages. Guarded by its namesake light, Prospect Harbor stretches along Route 186. Tiny Wonsqueak and Birch harbors flash after you exit Acadia. On the peninsula's most easterly shore, Corea is tucked away from it all on a small roundish harbor, the open ocean beyond.

GETTING HERE AND AROUND

Route 186 loops Schoodic Peninsula, intersecting with the U.S. Route 1 twice.

A seasonal passenger ferry travels Frenchman Bay between Bar Harbor and Winter Harbor, where visitors can connect with the seasonal free Island Explorer bus service to Acadia National Park's Schoodic District and nearby villages *(see the Getting Here and Around section of the Chapter Planner for more information)*. Route 195 runs down the middle of the peninsula from U.S. 1 to Prospect Harbor and continues east to Corea, where it ends.

VISITOR INFORMATION

CONTACTS Schoodic Chamber of Commerce. ✉ *Winter Harbor* 🌐 *schoodicchamber.com.*

Sights

For more information on the Schoodic District area of Acadia National Park, see the Acadia National Park chapter.

Restaurants

Lunch on the Wharf

$$ | **SEAFOOD** | **FAMILY** | A fisherman's wife owns this popular establishment, which buys lobster right off the boat and has covered tables spread about a deck atop a wharf. As stunning as the setting is, folks also come for the excellent food, including boiled lobster with sides; there are plenty of non-seafood choices, too, including pulled pork. **Known for:** BYOB; lobster rolls; whoopie pies. [$] *Average main: $18* ✉ *13 Gibbs La., Corea* ☎ *207/276–5262* 🌐 *www.corealunch.com.*

The Pickled Wrinkle

$ | **AMERICAN** | Regulars come from beyond Schoodic Peninsula to this fun Birch Harbor spot to order its namesake, a pickled protein-packed sea snail; this "Down East delicacy" isn't always on the menu. Visitors exiting Acadia National Park's Schoodic District stop here for fresh takes on traditional pub fare like burgers, wings, and pizzas (specialty or build your own), served in the spacious, woodsy, inside dining spaces or the eating area out front—both have bars. **Known for:** a dozen draft beers from craft breweries in the region; crab roll and crab flatbread made with fresh crab from local waters; Thursday steak night. [$] *Average main: $15* ✉ *9 E. Schoodic Dr., Gouldsboro* ☎ *207/963–7916* 🌐 *thepickledwrinkle.com* 🕒 *Closed Jan.–mid-Mar. Closed Mon. and Tues. mid-Mar.–Dec.*

Hotels

★ Acadia Oceanside Meadows Inn

$ | **B&B/INN** | **FAMILY** | A must for nature lovers, this lodging sits on a 200-acre preserve dotted with woods, streams, salt marshes, and ponds, with spacious guest rooms in two historic buildings overlooking a private white sand beach (rare for these parts); it's also home to Oceanside Meadows Innstitute for the Arts and Sciences, which holds lectures, musical performances, art exhibits, and other events in the restored barn. **Pros:** separate guest kitchen and picnic area with a grill; sea captain's home has three two-room suites that are ideal for families; laminated pamphlets with daily itineraries for exploring Schoodic Peninsula and beyond are available for guest use and purchase. **Cons:** beach is across the road; some dated baths; some third floor rooms. [$] *Rooms from: $199* ✉ *202 Corea Rd., Prospect*

Harbor ☎ *207/963–5557* 🌐 *gomaine.com* 🕒 *Closed mid-Oct.–late May* 🛏 *15 rooms* 🍴 *Free Breakfast.*

Elsa's Inn on the Harbor

$ | **B&B/INN** | Pretty period-style wallpaper and antiques add to the back-in-time, relaxed vibe at this lodging in an old home across from Prospect Harbor that offers six comfortable guest rooms, some with private entrances. **Pros:** two rooms can connect and roll-away beds are available; all the rooms have water views; innkeepers help guests plan outings. **Cons:** building partially obstructs water views; no restaurants or stores within immediate vicinity; no king beds. [$] *Rooms from: $175* ✉ *179 Main St. Prospect Harbor* ☎ *207/275–7441* 🌐 *www.elsasinnme.com* 🛏 *6 rooms* 🍴 *Free Breakfast.*

Shopping

U.S. Bells & Watering Cove Studios

CRAFTS | Hand-cast bronze doorbells and wind chimes are among the items sold at this longtime Prospect Harbor studio. You can also buy finely crafted quilts, wood-fired pottery, and fine cabinetry and furniture made by the owner's family, as well as cards, wild blueberry jam, jewelry, and such by other Maine artisans. Ask for a tour of the foundry—you might even catch a "pour," done several times a week. Open June to mid-October and otherwise by chance or appointment. ✉ *56 West Bay Rd., Prospect Harbor* ☎ *207/963–7184* 🌐 *www.usbells.com* 🕒 *Closed mid-Oct.–May.*

whopaints

ART GALLERIES | **FAMILY** | Wendilee Heath O'Brien's paintings in watercolor, oil, pastel, Asian ink, and *kinpakku* (Japanese traditional gold leaf) are sold at her studio gallery, where visitors often catch the artist at work and are welcome to listen in if she's teaching a class. Many works depict Down East landscapes, perhaps with people or children in the scene, but her repertoire includes abstract works, still lifes, and portraiture. A whimsical garden path leads to this year-round gallery behind the artist's home on Winter Harbor's Main Street. Notecards featuring her work (buy 10 and get one free!) and another artist's pottery are also sold. ✉ *316 Main St., Winter Harbor* ☎ *207/963–2076* 🌐 *www.whopaints.com.*

Activities

Sea Schoodic Kayak & Bike

BIKING | Near the entrance to Acadia National Park's Schoodic District, this outfitter rents only hybrid bikes as they're best suited for the park's gravel bike path network and Park Loop Road, which connects with it. Stop at the shop to get fitted for a personal flotation device and paddles so you can kayak at Jones Pond near U.S. 1 at the top of the peninsula, then head to what's in reality a lake: Sea Schoodic's rental kayaks are waiting for you there. You can also picnic and swim at Jones Pond. ✉ *8 Duck Pond Rd., Winter Harbor* ✥ *Off Rte. 186* ☎ *833/724–6634* 🌐 *www.seaschoodic.com* 🎟 *Bikes from $35; kayaks from $50.*

Chapter 10

DOWN EAST COAST

Updated by
Mary Ruoff

⊙ Sights	🍴 Restaurants	🛏 Hotels	🛍 Shopping	🍸 Nightlife
★★★★★	★★★☆☆	★★★☆☆	★★★☆☆	★★☆☆☆

WELCOME TO DOWN EAST COAST

TOP REASONS TO GO

★ **Bold Coast:** Memorable hikes along the cliffs with stupendous ocean views between Cutler and Lubec.

★ **Explore Campobello Island:** This Canadian island, across a short bridge from Lubec, Maine, is home to the must-visit Roosevelt Campobello International Park.

★ **Mingle with artisans:** Artists, artisans, and crafters selling fine works and wares have stories to tell about themselves, the region, and why they are here.

★ **Breakfast and beyond:** Innkeepers at Down East's traditional bed-and-breakfasts provide scrumptious breakfasts and all the travel highlights their guests need to know.

★ **Preserves a plenty:** Much of the coast is protected by private and public preserves and parks. Explore by trail or, at some, put in a kayak.

1 Milbridge Area. Take a puffin tour, grab a bite, or stock up in Milbridge. Visit Steuben, the "Blueberry Capital of the World," or check out Cherryfield's architecture.

2 Jonesport and Beals Island. A fishing village short on amenities, but with outstanding hiking preserves and great sunsets.

3 Machias Bay Area. Kayak in Machias Bay, hike the Down East Sunrise Trail, or visit the hidden gems of Jasper and Roque Bluffs beaches.

4 Lubec Area. More than a gateway to Campobello Island, this popular hiking destination has scenic trails and other coastal spots like the West Quoddy Head Light.

5 Campobello Island. Roosevelt International Park is home to President Franklin D. Roosevelt's former "summer cottage;" East Quoddy Head Light is nearby.

6 Eastport. Whale-watching tours, shops and galleries, and views of Canada.

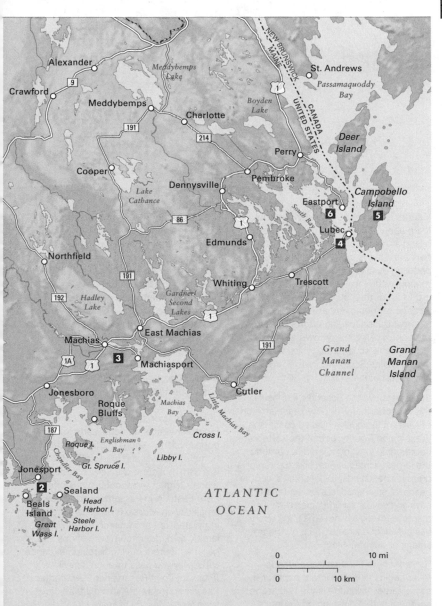

Slogans like "The Real Maine" ring true Down East, where the coast remains mostly raw and undeveloped. Even in July, you're likely to have rocky beaches and shady hiking trails all to yourself, and the slower pace is as calming as the sea breeze and the scenery—blueberry barrens, coastal bogs, and dark-purple and pink lupine-lined roads (late June).

Visitors are often surprised when they learn about all the region has to offer: hiking at national wildlife refuges, state parks and lands, and nature preserves; paddling on lakes, rivers, and bays; and museums on local history, culture, and art. Most of the country's remaining Atlantic salmon rivers are here, and so is an organization leading efforts to restore the fishery. And, many town centers have large granite sculptures, which are stops on the Maine Sculpture Trail (⊕ *www. schoodicsculpture.org*).

Situated above the Schoodic Peninsula, this most northerly, or down east, stretch of Maine's famously chiseled coast is in Washington County, one of the state's poorest and least populated but among the largest acreage-wise. Like the region's dramatic headlands, rocky shores, cobble beaches, splattered islands, and many bays and coves, communities here are quintessentially Maine—meaning each has a distinct character, be it on the artsy side or all-about-fishing.

Tucked where the tidal Narraguagus River begins to widen into the bay of the same name, Milbridge is the hub at the southern end of Washington County's coastal swath. Though the area isn't as well-known as destinations farther Down East, there's lots to explore, from popular hiking trails to vast blueberry barrens. Continuing Down East, fishing villages like Jonesport and its sister community across the bridge, Beals Island, are below U.S. 1. Above here a Revolutionary War naval battle was waged and won in the waters off Machias, Washington County's historic shire town and a regional hub, though thankfully not one big enough for big box stores. In and near Lubec, Maine's Bold Coast of granite cliffs is one of the premier coastal hiking destinations on the Eastern Seaboard. From the village, a bridge leads to Campobello Island, where the former summer home of Eleanor and Franklin D. Roosevelt is a park museum. Old Sow, one of the world's largest whirlpools, swirls offshore from Eastport in Passamaquoddy Bay. The small city on Moose Island has a welcoming waterfront and an architecturally rich, largely brick downtown with shops and galleries. Before driving across the granite causeway you pass through Sipayik (Pleasant Point Reservation), where the Passamaquoddy, a Wabanaki tribe, have lived for thousands of years.

Planning

Getting Here and Around

AIR

Bangor International Airport (BGR) in Bangor is the closest major airport to Down East. It's about 1¼ hours from there to Milbridge in the southern end of the region. Farther south along the coast, Portland International Airport (PWM) is 3¼ hours away. Renting a car is your best bet from either airport. The small regional Hancock County–Bar Harbor Airport (BHB) near Mount Desert Island is also an option for flying to the area and renting a car. Cape Air/JetBlue offer flights to and from here to Logan International Airport (BOS) in Boston.

CONTACTS Bangor International Airport.
☎ 207/992–4600 ⊕ www.flybangor.com. **Hancock County–Bar Harbor Airport.** (*BHB*) ✉ 143 Caruso Dr., Trenton ☎ 207/667–7329 ⊕ www.bhbairport.com. **Portland International Jetport.** (*PWM*) ✉ 1001 Westbrook St., Portland ☎ 207/774–7301 ⊕ www.portlandjetport.org.

CAR

Down East covers roughly a fifth of the state's coast as the crow flies from Portland. A car is essential for exploring this vast swath. Usually flowing slightly inland from the coast, U.S. 1 is the main transportation spine. Towns highlighted in the chapter are along this highway on area bays and rivers feeding into them.

Traveling the 125-mile National Scenic Bold Coast Byway (⊕ www.explore-maine.org/byways) is a great way to see the region. Cell phone reception may be spotty in places; if your phone shows Atlantic time in Eastport or Lubec, Canadian cell towers have picked up service (contact your carrier to have charges reversed). The inland countryside is sprinkled with lakes and rolling hills, so consider returning on a more inland route. At the southrn end of the coastal region and especially pretty in the fall, Maine Scenic Blackwoods Byway runs for 12½ miles west from Cherryfield on Route 182 and connects with U.S. 1 in Hancock.

FERRY

Downeast Water Taxi provides seasonal service between Lubec and Eastport, which are 3 miles apart by water and 38 miles by car ($25 per person round-trip; two-passenger minimum). A bridge connects Lubec with Campobello Island, New Brunswick, from which East Coast Ferries' seasonal car ferry runs to and from Canada's Deer Island from late June to mid-September (one-way fares are $24 car and driver, $5 per additional car passenger or passenger-only, bikes $2 extra). From Deer Island, you can continue to the Canadian mainland on the free government ferry to L'Etete near St. George. Deer Island and Campobello ferries run on Atlantic Time. Downeast Windjammer runs seasonal ferry service between Lubec and Eastport; check the website for information.

CONTACTS Downeast Water Taxi.
☎ 207/904–8029 ⊕ Facebook.com/Don-Baileywatertaxi. **Downeast Windjammer.** ⊕ www.downeastwindjammer.com/ferries. **East Coast Ferries Ltd..** ✉ Deer Island Point Rd. ☎ 506/747–2159, 877/747–2159 ⊕ www.eastcoastferriesltd.com.

Hotels

In the villages and along the back roads you can find wonderful bed-and-breakfasts run by innkeepers eager to share Down East's laidback charms and point you to both well-known and tucked-away locales of great natural beauty. Some of these inns are cozy places where you might feel you're staying in a friend's summer house, while others are more grand. You'll find lots of antique furnishings and often modern accommodations, perhaps with a kitchen, in a separate structure or wing. A few still have rooms with shared baths, and don't expect air conditioning—with cooling sea breezes it's not needed. Sure, there may be a couple days in the summer when it would be turned on if at hand, but fans are deployed in those cases. Don't write off anything called a cottage; many in this region are lovely. You won't find chain hotels, but there are well-kept roadside motels, mostly in larger towns. Many lodgings charge less than you might think, especially compared to similar accommodations in Bar Harbor.

Restaurants

You won't find fast-food chains Down East except in Machias and north of here in Calais on the Canadian border. If you don't have time to stop at a restaurant or a small town lacks one, you can grab a sandwich or slice of pizza at most convenience stores. Your only choice for a sit-down meal may be a casual establishment serving breakfast, lunch, and dinner, or lunch and dinner. Such places are big on seafood (it's not all fried) and often have offerings like wraps and Cobb salads, and like foodie spots, might well tout their use of local foods. Save room for dessert, often made right on the premises. Upscale dining establishments serving more creative cuisine are rare, but there are a few brewpubs about.

HOTEL AND RESTAURANT PRICES

Hotel prices in the reviews are the lowest cost of a standard double room in high season. Restaurant prices in the reviews are the average cost of a main course at dinner, or if dinner is not served, at lunch. Restaurant and hotel reviews have been shortened. For full information, visit Fodors.com.

What It Costs In U.S. Dollars			
$	$$	$$$	$$$$
RESTAURANTS			
under $18	$18–$24	$25–$35	over $35
HOTELS			
under $200	$200–$299	$300–$399	over $399

When to Go

Reservations are recommended in July and August, though you may find a last-minute room as long as it's not during one of the popular summer festivals, even in neighboring towns. Temperatures in summer average in the low 70s°F during the day. Nights are cool, so be sure to bring a light jacket. Fog is likely this time of year, so come prepared to appreciate its haunting beauty. Many establishments and businesses that rely on tourism are open from Memorial Day weekend through Indigenous Peoples Day/Columbus Day, but some seasonal businesses and typically small museums close earlier, say around Labor Day. A few folks trickle in for winter getaways—the scenery never disappoints, but you're unlikely to find a winter-sports outfitter.

FESTIVALS AND EVENTS

Eastport Pirate Festival. The weekend after Labor Day, a masquerade and pub crawl kick things off Thursday evening. Saturday there's a parade and fireworks. Folks in pirate attire rollick through Sunday at cutlass lessons and pirate encampments. Kids hop on a pirate boat ride. And there may be some pirate attacks. ⊕ *www.eastportpiratefestival.com.*

Eastport Salmon & Seafood Festival. Every Labor Day weekend, the festival has music, fish-theme kids activities, craft and farmers market, and, of course, a chance to eat and learn about seafood. On Saturday, chowders, crab rolls, and oysters are for lunch; on Sunday it's

Great Itineraries

If You Have 3 Days

On Day 1, travel north to Milbridge, where you can enjoy the Milbridge Historical Society and Museum, with displays on weir fishing and the town's shipbuilding heyday. In Cherryfield, follow the Narraguagus River while checking out the impressive Victorian homes. Next, tour historic Ruggles House in Columbia Falls. Continuing north, take the road to Jonesport. When you arrive, cross the bridge to Beals Island for a late-afternoon hike at the Great Wass Island Preserve. Spend the night in Jonesport or nearby in Machias. On day 2, take a morning puffin cruise from Jonesport, then, in the afternoon visit the historic Burnham Tavern Museum in downtown Machias and Ft. O'Brien State Historic Site in Machiasport. Before dining in Machias or East Machias, relax or stretch your legs—each town has a small riverside park. On day 3, take a walk on Jasper Beach where sea-polished stones glisten with jewel tones or hike on one of the many trails in Roque Bluffs State Park. Or, drive to Lubec and cross the bridge to New Brunswick's Campobello Island where you can tour the Roosevelt Cottage at Roosevelt Campobello International Park and, if tides allow, walk out to East Quoddy Head Lighthouse. Don't forget your passport.

If You Have 5 Days

Follow the three-day itinerary and on Day 4, drive to Lubec and cross the bridge to New Brunswick's Campobello Island. (Bring your passport.) Tour the Roosevelt Cottage at Roosevelt Campobello International Park and, if tides allow, walk out to East Quoddy Head Lighthouse. Then head to West Quoddy Head Light in Lubec to hike along the shore. Stay overnight in Lubec or on Campobello Island. On Day 5, visit downtown Lubec, checking out galleries and chocolate shops and taking a tour of the Historic McCurdy Smokehouse. Then head to Eastport for more galleries and water views and a visit to the Tides Institute & Museum of Art. Or, if returning south on U.S. 1, visit the handful of galleries in and near Machias or travel down to Roque Bluffs State Park for a hike or swim.

salmon barbeque—meal tickets include a boat ride to salmon pens on Cobscook Bay. ⊕ *www.eastportchamber.net/salmon.*

Machias Wild Blueberry Festival. Hosted by a local church the third weekend in August, this popular event offers a parade, craft fair, concerts, 5-mile run, blueberry farm tours, the Wild Blueberry Ball Saturday night, and plenty of blueberry dishes. ESPN paid a visit one year to broadcast the blueberry pie eating contest live! ⊕ *www.machiasblueberry.com.*

Visitor Information

CONTACTS DownEast & Acadia Regional Tourism. ✉ *Machias* ☎ *207/707–2057* ⊕ *www.discoverdowneastacadia.com.*

Milbridge Area

22 miles north of Hancock via U.S. 1.

Lumbering spurred the shipbuilding that thrived in Milbridge in the 1800s. Though small, it's a commercial hub for the area where you can stock up on groceries and

Down East: A Nautical Tale

Back when people mostly came and went from Maine by boat, "down east" was simply a nautical term that referred to sailing downwind (on the prevailing winds) along the Maine coast as it arcs in a northeasterly direction. Since those days, the term has blown into the vernacular language as a term for said coast. In keeping with its origins, it's often used in a relative sense, with someone farther down the coast referring to somewhere farther up as "Down East." A person in Bath, a mid-coast town 35 miles north of Portland, might say they're heading Down East, meaning Deer Isle, off the Blue Hill Peninsula, or nearby Bucksport, or Belfast south of there at the upper end of the mid-coast. Someone in Belfast, going to Mount Desert Island or a mainland town nearby, might say they're heading Down East. Increasingly but not exclusively, the term is used to refer to the coastal region of Washington County at the upper end of Maine's storied coast.

grab a bite. Driving through, look for a sign for easy-to-miss Milbridge Commons Wellness Park along Narraguagus Bay, with picnic area, paths, gardens, and an abstract granite sculpture on the Maine Sculpture Trail. West of Milbridge in Steuben, popular hiking trails await at a wildlife refuge and a preserve. Set back from U.S. 1, that town's tiny village is worth a drive-through: no amenities, just buy into the lost-in-time feel. The 1850s Greek Revival Steuben Union Church facing the green is a classic. Next door, the handsome Henry D. Moore Parish House (1910) is a library. Upriver from Milbridge, a rocky stretch of the Narraguagus River cuts through Cherryfield, the "Blueberry Capital of the World." Blueberry processing facilities are in town and wild blueberry barrens in the countryside. A lumbering center in the late 1800s, there are a surprising number of ornate Victorian-era homes for a small, remote New England village. The Cherryfield National Historic District has 52 buildings including Colonial Revival, Greek Revival, Italianate, Queen Anne, and Second Empire dwellings.

GETTING HERE AND AROUND

U.S. 1 enters Washington County in Steuben, then continues right through Milbridge and, after heading inland, Cherryfield. You can loop through Steuben's sleepy village alongside the road on Old Route 1/Village Road.

U.S. 1A splits off from U.S. 1 in Milbridge and reconnects with the highway in Harrington. This route is faster if traveling to towns further Down East such as Jonesport, Machias, Lubec, and Eastport, but it's worth taking the time to drive through historic Cherryfield, at least on one leg of your trip.

Sights

Catherine Hill Winery

WINERY | At this hillside winery outside Cherryfield along Black Woods Scenic Byway (Route 182), wines are made with local berries as well as grapes from beyond Maine, and artisanal methods are part of the winemaking process. The tasting room is in a restored barn with purple doors. Names of vintages like Cherryfield Blues and King Tunk play on local place names. Check the website for the winery's many special events and happenings. ✉ *661 Black Woods Rd., Cherryfield* ☎ *207/546–3426* 🌐 *www.cathillwinery.com* 🕒 *Closed Mon. and Tues. and Nov.–Apr.*

Milbridge Historical Society and Museum
HISTORY MUSEUM | The facade of this museum may lack period charm, but the interior more than makes up for it. Permanent exhibits document maritime industries past and present: shipbuilding, sardine canning, weir fishing, and lobstering. Each year there is a new exhibit, as well as a gallery that showcases local artists. On the second Tuesday of the month at 7 pm in-season, talks are held; check the website for details. ✉ *83 Main St., Milbridge* 🌐 *www.facebook.com/Milbridgehistoricalsociety* 🎟 *Free* 🕒 *Closed from Sept.–May, and Mon. and Wed.–Fri. from June–Aug.*

Petit Manan National Wildlife Refuge
WILDLIFE REFUGE | **FAMILY** | The refuge's 2,178-acre Petit Manan Point Division is a sanctuary of fields, forests, and rocky shorefront at the tip of a peninsula. In August, it's a popular spot for hand-picking wild blueberries. Whatever the time of year, you can explore here on two trails. Mostly a loop, the 1.7-mile Hollingsworth Trail has a gorgeous shore stretch on Pigeon Hill Bay where it's easy to head off path to clamor on the large granite ledges. Petit Manan Lighthouse—Maine's second tallest, on one of five lighthouse islands belonging to the refuge—towers in the distance beyond a wide cove. The 2.2-mile Birch Point Trail leads to salt marshes and mudflats on Dyer Bay, with side trails to a cove and rocky beach. ✉ *Pigeon Hill Rd., Steuben* ☎ *207/546–2124* 🌐 *www.fws.gov/refuge/petit-manan* 🎟 *Free.*

Pigeon Hill Preserve
TRAIL | **FAMILY** | At 317 feet, Pigeon Hill is the highest coastal point in Washington County, and it doesn't disappoint, rewarding hikers with panoramic views that stretch to Schoodic Peninsula, where Acadia National Park's mainland district is located; Petit Manan Lighthouse off the end of the narrow peninsula where this land rises; and island-splattered waters farther Down East. Hike up to the summit on the short historic trail, with some steep sections, that locals have used for generations. There are also longer, easier routes on the interconnected trail system, which was created when this became a Downeast Coastal Conservancy preserve. One trail traverses an old silver mine and another passes by a glacial erratic boulder. The 185-acre preserve's loop trail to Pigeon Hill Bay begins across the road from the parking area. ✉ *Pigeon Hill Rd., Steuben* ✥ *4½ miles below U.S. 1* 🌐 *www.downeastcoastalconservancy.org.*

🍴 Restaurants

44 Degrees North Restaurant & Pub
$$ | **AMERICAN** | With dishes like Parmesan-crusted baked haddock and seafood pasta, the dinner menu here isn't all about fried seafood, as steak and chicken dishes are available; the lunch menu features burgers, wraps, and sandwiches. The dining room has tables, booths, and bar seating, and a dessert case tempts; beyond here the pub, with a "steam-punk-inspired" compass rose mural by a local artist, offers bar tables and seating at the curved wood bar. **Known for:** several TVs in the pub increase the odds of seeing your team play; large selection of appetizers; prime-rib special on Friday and Saturday night. [$] *Average main: $22* ✉ *17 Main St., Milbridge* ☎ *207/546–4440* 🌐 *www.44-degrees-north.com* 🕒 *Closed Mon.; restaurant closed Sun.*

🛍 Shopping

Riverlily
HOUSEWARES | With clapboards and trim in contrasting shades of blue and a grand entrance, this year-round gift shop in an old storefront pops on Milbridge's

Main Street. Inside the large, beautifully arrayed store, offerings live up to
the expectations the exterior creates.
Many Maine-made items are among a
selection that includes premium bath
products, kitchen gadgets, fun socks,
books about Maine, and jewelry—check
out the store's own vintage-look Riverlily earrings. ⊠ *14 Main St. Milbridge*
☎ *207/546–7666* ⊕ *www.facebook.com/
riverlilymilbridge.*

Seadove Gallery

ART GALLERIES | Sweet hand-painted and
-lettered signs created with scrap wood
found along the coast from Maine to New-
foundland by owners Kim and Leon are
sold at this gallery. On the back, they write
where the wood was found. A "Loon" sign
has paintings of loon, a "Blueberry" sign
of blueberries, and so on, and some have
town names or say "Welcome," but all are
unique. Kim's original fiction and paintings,
which capture connections between the
Down East coast and the people who
make their living on it, are also sold, as are
her travel-inspired scenes of Ireland and
India. If you head this way consider continuing on back roads through Harrington and
Addison to Jonesport and Beals Island and
hiking at a preserve in the region as part
of the outing. ⊠ *60 Sunset Point Rd. Harrington* ✛ *From U.S. 1 in Harrington, take
Marshville Rd. 3 miles and turn right into
Sunset Point Campground and follow signs*
☎ *207/483–2005* ⊕ *www.seadovegallery.
com* ⊘ *Closed Oct.–late May.*

 Activities

TOURS

Robertson Sea Tours & Adventures

BOAT TOURS | **FAMILY** | Departing from
Milbridge Marina in a six-passenger
lobster boat, Robertson's offers a couple
of trip options as well as private charters.
The popular 2½-hour puffin and seabird
cruise heads out to Petit Manan Island
(no landings), a puffin nesting site and
home to a lighthouse of the same name.
In the fall, a three-hour lighthouse and

wildlife cruise takes in three lights—you'll
see the captain haul a lobster trap, too.
⊠ *57 Bayview St., Milbridge Marina*
☎ *207/461–7439* ⊕ *www.robertsonse-
atours.com* ⊗ *From $70 per person*
⊘ *Closed mid-Oct.–Apr.*

Jonesport and
Beals Island

*25 miles northeast of Milbridge via U.S. 1
and Rte. 187.*

Jonesport and Beals Island, a pair of
fishing villages joined by a bridge over
Moosabec Reach, are less geared toward
travelers than many coastal Maine
villages; there's no downtown, and what
few retail establishments there are, are
concentrated in Jonesport. Lobster traps
are piled in the yards, and a few stately
homes ring Sawyer Square, where Sawyer Memorial Congregational Church has
exquisite stained-glass windows. On a
summer evening, you may catch a beautiful sunset on the majestic waters while
driving to Beals and around the lanes
nestled just west of the bridge. Lobster-boat races on Moosabec Reach are
the highlight of the community's annual
Independence Day celebration.

The birding is superb in the area, and
there are a couple of great preserves
nearby, but you must hike to the shore
to experience what many liken to Acadia
National Park without the crowds. Up the
road in Columbia Falls on the Pleasant
River, where impressive homes sit on
hilly lanes, there is a cluster of museums. West of Jonesport in Addison, the
Pleasant River widens into an elongated
bay, drawing kayakers to its tidal waters.

GETTING HERE AND AROUND

In Columbia Falls, Route 187 loops down
to Jonesport, where a bridge leads to
Beals Island, then returns to U.S. 1 in
Jonesboro. The western stretch of Route
187 below Columbia Falls is Indian River

The fishing villages of Jonesport and Beals Island are connected by a bridge over the Moosabec Reach.

Road; the route is Main Street through the village; and between there and Jonesboro, Mason Bay Road.

Sights

Great Wass Island Preserve

NATURE PRESERVE | This wonderfully wild, ecologically unique 1,576-acre preserve takes up much of Great Wass Island, which is linked by causeway to Beals Island. Hiking here can be challenging, but the rewards may include spotting gray seals as you make your way among the rocks and boulders at Little Cape Point. Just beyond the only trailhead is the start of the 4½-mile loop to the point, made up of three trail sections. Plan six hours for the round-trip as hiking here is moderate to difficult. One half of the loop passes through woods with a deep rug of moss, a raised peat bog, and a sedge-shrub marsh. The other traverses a cove (likened to a fjord) before edging granite cliffs for about a mile, revealing "wow" views of neighboring islands. Nearing the point, trail follows a cobble beach. Stunted jack pines and rare plants like beachhead iris grow in the preserve's cool, humid climate, created by converging ocean waters. No pets are allowed though, and if it's been raining, it may be too wet for hiking. ⊠ *Black Duck Cove Rd., Beals* ✛ *Take Bay View Dr. to Black Duck Cove Rd., turn right and drive for about 2½ miles watching for the sign on left* ☎ *207/729–5181* ⊕ *www.nature.org/maine.*

Ingersoll Point

TRAIL | One of the joys of hiking here is arriving in South Addison, a fishing hamlet on a remote neck west of Jonesport. The wide harbor views in this sleepy village make you feel like you've discovered the real Maine. More magic moments of discovery await at this Downeast Coastal Conservancy preserve; the trailhead's at the village's Union Church, where hikers are allowed to park. The 145-acre preserve has a 3½-mile trail network that winds through the woods before hitting the coast and Carrying Place Cove and Wahoa Bay. ⊠ *Mooseneck Rd., Addison* ⊕ *downeastcoastalconservancy.org.*

★ **Ruggles House Museum**

HISTORIC HOME | Judge Thomas Ruggles, a wealthy lumber dealer, store owner, postmaster, and justice of the Court of Sessions, built this Federal-style home in 1818. The house's remarkable flying staircase, Palladian window, and intricate woodwork were crafted over three years by Massachusetts wood-carver Alvah Peterson. On guided tours you'll also learn about the outstanding collection of period furnishings, much of it original to the home. The museum includes displays in the excavated basement where the original kitchen was located. ✉ *146 Main St., Columbia Falls* ☎ *207/483–2131 off-season, 207/483–4637 in-season* 🌐 *www.ruggleshouse.org* 🎫 *$5* 🕒 *Closed Oct.–early July and Sat.–Mon. from early July–Sept.*

Wild Blueberry Heritage Center

SCIENCE MUSEUM | **FAMILY** | Formerly Wild Blueberry Land and built to resemble a giant blueberry, the museum's deep-blue geodesic dome is home to exhibits about the beloved crop that focus on the native plant's ecosystem; the canning of the fruit during the Civil War to help feed soldiers; local blueberry farmers; and research efforts to improve what is a managed wild crop. There's a blueberry-themed gift shop that sells items with a wild Maine blueberry theme or design like scented candles and blueberry socks; books about the crop and the culture it feeds; and foods featuring or made from the fruit such as Maine wild blueberry jam, vinegar, and chocolate truffles. ✉ *1067 U.S. 1, Columbia Falls* ☎ *207/483–2583* 🌐 *wildblueberryheritagecenter.org.*

Coffee and Quick Bites

Moosabec Video & Variety

$ | **AMERICAN** | **FAMILY** | Don't let this no-frills convenience shop's appearance deter you: lobster and crab rolls are among the homemade grab-and-go offerings in the summer, which also include sandwiches like pulled pork and fish burgers. If you're an early riser, don't miss the breakfast starting at 4 am (6 am Sunday) to join the fishermen. **Known for:** banana bread and cinnamon buns; community table sets a welcoming tone; one hot special daily such as mac-and-cheese or fish chowder. [$] *Average main: $7* ✉ *245 Main St. Jonesport* ☎ *207/497–2662.*

Hotels

★ **Pleasant Bay Bed & Breakfast**

$ | **B&B/INN** | **FAMILY** | A graciously welcoming, Cape Cod–style inn with three spacious guest rooms and a lovely suite, this appropriately named inn takes advantage of its location on a hilly farm aside a tidal river that widens into a bay offering visitors hiking paths and a tranquil place at the water's edge—and a chance to interact with llamas, goats, and other farm animals. **Pros:** nice for families, two guest rooms and suite have a pullout couch or extra bed; price and value can't be beat—this may be the best inn for the buck in America; innkeeper goes all out to adjust breakfast for special dietary needs. **Cons:** bit of a drive to restaurants and amenities; two rooms share a bath; off the beaten path (for some). [$] *Rooms from: $105* ✉ *386 West Side Rd., Addison* ☎ *207/483–4490* 🌐 *www.pleasantbay.com* 🔑 *4 rooms, 1 apartment* 🍴 *Free Breakfast.*

Activities

TOURS

Coastal Cruises

BOAT TOURS | Mistake Island, home to 72-foot Moose Peak Light, is a highlight of trips through ocean waters off Jonesport offered by this sister-and-brother team (she's the captain, he's the pilot). The 19-foot flat-bottom skiff can get close up to islands unlike large cruise boats, affording better wildlife views; passengers disembark, conditions allowing. You'll see Sealand, an abandoned island community where apple trees mark the sites of old homesteads; an anchorage Samuel de Champlain used when mapping lands for the King of France; and a site where huge blocks of granite were loaded onto schooners bound for New York and Boston. Custom trips are also offered. The captain recommends departing at 9 am. ⊠ *Jonesport Municipal Marina, Sawyer Sq.* ⚓ *Cruises depart from public marina near square* ☎ *207/598–7473* ⊕ *www.cruise-downeast.com* ⊠ *$225 for up to 3 people.*

Machias Bay Area

20 miles northeast of Jonesport.

The Machias area—Machiasport, East Machias, and Machias (Washington County's seat)—was the site of the Revolutionary War's first naval battle. Despite being outnumbered and out-armed, a small group of Machias men under the leadership of Jeremiah O'Brien captured the armed British schooner *Margaretta.* That battle, fought on June 12, 1775, is known as the "Lexington of the Sea." "Machias" is a Native American word meaning "bad little falls," for those falls crashing beside U.S. 1 as it curves into downtown below the University of Maine campus. If you only have a few minutes to watch the water churn through the rocky channel from the viewing platform or walking bridge at the small park here, do so. Better yet, picnic.

A few miles on, the village of East Machias flanks its namesake river, which flows into the Machias River above Machiasport and Machias Bay. Also linking Machias and East Machias is the multi-use Down East Sunrise Trail (⊕ *www.sunrise-trail.org*). Lakes streak the countryside, and the largest, Gardiner Lake, is outside the village of East Machias.

GETTING HERE AND AROUND

U.S. 1 runs right through Machias and ‾ast Machias. From downtown Machias, ⌐ute 92 leads to Machiasport.

VISITOR INFORMATION

CONTACTS Machias Bay Area Chamber of Commerce. ⊠ *2 Kilton La., in former train station, Machias* ☎ *207/255–4402* ⊕ *www.machiaschamber.org.*

 Sights

Burnham Tavern Museum

HISTORY MUSEUM | It was in this gambrel-roofed tavern home that the men of Machias laid the plans that culminated in the capture of the *Margaretta* in 1775. After the Revolutionary War's first naval battle, wounded British sailors were brought here. Period furnishings and household items show what life was like in Colonial times. On the National Register of Historic Places, the dwelling is among 21 in the country deemed most important to the Revolution. Tours by appointment in the off-season. ⊠ *14 Colonial Way, Machias* ☎ *207/255–6930* ⊕ *www.burnhamtavern.com* ⊠ *$5 suggested donation* ⊙ *Closed early Sept.–early July. Closed weekends early July–early Sept.*

Fort O'Brien State Historic Site

HISTORIC SIGHT | An active fort during the Revolutionary War, the War of 1812, and the Civil War, this site sits at the head of Machias Bay, where a naval battle was waged in 1775. Climb atop the grass-covered earthworks to take in the expansive water views. A panel display details the successive forts built here and relates the dramatic story of patriots, armed mostly with farm implements, who captured a British tender 2 miles offshore. A stone marker honors the site as a "birthplace" of the U.S. Navy. ⊠ *Fort O'Brien Point, Machiasport* ☎ *207/941–4014* ⊕ *www.maine.gov/dacf/parks* ⊠ *Free* ⊙ *Closed Oct.–late May.*

Nathan Gates House

HISTORY MUSEUM | The 1810 home-turned-museum contains an extensive collection of old photographs, period furniture, housewares, and other

Wild for Blueberries

Native only to northern New England, Atlantic Canada, and Quebec, wild blueberries have long been a favorite food and a key ingredient in cultural and economic life Down East. Maine's crop averages 85 million pounds annually, accounting for virtually all U.S. production and one-fourth of North America's. Washington County yields about 75% of Maine's crop, which is why the state's largest wild blueberry processors are here: Jasper Wyman & Son in Milbridge and the predecessor of what is now Cherryfield Foods in Cherryfield were founded shortly after the Civil War, during which Maine blueberries were shipped to Union soldiers.

Wild blueberries, which bear fruit every other year, thrive in the region's cold climate and sandy, acidic soil. Undulating blueberry barrens stretch for miles in Deblois and Cherryfield (the "Blueberry Capital of the World") and are scattered throughout Washington County. Look for tufts among low-lying plants along roadways. In spring, the fields shimmer as the small-leaf plants turn myriad shades of mauve, honey orange, and lemon yellow. White flowers appear in June. Fall transforms the barrens into a sea of otherworldly red.

Amid Cherryfield's barrens, a plaque on a boulder lauds the late J. Burleigh Crane for helping advance an industry that's not as wild as it used to be. Fields are irrigated, honeybees have been brought in to supplement native pollinators, and rocks and boulders are removed to literally "level" the field. In the past, barrens were typically burned to rid plants of disease and insects, reducing the need for pesticides to improve yield. Native Americans, who are still active in the industry, taught European settlers the practice, now used mostly by organic growers.

Most of the barrens in and around Cherryfield are owned by large blueberry processors. At least 90% of Maine's crop is harvested with machinery. That requires moving boulders, so the rest continues to be harvested by hand with blueberry rakes, which resemble large forks and pull the berries off their stems. Years ago, year-round residents did this work; today, it's mostly seasonal migrant workers.

Blueberries get their dark color from anthocyanins, which act as an antioxidant. Wild blueberries have more of these antiaging, anticancer compounds than their cultivated cousins; they're also smaller and more flavorful, and therefore mainly used in packaged foods, many of the frozen variety. Just 1% of the state's crop (some 500,000 pints) is consumed fresh, most of it in Maine. Look for fresh berries (usually starting in late July and lasting until early September) at roadside stands, farmers' markets, and supermarkets.

Find farm stores, stands, and markets statewide selling blueberries and blueberry jams and syrups at ⊕ *www. realmaine.com,* a Maine Department of Agriculture, Conservation and Forestry site that promotes Maine foods. Wild blueberries are the state's official berry and pies made with them are its official dessert.

memorabilia, including quilts and ship models. Operated by and headquarters for the Machiasport Historical Society, the building hugs Route 92 as it winds through the small pretty-as-a-picture village on Machias Bay. The Marine Room highlights the area's seafaring and shipbuilding past. A model schoolroom and post office, a display about the sardine canning industry here decades ago, and a large collection of carpentry tools occupy the adjacent Cooper House, a utilitarian building constructed in 1850. ✉ *344 Port Rd., Machiasport* 🌐 *www.machiasporthistoricalsociety.org* 🎟 *Donations encouraged* 🕒 *Closed early Sept.–early July. Closed Sat.–Mon. early July–early Sept.*

Beaches

★ Jasper Beach

BEACH | FAMILY | Sea-polished stones fascinate with glistening tones—many reddish but also heather, bluish, and creamy white—at this mesmerizing rock beach; removing stones from the beach is illegal. Banked in unusual geologic fashion, you must walk up and over a rock dune to get to the beach. When you do, you know you have arrived at a special place. Stones graduate from gravel at the shore to palm-size further back. Reddish volcanic rhyolite stones were mistaken for jasper, hence the name. Stretching a half mile across the end the rectangular-ish Howard Cove, bedrock at both ends deems this a pocket beach, but it's not your typical small one. A saltmarsh and fresh and saltwater lagoons intrigue visitors, and there are sea caves in the bedrock (be careful if you tread that way—the rocks are slippery). Tucked between the hamlets of Bucks Harbor and Starboard, Jasper Beach has long been a place of respite for folks in these parts. **Amenities:** parking (free). **Best for:** walking; solitude. ✉ *Jasper Beach, Machiasport.*

Roque Bluffs State Park

BEACH | FAMILY | Down East's rock- and fir-bound shores give way to the 274-acre park's half-mile crescent-shaped sand and pebble beach: one with any sand is a rarity in the region, and expansive ocean views enhance this one's beauty. Just beyond the beach you'll find a freshwater pond that's ideal for swimming and kayaking—rent flatwater kayaks here—and stocked for fishing. The park has changing areas (no showers), picnic area with grills, and a playground. Miles of trails traverse woods, apple orchards, and blueberry fields. The trailhead is just before the park entrance at Roque Bluffs Community Church. **Amenities:** parking; toilets. **Best for:** swimming; solitude, walking. ✉ *145 Schoppee Point Rd., Roque Bluffs, Machias* ✥ *Follow signs from U.S. 1 in Jonesboro or Machias* ☎ *207/255–3475* 🌐 *www.maine.gov/dacf/park* 🎟 *$4 Maine residents, $6 nonresidents.*

Restaurants

Helen's Restaurant

$$ | AMERICAN | FAMILY | In business for many years, the look here is updated and fresh, as the family-run establishment was rebuilt after a fire in 2014; it serves lunch and dinner, with entrées as well as burgers, sandwiches, salads, and the like. While the menu is big on seafood, don't expect only fried: try choices like charbroiled salmon topped with a maple glaze made with mustard, maple syrup, and blueberry jam, all Maine-made. **Known for:** fish-and-chips; lunch or dinner on the riverside deck come summer; Maine wild blueberry pie. [$] *Average main: $20* ✉ *111 Main St., Machias* ☎ *207/255–8423* 🌐 *www.helensrestaurantmachias.com* 🕒 *Closed Sun. and Mon.*

Hotels

Micmac Farm

$ | B&B/INN | Grouped along the Machi-as River at this wonderfully secluded 50-acre property are three open-plan cabins with pine interiors, kitchenettes, and Adirondack chairs on the lawn and the historic center-chimney cape house B&B with a modern guest room with deck. **Pros:** hiking trails on the proper-ty; cottages have queen and full beds; discount for week or longer stays. **Cons:** only one guest room in historic B&B; continental breakfast for B&B only; no sitting area in cottages. Ⓢ *Rooms from: $140 ✉ 47 Micmac La., Machiasport, Machias* ☎ *207/255–3008, 207/777–6616 cell ⊕ www.micmacfarm.com/ ⊘ Closed mid-Oct.–mid-May* ⇰ *4 units.*

 Activities

TOURS

Sunrise Canoe and Kayak

GUIDED TOURS | FAMILY | Sunrise Canoe & Kayak offers four-hour sea kayaking day trips on Machias Bay that include visiting petroglyphs (many 1,500 to 3,000 years old) carved on sea ledges; paddlers also learn about the Revolution-ary War naval battle waged in the waters here. There are also six-hour trips on the Great Wass archipelago off Jonesport south of Machias, spread with more than 40 islands, and canoe trips north of Machias on the St. Croix River in the Calais area. The company also rents canoes, kayaks, and standup paddle-boards and leads overnight trips. ✉ *168 Main St., Machias* ☎ *207/255–3375, 877/980–2300 ⊕ www.sunrisecanoean-dkayak.com* ⇰ *Kayak trips from $75 per person, rentals from $25.*

Lubec Area

28 miles northeast of Machias via U.S. 1 and Rte. 189.

Lubec is one of the first places in the United States to see the sunrise and a popular destination for outdoors enthusiasts. The Bold Coast of high cliffs between here and the quaint fishing hamlet Cutler offers some of the best coastal hiking in the Eastern United States, with sweeping views and rocky beaches. But there are trails throughout the area, not just on the high Bold Coast, and many aren't especially difficult. Along with government parks and lands, many conservation groups have preserves in and near Lubec. Birding is renowned as many migratory seabirds head this way; mudflats, marshes, and headlands offer diverse habitats for observing birds.

Lubec is a good base for visiting New Brunswick's Campobello Island across the bridge from downtown—the only one to the island, so don't forget your passport! The village itself is perched at the end of a neck, so you can often see water in three directions. While there are some rundown buildings in and around the small downtown, there's also a small cluster of restaurants, inns, shops, and lively murals that reveal the spirit of this remote, peaceful, and beautiful place.

GETTING HERE AND AROUND

From U.S. 1 in Whiting, Route 189 runs 11 miles to Lubec. To travel here on a slightly longer scenic route through the seaside hamlet of Cutler, take Route 191 from U.S. 1 in East Machias to Route 189 in West Lubec. From Lubec to Eastport it's 3 miles by boat but 38 miles by the circuitous northerly land route. In summer, a water taxi links the towns, as does a seasonal ferry (*see the Getting Here and Around section of the Chapter Planner for more information*).

◉ Sights

Boot Head Preserve

NATURE PRESERVE | FAMILY | There are some steep sections on the 2-mile trail network here, but this lovely preserve provides easy access to the Bold Coast, and there's a viewing platform that looks over the Grand Manan Channel. This 700-acre preserve is owned by Maine Coast Heritage Trust, a large conservation group in Maine. Check their website to learn about their other preserves near Lubec and way Down East. ⊠ *Boot Cove Rd., Lubec* ✛ *1.9 miles from Rte. 191* ⊕ *www.mcht.org/preserve/boot-head.*

Cobscook Shores

NATURE PRESERVE | FAMILY | Cobscook Bay is a mishmash of small coves and sub bays, as though a giant tried to claw his way inland from Lubec and Eastport. Even for Maine, the coast here is nooks and crooks, and a number of exceptional parcels on these wildly shaped waters have become part of a nonprofit, foundation-funded public park system with 15 parks that total about 15 miles of shore frontage. Park amenities include woodsy screened-in picnic shelters, restrooms, water fountains, and spiffy kiosks with large maps and information about the park's ecology and history. Old Farm Point Shorefront Park (⊠ *65 N. Lubec Rd.*) off Route 189 serves as an outdoor visitor center for Cobscook Shores and has a few short trails. Black Duck Cove and Race Point are two of the larger parks. The parks draw bikers and paddlers as well as hikers. ⊠ *Old Farm Point Shorefront, 65 N. Lubec Rd., Lubec* ⊕ *www.cobscookshores.org* ⊗ *Closed Nov.–Apr.*

★ Cutler Coast Public Land

NATURE PRESERVE | FAMILY | Views from this 12,234-acre state preserve above Cutler Harbor are likely to take your breath away, including 4½ miles of undeveloped Bold Coast between Cutler and Lubec. Here a wall of steep cliffs—some 150 feet tall—juts below ledges partially forested with spruce and fir; look for whales, seals, and porpoises while taking in views of cliff-ringed Grand Manan Island and the Bay of Fundy.

One of the East Coast's premier hiking destinations, the preserve's nearly 10 miles of interconnected trails offer hikes of about 3–10 miles, including loops. From the parking lot, the Coastal Trail runs 1.4 miles through woods to an ocean promontory, then follows the glorious Bold Coast for 3.4 miles. Revealing the area's unusual terrain inland from the coast, the 4½-mile Inland Trail passes by raised peat bogs, salt marshes, and swamps, and traverses meadows and forest. There are several primitive campsites. ⊠ *Rte. 191, Cutler* ⊕ *www.maine.gov/dacf/parks.*

Little River Lighthouse

LIGHTHOUSE | Hike in the state preserve in Cutler (Cutler Coast Public Land) for views of this lighthouse facing the ocean on a tiny, wooded island at the harbor's mouth. You can also kayak to its rocky, cliff-clad shores. Friends of Little River Lighthouse hosts open houses each summer, ferrying visitors over from the boat ramp in town, and offers overnight stays in the charming keeper's house. Check the website for details about overnight stays and the open houses. ⊠ *Little River Lighthouse, Cutler* ☎ *877/276–4682* ⊕ *www.littleriverlight.org.*

McCurdy Smokehouse Museum

HISTORIC SIGHT | Small buildings clustered on piers along the downtown waterfront are what remains of the nation's last herring smokehouse, which operated here from the 1890s until 1991. Restoration is ongoing, but you can take a guided tour of the skinning and packing sheds, which have exhibits about the smoking operation and the sardine canning industry that once thrived along the Down East coast; your guide might be someone who worked here years ago and is helping preserve this legacy. There are photos and a video about the industry. The museum, which is on the National Register of Historic Places, is part of Lubec Landmarks, whose Mulholland Market Gallery is next door with changing art exhibits. ✉ *50 S. Water St., Lubec* ☎ *207/733–2197* 🌐 *www.mccurdysmokehouse.org* 🎟 *$4* 🕒 *Closed Oct.–mid-June and Sun.–Tues. mid-June–Sept.*

West Quoddy Head Light/Quoddy Head State Park

STATE/PROVINCIAL PARK | FAMILY | Candy cane–stripe West Quoddy Head Light marks the easternmost point of land in the United States. One of Maine's most famous lighthouses, it guards Lubec Channel as it flows into much wider Atlantic waters that also demarcate Canada and the United States. Authorized by President Thomas Jefferson, the first light here was built in 1808. West Quoddy, just inside the park entrance, was constructed in 1858. You can't climb the tower, but the former lightkeeper's house is a seasonal museum; there are displays about the lighthouse and its former keepers, works by local artists, and a gift shop. Plan for more than a lighthouse visit at this enticing 541-acre Bold Coast park. Whales are often sighted offshore, the birding is world-famous, and there's a seaside picnic area. Visitors beachcomb, walk, or hike several miles of trails; a 2-mile trail along the cliffs yields magnificent views of Canada's cliff-clad Grand Manan Island, while the 1-mile roundtrip Bog Trail reveals arctic and subarctic plants rarely found south of Canada. Leading to a lookout with views of Lubec across the channel, the western leg of the 1-mile Coast Guard Trail is wheelchair accessible. In the off-season, visitors can park outside the gate and walk in. ✉ *973 S. Lubec Rd., Lubec* ☎ *207/733–0911* 🌐 *www.maine.gov/dacf/parks* 🎟 *$4* 🕒 *Closed mid-Oct.–mid-May.*

Beaches

Mowry Beach

BEACH | FAMILY | This 1.2-mile beach on the southern side of Lubec Neck has dramatic tides that produce excellent clamming conditions, and the shoreline is a hotspot for birds (migratory, nesting, and wintering) and birders. A short boardwalk leads through a heady mess of fragrant rugosa rose bushes out to the shore, from where you can see Lubec Channel Light—one of only three "spark plug" lighthouses in Maine—in these relatively shallow waters. **Amenities:** parking. **Best for:** solitude; sunrise; walking. ✉ *86–78 Pleasant St., Lubec* ☎ *207/255–4500* 🌐 *downeastcoastalconservancy.org.*

Restaurants

Water Street Tavern & Inn

$$$ | SEAFOOD | FAMILY | Perched on the water in a shingled building downtown, this popular restaurant serves some of the sweetest scallops you'll ever eat; *moqueca* (a Brazilian seafood stew); and filet mignon for those so inclined. It's also a great place to grab a glass of wine or a beer at the bar or a cup of coffee while gazing out at the water. **Known for:** laid-back, friendly atmosphere; specialty house-baked cake changes daily; also three guest rooms and a cozy suite. [$] *Average main: $25* ✉ *12 Water St., Lubec* ☎ *207/733–0122* 🌐 *www.watersttavernandinn.com* 🕒 *No lunch; closed late Oct.–late Apr.*

Hotels

★ Peacock House

$ | B&B/INN | Five generations of the Peacock family lived in this 1860 sea captain's home in the middle of the village before it was converted to an inn in 1989; with a large foyer, living room with fireplace, and cozy library, the white-clapboard house has plenty of places where you can relax—there's even a sunroom

Part of the Roosevelt Campobello International Park, the Franklin D. Roosevelt Summer Cottage is located on Campobello Island in New Brunswick, Canada.

that opens to a deck and gardens. **Pros:** guests welcome to play the instruments in the living room; four suites, including two on the first floor with sitting rooms and a primo open-plan one upstairs; innkeepers direct guests to area's tucked-away spots. **Cons:** not on the water; no self-check-in; one bedroom has slanted ceiling. $ *Rooms from: $175* ✉ *27 Summer St., Lubec* ☎ *207/733–2403, 888/305–0036* ⊕ *www.peacockhouse. com* ⤵ *7 rooms* ⭗ *Free Breakfast.*

West Quoddy Station

$ | B&B/INN | FAMILY | A former U.S. Coast Guard station on a hill overlooking Lubec Channel, this lodging offers a unique mix of accommodations in 14 buildings, some that were part of the station and others constructed this century by the historic-minded owner: the Keepers Cottage (sleeps four) has wonderful water views but no deck because it's a replica of the original 1808 lighthouse keeper's home that was at West Quoddy Head Light, just five minutes away by foot. **Pros:** all lodging units have kitchens

or kitchenettes; all guests can use the freestanding water-view deck and picnic/grill area; no charge for additional guests even though all units sleep at least four. **Cons:** one building lacks water views; no shops and restaurants in the immediate vicinity; few children's activities in Lubec. $ *Rooms from: $170* ✉ *Lubec* ☎ *877/535–4714* ⊕ *www.quoddyvacation.com* ⤵ *14 units* ⭗ *No Meals.*

Nightlife

SummerKeys

LIVE MUSIC | If you are walking in Lubec in the summertime and hear music playing it may be SummerKeys, which draws folks from far and wide here for summer music concerts that run June through August on Wednesday evenings at 7:30 pm. See the organization's website for more information. ✉ *Lubec's Congregational Christian Church, 46 Main St., Lubec* ☎ *207/733–2316* ⊕ *www.summerkeys.com.*

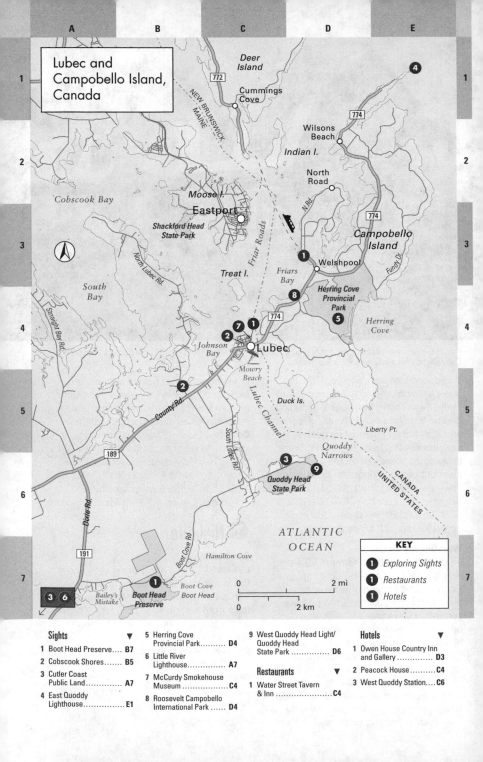

Shopping

★ Monica's Chocolates

CANDY | Taking in the appetizing scents in this shop is almost enough, but sinking your teeth into one of Monica's truffles, bonbons, crèmes, or caramels is pure heaven. Try a needham, a traditional Maine candy with a sugar, coconut, and potato filling, or a chocolate-shape moose or lobster. Conveniently on Route 189 at the turn for West Quoddy Head Light, it's owned by a Peruvian native (yes, Monica) and also carries clothing and accessories from her homeland. Indeed, some chocolates have a Peruvian filling. ⊠ *100 County Rd., Lubec* ☎ *866/952–4500* ⊕ *www.monicaschocolates.com* ⊗ *Closed Jan.–Mar.*

🏃 Activities

TOURS

Inn at the Wharf Boat Tours

BOAT TOURS | The 26-passenger *Tarquin* runs whale-watches out of Lubec, part of the offerings at Inn on the Wharf. There is indoor and outdoor seating on the boat, which cruises by lighthouses on the trips. They're part of the happenings at Inn on the Wharf, which has guest rooms in a renovated former sardine factory and a waterside restaurant. ⊠ *69 Johnson St., Lubec* ☎ *239/571–0208, 207/733–4400* ⊕ *www.theinnonthewharf.com* ☎ *From $60 per person.*

Campobello Island, Canada

Across the international bridge from downtown Lubec.

A popular excursion from Lubec, New Brunswick's Campobello Island has two small fishing villages, Welshpool and Wilson's Beach, but Roosevelt International Park, the former summer home of Franklin and Eleanor Roosevelt, is the big draw. If you have the time, you can take a whale-watching excursion, explore the large provincial park, or check out two lighthouses: Mulholland Point across from Lubec and East Quoddy just off the opposite end of the island. There are a few places to stay or grab a bite scattered around the lowkey island.

GETTING HERE AND AROUND

The only land route is the bridge from Lubec, but in summer a car ferry shuttles passengers from Campobello Island to Deer Island, where you can continue to the Canadian mainland on the free government ferry (*see the Getting Here and Around section of the Chapter Planner for more information*).

After coming across the bridge from Lubec, Route 774 runs from one end of the island to the other, taking you through the two villages and to Roosevelt Campobello International Park.

VISITOR INFORMATION

Campobello Island is part of New Brunswick, Canada, so U.S. Citizens will need their passports to get here.

CONTACTS Visit Campobello Island. ⊠ *Campobello* ⊕ *www.visitcampobello. com.*

👁 Sights

East Quoddy Lighthouse

(*Head Harbour Lighthouse*)

LIGHTHOUSE | **FAMILY** | Get an update on the tides before heading here if you want to walk out to the lighthouse (also known as Head Harbour Lighthouse) as you can only do so at low tide, via the ladders there—be careful on the wet rocks. On a tiny island off the eastern end of Campobello, this distinctive lighthouse is marked with a large red cross and is accessible only at and around low tide, but it's worth a look no matter the sea level. You may spot whales in the island-dotted waters off the small park on the rock-clad headland across from

East Quoddy Lighthouse, also known as Head Harbour Light, is the second oldest lighthouse in New Brunswick, Canada; it's only accessible at low tide.

the light. Seasonal tours of the light may be offered. ⊠ *East end of Rte. 774, Campobello.*

Herring Cove Provincial Park

STATE/PROVINCIAL PARK | FAMILY | The 1,049-acre park has camping, a restaurant, playgrounds, a 9-hole, par-36 Geoffrey Cornish golf course, a 1-mile beach, and six hiking trails, one of which follows a carriage and logging trail once used by the Roosevelts. ⊠ *136 Herring Cove Rd., Welshpool* ☎ *506/752–7010, 800/561–0123* ⊕ *parcsnbparks.ca* ✉ *Free.*

★ Roosevelt Campobello International Park

HISTORIC HOME | FAMILY | President Franklin D. Roosevelt and his family spent summers at this estate, which is now an international park with neatly manicured lawns that stretch out to the beach. Guided tours of the 34-room Roosevelt Cottage run every 15 minutes. Presented to Eleanor and Franklin as a wedding gift, the wicker-filled structure looks essentially as it did when the family was in residence. A visitor center has displays about the Roosevelts and Canadian-American

relations. In the neighboring Wells-Shober Cottage, Eleanor's Tea is held at 11 am (10 am EST) and 3 pm (2 pm EST) daily. A joint project of the American and Canadian governments, this park is crisscrossed with interesting hiking trails. Groomed dirt roads attract bikers. Eagle Hill Bog has a wooden walkway and signs identifying rare plants. ⊠ *459 Rte. 774, Welshpool* ☎ *506/752–2922, 877/851–6663* ⊕ *www.fdr.net* ✉ *Free* ⊘ *Roosevelt Cottage closed late Oct.–late May* ☞ *Islands are on Atlantic Time, which is an hour later than Eastern Standard Time.*

🛏 Hotels

Owen House Country Inn and Gallery

$ | B&B/INN | With glorious sea views, this 1835 house is full of antiques and original artwork by the owner, Joyce Morrell. **Pros:** a really peaceful haven, free of everyday distractions; many original features; several large sitting rooms. **Cons:** two rooms share a bathroom; the only TV is set up for video; not everyone likes a communal breakfast table. 🖄 *Rooms from: C$104* ✉ *11 Welshpool St., Welshpool* 🕾 *506/752–2977* ⊕ *www.owenhouse.ca* ⤳ *9 rooms* ⦿ *Free Breakfast.*

Eastport

38 miles northeast of Lubec via Rte. 189, U.S. 1, and Rte. 190.

Occupying Moose Island on Cobscook and Passamaquoddy bays, a causeway links Eastport to the mainland. "Island City" has wonderful island views, and downtown looks across Friar Roads (part of Passamaquoddy Bay) to Canada's Campobello Island. The water is so deep that whales are often spotted off the large municipal pier (a.k.a. the Breakwater), where you can eye fishing boats and freighters. Among the highest in the world, tides fluctuate as much as 28 feet—thus the ladders and steep gangways for accessing boats. Old Sow, the Western Hemisphere's largest whirlpool, is offshore.

Smuggling with British-controlled Canada thrived here in the early 1800s and sardine-canning at the century's end. Fishing, aquaculture, and a marine terminal are part of today's economy, as is tourism. Art galleries and interesting shops fill storefronts in the largely brick downtown; folks amble on a waterfront walkway with an amphitheater and sculptures. One with a granite-carved fish is on the Maine Sculpture Trail; there's also a tall, jolly fisherman and Nerida, a sweet bronze-cast mermaid. Known for artsy flair with a quirky twist, Eastport drops a sardine on New Year's Eve, plus a maple leaf for the Canadians. In September, buccaneers from Eastport and Lubec battle during the pirate festival (*see "When to Go, Festivals" in the Chapter Planner*).

GETTING HERE AND AROUND

From U.S. 1, Route 190 leads to Eastport, the only road to the city. Before the causeway over, it passes through Sipayik

(Pleasant Point) Passamaquoddy reservation. Continue on Washington Street to the water. In the summer, you can take a water taxi from here to Lubec—a few miles by boat but about 40 miles by land. There's also a seasonal ferry service (*see the Getting Here and Around section of the Chapter Planner for more information*).

VISITOR INFORMATION

CONTACTS Eastport Area Chamber of Commerce. ✉ *141 Water St., in Port Authority lobby, Eastport* 🕾 *207/853–4644* ⊕ *www. eastportchamber.net.*

Sights

National Historic Waterfront District

NEIGHBORHOOD | Anchoring downtown Eastport, this waterfront district extends from the Customs House down Water Street to Bank Square and the Peavey Memorial Library. Spanning such architectural styles as Federal, Victorian, Queen Anne, and Greek Revival, the district was largely built in the 19th century. A cannon sits on the lawn at the Romanesque Revival library, one of the many interesting structures. Benches are beside an iron drinking trough-turned-fountain in front of a bank-turned-museum, the Tides Institute & Museum of Art. ✉ *Eastport.*

Shackford Head State Park

STATE/PROVINCIAL PARK | FAMILY | At the parking area for this 90-acre park, placards and a stone memorial pay homage to wooden Civil War ships the federal government burned here for scrap years after the Civil War. Items salvaged from the ships are still about town. A trail from here leads through woods and past pocket beaches and coves to a headland where you can enjoy wonderful views of Cobscook Bay and over Passamaquoddy Bay to Campobello Island. You can also see the pens for Eastport's salmon-farming industry as well as Estes Head, where the city's cargo pier is located. The trail is part of an interconnected network totaling a few miles. There is also a short trail from the parking area to Cony Beach. ✉ *Off Rte. 190, Eastport* 🌐 *www.maine.gov/dacf/parks* 🎟 *$4.*

Tides Institute & Museum of Art

ART MUSEUM | In an 1887 landmark brick building where Water and Sea streets angle together, this museum's focus is art depicting or connected to the Passamaquoddy Bay region from the 1800s through the present. Changing exhibits in the modern gallery range from classic maritime paintings to abstract art created by institute artists-in-residence—you may spot them working in storefront studio space across Water Street. On the main floor of this former bank, where tall windows let in lots of light for viewing, works from the large permanent collection are displayed. The institute's other local preservation efforts include two early 1800s federal churches, Seaman's Church (26 Middle Street) and North Church (82 High Street), and a former Grand Army of the Republic meeting hall (6 Green Street) with patriotic wall art and veteran artifacts. Check out their exteriors on a walk and check the website for special events, like concerts. The institute also hosts artist talks and has a campus about a mile from downtown with a public waterfront park on Duck Cove Road. Information and maps about its properties are on the website. ✉ *43 Water St., Eastport* ☎ *207/853–4047* 🌐 *www.tidesinstitute.org* 🎟 *Free* 🕒 *Closed Mon. June–Sept.*

🍴 Restaurants

Horn Run Brewing

$ | **AMERICAN** | In this grand brick building in the center of downtown, huge arched windows flood light into this high-ceilinged brewpub, as do harbor-view windows in the back and glass doors to the water-view side deck. Passersby know things are happening here, and many turn right in for a craft brew, a bite from the simple pub food menu, and the local flavor. **Known for:** live music; large soft pretzel and cheese dip, made with the brewer's Ridge Road Red Beer; flatbread pizzas. [$] *Average main: $12* ✉ *75 Water St., Eastport* ☎ *207/853–7199* 🌐 *www.facebook.com/Hornrunbrewing* 🕒 *Closed Mon. and Tues. Oct.–Apr.*

☕ Coffee and Quick Bites

Bocephus

$ | **AMERICAN** | Modern takes on sandwich fare and salads at this convenient takeout at the north end of downtown are so beautifully prepared that you almost hate to take a bite. One popular offering is the Bocephus Banh Mi (slow-cooked, "Vietnamese style" pork loin served on a baguette with lightly pickled veggies, lettuce, cilantro, maple mayo, and house fish sauce for dipping). **Known for:** lobster sandwich on a brioche bun; local craft brews and wine from small-scale producers; crab sandwiches on a brioche bun. [$] *Average main: $16* ✉ *104 Water St., Eastport* ☎ *207/853–0600* 🌐 *www.facebook.com/biteintobocephus* 🕒 *Closed late Oct.–mid-June and Sun. and Thurs. from mid-Sept.–late Oct.*

Dastardly Dick's Wicked Good Coffee

$ | **CAFÉ** | **FAMILY** | The coffee isn't the only thing that's wicked good at this local café; homemade pastries, rich soups, and tasty sandwiches are all prepared daily, and the hot chocolate and chai are worth writing home about. There are nice murals on the walls, too. **Known for:** local gathering spot; daily soup specials; wicked good baked goods. [$] *Average main: $6* ✉ *62 Water St., Eastport* ☎ *207/853–2090* 🕒 *No lunch Sat. Closed Sun. and Mon. May–mid-Sept and Sat.–Mon. mid-Sept.–May.*

Hotels

The Kilby House Inn B&B

$ | B&B/INN | In this 1887 Queen Anne residence built by seaman Herbert Kilby, creamy white walls offset fine antique furnishings, for a brightening effect that evokes an old-fashioned summer home, especially as sea breezes blow through the large windows on a summer day; a carriage house can be booked for an extended stay. **Pros:** master bedroom has four-poster bed; rates adjusted for single occupancy; innkeeper goes all out to help guests plan outings, often to hidden gems beyond Eastport. **Cons:** carriage house only available weekly or longer; some small bathrooms; not on the water. [$] *Rooms from: $130* ✉ *122 Water St., Eastport* ☎ *207/214–6455, 207/853–0989* 🌐 *www.kilbyhouseinn.com* 🛏 *4 rooms* 🍴 *Free Breakfast.*

Shopping

The Commons Eastport

HOUSEWARES | In a striking 1886 brick building downtown with maroon wood banding on the front, this spacious, uncluttered, well-lit store features the works of many fine Maine artisans and artists as well as a nice selection of books including Passamaquoddy-theme children's books. Open year-round, it offers fine jewelry, bowls made from gourds, paintings, and Passamaquoddy baskets among many other decorative and useful items. Owned and operated by a trio of local women known as "The Women of the Commons," the property has vacation rentals with wonderful water views above the store. ✉ *51 Water St., Eastport* ☎ *207/853–4123* 🌐 *www.thecommonseastport.com* 🕒 *Closed Sun.*

Full Fathom Five

ART GALLERIES | There's lots of striking contemporary art in this large white-walled fine arts gallery, including the husband-and-wife owners' acrylic paintings (hers) and limited edition photographic prints (his), some of local waters. The gallery shows works in many mediums, including paintings and sculpture, by more than a dozen Maine artists. The gallery also has three vacation rentals, including lofts. ✉ *66 Water St., Eastport* ☎ *207/214–6818* 🌐 *www.fullfathomfivegallery.com* 🕒 *Closed Jan.–Mar.*

Sweeties Downeast

CANDY | FAMILY | Colorful gummies, circus peanuts, swirling lollipops, jelly beans, a chocolate lobster bake, homemade fudge, and much and much more fill the shelves and jars at this wacky fun candy store. Black-and-white patterns and bold colors combine in theatrical displays inside, outside, and in the store windows, making this shopfront hard to miss. ✉ *80 Water St., Eastport* ☎ *207/853–3120* 🌐 *www.facebook.com/sweetiesdowneast* 🕒 *Closed Jan.–mid-Apr.*

Activities

TOURS

Eastport Windjammers

BOAT TOURS | Run by a family that's plied these waters for generations, Eastport Windjammers offers whale-watching and deep-sea fishing trips as well as private charters on a 42-passenger boat that looks similar to a lobster boat. About 2½ hours long, whale-watches pass Old Sow whirlpool, one of the world's largest, and East Quoddy Lighthouse on Campobello Island. Along with whales, passengers spot seals, porpoises, osprey, and bald eagles; some lobster traps are hauled. Gear is provided for the three-hour fishing trips. Trips depart from Eastport Municipal Pier near the tour operator's ticket office and gift shop. ✉ *Eastport Municipal Pier, Eastport* ☎ *207/853–2500* 🌐 *www.eastportwindjammers.com* 🎟 *From $60* 🕒 *Closed mid-Oct.–May.*

Index

Photo Credits

Front Cover: Eye35 stock / Alamy Stock Photo [Description: Yachts moored in Camden Harbour Harbor Maine USA United States of America]. **Back cover, from left to right:** Try Media / iStockphoto. Natalia Bratslavsky/Shutterstock. haveseen / iStockphoto. **Spine:** SeanPavonePhoto / iStock. **Interior, from left to right:** Visit Maine (1). Sean Pavone/ Shutterstock (2-3). Doug Lemke/Shutterstock (5). **Chapter 1: Experience the Maine Coast:** f11photo/Shutterstock (6-7). Visit Maine (8-9). Visit Maine (9). Visit Maine (9). Warren Price Photography/Shutterstock (10). Visit Maine (10). Casco Bay Lines (10). Terry W Ryder/ Shutterstock (10). EQRoy/Shutterstock (11). Jackschultz50/Dreamstime (11). Visit Maine (12). Visit Maine (12). Demerzel21/Dreamstime (12). Courtesy of Coastal Maine Botanical Gardens (12). Visit Maine (13). Stillman Rogers / Alamy Stock Photo (13). Mathew Trogner/Allagash Brewing Company (18). Shannoní s Unshelled (18). Ron Gay/Flickr (18). Jennifer Bakos 2016 (18). Public Domain (18). Mia & Steve Mestdagh/Flickr (19). DAGphotog.com (19). The Highroller Lobster Co (19). due_mele/wikimedia.org (19). Kelsey Gayle (19). Darryl Brooks/Shutterstock (20). Magdalena Kucova/Shutterstock (20). Leonard Zhukovsky/ Shutterstock (20). Spwidoff/Shutterstock (20). David68967/Dreamstime (21). Marie Sonmez Photography/Shutterstock (22). Tim Jenkins/iStockphoto (23). Flickr/JRP (24). VisionsOfMaine/ iStockphoto (24). James Kirkikis/Shutterstock (24). Eric Urquhart/Shutterstock (25). Shanshan533/Dreamstime (25). Visit Maine (26). Allan Wood Photography/Shutterstock (27). flashbacknyc/Shutterstock (32). Sean Pavone/ Shutterstock (33). Maine State Museum (34). Allan Wood Photography/Shutterstock (34). Paul D. Lemke/iStockphoto (35). Bill Florence/ Shutterstock (36). Robert Campbell (37). Casey Jordan (37). Dave Johnston (37). Paul Dionne/iStockphoto (38). Doug Lemke/Shutterstock (38). Imel9000/iStockphoto (38). **Chapter 3: The Southern Coast:** David Leiter/Shutterstock (55). imagindiana (62). Martina Birnbaum/ iStockphoto (66). haveseen/Shutterstock (71). ejesposito (75). Jaclyn Vernace/Shutterstock (80). Ray Lewis/Shutterstock (83). Serena Folding (90). **Chapter 4: Portland:** jejim/ Shutterstock (93). EQRoy/Shutterstock (97). Appalachianviews/Dreamstime (104). Visit Maine (109). Visit Maine (114). CoreyTempleton/Flickr (126). Visit Maine (133). Rosko Photography/ Shutterstock (139). **Chapter 5: The Mid-Coast Region:** SharonCobo (143). Serena Folding (153). Maine Maritime Museum (161). Anthony Dolan/Shutterstock (162). Red's Eats (167). Coastal Maine Botanical Gardens (171). Logan Larabee/iStockphoto (181). Corey T Burns/ Shutterstock (190). **Chapter 6: Penobscot Bay:** Efaah0/Dreamstime (193). Visit Maine (201). Visit Maine (204). Visit Maine (213). Leerobin/Dreamstime (215). Edella/Dreamstime (224). Visit Maine (230). **Chapter 7: Blue Hill Peninsula and Deer Isle:** cdrin/Shutterstock (233). Ken Schulze/Shutterstock (242). Jaminnbenji/Shutterstock (244). Malachi Jacobs/Shutterstock (252). Enrico Della Pietra/Shutterstock (257). Steven Schremp/Shutterstock (258). **Chapter 8: Acadia National Park:** Try Media/iStockphoto (261). f11photo/Shutterstock (275). **Chapter 9: Acadia Region:** Randall Vermillion/Shutterstock (281). Visit Maine (293). Sandrafoyt/Dreamstime (296). f11photo/Shutterstock (308). Sara Winter/Shutterstock (312). Kcphotos/Dreamstime (315). **Chapter 10:Down East Coast:** Natalia Bratslavsky/Shutterstock (319). Igokapil/Dreamstime (329). Daniel M. Silva/Shutterstock (337). Ken R Morris Jr (340). **About Our Writers:** All photos are courtesy of the writers except for the following: Annie P. Quigley, courtesy of Greta Rybus.

Every effort has been made to trace the copyright holders, and we apologize in advance for any accidental errors. We would be happy to apply the corrections in the following edition of this publication.

Fodor's MAINE COAST

Publisher: Stephen Horowitz, *General Manager*

Editorial: Douglas Stallings, *Editorial Director;* Jill Fergus, Amanda Sadlowski, *Senior Editors;* Kayla Becker, Brian Eschrich, Alexis Kelly, *Editors;* Angelique Kennedy-Chavannes, *Assistant Editor*

Design: Tina Malaney, *Director of Design and Production;* Jessica Gonzalez, *Senior Designer;* Erin Caceres, *Graphic Design Associate*

Production: Jennifer DePrima, *Editorial Production Manager;* Elyse Rozelle, *Senior Production Editor;* Monica White, *Production Editor*

Maps: Rebecca Baer, *Senior Map Editor;* Mark Stroud (Moon Street Cartography), Andrew Murphy, *Cartographers*

Photography: Viviane Teles, *Senior Photo Editor;* Namrata Aggarwal, Neha Gupta, Payal Gupta, Ashok Kumar, *Photo Editors;* Eddie Aldrete, *Photo Production Intern;* Kadeem McPherson, *Photo Production Associate Intern*

Business and Operations: Chuck Hoover, *Chief Marketing Officer;* Robert Ames, *Group General Manager*

Public Relations and Marketing: Joe Ewaskiw, *Senior Director of Communications and Public Relations*

Fodors.com: Jeremy Tarr, *Editorial Director;* Rachael Levitt, *Managing Editor*

Technology: Jon Atkinson, *Director of Technology;* Rudresh Teotia, *Associate Director of Technology;* Alison Lieu, *Project Manager*

Writers: Andrew Collins, Alexandra Hall, Annie P. Quigley, Christine Burns Rudalevige, Mary Ruoff, Mimi Bigelow Steadman

Editors: Alexis Kelly (lead editor), Laura M. Kidder

Production Editor: Elyse Rozelle

4th edition

ISBN 978-1-64097-566-8

ISSN 1554-5830

All details in this book are based on information supplied to us at press time. Always confirm information when it matters, especially if you're making a detour to visit a specific place. Fodor's expressly disclaims any liability, loss, or risk, personal or otherwise, that is incurred as a consequence of the use of any of the contents of this book.

SPECIAL SALES

This book is available at special discounts for bulk purchases for sales promotions or premiums. For more information, e-mail SpecialMarkets@fodors.com.

PRINTED IN CANADA

10 9 8 7 6 5 4 3 2 1

About Our Writers

Former Fodor's staff editor **Andrew Collins** is based in Mexico City but spends a good bit of the year in northern New England. A longtime contributor to more than 200 Fodor's guidebooks, he's also written for dozens of mainstream and LGBTQ publications including *Travel + Leisure, New Mexico Magazine, AAA Living,*and *The Advocate.* Additionally, Collins teaches travel writing and food writing for New York City's Gotham Writers Workshop. Follow him on Instagram @TravelAndrew or at ⊕ *AndrewsTraveling. com.* He updated the Experience and Travel Smart chapters.

For more than two decades, **Alexandra Hall** has regularly covered food and travel for publications including *Condé Nast Traveler, The New York Times, Bon Appétit, The Portland Press Herald,* and *Down East Magazine.* She has also co-written two cookbooks and authored or co-authored 11 New England travel books. Since moving to Maine from Massachusetts she's relished exploring the state with her family of six and her three dogs. Find her on Instagram as @AlexHallEditor and read more of her work at ⊕ *alexandrahallwriter.com.* She updated the Portland chapter.

Annie P. Quigley is a writer, editor, and poet whose work has appeared in *The Wall Street Journal* and *Travel + Leisure.* She's the author of *Remodelista in Maine: A Design Lover's Guide to Inspired, Down-to-Earth Style,* published by Artisan Books, and a forthcoming book of poems. A graduate of New York University, she lives in Portland, Maine. She updated the Southern Coast chapter. You can check out more of her work at her website ⊕ *anniepquigley.com* or at Instagram @anniepquigs.

Christine Burns Rudalevige is a seasoned food writer and cheese lover who lives in coastal Maine. Her work has appeared in national food publications including *Culture: the word on Cheese, Fine Cooking, Cooking Light,* and *Eating Well.* She's the editor of *edible MAINE* magazine. She updated the Blue Hill Peninsula and Deer Island chapter.

Freelance writer and former newspaper reporter **Mary Ruoff** has written travel articles about her adopted state for the *Portland Press Herald* and other publications. During her career, she's covered many other subjects too, including shoe retailing, veterans, and locally grown foods. A St. Louis native, Mary has several journalism awards and a Bachelor of Journalism from Missouri School of Journalism. Her go-to Mainer is her husband, Michael Hodsdon, a mariner and grandson of a Down East fisherman. They live in Belfast. She updated Acadia National Park, Acadia Region, and Down East.

From her home base on Maine's Mid-Coast, **Mimi Bigelow Steadman** writes regularly for AAA publications. She has also authored and co-authored New England guidebooks; served as an editor of *Down East* and other regional magazines; and hosted a weekly Maine Public TV show. While venturing farther afield, she has completely levitated in a midwinter gale in the Outer Hebrides; sailed the Bay of Bengal, Aegean, and Caribbean seas, and most of the U.S. East Coast; and kissed the Blarney Stone twice—she claims it helps her tell a good story. She updated Mid-Coast and Penobscot Bay.